THE BEST OF COUNTRY COOKING
SECOND EDITION

Editor: Julie Schnittka
Food Editor: Mary Beth Jung
Assistant Food Editor: Coleen Martin
Assistant Editor: Julie Buchsbaum
Art Director: Ellen Lloyd
Illustrations: Jim Sibilski
Cover Photo Food Photography Artist: Stephanie Marchese
Food Photography: Scott Anderson, Mike Huibregtse, Judy Anderson, Gilo
Photography, Grace Sheldon
Cover Photo Prop Stylist: Anne Schimmel

©1995, Reiman Publications, L.P.
5400 S. 60th Street, Greendale WI 53129
International Standard Book Number: 0-89821-187-5
Library of Congress Number: 95-71712
Printed in U.S.A.

Pictured above: Chocolate Dessert Waffles (p. 206).

Pictured on front cover: Clockwise from bottom right: **Marie's Chicken Bake**
(p. 87), **Fresh Vegetable Casserole** (p. 130), **Grandma's Oatmeal Bread**
(p. 157) and **Strawberry Shortcake** (p. 257).

Pictured on back cover: Clockwise from top: **Chunky Chili** (p. 36), **Spiced
Almond Cookies** (p. 173) and **Mexican Salad** (p. 54).

ENJOY A HEARTY SECOND HELPING OF THE
NO. 1 COOKING CLASSIC IN THE COUNTRY!

SEVERAL YEARS AGO, after months of sifting and sorting through recipes, we produced what's turned out to be our most popular cookbook ever—*The Best of Country Cooking*.

Filled with the top recipes published in the early issues of *Country*, *Country EXTRA*, *Country Woman*, *Reminisce* and *Reminisce EXTRA* magazines—plus the first few editions of our *A Taste of the Country* cookbooks—it quickly became the No. 1 source coast to coast for down-home delicious eating.

So what could we do for an "encore"? You're about to find out—with this gigantic *second edition* that picks up where the first edition left off!

We've again devoted months to sifting through issues of those magazines mentioned above—this time, the more recent ones—and through recent editions of *A Taste of the Country* to select the *very best* recipes shared there by great cooks from all over the country. So you can look forward to nearly *900 recipes*—almost 500 of them pictured in full color—that didn't appear in the first edition...plus a handful of special-favorite country standbys that every cook should have in her recipe file.

In fact, if it's possible, the recipes in this second edition are even tastier and easier to make than those in the first edition—they use only ingredients cooks keep right on hand. And, for sure, they're easier to find!

To make this second edition as trouble-free as possible to use, we've organized all the recipes *by category* for instant reference. Looking for a filling lunch everyone will warm up to? Turn to the Soups & Sandwiches chapter for page after page of ideas such as Potato Soup with Spinach Dumplings. It's a family favorite of Rosemary Flexman in Waukesha, Wisconsin.

Want to surprise your family by baking a new lip-smacking main dish? Country Herbed Meat Loaf, from Barbara Roy of Middletown, Pennsylvania, is just one of *109* tempting recipes in the Oven Meals chapter!

In the Breads, Coffee Cakes & Muffins chapter, Darlene Markel of Roseburg, Oregon is among those sharing their top recipes. Her Cherry/Nut Breakfast Rolls are so delectable that you'll eat them around the clock!

And Glazed Peach Pie—in the Pies & Desserts chapter—is a fresh and fruity dessert that brings Trudy Dunn raves in Dallas, Texas.

With an appealing assortment of beef, chicken, pork and seafood recipes, two other main meal chapters—Skillet Suppers and Grilling Ideas—join the Oven Meals chapter in providing plenty of hearty eating. And, along with tempting pies and desserts, a host of savory, sweet treats can be found in the Cookies & Bars and Cakes & Tortes chapters.

This big book also brings you countless recipes for hearty appetizers, filling sandwiches, refreshing salads, sure-to-please side dishes and tasty condiments and sauces.

But that's not all. You'll also enjoy:

• 18 complete meals in minutes menus that you can prepare in 30 minutes or less.

• Memorable meals from 16 country cooks that take you back to your roots in both time and taste.

• Recipes marked with a √ that use less salt, sugar and fat and that include Diabetic Exchanges.

• Dozens of proven helpful hints from great cooks to save you time, money and work in the kitchen.

• A sturdy hard cover that stands up to common kitchen spills...and to the test of time. Plus, the spiral binding lets this handy cookbook lie conveniently flat on your countertop. Best of all, each recipe is complete on a page—there's no stopping and turning the page to finish a dish.

It's *The Best of Country Cooking*—and, with this second edition, it just got better than ever.

CONTENTS

HERE ARE some spicy country specialties to keep your taste buds tantalized! Enjoy Spiced Lemonade over ice in the summer—or warmed in the winter—for a sweet, refreshing beverage. Served over crunchy corn chips, Chalupa Grande makes a meaty appetizer or light dinner. Don't forget to try Southwestern Mini Muffins by themselves or split in half and topped with thin slices of cheese or ham.

TEX-MEX MIX.
Clockwise from the top: **Spiced Lemonade**, **Chalupa Grande** (both recipes on page 7) and **Southwestern Mini Muffins** (recipe on page 150).

SNACKS & BEVERAGES

These hearty hot and cold appetizers and thirst-quenching drinks are a sure cure for an attack of the "munchies"!

SPICED LEMONADE

Kim Van Rheenen, Mendota, Illinois

(PICTURED AT LEFT)

6 cups water, *divided*
3/4 cup sugar
2 cinnamon sticks
6 whole cloves
1 large lime, thinly sliced
1 lemon, thinly sliced
3/4 cup fresh lemon juice

In a large saucepan, bring 4 cups water, sugar, cinnamon and cloves to a boil. Reduce heat; simmer 10 minutes. Remove from heat; discard cinnamon and cloves. Cool. Pour into a large pitcher. Stir in lime, lemon, lemon juice and remaining water. Chill at least 1 hour. Can also be served warm. **Yield:** about 2 quarts.

CHALUPA GRANDE

Cindy Bertrand, Floydada, Texas

(PICTURED AT LEFT)

1 pound dry pinto beans
1 pork roast (3 pounds), fat trimmed
7 cups water
1/2 cup chopped onion
2 garlic cloves, minced
2 to 3 teaspoons ground cumin
2 tablespoons chili powder
1 tablespoon salt
1 teaspoon dried oregano
1 can (4 ounces) chopped green chilies
Corn chips
Shredded cheddar cheese
Diced avocado
Diced tomatoes
Chopped green onions
Salsa

Place first 10 ingredients in a large kettle. (Beans do not need to be soaked.) Bring to a boil; reduce heat and simmer, covered, about 3 hours or until beans and roast are tender. Remove roast; cool slightly. Remove meat from bones; shred with a fork. Return meat to kettle. Cook, uncovered, until thick, about 30 minutes. Serve over corn chips. Pass remaining ingredients as toppings. **Yield:** 10-12 servings.

Quick & Easy

CRUNCHY CHEESE DIP

Deborah Hill, Coffeyville, Kansas

1 can (8 ounces) pineapple tidbits
2 packages (8 ounces *each*) cream cheese, softened
1 can (8 ounces) water chestnuts, drained and chopped
3 tablespoons chopped fresh chives
1 teaspoon seasoned salt
1/4 teaspoon pepper
1 cup chopped pecans
Fresh chopped parsley
Assorted crackers

Drain pineapple, reserving 1 tablespoon juice. In a small bowl, combine pineapple, cream cheese, water chestnuts, chives, salt, pepper and pecans. Stir in reserved juice; mix well. Garnish with parsley. Cover and chill. Serve with crackers. **Yield:** about 3-1/2 cups.

CRANBERRY MEATBALLS

Tammy Neubauer, Ida Grove, Iowa

(PICTURED ON PAGE 144)

MEATBALLS:
2 eggs, beaten
1 cup cornflake crumbs
1/3 cup ketchup
2 tablespoons soy sauce
1 tablespoon dried parsley flakes
2 tablespoons dehydrated onion
1/2 teaspoon salt
1/4 teaspoon pepper
2 pounds ground pork
SAUCE:
1 can (16 ounces) jellied cranberry sauce
1 cup ketchup
3 tablespoons brown sugar
1 tablespoon lemon juice

In a mixing bowl, combine meatball ingredients. Shape into 72 meatballs (1 in. each). Place in a 15-in. x 10-in. x 1-in. baking pan. Bake at 350° for 20-25 minutes or until done. Remove from the oven; drain on paper towels. In a large saucepan, combine sauce ingredients. Cook, stirring frequently, until the cran-

berry sauce is melted. Add the meatballs and heat through. **Yield:** 24 servings.

BREAKFAST GRANOLA

Wilma Beller, Hamilton, Ohio

4 cups old-fashioned rolled oats
1 cup chopped nuts
3/4 cup bran cereal
1 cup flaked coconut
1/3 cup honey *or* molasses
1/4 cup vegetable oil
1 teaspoon vanilla extract
1 cup raisins
1 cup chopped dates

Spread rolled oats on a 15-in. x 10-in. x 1-in. baking pan. Bake at 350° for 5 minutes. Stir; bake 5 more minutes. Remove from oven but leave heat on. Toss with nuts, cereal and coconut; set aside. In a saucepan, combine honey or molasses with oil. Heat but do not boil. Stir in vanilla; pour over oat mixture and toss well. Return to oven and bake for 20-25 minutes, stirring 3 times while baking. Remove from the oven. Add raisins and dates; stir well. Cool. Store in airtight containers. **Yield:** 8 cups.

Quick & Easy

SALMON SPREAD

Carolyn Stewart, Anchorage, Alaska

(PICTURED ON PAGE 189)

2 cans (15 ounces *each*) salmon, drained, boned and flaked
1 tablespoon minced onion
1 tablespoon prepared horseradish
1 tablespoon lemon juice
1 package (8 ounces) cream cheese, softened
2 to 3 tablespoons mayonnaise
1-1/2 teaspoons dried dill weed
1/2 teaspoon salt
1 cup (8 ounces) sour cream
Fresh dill *or* parsley, optional
Toasted bread rounds *or* crackers

In a mixing bowl, combine first eight ingredients; mix well. Spread on a serving platter and shape into a loaf or ball. Top with sour cream. Chill. Garnish with dill or parsley if desired. Serve with bread rounds or crackers. **Yield:** 8-10 servings.

CHICKARITOS

Nancy Coates, Oro Valley, Arizona

(PICTURED AT RIGHT)

3 cups finely chopped cooked chicken
1 can (4 ounces) diced green chilies
1/2 cup finely chopped green onions
1-1/2 cups (6 ounces) shredded sharp cheddar cheese
1 teaspoon hot pepper sauce
1 teaspoon garlic salt
1/4 teaspoon pepper
1/4 teaspoon ground cumin
1/4 teaspoon paprika
1 box (17-1/4 ounces) frozen puff pastry sheets, thawed *or* pie pastry for double-crust 10-inch pie
Water
Salsa
Guacamole

In a bowl, combine chicken, chilies, onions, cheese and seasonings. Mix well; chill until ready to use. Remove half of the pastry from refrigerator at a time. On a lightly floured board, roll to a 9-in. x 12-in. rectangle. Cut into nine small rectangles. Place about 2 tablespoons of filling across the center of each rectangle. Wet edges of pastry with water and roll pastry around filling. Crimp ends with a fork to seal. Repeat with remaining pastry and filling. Place, seam side down, on a lightly greased cookie sheet. Refrigerate until ready to heat. Bake at 425° for 20-25 minutes or until golden brown. Serve warm with salsa and guacamole. **Yield:** 18 servings.

CRISPY CHICKEN WINGS

Nancy Lesky, LaCrosse, Wisconsin

(PICTURED AT RIGHT)

2 pounds chicken wings
1/2 cup butter *or* margarine, melted
1/4 teaspoon garlic powder
1 cup dry bread crumbs
1/2 cup grated Parmesan cheese
2 tablespoons chopped parsley
1/2 teaspoon salt
1/4 teaspoon pepper

Cut chicken wings in two pieces, discarding the tips. In a small shallow bowl, combine butter and garlic powder. In another bowl, combine remaining ingredients. Dip chicken into butter mixture, then into crumb mixture. Place on a greased cookie sheet; bake at 350°

for 50-60 minutes or until done. **Yield:** about 20 appetizers.

MARINATED MUSHROOMS

Agnes Smith, Bristol, Maine

1 pound fresh mushrooms
1/2 cup sliced green onions
1/4 cup chopped sweet red pepper
2 tablespoons minced fresh parsley
1 bottle (8 ounces) Italian salad dressing

In a glass bowl, combine all ingredients and allow to marinate several hours or overnight. **Yield:** 6 servings.

Quick & Easy

ORANGE TEA

Sally Mueller, Loveland, Colorado

7 cups water
1 can (12 ounces) frozen orange juice concentrate
1/2 cup sugar
2 tablespoons lemon juice
5 teaspoons instant tea
1 teaspoon whole cloves

In a large saucepan, combine water, orange juice concentrate, sugar, lemon juice and tea. Tie the cloves in a small cheesecloth bag; add to saucepan. Simmer, uncovered, for 15-20 minutes. Remove spice bag. Serve hot. Store leftovers in glass container in refrigerator. **Yield:** 8 servings (2 quarts).

Quick & Easy

WHITE BEAN DIP

Linn Landry, Honeydew, California

(PICTURED ON PAGE 139)

✓ This tasty dish uses less sugar, salt and fat. Recipe includes *Diabetic Exchanges*.

1 can (15 to 16 ounces) cannellini beans *or* great northern beans, rinsed and drained
1 tablespoon lemon juice
2 tablespoons plain yogurt
2 tablespoons chopped fresh parsley
1/2 teaspoon freshly ground black pepper
1/4 teaspoon hot pepper sauce
2 to 3 garlic cloves
Salt to taste
Pita bread, corn chips *or* vegetable dippers

In a food processor or blender, combine all ingredients except for last one. Cover and process until smooth. Chill.

Serve with toasted pita bread triangles, corn chips or fresh vegetables. **Yield:** 1-1/4 cups. **Diabetic Exchanges:** One tablespooon serving (prepared with skim yogurt and no added salt) equals 1/2 starch; also, 29 calories, 78 mg sodium, trace cholesterol, 6 gm carbohydrate, 2 gm protein, trace fat.

OYSTER CHEESE APPETIZER LOG

Mrs. William Tracy, Jerseyville, Illinois

(PICTURED ON PAGE 66)

3 packages (8 ounces *each*) cream cheese, softened
2 tablespoons bottled steak sauce
1/4 cup creamy salad dressing
1 clove garlic *or* 1 teaspoon garlic powder
1 small onion, finely chopped
2 cans (3-3/4 ounces *each*) smoked oysters, well-drained and chopped
3 cups chopped pecans, *divided*
3 tablespoons chili powder
Chopped fresh parsley

In mixer bowl, blend together cheese, steak sauce, salad dressing, garlic and onion. Stir in oysters and 1 cup of pecans. Shape into long cylinder. Combine remaining pecans, chili powder and parsley on a cookie sheet. Roll log in mixture. **Yield:** 1 log.

POPCORN CARAMEL CRUNCH

Lucille Hermsmeyer, Scotia, Nebraska

4 cups popped popcorn
1 cup dry roasted peanuts
1 cup chow mein noodles
1/2 cup raisins
1 cup sugar
3/4 cup butter
1/2 cup light corn syrup
2 tablespoons water
1 teaspoon ground cinnamon

In a large greased bowl, combine first four ingredients. Set aside. In a large saucepan, combine sugar, butter, corn syrup and water. Cook over medium heat, stirring occasionally, until mixture reaches soft crack stage (280°-290°) with a candy thermometer. Remove from the heat. Stir in cinnamon. Pour over popcorn mixture; stir until all ingredients are evenly coated. Immediately pour onto a greased 15-in. x 10-in. x 1-in. pan. When cool enough to handle, break into pieces. Store in airtight containers. **Yield:** about 8 cups.

FEW FOODS, week in and week out, top chicken in popularity. But few things are as difficult to come by as a deliciously different chicken dish to serve a hungry bunch. If that's true for you, too, your problem's a thing of the past—beginning with the four flavorful chicken favorites featured here. Try each of them…there's lots of great-tasting country eating that awaits you and your family!

CHOICE CHICKEN.
Clockwise from the top: **Hot Chicken Salad** (recipe on page 41), **Hungarian Chicken** (recipe on page 103), **Chickaritos** and **Crispy Chicken Wings** (both recipes on page 8).

SAUSAGE-STUFFED MUSHROOMS

Beatrice Vetrano, Landenberg, Pennsylvania

12 to 15 large fresh mushrooms
2 tablespoons butter *or*
  margarine, *divided*
2 tablespoons chopped onion
1 tablespoon lemon juice
1/4 teaspoon dried basil
Salt and pepper to taste
4 ounces bulk Italian sausage
1 tablespoon chopped fresh
  parsley
2 tablespoons dried bread
  crumbs
2 tablespoons grated Parmesan
  cheese

Remove stems from the mushrooms. Chop stems finely; reserve caps. Place stems in paper towel and squeeze to remove any liquid. In a skillet, cook stems and onion in 1-1/2 tablespoons butter until soft. Add lemon juice, basil, salt and pepper; cook until almost all the liquid has evaporated. Cool. Combine mushroom mixture with sausage and parsley. Stuff into the mushroom caps. Combine crumbs and cheese; sprinkle over stuffed mushrooms. Dot each with remaining butter. Place in a greased baking pan and bake at 400° for 20 minutes. Baste occasionally with pan juices. Serve hot. **Yield:** 12-15 servings.

SPICY CHICKEN WINGS

Nonie Dean, Balzac, Alberta

1 can (6 ounces) frozen orange
  juice concentrate, thawed
1 can (6 ounces) tomato paste
1/4 cup honey *or* packed brown
  sugar
2 tablespoons lemon juice
2 tablespoons lime juice
2 to 3 garlic cloves, crushed
1 teaspoon grated lime peel
1 teaspoon grated lemon peel
1 teaspoon grated orange peel
1/2 teaspoon seasoned pepper
1/2 teaspoon salt
1/4 teaspoon thyme
Few drops hot pepper sauce
30 to 36 chicken wings *or*
  drumettes (about 3-1/2 pounds)

In a saucepan, combine all ingredients except chicken; heat and stir until blended. Cool to room temperature; reserve 1/3 cup. Place the chicken in a shallow baking pan; pour remaining sauce over. Cover and let marinate in the refrigerator 12-24 hours. To cook, remove chicken from the marinade and place on a broiler

pan. Discard marinade. Bake at 375° for about 40 minutes or until tender. Turn chicken and brush with reserved marinade occasionally. **Yield:** 12 servings.

 **Quick & Easy**

SNAPPY ASPARAGUS DIP

Debra Johnson, Bonney Lake, Washington

(PICTURED BELOW)

1 pound fresh asparagus,
  trimmed
1 cup (8 ounces) sour cream
1/2 cup salsa (mild, medium *or*
  hot)
Dash lime juice
Salt and pepper to taste
Dash cayenne pepper

Cook asparagus in a small amount of water until tender. Drain and cool. In a blender or food processor, puree asparagus until smooth. Stir in all the remaining ingredients. Chill. Serve with assorted raw vegetable dippers or tortilla chips. **Yield:** 2 cups.

PERFECT PUREE. Serve Snappy Asparagus Dip with your favorite veggies or chips!

 **Quick & Easy**

CHEESE AND SAUSAGE APPETIZERS

Debbie Hogan, Tsaile, Arizona

1 pound (4 cups) shredded
  cheddar cheese, room
  temperature
1 cup butter *or* margarine,
  softened
2 cups all-purpose flour
1/2 teaspoon salt
1/2 teaspoon black *or*
  cayenne pepper
8 ounces pork sausage, cooked
  and drained

In large mixing bowl, combine cheese, butter, flour, salt and pepper. Beat with

an electric mixer on medium-low speed. Stir in cooked sausage. Form dough into 1-in. balls; place on an ungreased baking sheet. Bake at 400° for 15-20 minutes or until light golden brown. Serve warm or cold. Store in refrigerator or freezer. **Yield:** about 5-1/2 dozen.

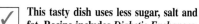

ZUCCHINI/HERB PATE

Melissa Sullivan, Iuka, Kansas

(PICTURED ON PAGE 132)

 This tasty dish uses less sugar, salt and fat. Recipe includes *Diabetic Exchanges*.

4 medium zucchini (about 1
  pound)
2 teaspoons tarragon vinegar
2 teaspoons sugar
2 teaspoons salt, *divided*
1/2 cup packed fresh parsley
  sprigs
1/2 cup snipped fresh chives *or*
  1/4 cup dried chives
1 package (8 ounces) cream
  cheese, softened
1/2 teaspoon pepper
Crackers

Line a mixing bowl with a double thickness of cheesecloth. Coarsely shred zucchini into prepared bowl. Sprinkle with vinegar, sugar and 1 teaspoon salt. Toss gently; cover with a towel and set aside for 1 hour. Meanwhile, in a food processor with the chopping blade, mince parsley and chives. Gather ends of cheesecloth, squeezing out as much liquid as possible. Add drained zucchini to food processor and process until pureed. Add cream cheese, pepper and remaining salt; process until smooth. Press pate into a small bowl. Cover and refrigerate overnight. Serve with crackers. **Yield:** 1-1/2 cups. **Diabetic Exchanges:** One serving (1 tablespoon) equals 1/2 vegetable, 1/2 fat; also, 29 calories, 280 mg sodium, 5 mg cholesterol, 3 gm carbohydrate, 2 gm protein, 2 gm fat.

PINEAPPLE PECAN CHEESE BALL

June Stone, Brewton, Alabama

(PICTURED ON PAGE 194)

2 packages (8 ounces *each*)
  cream cheese, softened
1 can (8 ounces) crushed
  pineapple, well drained
1/2 cup chopped green pepper
1/2 cup chopped green onions
1 teaspoon lemon pepper
  seasoning
1 teaspoon seasoned salt

2 cups chopped pecans, *divided*
Assorted crackers

In a mixing bowl, whip cream cheese until smooth. Gently stir in pineapple, green pepper, onions, seasonings and 1/2 cup nuts. Turn out onto a sheet of plastic wrap and shape into a ball. Refrigerate several hours or overnight. Before serving, roll cheese ball in remaining nuts. Serve with crackers. **Yield:** 12-14 servings.

CUCUMBER PARTY SANDWICHES

Rebecca Rose, Mount Washington, Kentucky

1 package (8 ounces) cream cheese, softened
1/2 envelope (2 teaspoons) dry Italian salad dressing mix
2 tablespoons mayonnaise
30 slices snack rye bread
30 thin slices cucumber
Fresh dill sprigs

In a bowl, combine the cream cheese, dressing mix and mayonnaise. Allow to stand at least 30 minutes. Spread on rye bread. Top with a slice of cucumber and a sprig of dill. Cover and refrigerate until serving time. **Yield:** 30 appetizers.

Quick & Easy

HOT CINNAMON COCOA

Norma Erne, Albuquerque, New Mexico

1/4 cup baking cocoa
1/4 cup sugar
1/8 teaspoon salt
1 cup boiling water
3 cups scalded milk
2 cinnamon sticks (about 3 inches *each*)
1 teaspoon vanilla extract

In the top of a double boiler, stir together cocoa, sugar and salt. Gradually add boiling water. Place over direct heat and boil for 2 minutes, stirring constantly. Add milk and cinnamon sticks and place over boiling water. Stir and heat 10 minutes. Remove sticks and stir in vanilla. Beat with a wire whisk to froth milk. Serve immediately. **Yield:** about 4 servings.

SALMON APPETIZERS

Evelyn Gebhardt, Kasilof, Alaska

1 can (15 ounces) salmon *or* 2 cups cooked salmon, flaked
1 package (8 ounces) cream cheese, softened

4 tablespoons mild *or* medium salsa
2 tablespoons chopped fresh parsley
1 teaspoon dried cilantro
1/4 teaspoon ground cumin, optional
8 flour tortillas (8 inches)

Drain salmon; remove any bones. In a small bowl, combine salmon, cream cheese, salsa, parsley, cilantro and cumin if desired. Spread about 2 tablespoons of the salmon mixture over each tortilla. Roll each tortilla up tightly and wrap individually with plastic wrap. Refrigerate 2-3 hours. Slice each tortilla into bite-size pieces. **Yield:** about 48 appetizers.

CONTINENTAL CHEESE SPREAD

Mrs. Wigglesworth, Absecon, New Jersey

1 package (8 ounces) cream cheese, softened
1 tablespoon milk
3 tablespoons grated Parmesan cheese
1 tablespoon minced fresh parsley
1 tablespoon minced green onion
1 garlic clove, minced
1/2 teaspoon dried thyme
1/8 teaspoon pepper

In a bowl, beat cream cheese and milk until fluffy. Add Parmesan cheese, parsley, onion, garlic, thyme and pepper. Mix until well blended. Spoon into a small container. Cover and refrigerate at least 1 hour. Store in refrigerator. **Yield:** 1 cup.

OLD-TIME POPCORN BALLS

LaReine Stevens, Ypsilanti, Michigan

2 quarts popped popcorn
1/2 cup molasses
1/2 cup sugar
1/3 cup water
1 tablespoon vinegar
1 tablespoon butter *or* margarine

1/4 teaspoon baking soda

Place popcorn in a large bowl and set aside. In a heavy saucepan, combine molasses, sugar, water, vinegar and butter. Cook, *without stirring*, over medium heat until the mixture reaches 235° on a candy thermometer (soft-ball stage). Add baking soda and stir well. Remove from heat and immediately pour over popcorn, stirring gently with a wooden spoon until well coated. When cool enough to handle, quickly shape into 3-in. balls, dipping hands in cold water to prevent syrup from sticking. **Yield:** 6-8 servings.

> **AVOID "OLD MAIDS"!** Store popcorn in the refrigerator until just before you're ready to put it in the hot oil. You'll find that most all of the kernels will pop.

Quick & Easy

ORANGE COLADA

Dotty Egge, Pelican Rapids, Minnesota

1 can (6 ounces) frozen orange juice concentrate, thawed
6 ounces frozen *non-alcoholic* pina colada mix, thawed
1 cup milk
2 tablespoons lemon juice
1-1/2 cups crushed ice
Orange slices for garnish

In a blender container, combine first four ingredients. Cover and process on high for 30 seconds. Add ice and continue to blend until ice is liquefied. Serve immediately with an orange slice. **Yield:** 6 servings.

Quick & Easy

CALIFORNIA FRESH FRUIT DIP

Nancy Cutright, San Jose, California

✓ This tasty dish uses less sugar, salt and fat. Recipe includes *Diabetic Exchanges*.

1 cup plain low-fat yogurt
2 tablespoons honey
2 tablespoons lime juice
1 teaspoon grated lime peel
1/4 teaspoon ground ginger

In a small bowl, combine all ingredients. Serve with fresh fruit. Cover and refrigerate leftovers. **Yield:** about 1 cup. **Diabetic Exchanges:** One serving (2 tablespoons) equals 1/4 fruit, 1/4 skim milk; also, 33 calories, 22 mg sodium, 1 mg cholesterol, 7 gm carbohydrate, 2 gm protein, trace fat.

WELCOME FRIENDS and family into your home during
the holidays with this fabulous spread of homemade foods.
Everyone will love nibbling on the assortment of satisfying snacks and
oven-fresh baked goods. And a steaming hot mug of
cappuccino will warm any weary traveler!

HOLIDAY BUFFET.
Clockwise from the lower left: **Three-in-One Cheese Ball**
(recipe on page 14), **Praline Sundae Topping** (recipe on page 143),
Fruitcake Cookies (recipe on page 172), **Sugar 'n' Spice Nuts**
(recipe on page 14), **Coconut Fruitcake** (recipe on page 188),
Cappuccino Mix (recipe on page 14),
Sweet-and-Sour Mustard (recipe on page 146)
and **Cheery Cherry Loaf** (recipe on page 158).

SUGAR 'N' SPICE NUTS

Debbi Baker, Green Springs, Ohio

(PICTURED ON PAGE 13)

3 cups lightly salted mixed nuts
1 egg white
1 tablespoon orange juice
2/3 cup sugar
1 tablespoon grated orange peel
1 teaspoon ground cinnamon
1/2 teaspoon ground ginger
1/2 teaspoon ground allspice

Place nuts in a large bowl. In a small bowl, beat egg white and orange juice with a fork until foamy. Add sugar, orange peel, cinnamon, ginger and allspice; mix well. Pour over nuts and stir to coat. Spread into an ungreased 15-in. x 10-in. x 1-in. baking pan. Bake at 275°, stirring every 15 minutes, for 45-50 minutes or until nuts are crisp and lightly browned. Cool completely. Store in an airtight container. **Yield:** 4 cups.

Quick & Easy

CAPPUCCINO MIX

Susan Prillhart, Rockledge, Florida

(PICTURED ON PAGE 13)

1 cup instant coffee creamer
1 cup instant chocolate drink mix
2/3 cup instant coffee crystals
1/2 cup sugar
1/2 teaspoon ground cinnamon
1/4 teaspoon ground nutmeg

Combine all ingredients; mix well. Store in an airtight container. To prepare one serving, add 3 tablespoons mix to 6 ozs. hot water; stir well. **Yield:** 3 cups dry mix.

THREE-IN-ONE CHEESE BALL

Mary Anne Marston, Almonte, Ontario

(PICTURED ON PAGE 12)

1 package (8 ounces) cream cheese, softened
4 cups (16 ounces) shredded cheddar cheese, room temperature
2 tablespoons milk
2 tablespoons minced onion
2 tablespoons Worcestershire sauce
Coarsely cracked black pepper
1/2 cup (2 ounces) crumbled blue cheese
Minced fresh parsley
1/4 teaspoon garlic powder
Finely chopped pecans
Assorted crackers

In a mixing bowl, beat cream cheese, cheddar cheese, milk, onion and Worcestershire sauce until mix is fluffy. If a smoother spread is desired, process in a food processor until creamy. Divide into thirds (about 1 cup each). Shape first portion into a ball; roll in cracked pepper. Add the blue cheese to the second portion; mix well. Shape into a ball; roll in parsley. Add garlic powder to the remaining portion; mix well. Shape into a ball; roll in nuts. Cover and refrigerate. Let stand at room temperature 1 hour before serving time. Serve with crackers. **Yield:** 3 cheese balls.

Quick & Easy

CHILI CHEESE DIP

Jerrie West, Oakhurst, California

1 can (15 ounces) chili con carne without beans
1 pound process American cheese, cubed
1 can (4 ounces) chopped green chilies
Tortilla chips

Combine chili, cheese and green chilies in a saucepan or fondue pot. Heat over medium-low, stirring frequently, until the cheese melts. Serve warm with tortilla chips. **Yield:** 12 servings.

Quick & Easy

FIESTA APPETIZER

Clarice Schweitzer, Sun City, Arizona

(PICTURED ON PAGE 138)

1 can (16 ounces) refried beans
1 package (1-1/4 ounces) taco seasoning
3 ripe avocados
1 tablespoon lemon juice
1/4 cup sour cream
1 can (2-1/4 ounces) sliced ripe olives, drained
1 can (4 ounces) chopped green chilies, drained
2 medium tomatoes, chopped
6 green onions, sliced
1 cup (4 ounces) shredded cheddar cheese
Tortilla chips

Combine beans and taco seasoning. Spread mixture on a round 12-in. serving platter. Mash avocados with lemon juice. Spread over beans. Spread sour cream over avocado. Sprinkle olives, chilies, tomatoes, onions and cheese over sour cream. Serve with tortilla chips. **Yield:** 8-10 servings.

FIRESIDE CHEESE SPREAD

Debbie Jones, California, Maryland

1 container (16 ounces) cheddar cheese spread, softened
2 packages (one 8 ounces, one 3 ounces) cream cheese, softened
3 tablespoons butter *or* margarine, softened
1 teaspoon Worcestershire sauce
1/2 teaspoon garlic powder
Paprika
Snipped fresh parsley
Assorted crackers

In a medium bowl, combine cheese spread, cream cheese, butter, Worcestershire sauce and garlic powder. Blend thoroughly. Chill at least 3 hours or overnight. Sprinkle with paprika and parsley. Serve with crackers. **Yield:** about 3-1/2 cups.

ADD ZIP TO DIP. Try adding a tablespoon of horseradish to a favorite vegetable dip. For the best flavor, be sure to refrigerate the dip for 24 hours before serving.

Quick & Easy

HOT AND SPICY CRANBERRY DIP

Dorothy Pritchett, Wills Point, Texas

1 can (16 ounces) jellied cranberry sauce
2 to 3 tablespoons prepared horseradish
2 tablespoons honey
1 tablespoon Worcestershire sauce
1 tablespoon lemon juice
1 garlic clove, minced
1/4 to 1/2 teaspoon ground cayenne pepper
Pineapple chunks
Orange sections
Mini precooked sausages, warmed

In a medium saucepan, combine first seven ingredients. Bring to a boil. Reduce heat and simmer, covered, 5 minutes. Serve warm with pineapple, oranges and sausages. **Yield:** 2 cups.

Winter Lemonade

A father's surprise turned a cold winter night into a warm memory that's lasted a lifetime.

By Carl Gregory, Higgins Lake, Michigan

The snow is coming down hard outside, but inside, the fireplace is crackling. I grab the afghan off the couch and wrap up snug and warm.

I start to read a book, but soon my mind wanders…back to a day more than half a century ago. The memory is so clear I can almost reach out and touch it.

It was 7:30 in the evening, February 6. My father came into the house carrying a "chunk", a large piece of firewood so knotty it couldn't be split.

I was puzzled—chunks were good for at least 3 hours of heat, but we generally went to bed by 9.

We couldn't afford to waste fuel, or anything else for that matter. Pa and Ma had just invested all their savings in a little cafe in a village several miles away. We were sure the business would take off, once word got out about Ma's home cooking!

Ma had already moved to the village. Pa stayed behind to help Clem Miller

"*Then Pa headed to the woodshed and brought in a real surprise!*"

harvest ice and was promised a few weeks' work at the gravel pit after that. Once school let out, we'd both join Ma.

Maneuvering the chunk into the stove, Pa muttered, "Looks like another cold one tonight. This morning the dipper was frozen tight in the water pail."

Good Night for Popcorn

He looked out the window at the big snowflakes floating down, then reached into his pocket and handed me a nickel. "Run up to Tom Allen's and get us a nickel's worth of popcorn," he told me. "We'll pop some tonight."

I brought back at least 5 lbs. of ears. We shelled them and Pa started cooking. Before long, he had a large bowl filled with snow-white kernels and another batch on the stove.

"That's enough popcorn for a family reunion," I said. But Pa kept right on popping, saying we could warm up the leftovers later.

Soon we had *heaps* of popcorn. "There's enough here to last through Decoration Day!" I laughed.

Just then the door burst open, and in came four of my closest friends, yelling, "*Happy birthday!*"

The Best Birthday Ever

I was completely surprised. And I was even more surprised with what Pa did next—he went out to the woodshed and returned with a pailful of fresh *lemonade!*

Pa knew I loved lemonade, and lemonade in the middle of winter—when lemons were scarce and expensive—was an extra-special treat. No batch of lemonade ever tasted any better than it did that night.

Even though there were no presents, no cake and no candles, that birthday party was one of the most memorable events of my life. Huddled around the stove, we ate all the popcorn we wanted, drank lemonade and laughed the evening away.

When the party broke up about 11 o'clock, the chunk was still glowing. As Pa closed the draft on the old stove, he said to me with a smile, "Quite a night, wasn't it?"

"It certainly was!" I said.

And I still feel the same today when I think about that winter lemonade. It certainly was quite a night.

Ken Novak

SURPRISE PARTY over 50 years ago lingers in mind of reader, who still savors memories of popcorn and lemonade his dad once made.

SAVOR the flavor of asparagus year-round. Rich in protein, vitamins, minerals—and taste—this vegetable provides a nutritious and delicious accent to any meal. Just look where it's cropped up!

AMAZING ASPARAGUS!
Clockwise from the top: **Asparagus Strata** (recipe on page 61), **Asparagus Appetizer Spread** (recipe on page 17), **Dilly Asparagus** (recipe on page 126) and **Creamy Asparagus Chowder** (recipe on page 36).

ASPARAGUS APPETIZER SPREAD

Linda Stotts, Lowell, Ohio

(PICTURED AT LEFT)

1 pound fresh asparagus, trimmed
1-1/2 cups (12 ounces) sour cream, *divided*
1 package (8 ounces) cream cheese, softened
1 envelope unflavored gelatin
1 cup finely chopped cooked ham
1 tablespoon chopped chives
1/2 teaspoon seasoned salt
1/8 teaspoon black pepper
Assorted crackers

Cook asparagus in a small amount of water until tender. Drain, reserving 1/4 cup liquid. Cool. Puree asparagus until smooth. Add 1 cup sour cream and the cream cheese; blend well. In a saucepan, combine gelatin and reserved liquid; heat slowly until the gelatin is dissolved. Remove from the heat; stir in the asparagus mixture, ham, chives, salt and pepper. Pour into a greased 1-qt. round-bottom bowl. Cover and chill until set, about 6 hours. Unmold onto a plate and spread with reserved sour cream. Garnish with additional chopped ham and cooked asparagus if desired. Serve with crackers. **Yield:** 6-8 servings.

RHUBARB PUNCH

Eleanor Martens, Rosenort, Manitoba

3 quarts diced fresh *or* frozen rhubarb
4-1/2 cups sugar
3 quarts water
1 can (6 ounces) frozen orange juice concentrate, thawed
3 tablespoons lemon juice
Lemon-lime soda

In a heavy saucepan, bring rhubarb, sugar and water to a boil. Boil for 15 minutes; cool and strain. Stir in orange and lemon juices. Refrigerate until well chilled. To serve, combine 1/2 cup rhubarb syrup to 1 cup soda. **Yield:** 24 servings (12 ozs. each).

ORANGE LEMONADE

Wendy Masters, Grand Valley, Ontario

(PICTURED ON PAGE 223)

2-1/2 cups water
1-3/4 cups sugar

1-1/2 cups fresh lemon juice (about 8 lemons)
1-1/2 cups fresh orange juice (about 5 oranges)
2 tablespoons grated lemon peel
2 tablespoons grated orange peel
Water

In a medium saucepan, combine water and sugar. Cook over medium heat, stirring occasionally, until sugar dissolves. Cool. Add juices and peel to cooled sugar syrup. Cover and let stand at room temperature 1 hour. Strain syrup, cover and refrigerate. To serve, fill glasses or pitcher with equal amounts of fruit syrup and water. Add ice and serve. **Yield:** 12 servings.

Quick & Easy

SPICY CRANBERRY WARMER

Marlene Cartwright, Sierra City, California

(PICTURED ON PAGE 145)

3 whole cloves
2 cinnamon sticks
2 whole allspice
4 cups apple cider
1/3 cup packed brown sugar
4 cups cranberry juice
Additional cinnamon sticks, optional

Place first three ingredients in a double thickness of cheesecloth. Bring up corners of cloth and tie with a string. Place with cider in a large saucepan. (Or, if desired, place loose spices in saucepan and strain before serving.) Simmer, covered, for 5 minutes. Stir in sugar and simmer for 5 minutes. Add cranberry juice and heat to simmering temperature. Serve hot in mugs. Garnish with cinnamon sticks if desired. **Yield:** 8-10 servings.

Quick & Easy

COUNTRY CHEESE SNACKS

Sandy Thorn, Sonora, California

1 cup mayonnaise
1 cup grated Parmesan cheese
1 package (8 ounces) cream cheese, softened
2 green onions with tops, minced

Snack-size rye bread slices *or* toasted English muffins *or* bagels
Parsley sprigs
Stuffed green olives, sliced

In a small bowl, combine first four ingredients. Spread on bread; place on a baking sheet. Broil 4 in. from the heat until golden and bubbly, about 1-2 minutes. Garnish with parsley and olives. Serve immediately. **Yield:** 2 cups spread.

Quick & Easy

FRESH CRANBERRY PUNCH

Deanna House, Portage, Michigan

(PICTURED ON PAGE 66)

4 cups fresh *or* frozen cranberries
3-1/2 quarts water
12 whole cloves
4 sticks cinnamon (3 inches each)
3/4 cup orange juice
2/3 cup fresh lemon juice
2 cups sugar

In Dutch oven or large kettle, combine cranberries, water, cloves and cinnamon. Bring to boil; cover, reduce heat and simmer for 12-15 minutes. Strain cooked juice through fine sieve or cheese cloth, squeezing gently. To strained juice, add orange juice, lemon juice and sugar; stir until sugar dissolves. Serve piping hot. **Yield:** 25 1/2-cup servings.

CRACK THE CASE. Before cracking nuts, try soaking them in salt water overnight. The nut meats will easily come out whole instead of in pieces, making them more attractive for a variety of your favorite recipes.

Quick & Easy

SPICED PECANS

Brenda Schneider, Armington, Illinois

1/2 cup sugar
1 tablespoon ground cinnamon
1/2 teaspoon salt
1 egg white
1 pound large pecan halves

Combine sugar, cinnamon and salt in a small bowl; set aside. In a large mixing bowl, lightly beat egg white. Add pecans; stir until coated. Sprinkle sugar mixture over pecans; mix well. Spread in a single layer on a baking sheet. Bake at 300° for 20 minutes. Remove nuts from baking sheet while warm to cool on waxed paper. **Yield:** about 6 cups.

TREAT your family or drop-in guests to some good down-home cooking that's guaranteed to hit the spot. Emily's Bean Soup freezes well and makes a quick, convenient meal with hot Italian Beef Sandwiches. And don't forget to serve up healthy portions of California Pasta Salad.

COUNTRY CLASSICS.
Top to bottom: **Emily's Bean Soup**, **Italian Beef Sandwiches** (both recipes on page 19) and **California Pasta Salad** (recipe on page 46).

SOUPS & SANDWICHES

For a simply satisfying lunch or dinner, nothing can beat the classic combination of a savory soup and filling sandwich.

ITALIAN BEEF SANDWICHES

Marjorie Libby, Madison, Wisconsin

(PICTURED AT LEFT)

1 beef sirloin tip roast (4 to 5 pounds)
Water
1/2 teaspoon salt
2 to 3 onions, thinly sliced
1 teaspoon onion salt
1 teaspoon garlic salt
1 teaspoon dried oregano
2 teaspoons Italian seasoning
1 teaspoon seasoned salt
1 teaspoon dried basil
3 beef bouillon cubes
7 to 8 hot banana peppers, seeded and sliced
Hard rolls

In a deep baking pan, place roast and 1 in. of water. Sprinkle with salt and cover with onions. Cover and bake at 350° for 1-1/2 hours or until meat is tender. Remove meat from baking pan; reserve and chill broth. Refrigerate meat until firm. Cut into thin slices. Place in a 13-in. x 9-in. x 2-in. baking pan; set aside. Meanwhile, in a saucepan, combine broth with remaining ingredients except rolls. Bring to a boil; reduce heat and simmer 10 minutes. Pour over meat. Cover and refrigerate for 24 hours. To re-heat, cover and bake, at 325° for 1 hour. Serve on hard rolls. **Yield:** 20-24 sandwiches.

EMILY'S BEAN SOUP

Emily Chaney, Penobscot, Maine

(PICTURED AT LEFT)

1/2 cup *each* great northern beans, kidney beans, navy beans, lima beans, butter beans, split green *or* yellow peas, pinto beans and lentils
Water
1 ham bone
2 chicken bouillon cubes
1 can (28 ounces) tomatoes with liquid, quartered
1 can (6 ounces) tomato paste
1 large onion, chopped

3 celery ribs, chopped
4 carrots, sliced
2 garlic cloves, minced
1/4 cup dried chives
3 bay leaves
2 tablespoons dried parsley
1 teaspoon dried thyme
1 teaspoon dry mustard
1/2 teaspoon ground red *or* cayenne pepper

Wash all beans thoroughly; drain and place in a 4-qt. kettle with 5 cups of water. Bring to a rapid boil; boil 2 minutes. Remove from heat and let stand, covered, for 1 hour. Meanwhile, place ham bone and 3 qts. of water in an 8-qt. soup kettle. Simmer until beans have stood for 1 hour. Drain beans and add to the ham stock; add remaining ingredients. Simmer 2-3 hours or until beans are tender. Discard bone; add additional water if desired. **Yield:** about 5-1/2 quarts.

> **PEPPY PEPPER.** Cayenne pepper (added a pinch at a time!) adds zip to soup.

NEW ENGLAND FISH CHOWDER

Dorothy Noonan, Quincy, Massachusetts

(PICTURED ON PAGE 92)

1/2 cup butter *or* margarine, *divided*
3 medium onions, sliced
5 medium potatoes, peeled and diced
4 teaspoons salt
1/2 teaspoon pepper
3 cups boiling water
2 pounds fresh *or* frozen haddock fillets, cut into large chunks
1 quart milk, scalded
1 can (12 ounces) evaporated milk

In a 6- to 8-qt. kettle, melt 1/4 cup butter over medium heat. Saute onions until tender but not browned. Add potatoes, salt, pepper and water. Top with fish. Simmer, covered, 25 minutes or until potatoes are fork-tender. Stir in scalded milk, evaporated milk and remaining butter; heat through. Season with additional salt and pepper if desired. **Yield:** about 4-1/2 quarts.

BUTTERMILK BISCUIT SAUSAGE PINWHEELS

Gladys Ferguson, Rossville, Georgia

(PICTURED ON PAGE 90)

1/4 cup shortening
2 cups unsifted self-rising flour
1 cup buttermilk
1 pound raw bulk pork sausage, room temperature

With a pastry blender, cut shortening into flour. Add buttermilk; mix. On a lightly floured board, knead for a few seconds, adding additional flour if necessary. Roll out onto a lightly floured board into a 12-in. x 9-in. rectangle. Spread sausage over dough. Roll up, jelly-roll style, starting from the short side. Chill. Cut into 1/2-in. slices. Place, cut side down, on a lightly greased baking sheet. Bake at 425° for 25 minutes or until lightly browned. **Yield:** about 9 servings.

Quick & Easy

CAULIFLOWER CHEESE SOUP

Mrs. Dave Barba, Downers Grove, Illinois

1/4 cup water
2 tablespoons butter *or* margarine
1/2 cup shredded carrots
1/4 cup chopped onion
2 cans (10-3/4 ounces *each*) condensed cream of potato soup, undiluted
2 cups milk
1 can (7 ounces) whole kernel corn, drained
1 to 2 cups fresh *or* frozen cauliflower florets, cooked just until tender
1 cup (4 ounces) shredded cheddar cheese
1/2 cup shredded Provolone *or* mozzarella cheese
1/8 teaspoon pepper

In a saucepan, heat first four ingredients until carrots are tender. Stir in soup, milk, corn and cauliflower. Heat through. Just before serving, stir in the cheeses and pepper. Serve immediately. **Yield:** 6-8 servings.

ASPARAGUS LEEK SOUP

Anne Landers, Louisville, Kentucky

(PICTURED ON PAGE 189)

3 large leeks, sliced into 1/2-inch
  pieces
1 large onion, chopped
3 tablespoons butter *or*
  margarine
4 medium potatoes, peeled and
  diced
3 medium carrots, thinly sliced
1 teaspoon salt
2-1/2 quarts chicken broth
1/2 cup uncooked long grain rice
1 pound fresh asparagus, cut
  into 1-inch pieces
1/2 pound fresh spinach,
  chopped into 1/2-inch pieces
1/4 teaspoon pepper
1 cup heavy cream

In a saucepan, saute leeks and onion in butter until tender. Add the potatoes, carrots, salt, broth and rice. Cover and bring to a boil; reduce heat and simmer for 25 minutes. Stir in asparagus. Cover and simmer for 10 minutes or until vegetables are tender. Add spinach, pepper and cream; heat through. **Yield:** 12-16 servings (4-1/2 quarts).

TOUGH IT OUT. Don't toss out the tough ends of asparagus spears. Save them for soup. Just simmer until tender, puree in a blender or food processor and add to soup broth.

SNAPPY BARBECUE BEEF SANDWICHES

Patricia Throlson, Hawick, Minnesota

(PICTURED ON PAGE 98)

1 beef chuck roast (4 pounds)
4 cups chopped celery
2 cups water
1 cup chopped onion
1 cup ketchup
1 cup barbecue sauce
2 tablespoons vinegar
2 tablespoons brown sugar
2 tablespoons Worcestershire
  sauce
1 teaspoon chili powder
1 teaspoon garlic powder
1 teaspoon salt
Rolls *or* buns

Place beef in a Dutch oven. Combine all remaining ingredients except the rolls; pour over beef. Cover and bake at 350° for 5 hours, turning beef occasionally. Shred beef with a fork. Serve on rolls or buns. **Yield:** about 24 servings.

FAMILY will say, "Thanks!" when you turn holiday turkey into savory soup (recipe below).

TURKEY SOUP

Carol Brethauer, Denver, Colorado

(PICTURED ABOVE)

✓ This tasty dish uses less sugar, salt and fat. Recipe includes *Diabetic Exchanges*.

1 turkey carcass
3 quarts water
2 cans (10-1/2 ounces *each*)
  low-sodium chicken broth
1/2 cup uncooked long grain rice
1 medium onion, finely chopped
4 celery ribs, finely chopped
2 carrots, grated
1 bay leaf
Dash poultry seasoning
Salt, optional
Pepper
Onion powder
Garlic powder

Place turkey carcass, water and broth in a large soup kettle. Simmer over low heat for 4-5 hours. Remove carcass from stock. Remove any meat and dice. Return to stock along with rice, onion, celery, carrots, bay leaf and poultry seasoning. Add remaining seasonings to taste. Simmer over medium-low heat until the rice is cooked. **Yield:** 8 servings (3 quarts). **Diabetic Exchanges:** One serving (prepared without salt; turkey meat estimated at 1 oz.) equals 1 lean meat, 1/2 starch; also, 95 calories, 54 mg sodium, 21 mg cholesterol, 9 gm carbohydrate, 10 gm protein, 2 gm fat.

CABBAGE AND BEEF SOUP

Ethel Ledbetter, Canton, North Carolina

1 pound lean ground beef
1/2 teaspoon garlic salt
1/4 teaspoon garlic powder
1/4 teaspoon pepper
2 celery ribs, chopped
1 can (16 ounces) kidney
  beans, undrained
1/2 medium head cabbage,
  chopped
1 can (28 ounces) tomatoes,
  chopped and liquid reserved
1 tomato can water
4 beef bouillon cubes
Chopped fresh parsley

In a Dutch oven, brown beef. Add all remaining ingredients except parsley; bring to a boil. Reduce heat and simmer, covered, for 1 hour. Garnish with parsley. **Yield:** 3 quarts.

POTATO SOUP WITH SPINACH DUMPLINGS

Rosemary Flexman, Waukesha, Wisconsin

(PICTURED ON PAGE 153)

2 cups cubed peeled potatoes
1/2 cup chopped onion
1/2 cup chopped sweet red pepper
2 tablespoons butter *or*
  margarine
3 cans (14-1/2 ounces *each*)
  chicken broth
1 package (10 ounces) frozen
  chopped spinach, thawed
1 cup seasoned dry bread
  crumbs
1 egg white, lightly beaten
Chopped fresh parsley

In a large saucepan, combine potatoes, onion, red pepper, butter and chicken broth; bring to a boil. Reduce heat; cover and simmer about 10 minutes or until the potatoes are tender. Remove from the heat. In a small bowl, combine the spinach, bread crumbs and egg white; let stand for 15 minutes. Shape into 1-in. balls; add to soup. Return to a boil; reduce heat and simmer 10-15 minutes or until dumplings are firm. Sprinkle with parsley. **Yield:** 4 servings.

Quick & Easy

CREAM OF VEGETABLE SOUP

Mary Parker, Copperas Cove, Texas

(PICTURED ON PAGE 52)

1 medium onion, chopped
3/4 cup butter *or* margarine
1/2 cup all-purpose flour
3 cans (10-1/2 ounces *each*)
  condensed chicken broth *or*
4 cups chicken broth
2 cups milk
2 cups light cream
1 teaspoon dried basil
1/2 teaspoon salt

1/2 teaspoon pepper
1/4 teaspoon garlic powder
5 cups chopped cooked mixed vegetables (such as broccoli, carrots and cauliflower)

In a large kettle or Dutch oven, saute onion in butter until tender. Add flour; cook and stir until bubbly. Gradually add chicken broth; cook and stir until thickened, about 5 minutes. Stir in the milk, cream, basil, salt, pepper and garlic powder. Add the vegetables; cook gently until heated through. **Yield:** 8-10 servings (about 3 quarts).

Quick & Easy

CALIFORNIA CHEESE SOUP

Darla Dockter, Fargo, North Dakota

1 quart water
2 chicken bouillon cubes
2-1/2 cups diced peeled potatoes
1 cup diced carrots
1 cup diced celery
1/2 cup diced onion
1 bag (16 ounces) frozen California Blend vegetables
2 cans (10-3/4 ounces *each*) condensed cream of chicken soup, undiluted
1 pound process American cheese, cut into cubes

Bring water to a boil in a large kettle; add next six ingredients. Reduce heat and simmer, covered, until all vegetables are tender, about 30 minutes. Stir in soup and cheese; cook until soup is heated through and the cheese is melted. **Yield:** 10-12 servings (3 quarts).

Quick & Easy

HEARTY CHICKEN BROCCOLI SOUP

Frankie Marie Gingrich, Palmyra, Pennsylvania

1/4 cup butter *or* margarine
1/2 cup chopped onion
1/2 cup chopped celery
3 tablespoons all-purpose flour
1 tablespoon dry mustard
1/2 teaspoon salt
1/4 teaspoon pepper
3 cups milk
2 teaspoons lemon juice
1-1/2 cups diced cooked chicken
2 packages (10 ounces *each*) cut broccoli in cheese sauce, thawed and chopped
Seasoned croutons, optional

In a large saucepan, melt butter over medium heat. Saute onion and celery until crisp-tender. Stir in flour, mustard, salt and pepper. Cook until mixture is smooth and bubbly. Gradually add milk;

cook and stir until mixture boils and thickens. Stir in the lemon juice, chicken and broccoli. Simmer, stirring occasionally, until heated through. Top with croutons if desired. **Yield:** 6-8 servings.

HARVEST CORN CHOWDER

Carolyn Lough, Medley, Alberta

1 medium onion, chopped
1 tablespoon butter *or* margarine
2 cans (14-1/2 ounces *each*) cream-style corn
4 cups whole kernel corn
4 cups diced peeled potatoes
1 can (10-3/4 ounces) condensed cream of mushroom soup, undiluted
1 jar (6 ounces) sliced mushrooms, drained
3 cups milk
1/2 medium green pepper, chopped
1/2 to 1 medium sweet red pepper, chopped
Pepper to taste
1/2 pound bacon, cooked and crumbled

In a saucepan, saute onion in butter until tender. Add cream-style corn, kernel corn, potatoes, soup and mushrooms. Stir in milk. Add green and red peppers. Season with pepper. Simmer for 30 minutes or until vegetables are tender. Garnish with bacon. **Yield:** about 12 servings (3-1/2 quarts).

CHICKEN NOODLE SOUP

Diane Edgecomb, Humboldt, South Dakota

1 stewing chicken (2 to 3 pounds)
2-1/2 quarts water
3 teaspoons salt
2 chicken bouillon cubes
1/2 medium onion, chopped
1/8 teaspoon pepper
1/4 teaspoon dried marjoram
1/4 teaspoon dried thyme
1 bay leaf
1 cup diced carrots
1 cup diced celery
1-1/2 cups uncooked fine noodles

In a large soup kettle, place chicken and all ingredients except noodles. Cover and bring to a boil; skim broth. Reduce heat; cover and simmer 1-1/2 hours or until chicken is tender. Re-

move chicken from broth; allow to cool. Debone chicken and cut into chunks. Skim fat from broth; bring to a boil. Add noodles; cook until noodles are done. Return chicken to kettle; adjust seasonings to taste. Remove bay leaf before serving. **Yield:** 8-10 servings.

CONFETTI CHOWDER

Rose Bomba, Lisbon, New Hampshire

3 tablespoons butter *or* margarine
1 cup diced carrots
1 cup diced zucchini
1 cup broccoli florets
1/2 cup chopped onion
1/2 cup chopped celery
1/4 cup all-purpose flour
1/2 teaspoon salt
1/2 teaspoon pepper
1/4 teaspoon sugar
3 cups milk
1 cup chicken broth
1 cup whole kernel corn
1 cup diced fully cooked ham
1/2 cup peas
1 jar (2 ounces) sliced pimientos, drained
1 cup (4 ounces) shredded cheddar cheese

Melt butter in a Dutch oven. Add carrots, zucchini, broccoli, onion and celery; cook and stir for about 5 minutes or until crisp-tender. Sprinkle flour, salt, pepper and sugar over vegetables; mix well. Stir in milk and chicken broth; cook and stir until thickened and bubbly. Add corn, ham, peas and pimientos; cook and stir until heated through. Remove from the heat; add cheese and stir until melted. Serve hot. **Yield:** 6-8 servings (2 quarts).

Quick & Easy

CHICKEN SALAD ON BUNS

Mary Jo Vander West, Grant, Michigan

2 cups diced leftover cooked chicken
1/4 pound process American cheese, diced
1 to 2 tablespoons pickle relish
1/4 cup salad dressing *or* mayonnaise
2 tablespoons chopped onion
2 tablespoons chopped green pepper
Kaiser rolls

In a bowl, combine first six ingredients; mix well. Spoon about 1/3 cup onto each roll. Wrap each tightly in foil. Bake at 300° for 20-30 minutes or until heated through. **Yield:** 6-8 servings.

SOUP is such a versatile menu item...from light first courses to hearty main meals. Hungarian Goulash and Chicken Barley Soups are so delicious, you'll want to share them with friends. For a quick yet satisfying meal, try Cheesy Vegetable Soup. And Fresh Fruit Soup is a great cool-down after spicy Mexican food.

SOUP'S ON!
Clockwise from the top: **Hungarian Goulash Soup**, **Cheesy Vegetable Soup**, **Fresh Fruit Soup** and **Chicken Barley Soup** (all recipes on page 23).

CHICKEN BARLEY SOUP

Diana Costello, Marion, Kansas

(PICTURED AT LEFT)

✓ This tasty dish uses less sugar, salt and fat. Recipe includes *Diabetic Exchanges*.

- 1 broiler-fryer chicken (2 to 3 pounds), cut up
- 2 quarts water
- 1-1/2 cups diced carrots
- 1 cup diced celery
- 1/2 cup barley
- 1/2 cup chopped onion
- 1 chicken bouillon cube, optional
- 1 teaspoon salt, optional
- 1 bay leaf
- 1/2 teaspoon poultry seasoning
- 1/2 teaspoon pepper
- 1/2 teaspoon dried sage

In a large kettle, cook chicken in water until tender. Cool broth and skim off fat. Bone the chicken and cut into bite-size pieces; return to kettle along with remaining ingredients. Simmer, covered, for at least 1 hour or until vegetables and barley are tender. Remove bay leaf. **Yield:** 5 servings (about 1-1/2 quarts). **Diabetic Exchanges:** One serving (prepared without bouillon and salt) equals 2-1/2 lean meat, 1 starch, 1 vegetable; also, 259 calories, 127 mg sodium, 89 mg cholesterol, 22 gm carbohydrate, 31 gm protein, 5 gm fat.

CHEESY VEGETABLE SOUP

Amy Sibra, Big Sandy, Montana

(PICTURED AT LEFT)

- 3 tablespoons butter *or* margarine
- 3 tablespoons all-purpose flour
- 2 cans (14-1/2 ounces *each*) chicken broth
- 2 cups coarsely chopped broccoli
- 3/4 cup chopped carrots
- 1/2 cup chopped celery
- 1 small onion, chopped
- 1/2 teaspoon salt
- 1/4 teaspoon garlic powder
- 1/4 teaspoon dried thyme
- 1 egg yolk
- 1 cup heavy cream
- 1-1/2 cups (6 ounces) shredded Swiss cheese

Melt butter in a heavy 4-qt. saucepan; add flour. Cook and stir until thick and bubbly; remove from the heat. Gradually blend in broth. Add next seven ingredients; return to the heat and bring to a boil. Reduce heat; cover and simmer for 20 minutes or until vegetables

are tender. In a small bowl, blend egg yolk and cream. Gradually blend in several tablespoonfuls of hot soup; return all to saucepan, stirring until slightly thickened. Simmer for another 15-20 minutes. Stir in cheese and heat over medium heat until melted. **Yield:** 8-10 servings (2-1/2 quarts).

HUNGARIAN GOULASH SOUP

Betty Kennedy, Alexandria, Virginia

(PICTURED AT LEFT)

- 3 bacon strips, diced
- 1 small green pepper, seeded and chopped
- 2 medium onions, chopped
- 1 large garlic clove, minced
- 1-1/2 pounds beef stew meat, cut into 1/2-inch cubes
- 2 tablespoons paprika
- 1-1/2 teaspoons salt
- Pepper to taste
- Dash sugar
- 1 can (14-1/2 ounces) stewed tomatoes, chopped
- 3 cups beef broth
- 2 large potatoes, peeled and diced
- 1/2 cup sour cream, optional

In a large kettle, cook bacon until almost crisp. Add green pepper, onions and garlic; cook until tender. Add beef cubes and brown on all sides. Sprinkle with paprika, salt, pepper and sugar; stir and cook for 2 minutes. Add tomatoes and broth. Cover and simmer for about 1-1/2 hours or until beef is tender. About 1/2 hour before serving, add the potatoes and cook until tender. Garnish each serving with a dollop of sour cream if desired. **Yield:** 8 servings (about 2 quarts).

COOL DOWN. Try a pinch of Hungarian paprika for soup-eaters who don't like "hot" seasonings. It adds flavor and color—without turning up the heat!

FRESH FRUIT SOUP

Jenny Sampson, Layton, Utah

(PICTURED AT LEFT)

- 1 can (12 ounces) frozen orange juice concentrate, thawed
- 1-1/2 cups sugar
- 1 cinnamon stick (2 inches)
- 6 whole cloves
- 1/4 cup cornstarch
- 2 tablespoons lemon juice
- 2 cups sliced fresh strawberries

- 2 bananas, sliced
- 2 cups halved green grapes

In a large saucepan, mix orange juice with water according to package directions. Remove 1/2 cup of juice; set aside. Add sugar, cinnamon stick and cloves to saucepan; bring to a boil. Reduce heat and simmer for 5 minutes. Blend cornstarch and reserved orange juice to form a smooth paste; stir into pan. Bring to a boil; cook and stir until thickened, about 2 minutes more. Remove from the heat and stir in lemon juice. Pour into a large bowl; cover and chill. Just before serving, remove the spices and stir in fruit. **Yield:** 8-10 servings (about 2-1/2 quarts).

KENTUCKY CHILI

Tina Sullivan, Corinth, Kentucky

- 1-1/2 pounds ground beef
- 1 medium onion, chopped
- 2 cans (32 ounces *each*) tomato juice
- 1 cup water
- 1 can (15 ounces) chili beans, undrained
- 1 tablespoon chili powder
- 1 teaspoon salt
- 1/2 teaspoon pepper
- 8 ounces uncooked spaghetti, broken in half

In a skillet, brown ground beef and onion; drain and set aside. In a large kettle, combine the tomato juice, water, chili beans, chili powder, salt and pepper. Bring to a boil; reduce heat and simmer 10-15 minutes. Stir in beef mixture; simmer an additional 10 minutes. Meanwhile, cook spaghetti according to package directions. Drain and stir into chili. **Yield:** 10-12 servings (3 quarts).

CHILLED RHUBARB SOUP

Laurel Anderson, Pinole, California

- 1 pint fresh strawberries, sliced
- 3 cups sliced fresh *or* frozen rhubarb (1/2-inch pieces)
- 1-1/4 cups orange juice
- 1/2 to 1 cup sugar
- Sliced oranges, kiwifruit *and/or* additional strawberries, optional

In a 3-qt. saucepan, bring strawberries, rhubarb and orange juice to a boil. Reduce heat; cover and simmer for 10 minutes. Remove from heat; stir in sugar to taste. In a blender or food processor, blend half the fruit mixture at a time until smooth. Chill. To serve, spoon into soup bowls and, if desired, garnish with oranges, kiwi and/or strawberries. **Yield:** about 1 quart.

EASY CHERRY FRUIT SOUP

Virginia Shellum, Nicollet, Minnesota

(PICTURED ON PAGE 231)

1 can (21 ounces) cherry
  pie filling
1 can (8 ounces) pineapple
  chunks in natural juices,
  undrained
2 cups water
2/3 cup chopped dried apricots
1 cup pitted prunes
1 tablespoon butter *or* margarine
2 lemon slices
1 teaspoon quick-cooking
  tapioca

In a 3-qt. casserole, combine all ingredients. Cover and bake at 325° for 1 hour. Serve warm. **Yield:** 6-8 servings.

Quick & Easy

PRONTO BEEF VEGETABLE SOUP

Dottie Casale, Ilion, New York

(PICTURED BELOW)

3 cups cubed cooked roast beef
1 cup diced carrots
1 cup diced peeled potatoes
1 cup corn
1 cup cut green beans
1/2 cup chopped onion
1 quart tomato sauce
1/2 teaspoon salt
1 teaspoon dried basil
1 teaspoon dried oregano
1 tablespoon chopped fresh
  parsley

In a large saucepan, combine all ingredients. Bring to a boil; reduce heat and simmer 30 minutes or until vegetables are tender. If necessary, add 1/2 to 1 cup water to thin soup. **Yield:** 6-8 servings.

Quick & Easy

TACOED EGGS

Mary Smith, Huntington, Indiana

(PICTURED ON PAGE 53)

8 eggs, beaten
1/2 cup shredded cheddar cheese
2 tablespoons finely chopped
  onion
2 tablespoons finely chopped
  green pepper
1 to 4 drops hot pepper sauce
1/2 cup cooked taco-seasoned
  ground beef
Flour tortillas, warmed, optional
Salsa, optional

In a bowl, combine eggs, cheese, onion, green pepper and hot pepper sauce. Cook and stir in a nonstick skillet until eggs begin to set. Add taco meat; cook until eggs are completely set. If desired, spoon onto a warmed tortilla and roll up; top with salsa. **Yield:** 4 servings.

ENGLISH PASTIES

Margaret Johnson, Yale, Michigan

PASTRY:
1-1/2 cups all-purpose flour
1/4 teaspoon salt
1/2 cup shortening
1/4 cup cold water *or* milk
FILLING:
1/2 pound boneless beef sirloin,
  cubed
1/4 pound boneless pork steak,
  cubed
2 medium potatoes, peeled and
  cubed
1 small onion, chopped
1/2 teaspoon salt
1/4 teaspoon pepper
1 tablespoon butter
1 egg, beaten, optional
2 teaspoons water

Combine flour and salt. Cut in shortening. Add enough water or milk to moisten dry ingredients. Shape into a ball. Cover and set aside. For filling, toss together beef, pork, potatoes, onion, salt and pepper. Divide the pastry in half and roll each into a 10-in. circle. Divide the filling over the center of each pastry; dot each with 1/2 tablespoon butter. Fold pastry over the filling, sealing edges tightly. Cut slits in the top of the pasties. If desired, brush tops with egg. Place on a greased baking sheet. Bake at 400° for 45 minutes. Spoon 1 teaspoon water per pasty in slits. Reduce heat to 350°; bake 15 minutes longer or until golden. **Yield:** 4 servings.

COMPANY ONION SOUP

Rose Marie Moore, Walla Walla, Washington

(PICTURED ON PAGE 97)

4 tablespoons unsalted butter
4 large sweet *or* Walla Walla
  onions, sliced
1 tablespoon sugar
6 cups beef broth, *divided*
2 tablespoons Worcestershire
  sauce
Salt and pepper to taste
4 thick slices French bread
Additional unsalted butter
Garlic salt *or* 1 garlic clove, halved
1 cup (4 ounces) shredded
  Gruyere *or* Swiss cheese

In a Dutch oven, melt butter over medium heat. Saute onions until tender. Sprinkle sugar over onions. Reduce heat and cook, stirring occasionally, until onions are caramelized, about 20 minutes. Add 3 cups broth; simmer 15 minutes. Add remaining broth, Worcestershire sauce, salt and pepper. Cover and simmer for 30-40 minutes. Meanwhile, spread both sides of the bread with additional butter; sprinkle with garlic salt or rub with the cut-side of garlic clove. Broil bread until golden brown, then turn and brown other side. Ladle soup into individual ovenproof soup bowls. Float a slice of bread in each bowl and sprinkle with cheese. Broil until cheese is melted and bubbly. Serve immediately. **Yield:** 4 servings.

STEAK SOUP

Mary Dice, Chemainus, British Columbia

(PICTURED ON PAGE 99)

 This tasty dish uses less sugar, salt and fat. Recipe includes *Diabetic Exchanges*.

2 tablespoons butter *or*
  margarine
2 tablespoons cooking oil
1-1/2 to 2 pounds lean round steak,
  cut into 1/2-inch cubes
1/4 cup chopped onion
3 tablespoons all-purpose flour

BOWL OVER family, friends with speedy soup (recipe above)—it's done beef-ore you know it!

1 tablespoon paprika
1 teaspoon salt, optional
1/4 teaspoon pepper
4 cups beef stock *or* broth
2 cups water
1 bay leaf
4 sprigs fresh parsley, chopped
2 sprigs celery leaves, chopped
1/2 teaspoon dried marjoram
1-1/2 cups cubed peeled potatoes
1-1/2 cups sliced carrots
1-1/2 cups chopped celery
1 can (6 ounces) tomato paste

In a Dutch oven, melt butter over medium heat; add oil. Brown beef and onion. Combine flour, paprika, salt and pepper; sprinkle over beef and mix well. Stir in stock and water. Add bay leaf, parsley, celery leaves and marjoram. Bring to a boil; reduce heat and simmer, covered, about 1 hour or until tender. Add potatoes, carrots and celery. Simmer, covered, for 30-45 minutes or until vegetables are tender and soup begins to thicken. Stir in tomato paste; simmer, uncovered, 15 minutes. Remove bay leaf before serving. **Yield:** 6 servings. **Diabetic Exchanges:** One serving (without added salt) equals 3-1/2 meat, 1 starch, 1 vegetable; also, 347 calories, 682 mg sodium, 93 mg cholesterol, 17 gm carbohydrate, 33 gm protein, 16 gm fat.

BASQUE VEGETABLE SOUP
Norman Chegwyn, Richmond, California

3/4 pound Polish sausage, sliced
1 broiler-fryer chicken
   (2 to 3 pounds)
8 cups water
2 leeks, sliced
2 carrots, sliced
1 large turnip, peeled and
   cubed
1 large onion, chopped
1 large potato, peeled and
   cubed
1 garlic clove, minced
1-1/2 teaspoons salt
1/2 teaspoon pepper
1 tablespoon snipped fresh
   parsley
1 teaspoon dried thyme
1 cup shredded cabbage
2 cups cooked navy *or* great
   northern beans

In a skillet, cook the sausage until done. Drain on paper towels; set aside. In a large Dutch oven, cook chicken in water until tender. Remove chicken; let cool. Strain broth and skim off fat. Return broth to Dutch oven. Add leeks, carrots, turnip, onion, potato, garlic, salt, pepper, parsley and thyme. Bring to a boil. Reduce heat; cover and simmer for 30 minutes. Meanwhile, remove chicken from bones and cut into bite-size pieces; add to the Dutch oven. Add cabbage, beans and cooked sausage. Simmer, uncovered, for about 30 minutes or until vegetables are tender. **Yield:** 10-12 servings.

LEFTOVER MASHED POTATOES make delicious and easy potato soup. Just simmer some chopped onion and celery in a little water until tender. Then add leftover mashed potatoes, milk and salt and pepper to taste. Minced parsley—or a shake of Parmesan cheese—adds a nice touch.

GARDEN HARVEST CHILI
Judy Sloter, Charles City, Iowa
(PICTURED ON PAGE 132)

 This tasty dish uses less sugar, salt and fat. Recipe includes *Diabetic Exchanges*.

2 tablespoons cooking oil
2 garlic cloves, minced
1 medium green pepper,
   chopped
1 medium sweet red pepper,
   chopped
1-1/2 cups sliced fresh mushrooms
1/2 cup chopped onion
1 can (28 ounces) whole
   tomatoes, cut up, undrained
1 can (15 ounces) tomato sauce
2 tablespoons chili powder
2 teaspoons sugar
1 teaspoon ground cumin
1 can (16 ounces) kidney beans,
   rinsed and drained
2 cups sliced zucchini
1 package (10 ounces) frozen
   sweet corn, defrosted
1-1/2 cups (6 ounces) shredded
   cheddar cheese, optional

In a skillet, heat oil over medium-high heat. Saute garlic, peppers, mushrooms and onion until tender. Add tomatoes with liquid, tomato sauce, chili powder, sugar and cumin; heat to boiling. Reduce heat to low; add beans, zucchini and corn. Simmer, uncovered, about 10 minutes or until zucchini is tender. Spoon into bowls; sprinkle with cheese if desired. **Yield:** 6 servings (2-1/2 quarts). **Diabetic Exchanges:** One serving (prepared with low-salt tomato sauce and no cheese) equals 2 starch, 2 vegetable, 1 fat; also, 252 calories, 675 mg sodium, 0 mg cholesterol, 44 gm carbohydrate, 10 gm protein, 7 gm fat.

DANISH POTATO SOUP
Sandra Halter, Akron, Ohio

1 ham bone
Water
2 potatoes, peeled and diced
6 green onions, sliced
3 celery ribs, chopped
1/4 cup minced fresh parsley
2 cups chopped cabbage
2 carrots, diced
3 tablespoons all-purpose flour
1 cup light cream
Ground nutmeg

In a soup kettle, bring ham bone and 2 quarts water to a boil. Reduce heat and simmer 1 hour or until meat pulls away from the bone. Remove ham bone. When cool enough to handle, trim any meat and dice. Discard bone. Return ham to kettle along with potatoes, onions, celery, parsley, cabbage and carrots; cook 40 minutes. In a small bowl, combine flour and 1/4 cup cold water. Slowly pour into the soup, stirring constantly. Bring soup to a boil; cook 2 minutes. Reduce heat; stir in cream. Remove from the heat. Sprinkle a dash of nutmeg on each bowlful just before serving. **Yield:** 6 servings.

Quick & Easy

BLACK-EYED PEA CHOWDER
Brenda Bates, Mesquite, Texas
(PICTURED ON PAGE 138)

1 pound bacon
1 cup chopped celery
1 cup chopped onion
1 cup chopped green pepper
2 cans (16 ounces *each*) black-
   eyed peas, rinsed and drained
1 can (10-1/2 ounces) beef
   consomme
2 cans (14-1/2 ounces *each*)
   stewed tomatoes

In a saucepan, cook bacon until crisp. Remove bacon; crumble and set aside. Discard all but 2 tablespoons of drippings; saute celery, onion and green pepper until tender. Add bacon and all remaining ingredients; heat through. **Yield:** 2-1/4 quarts.

SOUP AND LOVE. Sometimes it's not what's in the soup that makes it so special, but who you're with when sharing a bowl.

Cousin Flora's Secret Recipe

The soup held the magic of this little girl's lunches with her cousin.

By Linda Batt, Sandy Hook, Connecticut

TWO OR THREE times every year, Mom, Dad and I would set off for York, Pennsylvania to visit my father's Cousin Flora and Great-Aunt Lucy.

Aunt Lucy was chronically ill and had to remain in bed, so Cousin Flora took loving care of her.

When we arrived at the house, Mom and Dad would climb the stairs to the hush of Aunt Lucy's room. Meanwhile, Flora took me to the kitchen. This warm pleasant room was where Flora spent most of her time. Unlike the dim parlors and gloomy hallways in the rest of the house, the kitchen was bright and cheery, with old-fashioned wooden cabinets painted yellow to match the walls.

At lunchtime, Mom and Dad ate upstairs with Aunt Lucy. Flora stayed in the kitchen to make some of her special chicken soup just for me.

Bowlful of Wonder

I loved her soup. Flora always told me she made it with small noodle "wonders" and crisp corn "surprises".

We'd dip out steaming bowls, get a package of saltine crackers from one of the high kitchen cabinets and take them to our places.

The table was covered with oil-cloth, so a little girl's spills weren't a concern. I'd put my crackers in my soup and let them sit for a while to get soggy before slurping them up. Flora didn't complain about my table manners.

In fact, while we enjoyed our lunch together, Flora never corrected me. Many adults said things to me like "stop talking and eat" or "children should be seen and not heard". Cousin Flora never said those things.

Childhood Confidant

Instead, she told me about a pet dog she had when she was young, or about how the old black car she owned would groan when she started it to drive to the market. Then she would make me laugh by imitating the funny way the milkman twirled his mustache!

I told her about my cherry business and how I picked the fruit from a tree at a deserted farm. I explained that I sold the sour fruit door-to-door in wooden quart containers.

I showed her pictures of my cat and told her about my childhood nemesis, Dennis Mitchel. I didn't explain how he tried to steal a kiss from me, but only that he had freckles.

Those lunches were special times for me, and Flora's special soup seemed like a magic potion. Every time I visited Flora, I'd ask for her recipe.

"It's a secret," she'd say. "I'll tell you when you're older."

Shortly before I turned 16, Flora passed away. Among her personal belongings was an envelope addressed to me. Inside was the recipe for the soup, written in Flora's own distinctive hand: *Just cook a box of Lipton Chicken Noodle Soup and add a package of frozen corn when it reaches a boil.*

Beneath the recipe, that wise woman added these words: *The secret to making something special is adding together the ordinary.*

REUBEN LOAF

Armetta Keeney, Carlisle, Iowa

3-1/4 to 3-3/4 cups all-purpose flour
1 package (1/4 ounce) active dry yeast
1 tablespoon sugar
1 tablespoon butter *or* margarine, softened
1 teaspoon salt
1 cup warm water (120° to 130°)
1/4 cup Thousand Island salad dressing
6 ounces thinly sliced corned beef
4 ounces sliced Swiss cheese
1 can (8 ounces) sauerkraut, drained
1 egg white, beaten
Poppy seeds

In a mixing bowl, combine 2-1/4 cups flour, yeast, sugar, butter and salt. Stir in warm water and mix until a soft dough forms. Add remaining flour if necessary. Turn out onto a lightly floured surface; knead until smooth, about 4 minutes. On a lightly greased baking sheet, roll dough to a 14-in. x 10-in. rectangle. Spread dressing down the middle of one half of dough, leaving a 3/4-in. space along edges. Top with layers of beef, cheese and sauerkraut. Fold the remaining half of dough over the meat mixture. Pinch edges together to seal. Cut small slits in the dough to vent steam. Cover and let rise in a warm place for 15 minutes. Brush with egg white and sprinkle with poppy seeds. Bake at 400° for 25 minutes or until lightly browned. Serve immediately; refrigerate leftovers. **Yield:** 6-8 servings.

SHAKER BEAN SOUP

Deborah Amrine, Grand Haven, Michigan

(PICTURED ON PAGE 113)

1 pound dry great northern beans
Water
1 meaty ham bone *or* 2 smoked ham hocks
1 large onion, chopped
3 celery ribs, diced
2 carrots, shredded
Salt to taste
1/2 teaspoon pepper
1/2 teaspoon dried thyme
1 can (28 ounces) crushed tomatoes in puree
2 tablespoons brown sugar
1-1/2 cups finely shredded fresh spinach leaves

Sort and rinse beans. Place in a Dutch oven or soup kettle; cover with water and bring to a boil. Boil 2 minutes. Remove from the heat; let stand 1 hour.

Drain beans and discard liquid. In the same kettle, place ham bone or hocks, 3 qts. water and beans. Bring to a boil; reduce heat and simmer, covered, 1-1/2 hours or until meat easily falls from the bone. Remove bones from broth and, when cool enough to handle, trim meat. Discard bones. Add ham, onion, celery, carrots, salt, pepper and thyme. Simmer, covered, 1 hour or until beans are tender. Add tomatoes and brown sugar. Cook for 10 minutes. Just before serving, add spinach. **Yield:** 5 quarts.

BEEF AND BARLEY SOUP

Phyllis Utterback, Glendale, California

(PICTURED ON PAGE 70)

1 tablespoon cooking oil
2 pounds beef short ribs
2 medium onions, coarsely chopped
3 large carrots, sliced
3 celery ribs, sliced
1 can (28 ounces) whole tomatoes with liquid, chopped
2 quarts water
4 chicken bouillon cubes
1/3 cup medium pearl barley

In a large Dutch oven or kettle, heat oil over medium-high. Brown beef. Add onions, carrots, celery, tomatoes, water and bouillon; bring to a boil. Cover and simmer for about 2 hours or until beef is tender. Add barley; simmer another 50-60 minutes or until the barley is done. **Yield:** 10-12 servings (3-1/2 quarts).

SOUTHWESTERN CHICKEN SOUP

Joe Greenough, Bedford, Texas

✓ This tasty dish uses less sugar, salt and fat. Recipe includes *Diabetic Exchanges.*

1 can (10-1/2 ounces) condensed beef broth
1 can (12 ounces) tomato paste
1 can (15-1/2 ounces) kidney beans, rinsed and drained
1 can (11 ounces) Mexicorn, drained
1-1/2 cups diced cooked chicken
3 green onions, sliced
2 to 3 tablespoons chili powder
1 can (4 ounces) chopped green chilies
1-2/3 cups water

In a large saucepan, combine beef broth and tomato paste. Add remaining ingredients. Cover and simmer for 20 minutes. **Yield:** 6 servings. **Diabetic Exchanges:** One serving (prepared with low-sodium beef broth and salt-free tomato paste) equals 1-1/2 starch, 1-1/2 lean meat, 1

vegetable; also, 224 calories, 631 mg sodium, 21 mg cholesterol, 32 gm carbohydrate, 20 gm protein, 3 gm fat.

FALAFELS

Jodi Sykes, Lake Worth, Florida

2 cans (15 ounces *each*) garbanzo beans, rinsed and drained
1 cup fresh bean sprouts
1/4 cup hulled sunflower seeds
1/4 cup dry bread crumbs
1 egg
1/2 teaspoon garlic powder
1/4 teaspoon salt
1/4 teaspoon pepper
2 tablespoons soy sauce
2 tablespoons Worcestershire sauce
3 green onions, minced, *divided*
2 tablespoons cooking oil
2 cups (16 ounces) plain yogurt
1 tablespoon fresh dill weed
1 garlic clove, minced
9 pita bread halves
1 tomato, sliced
1 red onion, sliced
Lettuce leaves

In a food processor, combine first 10 ingredients; add 2 green onions. Process until smooth and well mixed. If mixture is moist, add a few more bread crumbs. Using a 1/3 cup measure, shape mixture into patties. In a skillet, heat oil over medium-high. Fry patties until golden brown on both sides. Meanwhile, combine yogurt, dill, garlic and remaining green onion. Stuff pita halves with patties, tomato, onion and lettuce. Spoon yogurt sauce into pitas. Serve immediately. **Yield:** 9 servings.

CRANBERRY SLOPPY JOES

Alice Davis, Wilmington, Delaware

1 pound ground beef
1 cup chopped celery
1 cup chopped onion
1 can (10-3/4 ounces) condensed tomato soup, undiluted
1 can (8 ounces) jellied cranberry sauce
1/2 teaspoon salt
1/4 teaspoon chili powder
Dash hot pepper sauce
Hamburger buns, split and toasted

In a skillet, cook beef, celery and onion until meat is brown and vegetables are tender. Drain. Stir in soup, cranberry sauce, salt, chili powder and hot pepper sauce. Simmer, uncovered, about 30 minutes, stirring occasionally. Spoon onto buns. **Yield:** 8 servings.

Quick & Easy

CLAM CHOWDER

Rosemary Peterson, Archie, Missouri

2 cans (6-1/2 ounces *each*) minced clams
6 potatoes, peeled and diced
6 carrots, diced
1/2 cup chopped onion
1/2 cup butter *or* margarine
1-1/2 cups water
2 cans (10-3/4 ounces *each*) condensed cream of mushroom soup, undiluted
2 cans (12 ounces *each*) evaporated milk
1 teaspoon salt
1/2 teaspoon pepper

Drain clams, reserving liquid. Set the clams aside. In a large kettle, combine clam juice, potatoes, carrots, onion, butter and water. Cook over medium heat for 15 minutes or until the vegetables are tender. Stir in soup, milk, salt and pepper; simmer until heated through. Stir in clams. **Yield:** 10-12 servings (3 quarts).

Quick & Easy

MOCK HAM SALAD SANDWICHES

Betty Follas, Morgan Hill, California

(PICTURED AT RIGHT)

1 pound chunk bologna, ground
2 hard-cooked eggs, finely chopped
1/2 small onion, finely chopped
1/3 cup finely chopped sweet pickles
1/2 cup mayonnaise
Leaf lettuce, optional
8 to 10 sandwich buns, split

In a mixing bowl, combine bologna, eggs, onion and pickles. Add mayonnaise; toss lightly until combined. Cover and chill. To serve, place a lettuce leaf on each sandwich bun, if desired, and top with about 1/3 cup ham salad; replace bun tops. **Yield:** 8-10 servings.

CHICKEN AND OKRA GUMBO

Catherine Bouis, Palm Harbor, Florida

(PICTURED ON PAGE 114)

1 broiler-fryer chicken (2-1/2 to 3 pounds), cut up
2 quarts water
1/4 cup cooking oil *or* bacon drippings
2 tablespoons all-purpose flour
2 medium onions, chopped
2 celery ribs, chopped

1 green pepper, chopped
3 garlic cloves, minced
1 can (28 ounces) tomatoes, drained
2 cups sliced fresh *or* frozen okra (1-inch pieces)
2 bay leaves
1 teaspoon dried basil
1 teaspoon salt
1/2 teaspoon pepper
1 to 2 teaspoons hot pepper sauce
2 tablespoons sliced green onions
Chopped fresh parsley
Cooked rice

Place chicken and water in a large kettle. Cover and bring to a boil. Reduce heat to simmer; cook until chicken is tender, about 30-45 minutes. Remove chicken and reserve broth. Bone and cube chicken; set aside. In an 8-qt. kettle, combine oil or drippings and flour until smooth. Cook over medium-high heat for 5 minutes, stirring constantly. Reduce heat to medium. Cook and stir about 5 minutes more or until mixture is reddish-brown (the color of a penny). Turn the heat to high. Stir in 2 cups of reserved broth, mixing well. Cook and stir until thickened. Add onions, celery, green pepper and garlic; cook and stir for 5 minutes. Add tomatoes, okra, bay leaves, basil, salt, pepper and hot pepper sauce. Simmer 1-1/2 to 2 hours; add additional seasonings to taste. Stir in chicken; heat through. Garnish with green onions and parsley. Serve with rice. **Yield:** 8-10 servings.

TACO SOUP

Tonya Jones, Sundown, Texas

(PICTURED ON PAGE 138)

2 pounds lean ground beef
1 small onion, chopped
3 cans (4 ounces *each*) chopped green chilies
1 teaspoon salt
1 teaspoon pepper
1 can (15 to 16 ounces) pinto beans, rinsed and drained
1 can (16 ounces) lima beans, rinsed and drained
1 package (1-1/4 ounces) taco seasoning
1-1/2 cups water
1 package (1 ounce) ranch dressing mix
1 can (14-1/2 ounces) hominy, drained
3 cans (14-1/2 ounces *each*) stewed tomatoes
1 can (15 to 16 ounces) red kidney beans, rinsed and drained
Shredded cheddar cheese, optional
Tortilla chips, optional

In a large Dutch oven or kettle, brown beef and onion. Drain. Add all remaining ingredients except cheese and chips; bring to a boil. Reduce heat and simmer 30 minutes. Top with cheese and serve with chips if desired. **Yield:** 10 servings.

BARBECUED BEEF SANDWICHES

Karen Ann Bland, Gove, Kansas

1 boneless beef brisket (2-1/2 pounds)
1/2 cup vegetable oil
1/3 cup ketchup
1/4 cup red wine vinegar
1/4 cup minced onion
1 tablespoon Worcestershire sauce
1-1/2 teaspoons salt
1 teaspoon dried oregano
1/2 teaspoon dry mustard
1/4 teaspoon cayenne pepper
1/4 teaspoon pepper
1/2 cup water
1 bottle (18 ounces) barbecue sauce
Hamburger buns

Place brisket in a large Dutch oven or soup kettle. Combine next 10 ingredients; pour over brisket. Add water; bring to a boil. Reduce heat; cover and simmer for 4-1/2 to 5 hours or until meat is tender. Remove brisket and discard marinade. Shred meat; return to Dutch oven. Add barbecue sauce and cook until heated through, stirring frequently. To serve, spoon onto hamburger buns. **Yield:** 10-12 servings.

Quick & Easy

PRONTO POTATO SOUP

Elaine Rutschke, Spruce View, Alberta

8 bacon strips, cut into pieces
1 small onion, chopped
1-1/2 to 2 cups mashed potatoes
1 can (10-3/4 ounces) condensed cream of chicken soup
1 to 2 soup cans of milk
1/2 teaspoon salt
Dash pepper
2 tablespoons chopped parsley

In small frying pan, brown bacon until crisp. Remove and let drain on paper towel. Add onion to drippings in pan and saute 2-3 minutes. Drain fat off. Meanwhile, in a 3-qt. saucepan, mix cold mashed potatoes and soup until smooth. Add milk gradually to desired consistency, stirring constantly. Add bacon and onions. Season with salt, pepper and parsley. Heat through. **Yield:** 3-4 generous servings.

IT'S SUMMER! So, why not pack a picnic and head outdoors? Hearty helpings of Mock Ham Salad Sandwiches will surely satisfy your hungry clan. Down-home Barbecue Beans and Pineapple Coleslaw are perfect for potlucks. And for dessert, folks will agree that this from-scratch chocolate cake is the best they've ever tasted.

POTLUCK POSSIBILITIES.
Clockwise from the bottom: **Mock Ham Salad Sandwiches** (recipe on page 28), **Barbecue Beans** (recipe on page 123), **Pineapple Coleslaw** (recipe on page 42) and **Classic Chocolate Cake** (recipe on page 187).

FAST FEAST—for eyes as well as stomach —results if you rustle up Italian Vegetable Soup.

Quick & Easy

ITALIAN VEGETABLE SOUP

Janet Frieman, Kenosha, Wisconsin

(PICTURED ABOVE)

- 1 pound bulk Italian sausage
- 1 medium onion, sliced
- 1 can (16 ounces) whole tomatoes with liquid, chopped
- 1 can (15 ounces) garbanzo beans, drained
- 1 can (14-1/2 ounces) beef broth
- 1-1/2 cups water
- 2 medium zucchini, cut into 1/4-inch slices
- 1/2 teaspoon dried basil
Grated Parmesan cheese

In a 3-qt. saucepan, cook sausage and onion; drain fat. Stir in tomatoes, beans, broth, water, zucchini and basil. Bring to a boil. Reduce heat and simmer 5 minutes or until the zucchini is tender. Sprinkle each serving with cheese. **Yield:** 6-8 servings (2 quarts).

CORN AND SAUSAGE CHOWDER

Joanne Watts, Kitchener, Ontario

(PICTURED ON PAGE 82)

- 3 ears fresh corn, husked and cleaned
- 4 cups heavy cream
- 2 cups chicken broth
- 4 garlic cloves, minced
- 10 fresh thyme sprigs
- 1 bay leaf
- 1-1/2 medium onions, finely chopped, *divided*

- 1/2 pound hot Italian sausage links
- 2 tablespoons butter *or* margarine
- 2 teaspoons minced jalapeno peppers with seeds
- 1/2 teaspoon ground cumin
- 2 tablespoons all-purpose flour
- 2 medium potatoes, peeled and cut into 1/2-inch cubes
Salt and pepper to taste
- 1-1/2 teaspoons snipped fresh chives

Using a small sharp knife, cut corn from cobs; set corn aside. Place the corncobs, cream, broth, garlic, thyme, bay leaf and one-third of the onions in a large saucepan. Heat almost to boiling; reduce heat and simmer, covered, for 1 hour, stirring occasionally. Remove and discard corncobs. Strain cream mixture through a sieve set over a large bowl, pressing solids with back of spoon; set aside. Meanwhile, brown sausage in a large skillet. Cool and cut into 1/2-in. slices. In a large saucepan, melt butter. Add jalapenos, cumin and remaining onions; cook 5 minutes. Stir in flour; cook and stir 2 minutes. Gradually add corn stock. Add sausage and potatoes. Cover and cook until potatoes are tender, about 25 minutes. Add corn and cook just until tender, about 5 minutes. Remove bay leaf. Season with salt and pepper. For a thinner chowder, add additional chicken broth. Sprinkle with chives before serving. **Yield:** 8 servings (2 quarts).

BARLEY BORSCHT

Blanche Babinski, Minto, North Dakota

✓ This tasty dish uses less sugar, salt and fat. Recipe includes *Diabetic Exchanges*.

- 2 pounds beef bones
- 1 medium onion, chopped
- 1 bay leaf
- 1 teaspoon salt
- 10 whole peppercorns
- 6 cups water
- 1 medium rutabaga (about 1 pound), diced
- 3 cups fresh diced beets (about 1-1/2 pounds)
- 2 cups chopped celery
- 1 small head cabbage (about 1 pound), shredded
- 2-1/2 cups diced carrots (about 1 pound)
- 2-1/2 cups diced peeled potatoes (about 1 pound)
- 3/4 cup pearl barley
- 1 can (14-1/2 ounces) tomatoes with liquid, cut up
- 1/4 cup vinegar
Sour cream, optional
Fresh dill

In a Dutch oven, combine beef bones, onion, bay leaf, salt, peppercorns and water. Bring to a boil; reduce heat. Cover and simmer for 2 hours. Strain broth; discard bones, onion and seasonings. Skim fat and return broth to the kettle. Add rutabaga, beets, celery, cabbage, carrots, potatoes and barley. Return to a boil; reduce heat. Cover and simmer 50 minutes or until vegetables are almost tender and barley is cooked. Stir in tomatoes with liquid and vinegar; heat through. Ladle into serving bowls. Top with a dollop of sour cream if desired. Sprinkle with dill. **Yield:** 16 servings. **Diabetic Exchanges:** One serving (1 cup, without sour cream) equals 1 starch, 1 vegetable; also, 110 calories, 227 mg sodium, 0 mg cholesterol, 26 gm carbohydrate, 3 gm protein, 1 gm fat.

POTATO/CUCUMBER SOUP

Janet Flower, Portland, Oregon

- 3 cups cold water
- 6 medium potatoes (about 2 pounds), peeled and cubed
- 1-1/2 teaspoons salt
- 1/4 teaspoon pepper
- 1 cup heavy cream
- 1 cup milk
- 1 teaspoon grated onion
- 1 large *or* 2 medium cucumbers, peeled, seeded and diced
- 1 tablespoon finely chopped fresh dill *or* 1 teaspoon dried dill weed

In a large saucepan, bring water, potatoes, salt and pepper to a boil. Reduce heat to simmer. Cook, uncovered, until potatoes are tender. Cool. Puree in a food processor or blender until smooth. Return to the saucepan. Stir in cream, milk, onion and cucumber. Add additional milk if soup is too thick. Simmer over low heat, stirring occasionally, for 5 minutes. Season with dill. **Yield:** 2 quarts.

GARDEN-FRESH TOMATO SOUP

Charlotte Goldbery, Honey Grove, Pennsylvania

- 1/2 cup butter *or* margarine
- 2 tablespoons olive oil
- 1 large onion, sliced
- 2 sprigs fresh thyme *or* 1/2 teaspoon dried thyme
- 4 fresh basil leaves *or* 1/2 teaspoon dried basil
- 1 teaspoon salt
- 1/4 teaspoon freshly ground black pepper

2-1/2 pounds diced fresh ripe tomatoes *or* 2 cans (16 ounces *each*) Italian-style tomatoes with juice
3 tablespoons tomato paste
1/4 cup all-purpose flour
3-3/4 cups chicken broth, *divided*
1 teaspoon sugar
1 cup heavy cream

CROUTONS:
8 slices day-old French *or* Italian bread
1 large garlic clove, sliced lengthwise
2 tablespoons olive oil

In a large kettle, heat butter and olive oil over medium-high. Add onion and seasonings. Cook, stirring occasionally, until the onion is soft. Add the tomatoes and paste. Stir to blend. Simmer 10 minutes. Place the flour in a small mixing bowl and stir in 1/4 cup chicken broth. Stir into the tomato mixture. Add the remaining broth. Simmer 30 minutes, stirring frequently. Allow mixture to cool and run through a sieve, food mill or food processor. Return the pureed mixture to the kettle. Add the sugar and cream. Heat through, stirring occasionally. To prepare the croutons, rub the garlic over both sides of the bread. Brush with olive oil and place on a baking sheet. Bake at 350° for 10-12 minutes or until toasted. Turn and toast other side 2-3 minutes. Just before serving, top each bowl with one or two croutons. **Yield:** 8 servings.

SAUSAGE BROCCOLI CHOWDER

Donald Roberts, Amherst, New Hampshire

1 pound bulk Italian sausage
1 medium onion, chopped
3 garlic cloves, minced
8 ounces fresh mushrooms, sliced
2 tablespoons butter *or* margarine
2 cups broccoli florets
2 to 3 carrots, diced
2 cans (14-1/2 ounces *each*) chicken broth
1 can (10-3/4 ounces) condensed cream of mushroom soup, undiluted
9 ounces cheese tortellini, cooked and drained
1/2 teaspoon pepper
1/2 teaspoon dried basil
1/2 teaspoon dried thyme
2 quarts light cream
1/2 cup grated Romano cheese

In a skillet, cook and crumble sausage until no longer pink. Remove to paper towels to drain; set aside. In the same skillet, saute onion, garlic and mushrooms in butter until tender; set aside. In a Dutch oven, cook the broccoli and carrots in chicken broth until tender. Stir in sausage and the mushroom mixture. Add soup, tortellini, pepper, basil and thyme; heat through. Stir in cream and Romano cheese; heat through. **Yield:** 12-16 servings (4 quarts).

  Quick & Easy

CHICKEN CHILI

Nancy Robinsion, Kansas City, Kansas

2 tablespoons vegetable oil
1 cup chopped onion
1 cup chopped green pepper
2 garlic cloves, minced
4-1/2 cups diced cooked chicken
2 cans (14-1/2 ounces *each*) stewed tomatoes
1 can (15 ounces) pinto beans, drained
2/3 to 3/4 cup mild *or* medium picante sauce
1 teaspoon chili powder
1 teaspoon ground cumin
1/2 teaspoon salt

Optional toppings: shredded cheddar cheese, diced avocado and sour cream

In a Dutch oven, heat oil on medium. Saute onion, green pepper and garlic until tender. Add chicken, tomatoes, beans, picante sauce and seasonings; bring to a boil. Reduce heat; simmer for 20 minutes. Ladle into soup bowls. Top with cheese, avocado and sour cream if desired. **Yield:** 6-8 servings.

CHEESE/PEPPER SOUP

Gay Nicholas, Henderson, Texas

(PICTURED ON PAGE 197)

1/3 cup finely chopped carrots
1/3 cup finely chopped celery
1 cup thinly sliced green onions
2 cups water
1 medium onion, chopped
3/4 cup butter *or* margarine
1 cup plus 2 tablespoons all-purpose flour
4 cups milk
4 cups chicken broth
1 jar (16 ounces) process cheese spread
1/8 teaspoon cayenne pepper *or* to taste
1 tablespoon prepared mustard

Salt and pepper to taste, optional

Combine carrots, celery and green onion in water; cook until tender. Set vegetables and broth aside. Saute onion in butter until limp; stir in the flour and blend well. *Do not brown.* Combine milk and chicken broth; bring to a boil.

Whisk in onion/flour mixture. Add cheese spread, cayenne, mustard and salt and pepper if desired. Slowly stir in vegetables and water they were cooked in. Bring just to a boil; serve immediately. Add additional cayenne if desired. **Yield:** 12 servings.

PASTA/SAUSAGE SOUP

Alice Rabe, Beemer, Nebraska

1-1/2 pounds hot *or* sweet Italian sausage
1 medium onion, chopped
1 medium green pepper, cut into strips
1 garlic clove, minced
1 can (28 ounces) tomatoes, chopped, liquid reserved
2 to 2-1/2 cups uncooked bow tie pasta
6 cups water
1 tablespoon sugar
1 tablespoon Worcestershire sauce
2 chicken bouillon cubes
1 teaspoon dried basil
1 teaspoon dried thyme
1 teaspoon salt

Remove casings from the sausages and cut into 1-in. pieces. In a Dutch oven, brown sausage over medium heat. Remove sausage and drain all but 2 tablespoons of the drippings. Saute onion, pepper and garlic until tender. Add sausage and all remaining ingredients. Simmer, uncovered, stirring occasionally, until pasta is tender, about 15-20 minutes. **Yield:** 3 quarts.

Quick & Easy

MOM'S MONDAY LUNCH POTATO SOUP

Evelyn Bonar, Pensacola, Florida

8 bacon strips, diced
1 small onion, chopped
1-1/2 cups mashed potatoes
1 can (10-3/4 ounces) condensed cream of chicken soup, undiluted
2 cups milk
1/2 teaspoon salt, optional
1/8 teaspoon pepper
2 tablespoons chopped fresh parsley

In a 3-qt. saucepan, cook bacon until crisp; remove to paper towels to drain. Saute onion in the drippings until tender. Add the potatoes and soup and stir until smooth. Gradually stir in milk. Cook over medium heat, stirring constantly. Stir in bacon, salt if desired and pepper. Cook until heated through. Garnish with parsley. **Yield:** 3-4 servings.

AAH…on a cold day, can anything compare with a pot of homemade soup simmering away on the stove? Whether it's stocked with chicken, beef or produce— or loaded with rice or noodles—you'll appreciate this hearty assortment of guaranteed-to-please favorites. So, it's easy to treat your family…*year-round!*

SIMPLY SOUPERIOR.
Clockwise from lower left: **Wild Rice Soup**, **Spiced Tomato Soup**, **Buttery Onion Soup**, **Mom's Chicken Noodle Soup**, **Beef Lentil Soup**, **Chili Con Carne**, **Mushroom/Onion Soup** and **Split Pea Vegetable Soup** (all recipes on pages 34 and 35).

CHILI CON CARNE

Janie Turner, Tuttle, Oklahoma

(PICTURED ON PAGE 33)

> 2 pounds ground beef
> 2 tablespoons olive oil
> 2 garlic cloves, minced
> 2 medium onions, chopped
> 1 green pepper, chopped
> 2 tablespoons chili powder
> 1-1/2 teaspoons salt
> 1/8 teaspoon cayenne pepper
> 1/4 teaspoon ground cinnamon
> 1 teaspoon ground cumin
> 1 teaspoon dried oregano
> 2 cans (16 ounces *each*) tomatoes with liquid, chopped
> 3 beef bouillon cubes
> 1 cup boiling water
> 1 can (16 ounces) kidney beans, undrained

In a large kettle, brown ground beef. Drain and set aside. In the same kettle, heat oil; saute garlic and onions over low heat until onions are tender. Stir in green pepper, chili powder, salt, cayenne pepper, cinnamon, cumin and oregano. Cook for 2 minutes, stirring until well mixed. Add beef and tomatoes with liquid. Dissolve bouillon in water and add to soup. Simmer, covered, for about 1 hour. Add kidney beans; simmer 30 minutes longer. **Yield:** 8-10 servings (about 2-1/2 quarts).

MOM'S CHICKEN NOODLE SOUP

Marlene Doolittle, Story City, Iowa

(PICTURED ON PAGE 33)

> 1 broiler-fryer chicken (2 to 3 pounds), cut up
> 2 quarts water
> 1 onion, chopped
> 2 chicken bouillon cubes
> 2 celery ribs, diced
> 2 carrots, diced
> 2 medium potatoes, peeled and cubed
> 1-1/2 cups fresh *or* frozen cut green beans
> 1 teaspoon salt
> 1/4 teaspoon pepper
> **NOODLES:**
> 1 cup all-purpose flour
> 1 egg, beaten
> 1/2 teaspoon salt
> 1 teaspoon butter *or* margarine, softened
> 1/4 teaspoon baking powder
> 2 to 3 tablespoons milk

In a large kettle, cook chicken in water. Cool broth and skim off fat. Skin and bone chicken and cut into bite-size pieces; add to broth with remaining ingredients except noodles. Bring to a boil. Reduce heat and simmer, uncovered, for 50-60 minutes or until vegetables are tender. Meanwhile, for noodles, place flour on a bread board or countertop and make a well in the center. In a small bowl, stir together remaining ingredients; pour into well. Working the mixture with your hands, fold flour into wet ingredients until dough can be rolled into a ball. Knead for 5-6 minutes. Cover and let rest for 10 minutes. On a floured surface, roll dough out to a square, 1/16 to 1/8 in. thick, and cut into 1/4-in.-wide strips. Cook noodles in boiling salted water for 2-3 minutes or until done. Drain and add to soup just before serving. **Yield:** 4-6 servings (1-1/2 quarts).

SPICED TOMATO SOUP

Lois DeMoss, Kingsburg, California

(PICTURED ON PAGE 32)

> 2 cups water
> 5 pounds fresh tomatoes, quartered
> 3/4 cup sugar
> 2 tablespoons salt
> 1 tablespoon mixed pickling spice, tied in a cheesecloth bag
> 3 large onions, chopped
> 1 bunch parsley, chopped
> 1 celery rib, sliced
> 2 tablespoons butter *or* margarine
> 2 tablespoons all-purpose flour
> 5 bacon strips, cooked and crumbled
> **Unsweetened whipped cream**
> **Toasted slivered almonds**

In a large kettle, bring first eight ingredients to a boil. Reduce heat and simmer for 1-1/2 to 2 hours or until vegetables are soft. Remove from the heat and cool slightly; discard spice bag. Press mixture through a food mill; return juice to kettle. In a small saucepan over medium heat, melt butter. Add flour and cook, stirring, until browned and bubbly; stir into soup. Add bacon and heat through. Top individual servings with a dollop of whipped cream and sprinkle with almonds. **Yield:** 8-10 servings (2-1/2 quarts).

WILD RICE SOUP

Elienore Myhre, Balaton, Minnesota

(PICTURED ON PAGE 32)

> 1/3 cup uncooked wild rice
> 1 tablespoon vegetable oil
> 1 quart water
> 1 medium onion, chopped
> 1 celery rib, finely chopped
> 1 carrot, finely chopped
> 1/2 cup butter *or* margarine
> 1/2 cup all-purpose flour
> 3 cups chicken broth
> 2 cups light cream
> 1/2 teaspoon dried rosemary
> 1 teaspoon salt

Rinse rice; drain. In a medium saucepan, combine rice, oil and water; bring to a boil. Reduce heat; cover and simmer for 30 minutes. Meanwhile, in a large kettle, cook onion, celery and carrot in butter until vegetables are almost tender. Blend in flour; cook and stir for 2 minutes. Add broth and *undrained* rice. Bring to a boil; cook and stir until slightly thickened. Stir in cream, rosemary and salt. Reduce heat and simmer, uncovered, for about 20 minutes or until rice is tender. **Yield:** 8 servings (about 2 quarts).

BEEF LENTIL SOUP

Constance Turnbull, Arlington, Massachusetts

(PICTURED ON PAGE 33)

> ✓ This tasty dish uses less sugar, salt and fat. Recipe includes *Diabetic Exchanges*.

> 1 pound ground beef
> 1 quart water
> 1 can (48 ounces) tomato juice
> 1 cup dried lentils, rinsed
> 2 cups chopped cabbage
> 1 cup sliced carrots
> 1 cup sliced celery
> 1 cup chopped onion
> 1/2 cup diced green pepper
> 1/2 teaspoon pepper
> 1/2 teaspoon dried thyme
> 1 bay leaf
> 1 teaspoon salt, optional
> 2 beef bouillon cubes, optional
> 1 package (10 ounces) frozen chopped spinach, thawed

In a large kettle, brown ground beef. Drain. Add water, tomato juice, lentils, cabbage, carrots, celery, onion, green pepper, pepper, thyme and bay leaf. Also add salt and bouillon if desired. Bring to a boil. Reduce heat and simmer, uncovered, for 1 to 1-1/2 hours or until the lentils and vegetables are tender. Add spinach and heat through. Remove bay leaf. **Yield:** 6 servings (2-

1/2 quarts). **Diabetic Exchanges:** One serving (prepared without bouillon and salt) equals 2 meat, 2 vegetable, 1-1/2 starch; also, 317 calories, 128 mg sodium, 45 mg cholesterol, 38 gm carbohydrate, 28 gm protein, 7 gm fat.

BUTTERY ONION SOUP

Sharon Berthelote, Sunburst, Montana

(PICTURED ON PAGE 32)

2 cups thinly sliced onions
1/2 cup butter *or* margarine
1/4 cup all-purpose flour
2 cups chicken broth
2 cups milk
1-1/2 to 2 cups (6 to 8 ounces) shredded mozzarella cheese
Salt and pepper to taste
Croutons, optional

In a large kettle, saute onions in butter over low heat until tender and transparent, about 20-30 minutes. Blend in flour. Gradually add broth and milk; cook and stir over medium heat until bubbly. Cook and stir for 1 minute more; reduce heat to low. Add mozzarella cheese and stir constantly until melted (do not boil). Season to taste with salt and pepper. Serve with croutons if desired. **Yield:** 6 servings (about 1-1/2 quarts).

MUSHROOM/ONION SOUP

Nancy Kuczynski, Holmen, Wisconsin

(PICTURED ON PAGE 33)

 This tasty dish uses less sugar, salt and fat. Recipe includes *Diabetic Exchanges*.

2 cups (8 ounces) fresh mushrooms
3 tablespoons butter *or* margarine
2 medium onions, chopped
2 tablespoons all-purpose flour
5 cups chicken broth
1/2 teaspoon salt, optional
Dash pepper
1/3 cup uncooked long grain rice
1 bay leaf
2 tablespoons chopped fresh parsley

Trim mushroom stems level with the caps; finely chop stems and thinly slice caps. In a large saucepan, melt butter; add mushrooms and onions. Cook and stir over low heat for 5 minutes. Blend in flour; add broth, salt and pepper. Cook,

stirring constantly, until mixture boils. Reduce heat. Add rice and bay leaf; cover and simmer for 15-20 minutes or until the rice is tender. Discard bay leaf. Sprinkle with parsley. **Yield:** 4 servings (about 1-1/2 quarts). **Diabetic Exchanges:** One serving (prepared with margarine, low sodium broth and no added salt) equals 1 vegetable, 1 fat, 1/2 starch; also, 118 calories, 126 mg sodium, 1 mg cholesterol, 10 gm carbohydrate, 8 gm protein, 5 gm fat.

SPLIT PEA VEGETABLE SOUP

Maureen Ylitalo, Wahnapitae, Ontario

(PICTURED ON PAGE 32)

1-1/2 cups dry split peas, rinsed
2-1/2 quarts water
7 to 8 whole allspice, tied in a cheesecloth bag
2 teaspoons salt
1/2 teaspoon pepper
6 large potatoes, peeled and cut into 1/2-inch cubes
6 carrots, chopped
2 medium onions, chopped
2 cups cubed cooked ham
1/2 medium head cabbage, shredded

In a large kettle, combine peas, water, allspice, salt and pepper; bring to a boil. Reduce heat; cover and simmer for 1 hour. Stir in potatoes, carrots, onions, ham and cabbage; return to a boil. Reduce heat; cover and simmer for about 30 minutes or until vegetables are tender, stirring occasionally. Discard allspice. **Yield:** 16-20 servings (about 5 quarts).

POTATO SOUP WITH SAUSAGE

Dorothy Althause, Magalia, California

1 pound pork sausage links, cut into 1/4-inch slices
1 cup sliced celery
1/2 cup chopped onion
1/2 teaspoon dried thyme
1/2 teaspoon salt
2 tablespoons all-purpose flour
1 can (14-1/2 ounces) chicken broth
1/2 cup water
4 medium potatoes, peeled and diced (about 4 cups)
1 cup milk
1 cup sliced green beans, partially cooked
Fresh chopped parsley

In a heavy skillet, brown sausage over medium heat. Remove sausage and set aside. Drain all but 1 tablespoon fat; saute celery, onion, thyme and salt.

Cook until onion is tender. Stir in flour; cook 1 minute. Gradually add broth and water, stirring until the mixture comes to a boil. Add potatoes; cover and simmer 25 minutes or until potatoes are tender. Allow soup to cool. Puree 2 cups in blender or food processor; return to kettle. Add milk, beans and sausage; heat through. Garnish with parsley. **Yield:** 6 servings.

SANDWICH ROLLS. For a change of pace, trim the crust off a slice of bread and roll the bread flat. Add meat, cheese and a favorite spread, roll up and secure with a pretzel stick or toothpick.

STUFFED SPINACH LOAF

Anita Harmala, Howell, Michigan

(PICTURED BELOW)

1 pound bulk Italian sausage
1/2 teaspoon salt
1/2 teaspoon dried basil
1 loaf (1 pound) frozen bread dough, thawed
1 package (10 ounces) frozen spinach, thawed and well-drained
2 cups (8 ounces) shredded mozzarella cheese

In a skillet, brown sausage. Drain; sprinkle with salt and basil. Roll out bread dough to a 13-in. x 10-in. rectangle. Sprinkle meat on top of dough. Place spinach on top of meat; top with cheese. Roll up from one of the long sides; seal seams and ends. Using a spatula, carefully place loaf on a greased baking sheet or jelly roll pan. Bake at 350° for 25-30 minutes or until the crust is golden brown. Serve warm. Refrigerate leftovers. **Yield:** 10 servings.

A SPECIAL SURPRISE awaits folks inside fast, filling sandwich loaf (recipe above).

CHUNKY CHILI

Verna Hofer, Mitchell, South Dakota

(PICTURED ON BACK COVER AND AT RIGHT)

 This tasty dish uses less sugar, salt and fat. Recipe includes *Diabetic Exchanges*.

1-1/2 pounds lean chuck *or* round
    steak, cut into bite-size pieces
1 tablespoon cooking oil
2 garlic cloves, minced
2 green peppers, chopped
1 large onion, chopped
1 to 3 tablespoons chili powder
2 teaspoons ground cumin
1 teaspoon dried oregano
1 can (28 ounces) tomatoes
    with liquid, chopped
1 can (16 ounces) kidney
    beans, rinsed and drained
Crusty round French rolls, optional

In a large heavy saucepan, cook meat in oil until lightly browned. Add remaining ingredients except kidney beans; bring to a boil. Reduce heat and simmer, covered, for 2-1/2 to 3 hours or until meat is tender. Stir in beans during the last 30 minutes of cooking. If desired, serve in "bread bowls" by hollowing out rolls and spooning chili into center. **Yield:** 6 servings. **Diabetic Exchanges:** One serving (without roll) equals 3 meat, 2 vegetable, 1 starch; also, 361 calories, 663 mg sodium, 66 mg cholesterol, 27 gm carbohydrate, 27 gm protein, 17 gm fat.

MEXICAN CARNITAS

Patricia Collins, Imbler, Oregon

(PICTURED ON PAGE 222)

1 boneless pork blade *or*
    shoulder roast (3 to 4 pounds),
    cut into 1-inch cubes
6 large garlic cloves, minced
1/2 cup fresh cilantro, chopped
1 teaspoon salt
Pepper to taste
3 large oranges, *divided*
1 large lemon
Oil for frying
Warm flour tortillas
Shredded cheddar cheese
Salsa
Guacamole

Place meat in a medium-size roasting pan. Sprinkle with garlic and cilantro. Season with salt and pepper. Squeeze the juice from one orange and the lemon over the meat. Slice the remaining oranges and place over the meat. Cover and bake at 350° for about 2 hours or until meat is tender. With a slotted spoon, remove meat and drain well on paper towels. Heat a small amount of oil in a skillet and fry meat 1 lb. at a time until brown and crispy. Serve warm in flour tortillas garnished with cheese, salsa and guacamole. **Yield:** 12-16 servings.

CREAMY ASPARAGUS CHOWDER

Shirley Beachum, Shelby, Michigan

(PICTURED ON PAGE 16)

1/4 cup butter *or* margarine
2 medium onions, chopped
2 cups chopped celery
1 garlic clove, minced
1/2 cup all-purpose flour
1 large potato, peeled and cut
    into 1/2-inch cubes
4 cups milk
4 cups chicken broth
1/2 teaspoon dried thyme
1/2 teaspoon dried marjoram
4 cups chopped fresh asparagus,
    cooked and drained
Salt and pepper to taste
Sliced almonds
Shredded cheddar cheese
Chopped fresh tomato

In a Dutch oven, melt butter; saute onions, celery and garlic until tender. Stir in flour. Add potato, milk, broth and herbs; cook over low heat, stirring occasionally, until the potato is tender and soup is thickened, about 20-30 minutes. Add asparagus, salt and pepper; heat through. To serve, sprinkle with almonds, cheese and the chopped tomato. **Yield:** about 2-1/2 quarts.

DILLED CHICKEN SOUP

Estelle Keefer, Allegany, New York

 This tasty dish uses less sugar, salt and fat. Recipe includes *Diabetic Exchanges*.

1 chicken (4 to 5 pounds),
    quartered
3 carrots, peeled
1 small sweet potato, peeled
4 celery ribs with leaves, cut up
1 small parsnip, peeled and
    sliced
1 large onion, peeled and
    quartered
Few sprigs fresh dill
Water
Salt and pepper to taste
8 ounces thin egg noodles,
    cooked and drained

Place chicken, vegetables and dill in a large kettle. Add water to cover, about 2-1/2 qts. Cover and bring to a boil over high heat. Skim foam. Add salt and pepper; simmer, covered, for 2 hours. Remove chicken and vegetables; set aside to cool. Pour the broth through a strainer. Slice carrots and dice chicken; return to broth. Discard all other vegetables and bones. Add noodles to soup and heat through. **Yield:** 10 servings. **Diabetic Exchanges:** One serving (without salt) equals 3-1/2 meat, 1 starch, 1 vegetable; also, 328 calories, 65 mg sodium, 127 mg cholesterol, 19 gm carbohydrate, 29 gm protein, 10 gm fat.

CHILI VERDE

Sherrie Scettrini, Salinas, California

(PICTURED ON PAGE 75)

4 tablespoons cooking oil,
    divided
4 pounds boneless pork, cut
    into 3/4-inch cubes
1/4 cup all-purpose flour
1 can (4 ounces) chopped
    green chilies
1/2 teaspoon ground cumin
1/4 teaspoon salt
1/4 teaspoon pepper
3 garlic cloves, minced
1/2 cup chopped fresh cilantro *or*
    parsley
1/2 to 1 cup salsa
1 can (14-1/2 ounces) chicken
    broth
Flour tortillas, warmed

In a Dutch oven, heat 1 tablespoon oil over medium-high. Add 1 pound of pork; cook and stir until lightly browned. Remove and set aside. Repeat with remaining meat, adding more oil as needed. Return all of the meat to Dutch oven. Sprinkle flour over meat; mix well. Add chilies, cumin, salt, pepper, garlic, cilantro or parsley, salsa and chicken broth. Cover and simmer until pork is tender and chili reaches desired consistency, about 1-1/2 hours. Serve with warmed tortillas. **Yield:** 6-8 servings.

SPEEDY BEAN SOUP

Kathleen Drott, Pineville, Louisiana

2 cans (11-1/2 ounces *each*)
    condensed bean and bacon
    soup, undiluted
1 soup can water
3 cans (16 ounces *each*)
    great northern *or* navy
    beans, undrained
1 can (15 ounces) jalapeno
    pinto beans, undrained
1 medium onion, finely
    chopped
1 teaspoon salt
1/2 teaspoon garlic powder
1/4 teaspoon pepper

In a large Dutch oven or soup kettle, combine all ingredients. Simmer about 20 minutes. **Yield:** 3 quarts.

TAKE control of your hurried weekends by
having a kettle of satisfying Chunky Chili
simmering on the back burner and a refreshing
Mexican Salad chilling in the refrigerator.
After enjoying that great combination,
nibble on delicious Spiced Almond Cookies.

CHILI WARM-UP.
Clockwise from the top: **Chunky Chili** (recipe on
page 36), **Spiced Almond Cookies**
(recipe on page 173) and **Mexican Salad**
(recipe on page 54).

PEORIA CHILI

Norma Erne, Albuquerque, New Mexico

 This tasty dish uses less sugar, salt and fat. Recipe includes *Diabetic Exchanges*.

2 pounds ground beef
1 medium onion, chopped
1 can (28 ounces) whole tomatoes with liquid, chopped
1 can (46 ounces) tomato juice
1 to 2 tablespoons chili powder
1 tablespoon sugar
Salt and pepper to taste
2 cans (15 ounces *each*) red kidney beans, rinsed and drained
Shredded cheddar cheese, optional

In a large kettle or Dutch oven, brown beef and onion. Drain off fat; add all remaining ingredients except beans and cheese. Cover and simmer 2-3 hours. Adjust seasonings, if necessary. Stir in beans and heat through. Before serving, top with shredded cheddar cheese if desired. **Yield:** 10 servings. **Diabetic Exchanges:** One serving equals 3 lean meat, 1-1/2 starch, 1 vegetable; also, 288 calories, 826 mg sodium, 64 mg cholesterol, 28 gm carbohydrate, 26 gm protein, 9 gm fat.

KIELBASA BEAN SOUP

Mary E. Cordes, Omaha, Nebraska

2 cups water
1 medium potato, peeled and diced
2 carrots, peeled and sliced
1 medium onion, chopped
1/3 cup chopped celery
8 ounces smoked kielbasa, thinly sliced
1 can (11-1/2 ounces) bean with bacon soup, undiluted
Chopped fresh parsley, optional

In a large saucepan, bring water and vegetables to a boil. Simmer 10 minutes or until vegetables are tender. Add kielbasa and soup. Heat through. Garnish with parsley if desired. **Yield:** 6 servings.

TURKEY WILD RICE SOUP

Doris Cox, New Freedom, Pennsylvania

1 medium onion, chopped
1 can (4 ounces) sliced mushrooms, drained

2 tablespoons butter *or* margarine
3 cups water
2 cups chicken broth
1 package (6 ounces) long grain and wild rice mix
2 cups diced cooked turkey
1 cup heavy cream
Chopped fresh parsley

In a large saucepan, saute onion and mushrooms in butter until onion is tender. Add water, broth and rice mix with seasoning; bring to a boil. Reduce heat; simmer for 20-25 minutes or until rice is tender. Stir in turkey and cream and heat through. Sprinkle with parsley. **Yield:** 6 servings.

CORNY GOOD CHILI

Mary Wolfe, LaCrete, Alberta

1 pound ground beef
1 medium onion, chopped
1/4 cup chopped celery
1 can (16 ounces) pork and beans, undrained
1 can (15-1/2 ounces) kidney beans, rinsed and drained
1 can (12 ounces) whole kernel corn, undrained
1 can (10-3/4 ounces) condensed tomato soup, undiluted
1 can (10-3/4 ounces) condensed vegetable soup, undiluted
1/4 cup water
1/4 cup packed brown sugar, optional
1 tablespoon vinegar
2 to 3 tablespoons chili powder

In a Dutch oven, brown ground beef, onion and celery; cook until tender. Drain. Add remaining ingredients; simmer until heated through. **Yield:** 6-8 servings.

STEW IT OVER. Meatballs make a fun substitute for stew meat in beef vegetable soup. Combine 1 lb. ground beef, 1 egg, 1-1/2 cups bread crumbs, salt, pepper and nutmeg to taste. Mix well; shape into 1/2-in. meatballs. Add to soup base, along with your vegetables, and cook for 30 minutes.

BEEF AND SAUSAGE SOUP

Darlene Dickinson, Lebec, California

1 tablespoon cooking oil
1 pound beef stew meat, cut into 1/2-inch cubes
1 pound bulk Italian sausage, shaped into balls

1 can (28 ounces) tomatoes with liquid, chopped
3-1/2 cups water
1 cup chopped onion
1 teaspoon salt
1/2 teaspoon Italian seasoning
1 tablespoon Worcestershire sauce
2 cups cubed peeled potatoes
1 cup sliced celery

In a Dutch oven, heat oil over medium-high. Brown beef on all sides. Remove with a slotted spoon and set aside. Brown sausage on all sides. Drain fat. Return beef to Dutch oven and add remaining ingredients except potatoes and celery. Bring to a boil; reduce heat and simmer, covered, until beef is tender, about 1-1/2 hours. Add the potatoes and celery. Simmer, covered, until vegetables are tender, about 30 minutes. **Yield:** 6-8 servings.

ZUCCHINI/POTATO SOUP

Christine Gibson, Fontana, Wisconsin

5 cups chicken broth
4 small zucchini (about 1 pound), thinly sliced
1 large potato, peeled, halved and thinly sliced
1 large onion, thinly sliced
3 eggs
2 tablespoons lemon juice
2 teaspoons dried dill weed
Salt and pepper to taste

In a saucepan, bring broth to a boil. Stir in zucchini, potato and onion. Reduce heat and simmer, covered, 15 minutes or until vegetables are tender. In a small bowl, beat eggs; blend in lemon juice and 1/2 cup hot broth. Stir back into the saucepan. Heat over medium for 1 minute, stirring constantly. Do not boil. Stir in dill; season with salt and pepper. Serve immediately. **Yield:** about 2 quarts.

GAZPACHO

Sharon Balzer, Phoenix, Arizona

2 cans (14-1/2 ounces *each*) tomatoes with liquid, minced
2 cups vegetable juice
2 tablespoons red wine vinegar
1 garlic clove, minced
1 teaspoon salt
1/2 teaspoon pepper
8 to 10 drops hot pepper sauce
1 package (6 ounces) seasoned croutons
1 medium cucumber, peeled and diced

1 medium green pepper, diced
1 bunch green onions with
tops, sliced

In a large bowl, combine first seven ingredients. Cover and refrigerate overnight. Stir well; ladle into soup bowls and garnish as desired with croutons, cucumbers, peppers and green onions. **Yield:** 6-8 servings.

 Quick & Easy

BEEF RAVIOLI SOUP

Marian Platt, Sequim, Washington

1 cup sliced celery
1/2 cup chopped onion
1 cup sliced carrots
2 tablespoons vegetable oil
4 cups beef broth
1/8 teaspoon pepper
1/4 teaspoon crushed red
pepper flakes
1 can (15 ounces) beef ravioli
1/4 cup chopped fresh parsley
Grated Parmesan cheese

In a large kettle, saute celery, onion and carrots in oil for 3 minutes; add broth and seasonings. Bring to a boil; reduce heat and simmer, covered, about 15 minutes or until the vegetables are tender. Stir in the ravioli and heat through. Garnish with parsley and Parmesan cheese. **Yield:** 4-6 servings (1-1/2 quarts).

SAUSAGE LENTIL SOUP

Catherine Rowe, Berthoud, Colorado

1/2 pound bulk Italian sausage
1 large onion, finely chopped
1 small green pepper, finely
chopped
1 small carrot, finely chopped
1 large garlic clove, finely
minced
1 bay leaf
2 cans (14-1/2 ounces *each*)
chicken broth
1 can (14-1/2 to 16 ounces)
whole tomatoes with liquid,
coarsely chopped
1 cup water
3/4 cup dry lentils
1/4 cup country-style *or* regular
Dijon mustard

In a Dutch oven, brown sausage. Drain the fat and crumble sausage; return to Dutch oven along with remaining ingredients except mustard. Simmer, covered, 1 hour or until lentils and vegetables are tender. Stir in the mustard. Remove and discard bay leaf before serving. **Yield:** 6 servings.

HOT ITALIAN ROAST BEEF SANDWICHES

Betty Claycomb, Alverton, Pennsylvania

(PICTURED ON PAGE 194)

✓ This tasty dish uses less sugar, salt and fat. Recipe includes *Diabetic Exchanges*.

1 tablespoon butter *or* margarine
1 boneless sirloin tip beef roast
(5 pounds)
1 can (28 ounces) tomatoes
with juice, cut up
1/3 cup water
1 tablespoon ground thyme
1 to 3 teaspoons crushed dried
red pepper
1 teaspoon salt
Semi-hard rolls

In a Dutch oven, melt butter over medium heat. Brown roast on all sides. Add remaining ingredients except rolls; cover and simmer until the roast is tender, about 3-1/2 to 4 hours. Add additional water, if necessary, to keep roast simmering in broth. Remove meat from broth and reserve broth. Let the meat stand 20 minutes. Trim any fat and thinly slice meat. When ready to serve, reheat sliced beef in broth. Serve on rolls. **Yield:** about 20 sandwiches. **Diabetic Exchanges:** One serving (without roll) equals 2 lean meat, 1/2 vegetable; also 129 calories, 244 mg sodium, 49 mg cholesterol, 3 gm carbohydrate, 18 gm protein, 5 gm fat.

BLACK BEAN SOUP

Mrs. Albert Lopez, Riverside, California

2 cups dry black beans
2 quarts water
1 medium onion, chopped
1/2 pound lean pork cubes
2 teaspoons salt
3 garlic cloves, minced
1 teaspoon dried oregano
1 can (6 ounces) tomato paste
Optional toppings: thinly sliced
radishes, finely shredded cabbage,
minced fresh chili peppers and
sour cream

Rinse beans. In a Dutch oven, combine beans and water. Bring to a boil. Reduce heat; cover and simmer until beans wrinkle and crack, about 1-1/2 hours. Add onion, pork, salt, garlic and oregano. Simmer, covered, 1-1/2 to 2 hours, or until beans and pork are tender. Stir in tomato paste; heat through. Ladle into soup bowls. If desired, top with radishes, cabbage, peppers and sour cream. **Yield:** 2 quarts.

FANTASTIC FLAVOR. Add a little curry powder and a large slice of lemon to the pot of your favorite vegetable soup when simmering. You'll get rave reviews about the soup's special taste.

Quick & Easy

MINESTRONE IN MINUTES

Sherrie Pfister, Hollandale, Wisconsin

(PICTURED BELOW)

3 links sweet *or* hot Italian
sausage, sliced
1 cup chopped onion
1 can (16 ounces) tomatoes
with liquid, chopped
2 small zucchini, cubed
3 beef bouillon cubes
3 cups water
2 cups finely chopped cabbage
1 can (16 ounces) great
northern beans, undrained
1 teaspoon dried basil
2 tablespoons chopped fresh
parsley
Grated Parmesan cheese

In a Dutch oven or soup kettle, brown sausage and onion until onion is tender. Add all remaining ingredients except cheese. Simmer 1 hour. Sprinkle with cheese. **Yield:** 2 quarts.

SOUP'S ON—THE DOUBLE! Making this minestrone (recipe above) is a quick trick.

THE FOCAL POINT of a meal isn't always the main course...as these recipes prove! Mustard dressing and peanuts add a tasty new twist to traditional coleslaw. Cheesy Scalloped Potatoes and rich Oven-Baked Beans are sure to please. And sweet Apple Cherry Cobbler will bring back many memories of dinners on the farm.

OLD-TIME FAVORITES.
Clockwise from the bottom: **Coleslaw with Mustard Dressing** (recipe on page 41), **Scalloped Potatoes** (recipe on page 140), **Oven-Baked Beans** (recipe on page 134) and **Apple Cherry Cobbler** (recipe on page 229).

GARDEN-FRESH SALADS

Whether you serve them as a meaty main meal or lighter side dish, refreshing salads add festive flair to any table.

COLESLAW WITH MUSTARD DRESSING

Eleanore Hill, Fresno, California

(PICTURED AT LEFT)

2 eggs
1/2 cup light cream
2 tablespoons sugar
1/2 teaspoon dry mustard
1/2 teaspoon paprika
1/2 teaspoon salt
1/3 cup cider vinegar
2 tablespoons vegetable oil
2 tablespoons water
Shredded cabbage
Salted peanuts

In a small mixing bowl, beat eggs and cream; set aside. In a small saucepan, bring sugar, mustard, paprika, salt, vinegar, oil and water to a boil, stirring constantly. Remove from the heat; very slowly add to egg mixture, stirring constantly. Return all to saucepan. Cook and stir over low heat until mixture thickens enough to coat a spoon. Cool. Just before serving, pour dressing over cabbage and toss. Sprinkle with peanuts. **Yield:** 1-1/3 cups dressing.

SEAFOOD MACARONI SALAD

Frances Harris, Coeur d'Alene, Idaho

3 cups (about 10 ounces) uncooked elbow macaroni
6 ounces peeled and deveined cooked shrimp, rinsed and drained
1 can (6 ounces) crabmeat, drained and flaked
2 cups sliced celery
1/2 small onion, finely chopped
3 to 4 hard-cooked eggs, coarsely chopped
1 cup mayonnaise
3 tablespoons sweet pickle relish *or* finely chopped sweet pickles
1 tablespoon prepared mustard
1 tablespoon vinegar
1 teaspoon paprika
Salt and pepper to taste

Cook macaroni in boiling salted water until tender; drain and cool. In a large bowl, combine macaroni, shrimp, crabmeat, celery, onion and eggs; set aside. In a small bowl, mix the mayonnaise, pickle relish, mustard, vinegar and paprika. Add to macaroni mixture; toss lightly. Season with salt and pepper. Cover and chill. **Yield:** 8 servings.

GERMAN POTATO SALAD

Mae Wagner, Pickerington, Ohio

1-1/2 to 2 pounds bacon
3-1/2 pounds potatoes, boiled, peeled and diced (about 7 cups)
1-1/2 cups chopped onion
1/4 cup all-purpose flour
1/4 cup sugar
1-1/2 cups water
1/4 cup cider vinegar
1-1/2 teaspoons salt
1/4 teaspoon pepper
1/2 cup light cream

In a large skillet, cook the bacon until crisp. Drain, reserving 3 tablespoons drippings. Crumble bacon. In a large bowl, toss bacon with potatoes and onion; set aside. In the drippings, combine flour and sugar. Combine water, vinegar, salt and pepper; stir into skillet. Cook and stir until thickened and bubbly. Stir in cream. Pour over potato mixture; toss gently to coat. Serve warm. **Yield:** 12 servings.

HOT CHICKEN SALAD

Michelle Wise, Spring Mills, Pennsylvania

(PICTURED ON PAGE 9)

✓ This tasty dish uses less sugar, salt and fat. Recipe includes *Diabetic Exchanges.*

2-1/2 cups diced cooked chicken
1 cup diced celery
1 cup sliced fresh mushrooms
1 tablespoon minced onion
1 teaspoon lemon juice
1/2 teaspoon crushed rosemary
1/4 teaspoon pepper
1 can (8 ounces) sliced water chestnuts, drained

2 cups cooked rice
3/4 cup light mayonnaise
1 can (10-3/4 ounces) cream of chicken soup, undiluted
TOPPING:
3 tablespoons butter *or* margarine
1/2 cup cornflake crumbs
1/2 cup slivered almonds

In a 2-1/2-qt. casserole, combine first nine ingredients. Blend mayonnaise and soup; toss with chicken mixture. Spoon into a greased 2-qt. casserole. In a skillet, melt butter and combine with the cornflakes and almonds. Top casserole with crumb mixture. Bake at 350° for 30 minutes. **Yield:** 6 servings. **Diabetic Exchanges:** One serving (prepared without topping) equals 2 lean meat, 1-1/2 starch, 1 vegetable, 1 fat; also, 272 calories, 522 mg sodium, 40 mg cholesterol, 29 gm carbohydrate, 21 gm protein, 12 gm fat.

LAYERED FRESH FRUIT SALAD

Page Alexander, Baldwin City, Kansas

(PICTURED ON PAGE 102)

CITRUS SAUCE:
2/3 cup fresh orange juice
1/3 cup fresh lemon juice
1/3 cup packed brown sugar
1 cinnamon stick
1/2 teaspoon grated orange peel
1/2 teaspoon grated lemon peel
FRUIT SALAD:
2 cups cubed fresh pineapple
1 pint fresh strawberries, hulled and sliced
2 kiwifruit, peeled and sliced
3 medium bananas, sliced
2 oranges, peeled and sectioned
1 red grapefruit, peeled and sectioned
1 cup seedless red grapes

In a saucepan, bring all sauce ingredients to a boil; simmer 5 minutes. Cool. Meanwhile, in a large clear glass salad bowl, layer fruit in order listed. Remove cinnamon stick from the sauce and pour sauce over fruit. Cover and refrigerate several hours. **Yield:** 10-12 servings.

SESAME BEEF AND ASPARAGUS SALAD

Tamara Steeb, Issaquah, Washington

(PICTURED ON PAGE 79)

✓ This tasty dish uses less sugar, salt and fat. Recipe includes *Diabetic Exchanges.*

1 pound top round steak
4 cups sliced fresh asparagus (cut in 2-inch pieces)
3 tablespoons soy sauce
2 tablespoons sesame oil
1 tablespoon rice wine vinegar
1/2 teaspoon grated gingerroot
Sesame seeds
Lettuce leaves, optional

Broil steak to desired doneness. Cool and cut into thin diagonal strips. Cook asparagus in a small amount of water 30-60 seconds. Drain and cool. Combine beef and asparagus. Blend all remaining ingredients except the sesame seeds and lettuce; pour over beef and asparagus. Sprinkle with sesame seeds and toss lightly. Serve warm or at room temperature on lettuce leaves if desired. **Yield:** 6 servings. **Diabetic Exchanges:** One serving equals 2 lean meat, 1-1/2 vegetable, 1/2 fat; also 179 calories, 696 mg sodium, 48 mg cholesterol, 6 gm carbohydrate, 21 gm protein, 8 gm fat.

Quick & Easy

PINEAPPLE COLESLAW

Betty Follas, Morgan Hill, California

(PICTURED ON PAGE 29)

3/4 cup mayonnaise
2 tablespoons vinegar
2 tablespoons sugar
1 to 2 tablespoons milk
4 cups shredded cabbage
1 can (8 ounces) pineapple tidbits, well drained
Paprika, optional

In a mixing bowl, combine mayonnaise, vinegar, sugar and milk. Place cabbage and pineapple in a large salad bowl; add dressing and toss. Chill. Sprinkle with paprika before serving if desired. **Yield:** 8 servings.

GRANDMA'S GELATIN FRUIT SALAD

Wilma McLean, Medford, Oregon

2 cups boiling water, *divided*
1 package (3 ounces) lemon-flavored gelatin
2 cups ice cubes, *divided*

1 can (20 ounces) crushed pineapple, liquid drained and reserved
1 package (3 ounces) orange-flavored gelatin
2 cups miniature marshmallows
3 large bananas, sliced
1/2 cup finely shredded cheddar cheese
COOKED SALAD DRESSING:
1 cup reserved pineapple juice
1/2 cup sugar
1 egg, beaten
2 tablespoons cornstarch
1 tablespoon butter *or* margarine
1 cup whipped topping

In a mixing bowl, combine 1 cup water and lemon gelatin. Add 1 cup ice cubes, stirring until melted. Add pineapple. Pour into a 13-in. x 9-in. x 2-in. baking pan; refrigerate until set. Repeat with orange gelatin, remaining water and ice. Stir in marshmallows. Pour over lemon layer; refrigerate until set. For dressing, combine pineapple juice, sugar, egg, cornstarch and butter in a saucepan. Cook over medium heat, stirring constantly, until thickened. Cover and refrigerate overnight. The next day, arrange bananas over gelatin. Combine dressing with whipped topping; spread over bananas. Sprinkle with cheese. **Yield:** 12-15 servings.

CALICO POTATO SALAD

Christine Hartry, Emo, Ontario

(PICTURED ON PAGE 108)

✓ This tasty dish uses less sugar, salt and fat. Recipe includes *Diabetic Exchanges.*

DRESSING:
1/2 cup olive oil
1/4 cup vinegar
1 tablespoon sugar
1-1/2 teaspoons chili powder
1 teaspoon salt, optional
Dash hot pepper sauce
SALAD:
4 large red potatoes (about 2 pounds), peeled and cooked
1-1/2 cups cooked whole kernel corn
1 cup shredded carrot
1/2 cup chopped red onion
1/2 cup diced green pepper
1/2 cup diced sweet red pepper
1/2 cup sliced pitted ripe olives

In a small bowl or jar, combine all dressing ingredients; cover and chill. Cube potatoes; combine with corn, carrot, onion, peppers and olives in a salad bowl. Pour dressing over; toss lightly. Cover and chill. **Yield:** 14 servings. **Diabetic Exchanges:** One serving (prepared without added

salt) equals 1-1/2 fat, 1 starch; also, 146 calories, 212 mg sodium, 0 cholesterol, 17 gm carbohydrate, 2 gm protein, 9 gm fat.

FRENCH DRESSING WITH TOMATOES

Dana Barnes, Beaufort, South Carolina

1 can (10-3/4 ounces) tomato soup, undiluted
1 cup vegetable oil
1/2 cup vinegar
1/2 cup sugar
1 tablespoon Worcestershire sauce
1 tablespoon prepared mustard
2 to 3 teaspoons pepper
1 teaspoon salt
1/4 teaspoon garlic powder
Tomatoes, cut into wedges
Lettuce leaves

In a jar or airtight container, place all ingredients except last two. Shake well. In a bowl, place tomatoes and enough dressing to cover. Let stand several hours at room temperature. To serve, remove tomatoes from dressing with a slotted spoon; place on lettuce leaves. Drizzle with dressing. **Yield:** 3 cups dressing.

Quick & Easy

MIXED GREENS WITH BLUE CHEESE DRESSING

Peggy Hughes, Albany, Kentucky

(PICTURED ON PAGE 180)

✓ This tasty dish uses less sugar, salt and fat. Recipe includes *Diabetic Exchanges.*

1 small head cauliflower, broken into florets
2 quarts mixed salad greens
4 slices red onion, separated into rings
1/4 cup sliced stuffed green olives
BLUE CHEESE DRESSING:
2 ounces blue cheese, crumbled
1/3 cup salad oil
2 tablespoons lemon juice
1/2 teaspoon sugar
1/4 teaspoon salt
2 tablespoons chopped parsley
3 tablespoons chopped green onion

In large salad bowl, combine first four ingredients. Chill until ready to serve. Combine dressing ingredients; toss with greens mixture just before serving. **Yield:** 8 servings. **Diabetic Exchanges:** One serving equals 1/2 meat, 2 vegetable, 2 fat; also, 181 calories, 310 mg sodium, 5 mg cholesterol, 9 gm carbohydrate, 6 gm protein, 13 gm fat.

IT WAS mid-morning, and I was a hungry 5-year-old.

Never mind the fact I'd earlier put away a farm breakfast of one country ham biscuit and one plum jam biscuit (each as big as a pancake), washed down with a foamy glass of fresh milk from "Bessie", Grandma's gentle cow.

Since lunch would not be served for a long time, I knew what I had to do—visit Grandma's garden for a taste of her wonderful red ripe "maters"!

Had Farm Fun

Homegrown tomatoes were a favorite part of summertime visits to my grandparents' farm during the 1930s. I was also enthralled with the space, the animals, the peace, Grandpa's dedication to the land and Grandma's contentment with her home.

Grandpa had built me a tree house in an old oak just outside the house, and that's where I was when my mid-morning hunger pangs hit.

I clambered down and scampered to the house. Bounding up the steps, I glanced beneath them to spy "Queenie" and her litter of kittens relaxing in the shade.

The screen door squeaked as I pulled it open. Grandma was standing at the sink, humming as she cleaned a chicken to fry for our lunch.

"Can I have some salt, please?" I innocently asked.

"Sure, honey. But don't go filling up on tomatoes before lunch," Grandma said in her best "you-don't-fool-me" tone.

I Recall Grandma's Red Ripe 'Maters'

A homegrown tomato eaten fresh from the vine was a summer pleasure to savor!

By Jane Wood
Wilson, North Carolina

I took a handful of salt and dashed out the door. I was so happy I skipped down the path to the garden, my bare feet slapping the warm earth and sending up little puffs of dust.

I sang to myself as I skipped, "To the garden hippy-hop, to the garden

ready or not, to the garden for maters so red, I don't care what Grandma said!"

Took Her Pick

The garden was laid out in perfect rows, and the tomato plants were neatly tied to wooden stakes. Their crimson fruit decorated the lush green vines like red ornaments at Christmas.

Grandma's tomatoes grew in all sizes, but I preferred only the *tiniest* ones, not much bigger than my brother's marble shooter. I picked six of these tasty morsels, put them in the pocket of my feed sack dress and set off for the barn to feast in privacy.

Once inside, I flopped atop a pile of plant bed sheeting and took a tomato out of my pocket. I carefully wiped the tantalizing treat on my skirt to remove any dirt or dust.

Then, holding the tomato by the stem with my little finger extended like a lady holding a teacup, I took a small bite out of the bottom to make the juice flow.

Quickly I dipped the dripping tomato into the salt in my left hand and popped it into my mouth. I closed my eyes to savor the flavor as the red juice, still warm from the August sun, bathed my taste buds with garden goodness.

One gulp and it was gone!

Dusting off tomato number two, I again sang my happy little tomato rhyme to myself…and wondered how long it would be before Grandma would call me and Grandpa inside for lunch!

WHEN the clan comes for dinner, you can bet
they'll be hungry! So it pays to have an appealing array of
side dishes, oven entrees and desserts on hand.
And no one will be able to resist the crunchy Broccoli Bacon Salad and cool
and creamy Autumn Apple Salad.
Why not try some of these recipes today?

COME AND GET IT!
Clockwise from lower left: **Blackberry Dumplings** (recipe on page 214),
Sour Cream 'n' Dill Chicken (recipe on page 64), **Pecan-Chocolate
Chip Pound Cake** (recipe on page 193), **Creamy Carrot Casserole**
(recipe on page 124), **Broccoli Bacon Salad** (recipe on page 46),
Cheddar Parmesan Potatoes (recipe on page 141), **Autumn
Apple Salad** (recipe on page 46) and **One-Dish
Pork Chop Dinner** (recipe on page 62).

AUTUMN APPLE SALAD

Melissa Bowers, Sidney, Ohio

(PICTURED ON PAGE 45)

1 can (20 ounces) crushed
  pineapple, undrained
2/3 cup sugar
1 package (3 ounces)
  lemon-flavored gelatin
1 package (8 ounces) cream
  cheese, softened
1 cup diced unpeeled apples
1/2 to 1 cup chopped nuts
1 cup chopped celery
1 cup whipped topping
Lettuce leaves

In a saucepan, combine pineapple and sugar; bring to a boil and boil for 3 minutes. Add gelatin; stir until dissolved. Add cream cheese; stir until mixture is thoroughly combined. Cool. Fold in apples, nuts, celery and whipped topping. Pour into a 9-in. square baking pan. Chill until firm. Cut into squares and serve on lettuce leaves. **Yield:** 9-12 servings.

Quick
& Easy

BROCCOLI BACON SALAD

Joyce Blakley, Windsor Locks, Connecticut

(PICTURED ON PAGE 45)

1 large bunch broccoli,
  separated into florets
1 small red onion,
  coarsely chopped
1 cup raisins
10 to 12 bacon strips, cooked
  and crumbled
DRESSING:
3 tablespoons vinegar
1/3 cup mayonnaise
1/3 cup sugar

In a large serving bowl, combine the broccoli, onion, raisins and bacon; set aside. In a mixing bowl, combine dressing ingredients. Just before serving, pour dressing over broccoli mixture; toss to coat. **Yield:** 6-8 servings.

CALIFORNIA PASTA SALAD

Jeanette Krembas, Laguna Niguel, California

(PICTURED ON PAGE 18)

1 pound thin spaghetti *or*
  vermicelli, broken into 1-inch
  pieces, cooked
3 large tomatoes, diced
2 medium zucchini, diced
1 large cucumber, diced
1 medium green pepper, diced
1 sweet red pepper, diced

1 large red onion, diced
2 cans (2-1/4 ounces *each*) sliced
  ripe olives, drained
1 bottle (16 ounces) Italian
  salad dressing
1/4 cup grated Parmesan *or*
  Romano cheese
1 tablespoon sesame seeds
2 teaspoons poppy seeds
1 teaspoon paprika
1/2 teaspoon celery seed
1/4 teaspoon garlic powder

Combine all ingredients in a large bowl; cover with plastic wrap and refrigerate overnight to blend flavors. **Yield:** 10-15 servings.

SPICY COLESLAW

Valerie Jones, Portland, Maine

(PICTURED ON PAGE 63)

☑ This tasty dish uses less sugar, salt and fat. Recipe includes *Diabetic Exchanges*.

6 cups shredded cabbage
1 cup chopped unpeeled
  cucumber
1 cup chopped tomato
1 cup chopped green pepper
1 cup sliced green onions
2/3 cup spicy vegetable juice
1/4 cup red wine vinegar
2 teaspoons sugar
1 teaspoon celery seed
1/2 teaspoon pepper
1/4 teaspoon salt, optional

In a large bowl, combine cabbage, cucumber, tomato, green pepper and green onions; set aside. In a small bowl, combine remaining ingredients; mix well. Pour over cabbage mixture and toss gently. Cover and chill for 2 hours; stir before serving. **Yield:** 12 servings.
Diabetic Exchanges: One 3/4-cup serving (prepared without added salt) equals 1 vegetable; also, 26 calories, 105 mg sodium, 0 cholesterol, 5 gm carbohydrate, 1 gm protein, trace fat.

MARINATED ZUCCHINI SALAD

Billie Blanton, Kingsport, Tennessee

(PICTURED ON PAGE 73)

6 small zucchini (about 1-1/4
  pounds), thinly sliced
1/2 cup chopped green pepper
1/2 cup diced celery
1/2 cup diced onion
1 jar (2 ounces) diced pimiento,
  drained
2/3 cup vinegar
1/3 cup vegetable oil

1/2 cup sugar
3 tablespoons white wine
  vinegar
1/2 teaspoon salt
1/2 teaspoon pepper

Combine zucchini, green pepper, celery, onion and pimiento in a medium bowl; set aside. Combine remaining ingredients in a jar; cover tightly and shake vigorously. Pour marinade over vegetables; toss gently. Cover and chill 8 hours or overnight. Serve with a slotted spoon. **Yield:** 8 servings.

Quick
& Easy

SPINACH SALAD

Irene Leopold, Colby, Kansas

(PICTURED ON PAGE 97)

DRESSING:
1/2 cup packed brown sugar
1/2 cup vegetable oil
1/3 cup vinegar
1/3 cup ketchup
1 tablespoon Worcestershire
  sauce
SALAD:
2 quarts fresh spinach
  leaves, torn
1 can (16 ounces) bean
  sprouts, drained *or* 2 cups
  fresh bean sprouts
1 can (8 ounces) sliced water
  chestnuts, drained
4 hard-cooked eggs, peeled
  and diced
6 bacon strips, cooked and
  crumbled
1 small onion, thinly sliced

In a bottle or jar, combine all dressing ingredients. Shake well to mix. Set aside. In a large salad bowl, toss all salad ingredients. Just before serving, pour dressing over salad and toss. **Yield:** 8 servings.

CRANBERRY SALAD

Nell Bass, Macon, Georgia

(PICTURED ON PAGE 128)

1 cup sugar
1 cup water
1 package (6 ounces) lemon-
  flavored gelatin
4 cups fresh cranberries,
  ground

2 large unpeeled apples, cored
   and ground
1 unpeeled orange, seeded and
   ground
1/2 cup chopped pecans
Lettuce leaves, optional
Mayonnaise, optional

In a saucepan, bring sugar and water to a boil, stirring constantly. Remove from the heat; immediately stir in gelatin until dissolved. Chill until mixture is the consistency of unbeaten egg whites. Fold in the cranberries, apples, orange and pecans. Spoon into oiled individual salad molds, a 6-1/2-cup ring mold or an 11-in. x 7-in. x 2-in. dish. Chill until firm. If desired, serve on lettuce leaves and top with a dollop of mayonnaise. **Yield:** 12-15 servings.

Quick & Easy

SOUR CREAM CUCUMBER SALAD

Lydia Robotewskyj, Franklin, Wisconsin

(PICTURED ON PAGE 226)

✓ This tasty dish uses less sugar, salt and fat. Recipe includes *Diabetic Exchanges*.

3 medium cucumbers, peeled
   and thinly sliced
1/2 teaspoon salt
1/2 cup finely chopped green
   onions
1 tablespoon white vinegar
Dash white pepper
1/4 cup sour cream

Sprinkle the cucumbers with salt. Let stand 15 minutes. Drain liquid. Add onions, vinegar and pepper. Just before serving, stir in sour cream. **Yield:** 6 servings. **Diabetic Exchanges:** One serving (prepared with light sour cream) equals 1 vegetable; also, 35 calories, 197 mg sodium, 2 mg cholesterol, 6 gm carbohydrate, 2 gm protein, 1 gm fat.

CHERRY PINEAPPLE SALAD

Leona Luecking, West Burlington, Iowa

3 packages (3 ounces *each*)
   cherry-flavored gelatin
2-1/3 cups boiling water
1 can (20 ounces) pineapple
   tidbits, liquid drained and
   reserved
2 cans (16-1/2 ounces *each*)
   pitted dark sweet cherries,
   liquid drained and reserved
1/3 cup lemon juice
1/3 cup whipping cream
1/3 cup mayonnaise
2 packages (3 ounces *each*)
   cream cheese, softened

Dash salt
1/2 cup coarsely chopped nuts

In a mixing bowl, dissolve gelatin in water. Combine pineapple and cherry juices to measure 2-1/2 cups; add along with lemon juice to gelatin. Divide gelatin in half. Set half of the gelatin aside and chill other half until partially set. Fold pineapple into chilled gelatin; pour into a 13-in. x 9-in. x 2-in. pan. Chill until almost firm. Whip cream, mayonnaise, cream cheese and salt until light and fluffy. Spread over chilled gelatin layer. Refrigerate until firm. Chill remaining gelatin mixture until partially set. Fold in cherries and nuts; spread over cream cheese layer. Chill for at least 3 hours. **Yield:** 12-16 servings.

SWISS CHEESE SALAD

Laverne Branomeyer, San Antonio, Texas

1 cup sliced green onions
1 cup sliced celery
1 cup diced green pepper
1 cup sliced stuffed green olives
1/3 cup vegetable oil
2 tablespoons red wine vinegar
1 tablespoon Dijon mustard
Salt and pepper to taste
6 cups shredded lettuce
2 cups (8 ounces) shredded
   Swiss cheese

In a small bowl, combine onions, celery, green pepper and olives. In another bowl, whisk together oil, vinegar, mustard, salt and pepper. Pour over vegetables and refrigerate several hours or overnight. Just before serving, place lettuce in a large salad bowl; add the cheese and dressing with vegetables. Toss lightly. **Yield:** 6-8 servings.

EASY AND CHEESY. To make hot cheesy potato salad, add 1 cup mayonnaise, 1 pound process cheese and 1/2 cup chopped onion to 8 sliced cooked potatoes. Top with 5 to 6 slices of bacon; bake at 325° for 1 hour.

CURRIED CHICKEN FRUIT SALAD

Carol Mead, Los Alamos, New Mexico

1 can (11 ounces) mandarin
   oranges, drained
1 can (8 ounces) pineapple
   tidbits, drained
1 can (8 ounces) water
   chestnuts, drained

4 cups cubed cooked chicken
2 cups seedless red *or* green
   grapes, halved
1 cup chopped celery
Lettuce leaves
Sliced almonds
DRESSING:
1-1/2 cups mayonnaise
1 tablespoon soy sauce
1 tablespoon lemon juice
1-1/2 teaspoons curry powder

In a large bowl, combine the oranges, pineapple, water chestnuts, chicken, grapes and celery. In a small bowl, combine all dressing ingredients. Pour over salad; toss well to coat. Chill 1 hour. Serve on a bed of lettuce; sprinkle with almonds. **Yield:** 8 servings.

CROWD-PLEASING POTATO SALAD

Marcille Meyer, Battle Creek, Nebraska

(PICTURED BELOW)

1 gallon potatoes (about 16
   large), cooked, peeled and
   sliced
10 hard-cooked eggs
1 cup chopped onion
2 cups salad dressing *or*
   mayonnaise
1 cup light cream
1/3 cup vinegar
1/3 cup sugar
3 tablespoons prepared
   mustard
1/2 teaspoon salt

Place potatoes in a large salad bowl. Separate eggs. Chop whites and add to potatoes with onion. Toss gently. In another bowl, mash yolks with salad dressing, cream, vinegar, sugar, mustard and salt. Pour over potatoes and stir to coat. Cover and chill. **Yield:** 16-20 servings.

MAKE YOUR MARK. Potato salad will become your trademark at potlucks, picnics.

MAKE THIS mouth-watering meat-and-potatoes meal for your family…and don't be surprised if it becomes a regular favorite! For starters, California Green Salad—made with chunks of avocado and almonds—will wake up tastebuds. It's a fitting accompaniment to the juicy, tomato-topped Country Herbed Meat Loaf and creamy Confetti Scalloped Potatoes.

TANTALIZING TRIO.
Top to bottom: **California Green Salad** (recipe on page 49), **Confetti Scalloped Potatoes** (recipe on page 134) and **Country Herbed Meat Loaf** (recipe on page 62).

Quick & Easy

CALIFORNIA GREEN SALAD

Mrs. W. Ellermeyer, Walnut Creek, California

(PICTURED AT LEFT)

DRESSING:
- 1/2 cup vegetable *or* olive oil
- 2 tablespoons vinegar
- 2 tablespoons lemon juice
- 1/4 to 1/2 teaspoon salt
- 1/4 teaspoon dry mustard
- 1/4 teaspoon paprika

SALAD:
- 1 large head romaine, torn into pieces
- 1 avocado, diced
- 4 green onions with tops, sliced
- 1/4 cup slivered almonds, toasted
- 1/4 cup crumbled blue cheese

Dash seasoned salt

In a jar, combine all dressing ingredients; shake well. Cover and refrigerate. Just before serving, toss together romaine, avocado, onions, almonds and blue cheese in a large salad bowl. Sprinkle with seasoned salt. Pour the dressing over salad; toss well to coat. Serve immediately. **Yield:** 6 servings.

MACARONI SALAD WITH BASIL DRESSING

Christine Gibson, Fontana, Wisconsin

(PICTURED ON PAGE 116)

 This tasty dish uses less sugar, salt and fat. Recipe includes *Diabetic Exchanges*.

- 1 cup loosely packed fresh basil leaves
- 3 garlic cloves
- 1/2 teaspoon pepper
- 1/2 teaspoon salt, optional
- 2/3 cup olive oil
- 1 tablespoon red wine vinegar
- 3 medium tomatoes, seeded and diced
- 2 to 3 medium zucchini, cut into 1/4-inch slices
- 7 to 8 ounces elbow macaroni, cooked and drained
- 2 cups (8 ounces) shredded cheddar cheese *or* low-fat mozzarella

In a blender container or food processor, combine the basil, garlic, pepper, and salt if desired. Process until finely chopped. Add oil and vinegar; process until well blended. Set aside. In a 4-qt. salad bowl, combine tomatoes, zucchini, macaroni and cheese; toss lightly. Pour dressing over all; toss to coat. Cover and refrigerate at least 2 hours or overnight. **Yield:** 10 servings. **Diabetic Exchanges:** One serving (prepared with low-fat mozzarella

and without added salt) equals 3 fat, 1 starch, 1 vegetable, 1 meat; also, 273 calories, 126 mg sodium, 12 mg cholesterol, 21 gm carbohydrate, 10 gm protein, 18 gm fat.

MOLDED ASPARAGUS SALAD

Bernice Morris, Marshfield, Missouri

(PICTURED ON PAGE 79)

- 1 cup sliced fresh asparagus
- 1 can (10-3/4 ounces) cream of asparagus soup, undiluted
- 1 package (8 ounces) cream cheese, softened
- 1 package (3 ounces) lemon-flavored gelatin
- 1 cup boiling water
- 1/2 teaspoon lemon extract
- 1/2 cup diced celery
- 1/2 cup diced green pepper
- 2 teaspoons minced onion
- 2 teaspoons minced pimiento
- 1/2 cup finely chopped pecans
- 1/2 cup mayonnaise

Celery leaves
Chopped pimiento
Lemon slice

Cook asparagus in a small amount of water. Drain and set aside to cool. In a saucepan, heat soup and cream cheese, stirring until well blended. Dissolve the gelatin in boiling water; add the extract. Cool. Combine gelatin, asparagus, celery, green pepper, onion, minced pimiento, pecans, mayonnaise and soup mixture. Pour into greased 5- to 6-cup mold. Chill until firm, about 4-6 hours. Unmold; garnish with celery leaves, pimiento pieces and lemon slice. **Yield:** 6-8 servings.

CATHY'S TOMATO AND BEAN SALAD

Cathy Meizel, Flanders, New York

(PICTURED ON PAGE 113)

 This tasty dish uses less sugar, salt and fat. Recipe includes *Diabetic Exchanges*.

- 1 can (15 ounces) garbanzo beans, rinsed and drained
- 4 large ripe tomatoes, sliced thick
- 1 cup thinly sliced red onion
- 1 can (6 ounces) medium pitted ripe olives, drained and halved
- 1/2 cup olive oil

- 5 to 6 large fresh basil leaves, snipped *or* 1 tablespoon dried basil
- 1/2 teaspoon dried oregano
- 1/4 teaspoon pepper

Salt to taste
- 1/8 teaspoon garlic powder

In a large salad bowl, layer beans, tomatoes, onion and olives. Combine all remaining ingredients; pour over vegetables. Cover and chill at least 3 hours or overnight. Serve chilled or at room temperature. **Yield:** 8 servings. **Diabetic Exchanges:** One serving (prepared without added salt) equals 1 starch, 1 vegetable, 2 fat; also, 178 calories, 333 mg sodium, 0 mg cholesterol, 19 gm carbohydrate, 4 gm protein, 10 gm fat.

PENNSYLVANIA DUTCH COLESLAW

Deb Darr, Falls City, Oregon

(PICTURED ON PAGE 86)

- 1 medium head green cabbage, shredded (about 8 cups)
- 1 cup shredded red cabbage
- 4 to 5 carrots, shredded
- 1 cup mayonnaise
- 2 tablespoons cider vinegar
- 1/2 cup sugar
- 1 teaspoon salt
- 1/4 teaspoon pepper

In a large bowl, combine cabbage and carrots; set aside. In a small bowl, combine all remaining ingredients; pour over cabbage mixture. Toss well and refrigerate overnight. **Yield:** 12-16 servings.

ROSY RHUBARB SALAD

Wanda Rader, Greeneville, Tennessee

(PICTURED ON PAGE 209)

- 3 cups sliced fresh *or* frozen rhubarb (1-inch pieces)
- 1 tablespoon sugar
- 1 package (3 ounces) raspberry-flavored gelatin
- 1 cup unsweetened pineapple juice
- 1 teaspoon lemon juice
- 1 cup diced peeled apples
- 1 cup diced celery
- 1/4 cup chopped pecans

In a medium saucepan, cook and stir rhubarb and sugar over medium-low heat until rhubarb is soft and tender. Remove from the heat; add gelatin and stir until dissolved. Stir in pineapple and lemon juices. Chill until partially set. Stir in apples, celery and pecans. Pour into a 4-1/2-cup mold or glass bowl. Chill several hours or overnight. **Yield:** 8 servings.

SPECIAL SALAD. Family, friends will be tickled pink when presented Cranberry Delight.

CRANBERRY DELIGHT

Edna Olson, Rancho Murieta, California

(PICTURED ABOVE)

- 1 can (20 ounces) crushed pineapple, juice drained and reserved
- 1 cup water
- 1 package (6 ounces) strawberry-flavored gelatin
- 1 can (16 ounces) whole-berry cranberry sauce
- 3 tablespoons lemon juice
- 1 teaspoon grated lemon peel
- 1/2 teaspoon ground nutmeg
- 2 cups (16 ounces) sour cream
- 1/2 cup chopped pecans
Fresh strawberries, optional

Combine pineapple juice and water in a 2-qt. saucepan; heat to boiling. Remove from heat; add gelatin and stir until it dissolves. Stir in cranberry sauce, lemon juice, peel and nutmeg. Chill until mixture thickens slightly. Add sour cream; stir until thoroughly combined. Fold in pineapple and pecans. Pour into an 8-cup mold; chill until firm. Unmold onto a serving plate. Garnish with fresh strawberries if desired. **Yield:** 12 servings.

CARROT/LENTIL SALAD

Monica Wilcott, Sturgis, Saskatchewan

(PICTURED ON PAGE 138)

✓ This tasty dish uses less sugar, salt and fat. Recipe includes *Diabetic Exchanges*.

- 1 cup dry lentils
- 1 cup diced carrots
- 2 garlic cloves, minced
- 1 bay leaf
DRESSING:
- 1/2 cup finely chopped celery
- 1/4 cup finely chopped fresh parsley

- 1/4 cup olive oil
- 1/4 cup lemon juice
- 1 teaspoon salt
- 1/2 teaspoon dried thyme
- 1/4 teaspoon pepper

In a Dutch oven, combine lentils, carrots, garlic and bay leaf. Cover with 1 in. of water. Bring to a boil, then simmer 15-20 minutes or until lentils are tender. Remove bay leaf; drain and cool. Meanwhile, combine all dressing ingredients. Pour over lentil mixture. Cover and refrigerate several hours. **Yield:** 6 servings. **Diabetic Exchanges:** One serving equals 1-1/2 vegetable, 1 starch, 2 fat; also, 202 calories, 403 mg sodium, 0 mg cholesterol, 23 gm carbohydrate, 8 gm protein, 9 gm fat.

Quick & Easy

CRAB SALAD SUPREME

Mrs. A. Mayer, Richmond, Virginia

- 2 cups crabmeat
- 1/2 cup minced green onions
- 1/2 cup diced celery
- 1/2 cup minced green pepper
- 1 tablespoon dry mustard
- 1 teaspoon salt
- 1/4 teaspoon pepper
- 2 teaspoons celery seed
Shredded lettuce
- 4 hard-cooked eggs, sliced
- 4 tomatoes, cut into wedges
SAUCE:
- 1/3 cup mayonnaise
- 1/3 cup sour cream
- 1/3 cup chili sauce
- 2 teaspoons lemon juice

Combine first eight ingredients. Combine sauce ingredients; pour over salad and toss. Spoon onto lettuce on individual plates or a serving platter; garnish with eggs and tomatoes. Refrigerate until serving. **Yield:** 4-6 servings.

MOLDED LIME SALAD

Jean Parsons, Sarver, Pennsylvania

- 2 cups boiling water
- 1 package (6 ounces) lime-flavored gelatin
- 1 cup cold water
- 1 tablespoon vinegar
Dash salt
Dash white pepper, optional
- 3/4 cup mayonnaise
- 1/2 cup shredded carrots
- 1/2 cup finely chopped peeled cucumber
- 1/2 cup finely chopped celery
- 1/2 cup finely chopped green pepper
- 2 tablespoons finely chopped onion
Carrot curls, optional

In a mixing bowl, pour boiling water over gelatin. Stir to dissolve. Add cold water, vinegar, salt and pepper if desired. Pour 1 cup of mixture into a 6-cup mold; set aside. Chill remaining gelatin for 30 minutes, then add mayonnaise and blend with a rotary beater until smooth. Chill until almost set. Meanwhile, chill gelatin in mold until almost set. Turn mayonnaise/gelatin mixture into a bowl and whip until fluffy. Fold in shredded carrots, cucumber, celery, green pepper and onion. Spoon into mold. Chill until firm. Unmold to serve. Garnish with carrot curls if desired. **Yield:** 8-10 servings.

ZUCCHINI HARVEST SALAD

Marie Wellman, Seattle, Washington

(PICTURED ON PAGE 136)

✓ This tasty dish uses less sugar, salt and fat. Recipe includes *Diabetic Exchanges*.

- 4 cups thinly sliced zucchini
- 1 cup sliced celery
- 1/2 cup sliced fresh mushrooms
- 1/2 cup sliced ripe olives
- 1/4 cup chopped green pepper
- 1/4 cup chopped sweet red pepper
- 1 cup mild *or* medium picante sauce *or* salsa
- 1/2 cup vinegar
- 3 tablespoons olive oil
- 3 tablespoons sugar
- 1/2 teaspoon oregano
- 1 garlic clove, minced
Lettuce leaves

In a large mixing bowl, combine first six ingredients, toss to mix. In a small bowl or jar, combine all remaining ingredients except lettuce and shake or mix well. Pour over vegetables. Cover and chill several hours or overnight. Serve in a large salad bowl lined with lettuce or in individual lettuce "cups". **Yield:** 8 servings. **Diabetic Exchanges:** One serving equals 1-1/2 vegetable, 1-1/2 fat; also, 113 calories, 37 mg sodium, 0 mg cholesterol, 13 gm carbohydrate, 2 gm protein, 7 gm fat.

NORWEGIAN COLESLAW

Gerry Beveridge, Beaufort, North Carolina

- 1 medium head cabbage
- 1 tablespoon salt
- 1-1/2 cups sugar
- 1 cup vinegar
- 1 teaspoon mustard seed
- 1 teaspoon celery seed
- 2 cups chopped celery
- 1 small green pepper, chopped
- 1 small sweet red pepper, chopped
- 2 carrots, shredded

Shred cabbage and toss with salt. Cover and refrigerate at least 2 hours. In a saucepan, heat sugar, vinegar, mustard and celery seed. Cook until the sugar dissolves, about 10 minutes. Cool completely. Add to the cabbage along with remaining vegetables; toss. Cover and refrigerate at least 1 week before serving. Keeps for 4-6 weeks in the refrigerator. **Yield:** 12-16 servings.

FRESH CORN SALAD
Carol Shaffer, Cape Girardeau, Missouri
(PICTURED ON PAGE 82)

 This tasty dish uses less sugar, salt and fat. Recipe includes *Diabetic Exchanges*.

8 ears fresh corn, husked and cleaned
1/2 cup vegetable oil
1/4 cup cider vinegar
1-1/2 teaspoons lemon juice
1/4 cup minced fresh parsley
2 teaspoons sugar
1 teaspoon salt, optional
1/2 teaspoon dried basil
1/8 to 1/4 teaspoon cayenne pepper
2 large tomatoes, seeded and coarsely chopped
1/2 cup chopped onion
1/3 cup chopped green pepper
1/3 cup chopped sweet red pepper

In a large saucepan, cook corn in enough boiling water to cover for 5-7 minutes or until tender. Drain, cool and set aside. In a large bowl, mix the oil, vinegar, lemon juice, parsley, sugar, salt if desired, basil and cayenne pepper. Cut cooled corn off the cob (should measure 4 cups). Add corn, tomatoes, onion and peppers to the oil mixture. Mix well. Cover and chill for several hours or overnight. **Yield:** 10 servings. **Diabetic Exchanges:** One serving (prepared without added salt) equals 1 starch, 1/2 vegetable, 1/2 fat; also, 102 calories, 251 mg sodium, 0 cholesterol, 21 gm carbohydrate, 3 gm protein, 2 gm fat.

SOUTHWESTERN SALAD
Carolyn Oler, Gilbert, Arizona

1 can (15 ounces) pinto beans, rinsed and drained
1 bunch green onions with tops, sliced
1 large tomato, seeded and chopped
1 avocado, chopped
1 bottle (8 ounces) Catalina salad dressing, *divided*
2 cups (8 ounces) shredded cheddar cheese

1 medium head lettuce, torn into bite-size pieces
4 cups corn chips

In a large salad bowl, toss together the beans, green onions, tomato, avocado and half of the Catalina dressing. Top with cheese and then lettuce. Refrigerate. Just before serving, add corn chips to salad and toss. Pass the remaining dressing. **Yield:** 8-10 servings.

GARDEN PASTA SALAD
Bernie Bellin, Franklin, Wisconsin

8 ounces corkscrew *or* cartwheel pasta
3 cups assorted chopped fresh *or* frozen vegetables
1 bottle (16 ounces) zesty Italian salad dressing, *divided*
1 cup cubed cooked chicken, turkey *or* ham
1 cup cubed cheddar, mozzarella *or* Monterey Jack cheese
1 can (2-1/2 ounces) sliced ripe olives, drained
Minced fresh parsley *or* basil, optional

Cook pasta according to package directions. Drain but do not rinse. Put pasta back into the kettle. While pasta is hot, toss with the vegetables. Cover for 3-5 minutes. Vegetables will lightly steam in pasta. Place pasta in a large salad bowl. Top with 3/4 of the dressing and lightly toss. Chill several hours or overnight. If pasta is dry, add remaining dressing along with meat, cheese, olives, and parsley or basil if desired. Chill until ready to serve. **Yield:** 6-8 servings.

SUNDAY LAYERED SALAD
Mildred Sherrer, Bay City, Texas

1 head iceberg lettuce, chopped
1 package (10 ounces) frozen peas, thawed
1/4 cup chopped red onion
1/2 cup chopped celery
1/2 cup diced green pepper
1 can (8 ounces) sliced water chestnuts, drained
2 cups salad dressing *or* mayonnaise
2 tablespoons sugar
1/4 cup grated Parmesan cheese
8 bacon strips, cooked and crumbled

In a 13-in. x 9-in. x 2-in. baking pan, layer all ingredients in order given. Cover and refrigerate until serving time. Do not toss. Cut into squares to serve. Will keep for several days. **Yield:** 8-10 servings.

ASPARAGUS AND TOMATO SALAD
Nanci Brewer, San Jose, California
(PICTURED ON PAGE 78)

 This tasty dish uses less sugar, salt and fat. Recipe includes *Diabetic Exchanges*.

1/4 cup water
1/4 teaspoon onion powder
1 pound fresh asparagus, trimmed
8 to 16 lettuce leaves
2 to 3 large tomatoes, sliced
1 ripe avocado, sliced, optional
DRESSING:
1/2 cup mayonnaise
1/2 cup sour cream
2 teaspoons prepared mustard
1 teaspoon catsup
Salt and pepper to taste

Combine the water and onion powder; bring to a boil. Add the asparagus and cook 3-5 minutes or until asparagus is crisp-tender and bright green. Drain; cool to room temperature. Place 1-2 lettuce leaves per serving on a large platter or individual salad plates. Halve the tomato slices and arrange over lettuce. Top tomatoes with spears of asparagus and slices of avocado if desired. Combine all dressing ingredients; top each salad serving with a generous dollop. **Yield:** 8 servings. **Diabetic Exchanges:** One serving (prepared with light mayonnaise and sour cream) equals 1-1/2 vegetable, 1 fat; also 96 calories, 134 mg sodium, 9 mg cholesterol, 9 gm carbohydrate, 3 gm protein, 6 gm fat.

ICEBOX VEGETABLE SALAD
Mary Anger, St. Clair Shores, Michigan

1 can (16 ounces) cut green beans, drained
1 can (17 ounces) tiny peas, drained
1 can (16 ounces) whole kernel corn *or* shoe peg corn, drained
1 jar (4 ounces) chopped pimientos, drained
1 cup finely chopped celery
1 medium onion, finely chopped
1 medium green pepper, finely chopped
1 cup sugar
1/2 cup vinegar
1/2 cup vegetable oil
1 teaspoon salt
1/2 teaspoon pepper

Combine all vegetables in a large glass bowl; set aside. In a saucepan, combine sugar, vinegar, oil, salt and pepper; bring to a boil. Cool slightly and pour over vegetables. Cover and refrigerate overnight. **Yield:** 6-8 servings.

YOU'LL harvest a bushel of compliments—instead of groans—when you present this spread of super dishes that are all made with... leftovers. *Yes*, leftovers! One taste and you'll agree that second-time-around food *can* have first-rate flavor!

SECONDS, PLEASE!
Clockwise from upper left: **Turkey Almond Salad** (recipe on page 54), **Cream of Vegetable Soup** (recipe on page 20), **Crunchy Pork and Rice Salad** (recipe on page 54), **Breakfast Oatmeal Muffins** (recipe on page 158), **Meat Loaf-Stuffed Peppers** (recipe on page 68), **Tacoed Eggs** (recipe on page 24), **Raisin/Date Bread Pudding** (recipe on page 227) and **Pineapple Ham Balls** (recipe on page 87).

TURKEY ALMOND SALAD

Donna Rear, Olds, Alberta

(PICTURED ON PAGE 52)

3 cups cubed cooked turkey
2 cups shredded cabbage
3/4 cup diced celery
1/4 cup sliced green onions
1-1/2 cups chow mein noodles
1/2 cup slivered almonds,
  toasted
2 tablespoons sesame seeds,
  toasted
DRESSING:
2/3 cup salad dressing *or*
  mayonnaise
1 tablespoon milk
2 teaspoons prepared mustard
1-1/2 teaspoons sugar
1/2 teaspoon salt
1/4 teaspoon pepper

In a large bowl, toss together turkey, cabbage, celery and green onions. In another bowl, combine dressing ingredients. Pour over the turkey mixture. Chill for several hours. Just before serving, add the chow mein noodles, almonds and sesame seeds; toss to mix. **Yield:** 6 servings.

CRUNCHY PORK AND RICE SALAD

Susan Kemmerer, Telford, Pennsylvania

(PICTURED ON PAGE 52)

1 head Chinese *or* green
  cabbage, shredded
  (about 6 cups)
2 cups cubed cooked pork
  roast
1-1/2 cups cooked rice
1 package (10 ounces)
  frozen peas, thawed
1 can (8 ounces) sliced water
  chestnuts, drained
DRESSING:
1/2 cup sour cream
1/2 cup mayonnaise
1 teaspoon celery seed
1/2 teaspoon salt

In a large bowl, toss together cabbage, pork, rice, peas and water chestnuts. In a small bowl, combine dressing ingredients; mix well. Pour over the salad and stir gently to mix. Chill for several hours. **Yield:** 8-10 servings.

ORANGE BUTTERMILK SALAD

Juanita Hutto, Mechanicsville, Virginia

1 can (20 ounces) unsweetened
  crushed pineapple, undrained
3 tablespoons sugar
1 package (6 ounces) orange-
  flavored gelatin
2 cups buttermilk
1 carton (8 ounces) frozen
  whipped topping, thawed
1 cup chopped nuts

In a saucepan, combine pineapple and sugar; bring to a boil, stirring occasionally. When mixture boils, immediately add gelatin and stir until dissolved. Cool slightly. Stir in buttermilk. Chill until partially set. Fold in whipped topping and nuts. If necessary, chill until mixture mounds slightly. Pour into a lightly oiled 8-1/2-cup mold. Chill overnight. **Yield:** 12-16 servings.

SWEET POTATO SALAD

Lettie Baker, Pennsboro, West Virginia

✓ This tasty dish uses less sugar, salt and fat. Recipe includes *Diabetic Exchanges*.

3 pounds sweet potatoes,
  cooked, peeled and cubed
1/2 cup finely chopped onion
1 cup chopped green pepper
1-1/2 teaspoons salt, optional
1/4 teaspoon pepper
1-1/2 cups light *or* regular
  mayonnaise
Dash hot pepper sauce

Combine first five ingredients in a large bowl. Stir in mayonnaise and hot pepper sauce; mix well. Cover and refrigerate at least 1 hour before serving. **Yield:** 10 servings. **Diabetic Exchanges:** One serving (prepared with light mayonnaise and without added salt) equals 2 starch, 1-1/2 fat; also, 217 calories, 167 mg sodium, 5 mg cholesterol, 38 gm carbohydrate, 4 gm protein, 7 gm fat.

Quick & Easy

CHICKEN SALAD

Cathy Rauen, Ridgway, Colorado

2-1/2 cups diced cooked chicken
4 bacon strips, cooked and
  crumbled
1 can (8 ounces) sliced water
  chestnuts, drained
1/2 cup thinly sliced celery

1 cup halved green grapes
3/4 cup salad dressing *or*
  mayonnaise
1 to 2 tablespoons dried
  parsley flakes
2 teaspoons finely minced
  onion
1 teaspoon lemon juice
1/4 teaspoon ground ginger
Dash Worcestershire sauce
Salt and pepper to taste

Combine chicken, bacon, water chestnuts, celery and grapes in a large bowl; set aside. In another bowl, whisk together remaining ingredients; add to salad and toss to coat. Chill until serving. **Yield:** 4-6 servings.

Quick & Easy

MEXICAN SALAD

Bernice Brown, Paradise, California

(PICTURED ON BACK COVER AND PAGE 37)

2 quarts salad greens
2 medium tomatoes, cut into
  wedges
1 bunch green onions, sliced
1 can (2-1/4 ounces) sliced ripe
  olives, drained
1 to 2 cups corn chips
AVOCADO DRESSING:
1 small ripe avocado, peeled
2 tablespoons lemon juice
1/2 cup sour cream
1/4 cup vegetable oil
1/2 teaspoon seasoned salt
1/2 teaspoon dried red pepper
  flakes
1/2 teaspoon sugar

In a large bowl, mix together first four ingredients; cover and chill. For dressing, mash avocado with a fork in a small mixing bowl. Stir in the lemon juice, sour cream, oil, seasoned salt, red pepper flakes and sugar; mix well. Just before serving, add corn chips to salad; pour dressing over and toss. **Yield:** 6-8 servings.

MOLDED CRANBERRY SALAD

Patricia Baxter of Great Bend, Kansas

(PICTURED ON PAGE 166)

8 cups fresh cranberries
2-1/2 cups sugar
2 tablespoons unflavored gelatin
1/3 cup orange juice
2 cups diced apples
1 cup chopped nuts
Leaf lettuce and mayonnaise for
  garnish

Finely grind the cranberries in a food chopper. Add sugar and mix thoroughly.

Let stand 15 minutes, stirring occasionally. (If using frozen berries, let them stand until the mixture is at room temperature.) Place the gelatin and orange juice in the top of a double boiler; stir over hot water until gelatin is dissolved. Add to cranberries along with apples and nuts; place in a 7-cup mold that has been rinsed in cold water. Chill until set. Unmold onto leaf lettuce. Garnish with mayonnaise. **Yield:** 12 servings.

MINTY RICE SALAD
Naomi Giddis, Grawn, Michigan

 This tasty dish uses less sugar, salt and fat. Recipe includes *Diabetic Exchanges*.

- 2 cups cooked brown *or* wild rice
- 3 medium tomatoes, seeded and finely chopped
- 1 cup fresh *or* frozen peas
- 1 cucumber, seeded and finely chopped
- 1 green pepper, finely chopped
- 1/2 cup sliced green onions
- 1/2 cup sliced radishes
- 1/3 cup olive oil
- 3 tablespoons lemon juice
- 1/2 teaspoon salt, optional
- 2 tablespoons chopped fresh mint
- 1/4 teaspoon pepper

In a large bowl, combine rice, tomatoes, peas, cucumber, green pepper, green onions and radishes; set aside. In a small bowl, combine remaining ingredients. Pour over rice and vegetables; mix well. Chill for at least 1 hour. Serve cold. **Yield:** 6 servings. **Diabetic Exchanges:** One serving (prepared with brown rice and without added salt) equals 2 fat, 1-1/2 starch, 1 vegetable; also, 231 calories, 225 mg sodium, 0 cholesterol, 27 gm carbohydrate, 5 gm protein, 12 gm fat.

GRANDMA'S POTATO SALAD
Karla Retzer, Grantsburg, Wisconsin

(PICTURED ON PAGE 194)

- 1-1/2 quarts salad dressing *or* mayonnaise
- 1/4 cup packed brown sugar
- 1 tablespoon sugar
- 1-1/2 teaspoons vanilla extract
- 1/2 teaspoon prepared mustard
- 1/2 cup milk
- 10 pounds salad potatoes, cooked, peeled and cubed
- 1 dozen hard-cooked eggs, chopped

- 4 celery ribs, chopped
- 5 radishes, sliced
- 1 medium onion, chopped
- 1/3 cup chopped green pepper
Salt and pepper to taste
Leaf lettuce
Paprika
Chopped parsley

In a large mixing bowl, combine salad dressing, sugars, vanilla and mustard. Stir in milk. Gently fold in potatoes, eggs, celery, radishes, onion, green pepper, salt and pepper. Chill several hours or overnight. Serve in a bowl lined with lettuce leaves. Sprinkle paprika and parsley on top. **Yield:** 6 quarts.

MOZZARELLA PASTA SALAD
Violet Kycek, Austin, Minnesota

(PICTURED ON PAGE 197)

- 2 cups corkscrew (twist) pasta, cooked and drained
- 10 ounces fresh spinach, washed, drained and torn in bite-size pieces
- 2 cups chopped cooked ham *or* bacon
- 1 can (4 ounces) diced green chilies, drained
- 2 cups cubed mozzarella cheese
- 3/4 cup shredded cheddar cheese
- 1 can (5-3/4 ounces) black olives, sliced *or* whole
PARMESAN DRESSING:
- 1 cup vegetable oil
- 1/2 cup grated Parmesan cheese
- 1/4 cup white wine vinegar *or* white vinegar
- 1/2 teaspoon black pepper
- 1/4 teaspoon ground cloves
- 1 to 2 cloves garlic, minced

Toss together first seven ingredients; cover and chill. To make dressing, place ingredients in blender; blend until smooth. Pour dressing over salad ingredients; toss to coat. Serve immediately. Chill leftovers. (If salad dressing is made in advance, keep chilled till used.) **Yield:** 12 servings.

CANTALOUPE WITH CHICKEN SALAD
Elsie Trude, Keizer, Oregon

(PICTURED ON PAGE 162)

 This tasty dish uses less sugar, salt and fat. Recipe includes *Nutritional Details*.

- 2 cups cubed cooked chicken
- 1-1/2 to 2 cups fresh blueberries
- 1 cup sliced celery

- 1 cup seedless green grapes, halved
- 1/2 cup sliced almonds
- 3 cantaloupe, halved and seeded
DRESSING:
- 1/2 cup mayonnaise
- 1/4 cup sour cream
- 1 tablespoon fresh lemon juice
- 1-1/2 teaspoons grated lemon peel
- 1-1/2 teaspoons sugar *or* sugar substitute to equal 1-1/2 teaspoons
- 1/2 teaspoon ground ginger
- 1/4 teaspoon salt, optional

In a large bowl, combine chicken, blueberries, celery, grapes and almonds. In a small bowl, mix dressing ingredients. Pour over the chicken mixture and toss gently. Spoon into cantaloupe halves. **Yield:** 6 servings. **Nutritional Details:** One serving (prepared with sugar substitute, light mayonnaise and sour cream and without added salt) equals 285 calories, 87 mg sodium, 36 mg cholesterol, 37 gm carbohydrate, 18 gm protein, 9 gm fat.

TOMATO VINAIGRETTE
Donna Aho, Fargo, North Dakota

This tasty dish uses less sugar, salt and fat. Recipe includes *Diabetic Exchanges*.

- 12 thick tomato slices
- 1/2 cup olive oil
- 2 to 3 tablespoons red wine vinegar
- 1 garlic clove, minced
- 1 teaspoon snipped fresh oregano
- 1/2 teaspoon salt
- 1/4 teaspoon pepper
- 1/4 teaspoon dry mustard
- 6 large lettuce leaves
Minced green onions
Minced fresh parsley

Arrange tomato slices in an 8-in. square dish; set aside. In a small bowl, whisk together oil, vinegar, garlic, oregano, salt, pepper and mustard. Pour over tomatoes. Cover and chill for 1-2 hours. To serve, place each lettuce leaf on an individual plate and top with two tomato slices. Drizzle with dressing. Sprinkle with onions and parsley. **Yield:** 6 servings. **Diabetic Exchanges:** One serving equals 3 fat, 1 vegetable; also, 174 calories, 197 mg sodium, 0 cholesterol, 3 gm carbohydrate, 1 gm protein, 18 gm fat.

A MORE SAVORY SALAD. Perk up your favorite tuna salad by adding 1/8 teaspoon of garlic powder for salad made with two cans of tuna. Your family will love the added flavor.

FROZEN CRANBERRY SALAD

Beverly Mix, Missoula, Montana
(PICTURED AT RIGHT)

- 4 packages (3 ounces *each*) cream cheese, softened
- 1/4 cup salad dressing *or* mayonnaise
- 2 tablespoons sugar
- 1 carton (16 ounces) frozen whipped topping, thawed
- 2 cans (20 ounces *each*) crushed pineapple, drained
- 2 cups chopped walnuts
- 2 cups flaked coconut
- 2 cans (16 ounces *each*) whole-berry cranberry sauce
- 1 cup fresh *or* frozen cranberries, chopped, optional
- Lettuce leaves

In a medium bowl, blend cream cheese, salad dressing and sugar. Fold in the whipped topping; set aside. In a large mixing bowl, combine pineapple, nuts, coconut and cranberry sauce. Add cranberries if desired. Gently combine with cream cheese mixture. Spread into a 13-in. x 9-in. x 2-in. glass baking dish or three foil-lined 8-in. x 4-in. x 2-in. loaf pans. Cover and freeze. Remove from freezer 10-15 minutes before serving. Cut into squares or slices. Serve on lettuce leaves. **Yield:** 24 servings.

HOT BEEF AND HAZELNUT SALAD

Ruth Gooding, Los Angeles, California
(PICTURED ON PAGE 99)

 This tasty dish uses less sugar, salt and fat. Recipe includes *Diabetic Exchanges.*

- 1 pound sirloin steak, sliced across grain into thin strips
- **MARINADE:**
- 1/4 cup sliced green onions
- 2 garlic cloves, minced
- 2 tablespoons light *or* regular soy sauce
- 1 tablespoon vegetable oil
- 1 tablespoon water
- **DRESSING:**
- 2 tablespoons cider vinegar
- 2 tablespoons light *or* regular soy sauce
- 2 tablespoons vegetable oil
- 1 garlic clove, minced
- 1 teaspoon sugar
- 1/4 teaspoon curry powder
- 1/4 teaspoon ground ginger

- 8 to 10 cups torn salad greens
- 1/4 cup coarsely chopped hazelnuts, toasted

Sliced green onions
Chopped sweet red *or* green peppers

Place beef in a glass mixing bowl. Combine marinade ingredients; pour over beef. Allow to stand at room temperature 30 minutes. Meanwhile, combine dressing ingredients; set aside. Place greens in a large salad bowl; refrigerate. In a skillet over high heat, brown half the beef and marinade. Remove and then brown remaining beef. Drain and add all beef to greens. In the same skillet, heat dressing. Pour over salad and quickly toss. Top with hazelnuts, onions and peppers. Serve immediately. **Yield:** 4 servings. **Diabetic Exchanges:** One serving (prepared with light soy sauce) equals 3-1/2 meat, 1 vegetable, 1 fat; also, 329 calories, 423 mg sodium, 70 mg cholesterol, 6 gm carbohydrate, 28 gm protein, 22 gm fat.

GREEN SALAD WITH POPPY SEED DRESSING

Toni Garman, Spokane, Washington

- 1 head lettuce, torn into bite-size pieces
- 1 small cucumber, sliced
- 1/4 red onion, sliced
- **DRESSING:**
- 1 cup honey
- 1 cup vinegar
- 1 cup vegetable oil
- 1 tablespoon poppy seeds
- 2 slices red onion, finely diced

In a large salad bowl, toss together lettuce, cucumber and red onion; set aside. In a glass jar with a tight-fitting lid, combine all dressing ingredients; shake until well blended. Just before serving, pour about 1/2 cup of dressing over salad; toss lightly. Cover and refrigerate remaining dressing for up to 1 week. **Yield:** 3 cups dressing.

CHRISTMAS VEGETABLE SALAD

Mary Dean, Eau Claire, Wisconsin
(PICTURED ON PAGE 66)

- **DRESSING:**
- 1-1/2 tablespoons fresh lemon juice
- 1-1/2 tablespoons white wine vinegar
- 4 tablespoons vegetable oil
- 1 teaspoon salt
- 1/2 teaspoon sugar
- Freshly ground black pepper
- **SALAD:**
- 2 cups thinly sliced cauliflower

- 1/2 cup sliced stuffed green olives
- 1/3 cup chopped green pepper
- 1/3 cup chopped red pepper

Put all dressing ingredients in jar; shake well. Combine cauliflower, olives and peppers in glass bowl; pour dressing over all. Marinate in refrigerator for several hours or overnight. **Yield:** 6-8 servings.

TURKEY PASTA SALAD

Karen Harris, Lewisville, Indiana

- 2 cups uncooked corkscrew pasta
- 1 cup chopped cooked turkey
- 1 cup chopped celery
- 1 medium red onion, chopped
- 1 medium green pepper, chopped
- 1 package (1 ounce) ranch dressing mix
- 1 cup (8 ounces) sour cream
- 1 cup salad dressing *or* mayonnaise
- 1 teaspoon garlic salt
- 1/2 cup slivered almonds
- 1 teaspoon paprika
- Green pepper rings and tomato slices, optional

Cook pasta according to package directions; drain and rinse. Place in a 2-1/2-qt. salad bowl. Add turkey, celery, onion and green pepper; toss to mix. Combine dressing mix, sour cream, salad dressing and garlic salt. Add to pasta mixture and mix well. Sprinkle with almonds and paprika. Garnish with pepper rings and tomato slices if desired. **Yield:** 6-8 servings.

BLACK BEAN AND CORN SALAD

Darlene Temple, Culpeper, Virginia

- 1 can (15 ounces) black beans, rinsed and drained
- 4 ounces Monterey Jack cheese, cut into 1/4-inch cubes
- 1 can (8-3/4 ounces) whole kernel corn, drained
- 1/4 cup sliced green onions with tops
- 3/4 cup thinly sliced celery
- 1 small sweet red pepper, diced
- 3/4 cup picante sauce
- 2 tablespoons olive oil
- 2 tablespoons lemon juice
- 1/2 to 1 teaspoon ground cumin
- 1 garlic clove, minced

Combine all ingredients in a large bowl; mix well. Cover and chill several hours or overnight. **Yield:** 8 servings.

WHETHER you're planning a special-occasion supper with family or a festive gathering with friends, you're bound to reach for this menu often. Frozen Cranberry Salad is a cool and tangy complement to Cornish Hens with Wild Rice. Top off the meal with Maple-Glazed Apple Pie, a spicy twist on a down-home favorite.

COMPANY'S COMING!
Clockwise from top: **Maple-Glazed Apple Pie** (recipe on page 215), **Cornish Hens with Wild Rice** (recipe on page 64) and **Frozen Cranberry Salad** (recipe on page 56).

ORANGE AND RED ONION SALAD

Nancy Schmidt, Gustine, California

(PICTURED ON PAGE 223)

✓ This tasty dish uses less sugar, salt and fat. Recipe includes *Diabetic Exchanges*.

- 1 tablespoon butter *or* margarine
- 1 cup sliced almonds, optional
- 2 tablespoons fresh lemon juice
- 1 teaspoon Dijon mustard
- 1/2 teaspoon sugar
- 1/2 teaspoon salt
- 1/4 teaspoon white pepper
- 1/2 cup vegetable oil
- 1 bunch romaine lettuce, torn into bite-size pieces
- 2 medium oranges, peeled and sectioned
- 1 small red onion, thinly sliced

In a skillet, melt butter over medium heat. Saute the almonds until golden brown. Remove almonds to paper towels to drain. Combine next five ingredients. Beat in oil. Combine lettuce, orange sections, onion slices and almonds. Toss with dressing. Serve immediately. **Yield:** 6 servings. **Diabetic Exchanges:** One serving (prepared without almonds) equals 1 vegetable, 3-1/2 fat; also, 193 calories, 207 mg sodium, 0 mg cholesterol, 8 gm carbohydrate, 1 gm protein, 18 gm fat.

TANGY POTATO SALAD

Monika Grotegeer, Elmendorf AFB, Alaska

- 12 medium red potatoes (about 4 pounds)
- 1 medium onion, finely chopped
- 3 hard-cooked eggs, chopped
- 2 dill pickles, finely chopped
- 2 tablespoons snipped fresh parsley
- 3/4 cup chicken broth
- 3/4 cup salad dressing *or* mayonnaise
- 1-1/2 teaspoons salt
- 1/2 teaspoon pepper
- 1/4 teaspoon garlic powder
- 2 tomatoes, cubed
- 6 bacon strips, cooked and crumbled

Cook potatoes in boiling salted water until tender. Drain; cool slightly. Peel and slice potatoes; combine with onion, eggs, pickles and parsley in a large salad bowl. Set aside. Heat chicken broth until warm; remove from the heat. Add salad dressing, salt, pepper and garlic powder; mix until smooth. Pour over potato mixture and mix lightly.

Cover and chill. Just before serving, gently stir in tomatoes and bacon. **Yield:** 10-12 servings.

Quick & Easy

STRAWBERRY SPINACH SALAD

Jamie Stoneman
Winston-Salem, North Carolina

- 2 bunches fresh spinach, washed and dried
- 1 pint fresh strawberries, hulled and sliced
- 1/2 cup sugar
- 2 tablespoons sesame seeds
- 1 tablespoon poppy seeds
- 1-1/2 teaspoons finely chopped onion
- 1/4 teaspoon Worcestershire sauce
- 1/4 teaspoon paprika
- 1/2 cup vegetable oil
- 1/4 cup cider vinegar

Arrange spinach and strawberries on individual salad plates or in a large salad bowl. Place the next six ingredients in a blender or food processor. With unit running, add oil and vinegar in a steady stream. Blend until thickened. Drizzle over salad; serve immediately. **Yield:** 6-8 servings.

GREEK CHICKEN SALAD

Donna Smith, Palisade, Colorado

✓ This tasty dish uses less sugar, salt and fat. Recipe includes *Diabetic Exchanges*.

- 3 cups cubed cooked chicken
- 2 medium cucumbers, peeled, seeded and chopped
- 1 cup crumbled feta cheese
- 2/3 cup sliced pitted black olives
- 1/4 cup minced fresh parsley
- 1 cup mayonnaise
- 3 garlic cloves, minced
- 1/2 cup plain yogurt
- 1 tablespoon dried oregano

Combine the first five ingredients. Set aside. In a small bowl, combine remaining ingredients. Toss with chicken mixture. Cover and chill for several hours. **Yield:** 7 servings. **Diabetic Exchanges:** One serving (prepared with light mayonnaise) equals 2-1/2 meat, 2 vegetable, 1 fat; also, 288 calories, 566 mg sodium, 80 mg cholesterol, 11 gm carbohydrate, 23 gm protein, 17 gm fat.

SPICE IT UP. When simmering chicken to be used in a salad, make it extra-special by adding salt, dried rosemary and onion powder to the water.

CHINESE NOODLE SLAW

Wilma Beller, Hamilton, Ohio

- 1 medium head cabbage, chopped (about 10 cups)
- 5 green onions with tops, chopped
- 2 packages (3 ounces *each*) Ramen noodles
- 1/2 cup butter *or* margarine
- 1 tablespoon sesame seeds
- 1/2 cup slivered almonds

DRESSING:
- 1/2 cup vegetable oil
- 1 tablespoon soy sauce
- 1/3 cup sugar
- 1/4 cup vinegar

In a large bowl, combine cabbage and onions. Chill. Meanwhile, break the noodles into small pieces (save the seasoning packets for another use). In a saucepan, melt butter over medium-low heat; brown noodles, sesame seeds and almonds, stirring frequently. Drain on paper towels; keep at room temperature. Combine all dressing ingredients in a mixing bowl; blend with a wire whisk. Twenty minutes before serving, toss noodle mixture with cabbage and onions. Pour dressing over and toss well. **Yield:** 10 servings.

CRANBERRY WALDORF SALAD

Faye Huff, Longview, Washington

(PICTURED ON PAGE 200)

- 1/2 pound fresh *or* frozen cranberries, halved
- 3/4 cup sugar
- 3 cups miniature marshmallows
- 2 cups chopped apples
- 1/2 cup chopped nuts
- 1 can (8 ounces) pineapple tidbits, drained
- 1 cup halved seedless grapes
- 1 cup whipping cream, stiffly beaten

In a large mixing bowl, combine cranberries and sugar; let stand 30 minutes. Add next five ingredients and mix well. Gently fold in the whipped cream; chill before serving. **Yield:** 10-12 servings.

OVERNIGHT SALAD

Susan Richardson, Racine, Wisconsin

- 1 can (8 ounces) pineapple tidbits
- 1 can (11 ounces) mandarin oranges
- 3 tablespoons lemon juice

1 tablespoon water
1 package (3-1/2 ounces) cook-and-serve vanilla pudding mix
1 cup miniature marshmallows
1 cup whipped topping
1 banana, sliced

Drain pineapple and oranges, reserving juices. Place juices in a saucepan with lemon juice and water; stir in pudding mix. Cook and stir over medium heat until mixture comes to a full boil. Remove from the heat; cool. Add pineapple, oranges and marshmallows. Fold in whipped topping. Chill overnight. Just before serving, fold in banana. **Yield:** 6-8 servings.

ZUCCHINI COLESLAW

Aloma Hawkins, Bixby, Missouri

 This tasty dish uses less sugar, salt and fat. Recipe includes *Diabetic Exchanges*.

2 cups coarsely shredded zucchini
2 cups shredded cabbage
1 medium carrot, shredded
2 green onions, sliced
1/2 cup thinly sliced radishes
1/3 cup light mayonnaise
1/3 cup mild picante sauce
1/2 teaspoon ground cumin

Drain zucchini by pressing between layers of paper towels. Place in a large bowl and combine with cabbage, carrot, onions and radishes. In a small bowl, combine remaining ingredients. Pour over vegetables and toss well. Cover and chill at least 1 hour. **Yield:** 8 servings. **Diabetic Exchanges:** One serving equals 1 vegetable, 1/2 fat; also, 55 calories, 154 mg sodium, 2 mg cholesterol, 7 gm carbohydrate, 1 gm protein, 3 gm fat.

BEET SALAD

Lani Hasbrouck, Cascade, Idaho

1 can (16 ounces) diced *or* julienned beets
1 package (6 ounces) lemon-flavored gelatin
1-1/2 cups cold water
2 tablespoons finely chopped onion
1 to 2 tablespoons prepared horseradish
4 teaspoons vinegar
1/4 teaspoon salt
1-1/2 cups chopped celery
1/4 cup sliced stuffed green olives
Lettuce leaves, mayonnaise and whole stuffed olives for garnish, optional

Drain beets, reserving liquid; add water to reserved liquid to equal 2 cups. In a

---

saucepan, bring liquid to a boil. Remove from the heat; stir in gelatin until dissolved. Add cold water, onion, horseradish, vinegar and salt. Chill until partially set. Stir in the beets, celery and sliced olives. Pour into an 8-in. square dish. Chill until firm, about 3 hours. Cut salad into squares. If desired, serve on a lettuce-lined plate and top with a dollop of mayonnaise and an olive. **Yield:** 9-12 servings.

CREAMED CUCUMBERS

Diane Maughan, Cedar City, Utah

5 cucumbers, peeled and thinly sliced
1 bunch green onions with tops, chopped
1 cup mayonnaise
1/4 cup evaporated milk
1/4 cup vinegar
1/4 cup sugar
2 drops hot pepper sauce
1 teaspoon dried parsley flakes
1 teaspoon salt
1/4 teaspoon pepper
1/4 teaspoon garlic salt
1/4 teaspoon onion salt

Combine cucumbers and green onions in a large bowl. Cover and let stand for 1 hour. Combine all remaining ingredients; pour over cucumber mixture and mix well. Refrigerate for several hours. **Yield:** 10-12 servings.

 Quick & Easy

RED GRAPE SALAD

Lorraine Black, Barnum, Iowa

1 can (20 ounces) pineapple tidbits
2 packages (3 ounces *each*) cream cheese, softened
2 tablespoons mayonnaise
3 cups miniature marshmallows
2 cups seedless red grapes, halved
1 cup heavy cream, whipped

Drain the pineapple, reserving 2 tablespoons juice; set pineapple aside. In a mixing bowl, beat juice, cream cheese and mayonnaise until fluffy. Stir in pineapple, marshmallows and grapes. Fold in whipped cream. Serve immediately or refrigerate. **Yield:** 10-12 servings.

FRUITED CHICKEN SALAD

Marilyn Hamilton, Kearsarge, New Hampshire

3 tablespoons vegetable oil
3 tablespoons red wine vinegar
2 tablespoons sugar
3 tablespoons orange juice
1 teaspoon dry mustard
1 tablespoon poppy seeds
10 cups torn fresh spinach
2 cans (11 ounces *each*) mandarin oranges, drained
2 cups fresh strawberries, hulled and halved
1-1/2 cups cubed cooked chicken

Combine first six ingredients in a jar with a tight-fitting lid; shake well. Chill for at least 2 hours. Just before serving, combine spinach, mandarin oranges, strawberries and chicken in a large salad bowl. Pour dressing over and toss lightly. **Yield:** 4 servings.

COUNTRY RICE SALAD

Arlyn Kramer, El Campo, Texas

This tasty dish uses less sugar, salt and fat. Recipe includes *Diabetic Exchanges*.

DRESSING:
1/2 cup mayonnaise
1/4 cup prepared mustard
2 tablespoons sugar
1 teaspoon vinegar
1/4 teaspoon salt
1/8 teaspoon pepper
1 to 2 tablespoons milk, if necessary

SALAD:
3 cups cooked rice, chilled
1/4 cup sweet pickle relish
1 jar (2 ounces) chopped pimiento, drained
1/3 cup finely chopped green onions (including tops)
1/4 cup finely chopped green pepper
1/4 cup finely chopped celery
3 hard-cooked eggs, diced
Fresh parsley
Cherry tomatoes

Combine all dressing ingredients except the milk; set aside. In a large salad bowl, combine all salad ingredients except parsley and tomatoes. Pour dressing over rice mixture; stir gently. Add milk if mixture is dry. Chill several hours before serving. Garnish with parsley and cherry tomatoes. **Yield:** 10 servings. **Diabetic Exchanges:** One serving (prepared with light mayonnaise) equals 1 starch, 1 fat, 1/2 vegetable; also, 144 calories, 280 mg sodium, 85 mg cholesterol, 20 gm carbohydrate, 3 gm protein, 5 gm fat.

SUNDAY MEALS are a time for your family's favorite dishes. You're sure to satisfy your hungry brood when you serve Perfect Pot Roast or Golden Ham Croquettes with fresh-from-the-oven Freeze-and-Bake Rolls. And for dessert, get ready to dish out second helpings of deliciously sweet Apple Roly-Poly.

SUNDAY SPREAD.
Clockwise from the bottom: **Golden Ham Croquettes** (recipe on page 61), **Apple Roly-Poly** (recipe on page 221), **Freeze-and-Bake Rolls** (recipe on page 158) and **Perfect Pot Roast** (recipe on page 61).

OVEN MEALS

An endless array of delicious one-dish dinners is at your fingertips with these beef, pork, fowl and seafood recipes.

PERFECT POT ROAST

Melody Sroufe, Wichita, Kansas

(PICTURED AT LEFT)

- 1 teaspoon seasoned salt
- 1/2 teaspoon onion powder
- 1/4 teaspoon pepper
- 1/8 teaspoon garlic powder
- 1 beef chuck pot roast (3 to 4 pounds)
- 1 tablespoon olive oil
- 3/4 cup water
- 1 large onion, chopped
- 1/4 cup chopped green pepper
- 2 garlic cloves, minced
- 2 bay leaves
- 2 teaspoons dried parsley flakes
- 1/4 teaspoon dried thyme

All-purpose flour

Combine first four ingredients; rub on-to roast. In a skillet, brown roast in oil. Place in a roasting pan. Add water, onion, green pepper and seasonings. Cover and bake at 325° for 2-1/2 to 3 hours or until roast is tender. Remove and keep warm. Discard bay leaves. Skim fat from pan juices. Measure juices and return to pan. For each cup of juices, combine 1 tablespoon flour with 2 tablespoons water; mix well. Stir flour mixture into pan; cook over medium heat, stirring constantly, until thickened and bubbly. Serve gravy with roast. **Yield:** 8-10 servings.

GOLDEN HAM CROQUETTES

Peggy Anderjaska, Haigler, Nebraska

(PICTURED AT LEFT)

- 3 tablespoons butter *or* margarine
- 1/4 to 1/2 teaspoon curry powder
- 1/4 cup all-purpose flour
- 3/4 cup milk
- 2 to 3 teaspoons prepared mustard
- 1 teaspoon grated onion
- 2 cups coarsely ground fully cooked ham
- 2/3 cup dry bread crumbs
- 1 egg, beaten
- 2 tablespoons water

Cooking oil for deep-fat frying
CHEESE SAUCE:
- 2 tablespoons butter *or* margarine
- 2 tablespoons all-purpose flour
- 1/4 teaspoon salt
Dash pepper
- 1-1/4 cups milk
- 1/2 cup shredded cheddar cheese
- 1/2 cup shredded Swiss cheese

In a saucepan, melt butter; stir in curry powder and flour. Gradually add milk; cook and stir until bubbly. Cook and stir 2 minutes more. Remove from the heat. Stir in mustard and onion; add ham and mix well. Cover and chill thoroughly. With wet hands, shape mixture into 10 balls. Roll balls in bread crumbs; shape each into a cone. Whisk together egg and water. Dip cones into egg mixture; roll again in crumbs. Heat oil in a deep-fat fryer to 365°. Fry croquettes, a few at a time, for 2 to 2-1/2 minutes or until golden brown. Drain on paper towels; keep warm. For the cheese sauce, melt butter in a saucepan; stir in flour, salt and pepper. Gradually add milk; cook and stir until thickened and bubbly. Cook and stir 2 minutes more. Add cheeses; heat and stir until melted. Spoon over croquettes. **Yield:** 5 servings.

ASPARAGUS STRATA

Ethel Pressel, New Oxford, Pennsylvania

(PICTURED ON PAGE 16)

- 12 slices white bread
- 12 ounces sharp process cheese, diced
- 1-1/2 pounds fresh asparagus, trimmed
- 2 cups diced cooked ham
- 6 eggs
- 3 cups milk
- 2 tablespoons minced onion
- 1/2 teaspoon salt
- 1/4 teaspoon dry mustard

Using a doughnut cutter, cut 12 circles and holes from bread; set aside. Tear remaining bread in pieces and place in a greased 13-in. x 9-in. x 2-in. baking pan. Layer cheese, asparagus and ham over torn bread; arrange bread circles and holes on top. Lightly beat eggs with milk. Add onion, salt and mustard; mix well. Pour egg mixture over bread cir-

cles and holes. Cover and refrigerate at least 6 hours or overnight. Bake, uncovered, at 325° for 55 minutes or until top is light golden brown. Let stand 10 minutes before serving. **Yield:** 6-8 servings.

CHILIES RELLENOS

Irene Martin, Portales, New Mexico

- 1 can (7 ounces) whole green chilies
- 2 cups (8 ounces) shredded Monterey Jack cheese
- 2 cups (8 ounces) shredded cheddar cheese
- 3 eggs
- 3 cups milk
- 1 cup biscuit mix
Seasoned salt to taste
Salsa

Split chilies; rinse and remove seeds. Dry on paper towels. Arrange chilies on the bottom of an 11-in. x 7-in. x 1-1/2-in. baking dish. Top with cheeses. In a bowl, beat eggs; add milk and biscuit mix. Blend well; pour over cheese. Sprinkle with salt. Bake at 325° for 50-55 minutes or until golden brown. Serve with salsa. **Yield:** 8 servings.

ITALIAN CHICKEN

Sherry Adams, Mount Ayr, Iowa

- 1 broiler/fryer chicken (2-1/2 to 3 pounds), cut up
- 1/4 cup grated Parmesan cheese
- 1 jar (30 ounces) spaghetti sauce
- 1/2 cup sliced fresh mushrooms
- 1/2 cup sliced black olives
- 2/3 cup shredded mozzarella cheese
Cooked spaghetti

Place chicken in a 13-in. x 9-in. x 2-in. baking pan. Bake, uncovered, at 350° for 40 minutes. Drain. Sprinkle chicken with Parmesan cheese. Combine spaghetti sauce, mushrooms and olives. (If the sauce is thick, add water.) Pour over chicken; bake for another 20 minutes or until chicken is done. Sprinkle with mozzarella cheese; return to oven just until cheese melts. Serve with spaghetti. **Yield:** 6 servings.

PARMESAN CHICKEN

Wendy Masters, Grand Valley, Ontario

(PICTURED AT RIGHT)

 3/4 cup coarsely crushed saltines
 1/3 cup grated Parmesan cheese
 1/2 teaspoon salt
 1/2 teaspoon celery salt
 1/2 teaspoon paprika
 1/4 teaspoon onion salt
  3 tablespoons evaporated milk
  3 tablespoons vegetable oil
  1 broiler-fryer chicken (about
    3-1/2 pounds), cut up

Combine first six ingredients in a shallow dish. In another dish, combine milk and oil. Dip chicken pieces into milk mixture, then roll in the Parmesan mixture. Place chicken, skin side up, in a shallow baking pan. Bake, uncovered, at 375° for 1 hour or until chicken is tender and no longer pink. **Yield:** 4-6 servings.

SWISS AND HAM PIE

Florence Ladwig, Monroe, Wisconsin

  1 unbaked pastry shell (9 or 10
    inches
  1 tablespoon butter or
    margarine
 1/4 cup finely chopped onion
  1 cup chopped cooked ham
1-1/2 cups (6 ounces) shredded
    Swiss cheese
  1 tablespoon all-purpose flour
  3 eggs, lightly beaten
1-1/2 cups milk
  1 teaspoon dry mustard
 1/8 teaspoon pepper

Bake pastry at 450° for 7 minutes or just until lightly browned. Remove from oven and reduce heat to 325°. Melt butter in a skillet; cook onion until tender. Remove from the heat and stir in ham. Place in prepared pie shell. In a bowl, toss together cheese and flour. Add eggs, milk, mustard and pepper; pour over ham. Bake for 35-40 minutes or until a knife inserted near the center comes out clean. Let stand 10-15 minutes before cutting. **Yield:** 6 servings.

ONE-DISH
PORK CHOP DINNER

Pat Waymire, Yellow Springs, Ohio

(PICTURED ON PAGE 45)

 This tasty dish uses less sugar, salt and fat. Recipe includes *Diabetic Exchanges*.

  8 pork chops (1/2 inch thick)
 1/3 cup all-purpose flour

 1/4 cup butter or margarine
Salt and pepper to taste, optional
  2 cups apple juice, *divided*
  2 pounds small red potatoes
  1 pound or 1 jar (16 ounces)
    small whole onions, drained
  1 pound carrots, peeled and
    cut into 3-inch pieces
  6 to 8 cups shredded cabbage

Coat pork chops in flour; reserve excess flour. In a large Dutch oven, melt butter over medium-high heat. Brown chops on both sides. Season with salt and pepper if desired. Remove and set aside. Stir reserved flour into pan; cook and stir until a paste forms. Gradually whisk in 1-1/2 cups apple juice; blend until smooth. Return chops to Dutch oven; cover and bake at 350° for 30 minutes. Add potatoes, onions, carrots and remaining apple juice. Cover and bake 30 minutes longer. Top with cabbage; cover and bake for 1 to 1-1/2 hours or until the pork chops are tender, basting occasionally with juices. **Yield:** 8 servings. **Diabetic Exchanges:** One serving (prepared with margarine and without additional salt) equals 2 meat, 2 starch, 2 vegetable, 2-1/2 fat; also, 464 calories, 333 mg sodium, 56 mg cholesterol, 43 gm carbohydrate, 19 gm protein, 24 gm fat.

COUNTRY HERBED
MEAT LOAF

Barbara Roy, Middletown, Pennsylvania

(PICTURED ON PAGE 48)

HERB SAUCE:
 1/4 cup olive oil
  8 ounces fresh mushrooms,
    chopped
  1 large onion, finely chopped
  1 garlic clove, minced
  1 can (28 ounces) tomatoes,
    crushed
  1 can (6 ounces) tomato paste
  1 teaspoon salt
 1/8 teaspoon pepper
  2 teaspoons sugar
  1 cup water
  1 bay leaf
  2 tablespoons chopped fresh
    basil or 2 teaspoons dried basil
MEAT LOAF:
  2 pounds ground beef or
    combination of ground beef,
    pork and veal
  1 cup seasoned dry bread
    crumbs
  3 tablespoons milk
  2 eggs, beaten

In a skillet, heat oil over high heat. Saute the mushrooms, onion and garlic. Add tomatoes, tomato paste, salt, pepper and sugar. Remove 1-1/2 cups. Add water, bay leaf and basil to skillet. Simmer,

uncovered, for 45 minutes, stirring occasionally. Meanwhile, combine all meat loaf ingredients with 1-1/2 cups reserved sauce. Press into a 9-in. x 5-in. x 3-in. loaf pan lined with waxed paper. Unmold onto a roasting pan. Bake at 350° for 45 minutes. Remove from oven; drain. Spread 1/2 cup of herb sauce over top of meat loaf. Return to oven for 15 minutes. Discard bay leaf and serve remaining sauce over individual servings. **Yield:** 8-10 servings.

MOIST MEAT LOAF. For tender, juicy meat loaf, first mix all ingredients except the ground beef. Then add meat and mix lightly. When shaping loaf, handle only as much as necessary.

LASAGNA ROLLS

Mary Lee Thomas, Logansport, Indiana

  6 lasagna noodles
  1 pound ground beef
  1 jar (15-1/2 ounces) spaghetti
    sauce
  1 teaspoon fennel seeds,
    optional
  1 package (8 ounces) shredded
    mozzarella cheese, *divided*

Cook lasagna noodles according to package directions. Meanwhile, in a skillet, brown beef and drain excess fat. Stir in spaghetti sauce, then fennel seeds if desired; simmer 5 minutes. Drain noodles. Spread 1/4 cup meat sauce on each noodle; top with 1-2 tablespoons cheese. Carefully roll up each noodle and place, seam side down, in a 9-in. x 9-in. baking dish. Spoon remaining sauce over each roll and sprinkle with remaining cheese. Bake at 400° for 10-15 minutes or until heated through. **Yield:** 6 servings.

HOT KIPPERED SALMON

Barbara Njaa, Nikiski, Alaska

  2 salmon fillets (about 2
    pounds *each*)
  4 teaspoons salt
Pepper to taste
  2 tablespoons plus 2 teaspoons
    brown sugar
  2 tablespoons liquid smoke

Place fillets skin side down, side by side, in a greased shallow baking pan. Sprinkle with salt, pepper and brown sugar; drizzle with liquid smoke. Cover and refrigerate 4-8 hours. Drain any liquid. Bake at 350° for 30-45 minutes or until fish flakes with a fork. **Yield:** 8 servings.

COMING UP with original recipes for family picnics, barbecues and potlucks can be a challenge. Next time, add some variety (and flavor!) to your menu by making cool Spicy Coleslaw and oven-fried Parmesan Chicken. Then please your gang by serving warm Caramel Apple Bars topped with a dollop of whipped cream.

CROWD-PLEASERS.
Clockwise from the top: **Parmesan Chicken** (recipe on page 62), **Spicy Coleslaw** (recipe on page 46) and **Caramel Apple Bars** (recipe on page 172).

PRODUCE a bushel of "Mmms!" with this robust California Casserole (recipe below).

CALIFORNIA CASSEROLE

Hope LaShier, Amarillo, Texas

(PICTURED ABOVE)

- 2 pounds ground beef
- 1 medium green pepper, chopped
- 3/4 cup chopped onion
- 1 can (16-1/2 ounces) cream-style corn
- 1 can (8 ounces) tomato sauce
- 1 can (10-3/4 ounces) condensed tomato soup, undiluted
- 1 can (4 ounces) mushrooms, undrained
- 1 can (10 ounces) tomatoes with green chilies, undrained
- 1 can (2-1/4 ounces) sliced ripe olives, drained
- 1 jar (4 ounces) chopped pimiento, drained
- 1-1/2 teaspoons celery salt
- 1/2 teaspoon chili powder
- 1/2 teaspoon dry mustard
- 1/4 teaspoon pepper
- 8 ounces wide egg noodles, cooked and drained
- 2 cups (8 ounces) shredded cheddar cheese

In a large skillet, cook ground beef with green pepper and onion until the meat is browned and the vegetables are tender; drain. Add next 11 ingredients; mix thoroughly. Add noodles; mix well. Pour into a Dutch oven or large baking dish. Cover and bake at 350° for 50 minutes. Sprinkle with cheese; return to the oven for 10 minutes or until the cheese melts. **Yield:** 12-16 servings.

SOUR CREAM 'N' DILL CHICKEN

Rebekah Brown, Three Hills, Alberta

(PICTURED ON PAGE 44)

- 8 to 10 chicken pieces, skinned
- Pepper to taste
- 1 can (10-3/4 ounces) condensed cream of mushroom soup, undiluted
- 1 envelope dry onion soup mix
- 1 cup (8 ounces) sour cream
- 1 tablespoon lemon juice
- 1 tablespoon fresh dill, chopped *or* 1 teaspoon dried dill weed
- 1 can (4 ounces) sliced mushrooms, drained
- Paprika
- Cooked wide egg noodles, optional

Place chicken in a single layer in a 13-in. x 9-in. x 2-in. baking pan. Sprinkle with pepper. Combine soup, soup mix, sour cream, lemon juice, dill and mushrooms; pour over chicken. Sprinkle with paprika. Bake, uncovered, at 350° for 1 hour or until chicken is tender. Serve over egg noodles if desired. **Yield:** 4-6 servings.

 Quick & Easy

PINTO BEAN AND RICE CASSEROLE

Linda Emery, Tuckerman, Arkansas

- 1 can (15 ounces) pinto beans, rinsed and drained
- 1/2 cup mild *or* hot picante sauce
- 1 can (15 ounces) Spanish rice
- 1 pound lean ground beef, cooked and drained
- 1 cup (4 ounces) shredded cheddar cheese, *divided*
- Tortilla chips, optional

In a 1-1/2-qt. casserole, combine the beans, picante sauce, rice, beef and half the cheese. Bake, uncovered, at 350° for 20-25 minutes or until heated through. Sprinkle with remaining cheese. Serve with tortilla chips if desired. **Yield:** 4-6 servings.

CORNISH HENS WITH WILD RICE

Evelyn Panka, Canby, Minnesota

(PICTURED ON PAGE 57)

- 1 can (10-3/4 ounces) condensed cream of mushroom soup, undiluted
- 2/3 cup milk
- 1 cup (4 ounces) shredded cheddar cheese
- 3 slices bacon
- 1 cup finely chopped onion
- 1/2 cup chopped green pepper
- 4-1/2 cups cooked wild rice
- 1 cup all-purpose flour
- 1 teaspoon salt
- 1/2 teaspoon paprika
- 1/4 teaspoon pepper
- 3 Cornish game hens, halved
- 4 tablespoons shortening
- Finely chopped parsley

In a saucepan, combine soup and milk. Cook over medium heat until smooth; stir in cheese. Meanwhile, in a skillet, fry bacon until crisp. Remove bacon; crumble and set aside. In drippings, saute onion and green pepper until tender. Add to soup mixture along with wild rice; mix well. Pour into a greased 15-in. x 10-in. x 2-in. baking dish; top with bacon. Combine flour, salt, paprika and pepper in a heavy plastic bag; place one or two hens at a time in bag and shake to coat well. In another skillet, melt shortening. Brown hens on all sides. Arrange on top of rice mixture. Bake, uncovered, at 350° for 45 minutes or until meat is tender. Sprinkle with parsley. **Yield:** 6 servings.

OVEN-BARBECUED PORK CHOPS

Teresa King, Whittier, California

- 6 to 8 loin *or* rib pork chops (3/4 inch thick)
- 1 tablespoon Worcestershire sauce
- 2 tablespoons vinegar
- 2 teaspoons brown sugar
- 1/2 teaspoon pepper
- 1/2 teaspoon chili powder
- 1/2 teaspoon paprika
- 3/4 cup ketchup
- 1/3 cup hot water

Place chops in a heavy cast-iron skillet. Combine all remaining ingredients; pour over chops. Bake, uncovered, at 375° for 1 hour. **Yield:** 6-8 servings.

BAKED BEEF STEW

Sue Hecht, Roselle Park, New Jersey

 This tasty dish uses less sugar, salt and fat. Recipe includes *Diabetic Exchanges*.

- 2 pounds lean beef stew meat, cut into 1-inch cubes
- 1 cup canned tomatoes, cut up
- 6 carrots, cut into strips
- 3 medium potatoes, peeled and quartered
- 1/2 cup thickly sliced celery

1 medium onion, sliced and
  separated into rings
3 tablespoons quick-cooking
  tapioca
1 slice bread, crumbled
1 cup water

In large bowl, combine all ingredients. Spoon into greased 3-qt. casserole. Cover and bake at 325° for 3-1/2 hours. **Yield:** 6 servings. **Diabetic Exchanges:** One serving equals 4 lean meat, 1-1/2 starch, 1 vegetable; also, 356 calories, 241 mg sodium, 97 mg cholesterol, 27 gm carbohydrate, 35 gm protein, 12 gm fat.

MY MOTHER'S MAC AND CHEESE

Phyllis Burkland, Portland, Oregon

2 cups elbow macaroni, cooked
  and drained
1 can (28 ounces) tomatoes with
  liquid, cut up
1/2 teaspoon onion salt, optional
1/4 teaspoon pepper
2 cups (8 ounces) shredded
  cheddar cheese, *divided*
2 tablespoons butter *or*
  margarine

In a bowl, combine macaroni, tomatoes, onion salt if desired, pepper and 1-1/2 cups cheddar cheese. Pour into a greased 2-qt. baking dish. Dot with butter. Bake, uncovered, at 350° for 45 minutes. Sprinkle with remaining cheese; bake 15 minutes longer. **Yield:** 4 servings.

QUICHE ITALIANO

Caryn Wiggins, Columbus, Indiana

(PICTURED ON PAGE 151)

Pastry for 1 pie shell (10 inches),
  unbaked
2-1/2 ounces (1/2 cup) pepperoni,
  thinly sliced and halved
3 tablespoons chopped green
  pepper
2 tablespoons chopped onion
1 jar (2-1/2 ounces) sliced
  mushrooms, drained
1 tablespoon butter *or*
  margarine

1/2 teaspoon crushed, dried
  oregano
1/2 teaspoon fennel seed
1-1/4 cups (5 ounces) shredded
  mozzarella cheese, *divided*
3 eggs
1-1/2 cups light cream
1/2 teaspoon salt
1/8 teaspoon pepper
1 tomato, cut in wedges

Line pie plate with pastry. Trim edges and flute. *Do not prick shell.* Bake crust at 425° for 5 minutes. Remove from the oven and set aside. Reduce heat to 375°. In a small skillet, cook pepperoni, green pepper, onion and mushrooms in butter until tender. Stir in oregano and fennel seed. In pastry shell, layer 1 cup mozzarella cheese; top with pepperoni mixture. In medium bowl, combine eggs, cream, salt and pepper. Beat with fork or whisk until mixed well but not frothy. Pour over pepperoni mixture. Bake for 25-30 minutes or until a knife inserted near the center comes out clean. Top with tomato wedges. Sprinkle with remaining mozzarella cheese. Bake 2 minutes longer or until cheese melts. Let stand 5 minutes before serving. **Yield:** 4-6 servings.

> **EASY CLEANUP.** Keep your oven clean when baking casseroles. Simply place an aluminum pan sprayed with nonstick cooking spray under the casserole dish to catch any spills.

COUNTRY CHICKEN CASSEROLE

Frances Gleichmann, Baltimore, Maryland

1/2 pound fresh mushrooms,
  quartered
2 medium onions, chopped
5 tablespoons butter *or*
  margarine, *divided*
2 cups cubed cooked chicken
2 cups diced cooked peeled
  potatoes
1 jar (2 ounces) pimientos,
  drained
1/4 cup chopped fresh parsley
1 cup light cream
1 teaspoon instant chicken
  bouillon granules
1 teaspoon salt
1/2 teaspoon dried rosemary,
  crushed
1/8 teaspoon pepper
1 cup soft bread crumbs
Additional parsley, optional

In a skillet, saute the mushrooms and onions in 3 tablespoons butter until tender. Add chicken, potatoes, pimientos, parsley, cream, bouillon, salt, rosemary and pepper; heat through. Spoon

into a greased 2-qt. casserole. Melt remaining butter; combine with the bread crumbs and sprinkle over casserole. Bake, uncovered, at 350° for 20-25 minutes or until crumbs are toasted. Garnish with parsley if desired. **Yield:** 6 servings.

FLORIDA SEAFOOD CASSEROLE

Lucille Pennington, Ormond Beach, Florida

(PICTURED BELOW)

1/3 cup minced onion
1/4 cup butter *or* margarine
1/4 cup all-purpose flour
1 cup milk
1 cup light cream
1/2 teaspoon salt
1/2 teaspoon pepper
1 tablespoon chopped
  pimientos
1 can (8 ounces) sliced water
  chestnuts, drained
2 tablespoons lemon juice
1 tablespoon snipped fresh
  parsley
1 cup flaked cooked crabmeat
1 cup peeled cooked shrimp
3 cups cooked rice
1 cup (4 ounces) shredded
  cheddar cheese, *divided*

In a saucepan, saute onion in butter until tender; blend in flour. Add milk and cream; cook and stir until thick and bubbly. Remove from the heat; stir in salt, pepper, pimientos, water chestnuts, lemon juice, parsley, crabmeat, shrimp, rice and half of the cheese. Spoon into a 2-1/2-qt. casserole. Bake at 350° for 25 minutes or until heated through. Sprinkle with remaining cheese just before serving. **Yield:** 6 servings.

FISHING for flavorful food? Florida Seafood Casserole (recipe above) really pleases.

LIGHT the candles, turn up the carols and put the finishing touches on your Christmas Eve buffet. After weeks of anticipation and hours of preparation, it's finally time to enjoy the warmth and love of a country Christmas. Gather friends and family around a sparkling table filled with such distinctive ethnic holiday favorites as cheese- or potato-stuffed Pierogi, saucy Mostaccioli and spiced Swedish Meatballs. Or expand your holiday horizons with regional favorites like crab pie, oyster cheese log, vegetable salad and cranberry punch. They're all filled with traditional flavors that link generations!

CANDLELIGHT DELIGHTS.
Clockwise from lower left: **Oyster Cheese Appetizer Log** (recipe on page 8), **Christmas Vegetable Salad** (recipe on page 56), **Celery En Casserole** (recipe on page 127), **Fresh Cranberry Punch** (recipe on page 17), **Swedish Meatballs** (recipe on page 95), **Mostaccioli** (recipe on page 68), **Polish Pierogi** (recipe on page 96) and **Swiss 'n' Crab Supper Pie** (recipe on page 68).

HAM LOAF with sauce (recipe below) tastes just like Mom's down-home country cooking.

HAM LOAF WITH GOLDEN SAUCE

Donna Smith, Palisade, Colorado

(PICTURED ABOVE)

- 1 pound ground fully cooked ham
- 1 pound ground pork
- 2 cups soft bread crumbs
- 1/3 cup pineapple juice
- 2 eggs, lightly beaten
- 1/2 cup chopped onion
- 1/4 cup packed brown sugar
- 2 tablespoons chopped fresh parsley
- 2 tablespoons cider vinegar
- 1/4 teaspoon ground cloves

SAUCE:
- 2 cups pineapple juice
- 3 tablespoons cornstarch
- 1 to 2 tablespoons brown sugar
- 2 teaspoons lemon juice
- 1/4 to 1/2 teaspoon ground ginger

In a large bowl, combine first 10 ingredients. Pack into a 9-in. x 5-in. x 3-in. loaf pan. Bake at 350° for 1-1/2 hours. Meanwhile, combine all sauce ingredients in a saucepan. Slowly bring to a boil, stirring constantly until thickened and translucent. Allow loaf to stand for 5 minutes. Remove loaf from pan and serve sauce over it. **Yield:** 6-8 servings.

COUNTRY CASSOULET

Roberta Strohmaier, Lebanon, New Jersey

(PICTURED ON PAGE 139)

- 3 cups water
- 3/4 pound dry navy beans
- 1 bay leaf
- 1 teaspoon salt
- 1/4 teaspoon pepper
- 1 can (14-1/2 ounces) chicken broth
- 1/4 pound bacon, diced
- 4 chicken legs *or* thighs
- 2 carrots, quartered
- 2 medium onions, quartered
- 1/4 cup coarsely chopped celery with leaves
- 1 can (8 ounces) tomatoes, chopped, liquid reserved
- 2 garlic cloves, crushed
- 1/2 teaspoon dried marjoram leaves
- 1/2 teaspoon ground sage
- 1 teaspoon whole cloves
- 1/2 pound smoked sausage, cut into 2-inch pieces

Chopped fresh parsley

In a large skillet, combine water, beans, bay leaf, salt and pepper. Bring to a boil; boil, uncovered, for 2 minutes. Remove from the heat. Cover and let soak for 1 hour. Add chicken broth; cover and cook 1 hour. Meanwhile, fry bacon until crisp. Remove bacon and reserve 2 tablespoons of the drippings. Brown chicken in drippings; set aside. In a 3-qt. casserole, mix beans and cooking liquid, bacon, carrots, onions, celery, tomatoes, garlic, marjoram and sage. Sprinkle with cloves; top with chicken. Cover and bake at 350° for 1 hour. Add sausage. Uncover; bake about 30 minutes more or until beans are tender. Discard bay leaf. Garnish with chopped parsley. **Yield:** 4 servings.

SWISS 'N' CRAB SUPPER PIE

Kathy Crow, Cordova, Alaska

(PICTURED ON PAGE 67)

- 1 unbaked 9-in. pie crust *or* pastry-lined 9-1/2-in. tart pan with removable bottom
- 1 can (7-1/2 ounces) crab, drained, flaked and cartilage removed
- 1 cup shredded Swiss cheese
- 2 green onions, thinly sliced
- 3 eggs, beaten
- 1 cup light cream *or* evaporated milk
- 1/2 teaspoon salt
- 1/2 teaspoon grated lemon peel
- 1/4 teaspoon dry mustard

Dash mace
- 1/4 cup sliced unblanched almonds

Bake crust at 425° for 5 minutes. Remove from the oven and set aside. Reduce heat to 325°. Arrange crab evenly over partially baked crust. Top with cheese and green onions. Combine eggs, cream or milk, salt, lemon peel, dry mustard and mace; pour over base. Top with almonds. Bake for 45 minutes or until a knife inserted near the center comes out clean. Remove from oven; let stand 10 minutes before serving. **Yield:** 10 servings.

MOSTACCIOLI

Nancy Mundhenke, Kinsley, Kansas

(PICTURED ON PAGE 67)

- 1-1/2 pounds bulk Italian sausage
- 4 cups meatless spaghetti sauce
- 1 pound mostaccioli, cooked and drained
- 1 beaten egg
- 15 ounces ricotta cheese
- 8 ounces shredded mozzarella cheese
- 1/2 cup freshly grated Romano cheese

Chopped fresh basil, optional

In a Dutch oven, brown sausage; drain. Stir in spaghetti sauce and mostaccioli; set aside. In a bowl, combine egg, ricotta and mozzarella. In a 13-in. x 9-in. x 2-in. baking pan or 2-1/2- to 3-qt. casserole, spread *one-half* of the mostaccioli mixture; layer cheese mixture over all; top with remaining mostaccioli mixture. Cover and bake at 375° for 40 minutes. Top with Romano cheese; bake 5 minutes more or until mixture is heated through. Garnish with fresh basil if desired. **Yield:** 10-12 servings.

MEAT LOAF-STUFFED PEPPERS

Kim Barker, Richmond, Texas

(PICTURED ON PAGE 53)

- 6 large green peppers
- 1 jar (27 to 32 ounces) spaghetti sauce *or* 3 cups leftover spaghetti sauce, *divided*
- 2 cups cubed cooked meat loaf
- 1 to 1-1/2 cups cooked rice
- 1/4 cup chopped onion
- 1/4 cup chopped green pepper
- 3/4 cup shredded cheddar cheese

Remove tops and seeds from peppers. Immerse in boiling water for 3 minutes; drain. Pour 1 cup of spaghetti sauce into the bottom of a shallow baking dish; set aside. In a saucepan, combine meat loaf, rice, onion, chopped green pepper and remaining spaghetti sauce. Cook and stir over medium-high heat for 5-10 minutes or until heated through. Stuff each pepper with meat loaf mixture;

place on sauce in baking dish. Bake, uncovered, at 375° for 15-20 minutes or until heated through. Sprinkle with the cheese and let stand until melted. **Yield:** 6 servings.

Quick & Easy

TURKEY DRESSING PIE

De De Boekelheide, Northville, South Dakota

(PICTURED ON PAGE 125)

3-1/2 to 4 cups cooked turkey dressing
1/2 cup turkey *or* chicken broth
2 tablespoons butter *or* margarine, melted
1 egg, beaten
1/2 cup chopped onion
1 tablespoon cooking oil
3 cups diced cooked turkey
1 cup turkey gravy
1 cup peas, optional
2 tablespoons dried parsley flakes
2 tablespoons diced pimientos
1 teaspoon Worcestershire sauce
1/2 teaspoon dried thyme
4 slices process American cheese, optional

In a large bowl, combine dressing, broth, butter and egg; mix well. Press into the bottom and up the sides of an ungreased 10-in. pie plate; set aside. In a large skillet, saute onion in oil until tender. Stir in turkey, gravy, peas if desired, parsley, pimientos, Worcestershire sauce and thyme; heat through. Pour over crust. Bake at 375° for 20 minutes or until golden. If desired, arrange cheese slices on top of pie and return to oven for 5 minutes or until cheese is melted. **Yield:** 6 servings.

SHIPWRECK STEW

Estelle Bates, Fallbrook, California

 This tasty dish uses less sugar, salt and fat. Recipe includes *Diabetic Exchanges*.

1 pound ground beef
1 cup chopped onion
3 cups peeled cubed potatoes
3 medium carrots, peeled and sliced
1 cup chopped celery
1/4 cup minced fresh parsley
1 package (9 ounces) frozen cut green beans, defrosted
1 can (15 ounces) kidney beans, rinsed and drained
1 can (8 ounces) tomato sauce
1/4 cup uncooked long-grain rice
1 teaspoon salt

1 teaspoon Worcestershire sauce
1/2 to 1 teaspoon chili powder
1/4 teaspoon ground pepper
1 cup water

In a skillet, brown beef with onion over medium heat. Drain fat. In a 3-qt. casserole, combine beef mixture with all remaining ingredients. Cover and bake at 350° for about 1 hour or until rice and potatoes are tender. **Yield:** 10 servings. **Diabetic Exchanges:** One serving equals 1-1/2 lean meat, 1-1/2 starch, 1 vegetable; also, 204 calories, 390 mg sodium, 32 mg cholesterol, 28 gm carbohydrate, 15 gm protein, 4 gm fat.

CARAWAY BEEF ROAST

Beverly Swanson, Red Oak, Iowa

(PICTURED ON PAGE 94)

3 tablespoons cooking oil
1 beef rump *or* chuck roast (3 pounds)
1 cup hot water
1-1/2 teaspoons instant beef bouillon
1/4 cup ketchup
1 tablespoon Worcestershire sauce
1 tablespoon instant minced onion
1 teaspoon salt
1/2 teaspoon pepper
2 teaspoons caraway seeds
2 bay leaves
2 tablespoons all-purpose flour
1/4 cup water
Cooked potatoes and carrots, optional

In a Dutch oven, heat oil over medium-high heat. Brown roast on all sides. Drain. Combine water, bouillon, ketchup, Worcestershire sauce, onion, salt, pepper and caraway. Pour over roast. Add bay leaves. Cover and bake at 325° for 3 hours or until tender. Remove roast to a warm serving platter. Combine flour and water. Stir into pan juices. Bring to a boil, stirring constantly. Cook until thickened, adding additional water if necessary. Remove bay leaves. Serve with cooked potatoes and carrots if desired. **Yield:** about 12 servings.

CHEDDAR CHICKEN POTPIE

Sandra Cothran, Ridgeland, South Carolina

(PICTURED BELOW)

CRUST:
1 cup all-purpose flour
1/2 teaspoon salt
5 tablespoons chilled butter *or* margarine, cut into pieces
3 tablespoons cold water
FILLING:
1-1/2 cups chicken broth
2 cups peeled cubed potatoes
1 cup sliced carrots
1/2 cup sliced celery
1/2 cup chopped onion
1/4 cup all-purpose flour
1-1/2 cups milk
2 cups (8 ounces) shredded sharp cheddar cheese
4 cups diced cooked chicken
1/4 teaspoon poultry seasoning
Salt and pepper to taste

For crust, combine flour and salt in a mixing bowl. Cut butter into flour until the mixture resembles a coarse meal. Gradually add the water, mixing gently with a fork. Gather into a ball. Cover with plastic wrap and chill at least 30 minutes. For filling, heat broth to a boil in a Dutch oven or large saucepan. Add vegetables; simmer 10-15 minutes or until tender. Blend flour with milk; stir into broth mixture. Cook and stir over medium heat until slightly thickened and bubbly. Stir in cheese, chicken, poultry seasoning, salt and pepper. Heat until cheese melts. Spoon into a 10-in. (2-1/2- to 3-qt.) casserole. Set aside. On a lightly floured board, roll crust to fit top of casserole, trimming edges as necessary. Place in casserole over filling; seal edges. Make several slits in center of crust for steam to escape. Bake at 425° for 40 minutes or until golden. **Yield:** 6 servings.

WHY NOT pop into the oven a cheesy chicken potpie (recipe above) for dinner tonight?

WHEN chilly winds blow, warm your family's hearts and stomachs with a robust meal. For starters, serve savory Beef and Barley Soup. Meat and potato lovers will want to prepare the New England Lamb Bake or Sweet-and-Sour Pork Chops. And for dessert, what could be more appealing than old-fashioned Apple Crisp?

COME IN FROM THE COLD.
Clockwise from the top: **Beef and Barley Soup**
(recipe on page 27), **Apple Crisp** (recipe on page 219),
Sweet-and-Sour Pork Chops and
New England Lamb Bake
(both recipes on page 71).

SWEET-AND-SOUR PORK CHOPS

Ophelia Williams, Otterville, Missouri

(PICTURED AT LEFT)

- 6 pork loin chops (about 3/4 inch thick)
- 1/2 cup pineapple juice
- 1/2 cup ketchup
- 2 tablespoons honey
- 2 tablespoons white wine vinegar
- 1-1/2 teaspoons Dijon mustard
- 1/4 teaspoon salt
- 4 teaspoons cornstarch
- 2 tablespoons water

Place pork chops in a 13-in. x 9-in. x 2-in. baking dish. In a bowl, combine pineapple juice, ketchup, honey, vinegar, mustard and salt. Pour over the chops. Cover and bake at 350° for 30 minutes. Uncover and bake about 30 minutes longer or until the meat is tender. Remove chops to a serving platter and keep warm. Strain pan juices into a saucepan. Combine cornstarch and water; add to pan juices. Cook and stir until thickened and bubbly; cook and stir 2 minutes longer. Serve immediately over chops. **Yield:** 6 servings.

NEW ENGLAND LAMB BAKE

Frank Grady, Fort Kent, Maine

(PICTURED AT LEFT)

- 1 tablespoon cooking oil
- 2 pounds boneless lean lamb, cubed
- 1 large onion, chopped
- 1/4 cup all-purpose flour
- 5 cups chicken broth
- 2 large carrots, sliced
- 2 large leeks, cut into 2-inch pieces
- 2 tablespoons minced fresh parsley, *divided*
- 1 bay leaf
- 1/2 teaspoon dried rosemary
- 1/4 teaspoon dried thyme
- 1/2 teaspoon salt
- 1/4 teaspoon pepper
- 3 large potatoes, peeled and sliced
- 1/4 cup butter *or* margarine

In a large Dutch oven, heat oil. Brown lamb and onion. Stir in flour; mix well. Gradually add broth. Bring to a boil, stirring to remove browned bits from pan. Add carrots, leeks, 1 tablespoon parsley, bay leaf, rosemary, thyme, salt and pepper. Spoon into a greased 3-qt. casserole. Cover with potatoes and dot with butter. Bake at 375° for 1-1/2 to 2 hours

or until the meat is tender and the potatoes are golden brown. Garnish with remaining parsley. **Yield:** 6-8 servings.

WILD RICE HOT DISH

Sandra McWithey, South St. Paul, Minnesota

- 3 cups boiling water
- 1 cup uncooked wild rice
- 1-1/2 pounds ground beef
- 1 medium onion, chopped
- 2 cans (10-3/4 ounces *each*) condensed cream of chicken soup, undiluted
- 2 cans (4 ounces *each*) sliced mushrooms, undrained
- 1 can (28 ounces) bean sprouts, drained
- 1 can (10-1/2 ounces) condensed beef broth
- 1-1/3 cups water
- 1/4 cup soy sauce
- 1 bay leaf, crushed
- 1 tablespoon dried parsley flakes
- 1/4 teaspoon *each* celery salt, onion salt, poultry seasoning, garlic powder, paprika and pepper
- 1/8 teaspoon dried thyme
- 1/2 cup sliced almonds

In a large bowl, pour water over rice; let stand for 15 minutes. Drain and set aside. In a skillet, brown ground beef and onion. Drain; add to rice with remaining ingredients except almonds. Transfer to a 13-in. x 9-in. x 2-in. baking dish. Cover and bake at 350° for 2 hours. Sprinkle almonds on top; bake, uncovered, 30 minutes longer. **Yield:** 8-12 servings.

SAVORY MEATBALLS

Delores Jordan, Oregon, Illinois

- 2 eggs, lightly beaten
- 3/4 cup milk
- 1/3 cup cornmeal
- 1 medium onion, chopped
- 2 teaspoons dry mustard
- 1 teaspoon salt
- 1/2 teaspoon pepper
- 1/2 teaspoon poultry seasoning
- 2 pounds ground beef
- 3 tablespoons shortening
- 2 cans (10-3/4 ounces *each*) cream of mushroom soup, undiluted
- 1-1/2 cups water

In a mixing bowl, combine the first eight ingredients. Add beef and mix well. Shape into 2-in. balls. In a skillet, melt the shortening over medium-high heat. Brown meatballs. Place in a casserole dish. Combine soup and water; pour over

meatballs. Bake, uncovered, at 350° for 45-50 minutes. **Yield:** about 8 servings.

BARBECUED RIBS

Frances Campbell, Charlotte, North Carolina

- 3 to 3-1/2 pounds pork spareribs
- 2 tablespoons cooking oil
- 1 medium onion, chopped
- 1 cup ketchup
- 1 cup hot water
- 2 tablespoons vinegar
- 1 tablespoon Worcestershire sauce
- 1 teaspoon dry mustard
- 1/2 teaspoon salt
- 1 tablespoon brown sugar
- 1/4 teaspoon cayenne pepper
- 1/4 teaspoon pepper

Place ribs on a jelly roll pan. Cover tightly with foil; bake at 450° for 45 minutes or until tender. Drain off any fat. In a saucepan, combine all remaining ingredients and bring to a boil. Pour over ribs. Reduce heat to 350°; bake, uncovered, for 1 hour, basting frequently. **Yield:** 6 servings.

CHICKEN AND OYSTER PIE

Mrs. Vernon Gergley, Lititz, Pennsylvania

- 1/4 cup all-purpose flour
- 3 cups chicken broth, *divided*
- 4 cups cubed cooked peeled potatoes
- 3 cups chopped cooked chicken
- 1 pint shucked oysters, drained and chopped *or* 2 cans (8 ounces *each*) whole oysters, drained and chopped
- 1 package (16 ounces) frozen peas, thawed
- 1/2 cup chopped celery
- 2 hard-cooked eggs, chopped
- 1 tablespoon snipped fresh parsley

Butter *or* **margarine**
Pastry for double-crust pie

In a large saucepan, stir flour and 1/2 cup chicken broth until smooth. Add remaining broth; cook and stir until thickened and bubbly. Cook and stir 1 minute more. Remove from the heat. Add the potatoes, chicken, oysters, peas, celery, eggs and parsley; mix gently. Pour into a greased 13-in. x 9-in. x 2-in. baking dish. Dot with butter. Roll pastry into a 14-in. x 10-in. rectangle; place over chicken mixture. Seal pastry edges to sides of baking dish. Cut steam vents in top of pastry. Bake at 425° for 35 minutes or until golden brown. **Yield:** 8-10 servings.

SQUASH-STUFFED CHICKEN

Bernadette Romano, Shaftsbury, Vermont

(PICTURED AT RIGHT)

- 3 tablespoons butter *or* margarine
- 1/2 small onion, chopped
- 1 tablespoon chopped fresh parsley
- 1/2 teaspoon dried basil
- 2 medium zucchini, shredded (about 2-1/2 cups)
- 3 slices white bread, torn into coarse crumbs
- 1 egg, beaten
- 3/4 cup shredded Swiss cheese
- 1/2 teaspoon salt
- 1/8 teaspoon pepper
- 4 chicken breast halves (with bones and skin)

In a skillet, melt butter over medium-high heat. Saute onion, parsley and basil until the onion is tender. Add zucchini and continue to cook for 2 minutes. Remove from the heat; stir in bread crumbs, egg, cheese, salt and pepper. Carefully loosen the skin of the chicken on one side to form a pocket. Stuff each breast with the zucchini mixture. Bake at 375° for 50-60 minutes or until chicken is done. **Yield:** 4 servings.

CHEESY FISH FILLETS WITH SPINACH

Marla Brenneman, Goshen, Indiana

(PICTURED ON PAGE 196)

 This tasty dish uses less sugar, salt and fat. Recipe includes *Diabetic Exchanges*.

- 2 tablespoons butter *or* margarine
- 2 tablespoons all-purpose flour
- 1 teaspoon instant chicken bouillon
- Dash nutmeg
- Dash cayenne pepper
- Dash white pepper
- 1 cup milk
- 2/3 cup shredded Swiss *or* cheddar cheese
- 1 package (10 ounces) frozen chopped spinach, thawed and well drained
- 1 tablespoon lemon juice
- 1 pound fish fillets, cut into serving pieces
- 1/2 teaspoon salt
- 2 tablespoons grated Parmesan cheese
- Paprika

Heat butter over low heat until melted. Stir in flour, bouillon, nutmeg, cayenne pepper and white pepper; cook over low heat, stirring constantly, until mixture is smooth and bubbly. Stir in milk; heat to boiling and cook, stirring constantly, for 1 minute. Add cheese and cook, stirring constantly, just until cheese melts. Set aside. Place spinach in an ungreased 12-in. x 7-1/2-in. baking dish or 8-in. square baking dish. Sprinkle with the lemon juice. Arrange fish on spinach; sprinkle with salt. Spread sauce over fish and spinach. Bake, uncovered, at 350° until fish flakes easily with a fork, about 20 minutes. Sprinkle with the Parmesan cheese and paprika; return to oven for 5 minutes. **Yield:** 4 servings. **Diabetic Exchanges:** One serving equals 4 protein, 2 vegetable, 1 fat; also, 307 calories, 860 mg sodium, 108 mg cholesterol, 10 gm carbohydrate, 31 gm protein, 16 gm fat.

MEXICAN PIZZA

Gail Reino, Franklinville, New York

- 1 tube (8 ounces) refrigerated crescent rolls
- 2 cups thick chili
- 1/2 cup sliced ripe olives
- 1/4 cup chopped onion
- 3/4 cup shredded cheddar cheese
- 1/2 cup crushed corn chips
- Avocado slices, shredded lettuce, chopped tomatoes *and/or* sour cream, optional

Unroll the crescent roll dough; pat into the bottom and up the sides of an ungreased 13-in. x 9-in. x 2-in. baking pan. Pinch edges together to seal. Bake at 400° for 10 minutes. In a bowl, combine the chili, olives and onion. Spread evenly over baked crust. Sprinkle with cheese and corn chips. Bake for 8-10 minutes or until bubbly. Top with avocado, lettuce, tomatoes and/or sour cream if desired. **Yield:** 6-8 servings.

POPPY SEED CHICKEN

Ernestin Plasek, Houston, Texas

- 1 tablespoon butter *or* margarine
- 8 ounces sliced fresh mushrooms
- 5 cups cubed cooked chicken
- 1 can (10-3/4 ounces) cream of chicken soup, undiluted
- 1 cup (8 ounces) sour cream
- 1 jar (2 ounces) pimiento, drained and diced

TOPPING:
- 1/2 cup butter *or* margarine, melted
- 1-1/3 cups finely crushed butter-flavored crackers
- 2 teaspoons poppy seeds

In a skillet, melt butter. Saute mushrooms until tender. Stir in chicken, soup, sour cream and pimiento; mix well. Spoon mixture into a greased 2-qt. casserole. In a small bowl, combine topping ingredients. Sprinkle over the chicken. Bake at 350° for 20 minutes. **Yield:** 6 servings.

HAM AND POTATOES AU GRATIN

Novella Cook, Hinton, West Virginia

- 2 cups sliced peeled potatoes, cooked
- 1 cup diced fully cooked ham
- 1 tablespoon minced onion
- 1/3 cup butter *or* margarine
- 3 tablespoons all-purpose flour
- 1-1/2 cups milk
- 1 cup (4 ounces) shredded cheddar cheese
- 3/4 teaspoon salt
- Dash white pepper
- Chopped fresh parsley

Combine potatoes, ham and onion in a greased 1-qt. casserole; set aside. In a saucepan, melt butter over medium heat; stir in flour until smooth. Gradually add milk, stirring constantly until mixture thickens and bubbles. Add cheese, salt and pepper; stir until cheese melts. Pour over potato mixture and stir gently to mix. Bake at 350° for 35-40 minutes or until bubbly. Garnish with parsley. **Yield:** 2 servings.

PORK CHOP AND CHILIES CASSEROLE

Mickey O'Neal, Chula Vista, California

- 1 tablespoon cooking oil
- 4 rib pork chops (3/4 to 1 inch thick)
- 1 medium onion, chopped
- 1 can (4 ounces) chopped green chilies
- 1/2 cup chopped celery
- 1-1/2 cups uncooked instant rice
- 1 can (10-3/4 ounces) cream of mushroom soup, undiluted
- 1 soup can water
- 3 tablespoons soy sauce

In a skillet, heat oil over medium-high. Brown pork chops on both sides. Remove and set aside. In the same skillet, saute onion, chilies and celery until onion is tender. Stir in rice; saute until lightly browned. Add soup, water and soy sauce; blend well. Place in a greased 2-qt. casserole. Top with pork chops. Bake at 350° for about 30 minutes or until rice is tender. **Yield:** 4 servings.

TOO MUCH of a good thing—that's what an annual abundance of squash seems to bring…and bring…and *bring*. What's a country cook to do? Turn to the delicious dishes here and see how you can use your surplus of squash in all sorts of flavorful new ways—from a(corn) to z(ucchini). So start cooking… and turn "excess" into "exciting" at your table!

GOURDGEOUS!
Clockwise from the top: **Cheddar/Squash Cloverleaf Rolls** (recipe on page 154), **Squash-Stuffed Chicken** (recipe on page 72), **Butternut Apple Crisp** (recipe on page 224) and **Marinated Zucchini Salad** (recipe on page 46).

WILD RICE QUICHE

Dotty Egge, Pelican Rapids, Minnesota

(PICTURED AT RIGHT)

- 1 unbaked pastry shell (9 inches)
- 1/3 cup chopped Canadian bacon *or* fully cooked ham
- 1 small onion, finely chopped
- 1 tablespoon butter *or* margarine
- 1 cup (4 ounces) shredded Monterey Jack cheese
- 1 cup cooked wild rice
- 3 eggs
- 1-1/2 cups light cream
- 1/2 teaspoon salt
- Snipped parsley, optional

Bake crust at 425° for 5 minutes. Remove from the oven and set aside. Reduce heat to 325°. In a skillet, saute Canadian bacon or ham and onion in butter until onion is tender. Spoon into the crust. Sprinkle with cheese and wild rice. In a small bowl, beat eggs, cream and salt. Pour over all. Bake at 325° for 35 minutes or until a knife inserted near the center comes out clean. Let stand 10 minutes before cutting. Garnish with parsley if desired. **Yield:** 6-8 servings.

SPICY STUFFED PEPPERS

Adele Bernard, Clinton, Missouri

(PICTURED AT RIGHT)

- 4 green peppers, tops and seeds removed
- 1 pound lean ground beef
- 1 cup finely chopped onion
- 1/2 cup cooked rice
- 1 teaspoon celery salt
- 1/2 teaspoon salt
- 1/4 teaspoon pepper
- Dash cayenne pepper
- 1 jar (8 ounces) picante sauce

Cook peppers in boiling salted water for 3 minutes. Drain and rinse with cold water. Combine ground beef, onion, rice and seasonings; spoon into peppers. Place in a greased baking dish; top with picante sauce. Bake, uncovered, at 375° for 35-40 minutes or until meat is no longer pink. **Yield:** 4 servings.

MEXICAN LASAGNA

Ellene Whitworth, Weatherford, Texas

- 1 pound lean ground beef
- 1 can (16 ounces) refried beans
- 2 teaspoons dried oregano
- 1 teaspoon ground cumin
- 3/4 teaspoon garlic powder
- 12 uncooked lasagna noodles
- 2-1/2 cups water
- 2-1/2 cups picante sauce *or* salsa
- 2 cups (16 ounces) sour cream
- 3/4 cup finely sliced green onions
- 1 can (2.2 ounces) sliced black olives, drained
- 1 cup (4 ounces) shredded Monterey Jack cheese

Combine beef, beans, oregano, cumin and garlic powder. Place four of the uncooked lasagna noodles in the bottom of a 13-in. x 9-in. x 2-in. baking pan. Spread half the beef mixture over the noodles. Top with four more noodles and the remaining beef mixture. Cover with remaining noodles. Combine water and picante sauce. Pour over all. Cover tightly with foil; bake at 350° for 1-1/2 hours or until noodles are tender. Combine sour cream, onions and olives. Spoon over casserole; top with cheese. Bake, uncovered, until cheese is melted, about 5 minutes. **Yield:** 12 servings.

TURKEY LEGS WITH MUSHROOM GRAVY

Wanda Swenson, Lady Lake, Florida

✓ This tasty dish uses less sugar, salt and fat. Recipe includes *Diabetic Exchanges*.

- 4 turkey legs (about 12 ounces each)
- 1/4 cup lemon juice
- 2 tablespoons cooking oil
- 1 teaspoon dried oregano
- 1 teaspoon dried basil
- 1 teaspoon garlic powder
- 1/4 teaspoon salt
- 1/4 teaspoon pepper

MUSHROOM GRAVY:

- 1 cup water
- 1 tablespoon cornstarch
- 1 can (4 ounces) sliced mushrooms, drained
- 1 can (10-1/2 ounces) mushroom gravy
- 1 teaspoon minced onion
- 1 tablespoon minced fresh parsley
- 1 teaspoon garlic powder

Place turkey legs in a roasting pan. In a small bowl, combine lemon juice, oil and seasonings. Pour over turkey legs. Bake, uncovered, at 375° for 45 minutes or until lightly browned. Turn legs twice and baste occasionally. Remove from the oven. For the gravy, combine water and cornstarch in a saucepan. Stir in remaining ingredients and bring to a boil over medium heat. Spoon over turkey legs. Cover loosely with foil. Bake, basting frequently, for 1 hour or until legs are tender. **Yield:** 4 servings. **Diabetic Ex-**

changes: One serving equals 4 lean meat, 1-1/2 fat, 1 vegetable, 1/2 starch; also, 357 calories, 703 mg sodium, 97 mg cholesterol, 11 gm carbohydrate, 36 gm protein, 18 gm fat.

HARVEST HAMBURGER CASSEROLE

Grace Hagen, Raggen, Colorado

- 1 pound lean ground beef, browned and drained
- 1 cup minced onion
- 1 can (28 ounces) tomatoes with liquid, cut up
- 1 tablespoon Worcestershire sauce
- 1 teaspoon salt
- 2 cups sliced potatoes
- 1/3 cup all-purpose flour
- 1 package (10 ounces) frozen corn, thawed
- 1 package (10 ounces) frozen lima beans, thawed
- 1 green pepper, cut into strips
- 1-1/2 cups (6 ounces) shredded cheddar cheese

In a mixing bowl, combine beef, onion, tomatoes with liquid, Worcestershire sauce and salt. Spoon into a greased 3-qt. casserole. Layer the potatoes, flour, corn, lima beans and green pepper on top. Cover and bake at 375° for 45 minutes. Sprinkle with cheese and continue baking, uncovered, for 30 minutes. **Yield:** 8 servings.

HAM AND CHEESE SOUFFLE

Airy Murray, Williamsport, Maryland

- 16 slices white bread (crusts removed), cubed
- 16 slices (about 1 pound) ham, cut into bite-size pieces
- 2 cups (8 ounces) shredded cheddar cheese
- 2 cups (8 ounces) shredded Swiss cheese
- 5 eggs, beaten
- 3 cups milk
- 1 teaspoon dry mustard
- 1/2 teaspoon onion salt
- 2-1/2 cups crushed cornflakes
- 1/3 cup butter *or* margarine, melted

In a greased 13-in. x 9-in. x 2-in. baking dish, layer half of the bread, ham, cheddar cheese and Swiss cheese. Repeat. Combine eggs, milk, mustard and onion salt; pour over layered mixture. Cover and refrigerate overnight. Combine cornflakes and butter; sprinkle on top. Bake at 375° for 40 minutes or until hot and bubbly. **Yield:** 8-10 servings.

DELIGHT your hungry clan by
dishing out this tempting fare. Everyone will
surely enjoy hearty helpings of savory Wild Rice Quiche and
Chili Verde. And highlight the fantastic flavor of produce with
Fresh Vegetable Casserole and Spicy Stuffed Peppers.

MMM-MARVELOUS MENU!
Clockwise from the bottom: **Wild Rice Quiche**, **Spicy Stuffed
Peppers** (both recipes on page 74), **Fresh Vegetable
Casserole** (recipe on page 130) and
Chili Verde (recipe on page 36).

CREAMY Chicken Tetrazzini (recipe at right) makes a nice change-of-pace pasta dinner.

PORK STUFFED WITH CORN BREAD DRESSING

Fern Kleeman, Tell City, Indiana

(PICTURED ON PAGE 200)

1/4 cup boiling water
1/4 cup raisins
  2 slices bacon, cut up
1/2 cup diced celery
  2 tablespoons diced onion
  1 egg, beaten
  1 teaspoon salt
1/4 teaspoon pepper
2-1/2 cups corn bread crumbs
  6 center cut pork chops (1-1/4 inches thick) *or* 1 pork blade roast (3 to 4 pounds), boned for stuffing

Pour water over raisins; set aside. In a saucepan, cook bacon until crisp; add celery and onion. Cook and stir for 2 minutes; remove from the heat. In a medium bowl, combine egg, salt, pepper and bacon and raisin mixtures. Stir in crumbs; toss lightly. If stuffing pork chops, cut a pocket in each chop by slicing from the fat side almost to the bone. Spoon about 1/3 cup stuffing into each chop; place on a rack in a shallow roasting pan. Bake at 375° for 40-50 minutes or until the meat is no longer pink. If stuffing a roast, fill pocket in roast with stuffing. Tie roast with string and place on a rack in a shallow roasting pan. Insert meat thermometer into center of meat. Roast at 325° for 1-3/4 to 2-1/4 hours or until the thermometer registers 160° for medium-well or 170° for well-done. Cover and let stand 10 minutes before carving. **Yield:** 6 servings (chops) or 8-10 servings (roast).

CHICKEN TETRAZZINI

Martha Sue Stroud, Clarksville, Texas

(PICTURED AT LEFT)

  1 package (16 ounces) uncooked spaghetti
  2 tablespoons butter *or* margarine
  1 medium green pepper, chopped
  1 medium onion, chopped
  2 cups cubed cooked chicken
  2 cans (4 ounces *each*) mushrooms, drained
  1 jar (2 ounces) diced pimiento, drained
  1 can (10-3/4 ounces) condensed cream of mushroom soup, undiluted
  2 cups milk
1/2 teaspoon garlic powder
1/2 teaspoon salt
  1 to 1-1/2 cups (4 to 6 ounces) shredded cheddar cheese

Cook spaghetti according to package directions. Meanwhile, melt butter in a large Dutch oven; saute green pepper and onion until peppers are crisp-tender. Stir in chicken, mushrooms, pimiento, soup, milk, garlic powder and salt. Drain spaghetti and add to mixture; toss. Pour into a greased 13-in. x 9-in. x 2-in. baking dish. Bake at 350° for 50-60 minutes or until hot and bubbly. Sprinkle with cheese; bake 10 minutes longer or until cheese is melted. **Yield:** 10-12 servings.

SAUCY CHICKEN CASSEROLE

Jacki Remsberg, La Canada, California

(PICTURED ON PAGE 180)

  1 can (10-3/4 ounces) cream of chicken soup, undiluted
  1 can (10-3/4 ounces) cream of mushroom soup, undiluted
  2 cups (16 ounces) sour cream
3/4 cup dry white wine *or* chicken broth
1/2 medium onion, chopped
  1 cup sliced fresh mushrooms
1/2 teaspoon garlic powder
1/2 teaspoon salt
1/2 teaspoon poultry seasoning
1/4 teaspoon ground black pepper
  6 boneless chicken breast halves
Cooked noodles *or* **rice**
Chopped parsley

In a 13-in. x 9-in. x 2-in. baking pan, combine soups, sour cream, wine or broth, onion, mushrooms and seasonings. Arrange chicken on top of sauce. Bake, uncovered, at 350° for 1 hour or until chicken is tender. Serve chicken and sauce over noodles or rice. Garnish with parsley. **Yield:** 6 servings.

CITRUS-BAKED CORNISH HENS

Mary-Lynne Mason, Janesville, Wisconsin

(PICTURED ON PAGE 223)

  4 Cornish game hens
SAUCE:
1/4 cup apricot preserves
  2 tablespoons grated onion
  1 tablespoon butter *or* margarine
  1 tablespoon Dijon mustard
  1 garlic clove, minced
Juice and grated peel of 1 lemon
Juice and grated peel of 1 orange

Remove giblets and necks from hens. Tie the legs of the hens together and turn the wing tips under the backs. In a saucepan, combine all sauce ingredients. Simmer 5 minutes. Brush the hens with the sauce and arrange, breast side up, on a rack in a large roasting pan. Bake at 350° for about 1-1/4 hours or until tender. Brush hens occasionally with sauce. **Yield:** 4-8 servings.

DINNER FOR TWO? When cooking for one or two people, divide casserole ingredients into two smaller dishes and freeze one for later use. You'll appreciate the ready-to-make meal on hectic days.

Quick & Easy

SAUSAGE AND SAUERKRAUT CASSEROLE

Deltie Tackette, Eubank, Kentucky

  2 cups uncooked elbow macaroni
  1 pound bulk pork sausage
  1 can (16 ounces) tomatoes with liquid, cut up
  1 cup sauerkraut
  1 teaspoon sugar
  4 to 5 tablespoons shredded cheddar cheese

Cook macaroni according to package directions. Meanwhile, brown sausage in a skillet; drain, reserving 1 tablespoon drippings. Add tomatoes, sauerkraut and sugar to sausage and cook for 2 minutes. Drain macaroni; stir into skillet along with cheese. Spoon into a greased 8-in. square baking dish. Bake, uncovered, at 350° for 20 minutes. **Yield:** 4-6 servings.

ITALIAN SAUSAGE AND SPINACH PIE

Teresa Johnson, Peru, Illinois

(PICTURED ON PAGE 189)

- 1 pound bulk Italian sausage
- 1 medium onion, chopped
- 6 eggs, beaten
- 2 packages (10 ounces *each*) frozen chopped spinach, thawed and well drained
- 4 cups (16 ounces) shredded mozzarella cheese
- 1 cup ricotta cheese
- 1/2 teaspoon garlic powder
- 1/4 teaspoon pepper
- Pastry for a two-crust pie (10 inches)
- 1 tablespoon water

In a skillet, brown sausage and onion until the sausage is done and onion is tender. Drain. Separate 1 egg and set aside the yolk. In a mixing bowl, beat the remaining egg white and whole eggs. Stir in the sausage and onion, spinach, mozzarella, ricotta, garlic powder and pepper. Line a 10-in. pie plate with bottom pastry. Add filling. Top with upper crust; seal and flute edges. Cut slits in top crust. Combine water with reserved egg yolk; brush over top crust. Bake at 375° for 50 minutes or until golden brown. Let stand 10 minutes before serving. **Yield:** 8 servings.

BEEF OR CHICKEN ENCHILADAS

Pam Tangbakken, Genesee, Idaho

- 1 tablespoon butter *or* margarine
- 2 medium onions, chopped
- 1 garlic clove, minced
- 2 tablespoons all-purpose flour
- 1 cup chicken broth
- 1 cup milk
- 2 cans (4 ounces *each*) chopped green chilies
- 1/4 teaspoon salt
- 1/4 teaspoon ground cumin
- 12 flour *or* corn tortillas
- 1-1/2 cups shredded cooked beef *or* chicken
- 1 cup (4 ounces) shredded Monterey Jack cheese
- 1 cup (4 ounces) shredded cheddar cheese
- 2 green onions with tops, thinly sliced
- Sour cream
- Salsa

In a saucepan, melt butter over medium heat. Saute onion and garlic until onion is tender. Blend in flour. Stir in broth, milk, chilies, salt and cumin. Cook and stir until thickened and bubbly. Reduce heat; simmer 5 minutes, stirring occasionally. Set aside. Grease a 13-in. x 9-in. x 2-in. baking dish. Spoon a little sauce in the center of each tortilla; spread to edges. Place about 2 tablespoons meat down the center of each tortilla. Combine cheeses; sprinkle 1-2 tablespoons on top of meat. Roll up tortillas and place in baking dish, seam-side down. Pour remaining sauce over. Sprinkle with green onions and remaining cheese. Bake, uncovered, at 350° for 20-30 minutes or until hot and bubbly. Serve with sour cream and salsa. **Yield:** 6 servings.

BRUNCH EGG CASSEROLE

Lelia Brown, Annandale, Virginia

- 2 cups unseasoned croutons
- 1 cup (4 ounces) shredded cheddar cheese
- 4 eggs, beaten
- 2 cups milk
- 1/2 teaspoon salt
- 1/2 teaspoon dry mustard
- 1/8 teaspoon onion powder
- Dash pepper
- 4 slices bacon, fried, drained and crumbled

Place croutons and cheese in the bottom of a greased 10-in. x 6-in. x 1-3/4-in. baking dish. Combine eggs, milk and seasonings; pour into baking dish. Sprinkle with bacon. Bake at 325° for 1 hour or until set. Serve immediately. **Yield:** 6 servings.

CHICKEN FEED

Jill Kinder, Richlands, Virginia

- 1 small onion, sliced
- 2 cups fresh mushrooms, sliced
- 1 garlic clove, minced
- 1/2 teaspoon dried thyme, *divided*
- 1 tablespoon butter *or* margarine
- 4 cups cubed cooked chicken
- 4 cups prepared gravy
- 1 teaspoon instant chicken bouillon granules
- Dash pepper
- 3 cups mashed potatoes

In a skillet, saute the onion, mushrooms, garlic and 1/4 teaspoon thyme in butter. Stir in the chicken, gravy, bouillon and pepper; spoon into a greased 3-qt. casserole. Combine potatoes and remaining thyme; spoon over mixture. Bake, uncovered, at 350° for 45 minutes. **Yield:** 6-8 servings.

CHURCH SUPPER HOT DISH

Norma Turner, Haslett, Michigan

- 1 pound ground beef
- 2 cups sliced peeled potatoes
- 2 cups finely chopped celery
- 3/4 cup finely chopped carrots
- 1/4 cup finely chopped green pepper
- 1/4 cup finely chopped onion
- 2 tablespoons butter *or* margarine
- 1 cup water
- 2 cans (10-3/4 ounces *each*) condensed cream of mushroom soup, undiluted
- 1 can (5 ounces) chow mein noodles, *divided*
- 1 cup (4 ounces) shredded cheddar cheese

In a skillet, brown beef. Drain and set aside. In a large saucepan or another skillet, saute potatoes, celery, carrots, green pepper and onion in butter for 5 minutes. Add water; cover and simmer for 10 minutes. Add soup and cooked ground beef; mix well. Sprinkle half of the chow mein noodles into a greased shallow 2-qt. baking dish. Spoon meat mixture over noodles. Cover and bake at 350° for 20 minutes. Top with the cheese and remaining noodles. Bake, uncovered, 10 minutes longer or until heated through. **Yield:** 8 servings.

POOR MAN'S FILET MIGNON

Gayle Mollenkamp, Russell Springs, Kansas

- 2 pounds extra-lean ground beef
- 4 slices bread, crumbed
- 2 eggs, beaten
- 1/2 cup milk
- 2 teaspoons salt
- 1 tablespoon minced onion
- 2 teaspoons dried celery flakes
- 1/2 teaspoon chili powder
- 1 bottle (18 ounces) smoke-flavored barbecue sauce, *divided*
- 12 slices uncooked bacon

Combine first eight ingredients and 2 tablespoons barbecue sauce. Form into 12 thick patties. Wrap a bacon slice around the sides of each patty and secure with a toothpick. Bake on a rack at 350° for 50-60 minutes or until desired doneness is reached. Baste frequently with remaining barbecue sauce the last 30 minutes. **Yield:** 12 servings.

FOR food that's full of freshness, what could possibly top asparagus? Those tender little spears are big on flavor in the tasty recipes featured here. What variety you'll find: refreshing salads, meaty main courses...even sure-to-please brunch recipes!

DON'T SPARE ASPARAGUS!
Clockwise from lower left: **Ham and Asparagus Au Gratin** (recipe on page 80), **Asparagus Quiche** (recipe on page 80), **Pasta with Asparagus** (recipe on page 100), **Sesame Beef and Asparagus Salad** (recipe on page 42), **Asparagus, Chicken, Wild Rice Casserole** (recipe on page 80), **Bacon and Asparagus Frittata** (recipe on page 104), **Molded Asparagus Salad** (recipe on page 49) and **Asparagus and Tomato Salad** (recipe on page 51).

THIS MAKE-AHEAD egg casserole (recipe below) is perfect for morning company.

OVERNIGHT EGG CASSEROLE

La Vonne Propst, Sweet Home, Oregon

(PICTURED ABOVE)

8 slices bread, cubed
3/4 pound cheddar cheese, shredded
1-1/2 pounds bulk pork sausage or Italian sausage
4 eggs
2-1/2 cups milk
1 tablespoon prepared mustard
1 can (10-3/4 ounces) condensed cream of mushroom soup, undiluted
1/4 cup chicken broth

Place bread cubes in a greased 13-in. x 9-in. x 2-in. baking dish. Sprinkle with cheese; set aside. In a skillet; brown sausage over medium heat; drain. Crumble sausage over cheese and bread. Beat eggs, milk, mustard, soup and broth; pour over sausage. Cover and refrigerate overnight or at least 2-3 hours before baking. Bake at 350° for 50-60 minutes or until a knife inserted near the center comes out clean. **Yield:** 6-8 servings.

ASPARAGUS, CHICKEN, WILD RICE CASSEROLE

Mary Drache, Roseville, Minnesota

(PICTURED ON PAGE 79)

1 cup uncooked wild rice, rinsed
2 cups chicken broth
1 can (4 ounces) mushrooms undrained
2 tablespoons butter or margarine
6 boneless chicken breast halves
1/2 package onion soup mix

1 can (10-3/4 ounces) cream of mushroom soup, undiluted
1-1/2 pounds fresh asparagus, trimmed
1/4 cup butter or margarine, melted
Paprika

Spread rice in a 11-in. x 7-in. x 1-1/2-in. baking pan. Add the chicken broth and mushrooms; dot with 2 tablespoons butter. Place chicken breasts in the center of the baking dish; sprinkle with the onion soup mix. Spoon mushroom soup over all. Bake, uncovered, at 350° for 1 hour. Arrange asparagus around outer edges of baking dish; brush with melted butter and sprinkle with paprika. Bake 15-20 minutes more or until asparagus is tender. **Yield:** 6 servings.

ASPARAGUS QUICHE

Edna Hoffman, Hebron, Indiana

(PICTURED ON PAGE 78)

1 unbaked pastry shell (9 inches)
1/2 pound fresh asparagus, trimmed
2 green onions, thinly sliced
1 tablespoon all-purpose flour
2 cups (8 ounces) shredded Swiss cheese
3 eggs, beaten
1 cup light cream
1/2 teaspoon salt
1/4 teaspoon basil
1/8 teaspoon cayenne pepper

Bake crust at 425° for 6-7 minutes. Remove from oven and set aside. Reduce heat to 325°. Cook the asparagus spears in a small amount of water until tender. Drain and cool. Reserve 3 whole spears for garnish; slice the remaining spears into 1/2-in. pieces. Toss together the asparagus pieces, onions and flour. Spread asparagus mixture into crust; sprinkle with cheese. Whisk together eggs, cream, salt, basil and cayenne pepper. Pour into crust. Bake at 325° for 25 minutes. Split the reserved asparagus spears lengthwise and arrange, cut side down, in a wheel pattern on top of filling. Bake 5-10 minutes longer or until a knife inserted near the center comes out clean. Let stand 10 minutes before cutting. **Yield:** 6 servings.

STUFFED BEEF TENDERLOIN

Norma Blank, Shawano, Wisconsin

1/4 cup butter or margarine
1 medium onion, chopped
1/2 cup diced celery

1 can (4 ounces) chopped mushrooms, drained
2 cups soft bread crumbs (about 3 slices)
1/2 to 1 teaspoon salt
1/8 teaspoon pepper
1/4 teaspoon dried basil or 1 teaspoon fresh basil
1/4 teaspoon dried parsley flakes or 1 teaspoon chopped fresh parsley
1 beef tenderloin (about 3 pounds), trimmed
4 slices bacon

In a small skillet, melt butter over low heat. Saute onion, celery and mushrooms until onion is soft and transparent. Meanwhile, in a mixing bowl, combine bread crumbs, salt, pepper, basil and parsley. Add onion mixture and mix well. Make a lengthwise cut 3/4 of the way through the tenderloin. Lightly place stuffing in the pocket; close with toothpicks. Place bacon strips diagonally across the top, covering the picks and pocket. Place meat, bacon side up, in a shallow roasting pan. Insert meat thermometer into meat, not stuffing. Bake, uncovered, at 350° until meat reaches desired degree of doneness: 140° for rare, 160° for medium and 170° for well-done. (Meat will need to bake approximately 1 hour for medium.) Remove from oven; let stand for 15 minutes. Remove toothpicks and slice. **Yield:** 10-12 servings.

HAM AND ASPARAGUS AU GRATIN

Dorothy Pritchett, Wills Point, Texas

(PICTURED ON PAGE 78)

6 slices baked ham
24 asparagus spears, cooked and drained
2 eggs
2 egg yolks
1-1/2 cups heavy cream
Salt and pepper to taste
2 tablespoons shredded Swiss cheese
2 tablespoons grated Parmesan cheese
Finely chopped fresh parsley, optional

Wrap each ham slice around 4 asparagus spears and place seam side down in a greased 11-in. x 7-in. x 1-1/2-in. baking pan. Beat together eggs, yolks, cream, salt and pepper. Pour over ham rolls. Bake at 350° for about 35 minutes or until top begins to brown and the tip of a knife inserted in the egg mixture comes out clean. Sprinkle with cheeses and parsley if desired. Serve immediately. **Yield:** 4-6 servings.

RHUBARB PORK CHOP CASSEROLE

Jeanie Castor, Decatur, Illinois

(PICTURED ON PAGE 209)

4 pork loin chops (3/4 inch thick)
1 tablespoon cooking oil
Salt and pepper to taste
2-1/2 to 3 cups soft bread crumbs
3 cups sliced fresh *or* frozen rhubarb (1-inch pieces)
1/2 cup packed brown sugar
1/4 cup all-purpose flour
1 teaspoon ground cinnamon

In a large skillet, brown pork chops in oil and season with salt and pepper. Remove to a warm platter. Mix 1/4 cup pan drippings with bread crumbs. Reserve 1/2 cup; sprinkle remaining crumbs into a 13-in. x 9-in. x 2-in. baking dish. Combine rhubarb, sugar, flour and cinnamon; spoon half over the bread crumbs. Arrange pork chops on top. Spoon remaining rhubarb mixture over chops. Cover with foil and bake at 350° for 30-45 minutes. Remove foil. Sprinkle with reserved bread crumbs. Bake 10-15 minutes longer or until chops test done. **Yield:** 4 servings.

TEXAS-STYLE LASAGNA

Effie Gish, Fort Worth, Texas

(PICTURED ON PAGE 164)

1-1/2 pounds ground beef
1 teaspoon seasoned salt
1 package (1-1/4 ounces) taco seasoning mix
1 can (14-1/2 ounces) diced tomatoes, undrained
1 can (15 ounces) tomato sauce
1 can (4 ounces) chopped green chilies
2 cups (16 ounces) small-curd cottage cheese
2 eggs, beaten
12 corn tortillas (6 inches), torn
3-1/2 to 4 cups shredded Monterey Jack cheese

In a large skillet, brown meat; drain. Add seasoned salt, taco seasoning mix, tomatoes, tomato sauce and chilies; mix

well. Simmer, uncovered, for 15 to 20 minutes. Combine cottage cheese and eggs. In a greased 13-in. x 9-in. x 2-in. baking dish, layer half of the meat sauce, half of the tortillas, half the cottage cheese mixture and half of Monterey Jack cheese. Repeat layers. Bake, uncovered, at 350° for 30 minutes or until bubbly. Let stand 10 minutes before serving. **Yield:** 10-12 servings.

LAZY-DAY LASAGNA. Don't spend extra time precooking noodles for lasagna or manicotti. Just add more sauce, cover pan with foil and cook slightly longer.

PLANTATION STUFFED PEPPERS

Sherry Morgan, Mansfield, Louisiana

8 medium green peppers, tops and seeds removed
1 pound ground beef
1 cup chopped onion
1 garlic clove, minced
2 teaspoons chili powder
1 teaspoon salt
1/2 teaspoon pepper
2 cans (10-3/4 ounces *each*) tomato soup, undiluted
2 cups (8 ounces) shredded cheddar cheese
1-1/2 cups cooked rice

In boiling salted water, cook peppers for 3-5 minutes. Remove and set aside. In a skillet, cook beef, onion and garlic until meat is done and onion is tender. Drain any fat. Add seasonings and soup; simmer, uncovered, for 10 minutes. Stir in cheese; cook and stir until melted. Stir in rice. Fill peppers; place in a shallow baking dish. Bake at 350° for 20 minutes. **Yield:** 8 servings.

BEEF AND NOODLE CASSEROLE

Mary Hinman, Escondido, California

1-1/2 pounds ground beef
1 tablespoon butter *or* margarine
1 large onion, chopped
1 cup chopped green pepper
1 tablespoon Worcestershire sauce
1 package (10 ounces) wide noodles, cooked and drained
2 cans (10-3/4 ounces *each*) cream of tomato soup, undiluted
1 can (10-3/4 ounces) cream of mushroom soup, undiluted
1 cup (4 ounces) shredded cheddar cheese

In a large skillet, brown beef. Remove beef and drain fat. In the same skillet, melt butter over medium-high heat. Saute onion and pepper until tender. Add beef, Worcestershire sauce, noodles and soups; mix well. Spoon into a greased 3-qt. casserole; top with cheese. Bake at 350° for 45 minutes. **Yield:** 8 servings.

HERBED MACARONI AND CHEESE

Nancy Raymond, Waldoboro, Maine

(PICTURED BELOW)

1 package (7 ounces) macaroni
2 tablespoons butter *or* margarine
2 tablespoons all-purpose flour
1/2 teaspoon Italian seasoning
1/4 teaspoon onion powder
Salt and pepper to taste
1 cup milk
1/4 cup sour cream
3/4 cup shredded cheddar cheese, *divided*
1/2 cup cubed Havarti *or* Muenster cheese
2 tablespoons grated Parmesan cheese
2 tablespoons Italian-style seasoned bread crumbs

Cook macaroni and drain well; place in a 1-1/2-qt. casserole and set aside. In a saucepan, melt butter over medium heat. Stir in the flour and seasonings; gradually add milk. Cook and stir until thickened. Remove pan from heat; add sour cream, 1/2 cup cheddar cheese and all the Havarti or Muenster. Stir until melted. Pour sauce over macaroni and mix well. Combine Parmesan cheese, bread crumbs and remaining cheddar cheese; sprinkle over casserole. Bake at 350° for 15-20 minutes. **Yield:** 6 servings.

GET READY to serve hearty helpings of marvelous herbed macaroni (recipe above).

VERSATILE is the best way to describe the
use of sweet, golden corn. Here the possibilities include
a tangy, colorful salad, appealing pork chops with corn dressing,
creamy chowder and hearty corn balls.

REFRESHING RECIPES.
Clockwise from the bottom: **Corn and Sausage Chowder**
(recipe on page 30), **Corn Balls** (recipe on page 131),
Fresh Corn Salad (recipe on page 51) and
Corn-Topped Chops (recipe on page 83).

CORN-TOPPED CHOPS
June Hassler, Sultan, Washington

(PICTURED AT LEFT)

1 egg, beaten
2 cups soft bread crumbs
1 can (17 ounces) whole kernel corn, drained *or* 1-1/2 cups cooked whole kernel corn
1/4 cup water
1/2 cup chopped green pepper
1 small onion, chopped
1 teaspoon Worcestershire sauce
2 tablespoons cooking oil
6 butterfly (boneless) pork chops (about 1 inch thick)
Salt and pepper to taste
1 can (10-3/4 ounces) condensed cream of mushroom soup, undiluted
1/2 soup can milk

In a bowl, combine egg, bread crumbs, corn, water, green pepper, onion and Worcestershire sauce; set aside. In a large ovenproof skillet or a Dutch oven, heat oil over medium-high. Lightly brown pork chops on both sides. Season with salt and pepper. Top with corn dressing mixture. Add enough water to cover bottom of pan. Bake, uncovered, at 350° for about 1 hour or until pork is tender. Add additional water to pan if necessary. Remove pork chops and dressing to a serving platter; keep warm. Add soup and milk to pan drippings. Cook and stir over medium heat until hot and bubbly. Serve with pork chops. **Yield:** 6 servings.

STEAK AND ONION PIE
Ardis Wirtz, Newburgh, Indiana

(PICTURED ON PAGE 153)

1 large onion, sliced
1/3 cup shortening
1/3 cup all-purpose flour
1 teaspoon salt
1 teaspoon pepper
1/2 teaspoon ground ginger
1-1/2 teaspoons ground allspice
1-1/2 pounds boneless round steak, cut into 1-inch cubes
2 cups boiling water
1-1/2 cups diced peeled potatoes
1 cup diced carrots
1 cup frozen peas
Pie pastry (9 to 10 inches)

In a Dutch oven, lightly brown onion in shortening. Meanwhile, combine flour, salt, pepper, ginger and allspice in a plastic bag. Place meat cubes in the bag, a few pieces at a time, and shake well to coat. Remove onion and set aside.

Brown beef on all sides. Add water; cover and simmer for 1 hour or until meat is tender, stirring occasionally. Add potatoes, carrots and reserved onions; cover and cook for 10 minutes. Stir in peas and continue cooking until all vegetables are tender, about 10 minutes. Spoon meat mixture into a 9-in. square baking pan. Roll pastry out to a 10-in. square; place over meat mixture and seal edges to pan. Cut several small steam vents in crust. Bake at 450° for 25-30 minutes or until pastry is browned. **Yield:** 6-8 servings.

SCRAMBLED EGG CASSEROLE
Mary Anne McWhirter, Pearland, Texas

(PICTURED ON PAGE 151)

2 tablespoons butter *or* margarine
2-1/2 tablespoons flour
2 cups milk
1/2 teaspoon salt
1/8 teaspoon pepper
1 cup American cheese, shredded
1 cup cubed ham
1/4 cup chopped green onion
3 tablespoons melted butter *or* margarine
1 dozen eggs, beaten
1 can (4 ounces) sliced mushrooms, drained
TOPPING:
2-1/4 cups soft bread crumbs
1/4 cup melted butter

In a saucepan, melt butter. Blend in flour and cook for 1 minute. Gradually stir in milk; cook until thick. Add salt, pepper and cheese; stir until cheese melts. Set aside. Saute ham and green onion in 3 tablespoons melted butter until onion is tender. Add eggs and cook over medium heat until eggs are set; stir in the mushrooms and cheese sauce. Spoon eggs into greased 13-in. x 9-in. x 2-in. baking pan. Combine topping ingredients; spread evenly over egg mixture. Cover; chill overnight. Bake, uncovered, at 350° for 30 minutes. **Yield:** 10-12 servings.

SUNDAY FRIED CHICKEN
Audrey Read, Fraser Lake, British Columbia

2 cups all-purpose flour
1/2 cup cornmeal
2 tablespoons salt
2 tablespoons dry mustard
2 tablespoons paprika
2 tablespoons garlic salt
1 tablespoon celery salt
1 tablespoon pepper

1 teaspoon ground ginger
1/2 teaspoon dried thyme
1/2 teaspoon oregano
1 broiler-fryer chicken (2-1/2 to 3-1/2 pounds), cut up
Cooking oil

Combine all ingredients except chicken and oil. Place about 1 cup flour mixture in a paper or plastic bag. Shake a few chicken pieces in the bag at a time, coating well. On medium-high, heat 1/4 in. of oil in a large skillet. Brown chicken on all sides; remove to a large shallow baking pan. Bake, uncovered, at 350° for 45-60 minutes or until done. Recipe makes enough coating for three chickens. Store unused mixture in an airtight container. **Yield:** 4-6 servings.

ASPARAGUS ENCHILADAS
Janet Hill, Sacramento, California

1/3 cup cooking oil
1 dozen flour tortillas (8 inches *each*)
1/2 cup butter *or* margarine
1/2 cup all-purpose flour
2 cans (15 ounces *each*) chicken broth
1 cup (8 ounces) sour cream
1/2 cup green taco sauce
3 cups shredded cooked chicken
3 cups (12 ounces) shredded Monterey Jack cheese, *divided*
1/2 cup chopped green onions, *divided*
2 pounds fresh asparagus, trimmed
1/3 cup grated Parmesan cheese
1/4 cup sliced ripe olives
Additional green taco sauce

In a skillet, heat oil over medium-high heat. Soften tortillas in the hot oil 30 seconds per side. Drain on paper towel; cool. In a large saucepan, melt butter over medium heat. Blend in flour. Whisk in chicken broth, cook and stir until thickened. Remove from the heat. Stir in sour cream and taco sauce. Keep warm but do not boil. Divide the chicken, 2-1/2 cups Monterey Jack cheese and all but 2 tablespoons of the onions over the 12 tortillas. Arrange asparagus over filling with the tips extending beyond the tortillas. Top each with 2 tablespoons sauce. Roll up and arrange, seam side down, in a 13-in. x 9-in. baking pan. Top with reserved sauce and the Parmesan cheese. Bake at 400° for 25 minutes or until bubbly. Sprinkle with remaining Monterey Jack cheese and return to the oven just until melted. Garnish with olives and reserved onions. Serve with additional green taco sauce. **Yield:** 12 servings.

SUPERBLY SEASONED brisket (recipe below) will become new-found family favorite.

COUNTRY BEEF BRISKET

Beth Blair, Kansas City, Missouri

(PICTURED ABOVE)

- 1 beef brisket (2-1/2 to 3 pounds), trimmed

MARINADE:
- 1/2 cup soy sauce
- 1 can (10-1/2 ounces) condensed beef broth
- 2-1/2 tablespoons lemon juice
- 1/2 teaspoon garlic powder
- Paprika

SEASONED BROTH:
- 1/4 cup vinegar
- 1/4 cup Worcestershire sauce
- 1/4 cup packed brown sugar
- 1/2 to 1 teaspoon liquid smoke

Place brisket in a shallow pan. Combine all marinade ingredients except paprika; reserve 1 cup and refrigerate. Pour remaining marinade over meat. Cover and refrigerate overnight. Drain meat. Place meat in a shallow baking pan; sprinkle with paprika. Cover tightly with foil. Bake at 325° for 3 hours or until meat is tender. Cool and refrigerate meat; discard cooking juices. When thoroughly chilled, slice meat and return to the baking pan. Combine seasoned broth ingredients and reserved marinade in a saucepan. Simmer for 10 minutes; pour over meat. Cover and bake at 300° for 1 hour. **Yield:** 10-12 servings.

ZUCCHINI QUICHE

Dorothy Collins, Winnsboro, Texas

- 1 unbaked pastry shell (9 inches)
- 2 tablespoons butter or margarine
- 1 pound zucchini, thinly sliced
- 1-1/2 cups (6 ounces) shredded mozzarella cheese
- 1 cup ricotta cheese or dry cottage cheese
- 1/2 cup light cream
- 3 eggs, lightly beaten
- 3/4 teaspoon salt
- 1/2 teaspoon dried oregano
- 1/2 teaspoon dried basil
- 1/4 teaspoon garlic powder
- Dash pepper
- Paprika

Prick bottom of pie crust with a fork and bake at 425° for 7 minutes. Remove crust from oven; set aside. Reduce heat to 350°. In a skillet, melt butter over medium-high heat; saute zucchini until tender. Drain. Place half the zucchini in the bottom of the crust. Sprinkle with mozzarella cheese. In a bowl, combine ricotta or cottage cheese, cream, eggs, salt, oregano, basil, garlic powder and pepper. Pour into crust. Arrange the remaining zucchini slices on top. Sprinkle with paprika. Bake about 45 minutes or until a knife inserted in the center comes out clean. **Yield:** 6-8 servings.

CHICKEN CANNELLONI

Barbara Nowakowski, N. Tonawanda, New York

- 1 small onion, sliced
- 1 garlic clove, minced
- 3/4 cup thinly sliced carrots
- 1/2 cup thinly sliced celery
- 1/2 cup sliced mushrooms
- 1 tablespoon cooking oil
- 1 can (6 ounces) tomato paste
- 1 can (8 ounces) tomatoes with liquid, cut up
- 1-1/2 teaspoons Italian seasoning, divided
- 1 teaspoon sugar
- 6 boneless skinless chicken breast halves
- 1/2 cup ricotta cheese
- 1/4 cup sliced green onions
- 3 tablespoons grated Parmesan cheese
- Dash pepper
- 1/2 cup mozzarella cheese
- Cooked pasta, optional

In a large saucepan, saute onion, garlic, carrots, celery and mushrooms in oil until onion is tender. Add tomato paste, tomatoes, 1 teaspoon Italian seasoning and sugar; bring to a boil. Reduce heat and simmer, uncovered, for 10 minutes. Meanwhile, pound chicken breasts to 1/4-in. thickness. Combine ricotta cheese, green onions, Parmesan cheese, pepper and remaining Italian seasoning; divide evenly and spoon on top of chicken breasts. Roll up; place seam side down in an 8-in. square baking dish. Spoon sauce over chicken. Bake, uncovered, at 375° for 25-30 minutes or until the chicken is tender. Sprinkle with mozzarella cheese; let stand for 5 minutes. Serve with pasta if desired. **Yield:** 4-6 servings.

CHICKEN/WILD RICE HOT DISH

Suzanne Greenslit, Merrifield, Minnesota

- 1 cup uncooked wild rice
- 3 cups boiling water
- 2-1/2 teaspoons salt, divided
- 1/4 cup butter or margarine
- 1 pound fresh mushrooms, sliced
- 1 medium onion, chopped
- 1/4 cup minced fresh parsley
- 1/4 teaspoon pepper
- 3 cups diced cooked chicken
- 1 jar (2 ounces) chopped pimiento, drained
- 1 cup chicken broth
- 1 cup heavy cream
- 1/4 cup grated Parmesan cheese
- 3/4 cup slivered almonds

Wash rice; place in a saucepan with water and 1 teaspoon salt. Cover and simmer 45-50 minutes or until tender. Drain if necessary. In a large skillet, melt butter over medium heat. Saute mushrooms, onion and parsley for 5 minutes. Stir in remaining 1-1/2 teaspoons salt, pepper, rice, chicken, pimiento, broth and cream. Place in a 13-in. x 9-in. x 2-in. baking dish. Top with cheese and almonds. Bake at 350° for 50-60 minutes. **Yield:** 8-10 servings.

STUFFED CROWN ROAST OF PORK

Marianne Severson, West Allis, Wisconsin

(PICTURED ON PAGE 220)

- 1 crown roast of pork (about 8 pounds)
- 1 pound ground pork
- 1/2 pound bulk pork sausage
- 3/4 cup finely chopped onion
- 3 tablespoons butter or margarine
- 1/2 cup diced peeled apple
- 1/4 cup finely chopped celery

1-1/2 cups soft bread crumbs
1/2 cup minced fresh parsley
1-1/2 teaspoons salt
1/2 teaspoon pepper
1/2 teaspoon dried sage
Spiced crab apples, optional

Tie roast and place on a rack in a large roasting pan. Cover the bone ends with foil. Insert meat thermometer. Roast at 350° for 2 hours. Meanwhile, in a large skillet, cook the pork and sausage until browned; drain and set aside. In the same skillet, saute onion in butter until tender. Add apple and celery; cook for 5 minutes. Remove from the heat. Add the cooked pork and sausage, crumbs, parsley, salt, pepper and sage; mix well. Remove roast from oven. Carefully press a double layer of foil down through open center of roast to form a base for stuffing. Spoon stuffing lightly into crown. Return to oven and bake for 1 hour more or until thermometer reads 160°. Transfer roast to serving platter. Garnish with spiced crab apples if desired. Cut between ribs to serve. **Yield:** 16-20 servings.

SPINACH SOUFFLE

Jeanie Perez, Fenton, Michigan

2 cups (16 ounces) cottage cheese
3 eggs, beaten
3 packages (10 ounces *each*) frozen spinach, thawed and drained
1-1/2 cups (6 ounces) shredded cheddar cheese, *divided*
1/2 teaspoon salt
Dash nutmeg

In large mixing bowl, combine cottage cheese and eggs. Add spinach, 1-1/4 cups cheddar cheese, salt and nutmeg. Spoon into a greased 12-in. x 7-1/2-in. x 2-in. baking pan. Bake at 350° for 45 minutes or until a knife inserted near the center comes out clean. Remove from oven. Sprinkle with remaining cheddar cheese and let stand 5 minutes. **Yield:** 6-8 servings.

COMPANY CASSEROLE

Suzann Verdun, Lisle, Illinois

1 package (6 ounces) wild rice, cooked
1 package (10 ounces) frozen chopped broccoli, thawed
1-1/2 cups cubed cooked chicken
1 cup cubed cooked ham
1 cup (4 ounces) shredded cheddar cheese
1 can (4 ounces) sliced

mushrooms, drained
1 cup mayonnaise
1 teaspoon prepared mustard
1/2 to 1 teaspoon curry powder
1 can (10-3/4 ounces) cream of mushroom soup, undiluted
1/4 cup grated Parmesan cheese

In a greased 2-qt. casserole, layer first six ingredients in order listed. Combine mayonnaise, mustard, curry and soup. Spread over casserole. Sprinkle with Parmesan cheese. Bake at 350° for 45-60 minutes or until top is light golden brown. **Yield:** 8 servings.

SCALLOPED CHICKEN

Rosella Bauer, Cissna Park, Illinois

1/2 loaf white bread, cubed
1-1/2 cups cracker crumbs, *divided*
3 cups chicken broth
3 eggs, lightly beaten
1 teaspoon salt
3/4 cup diced celery
2 tablespoons chopped onion
3 cups cubed cooked chicken
1 can (8 ounces) sliced mushrooms, drained
1 tablespoon butter *or* margarine

In a mixing bowl, combine bread cubes and 1 cup cracker crumbs. Stir in broth, eggs, salt, celery, onion, chicken and mushrooms. Spoon into a greased 2-qt. casserole. In a saucepan, melt butter; brown remaining cracker crumbs. Sprinkle over casserole. Bake at 350° for 1 hour. **Yield:** 6-8 servings.

CHICKEN ASPARAGUS DIVAN

Donna Stewart, West Chester, Ohio

4 boneless skinless chicken breast halves
Onion and celery with tops
Water
1/2 teaspoon salt
2 tablespoons chopped onion
1/2 cup grated Parmesan cheese, *divided*
1 can (10-3/4 ounces) cream of chicken soup, undiluted
1 pound fresh asparagus spears, cooked crisp-tender

1/3 cup whipping cream
1/3 cup mayonnaise

In a skillet, place chicken, onion, celery, water to cover and salt. Bring to a boil; reduce heat and simmer until chicken is tender. Drain and discard liquid. Combine chopped onion, 1/3 cup Parmesan cheese and soup. Spread half of the mixture in the bottom of a 13-in. x 9-in. x 2-in. baking pan. Top with asparagus, then chicken and remaining soup mixture. Cover and bake at 350° for 25 minutes or until heated through. Combine cream and mayonnaise. Spread over chicken. Sprinkle remaining Parmesan cheese on top. Brown lightly under broiler. Serve immediately. **Yield:** 4 servings.

CHICKEN ALOHA

Beth Corbin, Sarasota, Florida

(PICTURED BELOW)

6 to 8 chicken breast halves
1 bottle (14 ounces) catsup
1 can (10-3/4 ounces) cream of tomato soup, undiluted
1 green pepper, coarsely chopped
1/4 cup packed brown sugar
1/3 cup vinegar
1 teaspoon dry mustard
1 can (8 ounces) pineapple chunks with juice
Cooked rice

Place chicken in a greased 13-in. x 9-in. x 2-in. baking pan. Combine all remaining ingredients except rice; pour over chicken. Cover and bake at 375° for 1 hour. Uncover and bake 15 additional minutes. Serve with rice. **Yield:** 6-8 servings.

POULTRY IN MOTION. Chicken Aloha is a welcome way to cook a quick, delicious meal.

PULL up a chair, and dig into these delightful dishes with your family. Start with buttery chicken that's been dipped in bread crumbs and baked to a golden brown. Serve it alongside hearty helpings of coleslaw, and finish up with slices of light and airy Hot Milk Cake made in your well-seasoned cast-iron skillet.

DOWN-HOME DINNER.
Top to bottom: **Hot Milk Cake** (recipe on page 188),
Pennsylvania Dutch Coleslaw (recipe on page 49)
and **Marie's Chicken Bake**
(recipe on page 87).

MARIE'S CHICKEN BAKE

Marie Lully, Boulder, Colorado

(PICTURED ON FRONT COVER AND AT LEFT)

1 broiler/fryer chicken (2-1/2 to
  3 pounds), cut up
4 tablespoons butter *or*
  margarine, melted
1/2 cup grated Parmesan cheese
1/2 cup dry bread crumbs
1 teaspoon paprika
1/2 teaspoon dried thyme
2 tablespoons sesame seeds

Dip chicken pieces in butter. Combine remaining ingredients; dip chicken into this crumb mixture. Place on a greased 15-in. x 10-in. x 1-in. baking pan. Drizzle any remaining butter over chicken. Bake at 375° for 45-55 minutes or until chicken is done. **Yield:** 4-6 servings.

TEX-MEX QUICHE

Hazel Turner, Houston, Texas

1 unbaked pastry shell
  (9 inches)
1 teaspoon chili powder
1 cup (4 ounces) shredded
  cheddar cheese
1 cup (4 ounces) shredded
  Monterey Jack cheese
1 tablespoon all-purpose flour
3 eggs, beaten
1-1/2 cups light cream
1 can (4 ounces) chopped
  green chilies, well drained
1 can (2-1/2 ounces) sliced ripe
  olives, drained
1 teaspoon salt
1/4 teaspoon pepper

Sprinkle chili powder over the inside of the pie shell. Combine cheeses with flour and place in pie shell. Combine eggs, cream, chilies, olives, salt and pepper. Pour over cheese. Bake at 325° for 45-55 minutes or until a knife inserted near the center comes out clean. Let stand for 10 minutes before cutting. **Yield:** 6 servings.

BEEF-STUFFED SQUASH

Darlene R. Smith, Rockford, Illinois

3 small acorn squash, halved
  and seeded
1/2 cup water
FILLING:
1 pound lean ground beef
1 egg, beaten
1/2 cup Russian salad dressing

3/4 cup bread crumbs
1 medium onion, minced
1 tablespoon brown sugar
1 teaspoon lemon juice
3/4 teaspoon salt
GLAZE:
1/4 cup Russian salad dressing
1-1/2 teaspoons lemon juice
1-1/2 teaspoons brown sugar

Place squash cut-side down in a roasting pan and pour water in pan. Bake at 350° for 30 minutes. Meanwhile, in a medium bowl, combine filling ingredients. Remove squash from oven. Increase oven temperature to 375°. Lightly spoon filling into each squash cavity. Combine glaze ingredients and baste meat and top of squash. Bake 40-50 minutes, basting with glaze every 15 minutes. **Yield:** 6 servings.

CHICKEN POTPIES

Sonja Blow, Groveland, California

1 package (10 ounces) frozen
  peas and carrots
1/4 cup butter *or* margarine
1/2 cup chopped onion
1 can (4 ounces) mushroom
  pieces, drained
1/3 cup all-purpose flour
1/2 teaspoon salt
1/8 teaspoon pepper
1/4 teaspoon ground sage
3/4 cup milk
3 chicken bouillon cubes,
  crushed
2 cups water
3 cups cubed cooked chicken
  or turkey
1 jar (2 ounces) diced pimiento,
  drained
1/4 cup chopped fresh parsley
Pastry for double-crust pie

Cook frozen vegetables according to package directions. Drain. In a saucepan, melt butter over medium heat; saute onion and mushrooms until tender. Stir in flour, salt, pepper and sage. Combine milk, bouillon and water. Slowly pour into saucepan, stirring constantly. Cook and stir until mixture boils. Reduce heat and simmer 2 minutes. Stir in chicken, pimiento and parsley. Spoon into six individual casseroles. Roll and cut pastry into circles 1 in. smaller than top of casseroles. Place atop filling. Bake at 425° for 12-15 min-

utes or until the crust is lightly browned. **Yield:** 6 servings.

SPICED PORK ROAST WITH APPLESAUCE GLAZE

Lydia Robotewsky, Franklin, Wisconsin

(PICTURED ON PAGE 226)

1 rolled boneless pork loin
  roast (4 to 5 pounds)
1 garlic clove, cut into
  lengthwise strips
2 tablespoons all-purpose flour
1 teaspoon salt
1/2 teaspoon sugar
1 teaspoon prepared mustard
1/8 teaspoon pepper
1 cup applesauce
1/3 cup packed brown sugar
2 teaspoons vinegar
1/8 to 1/4 teaspoon ground cloves

Remove and discard all excess fat from roast. Cut slits in top of roast; insert garlic strips. Mix the flour with salt, sugar, mustard and pepper. Rub over the roast. Place the meat, fat side up, on a rack in a roasting pan. Bake at 325° for 30-40 minutes *per pound* or until the internal temperature reaches 160°-170°. Combine applesauce, brown sugar, vinegar and cloves; generously brush over roast during last half hour of baking. **Yield:** 12-15 servings.

PINEAPPLE HAM BALLS

Alice Whitlow, Didsbury, Alberta

(PICTURED ON PAGE 52)

3 cups ground fully
  cooked ham
1/2 pound ground pork
1 cup soft bread crumbs
2 eggs, beaten
1/4 teaspoon pepper
1 can (20 ounces) sliced
  pineapple
3/4 cup packed brown sugar
1/4 cup vinegar
1/2 teaspoon dry mustard

In a bowl, combine ham, pork, bread crumbs, eggs and pepper; mix well. Chill. Form into 10 balls; set aside. Drain pineapple, reserving 1/2 cup of juice. Place juice in a saucepan with sugar, vinegar and dry mustard; cook and stir over low heat until sugar is dissolved. Arrange pineapple slices in the bottom of an ungreased 13-in. x 9-in. x 2-in. baking dish. Place a ham ball on each pineapple slice. Pour sugar mixture over all. Cover and bake at 350° for 1 hour or until ham balls are thoroughly cooked. **Yield:** 4-5 servings.

The Old Cookstove Made Warm Childhood Memories

Stove left lasting impressions on reader...and especially on her brother!

I REMEMBER so many deep-freeze winters on our Pennsylvania farm, but most of those memories are warm ones, thanks to the wood-burning cookstove that stood in my mother's cozy kitchen.

Our winter lives revolved around that stove because of the wonderful warmth it provided for our 100-year-old farmhouse in lovely Muncy Valley.

Outside, the cold wind moaned restlessly and piled snowdrifts up to the windowsills. Inside, though, our kitchen was filled with warmth.

That old cookstove was an integral part of my childhood. Dad had always wanted Mother to have the best, and I remember the day he proudly brought that new cookstove home.

He pulled in the yard with the hulking black monster squatting in his empty produce wagon. But it was a handsome monster, trimmed in wide shiny bands of chrome. It even had little iron rosettes decorating its back and sides.

Toasted Our Toes

After a day of sledding, my brother and I would open its huge oven door and stick our feet inside, propping them on a hunk of wood, until the acrid odor of charred wood and toasted socks brought a stern warning from Mother.

I remember, too, spending a lot of my childhood in front of that stove in an old rocking chair with a camphorated cloth wrapped securely around my neck. That was Mother's remedy for anything from swollen glands to what she called the "grippe".

Today I love our central heating system, yet I still look back fondly at those old wood stove days with their chilly Saturday nights, because our bath ritual was unforgettable.

After bathing in a tub of water heated in the stove's reservoir, I huddled in front of that red-hot range with my face scorching and backside cooling! Then came the wonderful feeling of donning fresh long underwear that hugged my skinny legs tightly.

Other evenings, my brother and I would stay nice and warm next to that stove as we plodded through our homework by the light of a kerosene lamp.

By Allie Billman, Spring Hill, Florida

If we finished early we might get to play a game of checkers with Dad.

Felt "Bedtime Shivers"

It was sheer torture to leave the warmth of our kitchen "comfort zone" when bedtime rolled around. The lamp seemed to cast shadowy creatures on the walls as we climbed the stairway, and shivers—not entirely caused by the cold—chased up and down our spines.

With chattering teeth we scrambled

CHASED AWAY CHILLS. The good old cookstove was the center of the family's world in winter.

into our frigid bedrooms, where our breath rose in little plumes. We wasted no time burrowing down into cocoons of blankets and handmade quilts.

When morning came, it was downright difficult to crawl from the warmth of those covers and slip into *freezing-*cold clothes! And it was on a morning with record-breaking cold that one of my most vivid and *satisfying* childhood memories occurred.

Mother had just given her absolute final warning to rise and shine—or else! I poked my nose to the surface of the blankets, swung my feet onto the floor and immediately gasped from the cold. Grabbing my clothes, I made a wild dash downstairs in my long nightgown.

Running hard, I was determined to beat my older brother to the only spot in the house capable of warming both front and back on such a frosty morning.

She Lost That "Heat"

Too late! As I rounded the door into the kitchen I saw that he'd already squeezed in between the hot water heater and the stove. He was bigger than me, so no manner of threats, name-calling or pleading on my part was about to budge him from that privileged place.

Furious, I had to settle for a dressing spot in front of the oven door. Meanwhile, my brother grinned broadly, absorbing all that radiant energy.

In my state of self-pity I was determined not to even look at him—but when he suddenly let out a howl, I just *had to* look!

At first I didn't know what had happened. But as he kept howling and gingerly rubbing his posterior, I realized vengeance was mine—he had backed too near the range and was branded with a lovely rose tattoo!

As you can see, I have a lot of warm memories of that old stove and, likely, my brother does, too.

HONEY-BAKED CHICKEN

Lu Montezon, Campbellsport, Wisconsin

    1 broiler-fryer chicken
      (3 pounds), cut up
  1/3 cup butter *or* margarine,
      melted
  1/3 cup honey
    2 tablespoons prepared
      mustard
    1 teaspoon salt
    1 teaspoon curry powder
Cooked rice

Place chicken, skin side up, in a 13-in. x 9-in. x 2-in. baking pan. Combine all remaining ingredients except rice; pour over chicken. Bake at 350° for 1-1/4 hours, basting with the pan juices every 15 minutes. Serve with rice. **Yield:** 4-6 servings.

ZUCCHINI LASAGNA

Charlotte McDaniel, Williamsville, Illinois

    1 pound lean ground beef
  1/4 cup chopped onion
    1 can (15 ounces) tomato sauce
  1/2 teaspoon salt
  1/2 teaspoon dried oregano
  1/2 teaspoon dried basil
  1/4 teaspoon ground pepper
    4 medium zucchini (1-1/4 pounds)
    1 cup creamed cottage cheese
    1 egg, beaten
    3 tablespoons flour
    1 cup (4 ounces) shredded
      mozzarella cheese

In large skillet, brown beef and onion over medium heat; drain fat. Add tomato sauce and seasonings. Bring to boil; simmer 5 minutes. Meanwhile, slice zucchini crosswise, into 1/4-in. slices. In small bowl, combine cottage cheese and egg. In a greased 12-in. x 8-in. x 2-in. baking pan, place half the zucchini and sprinkle with half the flour. Top with cottage cheese mixture and half the meat mixture. Repeat layer of zucchini and flour. Sprinkle with mozzarella cheese and remaining meat mixture. Bake at 375° for about 40 minutes or until heated through. Remove from oven and sprinkle with additional cheese, if desired. To cut more easily, let stand 10 minutes before serving. **Yield:** 6-8 servings.

TROPICAL CHICKEN

Becky Palac, Escondido, California

    1 can (8 ounces) crushed
      pineapple, undrained
  1/3 cup lime juice
  1/4 teaspoon ground cloves

    4 boneless skinless chicken
      breast halves
  1/3 cup all-purpose flour
    1 teaspoon salt
    2 to 4 tablespoons cooking oil
  1/3 cup slivered almonds
  1/3 cup flaked coconut

In a bowl, combine pineapple, lime juice and cloves. Pound chicken to 1/4-in. thickness; add to marinade. Cover and refrigerate for at least 45 minutes. Drain, reserving marinade. Combine flour and salt; dredge chicken. In a skillet, brown chicken on both sides in oil. Place in a shallow baking dish. Add reserved marinade to skillet; cook until hot and bubbly. Pour over chicken. Sprinkle with almonds and coconut. Bake, uncovered, at 400° for 20-25 minutes. **Yield:** 4 servings.

CHICKEN ENCHILADAS

Mary Anne McWhirter, Pearland, Texas

    2 cups diced cooked chicken
    2 cups (8 ounces) shredded
      Monterey Jack cheese
    1 can (2-1/4 ounces) sliced ripe
      olives, drained
    2 teaspoons dried parsley flakes
  1/2 teaspoon garlic powder
  1/2 teaspoon salt
  1/8 teaspoon pepper
    6 to 8 flour tortillas (8 inches)
SAUCE:
    1 medium onion, diced
  1/2 green pepper, diced
    1 tablespoon cooking oil
    1 can (4 ounces) chopped
      green chilies
    1 can (15 ounces) tomato sauce
    2 teaspoons chili powder
    1 teaspoon sugar
  1/2 teaspoon garlic powder
    1 cup (4 ounces) shredded
      cheddar cheese

Combine first seven ingredients. Divide evenly among tortillas. Roll up and place, seam side down, in a 13-in. x 9-in. x 2-in. baking pan. For sauce, in a skillet, saute onion and green pepper in oil until tender. Add chilies, tomato sauce, chili powder, sugar and garlic powder; mix well. Pour over tortillas. Cover with foil. Bake at 350° for 30 minutes. Sprinkle with cheddar cheese and return to the oven for 10 minutes. **Yield:** 6-8 servings.

NOODLES WITH CREAMY MEAT SAUCE

May Nevenschwander, Dalton, Ohio

    2 pounds lean ground beef
    1 can (10-3/4 ounces)
      condensed cream of
      onion soup, undiluted

    1 can (10-3/4 ounces)
      condensed cream of
      mushroom soup, undiluted
    1 can (10-3/4 ounces)
      condensed golden
      mushroom soup, undiluted
Cooked egg noodles

Crumble uncooked ground beef into a large Dutch oven or casserole. Combine soups; pour over beef. Cover and bake at 350° for 1 to 1-1/4 hours or until the beef is no longer pink. Serve over noodles. **Yield:** 6-8 servings.

CHICKEN ASPARAGUS STROGANOFF

Linda Hutten, Hayden, Idaho

    1 can (10-3/4 ounces) cream
      of chicken soup, undiluted
  1/4 cup milk
  1/4 cup sour cream
    2 cups cooked sliced asparagus
    1 cup diced cooked chicken
  1/4 teaspoon rosemary
  1/4 cup shredded cheddar cheese
Cooked rice *or* noodles

Combine soup, milk and sour cream. Pour half the soup mixture into a greased 1-qt. casserole; top with asparagus, chicken and rosemary. Pour remaining soup over chicken. Sprinkle with cheese. Bake at 350° for 30 minutes. Serve with rice or noodles. **Yield:** 4 servings.

TUNA-CHIP CASSEROLE

Janis Plourde, Smooth Rock Falls, Ontario

    1 bag (7 ounces) plain potato
      chips, *divided*
    1 can (7 ounces) water-pack
      tuna, drained
    1 can (19 ounces) asparagus
      tips, drained *or* 10 ounces
      frozen asparagus tips,
      pre-cooked for 3 minutes,
      drained
SAUCE:
  2/3 cup evaporated milk
    1 tablespoon lemon juice
  1/4 teaspoon dry mustard
  1/8 teaspoon white pepper
TOPPING:
  1/4 cup shredded cheddar cheese
  1/2 cup sliced almonds

Crush chips and place *half* in greased 10-in. x 8-in. x 2-in. baking dish. Arrange tuna over chips; top with asparagus. Cover with the remaining chips. Combine sauce ingredients and pour over all. Sprinkle with cheese, then almonds. Bake at 325° for 20-25 minutes. Remove from oven; let stand 5 minutes before serving. **Yield:** 6 servings.

CELEBRATE the excitement of any special occasion by
preparing the recipes on this page. They'll win compliments
every time you serve them. Start your morning with a large platter of
hot Buttermilk Biscuit Sausage Pinwheels, or wait until brunch and
relish the great taste of Crab Quiche. For dinner, you'll love the
garlic- and herb-laced California Roast Lamb served with fresh artichokes. Plus,
leftover ham quickly disappears when you prepare hearty Iowa Ham Balls.

HELP YOURSELF!
Clockwise from the bottom: **Buttermilk Biscuit
Sausage Pinwheels** (recipe on page 19), **Crab Quiche**,
Iowa Ham Balls and **California Roast Lamb**
(all three recipes on page 91).

CRAB QUICHE

Michele Field, Burtonsville, Maryland

(PICTURED AT LEFT)

1/2 cup mayonnaise
2 tablespoons all-purpose flour
2 eggs, beaten
1/2 cup milk
2 cans (6 ounces *each*) flaked
   crabmeat, drained
1/3 cup chopped green onions
1 tablespoon finely chopped
   parsley
2 cups (8 ounces) shredded
   Swiss cheese
1 unbaked pastry shell (9 inches)

In a mixing bowl, combine mayonnaise, flour, eggs and milk. Stir in crab, onions, parsley and cheese. Spoon into the pastry shell. Bake at 350° for 1 hour or until a knife inserted near the center comes out clean. Let stand 10 minutes before serving. **Yield:** 6-8 servings.

IOWA HAM BALLS

Helen Koehler, Liscomb, Iowa

(PICTURED AT LEFT)

3-1/2 pounds ground ham
1-1/2 pounds ground beef
3 eggs, beaten
2 cups milk
3 cups graham cracker crumbs
2 cans (10-3/4 ounces *each*)
   condensed tomato soup,
   undiluted
3/4 cup vinegar
2-1/2 cups packed brown sugar
1 teaspoon prepared mustard

In a large mixing bowl, combine first five ingredients. Using a 1/3 cup measure, shape mixture into 2-in. balls. Place in two large shallow roasting pans. Combine all remaining ingredients; pour over balls. Bake at 325° for 1 hour, basting frequently with sauce. **Yield:** about 15 servings.

CALIFORNIA ROAST LAMB

Ann Eastman, Greenville, California

(PICTURED AT LEFT)

1 leg of lamb (4 to 5 pounds)
2 to 3 garlic cloves, halved
1 teaspoon seasoned salt
1 teaspoon pepper
1 teaspoon dried oregano
2 cans (8 ounces *each*) tomato
   sauce
1 cup water
Juice of 1 lemon

3 to 5 large fresh artichokes,
   quartered
Fresh lemon slices

Cut slits in lamb; insert garlic. Rub meat with salt, pepper and oregano. Roast at 400° for 30 minutes. Reduce heat to 350°; roast 1 hour more. Skim off any fat in pan; pour tomato sauce, water and lemon juice over lamb. Place artichokes around meat. Roast 1 hour longer or to desired doneness, basting occasionally with pan juices. Garnish with lemon. **Yield:** 10-12 servings.

CRANBERRY-GLAZED CORNISH HENS

Betty Nichols, Eugene, Oregon

1/2 cup jellied cranberry sauce
1 tablespoon Dijon mustard
1 can (10-1/2 ounces) chicken
   gravy
1 teaspoon grated orange peel
3 Cornish hens (1-1/2 pounds
   each), halved lengthwise
Salt and pepper to taste
Cooked wild rice
Orange slices, optional

In 1-qt. saucepan, combine the cranberry sauce, mustard, gravy and orange peel. Cook over low heat, stirring constantly, until smooth. Sprinkle hens with salt and pepper. Place on rack with drip pan, skin side down; brush generously with glaze. Bake at 400° for 15 minutes. Turn hens, brush with glaze, and bake 30 minutes more or until juices run clear, basting often with glaze. Serve over wild rice; garnish with orange slices if desired. **Yield:** 6 servings.

PORK LOIN ROAST WITH YAM-STUFFED APPLES

J. Wrigley, Lynden, Washington

1/4 teaspoon ground sage
1/4 teaspoon pepper
1-1/2 teaspoons salt, *divided*
1 boneless pork loin roast (3 to
   4 pounds)
8 to 10 large baking apples
1 can (24 ounces) yams, drained,
   liquid reserved
1/4 cup brown sugar
1/4 teaspoon cinnamon
1/2 cup slivered almonds, toasted,
   divided
1/4 cup butter
1/4 cup maple syrup

Combine sage, pepper and 1 teaspoon salt; rub over pork roast. Place roast, fat side up, on rack in open pan. Roast, uncovered, at 325° 2-1/2 to 3-1/4 hours or until meat thermometer registers 160°-170°. Meanwhile, core each apple, removing enough pulp to make 1-1/4-in. opening. Reserve pulp. Mash yams; combine with 1/4 cup reserved yam liquid, apple pulp, brown sugar, remaining salt, cinnamon and half the almonds. In saucepan, heat butter and maple syrup until butter melts. Drizzle half the butter mixture into apple cavities. Fill apples with yam mixture; garnish with remaining almonds. Place apples around roast or in separate baking dish, timing so that apples will bake 45-60 minutes and be done at the same time as the roast. Baste apples occasionally with remaining butter mixture. To serve, arrange roast and stuffed apples on heated platter. **Yield:** 8-10 servings.

CHICKEN OR TURKEY PIE

Joy Corie, Ruston, Louisiana

FILLING:
3 tablespoons butter *or*
   margarine
2 celery ribs, diced
2 carrots, peeled and diced
1 small onion, minced
1/4 cup all-purpose flour
1/2 teaspoon salt
1 cup milk
1 cup chicken broth
1 can (10-3/4 ounces) cream of
   mushroom soup, undiluted
4 cups cubed cooked chicken
   or turkey
CRUST:
1-1/2 cups all-purpose flour
3/4 teaspoon baking powder
1 teaspoon salt
3 tablespoons butter *or*
   margarine
1/2 cup milk
2 cups (8 ounces) shredded
   cheddar cheese

For filling, melt butter in a skillet; saute celery, carrots and onion until soft. Stir in flour and salt. Gradually add milk and broth, stirring constantly until sauce thickens. Fold in mushroom soup and chicken or turkey. Spoon mixture into a 13-in. x 9-in. x 2-in. baking pan; set aside. For crust, combine flour, baking powder and salt. Cut butter into flour mixture. Add milk and mix to form soft dough. Roll out to a 12-in. x 10-in. rectangle. Sprinkle with cheese and roll up, jelly-roll style, starting from long side. Slice into 1/2-in. wheels and place on chicken mixture. Bake at 350° for 35-40 minutes or until crust is lightly browned. **Yield:** 6-8 servings.

PERFECT for a blustery day, these cozy country recipes will
certainly drive the chill away! Enjoy a steaming cup or bowl of
New England Fish Chowder. You'll love its creamy broth and tender chunks of
potatoes. The Spanish Rice is a perfect spicy dish with your favorite roast or as a
meal all by itself. And, if you're looking for a real hearty hot dish, try the
Polish Poultry or the Bayou Country Seafood Casserole.

HOT IN A POT.
Top to bottom: **Spanish Rice** (recipe on page 135),
Bayou Country Seafood Casserole (recipe on page 93),
New England Fish Chowder (recipe on page 19) and
Polish Poultry (recipe on page 93).

BAYOU COUNTRY SEAFOOD CASSEROLE

Ethel Miller, Eunice, Louisiana

(PICTURED AT LEFT)

6 tablespoons butter *or* margarine
1 medium onion, chopped
1 medium green pepper, chopped
1 celery rib, chopped
1 garlic clove, minced
1 can (10-3/4 ounces) condensed cream of mushroom soup, undiluted
1 pound raw shrimp, peeled and deveined
1-1/2 cups cooked rice
2 cans (6 ounces *each*) crabmeat, drained and flaked with cartilage removed *or* 1-1/2 pounds cooked crabmeat
4 slices day-old bread, cubed
3/4 cup light cream *or* water
1/4 cup chopped green onion tops
1/2 teaspoon salt
1/4 teaspoon pepper
Dash cayenne pepper
TOPPING:
2 tablespoons butter *or* margarine, melted
1/3 cup dry bread crumbs
2 tablespoons snipped fresh parsley

In a skillet, melt butter over medium heat. Saute onion, green pepper, celery and garlic until tender. Add soup and shrimp. Cook and stir over medium heat 10 minutes or until shrimp turn pink. Stir in rice, crab, bread cubes, cream or water, onion tops and seasonings. Spoon into a greased 2-qt. baking dish. Combine topping ingredients; sprinkle over casserole. Bake at 375° for 30 minutes or until heated through. **Yield:** 8 servings.

POLISH POULTRY

Dorothea Kampfe, Gothenburg, Nebraska

(PICTURED AT LEFT)

1 medium onion, chopped
1 garlic clove, minced
1 teaspoon caraway seeds
1 can (27 ounces) sauerkraut, undrained
3/4 pound smoked Polish sausage, cut into 1-inch pieces
1 broiler/fryer chicken (2 to 3 pounds), cut up
1/2 teaspoon salt
1/4 teaspoon pepper
1/4 to 1/2 teaspoon dried thyme

In a mixing bowl, combine first four ingredients. Place on the bottom of a 13-in. x 9-in. x 2-in. baking dish. Top with sausage and chicken. Sprinkle with salt, pepper and thyme. Bake at 350° for 60-65 minutes or until chicken is tender, basting occasionally with pan juices. **Yield:** 6 servings.

CHURCH SUPPER HAM LOAF

Pat Habiger, Spearville, Kansas

HAM LOAF:
1 pound ground ham
1 pound lean pork sausage
2 cups soft bread crumbs
2 eggs, beaten
1 cup (8 ounces) sour cream
1/3 cup chopped onion
2 tablespoons lemon juice
1 teaspoon curry powder
1 teaspoon dry mustard
1 teaspoon ground ginger
1/8 teaspoon nutmeg
1/8 teaspoon paprika
BASTING SAUCE:
1/2 cup packed brown sugar
1/4 cup water
1/4 cup cider vinegar
1/8 teaspoon black pepper

In large mixing bowl, gently combine all ham loaf ingredients. Form into a loaf; place in shallow baking pan. Bake, uncovered, at 350° for 1 hour. Meanwhile, in small saucepan, combine all basting sauce ingredients; bring to a boil. Immediately drain any drippings from ham loaf and pour basting sauce over it. Continue baking ham loaf, basting occasionally with pan juices, for 15-30 minutes or until lightly browned. **Yield:** 8-10 servings.

HERBED PORK ROAST

Jean Harris, Central Point, Oregon

1/4 cup packed brown sugar
1 tablespoon dried thyme
1 teaspoon *each* garlic salt, pepper, dried rosemary and crushed sage
1 boneless pork loin roast (3 to 4 pounds)
1/4 cup all-purpose flour

Combine brown sugar, herbs and seasonings; rub over entire roast. Place roast, fat side up, on a rack in a roasting pan. Place in a 500° oven; immediately reduce heat to 325°. Bake, uncovered, for 2 hours or until a meat thermometer reads 160°. Remove roast from pan. Pour pan drippings into a large measuring cup; add water to equal 2 cups. Pour into a small saucepan; add flour. Cook and stir over medium heat until gravy comes to a boil; cook and stir 2 minutes more. Slice roast and serve with gravy. **Yield:** 6-8 servings.

CREAMY HAM ROLLS

Becky Carcich, Littleton, Colorado

1 medium onion, chopped
1/2 cup butter *or* margarine
1/2 cup all-purpose flour
1 teaspoon dill weed
1/2 teaspoon garlic salt
1/2 teaspoon pepper
1 can (14-1/2 ounces) chicken broth
1-1/2 cups light cream
1 tablespoon Dijon mustard
3 cups cooked wild rice
1 can (8 ounces) mushroom stems and pieces, drained
12 thin slices fully cooked ham (about 3/4 pound)
1/2 cup shredded cheddar cheese
Minced fresh parsley

In a large saucepan, saute onion in butter until tender. Stir in flour, dill, garlic salt and pepper until smooth and bubbly. Gradually add broth, cream and mustard; cook until thickened. Pour 1 cup into an ungreased 13-in. x 9-in. x 2-in. baking pan; reserve another cup for topping. To the remaining sauce, add rice and mushrooms; spoon 1/3 cup onto each ham slice. Roll up and place with seam side down over sauce in pan. Top with reserved sauce. Bake, uncovered, at 350° for 25-30 minutes or until heated through. Sprinkle with cheese and parsley; serve immediately. **Yield:** 12 servings.

CRISPY PICNIC CHICKEN

Joanie Elbourn, Gardner, Massachusetts

20 butter-flavored crackers, crushed
2/3 cup grated Parmesan cheese
2 teaspoons dried parsley flakes
3/4 teaspoon garlic powder
1/2 teaspoon paprika
1/8 teaspoon pepper
1 broiler-fryer chicken (3-1/2 to 4 pounds), cut up
1/3 cup butter *or* margarine, melted

In a small bowl, combine the first six ingredients. Dip chicken in butter and then roll in crumb mixture, coating both sides. Place in a greased 13-in. x 9-in. x 2-in. baking pan. Bake, uncovered, at 350° for 50 minutes or until chicken is tender and juices run clear. Serve hot or chilled. **Yield:** 4-6 servings.

FEW FOODS "stick to your ribs" like beef, and
these delicious dishes are designed to do just that.
Friends or family will be pleased to "meat" you at dinnertime
when you ladle up bowls of Beef Stew with Cheddar
Dumplings, serve savory Hungarian Short Ribs, offer easy-to-
make Caraway Beef Roast or pass the Italian Beef Roll-Ups.

GRADE A!
Clockwise from lower right: **Italian Beef Roll-Ups**,
Beef Stew with Cheddar Dumplings, **Hungarian
Short Ribs** (recipes on page 95) and
Caraway Beef Roast (recipe on page 69).

SKILLET SUPPERS

As these timeless stove-top specialties prove, it's easy to add some "sizzle" to everyday dinners and entertaining menus.

BEEF STEW WITH CHEDDAR DUMPLINGS

Jackie Riley, Garrettsville, Ohio

(PICTURED AT LEFT)

- 1/2 cup all-purpose flour
- 1/2 teaspoon salt
- 1/2 teaspoon pepper
- 2 to 3 pounds beef stew meat, cut into 1-inch pieces
- 2 tablespoons cooking oil
- 1/2 teaspoon onion salt
- 1/2 teaspoon garlic salt
- 1 tablespoon browning sauce
- 5 cups water
- 5 beef bouillon cubes
- 4 carrots, sliced
- 1 medium onion, cut into wedges
- 1 can (16 ounces) green beans, drained

DUMPLINGS:
- 2 cups buttermilk biscuit mix
- 1 cup (4 ounces) shredded cheddar cheese
- 2/3 cup milk

Combine flour, salt and pepper. Coat meat with flour mixture. In a Dutch oven, heat oil over medium-high. Brown meat on all sides. Add onion salt, garlic salt, browning sauce, water and bouillon. Bring to a boil; reduce heat, cover and simmer about 1 hour. Add carrots and onion. Cover and simmer until vegetables are tender. Stir in green beans. For dumplings, combine biscuit mix and cheese. Stir in enough milk to form a soft dough. Drop by tablespoonsful into bubbling stew. Cover and simmer 12 minutes (do not lift cover) or until dumplings test done. Serve immediately. **Yield:** 6-8 servings.

HUNGARIAN SHORT RIBS

Joanne ShewChuk, St. Benedict, Saskatchewan

(PICTURED AT LEFT)

- 2 to 3 tablespoons cooking oil
- 4 pounds short ribs with bones
- 2 medium onions, sliced
- 1 can (15 ounces) tomato sauce
- 2 cups water, *divided*
- 1/4 cup packed brown sugar

- 1/4 cup vinegar
- 1-1/2 teaspoons salt
- 1-1/2 teaspoons dry mustard
- 1-1/2 teaspoons Worcestershire sauce
- 1/4 teaspoon paprika

Cooked wide noodles

In a Dutch oven, heat oil over medium-high. Brown ribs on all sides. Add onions; cook until tender. Combine all remaining ingredients except noodles; pour over ribs. Reduce heat; cover and simmer until the meat is tender, about 3 hours. Thicken gravy if desired. Serve over noodles. **Yield:** 6-8 servings.

 Quick & Easy

BLACK BEANS AND SAUSAGE

Sharon Hunt, Spring Hill, Florida

- 1 tablespoon cooking oil
- 1 medium onion, chopped
- 1 can (14-1/2 ounces) stewed tomatoes
- 1 can (15 ounces) black beans, undrained
- 1 teaspoon dried oregano
- 1/2 teaspoon garlic powder

Salt to taste
- 1-1/2 cups uncooked instant brown rice
- 1 pound pork sausage links, cooked and sliced

In a skillet, heat oil. Cook onion until tender. Add the tomatoes, beans and seasonings. Bring to a boil. Stir in rice; reduce heat and simmer 5 minutes. Add sausage, cover and let stand 5 minutes. **Yield:** 6-8 servings.

ITALIAN BEEF ROLL-UPS

Lucia Johnson, Massena, New York

(PICTURED AT LEFT)

- 1-1/2 pounds thinly sliced round steak

Salt and pepper to taste
- 1 cup dry bread crumbs
- 1 cup grated Parmesan cheese
- 1/4 cup finely chopped fresh celery leaves
- 1 teaspoon dried parsley
- 1 teaspoon dried basil

- 1/2 teaspoon dried oregano
- 2 tablespoons vegetable *or* olive oil
- 4 cups spaghetti sauce

Cooked pasta

Pound meat to tenderize. Sprinkle with salt and pepper. Cut into 3-in. to 4-in. squares. Combine the bread crumbs, cheese, celery and herbs. Place a heaping spoonful of crumb mixture on each meat square and roll up. Secure with string or a toothpick. Roll meat in remaining crumb mixture. In a large skillet, heat oil over medium. Brown roll-ups on all sides. Pour spaghetti sauce over all; cover and simmer 1-1/2 hours or until meat is tender. Serve with pasta. **Yield:** about 6 servings.

SWEDISH MEATBALLS

Emily Gould, Hawarden, Iowa

(PICTURED ON PAGE 67)

- 1-2/3 cups evaporated milk, *divided*
- 2/3 cup chopped onion
- 1/4 cup fine dry bread crumbs
- 1/2 teaspoon salt
- 1/2 teaspoon allspice

Dash pepper
- 1 pound ground round
- 2 teaspoons butter *or* margarine
- 2 beef bouillon cubes
- 1 cup boiling water
- 1/2 cup cold water
- 2 tablespoons all-purpose flour
- 1 tablespoon lemon juice

Hot cooked noodles

Combine 2/3 cup evaporated milk, onion, crumbs, salt, allspice and pepper. Add meat; mix well, chill. Shape meat mixture into 1-in. balls. In large skillet, brown meatballs in butter. Dissolve bouillon cubes in boiling water; pour over meatballs and bring to boil over medium heat. Cover; simmer for 15 minutes. Meanwhile, blend together cold water and flour. Remove meatballs from skillet, skim fat from pan juices and reserve juices. Stir remaining evaporated milk and flour/water mixture into pan juices in skillet; cook, uncovered, over low heat, stirring until sauce thickens. Return meatballs to skillet. Stir in lemon juice. Serve over hot cooked noodles. **Yield:** 3-1/2 dozen 1-inch meatballs.

Quick & Easy

NORTH CAROLINA SHRIMP SAUTE

Teresa Hildreth, Stoneville, North Carolina

(PICTURED AT RIGHT)

1/4 cup butter *or* margarine
1 pound raw shrimp, peeled and deveined
1/2 pound fresh mushrooms, sliced
1 small green pepper, chopped
3 garlic cloves, minced
8 ounces linguini *or* spaghetti
1/2 cup grated Romano cheese
1/2 teaspoon salt
1/4 teaspoon pepper
Chopped fresh parsley
Lemon slices

In a skillet, melt butter over medium heat. Add shrimp, mushrooms, green pepper and garlic. Saute until shrimp turn pink, about 3-5 minutes. Meanwhile, cook pasta according to package directions; drain and place on a large serving platter. Top with shrimp mixture. Sprinkle with cheese, salt, pepper and parsley. Toss well; garnish with lemon. Serve immediately. **Yield:** 4 servings.

POLISH PIEROGI

Adeline Piscitelli, Sayreville, New Jersey

(PICTURED ON PAGE 67)

DOUGH:
4 cups all-purpose flour
2 eggs
1/2 cup sour cream
1 teaspoon salt
2/3 cup warm water
POTATO FILLING:
3 medium potatoes, cooked, drained and mashed, about 1 pound
1/2 medium onion, chopped
1/4 cup butter
Salt and pepper to taste
CHEESE FILLING:
1 pound dry cottage cheese
2 eggs, beaten
1/2 teaspoon salt
1/4 cup melted butter
SAUCE:
1 large onion, chopped
1/2 cup butter

To make dough, mix flour, eggs, sour cream, salt and water (a little at a time). Knead dough until firm and elastic; cover with a bowl and let rest 10 minutes. For potato filling, prepare potatoes; set aside. For cheese filling, combine ingredients and mix. Divide dough into 2 parts. On floured surface, roll dough to 1/8-in. thick; cut into 3-in. circles with cutter. Place a small spoonful of potato filling in center of half the circles; fold and press edges together firmly to seal. Repeat with the cheese filling and remaining circles. Drop pierogi in simmering chicken bouillon with 1 teaspoon oil. Do not crowd. Simmer for 15 minutes, stirring gently with wooden spoon to prevent sticking. Remove with slotted spoon; drain well. Saute onion and butter until golden. Placed drained pierogi in casserole and pour onion/butter mixture over all. Garnish with brown mushrooms. **Yield:** 7 dozen.

BEEF ROULADEN

Diana Schurrer, McHenry, Illinois

 This tasty dish uses less sugar, salt and fat. Recipe includes *Diabetic Exchanges*.

1 pound thin cut round steak, separated into 4 pieces
Coarse-ground prepared mustard
1/4 teaspoon dried thyme
Salt and pepper to taste
1 medium dill pickle, quartered lengthwise
3 carrots, cut into sticks, *divided*
1 small onion, cut into wedges
2 tablespoons all-purpose flour
1 tablespoon cooking oil
2 cups water
2 beef bouillon cubes
3 tablespoons ketchup
Hot cooked noodles

Spread steak pieces with mustard. Sprinkle with thyme, salt and pepper. Top one edge with a piece of pickle, carrot and a wedge of onion. Roll up and secure with a toothpick. Coat each roll with flour. In a skillet, heat oil over medium-high. Brown beef on all sides. Add water, bouillon, ketchup and remaining carrots. Cover and simmer 1 hour. Thicken gravy, if desired, and serve over noodles. **Yield:** 4 servings. **Diabetic Exchanges:** One serving (prepared without added salt) equals 3 lean meat, 1 vegetable, 1/2 starch, 1/2 fat; also, 250 calories, 1012 mg sodium, 70 mg cholesterol, 12 gm carbohydrate, 26 gm protein, 10 gm fat.

CHICKEN PAPRIKASH WITH SPAETZLE

John Niklasch, Terre Haute, Indiana

4 tablespoons butter *or* margarine
1 jar (16 ounces) whole onions, drained
1 large onion, chopped
1/2 cup all-purpose flour
2 tablespoons paprika, *divided*
1 broiler-fryer chicken (2-1/2 to 3 pounds), cut up
1/2 teaspoon salt
3 tablespoons chopped fresh parsley
1-1/4 cups chicken broth
1 cup (8 ounces) sour cream
3 tablespoons capers with juice
SPAETZLE:
2 eggs, well beaten
1-1/2 cups all-purpose flour
1/2 cup milk
3/4 teaspoon salt
1/4 teaspoon baking powder
1 tablespoon butter *or* margarine

In a heavy skillet, melt butter over medium-high heat. Saute whole onions until lightly browned. Remove and set aside. Saute chopped onion until tender. Set aside. Combine flour and 1-1/2 teaspoons paprika in a plastic bag. Place several chicken parts in flour mixture; shake to coat. Repeat until all chicken has been coated. Place chicken in skillet; brown on all sides. Add salt, parsley, broth and remaining paprika. Cover and cook over low heat until chicken is tender, about 45 minutes. Meanwhile, for spaetzle, bring a large kettle of salted water to a boil. Combine eggs, flour, milk, salt and baking powder. With a spoon, drop small dumplings into water. Reduce heat cover and simmer 10 minutes. Drain spaetzle and toss with butter. Remove chicken from skillet; stir in sour cream, capers with juice and onions. Return chicken to the skillet and gently heat through. Place spaetzle on a platter and top with chicken. Ladle the sauce over all. **Yield:** 6-8 servings.

Quick & Easy

TUNA ZUCCHINI CAKES

Billie Blanton, Kingsport, Tennessee

1 tablespoon butter *or* margarine
1/2 cup finely diced onion
1 can (6-1/8 ounces) tuna, drained and flaked
1 cup shredded zucchini
2 eggs, lightly beaten
1/3 cup snipped fresh parsley
1 teaspoon lemon juice
1/2 teaspoon salt
1/8 teaspoon pepper
1 cup seasoned bread crumbs, *divided*
2 tablespoons cooking oil

In a small saucepan, melt butter. Cook the onion until tender, but not brown. Remove from the heat. Add tuna, zucchini, eggs, parsley, lemon juice, salt, pepper and 1/2 cup bread crumbs. Stir until well combined. Shape into six 1/2-in.-thick patties; coat with remaining bread crumbs. In a medium skillet, heat oil and cook the patties 3 minutes on each side or until golden brown. **Yield:** 3 servings.

TREAT the family to a hearty new menu by serving the recipes on this page. Start off the meal with a generous serving of Company Onion Soup garnished with a thick slice of cheese-topped French bread, followed by a crisp Spinach Salad. For the main course, try the North Carolina Shrimp Saute—it's ready in minutes. And for the grand finale, pass the luscious Maple Cream Pie…guaranteed to keep them asking for more!

FOUR-COURSE FEAST.
Clockwise from lower left: **Company Onion Soup** (recipe on page 24), **Spinach Salad** (recipe on page 46), **Maple Cream Pie** (recipe on page 213) and **North Carolina Shrimp Saute** (recipe on page 96).

IN THE COUNTRY, appetites usually are brawny. And when they are, nothing satisfies better than hearty beef dishes! But best of all, beef also can break menu monotony…without doing the same to your budget.
From soups and stews to sandwiches and mouth-watering main courses (almost all calling for less-expensive cuts of meat), there are many months of imaginative and affordable eating in store for your family.
So let the beef feast begin at your table today!

PRIME BEEF.
Clockwise from top right: **Hot Beef and Hazelnut Salad** (recipe on page 56), **Oriental Beef and Cauliflower Stew** (recipe on page 100), **Steak Soup** (recipe on page 24), **Grilled Beef Kabobs** (recipe on page 117), **Santa Fe Stew** (recipe on page 100), **Old-World Sauerbraten** (recipe on page 100), **Round Steak Stroganoff** (recipe on page 100) and **Snappy Barbecue Beef Sandwiches** (recipe on page 20).

OLD-WORLD SAUERBRATEN

Phyllis Berenson, Cincinnati, Ohio

(PICTURED ON PAGE 98)

    2 tablespoons cooking oil
    1 beef rump roast (5 to 6
      pounds)
    2 onions, sliced
    1 cup vinegar
    2 cups water
 1/4 cup lemon juice
    3 bay leaves
    6 whole cloves
    2 teaspoons salt
 1/2 teaspoon pepper
    4 to 5 tablespoons ketchup
   12 gingersnaps, crumbled

In a Dutch oven, heat oil over medium-high. Brown beef on all sides. Add all remaining ingredients except gingersnaps; bring to a boil. Reduce heat; cover and simmer until beef is tender, about 3 hours. During the last 30 minutes, stir in gingersnaps. Remove meat; discard bay leaves and cloves. While slicing meat, bring gravy to a boil to reduce and thicken. **Yield:** 14-16 servings.

ROUND STEAK STROGANOFF

Brenda Read, Burns Lake, British Columbia

(PICTURED ON PAGE 98)

 1/2 cup all-purpose flour
    1 teaspoon salt
 1/2 teaspoon pepper
    1 teaspoon paprika
1-1/2 to 2 pounds round steak,
      trimmed and cut into thin
      strips
    3 tablespoons butter *or*
      margarine
    1 cup chopped onion
    1 garlic clove, minced
    1 can (10-1/2 ounces)
      condensed beef broth
 1/2 teaspoon dry mustard
    3 tablespoons chili sauce
    1 pound fresh mushrooms,
      sliced
    2 cups (16 ounces) sour cream
Cooked noodles
Chopped fresh parsley

Combine flour, salt, pepper and paprika in a plastic bag. Shake beef strips in bag until well coated. In a large skillet, melt butter over medium heat. Brown half the beef at a time. Remove. Add onion and garlic; cook until tender. Return beef to the skillet. Add broth, mustard, chili sauce and mushrooms; cover and simmer until the beef is tender,

about 1 hour. Just before serving, stir in sour cream. Heat gently but do not boil. Serve immediately over noodles. Garnish with chopped parsley. **Yield:** 6-8 servings.

ORIENTAL BEEF AND CAULIFLOWER STEW

Deborah Cole, Wolf Creek, Oregon

(PICTURED ON PAGE 99)

✓ This tasty dish uses less sugar, salt and fat. Recipe includes *Diabetic Exchanges.*

    2 tablespoons cooking oil
1-1/2 pounds lean round steak, cut
      into 1-inch cubes
    3 cups beef broth
    1 small head cauliflower,
      separated into florets
    1 green pepper, cut into chunks
 1/4 cup light *or* regular soy sauce
    1 garlic clove, minced
1-1/2 teaspoons grated fresh
      gingerroot, optional
    2 to 3 tablespoons cornstarch
 1/2 teaspoon sugar
 1/4 cup water
    1 cup sliced green onions
Cooked rice

In a skillet, heat oil over medium-high. Brown meat on all sides. Add broth; cover and simmer until beef is tender, about 1 hour. Add cauliflower, green pepper, soy sauce, garlic, and gingerroot if desired. Cover and simmer until the vegetables are tender, about 5-7 minutes. Combine cornstarch, sugar and water. Stir into meat mixture. Bring to a boil, stirring constantly; cook 2 minutes or until thickened. Stir in green onions. Serve on rice. **Yield:** 6 servings. **Diabetic Exchanges:** One serving (using light soy sauce) equals 2-1/2 lean meat, 1 vegetable; also, 165 calories, 771 mg sodium, 82 mg cholesterol, 8 gm carbohydrate, 23 gm protein, 4 gm fat.

SANTA FE STEW

Patti Henson, Linden, Texas

(PICTURED ON PAGE 99)

    2 tablespoons cooking oil
    1 lean beef roast (about 2 to 3
      pounds), cut into 1/2-inch
      cubes
    2 medium onions, sliced
    1 can (10 ounces) tomatoes
      with jalapenos* *or* 1 can (16
      ounces) tomatoes, cut up,
      liquid reserved
    1 can (15 ounces) pinto beans,
      rinsed and drained

    2 cans (4 ounces *each*)
      chopped green chilies
    1 can (10-1/2 ounces)
      condensed beef broth
    1 tablespoon sugar
    1 garlic clove, minced
    1 to 2 teaspoons ground cumin
    1 green pepper, chopped
    1 cup water
Salt to taste
Shredded Monterey Jack cheese

In a Dutch oven, heat oil over medium-high. Brown beef on all sides. Add all remaining ingredients except cheese; bring to a boil. Reduce heat; simmer 1-1/2 hours or until meat is tender. Serve in bowls topped with cheese. (*Look for tomatoes with jalapenos in the ethnic food section of your grocery store.) **Yield:** 6-8 servings.

PASTA WITH ASPARAGUS

Barbara Calhoun, Marquette Heights, Illinois

(PICTURED ON PAGE 78)

    2 pounds fresh asparagus,
      sliced diagonally into 1-inch
      pieces
    1 pound very thin spaghetti
    8 slices bacon, cut into 1-inch
      pieces
 1/2 cup sliced green onion
 1/2 teaspoon black pepper
 1/4 cup butter *or* margarine,
      softened
 1/2 cup light cream
 1/2 to 3/4 cup grated Parmesan
      cheese

Cook asparagus in boiling salted water 3 minutes. Drain and set aside. Cook spaghetti according to package directions. Drain and return to kettle to keep warm. Meanwhile, in a skillet, cook bacon until crisp. Remove to a paper towel. In bacon drippings, saute onion until soft. Add asparagus and pepper; heat through. Quickly toss together spaghetti, asparagus mixture, bacon, butter, cream and cheese. Serve immediately. **Yield:** 6-8 servings.

STUFFED CABBAGE ROLLS

Jean Parsons, Sarver, Pennsylvania

    1 large head cabbage
    1 cup quick-cooking rice,
      cooked and cooled
    1 pound lean ground beef
    1 medium onion, chopped
    2 tablespoons Worcestershire
      sauce
 1/2 teaspoon salt
 1/4 teaspoon pepper

1 can (10-3/4 ounces)
    condensed cream of tomato
    soup, undiluted, *divided*
1/2 cup water

Cook cabbage in boiling water only until leaves fall off head. Reserve 14-16 large leaves for rolls and set remaining cabbage aside. Combine rice, beef, onion, Worcestershire sauce, salt, pepper and 1/4 cup soup; mix well. Put 2 to 3 tablespoons meat mixture on each cabbage leaf. Fold in sides, starting at an unfolded edge, and roll up leaf completely to enclose meat. Repeat with remaining meat and leaves. Line a Dutch oven with leftover cabbage. Combine remaining soup and water; pour over cabbage. Stack cabbage rolls on top of sauce. Cover. Bring to a boil; reduce heat and simmer on low for 1 to 1-1/2 hours or until rolls are tender. Remove rolls and cabbage. If desired, sauce may be thickened by boiling over high heat. Spoon sauce over rolls and cabbage and serve immediately. **Yield:** 4-6 servings.

CORNMEAL SCRAPPLE

Mrs. Merlin Brubaker, Bettendorf, Iowa

    1 cup white *or* yellow cornmeal
    1 cup milk
    1 teaspoon sugar
    1 teaspoon salt
2-3/4 cups boiling water
    8 ounces bulk pork sausage,
        cooked, drained and crumbled
All-purpose flour
    2 tablespoons butter *or*
        margarine
Maple syrup, optional

In a saucepan, combine the cornmeal, milk, sugar and salt; gradually stir in water. Cook and stir until thickened and bubbly. Reduce heat; cover and cook 10 minutes longer or until very thick, stirring occasionally. Remove from the heat and stir in sausage. Pour into a greased 7-1/2-in. x 3-1/2-in. x 2-in. loaf pan (the pan will be very full). Cover with plastic wrap and refrigerate. To serve, unmold and cut into 1/3-in. slices. Dip both sides in flour. In a skillet, melt butter over medium heat; brown scrapple on both sides. Serve with maple syrup if desired. **Yield:** 6 servings.

ORANGE TURKEY STIR-FRY

Anne Frederick, New Hartford, New York

3/4 cup orange juice
1/4 cup orange marmalade
    2 tablespoons soy sauce
    2 tablespoons cornstarch

1/8 teaspoon ground ginger
1/8 teaspoon hot pepper sauce
1/4 cup all-purpose flour
    1 pound turkey cutlets, cut into
        1-inch strips
    2 tablespoons cooking oil,
        divided
    4 green onions, cut into 1-inch
        pieces
1/2 cup coarsely chopped green
        pepper
    1 seedless orange, peeled,
        sliced and halved
Cooked rice

In a small bowl, stir together first six ingredients; set aside. Place flour on a sheet of waxed paper; coat turkey strips, then shake off excess. In a 10-in. skillet, heat 1 tablespoon oil over medium-high heat. Cook turkey in three batches until strips are tender and lightly browned on all sides. Remove turkey and keep warm. Add remaining oil to skillet; cook and stir green onions and green pepper for 1 minute. Stir in orange juice mixture. Bring to a boil; reduce heat and simmer for 3 minutes. Add turkey and orange slices; heat through. Serve over rice. **Yield:** 4 servings.

EASY, HEARTY DINNER. Pour a 27-oz. can of sauerkraut into a Dutch oven. Top with a pork roast (3-4 lbs.) and another can of sauerkraut. Rinse cans; pour water over roast. Cover and cook over low heat for about 3 hours or until the roast is tender. Thicken juices if desired. Serve with mashed potatoes and rye bread.

Quick & Easy

CHICKEN AND APRICOT SAUTE

Carolyn Griffin, Macon, Georgia

✓ This tasty dish uses less sugar, salt and fat. Recipe includes *Diabetic Exchanges*.

    1 cup chicken broth
    1 tablespoon cornstarch
Pepper to taste
    1 tablespoon cooking oil
    1 pound boneless chicken
        breasts, cut into thin strips
    3 cups sliced celery
    2 garlic cloves, minced
    1 can (16 ounces) apricot
        halves in natural juice, drained
    6 ounces fresh *or* frozen snow
        peas
Cooked rice

Combine broth, cornstarch and pepper. Set aside. In a wok or large skillet, heat oil on high. Add chicken; stir-fry until chicken is no longer pink. Remove from pan. Add celery and garlic; stir-fry until the celery is crisp-tender, about 3 minutes. Stir in broth mixture. Cook, stirring

constantly until thick, about 1 minute. Add apricots, peas and cooked chicken. Stir-fry until heated through, about 1-2 minutes. Serve over rice. **Yield:** 6 servings. **Diabetic Exchanges:** One serving (prepared without rice) equals 2-1/2 lean meat, 1-1/2 vegetable, 1/2 fruit; also 204 calories, 114 mg sodium, 64 mg cholesterol, 14 gm carbohydrate, 25 gm protein, 5 gm fat.

PUEBLO GREEN CHILI STEW

Helen LaBrake, Rindge, New Hampshire

(PICTURED BELOW)

✓ This tasty dish uses less sugar, salt and fat. Recipe includes *Diabetic Exchanges*.

    2 pounds lean boneless pork,
        cut into 1-1/2-inch cubes
    1 tablespoon cooking oil
    3 cans (12 ounces *each*) whole
        kernel corn, drained
    2 celery ribs, chopped
    2 medium potatoes, peeled and
        chopped
    2 medium tomatoes, coarsely
        chopped
    3 cans (4 ounces *each*) chopped
        green chilies
    4 cups chicken broth
    2 teaspoons ground cumin
    1 teaspoon dried oregano
    1 teaspoon salt, optional

In a large Dutch oven, brown half of the pork at a time in oil. Add remaining ingredients. Cover and simmer for 1 hour or until pork is tender. **Yield:** 10 servings. **Diabetic Exchanges:** One serving (prepared with low-sodium chicken broth and without added salt) equals 2 lean meat, 1 starch, 1 vegetable; also, 196 calories, 561 mg sodium, 52 mg cholesterol, 25 gm carbohydrate, 13 gm protein, 7 gm fat.

STEWING over what to make for dinner? Family will warm up to Chili Stew (recipe above).

THE TANGY TASTE of citrus makes for some timeless treats. So, it's no wonder that citrus rates as a favorite of country cooks. And after one taste, your family will request this appealing assortment year after year...after year!

GOLDEN OPPORTUNITIES.
Clockwise from the bottom: **Orange Pork Chops** (recipe on page 103), **Fresh Grapefruit Cake** (recipe on page 199), **Golden Lemon Glazed Cheesecake** (recipe on page 224) and **Layered Fresh Fruit Salad** (recipe on page 41).

ORANGE PORK CHOPS

Elaine Fenton, Prescott, Arizona

(PICTURED AT LEFT)

☑ This tasty dish uses less sugar, salt and fat. Recipe includes *Diabetic Exchanges*.

6 pork loin chops (1/2 inch thick)
1 tablespoon cooking oil
3/4 cup water
1/2 teaspoon paprika
1/2 teaspoon pepper
1-1/4 teaspoons salt, *divided*
1 medium orange
1/2 cup sugar
1 tablespoon cornstarch
1/2 teaspoon ground cinnamon
12 whole cloves
1 cup fresh orange juice

In a large skillet, brown chops in oil on both sides. Add water, paprika, pepper and 1 teaspoon salt; bring to a boil. Reduce heat to low; cover and simmer about 35 minutes, turning once. Meanwhile, grate peel from the stem end of the orange, then cut six slices from the other end. Set aside. In a saucepan over medium-high, combine 1 tablespoon peel, sugar, cornstarch, cinnamon, cloves and remaining salt. Stir in juice. Cook and stir until thickened. Add orange slices, cover and remove from the heat. To serve, top chops with sauce and orange slices. **Yield:** 6 servings. **Diabetic Exchanges:** One serving equals 2-1/2 meat, 1/2 fruit; also, 208 calories, 522 mg sodium, 50 mg cholesterol, 9 gm carbohydrate, 18 gm protein, 11 gm fat.

HUNGARIAN CHICKEN

Crystal Garza, Shamrock, Texas

(PICTURED ON PAGE 9)

6 tablespoons all-purpose flour
Salt and pepper to taste
1 broiler-fryer chicken (about 3-1/2 pounds), cut up
1/4 cup butter *or* **margarine,** *divided*
1 large onion, chopped
2/3 cup tomato juice
1 to 2 tablespoons Hungarian *or* **regular paprika**
1 teaspoon sugar
1 teaspoon salt
1 bay leaf
2/3 cup chicken broth
2/3 cup sour cream
Parsley-buttered egg noodles

Combine flour, salt and pepper in a plastic bag. Shake chicken, a few pieces at a time, in flour mixture. Melt 1 tablespoon butter in a large skillet. Saute onion until tender. Remove from pan and set aside. In same skillet, melt remaining butter and brown chicken on all sides. Combine tomato juice, paprika, sugar and salt. Pour over chicken. Add bay leaf, broth and reserved onion. Cover and simmer 45-60 minutes or until chicken is tender. Remove chicken to a platter; keep warm. Reduce heat to low, remove bay leaf and stir in sour cream. Heat through 2-3 minutes. Do not boil. Pour sauce over chicken and noodles. Serve immediately. **Yield:** 4-6 servings.

 **Quick & Easy**

MEXICAN CORN SCRAMBLE

Brenda Spann, Granger, Indiana

1 small onion, chopped
3 tablespoons butter *or* **margarine**
1 can (11 ounces) whole kernel corn with peppers, drained
1 can (2-1/4 ounces) sliced ripe olives, drained
8 eggs, lightly beaten
1 cup cubed fully cooked smoked ham *or* **sausage**
3/4 cup shredded cheddar cheese
Tortilla chips
Picante sauce

In a medium skillet, saute onion in butter until tender. Stir in corn and olives. Add eggs; cook and stir over medium heat until eggs just begin to set. Add ham or sausage and cheese. Cook until eggs are fully cooked and cheese is melted. Serve with tortilla chips and picante sauce. **Yield:** 6 servings.

 **Quick & Easy**

SPEEDY STROGANOFF

Jo-Ann Knicely, Midland, Ontario

2 tablespoons cooking oil
2 cups cubed cooked roast beef
1 garlic clove, minced
1/3 cup chopped onion
2 tablespoons all-purpose flour
1 teaspoon salt
1/2 teaspoon paprika
1 can (10 ounces) mushroom stems and pieces, drained
1 can (10-3/4 ounces) cream of chicken soup, undiluted
1/2 cup water
1 cup (8 ounces) sour cream
Cooked wide egg noodles
Chopped fresh parsley

In a skillet, heat oil over medium-high. Saute beef, garlic and onion. When onion is tender, reduce heat to low; stir in flour, salt and paprika. Cook 5 minutes. Stir in mushrooms, soup and water. Simmer 10 minutes. Fold in sour cream; heat through but do not boil. Serve immediately over noodles. Garnish with parsley. **Yield:** 4-6 servings.

SKILLET LASAGNA

Lucinda Walker, Somerset, Pennsylvania

1-1/2 pounds lean ground beef
1 small onion, chopped
1 green pepper, chopped
1 jar (30 ounces) spaghetti sauce with mushrooms
1 teaspoon dried oregano
1 teaspoon dried basil
6 lasagna noodles, cooked and rinsed
3 cups (12 ounces) shredded mozzarella cheese, *divided*
1/2 cup grated Parmesan cheese

In a Dutch oven, brown beef, onion and pepper; drain fat. Stir in spaghetti sauce, oregano and basil. Simmer, uncovered, 10-15 minutes. In a 10-in. skillet, spread 1/4 cup of the meat sauce. Top with 3 noodles, cutting to fit as needed. Spread half the remaining sauce and half the mozzarella and Parmesan cheeses. Top with remaining noodles, meat sauce and Parmesan cheese. Cover and heat on medium for 3 minutes. Reduce heat to low; cook for 35 minutes. Sprinkle with remaining mozzarella and let stand 10 minutes with cover ajar. **Yield:** 6-8 servings.

SKILLET FRIED CHICKEN

Carolyn Burton, Evanston, Wyoming

3 cups all-purpose flour
2 to 3 teaspoons poultry seasoning
2 teaspoons paprika
2 to 3 teaspoons onion powder
1 to 2 teaspoons garlic powder
1/2 teaspoon salt
Dash pepper
2 eggs
1 tablespoon milk
2 broiler-fryer chickens (3 pounds *each***), cut up** *or* **16 of your favorite poultry pieces**
Cooking oil

Combine dry ingredients in a plastic bag. In a bowl, lightly beat eggs and milk. Dip chicken pieces in egg mixture and shake off excess. Shake a few chicken pieces in the bag at a time, coating well. In an electric skillet, heat 1/4 in. of oil to 350°; brown chicken on all sides. Reduce heat to 275° and continue cooking for 30 minutes. **Yield:** 6-8 servings.

BAVARIAN POT ROAST

Susan Robertson, Hamilton, Ohio

(PICTURED AT RIGHT)

- 1 boneless beef chuck pot roast (about 3 pounds)
- 2 tablespoons cooking oil
- 1-1/4 cups water
- 3/4 cup beer *or* beef broth
- 1 can (8 ounces) tomato sauce
- 1/2 cup chopped onion
- 2 tablespoons sugar
- 1 tablespoon vinegar
- 2 teaspoons salt
- 1 teaspoon ground cinnamon
- 1 bay leaf
- 1/2 teaspoon pepper
- 1/2 teaspoon ground ginger

Cornstarch and water, optional

In a Dutch oven, brown roast in hot oil. Combine water, beer or broth, tomato sauce, onion, sugar, vinegar, salt, cinnamon, bay leaf, pepper and ginger. Pour over meat and bring to a boil. Reduce heat; cover and simmer until meat is tender, about 2-1/2 to 3 hours. Remove meat. Discard bay leaf. If desired, thicken juices with cornstarch and water. **Yield:** 8-10 servings.

CREOLE JAMBALAYA

Ruby Williams, Bogalusa, Louisiana

 This tasty dish uses less sugar, salt and fat. Recipe includes *Diabetic Exchanges*.

- 3/4 cup chopped onion
- 1/2 cup chopped celery
- 1/4 cup chopped green pepper
- 2 garlic cloves, minced
- 2 tablespoons butter *or* margarine
- 2 cups cubed fully cooked ham
- 1 can (28 ounces) tomatoes with liquid, cut up
- 1 can (10-1/2 ounces) condensed beef broth
- 1 cup uncooked long grain white rice
- 1 cup water
- 1 teaspoon sugar
- 1 teaspoon dried thyme
- 1/2 teaspoon chili powder
- 1/4 teaspoon pepper
- 1-1/2 pounds fresh *or* frozen uncooked shrimp, peeled and deveined
- 1 tablespoon chopped fresh parsley

In a Dutch oven, saute onion, celery, green pepper and garlic in butter until tender. Add next nine ingredients; bring to a boil. Reduce heat; cover and simmer until

rice is tender, about 25 minutes. Add shrimp and parsley; simmer, uncovered, until shrimp are cooked, 7-10 minutes. **Yield:** 8 servings. **Diabetic Exchanges:** One serving (prepared with margarine and low-sodium tomatoes and beef broth) equals 3 lean meat, 1-1/2 starch, 1 vegetable; also, 310 calories, 464 mg sodium, 154 mg cholesterol, 28 gm carbohydrate, 31 gm protein, 8 gm fat.

GREEN PEPPER STEAK

Emmalee Thomas, Laddonia, Missouri

- 1 pound boneless beef sirloin steak
- 1/4 cup soy sauce
- 1/4 cup water
- 1 tablespoon cornstarch
- 2 to 3 tablespoons cooking oil, *divided*
- 2 small onions, thinly sliced and separated into rings
- 1 green pepper, cut into 1-inch pieces
- 2 celery ribs, sliced diagonally
- 2 tomatoes, cut into wedges

Cooked rice

Partially freeze beef. Thinly slice across the grain into bite-size strips; set aside. For sauce, combine soy sauce, water and cornstarch; set aside. Heat 1 tablespoon oil in a large skillet or wok over high heat. Stir-fry half of the beef until browned. Remove and repeat with remaining beef, adding additional oil as needed. Remove meat and keep warm. Add onions, green pepper and celery to pan; stir-fry until crisp-tender, about 3-4 minutes. Return beef to pan. Stir the sauce; add to pan. Cook and stir until thickened and bubbly. Cook and stir 2 minutes more. Add tomatoes; cook just until heated through. Serve over rice. **Yield:** 4 servings.

CHICKEN AND DUMPLINGS

Patricia Collins, Imbler, Oregon

 This tasty dish uses less sugar, salt and fat. Recipe includes *Diabetic Exchanges*.

- 1 broiler-fryer chicken (2-1/2 to 3 pounds), cut up
- 3 cups water
- 1 cup chopped onion

- 4 celery ribs, sliced
- 3 carrots, sliced
- 1 teaspoon celery seed
- 2 teaspoons sage, *divided*
- 1 teaspoon salt
- 1/4 teaspoon pepper
- 3 cups biscuit mix
- 3/4 cup plus 2 tablespoons milk
- 1 tablespoon minced fresh parsley

Place chicken and water in a Dutch oven. Cover and bring to a boil. Reduce heat to simmer; cook until chicken is tender, about 30-45 minutes. Remove chicken from kettle; bone and cube. Return chicken to kettle along with onion, celery, carrots, celery seed, 1 teaspoon sage, salt and pepper. Cover and simmer for 45-60 minutes or until the vegetables are tender. For dumplings, combine biscuit mix, milk, parsley and remaining sage to form a stiff batter. Drop by tablespoonsful into the simmering chicken mixture. Cover and simmer for 15 minutes. Serve immediately. **Yield:** 8 servings. **Diabetic Exchanges:** One serving equals 2 starch, 2 meat; also, 276 calories, 579 mg sodium, 29 mg cholesterol, 30 gm carbohydrate, 20 gm protein, 9 gm fat.

BACON AND ASPARAGUS FRITTATA

Gwen Clemon, Soldier, Iowa

(PICTURED ON PAGE 79)

- 12 ounces bacon
- 2 cups sliced fresh asparagus (cut in 1/2-inch pieces)
- 1 cup chopped onion
- 2 garlic cloves, minced
- 10 eggs, beaten
- 1/4 cup minced parsley
- 1/2 teaspoon seasoned salt
- 1/4 teaspoon black pepper
- 1 large tomato, thinly sliced
- 1 cup (4 ounces) shredded cheddar cheese

Cook bacon until crisp. Drain, reserving 1 tablespoon drippings. In a 9-in. or 10-in. ovenproof skillet, heat reserved drippings on medium-high. Add asparagus, onion and garlic; saute until onion is tender. Crumble bacon and set aside about a third for topping. In a large bowl, combine remaining bacon, eggs, parsley, salt and pepper. Pour egg mixture into skillet; stir. Top with tomato slices, cheese and remaining bacon. Cover and cook over medium-low for 10-15 minutes or until eggs are nearly set. Preheat broiler; place skillet 6 in. from heat for 2 minutes or until lightly browned. Serve immediately. **Yield:** 6 servings.

WHEN the days get shorter and the winds get colder, enjoy the aroma of a simmering Bavarian Pot Roast, rich with spices and tomato. You'll gladly heat up the oven for nutty Cinnamon Cranberry Muffins. For dessert, tangy Cran-Orange Delight will delight your family. Or make Caramel Custard and surprise everyone with their own individual treat!

FLAVOR OF FALL.
Clockwise from the top: **Cran-Orange Delight** (recipe on page 192), **Cinnamon Cranberry Muffins** (recipe on page 161), **Caramel Custard** (recipe on page 214) and **Bavarian Pot Roast** (recipe on page 104).

CRANBERRY/ORANGE CHICKEN

Sharon Parsons, Killingworth, Connecticut

(PICTURED AT RIGHT)

- 1/2 cup all-purpose flour
- 1/8 teaspoon salt
- 1 broiler-fryer chicken (about 3 pounds), cut up
- 4 tablespoons butter *or* margarine
- 2 cups whole fresh *or* frozen cranberries
- 1-3/4 cups sugar
- 1-1/4 cups orange juice
- 1/2 cup chopped onion
- 2 tablespoons grated orange peel
- 1/4 teaspoon ground ginger
- 1/4 teaspoon ground cinnamon
- Red food coloring, optional

Combine the flour and salt and place in a plastic bag. Shake chicken, a few pieces at a time, in flour mixture. Melt butter in a large skillet; brown chicken on all sides. In a saucepan, combine remaining ingredients except food coloring; bring to a boil and pour over chicken. Cover and simmer 1 hour. Remove chicken to a warm platter. Bring sauce to a boil and cook, stirring constantly, until thickened. Add a few drops red food coloring if desired. Serve sauce over chicken. **Yield:** 4-6 servings.

LENTIL/VEGETABLE STEW

Chris Moyers, Felton, California

- 2 cups dry lentils
- 3/4 cup uncooked brown rice
- 1 can (28 ounces) tomatoes with juice, chopped
- 1 can (48 ounces) tomato *or* vegetable juice
- 4 cups water
- 3 garlic cloves, minced
- 1 large onion, chopped
- 2 celery ribs, sliced
- 3 carrots, sliced
- 1 bay leaf
- 1 teaspoon dried basil
- 1 teaspoon dried oregano
- 1 teaspoon dried thyme
- 1/2 teaspoon pepper
- 3 tablespoons minced fresh parsley
- 1 zucchini, sliced
- 2 medium potatoes, peeled and diced
- 2 tablespoons lemon juice
- 1 teaspoon dry mustard
- Salt to taste

In a 6-qt. Dutch oven or soup kettle, combine first 15 ingredients. Bring to a boil. Reduce heat, cover and simmer, until rice and lentils are tender, 45-60 minutes. Add additional water or tomato juice if necessary. Stir in all of the remaining ingredients. Cover and continue to cook until vegetables are tender, about 45 minutes. **Yield:** 5 quarts.

APPLES 'N' CREAM PANCAKE

Ruth Schafer, Defiance, Ohio

- 1/2 cup milk
- 2 eggs
- 1/2 cup all-purpose flour
- 1/4 teaspoon salt
- 1 to 2 tablespoons butter *or* margarine
- 1/4 cup packed brown sugar
- 1 package (3 ounces) cream cheese, softened
- 1/2 cup sour cream
- 1/2 teaspoon vanilla extract
- 1-1/2 cups thinly sliced unpeeled apples
- 1/4 cup chopped walnuts

In a small mixing bowl, combine milk, eggs, flour and salt. Beat until smooth. Heat a cast-iron or ovenproof skillet in a 450° oven until hot. Add butter to the skillet; spread over entire bottom. Pour in batter; bake for 10 minutes or until golden brown. Meanwhile, combine sugar and cream cheese. Blend in sour cream and vanilla. Fill pancake with 3/4 cup cream cheese mixture and top with apples. Spread remaining cream cheese mixture over apples and sprinkle with nuts. Cut into wedges and serve immediately. **Yield:** 4-6 servings.

TURKEY MUSHROOM SUPREME

Jeanie Beers, Montgomery, New York

- 1/4 cup butter *or* margarine
- 1 cup diced green pepper
- 1 cup sliced fresh mushrooms
- 1/3 cup all-purpose flour
- 1/2 teaspoon salt
- 1/4 teaspoon pepper
- 1/8 to 1/4 teaspoon curry powder
- 1/8 to 1/4 teaspoon dried tarragon
- 1/8 teaspoon coriander
- 1 cup chicken broth
- 1/2 cup milk
- 2 cups diced cooked turkey *or* chicken
- 1/2 cup frozen peas, thawed
- 1 jar (4 ounces) sliced pimientos, drained
- 6 puff-pastry patty shells, baked

In a medium saucepan, melt butter over medium heat. Saute green pepper and mushrooms until peppers are crisp-tender. Meanwhile, mix together flour and seasonings; stir into vegetables. Cook and stir until flour is moistened. Stir in broth and milk. Cook, stirring constantly, until thickened. Add turkey and peas; heat through. Gently stir in pimientos. Spoon into shells and serve immediately. **Yield:** 6 servings.

ORANGE BEEF AND BROCCOLI STIR-FRY

Arly M. Schnabel, Ellendale, North Dakota

✓ This tasty dish uses less sugar, salt and fat. Recipe includes *Diabetic Exchanges*.

- 1 pound well-trimmed top sirloin, cut into thin strips
- 4 teaspoons soy sauce
- 2 teaspoons shredded fresh gingerroot *or* 1/2 teaspoon ground ginger
- 1 teaspoon finely grated orange peel
- 1 tablespoon vegetable oil
- 2 cups broccoli florets
- 1 small sweet red pepper, cut into strips
- 2/3 cup picante sauce
- 1/2 teaspoon sugar, optional
- 1/3 cup orange juice
- 1 tablespoon cornstarch
- 3 green onions with tops, cut diagonally into 1-inch pieces
- Sliced almonds, optional
- Hot cooked rice

Toss meat with soy sauce, ginger and orange peel; set aside for 10 minutes. Heat oil in a wok or large skillet on high. Stir-fry mixture just until meat is no longer pink; remove. To skillet, add broccoli, pepper, picante sauce and sugar if desired. Cover and reduce heat to simmer. Cook until vegetables are crisp-tender, about 3 minutes. Combine orange juice and cornstarch; add to skillet along with meat and onions. Cook and stir 1 minute or until sauce is thickened. Sprinkle with almonds if desired. Serve over hot cooked rice. **Yield:** 4-6 servings. **Diabetic Exchanges:** One serving (prepared without rice) equals 2 lean meats, 1 vegetable, 1/4 starch; also, 160 calories, 412 mg sodium, 52 mg cholesterol, 10 gm carbohydrate, 20 gm protein, 5 gm fat.

WITH their lively tart taste and crimson color, there's little wonder why cranberries have long had a place reserved on countless families' Thanksgiving and Christmas tables. So it isn't surprising these days to see this cheerfully bright fruit becoming a standby of country cooks no matter what the season! Cranberries are delicious in baked goods, of course…but there's also a fresh new main dish to add to your recipe file plus a truly different side dish. Red-y? Dig in!

VINE'S FINEST.
Clockwise from the top: **Rich Cranberry Coffee Cake** (recipe on page 152), **Cranberry/Orange Chicken** (recipe on page 106), **Cranberry Nut Swirls** (recipe on page 174) and **Cranberry Stuffing Balls** (recipe on page 137).

DON'T RESTRICT your use of corn to the cob! This sweet succulent vegetable lusciously livens up salads, muffins, side dishes, main meals and more! Plus, the pleasing golden kernels add a festive color to tables throughout the year.

CORNUCOPIA!
Clockwise from bottom center: **Hush Puppies** (recipe on page 129) **Colossal Cornburger** (recipe on page 121), **Calico Potato Salad** (recipe on page 42), **Corn Relish** (recipe on page 147), **Corn Muffins with Honey Butter** (recipe on page 154), **Company Vegetable Casserole** (recipe on page 127), **Corn and Chicken Dinner** (recipe on page 110) and **Fresh Corn Cakes** (recipe on page 110).

FRESH CORN CAKES

Gaynelle Fritsch, Welches, Oregon

(PICTURED ON PAGE 109)

1 cup all-purpose flour
1/2 cup yellow *or* blue cornmeal
1 tablespoon sugar
1 tablespoon baking powder
1/2 teaspoon salt
2 eggs, *separated*
1 cup milk
1/4 cup butter *or* margarine, melted
1 cup cooked whole kernel corn
4 green onions, thinly sliced
1/2 medium sweet red pepper, finely chopped
1 can (4 ounces) chopped green chilies
Butter, margarine *or* cooking oil for frying
Maple syrup, optional

In a medium bowl, combine flour, cornmeal, sugar, baking powder and salt. In a small bowl, beat egg yolks; blend in milk and butter. Add to dry ingredients; stir until just mixed. (Batter may be slightly lumpy). Stir in the corn, green onions, red pepper and green chilies; set aside. In a small mixing bowl, beat egg whites until stiff peaks form. Gently fold into batter. For each pancake, pour about 1/4 cup batter onto a lightly greased hot griddle; turn when bubbles form on tops of cakes. Cook second side until golden brown. Serve immediately with syrup if desired. **Yield:** 20 pancakes.

CORN AND CHICKEN DINNER

Doralee Pinkerton, Milford, Indiana

(PICTURED ON PAGE 109)

3 garlic cloves, minced, *divided*
1/2 cup butter *or* margarine, *divided*
3 pounds chicken legs and thighs (about 8 pieces)
3 ears fresh corn, husked, cleaned and cut into thirds
1/4 cup water
2 teaspoons dried tarragon, *divided*
1/2 teaspoon salt
1/4 teaspoon pepper
2 medium zucchini, sliced into 1/2-inch pieces

2 tomatoes, seeded and cut into chunks

In a Dutch oven or large skillet over medium-high heat, saute 2 of the garlic cloves in 2 tablespoons butter. Add the chicken and brown on both sides. Reduce heat. Add corn and water. Sprinkle with 1 teaspoon tarragon, salt and pepper. Cover and simmer for 20-25 minutes or until chicken is tender. Meanwhile, in a small saucepan, melt remaining butter. Add remaining garlic and tarragon; simmer for 3 minutes. Layer zucchini and tomatoes over the chicken mixture. Drizzle seasoned butter over all; cover and cook for 3-5 minutes. **Yield:** 6-8 servings.

STEW SECRET. Add chopped turnip to beef stew for a satisfying, slightly sweet taste.

NORWEGIAN MEATBALLS

Karen Hoylo, Duluth, Minnesota

(PICTURED ON PAGE 122)

1 egg
1/2 cup milk
1 tablespoon cornstarch
1 medium onion, finely chopped
1 teaspoon salt
Dash pepper
1/4 teaspoon ground nutmeg
1/4 teaspoon ground allspice
1/4 teaspoon ground ginger
1-1/2 pounds lean ground beef
3 to 4 tablespoons butter *or* margarine
GRAVY:
1 tablespoon butter *or* margarine
2 tablespoons all-purpose flour
1 cup beef broth
1/2 cup milk *or* light cream
Salt and pepper to taste
Minced fresh parsley, optional

In a mixing bowl, beat egg. Add milk, cornstarch, onion, salt, pepper, nutmeg, allspice and ginger. Add beef; mix well. Shape into 1-1/2-in. meatballs. (Mixture will be very soft. For easier shaping, rinse hands in cold water frequently.) In a large skillet over medium heat, brown the meatballs in butter, half at a time, for about 10 minutes or until no pink remains. Turn to brown evenly. Remove meatballs to paper towels to drain, reserving 1 tablespoon drippings in skillet. For gravy, add butter to drippings. Stir in flour. Add broth and milk or cream; cook and stir until thickened and bubbly. Cook and stir 1 minute more. Season with salt and pepper. Return meatballs to skillet; heat through on low. Garnish with parsley if desired. **Yield:** 6 servings.

POT ROAST WITH SPAGHETTI

Ellen Cote, Sealy, Texas

2 tablespoons cooking oil
2 tablespoons butter *or* margarine
1 chuck roast (2 to 3 pounds)
1 garlic clove, minced
1 small onion, chopped
2 teaspoons dried oregano
1 teaspoon dried thyme
1/2 teaspoon dried basil
1/8 teaspoon ground cinnamon
1-1/2 to 2 teaspoons salt
1/2 teaspoon pepper
3 cups hot water
3 cans (6 ounces *each*) tomato paste
1 pound spaghetti, cooked and drained
Grated Parmesan cheese, optional

Heat oil and butter in a Dutch oven; brown roast evenly on all sides. Remove and set aside. Add garlic, onion and seasonings. Cook slowly for about 5 minutes, stirring constantly. Stir in water and tomato paste; blend well. Return roast to Dutch oven and spoon sauce over it. Cover and simmer for 2-1/2 to 3 hours or until the meat is tender. Remove roast; cut into slices. Serve with spaghetti and sauce. Sprinkle with Parmesan cheese if desired. **Yield:** 6-8 servings.

CHIMICHANGAS

Laura Towns, Glendale, Arizona

1/4 cup bacon grease
2 cups chopped *or* shredded cooked beef, pork *or* chicken
1 medium onion, diced
2 garlic cloves, minced
2 medium tomatoes, chopped
2 cans (4 ounces *each*) chopped green chilies
1 large peeled boiled potato, diced
1 teaspoon salt
1-1/2 teaspoons dried oregano
1 to 2 teaspoons chili powder *or* to taste
2 tablespoons minced fresh cilantro
12 large flour tortillas, warmed
Vegetable oil
Shredded cheddar cheese
Sour cream
Guacamole
Salsa
Shredded lettuce
Chopped tomatoes
Sliced ripe olives

In a skillet, melt bacon grease over medium heat. Saute meat, onion, garlic, tomatoes, chilies and potatoes until the onion softens. Add salt, oregano, chili powder and cilantro; simmer 2-3 minutes. Place a scant 1/2 cup meat filling on each tortilla. Fold, envelope-style, like a burrito. Fry, seam side down, in 1/2 in. of hot oil (360°-375°) until crispy and brown. Turn and brown other side. Drain briefly on a paper towel. Place on a serving plate and top with shredded cheese, a dollop of sour cream, guacamole and salsa. Place shredded lettuce next to chimichanga and top with tomatoes and olives. Serve immediately. **Yield:** 12 servings.

 Quick & Easy

ROAST BEEF WITH MUSHROOM SAUCE

Rev. Arthur Tiffen, Williamsfield, Ohio

- 2 tablespoons butter *or* margarine
- 3/4 cup thinly sliced onion
- 1/4 pound fresh mushrooms, sliced
- 2 tablespoons all-purpose flour
- 1/4 teaspoon ground marjoram
- 1/4 teaspoon garlic salt
- Salt and pepper to taste
- 3/4 cup beef broth
- 1/4 cup ketchup
- 8 slices cooked roast beef

In a skillet, melt butter over medium heat. Saute onion for 5 minutes. Add mushrooms and saute 2-3 minutes. Stir in the flour and seasonings. Add broth and ketchup. Bring to a boil, stirring constantly. Reduce heat to low; simmer 10 minutes. Add beef and heat through. **Yield:** 4 servings.

SKILLET CHICKEN AND ARTICHOKES

Jody Steinke, Nekoosa, Wisconsin

- 4 large boneless chicken breast halves
- 3/4 teaspoon salt-free herb seasoning
- 1 jar (6 ounces) marinated artichoke hearts, drained and marinade reserved
- 1 tablespoon all-purpose flour
- 1/2 cup water

- 1/4 cup dry white wine *or* water
- 1 teaspoon chicken bouillon granules
- 12 small fresh mushrooms, cut in half
- 1 tablespoon chopped fresh parsley
- Cooked rice *or* noodles

Sprinkle chicken with herb seasoning. In a medium skillet, heat 3 tablespoons of the reserved artichoke marinade. Add chicken and brown 3-4 minutes per side. Drain all but 1 tablespoon of marinade in skillet. Push chicken to one side and stir in flour. Add water, wine and bouillon. Stir until mixture boils and sauce is lightly thickened. Stir in the artichokes and mushrooms. Cover and simmer on very low heat 20 minutes or until the chicken is tender. Sprinkle with parsley. Serve on a bed of rice or noodles. **Yield:** 4 servings.

 Quick & Easy

QUICK BEEF STEW

Valerie Cook, Hubbard, Iowa

- 2 cups diced cooked roast beef
- 1 can (16 ounces) mixed vegetables, liquid drained and reserved
- 1 can (10-3/4 ounces) cream of celery soup, undiluted
- 1 can (10-3/4 ounces) cream of mushroom soup, undiluted
- 1/2 teaspoon dried thyme, optional
- 1/4 teaspoon dried rosemary, optional
- Pepper to taste

In a saucepan, combine beef, vegetables, soups and seasonings. Heat through. If desired, add the reserved vegetable liquid to thin the stew. **Yield:** 4 servings.

SOUTHWESTERN SWISS STEAK

Myra Innes, Auburn, Kansas

- 1 pound round steak, cut into serving-size pieces
- 1/4 teaspoon salt
- 1/8 teaspoon pepper
- 2 tablespoons all-purpose flour
- 1 tablespoon cooking oil
- 10 onion slices
- 1 garlic clove, minced
- 1 can (16 ounces) tomatoes with liquid, chopped
- 1/4 cup mild, medium *or* hot picante sauce
- 1/4 cup beef broth

Sprinkle meat with salt and pepper. Using a mallet, pound all of the flour

---

into the meat. In a skillet, heat oil over medium-high. Brown the meat on both sides. Arrange onion slices over the meat. Combine remaining ingredients and pour over onions. Cover and simmer until the meat is tender, about 45 minutes. Remove meat and keep warm. Cook the sauce until it is reduced and thickened, about 5 minutes. Season to taste with additional salt and pepper if desired. Pour sauce over meat and serve immediately. **Yield:** 4 servings.

 Quick & Easy

CRANBERRY SWEET-AND-SOUR PORK

Gert Snyder, West Montrose, Ontario

(PICTURED BELOW)

- 1 can (8-3/4 ounces) pineapple tidbits, liquid drained, reserved
- 1 tablespoon cornstarch
- 1/2 cup barbecue sauce
- 1 cup whole-berry cranberry sauce
- 1 tablespoon cooking oil
- 1-1/2 pounds pork tenderloin, cut into 1/2-inch cubes
- 1/2 teaspoon salt
- 1/4 teaspoon pepper
- 1 medium green pepper, cut into strips
- Cooked rice or chow mein noodles

In a bowl, combine pineapple liquid and cornstarch. Stir in sauces and set aside. In a large skillet, heat oil over high heat. Add pork, salt and pepper; stir-fry for about 3 minutes or until meat is no longer pink. Add peppers and pineapple; stir-fry 2 minutes more. Stir cornstarch mixture and add to skillet. Cook, stirring constantly, over medium-high heat, until thickened. Serve over rice or noodles. **Yield:** 6 servings.

QUITE A STIR is quickly created by swift sweet-and-sour pork dish (recipe above).

SPICY RED BEANS AND RICE

Rebecca Michael, San Diego, California
(PICTURED AT RIGHT)

    1 pound dry red kidney beans
    2 teaspoons paprika
1/2 to 1 teaspoon cayenne pepper
    1 teaspoon freshly ground
      black pepper
    2 bay leaves
    1 teaspoon ground cumin
    1 quart water
    1 large smoked ham hock
  2 to 3 teaspoons salt
1-1/2 cups chopped celery
1-1/2 cups chopped onion
    2 garlic cloves, minced
  1/2 teaspoon hot pepper sauce
    3 tablespoons minced fresh
      parsley
Cooked rice

Sort and rinse beans. In a large Dutch oven or kettle, place all ingredients except parsley and rice. Bring to a boil, then cover and simmer 3 to 4 hours or until beans are tender. Stir occasionally, adding water as needed to make a thick gravy. Just before serving, remove bay leaves and stir in parsley. Serve over rice. **Yield: 8 servings.**

SUMMER STUFFED PEPPERS

Pat Whitaker, Lebanon, Oregon

 This tasty dish uses less sugar, salt and fat. Recipe includes *Diabetic Exchanges*.

    8 medium yellow, green *or*
      sweet red peppers
1-1/2 pounds lean ground beef
  1/2 garlic clove, minced
    1 medium onion, minced
  1/2 cup finely chopped cabbage
    1 medium carrot, shredded
  1/2 cup shredded zucchini
    1 can (28 ounces) tomatoes
      with liquid, cut up
  1/2 cup uncooked long-grain rice
    1 tablespoon brown sugar
  1/4 teaspoon dried basil
Pepper to taste

Cut the tops off each pepper and reserve. Cook peppers in boiling water until crisp-tender, about 2-3 minutes. Remove from water and rinse with cold water. Remove stems from pepper tops and chop enough of the tops to make 1/3 cup. In a large skillet, brown ground beef over medium heat. Add garlic, onion, cabbage, carrot, zucchini and reserved chopped peppers. Saute until vegetables are tender. Add tomatoes,

rice, sugar, basil and pepper. Cover and reduce heat to simmer. Cook until the rice is tender, about 20 minutes. Stuff hot meat mixture into peppers. Serve immediately. **Yield:** 8 servings. **Diabetic Exchanges:** One serving equals 3 lean meat, 2 vegetable, 1 starch, 1/2 fat; also, 315 calories, 234 mg sodium, 67 mg cholesterol, 25 gm carbohydrate, 28 gm protein, 12 gm fat.

(Quick & Easy)

SESAME BEEF

Kim Champlin, Miami, Florida

    1 pound sirloin steak, cut into
      1/8-inch strips
    2 tablespoons sugar
    3 tablespoons cooking oil,
      divided
    2 tablespoons soy sauce
  1/4 teaspoon pepper
    3 green onions, thinly sliced
    2 garlic cloves, minced
    1 tablespoon sesame seeds
Rice *or* chow mein noodles

Place beef in a glass bowl. Combine sugar, 2 tablespoons oil, soy sauce, pepper, onions, garlic and sesame seeds. Pour over beef and toss to coat. Let stand 15 minutes. In skillet or wok, heat remaining oil over high heat; add beef and marinade. Stir-fry until beef is brown and has reached desired doneness. Serve immediately over rice or noodles. **Yield:** 4 servings.

BRUNSWICK STEW

Alyce Ray, Forest Park, Georgia

    2 pork chops (about 1 pound)
    2 whole chicken breasts
    1 pound round steak, cut into
      bite-size pieces
1-1/2 quarts water
    1 can (8 ounces) tomato sauce
    2 teaspoons hot pepper sauce
      or to taste
  1/2 cup vinegar
  1/4 cup sugar
    2 cups chopped onion
  4 to 5 garlic cloves, minced
    2 cans (16 ounces *each*)
      tomatoes with liquid, chopped
    2 cans (16 ounces *each*)
      cream-style corn
    2 cans (16 ounces *each*) whole
      kernel corn, drained
    1 cup toasted bread crumbs
Salt and pepper to taste

In a Dutch oven or soup kettle, place pork chops, chicken breasts and round steak; cover with water. Cover and cook for about 1-1/2 hours or until meat

is tender. Strain stock into another large kettle; refrigerate overnight. Remove bones from meat; dice and place in a separate bowl. Cover and refrigerate overnight. The next day, skim fat from stock; add tomato sauce, hot pepper sauce, vinegar, sugar, onions, garlic and tomatoes. Simmer, uncovered, for about 45 minutes. Add cream-style and kernel corn, reserved meat and chicken; simmer for about 15 minutes or until thoroughly heated through. Stir in bread crumbs; season with salt and pepper. **Yield:** 6 quarts.

CAMPFIRE HASH

Janet Danilow, Winkelman, Arizona

    2 tablespoons cooking oil
    1 large onion, chopped
    2 garlic cloves, minced
    4 large potatoes, peeled and
      cubed (about 2 pounds)
    1 pound fully cooked smoked
      kielbasa, cubed
    1 can (4 ounces) chopped
      green chilies
    1 can (15 to 16 ounces) whole
      kernel corn, drained

In a Dutch oven, heat oil. Saute onion and garlic until tender. Add potatoes. Cook, uncovered, over medium heat for 20 minutes, stirring occasionally. Add kielbasa; cook and stir until potatoes are tender and well browned, about 10 minutes more. Stir in chilies and corn; cook until heated through. **Yield:** 6 servings.

CITRUS-TOPPED PORK CHOPS

Brenda Wood, Egbert, Ontario

    1 tablespoon cooking oil
    6 loin pork chops (1 inch thick)
Salt and pepper to taste
  1/4 teaspoon paprika
  1/2 cup apple jelly
    1 cup orange juice
  1/2 teaspoon lemon juice
    1 teaspoon dry mustard
Dash ground ginger
    6 orange slices
    6 lemon slices

In a large skillet, heat oil over medium-high. Brown chops on both sides. Season with salt, pepper and paprika. Combine jelly, juices, mustard and ginger. Pour over chops. Cover and simmer for 15 minutes. Turn chops; cover and simmer 15 minutes. Top each chop with an orange and lemon slice. Cover and cook 6-8 minutes longer or until chops are done. **Yield:** 6 servings.

COUNTRY COOKS have a special way of taking ordinary beans and turning them into extraordinary family favorites. Just glance at the imaginative dishes here for a robust helping of proof! These taste-tempters are bound to become tops at your dinner table.

BACK TO BASICS.
Clockwise from top right: **Maple Baked Beans** (recipe on page 124), **Shaker Bean Soup** (recipe on page 27), **Spicy Red Beans and Rice** (recipe on page 112) and **Cathy's Tomato and Bean Salad** (recipe on page 49).

ENJOY a year-round harvest of good eating from
your garden (and your grocer) with the recipes shown here.
Loaded with vegetables, both the Summer's End Stew
and Chicken and Okra Gumbo go nicely with freshly baked
bread. Serve the lip-smacking Bacon-Stuffed Burgers with
a generous helping of spicy Mission Baked Beans—
all guaranteed to please hearty appetites!

GARDEN VARIETY.
Clockwise from top: **Chicken and Okra Gumbo**
(page 28), **Summer's End Stew** (page 115),
Bacon-Stuffed Burgers (page 118),
Mission Baked Beans (page 130).

SUMMER'S END STEW

Laura Garton, Lenox, Massachusetts

(PICTURED AT LEFT)

✓ This tasty dish uses less sugar, salt and fat. Recipe includes *Diabetic Exchanges*.

- 1-1/2 pounds beef stew meat, trimmed
- 1 tablespoon cooking oil
- 8 to 12 medium fresh tomatoes, peeled and cut up
- 2 cups tomato juice *or* water
- 2 medium onions, chopped
- 1 garlic clove, minced
- 1/2 teaspoon pepper
- 2 teaspoons salt, optional
- 4 to 6 medium potatoes, peeled and quartered
- 3 to 5 carrots, sliced
- 2 cups frozen corn
- 2 cups fresh cut green beans
- 2 cups frozen peas
- 2 to 3 celery ribs, sliced
- 1 cup sliced summer squash
- 1/4 cup snipped fresh parsley
- 1 teaspoon sugar

In a Dutch oven, brown meat in oil over medium-high heat. Add tomatoes, tomato juice or water, onions, garlic, pepper, and salt if desired. Bring to a boil; reduce heat and simmer for 1 hour. Add potatoes, carrots, corn, green beans, peas and celery. Cover and simmer 30 minutes. Add squash; simmer 10-15 minutes or until meat and vegetables are tender. Stir in parsley and sugar. **Yield:** 16 servings. **Diabetic Exchanges:** One serving (1 cup, without added salt) equals 1 meat, 1 starch, 2 vegetable; also, 189 calories, 170 mg sodium, 32 mg cholesterol, 22 gm carbohydrate, 13 gm protein, 6 gm fat.

CHUCK WAGON CHOW

Ed Jones, Baker City, Oregon

- 1/2 cup all-purpose flour
- 1 teaspoon salt
- 1/4 teaspoon pepper
- 2 pounds beef round steak (1/2 inch thick), cut into 1/2-inch cubes
- 1/4 cup cooking oil
- 1 medium onion, chopped
- 1 green pepper, chopped
- 1 garlic clove, minced
- 1 tablespoon chili powder
- 1 teaspoon dried oregano
- 1 can (16 ounces) kidney beans, juice drained and reserved
- 1 can (16 ounces) whole kernel corn, juice drained and reserved

Combine flour, salt and pepper in a large plastic bag. Place beef cubes in bag and shake to coat evenly. In a Dutch oven or large skillet, brown beef in oil. Add onion, green pepper and garlic; cook until peppers are crisp-tender. Stir in chili powder, oregano and reserved vegetable liquid; bring to a boil. Reduce heat, cover and simmer until meat is tender, about 45-50 minutes. Stir in beans and corn; simmer 10 minutes or until heated through. **Yield:** 6-8 servings.

BEEF FLAUTAS

Maria Goclan, Katy, Texas

- 2 pounds beef brisket
- 1 medium onion, cut into fourths
- 1 teaspoon salt
- 1 teaspoon pepper
- 1 teaspoon dried oregano
- 1 teaspoon dried marjoram

Water
- 1 green pepper, finely chopped
- 18 to 24 corn tortillas

Cooking oil for deep-fat frying
Guacamole, sour cream and salsa, optional

In a Dutch oven, place brisket, onion, spices and enough water to cover. Cover and simmer about 2-1/2 hours or until meat is very tender. Finely shred beef and chop the onion; mix together with green pepper. Place a spoonful of meat mixture on each tortilla; roll up and secure with toothpicks. Deep-fry flautas in hot oil. Drain on paper towels. If desired, serve with guacamole, salsa and/or sour cream. **Yield:** 9-12 servings.

HERBED CHICKEN

Marshall Simon, Grand Rapids, Michigan

- 1 tablespoon olive *or* vegetable oil
- 1 medium onion, chopped
- 1 green *or* sweet red pepper, chopped
- 6 large fresh mushrooms, thinly sliced
- 1/3 cup chicken broth
- 2 tablespoons red wine vinegar
- 1 can (29 ounces) tomato sauce
- 2 garlic cloves, minced
- 1 teaspoon sugar
- 1/4 teaspoon salt
- 1/4 teaspoon pepper
- 1 pound boneless skinless chicken breasts, cut into chunks
- 2 tablespoons chopped fresh basil *or* 1 teaspoon dried basil
- 1 tablespoon chopped fresh sage *or* 1/2 teaspoon dried sage
- 1 pound dry linguini, cooked and drained
- 2 to 3 tablespoons grated Parmesan cheese
- 2 tablespoons chopped fresh parsley

In a skillet, heat oil over medium-high heat. Saute onion, pepper and mushrooms until tender. Add broth and vinegar; bring to a boil. Boil 2 minutes. Add tomato sauce, garlic, sugar, salt and pepper. Bring to a boil. Reduce heat; cover and simmer 25 minutes. Add chicken, basil and sage. Cook, uncovered, 15 minutes more or until chicken is done and sauce is slightly thickened. Serve chicken and sauce over pasta. Sprinkle with Parmesan cheese and parsley. **Yield:** 4 servings.

CHICKEN CACCIATORE

Barbara Roberts, Courtenay, British Columbia

- 1 broiler-fryer chicken (2-1/2 to 3 pounds), cut up
- 1/4 cup all-purpose flour
- 2 tablespoons olive oil
- 2 tablespoons butter *or* margarine

Salt and pepper to taste
- 1 large onion, chopped
- 2 celery ribs, sliced diagonally
- 1 large green pepper, cut into strips
- 1/2 pound fresh mushrooms, sliced
- 1 can (28 ounces) tomatoes, cut up and juice reserved
- 1 can (8 ounces) tomato sauce
- 1 can (6 ounces) tomato paste
- 1 cup dry red wine *or* water
- 1 teaspoon dried thyme
- 1 teaspoon dried rosemary
- 1 teaspoon dried oregano
- 1 teaspoon dried basil
- 3 garlic cloves, minced
- 1 tablespoon sugar

Cooked pasta
Grated Parmesan cheese

Dust chicken with flour. In a large skillet, heat the oil and butter on medium-high heat; brown chicken on all sides. Season with salt and pepper while cooking. Remove chicken to platter. Add fresh vegetables to skillet; cook and stir 5 minutes. Stir in tomatoes, sauce, paste and wine or water. Add herbs, garlic and sugar. Cover and simmer 30 minutes. Adjust seasonings if necessary and return chicken to skillet. Cover and simmer 1 hour or until chicken is tender. Serve over pasta and sprinkle with Parmesan cheese. **Yield:** 4-6 servings.

BARBECUING is a perfectly fun way to enjoy the outdoors, especially when the recipes are easy to make and delicious! Enjoy tangy Picante-Dijon Grilled Chicken with cool, refreshing Macaroni Salad with Basil Dressing. Rich, moist Fudgy Brownies are irresistible!

OUTDOOR EATING.
Clockwise from the bottom: **Picante-Dijon Grilled Chicken** (recipe on page 117), **Fudgy Brownies** (recipe on page 172) and **Macaroni Salad with Basil Dressing** (recipe on page 49).

GRILLING IDEAS

*Fun-filled outdoor gatherings with family and friends
begin with the main course picnic fixin's found here.*

PICANTE-DIJON GRILLED CHICKEN

Karen Page, St. Louis, Missouri

(PICTURED AT LEFT)

**8 chicken breast halves,
  skinned and boned
1-1/2 cups picante sauce
2 tablespoons Dijon mustard
1/4 cup packed brown sugar**

Pound chicken breasts to about 1/2-in. thickness; set aside. Combine picante sauce, mustard and sugar; mix well. Place chicken over medium-hot coals; brush generously with sauce. Grill about 6-8 minutes per side or until chicken is tender and no longer pink, brushing occasionally with remaining sauce. **Yield:** 8 servings.

GRILLED FLANK STEAK

Jenny Reece, Farwell, Minnesota

 This tasty dish uses less sugar, salt and fat. Recipe includes *Diabetic Exchanges.*

**1/4 cup soy sauce
2 tablespoons vinegar
1 green onion, sliced
1-1/2 teaspoons garlic powder
1-1/2 teaspoons ground ginger
3 tablespoons honey
3/4 cup vegetable oil
1 beef flank steak (about 1-1/2
  pounds)
1 pound fresh mushrooms,
  sliced
1 green pepper, cut into thin
  strips
1 yellow *or* sweet red pepper,
  cut into thin strips
3 carrots, cut into julienne strips**

In a glass baking dish, combine first seven ingredients. Set aside 1/4 cup. Place meat in remaining marinade; cover and refrigerate for 24 hours, turning once. Remove meat, discarding marinade. Grill meat over hot coals until cooked to your preference (about 15 minutes for medium). Meanwhile, in a skillet, saute vegetables in reserved marinade until tender. Slice meat at an angle into thin strips and serve with

vegetables. **Yield:** 5 servings. **Diabetic Exchanges:** One serving equals 3 lean meat, 2 vegetable, 1 fat; also, 265 calories, 173 mg sodium, 65 mg cholesterol, 11 gm carbohydrate, 28 gm protein, 12 gm fat.

GRILLED BEEF KABOBS

Dolores Lueken, Ferdinand, Indiana

(PICTURED ON PAGE 99)

**1 pound boneless sirloin steak,
  cut into 1-1/2-inch cubes
1 bottle (8 ounces) French *or*
  Russian salad dressing
2 tablespoons Worcestershire
  sauce
2 tablespoons lemon juice
1/8 teaspoon pepper
1/8 teaspoon garlic powder
8 to 10 bacon strips, cut in half
1 sweet red pepper, cut into
  chunks
1 green pepper, cut into chunks
2 small zucchini, cut into chunks
8 medium fresh mushrooms
1 large onion, quartered,
  optional**

Place beef in a shallow glass pan. Combine salad dressing, Worcestershire sauce, lemon juice, pepper and garlic powder. Reserve 1/3 cup marinade; set aside. Pour remaining marinade over beef. Cover and refrigerate 8-24 hours. Drain; wrap bacon around beef cubes. On metal or soaked wooden skewers, alternately thread beef and vegetables. Grill over hot coals for 10-15 minutes or until the desired doneness is reached. Baste frequently with reserved marinade. **Yield:** 4 servings.

MARINATED FLANK STEAK WITH PEPPERS

Sandra Wright, Embudo, New Mexico

**1 large garlic clove, minced
Juice and grated peel of 1 lime
2 teaspoons oregano
1-1/2 tablespoons olive oil *or*
  vegetable oil
1 teaspoon salt, optional**

**Freshly ground black pepper
1 beef flank steak (about 1-1/2
  pounds)
1 large green pepper
1 large sweet red pepper
1 large yellow pepper**

In a small bowl, combine first six ingredients, whisking to blend. Place steak in a heavy resealable plastic bag. Pour marinade over steak; turn to coat. Seal bag and refrigerate overnight. Drain steak, discarding marinade. Grill steak and char peppers over hot coals. Cook steak about 10 minutes per side for medium doneness. Turn peppers until skins are charred and blackened; remove from grill. Place peppers in paper sack, close and allow to steam for about 10 minutes. Remove skins; slice into strips and keep warm. Place steak on warm platter; let stand a few minutes before carving. Serve with peppers. **Yield:** 4 servings.

> **MARINADE REMINDER.** Always discard sauces used for marinating and basting uncooked meat. If you want to serve some sauce with dinner, set aside the desired amount before using it on raw meat.

BEEF AND BACON TWIRLS

Patricia Rutherford, Winchester, Illinois

**1-1/2 pounds round steak, trimmed
  of fat
Meat tenderizer
1/2 pound sliced bacon
1/4 to 1/2 teaspoon garlic powder
Salt and fresh-ground pepper to taste
2 tablespoons minced fresh
  parsley**

Pound steak to 1/2-in. thickness or less. Use meat tenderizer according to package directions. Cook bacon until nearly done *but not crisp.* Sprinkle the steak with garlic, salt, pepper and parsley. Place bacon strips lengthwise on steak. Roll up jelly-roll style, starting with narrow end. Skewer with wooden picks at 1-in. intervals. Cut in 1-in. slices with serrated knife. Grill over hot coals, 8-10 minutes, turning once. Remove wooden picks. **Yield:** 6 servings.

BACON-STUFFED BURGERS

Sandy McKenzie, Braham, Minnesota

(PICTURED ON PAGE 114)

- 4 bacon strips
- 1/4 cup chopped onion
- 1 can (4 ounces) mushroom pieces, drained and finely chopped
- 1 pound lean ground beef
- 1 pound bulk pork sausage
- 1/4 cup grated Parmesan cheese
- 1/2 teaspoon pepper
- 1/4 teaspoon garlic powder
- 2 tablespoons steak sauce
- 8 hamburger buns, split and toasted

Leaf lettuce, optional

Cook bacon until crisp. Remove bacon and discard all but 2 tablespoons drippings. Saute onion in drippings until tender. Crumble bacon; add with mushrooms to skillet and set aside. Meanwhile, combine beef, pork, cheese, pepper, garlic powder and steak sauce in a large bowl. Shape into 16 patties. Divide bacon mixture and place over eight of the patties. Place remaining patties on top and press edges tightly to seal. Grill over medium coals until *well-done* (pork sausage in burgers requires thorough cooking). Serve on buns with lettuce if desired. **Yield:** 8 servings.

SPIEDIS

Gertrude Skinner, Binghamton, New York

(PICTURED ON PAGE 136)

 This tasty dish uses less sugar, salt and fat. Recipe includes *Diabetic Exchanges*.

- 1 cup vegetable oil
- 2/3 cup cider vinegar
- 2 tablespoons Worcestershire sauce
- 1/2 medium onion, finely chopped
- 1/2 teaspoon salt
- 1/2 teaspoon sugar
- 1/2 teaspoon dried basil
- 1/2 teaspoon dried marjoram
- 1/2 teaspoon dried rosemary
- 2-1/2 pounds boneless lean pork, beef, lamb, venison, chicken *or* turkey, cut into 1-1/2- to 2-inch cubes

Italian rolls *or* hot dog buns

In a glass or plastic bowl, combine first nine ingredients. Add meat and toss to coat. Cover and refrigerate for 24 hours, stirring occasionally. Drain meat, discarding marinade. When ready to cook, thread meat on metal skewers and grill over hot coals until meat reaches desired doneness, about 10-15 minutes. Remove meat from skewers and serve on long Italian rolls or hot dog buns. **Yield:** 8 servings. **Diabetic Exchanges:** One serving of beef equals 3 lean meat, 1 fat; also, 205 calories, 104 mg sodium, 42 mg cholesterol, 1 gm carbohydrate, 22 gm protein, 12 gm fat.

Quick & Easy

MUSTARD GRILLED STEAKS

Sharon Kraeger, Plattsmouth, Nebraska

- 1/3 cup Dijon mustard
- 1 tablespoon chopped fresh parsley
- 2 tablespoons honey
- 1 tablespoon cider vinegar
- 1 tablespoon water
- 1/4 teaspoon hot pepper sauce
- 1/8 teaspoon coarsely ground pepper
- 2 beef top loin steaks (1 inch thick)
- 1 large onion, cut into 4 thick slices

Combine the first seven ingredients. Brush over both sides of the steaks and onion slices. Grill over hot coals, turning once, 15-20 minutes or until steaks have reached desired doneness and onion is tender. Brush occasionally with sauce during grilling. Serve onion slices alongside each steak. **Yield:** 2 servings.

SHRIMP KABOBS WITH VEGETABLE POCKETS

Mary Boyd, Mountainair, New Mexico

KABOBS:
- 8 bacon strips, cut into quarters
- 16 cherry tomatoes *or* Roma tomato chunks
- 32 medium fresh shrimp, shelled and cleaned (about 2 pounds)
- 2 cans (8 ounces *each*) button mushrooms, drained, reserving liquid

POCKETS:
- 8 sheets heavy-duty foil
- 1 sweet red pepper, sliced into thin strips
- 1 green pepper, sliced into thin strips
- 1 medium zucchini, peeled and cubed
- 1/2 cup chopped green onions
- 2 teaspoons salt
- 1 teaspoon pepper
- 4 teaspoons sesame seeds
- 4 teaspoons chopped fresh parsley
- 8 tablespoons butter *or* margarine

BASTING SAUCE:
- 1/4 cup vegetable oil
- 2 tablespoons reduced-sodium soy sauce
- 1 tablespoon lemon juice
- 1/2 teaspoon *each* pepper, thyme, basil and marjoram

Form kabobs by alternating bacon, tomatoes, shrimp and mushrooms on skewers. Cover and refrigerate. To prepare vegetable pockets, take a sheet of foil and fold in half; crimp sides tightly, leaving top of pocket open. Divide vegetables equally among pockets; sprinkle evenly with salt, pepper, sesame seeds and parsley. Dot each pocket with butter; add 2 tablespoons of reserved mushroom liquid to each. Fold tops over; crimp tightly. Prepare basting sauce by combining all ingredients. Grill pockets over medium-heat coals; cook for 10-15 minutes. After 3-5 minutes, put kabobs on grill; turn often, basting with sauce. Grill for 7-10 minutes or until shrimp are done. **Yield:** 8 servings.

PORK CHOPS WITH ROSEMARY/LEMON MARINADE

Peggy Gwillim, Strasbourg, Saskatchewan

- 2 garlic cloves, minced
- 1/2 cup lemon juice

Grated peel of 1 lemon
- 2 tablespoons olive oil
- 1 tablespoon chopped fresh rosemary *or* 1 teaspoon dried rosemary
- 1/8 teaspoon dried basil
- 1/8 teaspoon lemon pepper
- 4 pork chops, cut 1 inch thick

In a small bowl, whisk together first seven ingredients. Place pork chops in a heavy resealable plastic bag. Pour marinade over chops. Seal and refrigerate at least 2 hours or overnight, turning occasionally. Drain and discard marinade. Grill chops over medium-hot coals for about 6 minutes on each side or until no longer pink. **Yield:** 4 servings.

SIMPLE SOLUTION. Avoid the sticky situation of food getting stuck on your grill. Spray a *cold* grill rack—away from open flames—with nonstick cooking spray before beginning your barbecue.

Mother grew the sweetest melons ever, and I doubt anyone loved them as much as she did. She'd always pick a few early in the morning and put them in the spring to cool for later…but almost anytime was the right time to enjoy a fresh, sweet melon!

We sometimes ate melon in the morning, still moist with dew, and often carried melons to the field to refresh us in the midday sun. Occasionally, when Mother's patch reached its peak of perfection, she'd invite the neighbors for a "watermelon feast".

Treat After Work

But the best times of all were when we came in from the fields on a hot day to find several rows of juicy red slices, their seeds glistening like rows of black pearls, waiting in the shade of the front porch.

Mother's eyes would glow with pleasure as she came hurrying out of the door. "Now children, go inside and wash your hands, then come right on out here," she'd announce. "I've got the salt all ready, and you can put your rinds there in the tub."

We'd line up like so many crows in a row, down on our haunches with the juice running off our elbows. "Y'all gnaw those rinds right down to the pink," Mother would remind with a smile. "It'd be a real shame to waste anything as purely good as this!"

I don't think anything ever tasted quite as good as those thirst-quenching homegrown melons. When it seemed like none of us

Tom McCarthy/Unicorn Stock Photos

How Mama Loved Watermelon!

The sweetest memory for this reader is the pure pleasure her mother found "at the heart of the melon".

By Ruby Sentman, Tonawanda, New York

"FIRST ONE to the end of the row gets to open the melon!"

Whenever we heard that challenge from Mother, all five of us kids would return to our hoeing with vigor. The hot Virginia sun baked our backs as we leaned into our task, tools clinking against the stones in the loose earth.

"I'm out!" called my brother Marvin, throwing down his hoe and heading for the big, juicy watermelon cooling in the shade of an old oak. The rest of us weren't far behind, knowing that Marvin would soon have that melon smashed against a rock and the sweet, juicy heart in his hands. What a wonderful mid-morning treat we'd enjoy!

could eat another bite, Mother would sheepishly reach for that one last piece, explaining, "It seems a shame to let such a pleasure go to waste."

To an outsider, those hot summer days on our farm in southern Virginia might well have seemed uneventful and even harsh. We were poor, though I didn't realize it then. Now, when I look back on those days, my memory bathes them in a soft, shimmering light.

It was an era that had an entirely different measure of pleasure…a time when children had no more serious concerns than who would get to enjoy the heart of the melon.

HERE'S a cook-out classic you can serve family and friends
at your next grill-side gathering. To leave more time for visiting,
you can prepare the meaty kabobs ahead of time,
letting the marinade flavors blend overnight. Everyone will agree
this dish deliciously captures the taste of summer!

SCRUMPTIOUS SENSATION.
Steak and Vegetable Kabobs (recipe on page 121).

STEAK AND VEGETABLE KABOBS

Lorri Cleveland, Kingsville, Ohio

(PICTURED AT LEFT)

 This tasty dish uses less sugar, salt and fat. Recipe includes *Diabetic Exchanges*.

1/4 cup vegetable oil
1/4 cup lemon juice
1/4 cup soy sauce
1/4 cup packed brown sugar
2 garlic cloves, minced
3 whole cloves
Dash dried sweet basil
2-1/2 pounds sirloin steak, cut into 1-1/4-inch pieces
2 dozen cherry tomatoes
2 dozen fresh mushroom caps
1 large green *or* sweet red pepper, cut into 1-1/2-inch cubes
2 small zucchini, cut into 1-inch slices
1 medium onion, cut into wedges
Hot cooked rice

In a bowl, combine first seven ingredients for the marinade. Set aside. Assemble kabobs by threading meat and vegetables on metal skewers. Place in a large glass dish. Pour marinade over kabobs; cover and refrigerate 6 hours or overnight. Turn several times. To cook, grill kabobs over hot coals until the meat and vegetables have reached desired doneness. Remove from the skewers and serve with rice. **Yield:** 10 servings. **Diabetic Exchanges:** One serving equals 2 meat, 1-1/2 vegetable; also, 195 calories, 381 mg sodium, 49 mg cholesterol, 8 gm carbohydrate, 19 gm protein, 10 gm fat.

COLOSSAL CORNBURGER

Lesley Colgan, London, Ontario

(PICTURED ON PAGE 108)

1 egg, beaten
1 cup cooked whole kernel corn
1/2 cup coarsely crushed cheese crackers
1/4 cup sliced green onions
1/4 cup chopped fresh parsley
1 teaspoon Worcestershire sauce
2 pounds ground beef
1 teaspoon salt
1/2 teaspoon pepper
1/2 teaspoon ground sage

In a medium bowl, combine egg, corn, crackers, green onions, parsley and Worcestershire sauce; set aside. In a large bowl, combine ground beef and

seasonings. On sheets of waxed paper, pat half of the beef mixture at a time into an 8-1/2-in. circle. Spoon corn mixture onto one circle of meat to within 1 in. of the edge. Top with second circle of meat; remove top sheet of waxed paper and seal edges. Invert onto a well-greased wire grill basket; peel off waxed paper. Grill over medium coals, turning once, for 25-30 minutes or until burger reaches desired doneness. For oven method, place burger on a baking pan. Bake at 350° for 40-45 minutes or until burger reaches desired doneness. Cut into wedges to serve. **Yield:** 6 servings.

SWEET AND SOUR PORK KABOBS

Barbara Fossen, La Crescent, Minnesota

2 medium carrots, bias cut into 1-inch pieces
1 can (8 ounces) pineapple chunks, juice pack
1 tablespoon vegetable oil
1 garlic clove, minced
1/4 cup red wine vinegar
1 tablespoon soy sauce
1 teaspoon sugar
3/4 pound boneless pork, cut into 1-inch cubes
1 small green pepper, cut into 1-inch pieces
1 small sweet red pepper, cut into 1-inch pieces
Hot cooked rice

Cook carrots in boiling water for about 12 minutes; drain well. Drain pineapple and set aside, reserving 1/4 cup juice. Combine juice, oil, garlic, vinegar, soy sauce and sugar. Pour over pork; let stand for 30 minutes. On four skewers, alternate pork, carrots, green and red pepper and pineapple. Discard marinade. Grill over hot coals for about 12 minutes, turning once. Serve with rice. **Yield:** 4 servings.

KOREAN BEEF BARBECUE

Linda Miller, Buffalo, North Dakota

10 green onions with stems, minced, or 1/2 large white onion, chopped
3 garlic cloves, minced
1/4 cup reduced-sodium soy sauce
1/2 teaspoon salt, optional
1 large teaspoon Accent or MSG, optional
3 tablespoons toasted sesame seeds
1/2 teaspoon pepper

3 tablespoons sesame seed oil
3 tablespoons vegetable oil
2 tablespoons to 1/4 cup honey
2 tablespoons to 1/4 cup sugar
1 sirloin tip roast (4 pounds) *or* thick-cut round steak *or* sirloin steak, trimmed of fat

Combine first eleven ingredients in glass jar. Shake well. Cut meat into 1/8-in.-thick slices; pound to tenderize if desired. Place meat and marinade in a large resealable plastic bag. Seal; shake and turn to mix ingredients. Refrigerate overnight. Before grilling, drain excess moisture. Place a wire cooling rack over top of barbecue grill; lay meat strips on top of rack. Grill over medium coals for 5-8 minutes. Turn once. Serve hot or cold. **Yield:** 8-10 servings.

MILK KEEPS IT MOIST. To keep barbecued chicken tender and flavorful while grilling, first soak boneless skinless chicken breasts in evaporated milk overnight. Drain, discarding milk, and prepare as usual.

PHILLY BURGERS

Marjorie Carey, Belfry, Montana

1 pound ground beef
2 tablespoons Worcestershire sauce, *divided*
4 teaspoons Dijon mustard, *divided*
1 can (2.8 ounces) french-fried onions, *divided*
1 package (3 ounces) cream cheese, softened
1 jar (2-1/2 ounces) sliced mushrooms, drained
1 teaspoon parsley flakes
4 Kaiser rolls

In a large bowl, combine beef, 1 tablespoon Worcestershire sauce, 3 teaspoons mustard and half the onions. Form into four patties and grill until done. Meanwhile, in a small bowl, blend cream cheese, remaining Worcestershire sauce and mustard, mushrooms and parsley. Spread the cream cheese mixture on cooked patties; top with remaining onions. Grill 30 seconds more or until the onions are golden. Serve on Kaiser rolls. **Yield:** 4 servings.

THIS HOLIDAY, why not take a "taste tour" to Norway? Norwegian Meatballs and Sandbakkelse (Sand Tarts) are authentic treats that will truly tempt your clan. And ever-popular Cheese Potatoes and Merry Christmas Rice are always a welcome sight on a yuletide table!

KITCHEN TRADITIONS.
Clockwise from the bottom: **Sandbakkelse** (recipe on page 174), **Merry Christmas Rice** (recipe on page 123), **Norwegian Meatballs** (recipe on page 110) and **Cheese Potatoes** (recipe on page 123).

SIDE DISHES

Looking for mouth-watering ways to round out your meals?
Turn to these delectable vegetable, fruit, pasta and rice dishes.

CHEESE POTATOES

Karen Hoylo, Duluth, Minnesota

(PICTURED AT LEFT)

6 tablespoons butter *or*
  margarine
6 tablespoons all-purpose flour
3/4 teaspoon salt
1/4 teaspoon pepper
3 cups milk
12 ounces process American
  cheese, cubed
About 4 pounds potatoes, peeled,
  cooked and thinly sliced (8 cups)
Paprika

Melt butter in a saucepan; add flour, salt and pepper. Cook over low heat, stirring until mixture is smooth and bubbly. Add milk all at once; cook and stir over medium heat until thickened and bubbly. Cook and stir 1 minute more. Remove from the heat. Add cheese and stir until melted. Place potatoes in a large bowl; gently stir in cheese sauce. Transfer to a greased 2-1/2-qt. baking dish. Sprinkle with paprika. Bake, uncovered, at 350° for 30 minutes or until heated through. **Yield:** 6-8 servings.

Quick & Easy

PICNIC PEAS

Joyce Sander, Evansville, Indiana

1 tablespoon cooking oil
1 cup chopped green pepper
1 cup chopped onion
1 cup minced celery
1 tablespoon sugar
1 bay leaf
1 can (15 ounces) black-eyed
  peas, rinsed and drained
1 can (14-1/2 ounces) tomatoes,
  chopped, liquid reserved
1/2 teaspoon salt
1/4 teaspoon pepper
4 bacon slices, cooked and
  crumbled

In a skillet, heat oil over medium-high heat. Saute green pepper, onion and celery. Add sugar, bay leaf, peas, tomatoes, half the tomato liquid, salt and pepper. Reduce heat and simmer 15 minutes. Remove to a bowl and sprin-

kle with bacon. Serve hot or at room temperature. **Yield:** 6 servings.

 **Quick & Easy**

MERRY CHRISTMAS RICE

Karen Hoylo, Duluth, Minnesota

(PICTURED AT LEFT)

2 cups water, *divided*
1-1/3 cups sugar, *divided*
2 cups (1/2 pound) fresh *or*
  frozen cranberries
1-1/3 cups quick-cooking rice
1/4 teaspoon ground cinnamon
1/8 teaspoon salt
1 apple, peeled and sliced

In a saucepan, combine 1/2 cup water and 1 cup sugar; bring to a boil. Add the cranberries; return to boiling. Reduce heat; simmer for 10 minutes or until most of the berries pop, stirring occasionally. Add rice, remaining water, remaining sugar, cinnamon and salt. Bring to a boil. Reduce heat; cover and simmer for 10 minutes. Remove from the heat and stir in apple. Cover and let stand for 10 minutes. **Yield:** 6 servings.

 Quick & Easy

SKILLET VEGETABLE SIDE DISH

Ada Gendell, Claremont, New Hampshire

2 tablespoons olive oil
3 carrots, thinly sliced
1 large onion, chopped
1/2 medium head cabbage,
  chopped
1/2 medium green pepper, chopped
2 garlic cloves, minced
2 tablespoons Worcestershire
  sauce
1 tablespoon minced fresh
  parsley
1 teaspoon caraway seed
1 teaspoon dried Italian
  seasoning
1/2 teaspoon celery salt

In a large skillet, heat oil over medium-high heat. Cook and stir the carrots, onion, cabbage and green pepper for 5 minutes. Add remaining ingredients; cook and stir about 5 minutes longer or until the vegetables are cooked to desired doneness. **Yield:** 8 servings.

BARBECUE BEANS

Betty Follas, Morgan Hill, California

(PICTURED ON PAGE 29)

1/2 pound ground beef
1/2 large onion, chopped
1/4 medium green pepper,
  chopped
2 celery ribs, chopped
1/2 cup packed brown sugar
1/2 cup ketchup
1/2 teaspoon ground ginger
Dash ground cloves
2 cans (31 ounces *each*) pork
  and beans

In a large skillet, brown beef with onion, green pepper and celery until meat is browned and vegetables are tender. Drain fat. Stir in brown sugar, ketchup, ginger and cloves. Add beans and mix well. Spoon into a 2-1/2-qt. casserole. Bake, uncovered, at 350° for 1 to 1-1/2 hours or until beans are as thick as desired. **Yield:** 8-10 servings.

POTATO PANCAKES

Roseanna Budell, Dunnellon, Florida

✓ This tasty dish uses less sugar, salt and fat. Recipe includes *Diabetic Exchanges*.

3 cups finely shredded peeled
  potatoes, well drained
2 eggs, well beaten
1-1/2 tablespoons all-purpose flour
1/8 teaspoon baking powder
1/2 to 1 teaspoon salt
1/2 teaspoon grated onion
Applesauce *or* maple syrup,
  optional

In a mixing bowl, gently combine potatoes and eggs. Combine dry ingredients and onion; stir into potato mixture. Drop by tablespoonfuls onto a preheated greased skillet. Brown lightly on both sides. Serve with applesauce or syrup if desired. **Yield:** 12 (2-inch) pancakes. **Diabetic Exchanges:** One pancake (prepared without added salt) equals 1 starch; also, 77 calories, 21 mg sodium, 36 mg cholesterol, 15 gm carbohydrate, 3 gm protein, 1 gm fat.

POTATO PUFFS

June Mullins, Livonia, Missouri

(PICTURED AT RIGHT)

2 eggs, *separated*
2 cups mashed potatoes
2 tablespoons grated Parmesan cheese
1 tablespoon minced fresh parsley *or* chives
1 teaspoon dried minced onion
1/8 teaspoon garlic powder
2 to 3 tablespoons butter *or* margarine, melted

In a mixing bowl, beat egg yolks. Add potatoes, Parmesan cheese, parsley, onion and garlic powder; mix well. Beat egg whites until stiff; fold into the potato mixture. Brush eight muffin cups or small ramekins generously with melted butter. Divide potato mixture into cups. Brush remaining butter over potatoes. Bake at 375° for 30-35 minutes or until lightly browned. Serve immediately. **Yield:** 8 puffs.

CREAMY CARROT CASSEROLE

Laurie Heward, Fillmore, Utah

(PICTURED ON PAGE 45)

1-1/2 pounds carrots, peeled and sliced *or* 1 bag (20 ounces) frozen sliced carrots, thawed
1 cup mayonnaise
1 tablespoon grated onion
1 tablespoon prepared horseradish
1/4 cup shredded cheddar cheese
2 tablespoons buttered bread crumbs

In a saucepan, cook carrots just until crisp-tender; drain, reserving 1/4 cup cooking liquid. Place carrots in a 1-1/2-qt. baking dish. Combine mayonnaise, onion, horseradish and reserved cooking liquid; spread evenly over carrots. Sprinkle with cheese; top with bread crumbs. Bake, uncovered, at 350° for 30 minutes. **Yield:** 8-10 servings.

FRUITED RICE MIX

Lillian Justis, Belleplain, New Jersey

(PICTURED ON PAGE 142)

3 cups uncooked long grain rice
1 cup chopped dried apples
1/3 cup golden raisins

1/3 cup slivered almonds
1/4 cup chicken bouillon granules
3 tablespoons dried minced onion
4-1/2 teaspoons curry powder

Combine all ingredients and store in an airtight container. To prepare, combine 1 cup mix with 2 cups water and 2 tablespoons butter or margarine in a saucepan. Bring to a boil. Reduce heat; cover and simmer for 25-30 minutes or until water is absorbed. **Yield:** about 5 cups dry mix (each cup makes 4-6 servings).

WHITER RICE. A teaspoon of lemon juice added to each quart of water when cooking rice keeps the grains white and separated.

MAPLE BAKED BEANS

Cindy Huitema, Dunnville, Ontario

(PICTURED ON PAGE 113)

1 pound dry navy beans
4 quarts water, *divided*
6 bacon strips, cut up *or* 1 cup cubed cooked ham
1 medium onion, chopped
1 cup maple syrup *or* maple-flavored syrup
1/2 cup ketchup
1/4 cup barbecue sauce
5 teaspoons cider vinegar
1 teaspoon prepared mustard
1 teaspoon salt
1/2 teaspoon pepper

Sort and rinse beans; place in a 4-qt. Dutch oven. Cover with 2 qts. cold water. Bring to a boil; reduce heat and simmer for 2 minutes. Remove from the heat. Cover and let stand 1 hour. Drain and rinse beans. Return beans to Dutch oven; cover with remaining water. Bring to a boil; reduce heat and simmer for 30-40 minutes or until almost tender. Drain and reserve liquid. In a 2-1/2-qt. casserole or bean pot, combine beans with all remaining ingredients. Cover and bake at 300° for 2-1/2 hours or until tender. Stir occasionally; add reserved bean liquid if necessary. **Yield:** 10-12 servings.

TORTELLINI BAKE

Donald Roberts, Amherst, New Hampshire

1 package (10 ounces) refrigerated cheese tortellini

1 tablespoon olive oil
1 small zucchini, diced
1 yellow squash, diced
1 onion, diced
1 sweet red pepper, diced
1 teaspoon dried basil
1/2 teaspoon pepper
1/2 teaspoon salt
1 cup (4 ounces) shredded mozzarella cheese
1 cup light cream

Cook tortellini according to package directions. Meanwhile, heat oil in a skillet; cook zucchini, squash, onion, red pepper and spices until vegetables are crisp-tender. Drain tortellini and rinse in hot water; combine with vegetable mixture, mozzarella and cream in a 1-1/2-qt. baking dish. Bake, uncovered, at 375° for 20 minutes or until heated through. **Yield:** 6-8 servings.

CAULIFLOWER WITH ALMONDS

Patricia Baxter, Great Bend, Kansas

(PICTURED ON PAGE 166)

1 medium head cauliflower (about 1-1/2 pounds)
2 tablespoons butter *or* margarine
2 tablespoons all-purpose flour
1/4 teaspoon salt
1 cup milk
Shredded cheddar cheese
2 tablespoons sliced almonds, toasted
Paprika
Cooked green beans, optional

Trim leaves from cauliflower, leaving 1 in. of stem for support. Place in Dutch oven; add hot water that covers stem but does not touch head. Cover and steam until tender, about 12-15 minutes. Meanwhile, melt butter in a small saucepan; blend in flour and salt. Add milk. Cook and stir over medium heat until thickened and bubbly; cook and stir 1 minute longer. To serve, cut off stem and place cauliflower on a serving dish. Spoon the sauce over and sprinkle with cheese, almonds and paprika. Accompany with green beans if desired. **Yield:** 6-8 servings.

TIRED OF traditional uses for those Thanksgiving Day leftovers? Next time you have excess mashed potatoes, try preparing tasty Potato Puffs or Golden Potato Rolls—your family will be delighted! Turkey Dressing Pie turns extra meat and stuffing into a deliciously different dinner. And for a fantastic finale, prepare an easy yet elegant Pumpkin Trifle.

LIVELY LEFTOVERS.
Clockwise from the bottom: **Potato Puffs** (recipe on page 124), **Golden Potato Rolls** (recipe on page 161), **Pumpkin Trifle** (recipe on page 214) and **Turkey Dressing Pie** (recipe on page 69).

DILLY ASPARAGUS
Margot Foster, Hubbard, Texas

(PICTURED ON PAGE 16)

✓ This tasty dish uses less sugar, salt and fat. Recipe includes *Diabetic Exchanges*.

- 1 pound fresh asparagus, trimmed
- 1 jar (2 ounces) diced pimientos, drained
- 1/2 cup vinegar
- 1/4 cup olive oil
- 1 tablespoon sugar
- 1 tablespoon chopped fresh parsley
- 2 teaspoons dried minced onion
- 1 teaspoon dried dill weed
- 1/2 teaspoon salt
- 1/4 teaspoon coarse ground black pepper

Cook the asparagus in a small amount of water until crisp-tender. Drain. In a jar with a tight-fitting lid, combine all the remaining ingredients and shake well. Place asparagus in a shallow dish; pour marinade over asparagus. Cover and refrigerate 8 hours. To serve, remove asparagus and arrange on a platter; remove pimientos and onion from marinade with a slotted spoon and sprinkle over asparagus. **Yield:** 4 servings. **Diabetic Exchanges:** One serving equals 2-1/2 fat, 1 vegetable, 1/2 starch; also 173 calories, 299 mg sodium, 0 cholesterol, 11 gm carbohydrate, 3 gm protein, 14 gm fat.

EGGPLANT WITH TOMATO SAUCE
Theresa Grassi, St. Louis, Missouri

- 2 pounds eggplant, unpeeled
- 1 teaspoon salt
- 1 tablespoon olive oil
- 1 can (28 ounces) crushed tomatoes in puree
- 2 garlic cloves, minced
- 1 teaspoon dried basil
- 1 to 2 teaspoons sugar
- Salt and pepper to taste
- Olive oil *or* vegetable oil for frying
- 1/4 cup shredded Parmesan cheese

Cut eggplant into 1/2-in.-thick slices. Sprinkle with salt. Place in a deep dish; cover and let stand for 30 minutes. Rinse with cold water; drain and dry on paper towels. In a 2-qt. saucepan, heat olive oil over medium heat. Add tomatoes, garlic, basil and sugar; bring to a boil. Reduce heat and simmer, uncovered, about 45 minutes or until thickened, stirring occasionally. Season with salt and pepper. Keep warm while preparing eggplant. In a large skillet, heat about 1/4 cup oil; brown eggplant, a quarter at a time, adding more oil as needed. Place on a serving platter one row at a time. Cover with sauce and sprinkle with cheese. Serve warm. **Yield:** 8 servings.

MAKE-AHEAD CREAM CORN. In a large roaster, combine 8-10 cups corn cut from the cobs, 1 lb. butter or margarine and 1 pint of cream. Bake at 350° for 1 hour, stirring every 15 minutes. When cool, ladle into containers and freeze for a fast and flavorful addition to your meals.

    Quick & Easy

EASY BAKED CORN
Kim McLaughlin, New Concord, Ohio

- 1 egg, beaten
- 1 cup (8 ounces) sour cream
- 1 package (8-1/2 ounces) corn bread mix
- 1/2 teaspoon salt
- 1/4 teaspoon pepper
- 2 cans (16 ounces *each*) whole kernel corn, drained

In a mixing bowl, combine egg and sour cream; stir in corn bread mix, salt and pepper. Add corn; mix well. Pour into a greased 11-in. x 7-in. x 1-1/2-in. baking pan. Bake, uncovered, at 400° for 25-30 minutes or till golden. **Yield:** 8 servings.

CALICO RICE
Deborah Hill, Coffeyville, Kansas

- 1 medium green pepper, diced
- 1 medium yellow pepper, diced
- 1 medium sweet red pepper, diced
- 1 medium onion, diced
- 2 tablespoons butter *or* margarine
- 1-1/2 cups uncooked long grain rice
- 1 envelope dry onion soup mix
- 2 tablespoons picante sauce *or* salsa
- 1 tablespoon ground cumin
- 4 garlic cloves, minced
- 1/2 teaspoon salt
- 3 cups water
- Sour cream, optional

In a skillet or saucepan, saute peppers and onion in butter for 3 minutes. Stir in the rice, soup mix, picante or salsa, cumin, garlic, salt and water. Bring to a boil. Reduce heat; cover and simmer for 20-25 minutes or until rice is tender. Garnish with sour cream if desired. **Yield:** 6-8 servings.

POTATO/SPINACH CASSEROLE
Winifred Winch, Wetmore, Michigan

- 6 to 8 large potatoes, peeled, cooked and mashed
- 1 cup (8 ounces) sour cream
- 2 teaspoons salt
- 1/4 teaspoon pepper
- 2 tablespoons chopped chives *or* green onion tops
- 1/4 cup butter *or* margarine
- 1 package (10 ounces) frozen chopped spinach, thawed and well drained
- 1 cup (4 ounces) shredded cheddar cheese

In a large bowl, combine all ingredients except cheese. Spoon into a greased 2-qt. casserole. Bake, uncovered, at 400° for 15 minutes. Top with cheese and bake 5 minutes longer. **Yield:** 6-8 servings.

COUNTRY POTATO PANCAKES
Lydia Robotewsky, Franklin, Wisconsin

(PICTURED ON PAGE 226)

- 3 large potatoes (about 2 pounds), peeled
- 2 eggs, slightly beaten
- 1 tablespoon grated onion
- 2 tablespoons all-purpose flour
- 1 teaspoon salt
- 1/2 teaspoon baking powder
- Vegetable oil

Finely grate potatoes. Drain any liquid. Add eggs, onion, flour, salt and baking powder. In a frying pan, add oil to the depth of 1/8 in.; heat over medium-high heat (375°). Drop batter by heaping tablespoonfuls in hot oil. Flatten to form patties. Fry until golden brown then turn and cook other side. Serve immediately. **Yield:** about 24 pancakes.

HEAVENLY ONION CASSEROLE
Maryln Rose, Naples, Florida

- 2 tablespoons butter *or* margarine
- 3 medium sweet Spanish onions, sliced
- 8 ounces fresh mushrooms, sliced
- 1 cup (4 ounces) shredded Swiss cheese
- 1 can (10-3/4 ounces) condensed cream of mushroom soup, undiluted

1 can (5 ounces) evaporated
milk
2 teaspoons soy sauce
6 to 8 slices French bread
(1/2 inch thick)
6 to 8 thin slices Swiss
cheese (about 4 ounces)

In a large skillet, melt butter over medium-high heat. Saute onions and mushrooms until tender. Place in a 12-in. x 7-1/2-in. x 2-in. baking dish or 2-qt. casserole. Sprinkle shredded cheese on top. Combine soup, milk and soy sauce; pour over cheese. Top with bread slices and cheese slices. Cover and refrigerate 4 hours or overnight. Bake, loosely covered, at 375° for 30 minutes. Uncover and bake 15-20 minutes longer or until heated through. Let stand 5 minutes before serving. **Yield:** 6-8 servings.

CELERY EN CASSEROLE
Mary Lou Sipherd, Bishop, California
(PICTURED ON PAGE 66)

4-1/2 cups diagonally sliced celery
1 can (5 ounces) water
chestnuts, drained and sliced
1/4 cup diced pimientos
1/4 cup slivered almonds
1 can (10-3/4 ounces)
condensed cream of chicken
soup, undiluted
TOPPING:
1/2 cup dry bread crumbs
4 teaspoons melted butter
or margarine
2 tablespoons sesame seed
2 tablespoons grated Parmesan
cheese

Cook celery in enough water to cover for 5 minutes or until crisp-tender; drain. Add water chestnuts, pimientos, almonds and soup. Pour into a 1-1/2-qt. greased baking dish. Combine topping ingredients; sprinkle over casserole. Bake at 350° for 25 minutes or until crumbs are golden brown. **Yield:** 8 servings.

GRANDMA'S
POULTRY DRESSING
Norma Howland, Joliet, Illinois

1 pound bulk pork sausage
2 eggs, lightly beaten
1 cup milk, scalded
7 cups coarse dry bread crumbs
2 tablespoons diced onion
1 cup diced celery
2 to 3 tablespoons minced
fresh parsley
1/2 teaspoon salt or salt to taste

In a skillet, brown sausage. Drain and discard the drippings. In a large mixing bowl, combine sausage and remaining ingredients; mix well. Place in a greased 2-qt. casserole. Cover and bake at 350° for 40 minutes or until lightly browned. **Yield:** 6 cups (makes enough to stuff a medium-size turkey).

COMPANY
VEGETABLE CASSEROLE
Leora Clark, Lincoln, Nebraska
(PICTURED ON PAGE 109)

1 can (15 ounces) cut green
beans, drained or 2 cups
frozen cut green beans, thawed
1 can (15 ounces) whole kernel
corn, drained or 2 cups
cooked fresh or frozen
whole kernel corn
1 can (10-3/4 ounces)
condensed cream of celery
soup, undiluted
1/2 cup sour cream
1/2 cup shredded cheddar cheese
1/2 cup chopped onion
1/4 cup butter or margarine,
melted
3/4 cup saltine crumbs
1/4 cup sliced almonds, toasted

In a bowl, combine beans, corn, soup, sour cream, cheese and onion. Pour into an ungreased 2-qt. baking dish. Combine butter, crumbs and almonds; sprinkle over vegetables. Bake, uncovered, at 350° for 35-40 minutes or until bubbly. **Yield:** 6-8 servings.

APRICOT-GLAZED
SWEET POTATOES
Joan Huggins, Waynesboro, Mississippi
(PICTURED ON PAGE 200)

3 pounds sweet potatoes,
cooked, peeled and cut up
1 cup packed brown sugar
5 teaspoons cornstarch
1/4 teaspoon salt
1/8 teaspoon ground cinnamon
1 cup apricot nectar
1/2 cup hot water
2 teaspoons grated orange peel
2 teaspoons butter or
margarine
1/2 cup chopped pecans

Place sweet potatoes in a 13-in. x 9-in. x 2-in. baking dish; set aside. In a saucepan, combine sugar, cornstarch, salt and cinnamon; stir in apricot nectar, water and orange peel. Bring to a boil, stirring constantly. Cook and stir 2 minutes more. Remove from heat, stir in butter and pecans. Pour over sweet potatoes. Bake, uncovered, at 350° for 20-25 minutes or until heated through. **Yield:** 8-10 servings.

SCALLOPED CABBAGE
Freda Willoughby, Medical Lake, Washington

1/2 medium head cabbage,
chopped (about 4 cups)
3 tablespoons cooking oil
3 tablespoons all-purpose flour
1/2 teaspoon salt
Dash pepper
1 cup milk
1 cup (4 ounces) shredded
cheddar cheese
3/4 cup bread crumbs
2 tablespoons butter or
margarine, melted

Place cabbage in a greased 2-qt. casserole; set aside. In a saucepan, heat oil over medium heat. Stir in flour, salt and pepper; cook until bubbly. Gradually stir in milk; cook and stir until thickened. Fold in cheese. Pour over cabbage. Combine bread crumbs and butter; sprinkle on top. Bake, uncovered, at 350° for 20-30 minutes or until bubbly. Serve immediately. **Yield:** 4-6 servings.

HOPPING JOHN
Anne Creech, Kinston, North Carolina

1/2 pound bacon, cut into 1-inch
pieces
1/2 cup chopped green or sweet
red pepper
2 celery ribs, chopped
6 green onions, sliced
1 cup uncooked long grain rice
2 cups water
Salt and pepper to taste
1 teaspoon ground red pepper
1/2 teaspoon dried basil
1/4 teaspoon dried thyme
1/4 teaspoon dried oregano
1 bay leaf
1 can (15 ounces) black-eyed
peas, drained

In a skillet, cook bacon until crisp. Remove bacon, reserving 2 tablespoons of the drippings. Saute pepper, celery and onions in drippings until almost tender. Add rice, water and seasonings. Cover and simmer 10 minutes. Add peas and bacon; cook 10 minutes. Remove bay leaf. **Yield:** 4-6 servings.

CAPTURE the wonderful foods of the South with classics like Corn Bread Dressing with Oysters and Sweet Potato Bake. And for other perfect additions to any meal, you'll reach for the sweet, nutty Cranberry Salad and light Miracle Rolls recipes often.

SOUTHERN SIDES.
Clockwise from lower left: **Cranberry Salad** (recipe on page 46), **Corn Bread Dressing with Oysters** (recipe on page 129), **Miracle Rolls** (recipe on page 167) and **Sweet Potato Bake** (recipe on page 129).

CORN BREAD DRESSING WITH OYSTERS

Nell Bass, Macon, Georgia

(PICTURED AT LEFT)

8 to 10 cups coarsely crumbled corn bread
2 slices white bread, toasted and torn into small pieces
2 hard-cooked eggs, chopped
2 cups chopped celery
1 cup chopped onion
1 pint shucked oysters, drained and chopped *or* 2 cans (8 ounces *each*) whole oysters, drained and chopped
2 eggs, beaten
1 teaspoon poultry seasoning
5 to 6 cups turkey *or* chicken broth

Combine the first eight ingredients in a large bowl. Stir in enough broth until the mixture is very wet. Pour into a greased 13-in. x 9-in. x 2-in. baking dish or shallow 3-qt. baking dish. Bake, uncovered, at 400° for 45 minutes or until lightly browned. **Yield:** 12-15 servings.

SWEET POTATO BAKE

Nell Bass, Macon, Georgia

(PICTURED AT LEFT)

2 to 2-1/2 pounds sweet potatoes
1/4 cup butter *or* margarine, melted
1/4 to 1/2 cup sugar
1/4 cup raisins
1/3 cup chopped nuts
1/3 cup miniature marshmallows

Place sweet potatoes and enough water to cover in a large saucepan or Dutch oven. Cover and cook over medium-low heat for 25-35 minutes or just until tender. Drain; cool slightly and peel. In a large bowl, mash potatoes. Stir in butter, sugar and raisins. Place in a 2-qt. baking dish; sprinkle with nuts and marshmallows. Bake, uncovered, at 350° for 30 minutes or until heated through and marshmallows begin to brown. **Yield:** 8-10 servings.

Quick & Easy

SWEET CORN AND TOMATO SAUTE

Kim L'Hote, Neillsville, Wisconsin

1/4 cup butter *or* margarine
2 cups cooked whole kernel corn
1/4 cup chopped onion
1/4 cup chopped green pepper
2 tablespoons brown sugar

1/2 teaspoon salt
1 large tomato, diced

In a saucepan, melt butter. Add corn, onion, green pepper, brown sugar and salt. Cover and simmer 10 minutes. Stir in the tomato; simmer 5 minutes longer. **Yield:** 4 servings.

CAJUN CABBAGE

Florence Davis, Amesbury, Massachusetts

1 pound ground beef
2 small onions, chopped
1 green pepper, chopped
6 cups chopped cabbage
1-1/4 cups uncooked long grain rice
1 can (14-1/2 ounces) stewed tomatoes
1 can (8 ounces) tomato sauce
1 cup water
1 teaspoon sugar
1 teaspoon Cajun seasoning
1 teaspoon salt
1/2 teaspoon pepper

In a large Dutch oven, brown ground beef. Add onions and green pepper; cook until the onions are transparent. Add the cabbage, rice, tomatoes, tomato sauce, water, sugar and seasonings. Cover and bake at 375° for 50-60 minutes or until the cabbage is tender. **Yield:** 10-12 servings.

HARVARD BEETS

Stella Quade, Carthage, Missouri

3 cups sliced raw beets *or* 2 cans (16 ounces *each*) sliced beets
1/2 cup sugar
1 tablespoon all-purpose flour
1/2 cup white vinegar
1/2 teaspoon salt
2 tablespoons butter *or* margarine

Place raw beets and enough water to cover in a saucepan. Cook until tender, about 15-20 minutes. Drain, reserving 1/4 cup liquid. (If using canned beets, drain and reserve 1/4 cup juice.) In another saucepan, combine sugar, flour, vinegar and reserved beet juice. Cook over low heat until thickened. Stir in beets, salt and butter. Simmer for 10 minutes. **Yield:** 6-8 servings.

TWICE-BAKED POTATOES

Debbie Jones, California, Maryland

6 large baking potatoes
1/2 cup butter *or* margarine, softened
3/4 to 1 cup milk *or* cream
3 tablespoons crumbled cooked bacon

3 tablespoons minced onion
1 tablespoon snipped chives
1/2 teaspoon salt
Dash pepper
1-1/2 cups (6 ounces) shredded cheddar cheese, *divided*
Paprika

Bake potatoes at 400° for 60 minutes or until soft. Cut a lengthwise slice from the top of the potatoes. Scoop out the pulp and place in a bowl. Mash potatoes and butter. Blend in milk or cream, bacon, onion, chives, salt, pepper and 1 cup of cheese. Refill potato shells. Top with remaining cheese and sprinkle with paprika. Bake at 375° for 25-30 minutes or until heated through. **Yield:** 6 servings.

APPLES, BERRIES AND YAMS

Dixy Moore, Avalon, California

2 tablespoons butter *or* margarine
3 apples, peeled and cut into chunks
1 can (23 ounces) yams, drained
1/2 teaspoon ground nutmeg
1 can (16 ounces) whole-berry cranberry sauce
1/2 cup orange marmalade

In a skillet, melt butter over medium heat. Saute apples until crisp-tender. Place apples and yams in a greased 3-qt. casserole. Sprinkle with the nutmeg. Combine cranberry sauce and marmalade. Spoon over yams. Bake at 350° for 30 minutes. **Yield:** 8-10 servings.

HUSH PUPPIES

Karyl Goodhart, Geraldine, Montana

(PICTURED ON PAGE 109)

2 cups yellow cornmeal
1/2 cup all-purpose flour
2 tablespoons sugar
2 teaspoons baking powder
1 teaspoon salt
1/2 teaspoon baking soda
1 egg, beaten
3/4 cup milk
3/4 cup cream-style corn
Cooking oil for frying
Confectioners' sugar, optional

In a bowl, combine cornmeal, flour, sugar, baking powder, salt and baking soda. Add egg, milk and corn; stir just until mixed. In a deep-fat fryer, heat oil to 375°. Drop batter by teaspoonfuls into oil. Fry until golden brown. Allow to cool slightly and roll in confectioners' sugar if desired. Serve immediately. **Yield:** 12-15 servings.

MISSION BAKED BEANS

Mrs. Charles Lewis, Yucaipa, California

(PICTURED ON PAGE 114)

    8 bacon strips, cooked and
       crumbled
    1 can (28 ounces) pork and
       beans
    1 can (15-1/2 ounces) chili
       beans, undrained
  3/4 cup finely chopped onion
  1/2 cup packed dark brown sugar
    1 can (8 ounces) enchilada
       sauce
    1 tablespoon all-purpose flour
    2 teaspoons chili powder
    1 teaspoon ground cumin
  1/8 teaspoon garlic powder
    1 cup (4 ounces) shredded
       Monterey Jack cheese

Combine all ingredients except cheese; mix gently. Place in a greased 2-qt. casserole. Bake, uncovered, at 475° for 15 minutes. Reduce heat to 375°; bake for 30 minutes, stirring occasionally. Sprinkle with cheese; bake 15 minutes longer. **Yield:** 8-10 servings.

GOLDEN PINEAPPLE CASSEROLE

Beth Koehler, Mansfield, Pennsylvania

(PICTURED BELOW)

    2 cans (20 ounces *each*)
      crushed pineapple
  1/2 cup sugar
    2 tablespoons all-purpose
      flour
    3 eggs, beaten
    4 slices bread (crusts
      removed), buttered and
      cubed

SWEET SIDE DISH. Pineapple Casserole brings out flavor of ham and poultry dishes.

Drain pineapple, reserving 1 cup juice. In a mixing bowl, combine pineapple and juice with sugar, flour and eggs; mix well. Spoon into a 2-qt. baking dish; top with bread cubes. Bake at 350°, uncovered, for 45-50 minutes or until set and browned. **Yield:** 8 servings.

SWEET POTATOES FOR TWO

Flo Burtnett, Gage, Oklahoma

  2 to 3 sweet potatoes, cooked
     and peeled
  1/2 cup packed brown sugar
    2 tablespoons butter *or*
      margarine
    2 tablespoons water
  1/4 teaspoon salt
Dash ground nutmeg *or* ground mace

Slice sweet potatoes into an 8-in. pie plate; set aside. In a saucepan, combine brown sugar, butter, water and salt; bring to a boil. Pour hot syrup over potatoes. Bake, uncovered, at 350° for 30 minutes, basting occasionally, or until syrup thickens and potatoes are glazed. Sprinkle with nutmeg or mace. **Yield:** 2 servings.

FRESH VEGETABLE CASSEROLE

Audrey Thibodeau, Lancaster, New Hampshire

(PICTURED ON FRONT COVER AND PAGE 75)

    2 cups broccoli florets
1-1/2 cups sliced carrots
    1 cup mayonnaise
    1 cup (4 ounces) shredded
      cheddar cheese
  3 to 4 drops hot pepper sauce
  1/4 teaspoon pepper
  1/4 cup cooking sherry *or* dry
      white wine, optional
1-1/2 cups sliced zucchini
    1 cup sliced celery
  1/2 cup diced green pepper
  1/2 cup diced onion
    1 tablespoon minced fresh
      parsley
    1 tablespoon minced fresh basil
    3 tablespoons butter *or*
      margarine
  12 saltines, crushed
  1/3 cup grated Parmesan cheese

Steam broccoli and carrots until crisp-tender; drain and set aside. In a large bowl, mix together mayonnaise, cheddar cheese, hot pepper sauce, pepper and sherry if desired. Add broccoli, carrots, remaining vegetables, parsley and basil; stir gently to mix. Spoon into a greased 2-qt. baking dish. Melt butter in a small saucepan. Add crushed saltines; stir until browned. Remove from the heat and stir in Parmesan cheese; sprinkle over vegetables. Bake, uncovered, at 350° for 30-40 minutes. **Yield:** 6-8 servings.

DAD'S ONION RINGS

Connie Thurman, Monroe City, Missouri

    4 medium onions, sliced
      1/4 inch thick
Cold water
    1 egg, beaten
  2/3 cup milk
  3/4 cup all-purpose flour
    1 teaspoon sugar
  1/2 teaspoon salt
    1 tablespoon shortening,
      melted and cooled
Oil *or* shortening for deep-fat frying

Separate onion slices into rings; soak in water 30 minutes. Meanwhile, in a small bowl, beat egg, milk, flour, sugar, salt and shortening. Drain onions and pat dry. With a fork, dip rings into batter. Preheat oil to 375°. Fry in 1 in. of oil or shortening, a few rings at a time, for 2-3 minutes or until golden brown. Drain on paper towels. Keep warm in a 300° oven while frying remaining rings. **Yield:** 4-6 servings.

CRUNCHY POTATO BALLS

Nancy Eash, Gambier, Ohio

    2 cups very stiff mashed
      potatoes
    2 cups finely chopped fully
      cooked ham
    1 cup (4 ounces) shredded
      cheddar *or* Swiss cheese
  1/3 cup mayonnaise
    1 egg, beaten
    1 teaspoon prepared mustard
  1/4 teaspoon pepper
  2 to 4 tablespoons all-purpose
      flour
1-3/4 cups crushed cornflakes

In a bowl, combine the potatoes, ham, cheese, mayonnaise, egg, mustard and pepper; mix well. Add enough of the flour to make a stiff mixture. Chill. Shape into 1-in. balls; roll in cornflakes. Place on a greased baking sheet. Bake at 350° for 25 to 30 minutes. Serve hot. **Yield:** about 6 dozen.

SQUASH BAKE

Thelma Mefford, Wetumka, Oklahoma

8 cups sliced yellow squash
  (about 2 pounds)
1/2 cup chopped onion
3/4 cup shredded carrots
1/4 cup butter *or* margarine
1 can (10-3/4 ounces)
  condensed cream of
  chicken soup, undiluted
1/2 cup sour cream
2 cups herb-seasoned stuffing
  croutons, *divided*

Cook squash in lightly salted boiling water for 3 to 4 minutes or until crisp-tender; drain well. In a skillet, saute onion and carrots in butter until tender. Combine onion and carrots with soup, sour cream and 1-1/2 cups croutons. Add squash and mix lightly. Spoon into a lightly greased 12-in. x 8-in. x 2-in. baking dish or a 2-qt. casserole. Sprinkle with the remaining croutons. Bake, uncovered, at 350° for 25 minutes or until heated through. **Yield:** 8-10 servings.

Quick & Easy

CORN BALLS

Sharon Knicely, Harrisonburg, Virginia

(PICTURED ON PAGE 82)

1/2 cup chopped onion
1 cup chopped celery
1/2 cup butter *or* margarine
3-1/2 cups herb-seasoned stuffing
  croutons
3 cups cooked whole kernel
  corn
3 eggs, beaten
1/2 cup water
1/2 teaspoon salt
1/4 teaspoon pepper

In a saucepan, cook onion and celery in butter until tender; set aside to cool. In a bowl, combine croutons, corn, eggs, water, salt, pepper and onion mixture; mix well. Shape into eight to 10 balls. Place in an ungreased shallow baking dish. Bake, uncovered, at 375° for 25-30 minutes. **Yield:** 8-10 servings.

COPPER PENNIES

Agnes Circello, Belle Rose, Louisiana

2 pounds carrots, peeled and
  sliced into 1/4-inch coins
1/2 cup vegetable oil
1 cup sugar
1 large onion, diced
1 large green pepper, diced

1 can (5-1/2 ounces) tomato
  juice
3/4 cup red wine vinegar
1 teaspoon prepared mustard
1 teaspoon Worcestershire
  sauce
1 teaspoon salt
1/4 teaspoon pepper

Cook the carrots just until crisp-tender; drain. Combine all remaining ingredients in a large bowl; mix well. Add carrots and stir until well mixed. Cover and refrigerate at least 3-4 hours. Serve cold as a salad, or warm it and use as a side dish. Store in the refrigerator for up to 2 weeks. **Yield:** 8 cups.

BROCCOLI/CHEESE TWICE-BAKED POTATOES

Joyce Brown, Genesee, Idaho

6 medium baking potatoes
1/2 cup sour cream
3 tablespoons butter *or*
  margarine
1/2 teaspoon salt
1/4 teaspoon pepper
2 green onions, thinly sliced
1-1/2 cups cooked chopped broccoli
1 cup (4 ounces) shredded
  cheddar cheese, *divided*
Paprika

Bake potatoes at 425° for 45-60 minutes or until soft. Cut a lengthwise slice from the top of the potatoes. Scoop out pulp and place in bowl. Mash potatoes; add sour cream, butter, salt, pepper, onions, broccoli and 3/4 cup cheese. Re-fill potato shells; top with remaining cheese and sprinkle with paprika. Bake at 425° for 20-25 minutes or until heated through. **Yield:** 6 servings.

WINTER SQUASH CHEESE CASSEROLE

Alberta Goodrich, Portland, Connecticut

2 pounds winter squash,
  peeled, seeded and cut into
  1-inch cubes
1 tablespoon butter *or*
  margarine
1/2 cup chopped onion
2 cups (8 ounces) shredded
  cheddar cheese, *divided*
2 eggs
3/4 cup milk
Salt and pepper to taste
1/2 cup soft bread crumbs
Ground nutmeg to taste

In a saucepan, cook squash in enough water to cover until tender. Drain. In a skillet, melt butter over medium-high heat. Saute onion until tender. Place squash in a greased 2-qt. casserole. Top with the onion and half the cheese. Beat the eggs, milk, salt and pepper. Pour over the squash. Top with remaining cheese; sprinkle with bread crumbs and nutmeg. Bake at 325° for 30 minutes or until set and lightly browned. Serve immediately. **Yield:** 8 servings.

Quick & Easy

CAULIFLOWER AU GRATIN

Jacki Ricci, Ely, Nevada

6 tablespoons butter *or*
  margarine
1 to 2 garlic cloves, minced
4 ounces cooked ham, chopped
1 head cauliflower, broken into
  florets
2 tablespoons all-purpose flour
1-1/2 cups whipping cream
1/4 teaspoon salt
Pepper to taste
Pinch cayenne pepper
1-1/2 cups (4 to 6 ounces)
  shredded Swiss cheese
2 to 3 tablespoons chopped
  fresh parsley

Melt butter in a large skillet. Saute garlic and ham for 2 minutes. Add cauliflower and cook just until crisp-tender. Combine flour and cream; stir into skillet and blend well. Add salt, pepper and cayenne pepper. Cook and stir until thickened and bubbly; cook and stir 1 minute more. Pour into a 2-qt. baking dish. Sprinkle with cheese. Place under a preheated broiler until lightly browned, about 2-4 minutes. Sprinkle with parsley. Serve immediately. **Yield:** 6-8 servings.

Quick & Easy

RATATOUILLE

Donna Rushing, Belk, Alabama

3 tablespoons olive *or*
  vegetable oil
3 medium zucchini, cut into
  1/2-inch slices
2 large tomatoes, peeled and
  chopped
1 large onion, chopped
1 green pepper, cut into strips
1/4 cup minced fresh parsley
1 tablespoon minced fresh
  basil *or* 1 teaspoon dried
  basil
1/2 teaspoon salt
1/4 teaspoon pepper

In a large Dutch oven, heat oil over medium-high heat. Saute all ingredients for 5 minutes. Cover and simmer, stirring occasionally, 15 minutes or until vegetables are tender. **Yield:** 6-8 servings.

HEARTY, healthful squash isn't just for autumn anymore. It's popping up in plenty of savory recipes the whole family can enjoy year-round...from crispy fritters and a palate-pleasing pie to a simple-to-make casserole and a tasty stir-fry.

GOOD AND PLENTY.
Clockwise from lower left: **Zucchini/Herb Pate** (recipe on page 10), **Confetti Zucchini Relish** (recipe on page 147), **Spaghetti Squash Casserole** (recipe on page 134), **Zucchini Fritters** (recipe on page 134), **Squash Custard Pie** (recipe on page 221), **Winter Squash Squares** (recipe on page 175), **Garden Harvest Chili** (recipe on page 25) and **Squash and Broccoli Stir-Fry** (recipe on page 134).

SPAGHETTI SQUASH CASSEROLE

Glenafa Vrchota, Mason City, Iowa

(PICTURED ON PAGE 132)

- 1 medium spaghetti squash (about 8 inches)
- 1 cup water
- 1 tablespoon butter *or* margarine
- 1 cup chopped onion
- 2 garlic cloves, minced
- 1/2 pound fresh mushrooms, sliced
- 1 teaspoon dried basil
- 1/2 teaspoon dried oregano
- 1/4 teaspoon dried thyme
- 1/2 teaspoon salt
- 1/4 teaspoon pepper
- 2 fresh tomatoes, diced
- 1 cup (8 ounces) ricotta *or* cottage cheese
- 1 cup (4 ounces) shredded mozzarella cheese
- 1/4 cup finely chopped parsley
- 1 cup dry bread crumbs
- 1/4 cup grated Parmesan cheese

Slice the squash in half lengthwise and scoop out the seeds. Place squash, cut side down, in a baking dish. Add water and cover tightly with foil. Bake at 375° for 20-30 minutes or until easily pierced with a fork. Meanwhile, melt butter in skillet. Add the onion, garlic, mushrooms, herbs and seasonings; saute until onion is transparent. Add the tomatoes; cook until most of the liquid has evaporated. Set aside. Scoop out the squash, separating strands with a fork. Combine squash, tomato mixture and all remaining ingredients except Parmesan cheese. Pour into a greased 2-qt. casserole. Sprinkle with Parmesan cheese. Bake, uncovered, at 375° for 40 minutes or until heated through and top is golden brown. **Yield:** 6 servings.

Quick & Easy

SQUASH AND BROCCOLI STIR-FRY

Erlene Cornelius, Spring City, Tennessee

(PICTURED ON PAGE 132)

✓ This tasty dish uses less sugar, salt and fat. Recipe includes *Diabetic Exchanges.*

- 1 tablespoon lemon juice
- 2 teaspoons honey
- 2 tablespoons cooking oil
- 1 pound butternut squash, peeled, seeded and cut into 1/4-inch slices
- 1 garlic clove, minced
- 1/4 teaspoon ground ginger
- 1 cup fresh broccoli florets

- 1/2 cup bias-sliced celery
- 1/2 cup thinly sliced onion
- 2 tablespoons sunflower seeds

Combine lemon juice and honey; set aside. In a wok or large skillet, heat oil on medium-high heat. Add squash, garlic and ginger. Stir-fry about 3 minutes. Add the broccoli, celery and onion; stir-fry 3-4 minutes or until crisp-tender. Remove from heat and quickly toss with the honey mixture. Sprinkle with sunflower seeds. Serve immediately. **Yield:** 6 servings. **Diabetic Exchanges:** One serving equals 2 vegetable, 1-1/2 fat; also, 113 calories, 20 mg sodium, 0 mg cholesterol, 13 gm carbohydrate, 2 gm protein, 7 gm fat.

ZUCCHINI FRITTERS

Mary Dixson, Catlin, Illinois

(PICTURED ON PAGE 133)

- Vegetable oil
- 1/2 cup milk
- 1 egg, lightly beaten
- 1 cup all-purpose flour
- 1-1/2 teaspoons baking powder
- 1/2 of 1-ounce package ranch-style dip mix
- 2 cups (8 ounces) shredded zucchini

Fill a deep-fat fryer or skillet with oil to a 2-in. depth. Heat to 375°. Meanwhile, combine milk and egg in a mixing bowl. Stir together dry ingredients and add to egg mixture; blend well. Fold in zucchini. Drop batter by rounded teaspoonsful into hot oil. Fry until deep golden brown, turning once. Drain thoroughly on paper towels. **Yield:** 1-1/2 to 2 dozen.

Quick & Easy

YELLOW SQUASH CASSEROLE

Mae Kruis, Gallup, New Mexico

- 3 tablespoons butter *or* margarine
- 3 to 4 yellow summer squash, sliced
- 1 medium onion, chopped
- 1 can (4 ounces) chopped green chilies
- 8 to 10 saltine crackers, crushed
- Salt and pepper to taste
- 1-1/2 cups (6 ounces) shredded cheddar cheese

In a skillet, melt butter over medium-high heat. Saute squash and onion until crisp-tender. Remove from the heat; stir in chilies, crackers, salt and pepper. Spoon into a greased 1-1/2-qt. casse-

role. Top with cheese. Bake at 350° for 15-20 minutes. **Yield:** 4-6 servings.

OVEN BAKED BEANS

Eleanore Hill, Fresno, California

(PICTURED ON PAGE 40)

- 2 cups dry navy beans
- 8 cups cold water
- 1 teaspoon salt, *divided*
- 2/3 cup packed brown sugar
- 1 teaspoon dry mustard
- 1/2 cup dark molasses
- 1/4 teaspoon pepper
- 1/4 pound salt pork, cut up
- 1/2 cup finely chopped onion
- 1/2 cup finely chopped celery
- 1/2 cup finely chopped green pepper

Rinse beans; place in a Dutch oven with cold water. Bring to a boil; reduce heat and simmer for 2 minutes. Remove from the heat; cover and let stand for 1 hour. (Or, omit boiling and soak beans in water overnight.) Add 1/2 teaspoon salt to beans and soaking water. Bring to a boil. Reduce heat, cover and simmer for 1 hour. Drain, reserving cooking liquid. Combine brown sugar, mustard, molasses, pepper and remaining salt. Stir in 2 cups reserved cooking liquid; add to beans with salt pork, onion, celery and green pepper. Spoon into a 2-1/2-qt. baking dish. Cover and bake at 300° for 2-1/2 hours, stirring occasionally, or until beans are as thick as desired. Add more cooking liquid if necessary. **Yield:** 8-10 servings.

CONFETTI SCALLOPED POTATOES

Frances Anderson, Boise, Idaho

(PICTURED ON PAGE 48)

- 1/2 cup butter *or* margarine
- 1/2 cup chopped onion
- 1 package (16 ounces) frozen hash brown potatoes
- 1 can (10-3/4 ounces) cream of mushroom soup, undiluted
- 1 soup can milk
- 1 cup (4 ounces) shredded cheddar cheese
- 1 small green pepper, cut into strips
- 2 tablespoons chopped pimientos
- Dash pepper
- 1 cup cheese cracker crumbs, *divided*

In a skillet, melt butter over medium heat. Saute onion until tender. Stir in potatoes, soup and milk. Add cheese, green pepper, pimientos, pepper and 1/2 cup crumbs. Pour into a greased shallow casserole; top with remaining crumbs. Bake at 375° for 35-40 minutes. **Yield:** 6-8 servings.

SPANISH RICE

Beth Wool, Barnhart, Texas

(PICTURED ON PAGE 92)

 1/2 pound sliced bacon, diced
 2 cans (28 ounces *each*) tomatoes with liquid, diced
 1 can (10 ounces) tomatoes with green chilies with liquid, diced *or* 1 can (8 ounces) tomatoes with liquid, diced
 2 cans (4 ounces *each*) chopped green chilies
 1 can (8 ounces) tomato sauce
 1/2 teaspoon salt
 1/4 teaspoon pepper
 2 cups uncooked long-grain rice

In a Dutch oven, cook bacon until crisp. Drain fat. Add all remaining ingredients. Bring mixture to a boil; reduce heat. Simmer, uncovered, over medium-low heat, until rice is tender, about 35-40 minutes. Stir occasionally to prevent scorching. **Yield:** 12-14 servings.

 **Quick & Easy**

BAKED CORN CASSEROLE

Jackie Willingham, Pasadena, Texas

 1/4 cup butter *or* margarine
 2 packages (3 ounces *each*) cream cheese, softened
 1 can (17 ounces) whole kernel corn, drained
 1 can (16-1/2 ounces) cream-style corn
 1 can (4 ounces) chopped green chilies
 1/2 cup chopped onion
 1 can (2.8 ounces) french-fried onions, *divided*

In a large bowl, beat together butter and cream cheese. Stir in the kernel corn, cream-style corn, chilies and onion; mix well. Pour into a greased 8-in. square baking dish. Bake, uncovered, at 350° for 15 minutes. Remove from oven; stir in half of the fried onions. Sprinkle remaining fried onions on top. Bake 15 minutes longer. **Yield:** 8-10 servings.

CHEESY CHILI CASSEROLE

Phyllis Bidwell, Las Vegas, Nevada

 2 cups (8 ounces) shredded Monterey Jack cheese

 2 cups (8 ounces) shredded cheddar cheese
 2 cans (4 ounces *each*) whole green chilies, rinsed and seeded
 2 eggs
 2 tablespoons all-purpose flour
 1 can (12 ounces) evaporated milk
 1 can (8 ounces) tomato sauce *or* 1 cup salsa, *divided*

Combine cheeses. In a 10-in. x 6-in. x 2-in. baking dish, layer cheese and chilies. Combine eggs, flour and milk; pour over cheese mixture. Bake at 350° for 30 minutes. Top casserole with half the tomato sauce or salsa; bake 10 minutes longer. Let stand 5 minutes before serving. Serve with remaining sauce. **Yield:** 8 servings.

NELDA'S SAUSAGE AND RICE DRESSING

Nelda Moore, Moore, Oklahoma

 1 package (6 ounces) long grain and wild rice mix
 1/4 cup butter *or* margarine
 1 cup chopped onion
 1 cup chopped celery
 1 pound mild *or* hot bulk pork sausage, cooked and crumbled
 1 box (6 ounces) stuffing croutons
 1 can (2 ounces) mushroom pieces and stems
 2 eggs, beaten
 3 cups chicken broth
 1/2 cup chopped walnuts *or* pecans, toasted
 1/4 teaspoon seasoned pepper
Poultry seasoning to taste

Cook rice mix according to package directions. Set aside. In a skillet, melt butter. Saute the onion and celery until tender. Combine all remaining ingredients and place in a greased 13-in. x 9-in. x 2-in. baking pan. Bake at 350° for 45 minutes. **Yield:** 8-10 servings (makes enough to stuff a 12-lb. turkey).

CORN PUDDING

Peggy Burdick, Burlington, Michigan

 4 tablespoons butter *or* margarine, *divided*
 1 green pepper, chopped
 1 medium onion, chopped
 3 tablespoons all-purpose flour
 1 teaspoon salt
Dash pepper
 1-1/2 cups milk
 3 egg yolks, lightly beaten
 2 cups fresh *or* frozen corn

kernels
 2 jars (2 ounces *each*) chopped pimientos, drained
 1-2/3 cups cracker crumbs, *divided*

In a skillet, melt 3 tablespoons butter over medium heat. Saute pepper and onion until tender. Add flour, salt and pepper; stir until well blended. Gradually add milk; cook and stir until thickened. Slowly blend in egg yolks. Remove from the heat; fold in corn, pimientos and 1 cup crumbs. Pour into a greased 1-1/2-qt. casserole. Melt remaining butter and toss with remaining crumbs; sprinkle over casserole. Bake, uncovered, at 350° for 30-40 minutes. **Yield:** 6 servings.

 **Quick & Easy**

HOMINY CASSEROLE

Lila Thurman, Crossett, Arkansas

(PICTURED BELOW)

 1 medium onion, chopped
 1 garlic clove, minced
 1 tablespoon cooking oil
 1 cup (8 ounces) sour cream
 3/4 cup shredded cheddar cheese, *divided*
 1/4 cup milk
 1 can (4 ounces) chopped green chilies
 1/4 teaspoon ground cumin
 3 cans (15 ounces *each*) golden hominy, drained

In a small skillet, cook onion and garlic in oil until tender. Remove from heat. In a bowl, combine onion mixture, sour cream, half of the cheese, milk, chilies and cumin. Add hominy; mix well. Pour into a greased 2-qt. baking dish. Bake, uncovered, at 350° for 30 minutes or until heated through. Sprinkle with remaining cheese. Serve immediately. **Yield:** 8-10 servings.

GOLDEN MOMENTS. Bring a homey touch to your table with cheesy Hominy Casserole.

ADD SOME flair to your next warm-weather gathering with this fantastic menu. Folks will eagerly await hearty sandwiches of Spiedis served with spicy Zucchini Harvest Salad. Herb-topped Parmesan Potato Rounds are guaranteed to satisfy everyone. And celebrate the fresh fruits of summer with Cherry Berry Pie.

GET-TOGETHER GREATS.
Clockwise from top right: **Spiedis** (recipe on page 118), **Cherry Berry Pie** (recipe on page 228), **Zucchini Harvest Salad** (recipe on page 50) and **Parmesan Potato Rounds** (recipe on page 137).

PARMESAN POTATO ROUNDS

Terri Adrian, Lake City, Florida

(PICTURED AT LEFT)

1/3 cup butter *or* margarine, melted
1/4 cup all-purpose flour
1/4 cup grated Parmesan cheese
Salt and pepper to taste
6 medium potatoes, each sliced into 4 rounds
Italian seasoning to taste

Pour butter into a 15-1/2-in. x 10-1/2-in. x 1-in. baking pan. In a plastic bag, combine flour, cheese, salt and pepper. Shake a few potato slices at a time in the bag to coat with the flour mixture. Place potatoes in a single layer over the butter. Bake at 375° for 30 minutes. Turn slices and sprinkle with Italian seasoning. Bake for 30 minutes more or until tender. **Yield:** 6 servings.

STUFFED ZUCCHINI

Vonnie Elledge, Pinole, California

4 medium zucchini
2 tablespoons cooking oil
1 small onion, minced
2 eggs, lightly beaten
1/2 cup dry bread crumbs
1/4 cup grated Parmesan cheese
2 tablespoons minced parsley
Salt and pepper to taste

Cut zucchini in half lengthwise. Scoop out pulp, leaving a 3/8-in. shell. Reserve pulp. Parboil shells in salted water 2 minutes. Remove and drain. Set aside. Chop zucchini pulp. In a skillet, heat oil over medium-high heat. Saute the onion and chopped zucchini until tender. Remove from the heat and combine remaining ingredients. Fill shells. Place in a greased baking dish. Bake at 375° for 15 minutes or until heated through. **Yield:** 8 servings.

BROCCOLI-STUFFED ONIONS

Lori Gilbertoni, Fairbanks, Alaska

3 large sweet Spanish onions (3 to 4 inches)
1 package (10 ounces) frozen chopped broccoli, thawed
1/2 cup grated Parmesan cheese
1/3 cup mayonnaise
2 tablespoons lemon juice

2 tablespoons butter *or* margarine
2 tablespoons all-purpose flour
1/4 teaspoon salt
2/3 cup milk
1 package (3 ounces) cream cheese, cubed
Chopped fresh parsley
Additional Parmesan cheese

Peel and halve onions horizontally. Parboil in salted water for 10-12 minutes; drain. Leaving 3/4-in. edges, remove centers. Place onion shells in a greased 1-1/2-qt. shallow baking dish. Chop centers of onions to equal 1 cup. Combine chopped onion, broccoli, Parmesan cheese, mayonnaise and lemon juice; spoon into onion shells. In a saucepan, melt butter; stir in flour and salt. Gradually add milk; cook until thick, stirring constantly. Remove from the heat and blend in cream cheese. Spoon sauce over onions. Bake at 375° for 20 minutes. Sprinkle with parsley and additional Parmesan cheese. **Yield:** 6 servings.

AUTUMN BEANS

Mara McAuley, Hinsdale, New York

8 bacon strips, chopped
1/4 cup minced onion
1 cup apple cider
2 cans (16 ounces *each*) baked beans, undrained
1/4 to 1/2 cup raisins
1/2 teaspoon ground cinnamon

In a skillet, lightly fry bacon. Remove to paper towel to drain. Discard all but 2 tablespoons drippings. Saute onion in the drippings until tender. Add all remaining ingredients. Bring to a boil; reduce heat and simmer, uncovered, 20-25 minutes, stirring occasionally. **Yield:** 4 servings.

OVEN-ROASTED POTATOES

Margie Wampler, Butler, Pennsylvania

2 pounds small unpeeled red potatoes, cut into wedges
2 to 3 tablespoons vegetable *or* olive oil
2 garlic cloves, minced

1 tablespoon chopped fresh rosemary *or* 1 teaspoon dried rosemary
1/2 teaspoon salt
1/4 teaspoon pepper

Place potatoes in a 13-in. x 9-in. x 2-in. baking pan. Drizzle oil over. Sprinkle with garlic, rosemary, salt and pepper; toss gently to coat. Bake at 450° for 20-30 minutes or until potatoes are golden brown and tender when pierced with a fork. **Yield:** 6-8 servings.

CRANBERRY STUFFING BALLS

Bernadine Dirmeyer, Harpster, Ohio

(PICTURED ON PAGE 107)

1 pound bulk pork sausage
1/2 cup chopped celery
1/4 cup chopped onion
2 tablespoons minced fresh parsley
1 package (7 ounces) herb-seasoned stuffing croutons
3/4 cup fresh cranberries, halved
2 eggs, well beaten
1 to 1-1/2 cups chicken broth

In a skillet, cook sausage, celery and onion until sausage is done and vegetables are tender. Drain excess fat. In a large mixing bowl, combine the meat mixture with remaining ingredients and enough broth to hold mixture together. Shape into 8-10 balls. Place in a greased shallow baking dish. Bake at 325° for 30 minutes. **Yield:** 8-10 servings.

Quick & Easy

INSTANT PARTY POTATOES

Kathy Roosma, Zeeland, Michigan

3 cups water
4 tablespoons butter *or* margarine
1 teaspoon salt
3/4 cup milk
1 package (8 ounces) cream cheese, softened
1 cup (8 ounces) sour cream
1 teaspoon garlic powder
1 teaspoon dried minced onion
2-2/3 cups instant potato flakes
Paprika, optional

In a saucepan, bring water, butter and salt to a boil. Add milk, cream cheese, sour cream, garlic powder and minced onion; stir in potato flakes. Spoon into a greased 2-qt. baking dish. Sprinkle with paprika if desired. Bake, uncovered, at 350° for 30 minutes. **Yield:** 8-10 servings.

BEANS—a nutritious and delicious staple in country kitchens—
are perfect for hearty winter warm-ups as well as simple
summer meals. In skillets, bowls and casseroles, these easy bean dishes
are delightful, even as leftovers!

A BUSHEL OF IDEAS.
Clockwise from lower left: **Three Bean Casserole** (recipe on page
140), **Carrot/Lentil Salad** (recipe on page 50), **Taco Soup** (recipe on
page 28), **Black-Eyed Pea Chowder** (recipe on page 25), **Country
Cassoulet** (recipe on page 68), **Chili-Cheese Bake** (recipe on
page 140), **White Bean Dip** (recipe on page 8) and
Fiesta Appetizer (recipe on page 14).

THREE BEAN CASSEROLE
Georgia Hennings, Alliance, Nebraska

(PICTURED ON PAGE 138)

1 can (15 to 16 ounces) red
  kidney beans, rinsed and
  drained
1 can (15 ounces) garbanzo
  beans, rinsed and drained
1 can (16 ounces) lima beans,
  rinsed and drained
1 pound lean ground beef
1 large onion, chopped
1 garlic clove, minced
1/2 cup ketchup
1/4 cup water
1/4 cup packed brown sugar
2 tablespoons prepared mustard
1 tablespoon vinegar
1 teaspoon ground cumin
1/2 teaspoon salt
Dash pepper

In a 2-1/2-qt. casserole, combine beans; set aside. In a skillet, cook beef, onion and garlic until beef is no longer pink. Remove from the heat; drain. Add remaining ingredients to skillet; mix well. Stir beef mixture into beans. Bake at 350° for 45 minutes or until heated through. **Yield:** 6-8 servings.

CHILI-CHEESE BAKE
Rosemary West, Topsham, Maine

(PICTURED ON PAGE 139)

3 cups cooked rice
2 garlic cloves, minced
1 can (4 ounces) chopped
  green chilies
2 teaspoons chili powder
1/2 teaspoon salt
1 can (15 to 16 ounces) red
  kidney beans, rinsed and
  drained
1 medium onion, chopped
2 teaspoons ground cumin
1 teaspoon dried oregano
1 teaspoon Creole seasoning
2 cups (8 ounces) shredded
  cheddar cheese, *divided*

In a greased 2-qt. saucepan, combine all ingredients except cheese. Top with 1-1/2 cups of cheese. Cover and bake at 350° for 25 minutes. Top with remaining cheese. Bake, uncovered, 10 minutes more. **Yield:** 6 servings.

CIDER BAKED SQUASH
Christine Gibson, Fontana, Wisconsin

2 medium acorn squash, sliced
  into 1-inch circles and seeds

  removed
1/2 cup apple cider
1/4 cup packed brown sugar
1/2 teaspoon salt
1/8 teaspoon ground cinnamon
1/8 teaspoon ground mace

Place squash in a 15-in. x 10-in. x 1-in. baking pan. Pour cider over squash. Combine all remaining ingredients and sprinkle on top. Cover with foil. Bake at 325° for 45 minutes or until squash is tender. **Yield:** 6 servings.

RANCH-STYLE BAKED LENTILS
Linda Lewis, Coeur d'Alene, Idaho

2 cups dry lentils (4 cups
  cooked)
2 teaspoons salt
5 cups water, *divided*
1 pound lean ground beef
1 envelope dry onion soup mix
1 cup catsup
1 teaspoon prepared mustard
1 teaspoon vinegar

Rinse the lentils. In a heavy saucepan, bring lentils, salt and 4 cups water to a boil. Cover and simmer 20 minutes or until the water is absorbed and the lentils are tender. Meanwhile, brown beef in a skillet. Drain excess fat. Stir in soup mix, catsup, mustard, vinegar and remaining water. Gently stir in lentils. Spoon into a 2-qt. casserole. Bake, covered, at 400° for 30-35 minutes. **Yield:** 4-6 servings.

Quick & Easy

TEXAS-STYLE SPANISH RICE
Melissa Pride, Plano, Texas

1/4 cup chopped onion
1/4 cup chopped green pepper
2 tablespoons cooking oil
1 cup uncooked long grain rice
1/2 cup tomatoes with green
  chilies
1/4 teaspoon ground turmeric
1 teaspoon ground cumin
1/2 teaspoon salt
1/4 teaspoon garlic powder
2 cups water
2 to 3 tablespoons chopped
  fresh cilantro, optional

In a skillet, saute onion and green pepper in oil for about 2 minutes. Add rice and stir until coated with oil. Add tomatoes, turmeric, cumin, salt, garlic powder and water; bring to a boil. Reduce heat and simmer, covered, about 20 minutes or until liquid is absorbed. Add cilantro if desired. **Yield:** 6 servings.

SCALLOPED POTATOES
Eleanore Hill, Fresno, California

(PICTURED ON PAGE 40)

2 tablespoons butter *or*
  margarine
1 tablespoon all-purpose flour
1-1/2 cups milk
1 teaspoon salt
1/4 teaspoon pepper
4 cups thinly sliced peeled
  potatoes (about 2 pounds)
1 medium onion, finely chopped
1 small green pepper, finely
  chopped
Buttered bread crumbs
Shredded cheddar cheese

In a saucepan, melt butter; stir in flour. Add milk all at once, stirring constantly. Cook and stir over low heat until thickened and bubbly. Season with salt and pepper. In a greased 1-1/2-qt. baking dish, arrange half the potatoes, onion and green pepper in layers; cover with half of the sauce. Repeat layers. Cover and bake at 350° for 35 minutes. Sprinkle with buttered bread crumbs. Bake, uncovered, about 40 minutes longer or until potatoes are tender. Sprinkle with cheddar cheese. Let stand for 5 minutes before serving. **Yield:** 4-6 servings.

NORTHWOODS WILD RICE
Suzanne Caquelin, Minneapolis, Minnesota

1-1/2 cups uncooked wild rice,
  rinsed
4 cups water
1 teaspoon salt
4 slices bacon, diced
1/4 cup butter *or* margarine
1 small onion, chopped
1/2 cup celery, sliced
1/2 cup sliced fresh mushrooms
Seasoned salt to taste
1/4 teaspoon pepper
1/2 cup salted cashews

Place rice, water and salt in a heavy saucepan. Bring to a boil. Reduce heat to simmer; cook 45 minutes or until tender. Uncover and fluff with a fork. Simmer for 5 additional minutes. Drain any liquid. While rice is cooking, fry bacon until crisp. Drain on paper towels. In a skillet, melt butter and saute onion, celery and mushrooms until tender. Add rice, seasoned salt and pepper. Heat through. Just before serving, top with cashews and reserved bacon. For a make-ahead dish, place cooked rice mixture in a 2-qt. casserole; top with cashews and bacon. Refrigerate until ready to reheat. Bake at 350° for 20-30 minutes. **Yield:** 6-8 servings.

SWEET POTATO CASSEROLE
Marlene Sale, Naples, Florida

2 eggs
3 cups mashed sweet potatoes
1 cup sugar
1/2 cup butter *or* margarine,
    melted
1/3 cup milk
1 teaspoon vanilla extract
TOPPING:
3 cups cornflakes
2/3 cup butter *or* margarine,
    melted
1 cup packed brown sugar
1/2 cup chopped nuts
1/2 cup raisins

In large bowl, beat eggs. Add next five ingredients; mix well. Spoon into ungreased 13-in. x 9-in. x 2-in. baking dish. Combine topping ingredients; sprinkle over potatoes. Bake at 350° for 30-40 minutes. **Yield:** 6-8 servings.

POTATO STUFFING
Betty McCloskey, Pennsauken, New Jersey

1 large onion, finely chopped
2 to 3 celery ribs, finely chopped
6 tablespoons butter *or*
    margarine
2 slices white bread, torn
3 cups mashed potatoes
2 tablespoons minced fresh
    parsley

In a large saucepan, saute the onion and celery in butter until tender. Remove from the heat. Add bread, potatoes and parsley; mix well. Spoon into a greased 1-qt. casserole. Bake, uncovered, at 350° for 45 minutes or until top is lightly browned. **Yield:** 6 servings.

BLOCK PARTY BEANS
LaDonna Daley, Elyria, Ohio

2 pounds ground beef
2 cups chopped onion
1 cup chopped celery
1 can (10-3/4 ounces) cream
    of tomato soup, undiluted
1 can (6 ounces) tomato paste
1/2 cup ketchup
1 can (16 ounces) green
    beans, drained
1 can (17 ounces) lima beans,
    drained
1 can (15-1/2 ounces) wax
    beans, drained
1 can (15 to 16 ounces) chili
    beans, undrained
1 can (16 ounces) pork and
    beans, undrained

1/2 cup packed brown sugar
2 tablespoons prepared mustard

In a large Dutch oven, brown beef over medium-high heat. Drain fat. Add onion and celery; cook until tender. Stir in soup, tomato paste and ketchup; simmer 15-20 minutes. Spoon into a large kettle or roaster. Add all remaining ingredients; stir well. Bake, uncovered, at 350° for 1 hour. **Yield:** about 25 servings.

CHEDDAR PARMESAN POTATOES
Nellie Webb, Athens, Tennessee

(PICTURED ON PAGE 45)

1/4 cup butter *or* margarine
1/4 cup all-purpose flour
2 cups milk
1/2 teaspoon salt
1 cup (4 ounces) shredded
    cheddar cheese
1/2 cup grated Parmesan cheese
5 cups sliced cooked peeled
    potatoes (about 5 medium)
1/4 cup buttered bread crumbs

In a saucepan, melt butter over low heat. Stir in flour until smooth. Gradually add milk; cook and stir over medium heat until mixture thickens. Remove from the heat. Add the salt, cheddar cheese and Parmesan cheese; stir until cheeses melt. Add potatoes; stir gently to mix. Place in a greased 2-qt. baking dish. Sprinkle bread crumbs on top. Bake, uncovered, at 350° for 30-35 minutes. **Yield:** 6-8 servings.

BREADED TOMATOES
Marion Stanley, Gilroy, California

8 to 10 small to medium firm
    fresh tomatoes
1/2 cup butter *or* margarine,
    melted
1 cup crushed saltines
1 tablespoon grated Parmesan
    cheese
CHEESE SAUCE:
2 tablespoons butter *or*
    margarine
2 tablespoons all-purpose flour
1/4 teaspoon salt
Dash white pepper
1-1/2 cups milk
3 tablespoons grated Parmesan
    cheese

Peel and core tomatoes but leave them whole. Dip each whole tomato in melted butter. In a small bowl, combine saltine crumbs and Parmesan cheese. Roll tomatoes in crumb mixture, gently pressing crumbs onto tomato. Place tomatoes in a single layer in a greased shal-

low baking dish. If there are any crumbs or butter left, combine them and sprinkle over the tomatoes. Bake at 475° for 15 minutes or until tomatoes begin to brown and are heated through. Watch closely; they burn easily. Meanwhile, for cheese sauce, melt butter in a medium saucepan. Stir in flour, salt and pepper. Add milk all at once; cook and stir over medium heat until thickened and bubbly. Remove from the heat; stir in Parmesan cheese. Serve over tomatoes. **Yield:** 8-10 servings.

CALICO BEANS
Betty Claycomb, Alverton, Pennsylvania

(PICTURED BELOW)

4 ounces bacon, diced
1 pound lean ground beef
1/2 cup chopped onion
1 can (16 ounces) kidney
    beans, rinsed and drained
1 can (21 ounces) pork and
    beans
1 can (15 ounces) butter beans,
    rinsed and drained
1/2 cup ketchup
1/2 cup packed brown sugar
1 tablespoon vinegar
1 teaspoon prepared mustard
1 teaspoon salt

In a skillet, cook bacon until crisp. Remove to paper towels to drain. Discard drippings. In the same skillet, cook beef and onion until the beef is browned and the onion is tender. Drain fat. Combine ground beef and bacon with all remaining ingredients. Spoon into a 2-qt. casserole. Bake, uncovered, at 300° for 1 hour or until the beans are as thick as desired. Recipe can be easily doubled for a larger group. **Yield:** 8-10 servings.

DISH TO PASS. Calico Beans will become your best recipe to feed a flock of hungry folks!

MANY MAKINGS of a merry Christmas come right from the kitchen—sometimes one located quite a few miles away! Few gifts are as warmly appreciated as food homemade from treasured family recipes. And here, you can look forward to a hearty helping of such ideas for treating family and friends throughout the year.

SEASON'S BEST.
Clockwise from lower right: **Cranberry Chutney** (recipe on page 143), **Fruited Rice Mix** (recipe on page 124), **Angel Food Candy** (recipe on page 224) and **Christmas Wreaths** (recipe on page 163).

CONDIMENTS & SAUCES

You'll really relish this appealing assortment of pickles, jams, sauces and more...they deliciously top off your favorite foods!

CRANBERRY CHUTNEY

Alease Case, Summerland Key, Florida

(PICTURED AT LEFT)

- 1 pound fresh *or* frozen cranberries
- 2-1/4 cups packed brown sugar
- 1 cup raisins
- 1 cup water
- 1/2 cup chopped pecans *or* walnuts
- 1/4 cup candied ginger, chopped
- 1/4 cup lemon juice
- 1 teaspoon salt
- 1 teaspoon grated onion
- 1/4 teaspoon ground cloves

Combine all the ingredients in a Dutch oven; bring to a boil. Reduce heat and simmer for 20-30 minutes or until slightly thickened, stirring occasionally. Pour into hot sterilized jars, leaving 1/4-in. headspace. Adjust caps. Process in a boiling-water bath for 10 minutes. If not processed, store chutney in the refrigerator. **Yield:** 4-1/2 cups.

CALICO PICKLES

Bob Olsen, Grand Forks, North Dakota

- 4 cups sliced cucumbers (1-inch slices)
- 2-1/4 cups sliced carrots (1-inch slices)
- 2 cups sliced celery (1-inch slices)
- 2 cups cubed onion (1-inch cubes)
- 2 cups cubed sweet red pepper (1-inch cubes)
- 1 cup cubed green pepper (1-inch cubes)
- 1 medium head cauliflower, broken into florets (6 cups)
- 1 cup salt
- 4 quarts cold water
- 2 cups sugar
- 1/4 cup mustard seed
- 2 tablespoons celery seed
- 2 tablespoons dried whole black peppercorns
- 1 tablespoon dried cilantro
- 6-1/2 cups vinegar

Combine vegetables in a large bowl. Dissolve salt in water and pour over veg-etables. Soak for 15 to 18 hours in a cool place. Drain. In a large kettle, mix sugar, spices and vinegar. Bring to a boil and boil for 3-4 minutes. Add vegetables and simmer 5-7 minutes. Pack hot into eight hot pint jars, leaving 1/4-in. headspace. Remove air bubbles. Adjust caps; process 15 minutes in boiling-water bath. **Yield:** 8 pints.

CAN'T BE BEET. Don't throw away sweet pickle juice when the pickles are all gone. Instead, pour the juice into a kettle and add a can of drained, small whole beets. Bring to a boil, then simmer for about 5 minutes. Pour into a serving dish and refrigerate. Now you've got some quickly made pickled beets.

  Quick & Easy

PRALINE SUNDAE TOPPING

Valerie Cook, Hubbard, Iowa

(PICTURED ON PAGE 12)

- 1/4 cup butter *or* margarine
- 1-1/4 cups packed brown sugar
- 16 large marshmallows
- 2 tablespoons light corn syrup
- Dash salt
- 1 cup evaporated milk
- 1/2 cup chopped pecans, toasted
- 1 teaspoon vanilla extract
- Ice cream

Melt butter in a saucepan. Add brown sugar, marshmallows, corn syrup and salt. Cook and stir over low heat until marshmallows are melted and mixture comes to a boil. Boil for 1 minute. Remove from the heat; cool for 5 minutes. Stir in evaporated milk, pecans and vanilla; mix well. Serve warm or cold over ice cream. Store in the refrigerator. **Yield:** 2-1/2 cups.

BASIL BUTTER

Emily Chaney, Penobscot, Maine

- 1-1/2 cups loosely packed fresh basil leaves
- 3/4 pound butter (no substitutes), softened
- 1-1/2 teaspoons lemon juice
- 1-1/2 teaspoons white pepper

In a food processor, chop basil. Add butter, lemon juice and pepper; blend until smooth. Drop by half-tablespoons onto a cookie sheet; freeze. Remove from cookie sheet and store in freezer bags. Use to flavor chicken, fish or vegetables. **Yield:** 4 dozen butter balls.

CRANBERRY APPLE RELISH

Mary Guengerich, High River, Alberta

- 4 cups raw cranberries
- 2 apples, peeled and cored
- 2 oranges, quartered with peel, seeded
- 1 lemon, quartered with peel, seeded
- 2-1/2 cups sugar *or* 1-1/2 cups honey

Grind cranberries, apples, oranges and lemon. Stir in sugar or honey. Refrigerate several hours or up to several days. **Yield:** about 6 cups.

NORTHWEST CHERRY SALSA

Margaret Slocum, Ridgefield, Washington

(PICTURED ON PAGE 230)

✓ This tasty dish uses less sugar, salt and fat. Recipe includes *Diabetic Exchanges*.

- 1 cup fresh *or* frozen pitted dark sweet cherries, chopped
- 2 tablespoons chopped fresh basil
- 1 tablespoon finely chopped green pepper
- 1 teaspoon lemon juice
- 1/4 teaspoon Worcestershire sauce
- 1/4 teaspoon grated lemon peel
- 1/8 teaspoon salt
- Dash hot pepper sauce

Combine all ingredients; refrigerate at least 1 hour. Serve as a condiment with chicken, turkey or pork. **Yield:** 3/4 cup. **Diabetic Exchanges:** One serving (2 tablespoons) equals 1/2 fruit; also, 22 calories, 59 mg sodium, 0 mg cholesterol, 5 gm carbohydrate, 1 gm protein, 1/2 gm fat.

PUCKER UP for the pleasing, tart taste of cranberry in a variety of year-round recipes. Enjoy summer's cool Cranberry Sherbet or winter's Spicy Cranberry Warmer...try the Holiday Cranberry Jam with muffins or biscuits...or feast on a country favorite—Cranberry Meatballs. All of these cranberry dishes are bound to become popular among your family and friends. Whip up a cranberry creation today!

DANDY CRANBERRY!
Clockwise from lower left: **Apricot-Cranberry Chutney** (recipe on page 146), **Cranberry Meatballs** (recipe on page 7), **Cranberry Upside-Down Cake** (recipe on page 199), **Cranberry Sherbet** (recipe on page 218), **Cran-Apple Sauce** (recipe on page 146), **Spicy Cranberry Warmer** (recipe on page 17), **Cranberry Walnut Tart** (recipe on page 210) and **Holiday Cranberry Jam** (recipe on page 146).

HOLIDAY CRANBERRY JAM

Sandee Berg, Fort Saskatchewan, Alberta

(PICTURED ON PAGE 144)

**2 cups fresh *or* frozen
  cranberries
1 medium orange, peeled and
  broken into sections
1 carton (16 ounces) frozen
  sliced strawberries, thawed
3 cups sugar
1/2 of a 6-ounce package liquid
  fruit pectin**

In a food grinder or food processor, coarsely grind cranberries and orange sections. Place in a Dutch oven or large kettle with strawberries and sugar. Bring to a full rolling boil over high heat, stirring constantly. Boil for 1 minute. Remove from the heat and stir in the pectin. Quickly skim off the foam with a large metal spoon. Immediately pour into hot sterilized jars. Adjust caps. Process 10 minutes in a boiling-water bath. **Yield:** 5 half-pints.

Quick & Easy

APRICOT-CRANBERRY CHUTNEY

Joyce Vivian, Mitchell, Ontario

(PICTURED ON PAGE 144)

**3 cups fresh *or* frozen
  cranberries
1 cup chopped dried apricots
1/2 cup chopped dates
1/2 cup chopped onion
1/2 cup cider vinegar
1/2 cup light corn syrup
3/4 cup packed brown sugar
1 tablespoon grated orange peel
3/4 cup orange juice
1/2 teaspoon dry mustard
1/2 teaspoon salt
1/4 teaspoon ground ginger**

In a large heavy saucepan, combine all ingredients. Bring to a boil. Reduce heat and simmer, uncovered, for 15-20 minutes or until thickened and cranberries have popped. Chill. Serve as an accompaniment to turkey or pork. **Yield:** about 3-1/2 cups.

Quick & Easy

CRAN-APPLE SAUCE

**Stella Kalynchuk
Whitehorse, Yukon Territory**

(PICTURED ON PAGE 145)

**1 cup fresh *or* frozen
  cranberries
6 large apples, peeled, cored
  and coarsely chopped**

**1/2 cup sugar
1/3 cup apple juice
1/4 teaspoon ground mace
1/8 teaspoon ground coriander**

In a large saucepan, combine all ingredients. Bring to a boil. Reduce heat; cover and simmer for 10-15 minutes or until apples are tender. Remove from heat and cool slightly. Puree mixture in food processor. Cover and refrigerate. **Yield:** about 4 cups.

CORNCOB JELLY

Marge Hagy, Brewster, Washington

**12 large corncobs
4 cups water
1 box powdered fruit pectin
4 cups sugar
Yellow food coloring**

Cut corn kernels from cobs and reserve for another recipe. In a large kettle, place corncobs and water; bring to a boil. Boil for 10 minutes. Remove and discard the cobs; strain liquid through cheesecloth. Liquid should measure 3 cups. Add additional water if necessary. Return to the kettle and stir in pectin. Bring to a full rolling boil. Add sugar and bring back to a boil. Skim foam and add a few drops of food coloring. Pour into hot jars. Cool and refrigerate until ready to use. **Yield:** about 4 pints.

Quick & Easy

SWEET-AND-SOUR MUSTARD

Cheri White, Richland, Michigan

(PICTURED ON PAGE 13)

**1 cup packed brown sugar
1/2 cup cider *or* raspberry vinegar
1/3 cup dry mustard
2 tablespoons water
2 eggs, lightly beaten**

In a saucepan, whisk together all ingredients. Cook over low heat, stirring constantly, until thickened. Pour into small jars. Cover and refrigerate. **Yield:** 1-1/2 cups.

RHUBARB CHUTNEY

Mrs. Selmer Looney, Eugene, Oregon

(PICTURED ON PAGE 209)

**4 cups diced fresh *or* frozen
  rhubarb
2 cups diced peeled apples
1 orange
1 lemon
2 cups packed brown sugar**

**1 cup raisins
1 cup currants
1/2 cup diced candied citron
1/2 cup apple juice
1/2 teaspoon ground nutmeg
1/2 teaspoon ground allspice
1/2 teaspoon ground cloves
1/2 teaspoon ground cinnamon
1/4 teaspoon salt**

Place rhubarb and apples in a large Dutch oven or kettle. Grate the rind of the orange and lemon; add to kettle. Peel and section orange and lemon. Discard the seeds. Cut fruit into small pieces; stir into kettle. Add remaining ingredients. Bring to a boil. Reduce heat and simmer, uncovered, for 30-40 minutes or until thickened, stirring occasionally. Pour into half-pint jars and seal. Freeze or process for 15 minutes in a boiling-water bath. **Yield:** about 6 half-pints.

Quick & Easy

CHERRY/ALMOND HAM GLAZE

Julie Sterchi, Fairfield, Illinois

(PICTURED ON PAGE 230)

**1 jar (12 ounces) cherry
  preserves
1/4 cup vinegar
2 tablespoons corn syrup
1/4 teaspoon ground cinnamon
1/4 teaspoon ground cloves
1/4 teaspoon ground nutmeg
1/3 cup slivered almonds
3 tablespoons water**

In a saucepan, combine first six ingredients. Bring to a boil. Reduce heat; simmer 2 minutes, stirring frequently. Stir in the almonds. About 15 minutes before ham is done, spoon 1/4 to 1/3 cup glaze over ham. Repeat if desired. Stir water into remaining glaze; heat through and serve with ham. **Yield:** about 1-1/2 cups.

BREAD-AND-BUTTER PICKLES

Olivia Miller, Memphis, Tennessee

**16 cups sliced cucumbers
  (about 4 pounds)
6 cups thinly sliced onions
1/2 cup salt
Ice cubes
5 cups sugar
5 cups cider vinegar
1-1/2 teaspoons turmeric
1-1/2 teaspoons celery seed
1-1/2 teaspoons mustard seed**

Combine cucumber and onion slices in a large bowl. Layer with salt; cover with ice cubes. Let stand 1-1/2 hours. Drain and rinse. Place remaining ingredients in a kettle and bring to a boil. Add cucumbers and onions. Return to a boil. Pack hot into hot jars to within 1/4 in. of top. Remove any air bubbles. Adjust caps. Process 15 minutes in boiling-water bath. **Yield:** about 6 pints.

SPICED RHUBARB

Paula Pelis, Rocky Point, New York

(PICTURED ON PAGE 208)

10 cups diced fresh *or* frozen
  rhubarb
4-1/2 cups sugar
  1 cup cider vinegar
  2 teaspoons ground cinnamon
1/2 to 1 teaspoon ground cloves
1/2 to 1 teaspoon ground allspice

In a large Dutch oven or kettle, combine all ingredients. Bring to a rapid boil; reduce heat and simmer for 60-70 minutes. Pour into pint jars and refrigerate. Serve as a glaze for ham or spread on biscuits. **Yield:** about 4 pints.

 **Quick & Easy**

ZESTY LEMON CURD

Jean Gaines, Bullhead City, Arizona

(PICTURED ON PAGE 222)

  3 eggs, beaten
  2 cups sugar
1/2 pound butter (no substitutes),
  cut into tablespoon-size pieces
3/4 cup fresh lemon juice
Grated peel of 1 lemon

In the top of a double boiler, combine all ingredients. Cook and stir over boiling water until thickened like pudding. Remove from heat and cool. Chill until ready to serve. Spread on muffins or rolls, or serve over waffles or ice cream. Keeps well in the refrigerator up to 2 weeks. **Yield:** 3 cups.

SAUERKRAUT SALAD

Evelyn Clarke, Hackensack, New Jersey

  1 can (27 ounces) sauerkraut,
  undrained
  1 large green pepper, finely
  chopped
  1 medium onion, finely chopped
  1 cup finely chopped celery
  1 jar (2 ounces) sliced
  pimientos, drained
1-1/2 cups sugar
1/2 cup white wine vinegar
1/4 cup vegetable oil
1/2 teaspoon salt

In a large bowl, combine all ingredients. Cover and chill overnight. Drain before serving. Serve as a side dish or use as a relish on hot dogs or sandwiches. Salad will keep up to a week stored tightly covered in the refrigerator. **Yield:** 10-12 servings.

 **Quick & Easy**

DOUBLE HOT
HORSERADISH MUSTARD

Madeline Cole, Willow, Alaska

1/4 cup cider vinegar
1/4 cup dry mustard
  3 tablespoons white wine
  vinegar
  2 tablespoons mustard seed
  1 tablespoon prepared
  horseradish
1-1/2 teaspoons honey

Combine all ingredients in a blender container. Process on high until smooth. Transfer to a small jar and cover tightly. Store in the refrigerator. **Yield:** 1/2 cup.

HOT FUDGE SAUCE

Florence Herman, Fairbury, Nebraska

(PICTURED ON PAGE 216)

  3 ounces (3 squares)
  unsweetened chocolate
  5 tablespoons butter *or*
  margarine
  3 cups (14 ounces) sifted
  confectioners' sugar
1/8 teaspoon salt
  1 cup evaporated milk
  1 teaspoon vanilla

Melt chocolate and butter in saucepan over very low heat. Stir in sugar and salt alternately with milk; blend well with wire whisk. Bring mixture to boil over medium heat, stirring constantly. Stir while cooking until mixture becomes thick and creamy, about 8 minutes. Stir in vanilla. Serve warm over ice cream. **Yield:** about 1-1/2 pints.

CORN RELISH

Karen Smock, Girard, Pennsylvania

(PICTURED ON PAGE 108)

10 cups fresh whole kernel corn
  1 small head cabbage, shredded
  6 medium onions, chopped
  4 medium green peppers,
  chopped
  2 medium sweet red peppers,
  chopped
  1 quart cider vinegar
  4 cups sugar

2-1/2 teaspoons ground turmeric
2-1/2 teaspoons dry mustard
  2 teaspoons celery seed
  2 teaspoons salt

In a large Dutch oven, combine corn, cabbage, onions and peppers. In a bowl, stir together remaining ingredients. Pour over vegetables. Bring to a boil; reduce heat and simmer for 10 minutes. Ladle into hot sterilized jars, leaving 1/4-in. headspace. Adjust caps. Process in a boiling-water bath for 10 minutes. Let stand for at least 1 week to blend flavors. **Yield:** about 14 jars (12 ozs. each).

 **Quick & Easy**

BLACK BEAN SALSA

Susan Cochran, Anaheim, California

  1 can (15 ounces) black
  beans, *divided*
  2 tablespoons lime juice
  2 to 4 tablespoons chopped
  fresh cilantro
  1 medium onion, chopped
  1 garlic clove, minced
  3 plum tomatoes, seeded and
  chopped
Salt to taste
Tortilla chips

Drain beans, reserving 1 tablespoon liquid. In a mixing bowl, combine lime juice, half the beans and the reserved bean liquid. Mash until smooth. Stir in remaining beans, cilantro, onion, garlic, tomatoes and salt. Serve with tortilla chips. **Yield:** 4-6 servings.

CONFETTI
ZUCCHINI RELISH

Dodie Strobel, Grants Pass, Oregon

(PICTURED ON PAGE 132)

10 cups chopped zucchini
  4 cups chopped onion
  5 tablespoons salt
  1 sweet red pepper, chopped
  1 green pepper, chopped
  3 cups sugar
2-1/2 cups cider vinegar
  2 tablespoons cornstarch
  3 teaspoons turmeric
  2 teaspoons dry mustard
  2 teaspoons celery seed
1/2 teaspoon pepper

Combine zucchini, onion and salt; let stand overnight. Rinse and drain well. Place in a large kettle or Dutch oven along with remaining ingredients; cook until mixture thickens, stirring constantly. Do not overcook. Pack hot into hot sterilized jars, leaving 1/4-in. headspace. Adjust caps. Process 10 minutes in a boiling-water bath. **Yield:** 16 half-pints.

EACH ONE of the breads featured here is just right for
eating or wrapping up for gift-giving. Everyone will agree
they're irresistible. But you better watch out…
preparing these palate-pleasing recipes is apt to become
a regular tradition in your home all year long!

RISE TO THE OCCASION.
Top to bottom: **Christmas Stollen**, **Cranberry Christmas
Canes** and **Butter Rings** (all recipes on page 149).

BREADS, COFFEE CAKES & MUFFINS

*There's no better way to warmly welcome folks into your home
than with the tantalizing aroma of oven-fresh baked goodies.*

BUTTER RINGS

Florence McBride, Harvard, Illinois
(PICTURED AT LEFT)

1 package (1/4 ounce) active
  dry yeast
3 tablespoons sugar, *divided*
1/4 cup warm milk (110° to 115°)
4 cups all-purpose flour
1 teaspoon salt
1/2 cup butter *or* margarine
3 egg yolks
1 cup light cream, heated to
  lukewarm
Chopped nuts for garnish
ICING:
1 cup confectioners' sugar
1 tablespoon milk
1/4 teaspoon vanilla extract

Dissolve yeast and 2 teaspoons sugar in milk; set aside. Combine flour, salt and remaining sugar. Cut in butter as for pie crust. Beat egg yolks into cream; add to flour mixture along with yeast mixture. Blend well and form into ball. Place dough in greased bowl; cover and refrigerate overnight. Punch dough down; place on lightly floured board and divide into six balls. Roll each ball into a 24-in. rope. On a greased cookie sheet, twist two ropes together, then shape into a 6- to 8-in. ring. Pinch ends together and sprinkle with nuts. Repeat with remaining two rings. Cover and allow to rise until almost doubled, about 30-45 minutes. Bake at 350° for about 25 minutes or until golden brown. Place on wire racks. Combine icing ingredients; drizzle over warm rings. **Yield:** 3 coffee cakes.

CHRISTMAS STOLLEN

Jenny Nichols, Arlington, Texas
(PICTURED AT LEFT)

1-1/2 cups warm milk *or* water
  (110° to 115°)
2 packages (1/4 ounce *each*)
  active dry yeast
6-1/2 to 7-1/2 cups all-purpose
  flour, *divided*
1-1/2 cups butter *or* margarine
3/4 cup sugar
3 eggs
3/4 teaspoon salt

3/4 teaspoon grated lemon peel
1/2 pound raisins
1/2 pound chopped blanched
  almonds
1/2 cup chopped candied fruit
3 tablespoons butter *or*
  margarine, melted
LEMON GLAZE:
1-1/4 cups confectioners' sugar
1/4 cup lemon juice
1 teaspoon vanilla extract

Combine milk or water and yeast. Let stand 3-5 minutes. Add 1 cup flour; mix well. Cover and let rest in a warm place until light and foamy, about 1 hour. In a large mixing bowl, cream butter and sugar. Beat in eggs, one at a time. Add salt and lemon peel. Stir in the yeast mixture and enough remaining flour to form a soft dough. Knead until smooth and elastic, about 6-8 minutes. Place the dough in a greased bowl, cover and let rise in a warm place until doubled, about 1 hour. Punch dough down; knead in raisins, nuts and fruit. Divide into two parts; roll each into a 15-in. x 8-in. oval. Fold each in half lengthwise and place on a greased baking sheet. Brush with melted butter. Cover and allow loaves to rise until almost doubled in bulk, about 45 minutes. Bake at 350° for 30-40 minutes or until golden brown. Cool on wire racks. Combine all glaze ingredients; brush on tops of cooled loaves. **Yield:** 2 loaves.

CRANBERRY
CHRISTMAS CANES

Jan Malone, Arapaho, Oklahoma
(PICTURED AT LEFT)

FILLING:
1-1/2 cups finely chopped fresh *or*
  frozen cranberries
1/2 cup sugar
1/2 cup raisins
1/3 cup chopped pecans
1/3 cup honey
1-1/2 teaspoons grated orange peel
DOUGH:
1 cup milk
1 package (1/4 ounce) active
  dry yeast
1/4 cup warm water (110°-115°)
4 cups all-purpose flour
1/4 cup sugar

1 teaspoon salt
1 teaspoon grated lemon peel
1 cup butter *or* margarine
2 eggs, beaten
Confectioners' sugar icing, optional

In a saucepan, combine all filling ingredients. Bring to a boil; reduce heat and cook 5 minutes. Cool to room temperature. Meanwhile, for dough, scald milk and cool to lukewarm. Dissolve yeast in water; set aside. In a large mixing bowl, combine flour, sugar, salt and lemon peel. Cut in butter until mixture resembles a coarse meal. Add milk, yeast mixture and eggs. Combine to form a soft dough. Place dough in a greased bowl. Cover tightly with plastic wrap; refrigerate for at least 2 hours. Divide dough in half. On a well-floured board, roll out each half of the dough into an 18-in. x 15-in. rectangle. Divide the filling and spread on each rectangle. Fold each rectangle into thirds, starting with the 15-in. side. The dough will now measure 15 in. x 6 in. Cut each piece into 15 short strips. Twist each strip and shape into a candy cane. Place on greased cookie sheets. Bake at 375° for 15-18 minutes or until golden brown. Cool on wire racks. Frost with a confectioners' sugar icing if desired. **Yield:** 30 sweet rolls.

ZUCCHINI/OATMEAL
MUFFINS

Janet Bonarski, Perry, New York

2-1/2 cups all-purpose flour
1-1/2 cups sugar
1 cup chopped pecans
1/2 cup quick-cooking oats
1 tablespoon baking powder
1 teaspoon salt
1 teaspoon ground cinnamon
4 eggs
1 medium zucchini, shredded
  (about 3/4 cup)
3/4 cup vegetable oil

In a mixing bowl, combine first seven ingredients. Beat eggs; combine with zucchini and oil. Pour over dry ingredients, stirring just until moistened. Batter will be lumpy. Fill greased muffin cups 3/4 full. Bake at 400° for 25 minutes or until a toothpick inserted in the center comes out clean. Cool on wire rack. **Yield:** 1 dozen.

SOUTHERN PLANTATION CORN BREAD

Beverly Plymell, Keytesville, Missouri

(PICTURED AT RIGHT)

- 1 cup butter or margarine, *divided*
- 4 tablespoons all-purpose flour
- 1 pint half-and-half cream
- 4 slices American cheese
- 1 carton (8 ounces) whipping cream
- 1 egg, beaten
- 1 carton (8 ounces) sour cream
- 2 boxes (8-1/2 ounces *each*) corn muffin mix
- 6 ounces diced breakfast ham *or* 1-1/2 cups diced ham

In saucepan, melt 1/2 cup of butter. Add flour and cream; cook until slightly thickened. Crumble in cheese; blend. Cool. Add whipping cream, egg and sour cream; mix well. Melt remaining butter; add butter and corn muffin mix to cheese mixture. Fold in ham. Spread in 13-in. x 9-in. x 2-in. baking pan. Bake at 350° for 50-60 minutes or until set. *Do not overbake—bread should be moist.* **Yield:** 12-15 servings.

BUTTERMILK CRANBERRY MUFFINS

Jane Yunker, Rochester, New York

(PICTURED AT RIGHT)

- 1 heaping cup cranberries, coarsely chopped
- 3/4 cup sugar, *divided*
- 3 cups all-purpose flour
- 3-1/2 teaspoons baking powder
- 1/4 teaspoon baking soda
- 1/2 teaspoon salt
- 1/2 cup butter
- 1 egg
- 1-1/2 cups buttermilk, room temperature
- 2 tablespoons frozen orange juice concentrate, thawed

CRANBERRY BUTTER:
- 1 cup cranberries
- 1 cup confectioners' sugar
- 1/2 cup butter *or* margarine
- 1 tablespoon lemon juice

Combine cranberries and 1/4 cup sugar; set aside. Sift together flour, remaining sugar, baking powder, soda and salt. Cut in butter until mixture resembles coarse meal. Lightly beat together egg, buttermilk and orange juice. Add the liquid and sweetened cranberries to dry ingredients, stirring only until well-combined. Spoon batter into greased muffin cups, filling them two-thirds full.

Bake at 375° for 25 minutes. To make cranberry butter, puree cranberries in food processor or blender. Add sugar, butter and lemon juice; process until smooth. Refrigerate until ready to use. **Yield:** 18 muffins.

SOUTHWESTERN MINI MUFFINS

Jennifer Dise, Phoenix, Arizona

(PICTURED ON PAGE 6)

- 2 cups all-purpose flour
- 1 tablespoon baking powder
- 1/2 teaspoon seasoned salt
- 1/4 teaspoon freshly ground black pepper
- 1 cup (4 ounces) shredded cheddar cheese
- 1 can (4 ounces) chopped green chilies, drained
- 1 egg, beaten
- 4 tablespoons Dijon mustard
- 1 cup milk
- 1/4 cup butter *or* margarine, melted

In a large bowl, combine flour, baking powder, seasoned salt and pepper. Add cheese; toss well. Stir in chilies. In a small bowl, mix egg, mustard, milk and butter. Pour over flour mixture; stir until dry ingredients are moistened. Spoon into greased mini muffin cups. Bake at 350° for 20-25 minutes or until done. Turn out onto a rack to cool. **Yield:** 36 muffins.

RASPBERRY CREAM CHEESE COFFEE CAKE

Brenda Knautz, West Chicago, Illinois

(PICTURED ON PAGE 197)

COFFEE CAKE:
- 2-1/2 cups all-purpose flour
- 3/4 cup sugar
- 3/4 cup butter *or* margarine
- 1/2 teaspoon baking powder
- 1/2 teaspoon baking soda
- 1/4 teaspoon salt
- 3/4 cup sour cream
- 1 egg
- 1 teaspoon almond extract

FILLING:
- 1 package (8 ounces) cream cheese, softened
- 1/4 cup sugar

- 1 egg
- 1/2 cup raspberry jam

TOPPING:
- 1/2 cup sliced almonds

In a large bowl, combine flour and sugar; cut in the butter using a pastry blender until mixture resembles coarse crumbs. Remove 1 cup crumbs for topping. To remaining crumb mixture, add baking powder, soda, salt, sour cream, egg and almond extract; blend well. Spread batter over bottom and 2 in. up side of greased and floured 9-in. springform pan. (Batter should be 1/4 in. thick on sides.) For filling, in small bowl, combine cream cheese, sugar and egg; blend well. Pour over batter in the pan. Carefully spoon jam evenly over cheese filling. In a small bowl, combine 1 cup of reserved flour mixture and almonds; sprinkle over top. Bake at 350° for about 55-60 minutes or until cream cheese filling is set and crust is a deep golden brown. Cool 15 minutes. Remove sides of pan. Serve warm or cool. Cover and refrigerate leftovers. **Yield:** 16 servings.

APPLE CREAM COFFEE CAKE

Oriana Churchill, Londonderry, New Hampshire

- 1/2 cup chopped walnuts
- 2 teaspoons ground cinnamon
- 1-1/2 cups sugar, *divided*
- 1/2 cup butter *or* margarine, softened
- 2 eggs
- 1 teaspoon vanilla extract
- 2 cups all-purpose flour
- 1 teaspoon baking powder
- 1 teaspoon baking soda
- 1/2 teaspoon salt
- 1 cup (8 ounces) sour cream
- 1 medium apple, peeled, cored and thinly sliced

Combine nuts, cinnamon and 1/2 cup sugar; set aside. In a large mixing bowl, cream butter; gradually add remaining sugar, beating until light and fluffy. Add eggs, one at a time, beating well after each addition. Blend in vanilla. Combine dry ingredients; add to creamed mixture alternately with sour cream, beating well after each addition. Spread half of the batter in a well-greased 10-in. tube pan with a removable bottom. Top with apple slices; sprinkle with half of the nut mixture. Top with remaining batter, then with remaining nut mixture. Bake at 375° for 40 minutes or until cake tests done. Remove from oven; let stand 30 minutes. Loosen sides of cake; lift cake with removable bottom from pan. Cool. Before serving, carefully lift cake from pan. **Yield:** 12-16 servings.

HEARTY breakfasts—there's no better way to begin a country day! Your family will be glad for the good start these recipes give them. And you'll appreciate a handy aspect of these dishes—some of them can be made ahead of time. Plus, they satisfy assorted tastes to make the first meal of the day a mmm-memorable one!

BREAKFAST BREAKTHROUGHS.
Top to bottom: **Southern Plantation Corn Bread** (recipe on page 150), **Quiche Italiano** (recipe on page 65), **Scrambled Egg Casserole** (recipe on page 83) and **Buttermilk Cranberry Muffins** (recipe on page 150).

IRISH BREAD

Martha Glenn, Enid, Oklahoma

(PICTURED AT RIGHT)

2-3/4 cups all-purpose flour,
  divided
3 tablespoons sugar
1 package (1/4 ounce) active
  dry yeast
1/2 teaspoon salt
1/2 teaspoon baking soda
1 cup warm buttermilk
  (120° to 130°)
2 tablespoons butter *or*
  margarine, melted
3/4 cup raisins

In a mixing bowl, combine 2 cups flour, sugar, yeast, salt and baking soda. Combine buttermilk and butter; gradually add to dry ingredients and beat well. Turn out onto a lightly floured surface; knead in raisins and enough remaining flour to make a soft dough, about 6-8 minutes. Place in a greased bowl, turning once to grease top. Cover and let rise in a warm place until doubled, about 1-1/2 hours. Punch dough down. Knead on a lightly floured surface about 15 times, forming a smooth round ball. Place on a greased baking sheet. Press dough down to form an 8-in. circle. Cover and let rise until doubled, about 30 minutes. Sprinkle dough lightly with flour; cut a 4-in. cross about 1/4 in. deep on the top. Bake at 350° for 30 minutes or until bread tests done. Remove to a wire rack. **Yield:** 1 loaf.

HERB BREAD

Darlene Miller, Linn, Missouri

 This tasty dish uses less sugar, salt and fat. Recipe includes *Diabetic Exchanges*.

3 cups whole wheat flour
5 to 5-1/2 cups all-purpose
  flour, *divided*
2 packages (1/4 ounce *each*)
  active dry yeast
3 tablespoons sugar
1 tablespoon salt
1 teaspoon dried sage
1/2 teaspoon dried thyme
1/2 teaspoon dried marjoram
1 small onion, minced
3 tablespoons cooking oil
3 cups warm water (120° to 130°)
Milk
2 tablespoons grated Parmesan
  cheese

In a large mixing bowl, combine whole wheat flour, 1 cup all-purpose flour, yeast, sugar, salt, herbs, onion, oil and water. Beat with an electric mixer on low until moistened, then beat for 3 minutes

at medium. By hand, stir in enough of the remaining flour to form a stiff dough. Place in a greased bowl, turning once to grease top. Cover and allow to rise until doubled, about 1 hour. Punch dough down. Shape into two balls and place in two greased 2-qt. casseroles. Cover and let rise until almost doubled, about 45 minutes. Brush tops with milk and sprinkle with Parmesan cheese. Bake at 350° for 40-45 minutes. Remove from casseroles to cool on a wire rack. **Yield:** 2 loaves (40 slices). **Diabetic Exchanges:** One serving (one slice) equals 1-1/4 starch; also, 99 calories, 63 mg sodium, trace cholesterol, 21 gm carbohydrate, 3 gm protein, trace fat.

ORANGE MINI MUFFINS

Linda Clapp, Stow, Ohio

(PICTURED ON PAGE 223)

2 cups sugar, *divided*
1/2 cup fresh orange juice
1/2 cup butter *or* margarine,
  softened
3/4 cup sour cream
2 cups all-purpose flour
1 teaspoon baking soda
1 teaspoon salt
1 teaspoon grated orange peel
1/2 cup raisins
1/2 cup chopped nuts

Combine 1 cup sugar and the orange juice; set aside. Cream butter and remaining sugar; blend in sour cream. Combine dry ingredients and add to creamed mixture. Beat on low speed just until ingredients are combined. Stir in orange peel, raisins and nuts. The batter will be stiff. Spoon batter into greased mini muffin cups, filling each cup completely full. Bake at 375° for about 12 minutes or until done. While still warm, dip each muffin in reserved sugar/orange juice mixture. Cool on wire rack. **Yield:** 36 mini muffins.

RICH CRANBERRY
COFFEE CAKE

Mildred Schwartzentruber, Tavistock, Ontario

(PICTURED ON PAGE 107)

1 package (8 ounces) cream
  cheese, softened
1 cup butter *or* margarine
1-1/2 cups sugar
1-1/2 teaspoons vanilla extract

4 eggs
2-1/4 cups all-purpose flour,
  divided
1-1/2 teaspoons baking powder
1/2 teaspoon salt
2 cups fresh *or* frozen
  cranberries, patted dry
1/2 cup chopped pecans *or*
  walnuts
Confectioners' sugar

In a mixing bowl, beat cream cheese, butter, sugar and vanilla until smooth. Add eggs, one at a time, mixing well after each addition. Combine 2 cups flour, baking powder and salt; gradually add to butter mixture. Mix remaining flour with cranberries and nuts; fold into batter. Batter will be very thick. Spoon into a greased 10-in. fluted tube pan. Bake at 350° for 65-70 minutes or until cake tests done. Let stand 5 minutes before removing from the pan. Cool on a wire rack. Before serving, dust with confectioners' sugar. **Yield:** about 16 servings.

CINNAMON POTATO ROLLS

Mrs. Jonas Schwartz, Berne, Indiana

FILLING:
1-1/3 cups packed brown sugar
1/2 teaspoon ground cinnamon
3 tablespoons half-and-half
  cream
2 tablespoons butter *or*
  margarine, softened
ROLLS:
3/4 cup sugar
3/4 cup hot mashed potatoes
1-1/2 cups warm water (110° to 115°)
2 packages (1/4 ounce *each*)
  active dry yeast
1/2 cup butter *or* margarine,
  softened
2 eggs
2 teaspoons salt
6-1/2 cups all-purpose flour
Confectioners' sugar icing, optional

Combine filling ingredients and set aside. In a large mixing bowl, combine sugar and mashed potatoes. Add water and yeast; mix well. Cover and let rise in a warm place for 1 hour. Stir dough down; mix in butter, eggs and salt. Gradually stir in flour. Turn out onto a lightly floured surface; knead until smooth and elastic, about 6-8 minutes. Divide dough in half. On a floured surface, roll each portion into a 12-in. x 12-in. square. Divide filling and spread over each square to within 1 in. of the edges. Roll up jelly-roll style. Cut each roll into nine slices. Place in a greased 9-in. x 9-in. baking pan. Cover and let rise in a warm place until doubled, about 1 hour. Bake at 350° for 35-40 minutes or until golden. Drizzle with a confectioners' sugar icing if desired. **Yield:** 18 rolls.

WHO doesn't have warm memories of their mom's fresh-from-the-oven bread slathered with sweet, soft butter? Now you can recreate that mouth-watering memory with festive Irish Bread. Serve it with Potato Soup with Spinach Dumplings or Steak and Onion Pie for a truly tasty meal.

BAKED GOODNESS.
Clockwise from the bottom: **Steak and Onion Pie** (recipe on page 83), **Irish Bread** (recipe on page 152) and **Potato Soup with Spinach Dumplings** (recipe on page 20).

CHEDDAR/SQUASH CLOVERLEAF ROLLS

DeDe Waldmann, Monona, Wisconsin

(PICTURED ON PAGE 73)

2 tablespoons sugar
1/4 cup warm water (110° to 115°)
1 package (1/4 ounce) active
   dry yeast
1 cup warm milk (110° to 115°)
4 tablespoons butter *or*
   margarine, melted, *divided*
1 teaspoon salt
1 cup mashed cooked winter
   squash
3/4 cup shredded cheddar cheese
4 to 4-1/2 cups all-purpose flour
Sesame seeds, optional

In a large mixing bowl, dissolve sugar in water. Sprinkle the yeast over the water and stir gently. Let stand until light and foamy. Stir in milk, 3 tablespoons butter, salt, squash and cheese. Add enough flour to form a soft dough. Turn out onto a lightly floured surface; knead until the dough is no longer sticky, about 5 minutes. Form into a ball and place in a greased bowl, turning once to grease top. Cover and let rise in a warm place until doubled, about 1 hour. Meanwhile, lightly grease 24 muffin cups. Punch down dough. Break off small portions and roll into 1-in. balls. Put three balls into each cup. Cover and let rise in a warm place until doubled, about 30 minutes. Brush tops of rolls with remaining butter; sprinkle with sesame seeds if desired. Bake at 375° for 16-18 minutes or until golden. Serve warm. **Yield:** 2 dozen.

CORN MUFFINS WITH HONEY BUTTER

Marilyn Platner, Marion, Iowa

(PICTURED ON PAGE 109)

2 cups all-purpose flour
2 cups yellow cornmeal
1 cup dry milk powder
1/4 cup sugar
2 tablespoons baking powder
1 teaspoon salt
1/2 teaspoon baking soda
2-2/3 cups water
1/2 cup butter *or* margarine,
   melted
2 eggs, beaten
1 tablespoon lemon juice
HONEY BUTTER:
2 tablespoons honey
1/2 cup butter, softened
   (no substitutes)

In a bowl, combine flour, cornmeal, milk powder, sugar, baking powder, salt and

baking soda. Add water, butter, eggs and lemon juice; stir until dry ingredients are moistened. Spoon into 24 greased muffin cups. Bake at 425° for 13-15 minutes. In a small mixing bowl, beat together honey and softened butter. Serve with the muffins. **Yield:** 2 dozen.

SAVORY CHEDDAR BREAD

Carol Funk, Richard, Saskatchewan

(PICTURED ON PAGE 196)

2 cups all-purpose flour
4 teaspoons baking powder
1 tablespoon sugar
1/2 teaspoon onion salt
1/2 teaspoon oregano
1/4 teaspoon dry mustard
1-1/4 cups (5 ounces) shredded
   sharp cheddar cheese
1 egg, well beaten
1 cup milk
1 tablespoon butter *or*
   margarine, melted

Combine flour, baking powder, sugar, onion salt, oregano, dry mustard and cheese; set aside. Combine egg, milk and butter; add all at once to dry ingredients, stirring just until moistened. Spread batter in a greased 8-1/2-in. x 4-1/2-in. loaf pan. Bake at 350° for 45 minutes. **Yield:** 1 loaf.

CHERRY/NUT BREAKFAST ROLLS

Darlene Markel, Roseburg, Oregon

(PICTURED ON PAGE 231)

2 packages (1/4 ounce *each*)
   active dry yeast
1 cup warm water (110° to 115°)
1/2 cup butter *or* margarine,
   melted
1/2 cup sugar
3 eggs, beaten
1/2 teaspoon salt
4-1/2 to 5 cups all-purpose flour,
   divided
FILLING:
3 cups fresh *or* frozen pitted
   tart red cherries, chopped
2/3 cup sugar
1/3 cup finely chopped almonds
3 tablespoons cornstarch
1/4 teaspoon almond extract
Few drops red food coloring,
   optional
ICING:
1/2 cup confectioners' sugar
1/2 to 2 teaspoons milk
1/2 teaspoon butter *or*
   margarine, softened
1/2 teaspoon almond extract

In a large mixing bowl, dissolve yeast in water. Let stand 5 minutes. Stir in butter, sugar, eggs, salt and 3 cups flour. Add enough remaining flour to form a soft dough. Turn out onto a floured surface; knead until smooth and elastic, about 6-8 minutes. Place dough in a greased bowl, turning once to grease top. Cover and refrigerate 2 hours. Meanwhile, combine all filling ingredients in a saucepan. Bring to a boil; reduce heat and cook until thickened, stirring constantly. Cool. Turn dough out onto a lightly floured surface. Roll out to make a 14-in. x 16-in. rectangle. Spread with filling. Roll up, jelly-roll style, beginning with the long end. Cut into 12 slices. Place, cut side down, on a greased 13-in. x 9-in. x 2-in. baking pan. Cover and let rise until almost doubled, about 25 minutes. Bake at 375° for 25 minutes or until golden brown. Remove from pan; cool slightly. Combine all icing ingredients; drizzle over warm rolls. Serve immediately. **Yield:** 12 rolls.

Quick & Easy

MOM'S CORN BREAD

Norma Erne, Albuquerque, New Mexico

2 eggs, beaten
1-1/4 cups milk
1/4 cup shortening or bacon fat,
melted
1-1/2 cups yellow cornmeal
3/4 cup all-purpose flour
2 tablespoons sugar
2-1/4 teaspoons baking powder
1 teaspoon salt

Combine eggs, milk and shortening. Sift together all remaining ingredients and add to egg mixture; stir just until moistened. Pour into a greased 8-in. x 8-in. baking pan. Bake at 400° for 20-25 minutes, or until bread shrinks slightly from sides of the pan and begins to brown on the edges. **Yield:** about 9 servings.

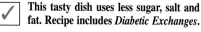

BEST BRAN MUFFINS

Suzanne Smith, Framingham, Massachusetts

✓ This tasty dish uses less sugar, salt and fat. Recipe includes *Diabetic Exchanges*.

1 cup all-purpose flour
1 cup whole wheat flour
1/2 cup rolled oats
1/2 cup all-bran cereal
1 teaspoon baking powder
1 teaspoon baking soda
1/2 teaspoon salt
1 egg, beaten
3/4 cup buttermilk
1/2 cup molasses
1/4 cup vegetable oil

1 can (8 ounces) crushed
    pineapple in natural juice,
    undrained
1/2 cup chopped nuts, dates *or*
    raisins

In a mixing bowl, combine first seven ingredients. Make a well in the center. Combine the egg, buttermilk, molasses, oil and pineapple with juice. Pour into well; mix until dry ingredients are moistened. Stir in nuts, dates or raisins. Fill 18 greased muffin cups 2/3 full. Bake at 400° for 12 minutes or until golden brown. **Yield:** 18 muffins. **Diabetic Exchanges:** One serving (prepared with nuts) equals 1 starch, 1/2 fruit, 1 fat; also, 151 calories, 221 mg sodium, 16 mg cholesterol, 22 gm carbohydrate, 4 gm protein, 6 gm fat.

CHOCOLATE CHIP OATMEAL MUFFINS

Cheryl Bohn, Dominion City, Manitoba

1/2 cup butter *or* margarine
3/4 cup packed brown sugar
1 egg
1 cup all-purpose flour
1 teaspoon baking powder
1/4 teaspoon baking soda
1/4 teaspoon salt
3/4 cup applesauce
1 cup rolled oats
1 cup (6 ounces) semisweet
    chocolate chips

In a large mixing bowl, cream butter and sugar. Beat in egg. Combine next four ingredients; add alternately with applesauce to the creamed mixture. Stir in oats and chips. Fill greased or paper-lined muffin tins 3/4 full. Bake at 350° for 25 minutes. **Yield:** 12 muffins.

> **COME OUT ON TOP.** For evenly rounded tops on muffins, grease cups on bottom and only 1/2-inch up sides.

ORANGE PECAN MUFFINS

Margie Schwartz, Sarasota, Florida

1-1/4 cups all-purpose flour
3/4 cup sugar
1-1/2 teaspoons baking soda
1 teaspoon salt
4 large oranges
Water
2 eggs, beaten
1/2 cup vegetable oil
4-1/2 cups raisin bran cereal
1 cup chopped pecans

In a large mixing bowl, combine first four ingredients. Set aside. Remove the peel from two of the oranges. Cut all four of the oranges into eighths and remove seeds; puree in a blender or food processor. If necessary, add enough water to puree to equal 2 cups. Stir oranges, eggs, oil, cereal and pecans into the dry ingredients. Blend just until mixed. Fill greased muffin tins 3/4 full. Bake at 375° for 20-25 minutes. **Yield:** 18 muffins.

ORANGE BOWKNOTS

Pam Hansen Taylor, Houston, Texas

1 cup milk
1/2 cup shortening
1/3 cup sugar
1 teaspoon salt
1 package (1/4 ounce) active
    dry yeast
1/4 cup warm water (110° to 115°)
2 eggs, beaten
1/4 cup orange juice
Grated peel of 2 oranges
5 to 6 cups all-purpose flour,
    divided
ORANGE GLAZE:
1 cup confectioners' sugar
2 tablespoons orange juice
2 teaspoons grated orange peel

In a saucepan, heat milk, shortening, sugar and salt. Cool to lukewarm. Dissolve yeast in water. In a large mixing bowl, combine yeast with milk mixture, eggs, juice, peel and 3 cups flour. Mix until smooth. Stir in enough remaining flour to form a soft dough. Knead until smooth and elastic, about 6-8 minutes. Place dough in a greased bowl; cover and let rise in a warm place until doubled, about 1-1/2 hours. Punch dough down; let rest 15 minutes. Roll dough into a 16-in. x 10-in. rectangle. Cut into 16 1-in. strips. Tie strips into knots; place on greased baking sheets. Cover and let rise until doubled, about 1 hour. Bake at 400° for about 10 minutes or until golden brown. Cool on wire rack. Combine all glaze ingredients; spread over rolls. **Yield:** 16 rolls.

RHUBARB COFFEE CAKE

Genelle Andrews, South Roxana, Illinois

1-1/2 cups packed brown sugar
1/2 cup shortening
1 egg
2 cups all-purpose flour
1 teaspoon baking soda
1/2 teaspoon salt
1 cup (8 ounces) sour cream
1-1/2 cups chopped rhubarb
TOPPING:
1/4 cup sugar
1/4 cup packed brown sugar
1/2 cup chopped pecans *or*
    walnuts

1 tablespoon butter *or*
    margarine
1 teaspoon ground cinnamon

In a mixing bowl, cream brown sugar and shortening. Add egg. Combine flour, baking soda and salt; add alternately with sour cream to the brown sugar/shortening mixture. Fold in rhubarb. Spread in a greased 13-in. x 9-in. x 2-in. baking pan. Combine all topping ingredients; sprinkle over batter. Bake at 350° for 45-50 minutes. Cool on wire rack. **Yield:** about 12 servings.

CHERRY/ALMOND QUICK BREAD

Nancy Reichert, Thomasville, Georgia

1 cup sugar
1/2 cup butter *or* margarine,
    softened
2 eggs
1 teaspoon almond extract
2 cups all-purpose flour
1 teaspoon baking soda
1/2 teaspoon salt
1 cup buttermilk
1 cup chopped almonds
1 jar (6 ounces) maraschino
    cherries, drained and chopped

In a large mixing bowl, cream sugar and butter. Add eggs, one at a time, beating well after each addition. Blend in extract. Combine dry ingredients; blend into creamed mixture alternately with the buttermilk. Stir in the almonds and cherries. Pour into a greased and floured 9-in. x 5-in. x 3-in. loaf pan. Bake at 350° for about 70 minutes or until loaf tests done. Remove from pan and cool on a wire rack. **Yield:** 1 loaf.

BREAKFAST BUNS

Dorothy McGinnis, West Haven, Connecticut

2 cups all-purpose flour
3/4 cup sugar, *divided*
1 tablespoon baking powder
3 tablespoons butter *or*
    margarine
2 eggs, lightly beaten
1 teaspoon vanilla extract
1/2 cup milk
1 cup raisins
1/2 teaspoon ground cinnamon

In a mixing bowl, stir together flour, 1/2 cup sugar and baking powder; cut in butter. Combine eggs, vanilla and milk; add to dry ingredients and stir just until moistened. Add raisins. Drop by tablespoonfuls onto greased baking sheet. Combine the cinnamon and remaining sugar; sprinkle over buns. Bake at 325° for 20-25 minutes or until light golden brown. Serve warm. **Yield:** 16 servings.

YOU'LL add fireworks to an Independence Day celebration with these four fantastic recipes. Start your day with piping hot Blueberry Cream Muffins or generous slices of Peachy Sour Cream Coffee Cake. After your meaty fare, serve Mountain Berry Pie with lots of cool and creamy hand-cranked ice cream. And pass the Lemon Filbert Tea Bars—they're perfect for a summer day!

FOR THE FOURTH.
Clockwise from the bottom: **Lemon Filbert Tea Bars** (recipe on page 185), **Peachy Sour Cream Coffee Cake** (recipe on page 157), **Blueberry Cream Muffins** (recipe on page 157) and **Ozark Mountain Berry Pie** (recipe on page 204).

BLUEBERRY CREAM MUFFINS

Lillian Van der Harst, Center Lovell, Maine

(PICTURED AT LEFT)

4 eggs
2 cups sugar
1 cup vegetable oil
1 teaspoon vanilla extract
4 cups all-purpose flour
1 teaspoon salt
1 teaspoon baking soda
2 teaspoons baking powder
2 cups (16 ounces) sour cream
2 cups fresh blueberries

In a mixing bowl, beat eggs. Gradually add sugar. While beating, slowly pour in oil; add vanilla. Combine dry ingredients; add alternately with the sour cream to the egg mixture. Gently fold in blueberries. Spoon into greased muffin tins. Bake at 400° for 20 minutes. **Yield:** 24 muffins.

PEACHY SOUR CREAM COFFEE CAKE

Alice Brandt, Marengo, Illinois

(PICTURED AT LEFT)

STREUSEL TOPPING/FILLING:
2 cups chopped pecans
1/3 cup packed brown sugar
3 tablespoons sugar
1 teaspoon ground cinnamon
CAKE:
1/2 cup butter-flavored shortening
1 cup sugar
2 eggs
2 cups all-purpose flour
1-1/2 teaspoons baking powder
1/2 teaspoon baking soda
1/2 teaspoon salt
1 cup (8 ounces) sour cream
1 teaspoon vanilla extract
2 cups sliced peeled fresh peaches

Combine streusel ingredients; set aside. In a large mixing bowl, cream shortening and sugar until fluffy. Beat in eggs. Combine dry ingredients; add alternately with sour cream and vanilla to creamed mixture. Beat until smooth. Pour half the batter into a 9-in. springform pan. Sprinkle with 1 cup streusel. Top with remaining batter and 1/2 cup streusel. Bake at 350° for 30 minutes. Arrange peaches over cake; sprinkle with remaining streusel. Bake an additional 30-40 minutes or until cake tests done. Cool cake 10 minutes before removing sides of pan. **Yield:** 12 servings.

GRANDMA'S OATMEAL BREAD

Marcia Hostetter, Ogdensburg, New York

(PICTURED ON FRONT COVER)

1-1/2 cups boiling water
1 tablespoon butter *or* margarine
2 teaspoons salt
1/2 cup sugar
1 cup rolled oats
2 packages (1/4 ounce *each*) active dry yeast
3/4 cup warm water (110° to 115°)
1/4 cup molasses
1/4 cup packed brown sugar
6 to 6-1/2 cups all-purpose flour, *divided*

In a small mixing bowl, combine boiling water, butter, salt and sugar. Stir in oats; cool to lukewarm. In a large mixing bowl, dissolve yeast in warm water. Stir in molasses, brown sugar and 1 cup flour. Beat until smooth. Add oat mixture and enough remaining flour to make a stiff dough. Turn out onto a floured board; knead until smooth and elastic, about 6-8 minutes. Shape into a ball. Place in a greased bowl, turning once to grease top. Cover and allow to rise until doubled, about 1-1/2 hours. Punch dough down; divide in half and shape into balls. Cover and let rest 10 minutes. Shape into loaves and place into two greased 9-in. x 5-in. x 3-in. loaf pans. Cover and let rise until nearly doubled, about 1 hour. Bake at 375° for 35 minutes. Cover loosely with foil the last 20 minutes if loaves are browning excessively. Remove from pans and cool on wire rack. **Yield:** 2 loaves.

ELEPHANT EARS

Jane Carlorsky, Delton, Michigan

1 package (1/4 ounce) active dry yeast
1/4 cup warm water (110° to 115°)
2 cups all-purpose flour
2 tablespoons sugar
1/2 teaspoon salt
1/2 cup butter *or* margarine
1/2 cup warm milk (110° to 115°)
1 egg
FILLING:
2 tablespoons butter *or* margarine, softened
1/2 cup sugar
1 teaspoon ground cinnamon
TOPPING:
1-1/2 cups sugar
1 teaspoon cinnamon
1/2 cup chopped walnuts, optional

Dissolve yeast in water. In a large mixing bowl, combine flour, sugar and salt. Cut butter into flour mixture as for pastry. Beat milk, egg and yeast mixture until smooth. Stir into the flour mixture and shape into a ball. Place in a greased bowl; cover and chill for at least 2 hours. Turn out onto a floured board; punch dough down. Cover with a towel and allow to rest 10 minutes. Roll into a 18-in. x 10-in. rectangle. Spread with softened butter. Combine remaining filling ingredients and sprinkle over butter. Starting with the long side, roll up dough jelly-roll style and pinch the edges to seal. Cut into 1-in. slices. Mix the topping ingredients and sprinkle a portion of the mixture on waxed paper. Place one slice of dough on top of the mixture and roll to a 5-in. circle, turning to coat both sides. Place on greased baking sheets. Repeat until all the circles are rolled and coated. Sprinkle tops of ears with leftover topping if desired. Bake at 375° for 10-12 minutes or until golden brown. Cool on wire racks. **Yield:** 1-1/2 dozen.

OLD-FASHIONED ROLLS

Martha Buhler, Dalles, Oregon

 This tasty dish uses less sugar, salt and fat. Recipe includes *Diabetic Exchanges*.

1 package (1/4 ounce) active dry yeast
1 teaspoon sugar
1/2 cup warm water (110° to 115°)
6 to 6-1/2 cups all-purpose flour
1 tablespoon salt
3/4 cup shortening, butter *or* margarine, melted and cooled
2 cups milk (110° to 115°)

Dissolve yeast and sugar in water; set aside. In a large mixing bowl, combine 3 cups flour, salt, shortening, milk and yeast mixture. Beat well. Add enough of the remaining flour to form a soft dough. Turn out onto a lightly floured board; knead until smooth and elastic, about 6-8 minutes. Dough should be soft. Place dough in a lightly greased bowl; cover and allow to rise in a warm place until doubled, about 1 hour. Punch dough down and divide into four pieces. Divide three of the pieces into eight pieces each; shape into smooth balls and place on greased baking sheets. Divide remaining dough into 24 balls. Press 1 small ball atop each larger ball. Cover and let rise until doubled, about 45 minutes. Bake at 375° for 30 minutes or until golden. **Yield:** 2 dozen. **Diabetic Exchanges:** One serving (prepared with shortening and skim milk) equals 2 starch, 1 fat; also, 186 calories, 299 mg sodium, 0 mg cholesterol, 27 gm carbohydrate, 4 gm protein, 6 gm fat.

CHERRY CREAM SCONES

Carrie Sherrill, Forestville, Wisconsin

(PICTURED AT RIGHT)

> 3/4 cup dried cherries
> 1 cup boiling water
> 3 cups all-purpose flour
> 3 tablespoons sugar
> 1 tablespoon baking powder
> 1/2 teaspoon salt
> 1/2 teaspoon cream of tartar
> 1/2 cup butter *or* margarine, room temperature
> 1 egg, *separated*
> 1/2 cup sour cream
> 3/4 cup half-and-half cream
> 1-1/2 teaspoons almond extract
> Additional sugar

Soak cherries in water for 10 minutes. Drain and set aside. In a large mixing bowl, combine the flour, sugar, baking powder, salt and cream of tartar. With a pastry blender, cut in the butter. Set aside. In a small bowl, combine egg yolk, sour cream, cream and extract. Add to flour mixture; stir until a soft dough forms. Turn out onto a lightly floured surface; knead gently six to eight times. Knead in cherries. Divide dough in half and shape into balls. Roll each ball into a 6-in. circle. Cut into six wedges. Repeat with remaining ball. Place on lightly greased baking sheet. Beat the egg white until foamy; brush tops of scones and sprinkle with sugar. Bake at 400° for 15-20 minutes. Serve warm. **Yield:** 12 scones.

CHEERY CHERRY LOAF

Mina Dyck, Boissevain, Manitoba

(PICTURED ON PAGE 12)

> 1 jar (6 ounces) red maraschino cherries
> 2-1/2 cups all-purpose flour
> 1 cup sugar
> 4 teaspoons baking powder
> 1/2 teaspoon salt
> 2 eggs
> 2/3 cup milk
> 1/3 cup butter *or* margarine, melted
> 1 jar (8 ounces) green maraschino cherries, drained and cut up
> 1/2 cup chopped pecans
> 1 tablespoon grated orange peel

Drain red cherries, reserving liquid; add water, if needed, to liquid to equal 1/3 cup. Cut up cherries; set cherries and liquid aside. In a large bowl, combine flour, sugar, baking powder and salt. In a small bowl, lightly beat eggs. Add milk,

butter and cherry liquid; stir into dry ingredients just until combined. Fold in red and green cherries, pecans and orange peel. Pour into a greased 9-in. x 5-in. x 3-in. loaf pan. Bake at 350° for 1 hour or until bread tests done. **Yield:** 1 loaf.

 **Quick & Easy**

FRUIT AND NUT MUFFINS

Dorothy Boltman, Shorewood, Minnesota

> 4 cups diced peeled tart baking apples (1/4-inch pieces)
> 1 cup sugar
> 1-1/2 cups raisins
> 1-1/2 cups chopped nuts
> 2 eggs
> 1/2 cup vegetable oil
> 2 teaspoons vanilla extract
> 2 cups all-purpose flour
> 1-1/2 teaspoons baking soda
> 2 teaspoons ground cinnamon
> 1/8 teaspoon salt

In a large mixing bowl, combine apples, sugar, raisins and nuts; set aside. In another bowl, beat eggs, oil and vanilla; stir into apple mixture. Combine dry ingredients; carefully fold into apple mixture. Do not overmix. Fill 18 greased muffin cups almost to the top. Bake at 375° for 18-20 minutes or until muffins test done. **Yield:** 1-1/2 dozen.

FREEZE-AND-BAKE ROLLS

Jayne Duce, Raymond, Alberta

(PICTURED ON PAGE 60)

> ✓ This tasty dish uses less sugar, salt and fat. Recipe includes *Diabetic Exchanges*.

> 2 packages (1/4 ounce *each*) active dry yeast
> 1-1/2 cups warm water (110° to 115°)
> 1/2 cup plus 2 teaspoons sugar, *divided*
> 1-1/2 cups warm milk (110° to 115°)
> 1/4 cup vegetable oil
> 4 teaspoons salt
> 7-1/2 to 8-1/2 cups all-purpose flour
> Butter *or* margarine, melted

In a large mixing bowl, dissolve yeast in water. Add 2 teaspoons sugar; let stand 5 minutes. Add milk, oil, salt and remaining sugar. Add enough flour to form stiff dough. Turn out onto a floured surface; knead until smooth and elastic, about 6-8 minutes. Place in a greased bowl, turning once to grease top. Cover and let rise in a warm place until doubled, about 1-1/2 hours. Punch dough down. Divide into four pieces. Cover three pieces with plastic wrap. Divide one piece into 12 balls. Roll each ball into a 10-in. rope; tie into a knot and pinch ends together. Repeat with remaining dough. Place rolls on

greased baking sheets; brush with melted butter. Cover and let rise until doubled, about 20-30 minutes. To serve immediately, bake at 375° for 15-18 minutes. To freeze for later use, partially bake at 300° for 15 minutes. Allow to cool; freeze. Reheat frozen rolls at 375° for 12-15 minutes or until browned. **Yield:** 4 dozen. **Diabetic Exchanges:** One roll (prepared with skim milk) equals 1-1/2 starch; also, 120 calories, 197 mg sodium, trace cholesterol, 24 gm carbohydrate, 3 gm protein, 1 gm fat.

 **Quick & Easy**

BREAKFAST OATMEAL MUFFINS

Edna Bowyer, Simcoe, Ontario

(PICTURED ON PAGE 53)

> 1 cup all-purpose flour
> 1 cup packed brown sugar
> 1 teaspoon baking powder
> 1 teaspoon baking soda
> 1/2 cup vegetable oil
> 2 eggs, lightly beaten
> 1 cup leftover oatmeal
> 1 cup raisins
> 1 teaspoon vanilla extract

In a large bowl, combine flour, brown sugar, baking powder and baking soda. In another bowl, combine oil, eggs, oatmeal, raisins and vanilla; add to dry ingredients and stir just until moistened (the batter will be thin). Spoon into 12 greased muffin cups. Bake at 350° for 18 minutes or until the muffins test done. **Yield:** 1 dozen.

 **Quick & Easy**

KATE SMITH COFFEE CAKE

Ruth Nast, Waterford, Connecticut

> 1 egg
> 1/4 cup butter *or* margarine, melted
> 1/3 cup milk
> 1 cup all-purpose flour
> 1/4 cup sugar
> 2 teaspoons baking powder
> 1/4 teaspoon salt
> 1 cup bran flakes, crushed
> **TOPPING:**
> 1/3 cup bran flakes, crushed
> 2 tablespoons brown sugar
> 2 teaspoons butter *or* margarine, softened

In a mixing bowl, combine egg, butter and milk. Combine flour, sugar, baking powder and salt; stir into batter. Add bran flakes. Spread into a greased 8-in. round baking pan. Combine topping ingredients; sprinkle over batter. Bake at 375° for 18-22 minutes or until cake tests done. Serve warm. **Yield:** 6 servings.

YOUR FAMILY will give four cheers—and more—for cherries when you offer these sweet treats featuring that delectable red fruit. Don't be surprised when these scrumptious dishes become much-requested menu items in your home!

CHERRY JUBILEE!.
Clockwise from top right: **Cherry Crisp** (recipe on page 204), **Cherry Cheesecake Tarts** (recipe on page 204), **Cherry/Rhubarb Cobbler** (recipe on page 204) and **Cherry Cream Scones** (recipe on page 158).

I Remember Mama's Manna

ONE OF the most indelible memories of my childhood is the wonderful aroma of baking bread. I enjoyed that unforgettable fragrance every Friday as Mama baked six big crusty brown loaves for us to enjoy.

On summer days when our doors and windows were open, the smell of baking bread permeated the neighborhood, attracting salesmen, the pump repairman and any nearby bachelors (Mama was a widow).

Anyone who stopped to visit on Friday could expect a warm slab of fresh bread to sample…and I mean a *slab*, not a slice, generously slathered with fresh sweet butter.

For me, the heel was the choicest part of all. I always hurried home from school on Fridays, lest someone beat me to that hot crusty morsel.

Baking was an all-day job for Mama. Early Friday morning I'd find her in the

The aroma of her homemade bread enriched a whole town.

By Louise Kohr
Olympia, Washington

kitchen, sleeves rolled to her elbows and flour on her nose, preparing her bread dough.

She had a little jingle she'd say as she stirred in the yeast, earnestly repeated as a part of the baking ritual:

Rise, rise,
Swell and swell,
Lift our lives
With taste and smell.

Mama always said that her bread wouldn't be good until the dough squeaked, so she kneaded until that dough "talked back". Her loaves were

huge, making today's bread seem puny by comparison.

That wonderful bread always won a prize at the county fair. One year, though, Mama was working away from home and didn't have time to bake, so my Aunt Jessie filled in, using Mama's recipe. She baked two loaves and entered one in her own name and one in Mama's. Mama won the premium, and Aunt Jessie came in second!

Mama sincerely believed that a woman's ability to turn out a good loaf of bread would go a long way toward ensuring a happy marriage. Her gift to new brides in town was a starter of yeast and instructions in the art of baking.

Raising a family without a husband was not an easy job for Mama, but she did love life. And her way of showing it was evident every Friday—in the aroma and great taste of her wonderful home-baked bread.

GOLDEN POTATO ROLLS
Noni Ruegner, Salt Lake City, Utah
(PICTURED ON PAGE 125)

 This tasty dish uses less sugar, salt and fat. Recipe includes *Diabetic Exchanges*.

1 package (1/4 ounce) active
  dry yeast
1/2 cup warm water (110° to 115°)
1 cup milk
3/4 cup shortening *or* margarine
1-1/4 cups mashed potatoes
1/2 cup sugar
2 teaspoons salt
8 to 8-1/2 cups all-purpose
  flour, *divided*
2 eggs, beaten

Dissolve yeast in water; set aside. In a saucepan, combine milk, shortening and potatoes; cook and stir over low heat just until shortening is melted. Remove from the heat and place in a large bowl with sugar, salt, 2 cups of flour and the yeast mixture. Add eggs; mix well. Cover loosely and allow to stand for 2 hours (the dough will be like a sponge). Stir in enough of the remaining flour to make a soft dough. Turn out onto a floured surface and knead until smooth and elastic, about 6 minutes. Place in a greased bowl, turning once to grease top. Cover and let rise in a warm place until doubled, about 1 hour. Punch down and divide into thirds. On a floured surface, roll each portion into a 12-in. circle. Cut each circle into 12 pie-shaped wedges. Beginning at the wide end, roll up each wedge. Place rolls, point side down, 2 in. apart on greased baking sheets. Cover and let rise 30 minutes or until nearly doubled. Bake at 400° for 15 minutes or until golden. **Yield:** 3 dozen. **Diabetic Exchanges:** One roll (prepared with skim milk and margarine) equals 1-1/2 starch, 1 fat; also, 170 calories, 168 mg sodium, 12 mg cholesterol, 28 gm carbohydrate, 4 gm protein, 5 gm fat.

CINNAMON CRANBERRY MUFFINS
Ronni Dufour, Lebanon, Connecticut
(PICTURED ON PAGE 105)

2 cups all-purpose flour
1 cup sugar
1-1/2 teaspoons baking powder
1 teaspoon ground nutmeg
1 teaspoon ground cinnamon
1/2 teaspoon baking soda
1/2 teaspoon ground ginger
1/2 teaspoon salt
2 teaspoons grated orange peel
1/2 cup shortening

3/4 cup orange juice
2 eggs, beaten
1 tablespoon vanilla extract
1-1/2 cups coarsely chopped
  cranberries
1-1/2 cups chopped pecans

In a large bowl, combine flour, sugar, baking powder, nutmeg, cinnamon, baking soda, ginger, salt and orange peel. Cut in shortening until crumbly. Stir in orange juice, eggs, and vanilla just until moistened. Fold in cranberries and nuts. Fill 18 greased or paper-lined muffin cups two-thirds full. Bake at 375° for 18-20 minutes or until golden. **Yield:** 1-1/2 dozen.

BLUEBERRY BUCKLE
Debbie Thackrah, Latrobe, Pennsylvania

1/2 cup shortening
1 cup sugar, *divided*
1 egg, beaten
2-1/2 cups all-purpose flour, *divided*
2-1/2 teaspoons baking powder
1/2 teaspoon salt
1/2 cup milk
2 cups fresh *or* frozen
  blueberries
2 teaspoons lemon juice
1/2 teaspoon ground cinnamon
1/4 cup butter *or* margarine

In a mixing bowl, cream shortening and 1/2 cup sugar. Add egg and mix well. Combine 2 cups flour, baking powder and salt; add to creamed mixture alternately with the milk. Spread into a greased 9-in. square baking pan. Toss blueberries with lemon juice; sprinkle over batter. In a small bowl, combine cinnamon and remaining sugar and flour; cut in butter until mixture is the size of peas. Sprinkle over berries. Bake at 350° for 60-65 minutes. **Yield:** 9-12 servings.

APRICOT BREAD
Ruth Jones, Maitland, Florida

1 cup snipped dried apricots
2 cups warm water
1 cup sugar
2 tablespoons butter *or*
  margarine, softened
1 egg
3/4 cup orange juice
2 cups all-purpose flour
2 teaspoons baking powder
1/4 teaspoon baking soda
1 teaspoon salt
3/4 cup chopped nuts

Soak apricots in warm water for 30 minutes. Meanwhile, in a mixing bowl, cream the sugar, butter and egg. Stir in orange juice. Combine flour, baking powder, baking soda and salt; stir into creamed mixture just until combined. Drain apricots well; add to batter with nuts. Pour into a greased 9-in. x 5-in. x 3-in. loaf pan. Bake at 350° for 55 minutes or until bread tests done. Cool 10 minutes in pan before removing to a wire rack. **Yield:** 1 loaf.

NEW ENGLAND BLUEBERRY COFFEE CAKE
Audrey Thibodeau, Lancaster, New Hampshire

1-1/2 cups all-purpose flour
1/2 cup sugar
1 tablespoon baking powder
1 teaspoon cinnamon
1/2 teaspoon salt
1-1/2 cups fresh blueberries
1 egg
1/2 cup milk
1/4 cup butter *or* margarine, melted
TOPPING:
1/4 cup butter *or* margarine, melted
3/4 cup packed brown sugar
1/2 cup chopped walnuts
1 tablespoon all-purpose flour

In a large mixing bowl, combine flour, sugar, baking powder, cinnamon and salt. Gently fold in blueberries. In a small bowl, whisk together the egg, milk and butter. Add to the flour mixture and stir carefully. Spread into a greased 8-in. x 8-in. baking pan. Combine all topping ingredients and sprinkle over batter. Bake at 425° for 20-25 minutes or until top is light golden brown. Serve warm or at room temperature. **Yield:** 12 servings.

COCONUT BREAD
Virginia Doyle, Pinedale, Wyoming

3 cups all-purpose flour
2 teaspoons baking powder
1/2 teaspoon baking soda
1/2 teaspoon salt
2 cups sugar
1 cup vegetable oil
4 eggs, lightly beaten
2 teaspoons coconut extract
1 cup buttermilk
1 cup shredded coconut
1 cup chopped walnuts

Combine flour, baking powder, baking soda and salt; set aside. In a large bowl, combine sugar, oil, eggs and coconut extract. Add dry ingredients alternately with buttermilk; stir just until moistened. Fold in coconut and nuts. Pour into two greased and floured 8-1/2-in. x 4-1/2-in. x 2-1/2-in. loaf pans. Bake at 325° for 1 hour or until breads test done. Cool 10 minutes in pans before removing to a wire rack to cool completely. **Yield:** 2 loaves.

HOT SUMMER DAYS call for lighter meals. For a refreshing yet hearty luncheon entree, Cantaloupe with Chicken Salad truly fills the bill. And for dessert, pass a variety of tempting treats, such as Pineapple Carrot Bread, Praline Peach Cobbler and Sour Cream Raisin Squares. Judge for yourself… is this the best spread you've ever sampled?

LUSCIOUS LUNCH.
Clockwise from the top: **Sour Cream Raisin Squares** (recipe on page 184), **Cantaloupe with Chicken Salad** (recipe on page 55), **Pineapple Carrot Bread** (recipe on page 163) and **Praline Peach Cobbler** (recipe on page 218).

PINEAPPLE CARROT BREAD

Paula Spink, Elkins Park, Pennsylvania

(PICTURED AT LEFT)

3 cups all-purpose flour
2 cups sugar
1 teaspoon baking soda
1 teaspoon ground cinnamon
3/4 teaspoon salt
3 eggs
2 cups shredded carrots
1 cup vegetable oil
1 can (8 ounces) crushed
   pineapple, drained
1 cup chopped pecans or
   walnuts
2 teaspoons vanilla extract
3/4 cup confectioners' sugar,
   optional
1 to 1-1/2 teaspoons milk,
   optional

In a large bowl, combine the flour, sugar, baking soda, cinnamon and salt. In another bowl, beat eggs; add carrots, oil, pineapple, nuts and vanilla. Stir into the dry ingredients just until moistened. Spoon into two greased and floured 8-1/2-in. x 4-1/2-in. x 2-1/2-in. loaf pans. Bake at 350° for 65-75 minutes or until loaves test done. Cool 10 minutes in pans before removing to wire racks. Cool completely. If desired, combine confectioners' sugar and milk; drizzle over loaves. **Yield:** 2 loaves.

CHRISTMAS WREATHS

Margaret Foreman, La Verne, California

(PICTURED ON PAGE 142)

FILLING:
9 ounces pitted prunes,
   cooked, drained and mashed
   (about 1-1/2 cups)
1-1/2 cups chopped peeled apples
3/4 cup finely chopped walnuts
3/4 cup packed brown sugar
1/3 cup sugar
1/2 teaspoon ground cinnamon
1/2 teaspoon salt
DOUGH:
1 cup warm milk (110° to 115°)
1/2 cup sugar
1 teaspoon salt
2 packages (1/4 ounce each)
   active dry yeast
2 eggs, lightly beaten
1/2 cup shortening
4-1/2 to 5 cups all-purpose flour
ICING:
2 cups confectioners' sugar
2 to 3 tablespoons milk
1 teaspoon vanilla extract
Candied cherries, optional

Combine all filling ingredients in a bowl; cover and refrigerate until ready to use. For dough, combine warm milk, sugar, salt and yeast in a mixing bowl. Let stand for 5 minutes. Add eggs, shortening and 3 cups flour; mix until smooth. Add enough of the remaining flour to form a soft dough. Turn out onto a floured surface; knead until smooth and elastic, about 6-8 minutes. Place in a greased bowl, turning once to grease top. Cover and let rise in a warm place until doubled, about 1 to 1-1/2 hours. Punch dough down; divide in half. Roll each half into an 18-in. x 9-in. rectangle. Spread each with half of the filling. Starting at the long end, roll up tightly and seal edges. Place on a greased baking sheet, sealing ends together and forming a ring. With a scissors, cut two-thirds of the way through the ring at 1-in. intervals. Carefully turn each section onto its side. Cover and let rise until nearly doubled, 30-45 minutes. Bake at 350° for 25-30 minutes or until golden. Cool for 20 minutes. Beat confectioners' sugar, milk and vanilla until smooth. Remove wreaths to a platter; drizzle with icing while warm. Decorate with candied cherries if desired. **Yield:** 2 loaves.

WALNUT-RAISIN BREAD

Charles Stuller, Winter Haven, Florida

2 cups all-purpose flour
1 teaspoon baking powder
1/2 teaspoon baking soda
1/2 teaspoon salt
1/2 cup butter or margarine,
   softened
3/4 cup sugar
1 egg
1/4 cup orange juice
1 can (8 ounces) crushed
   pineapple, undrained
1 cup raisins
1 cup chopped walnuts

In a mixing bowl, combine flour, baking powder, baking soda and salt; set aside. In another bowl, cream butter and sugar. Add egg and orange juice; beat well. Add 1/3 cup of flour mixture; beat until smooth. Mix in remaining flour mixture and the pineapple. Stir in raisins and walnuts. Pour into a greased 9-in. x 5-in. x 3-in. loaf pan. Bake at 350° for 60-70 minutes. Let cool in pan for 10 minutes. Remove to a wire rack to cool completely. **Yield:** 1 loaf.

SOFT PRETZELS

Karen Stewart-Linkhart, Xenia, Ohio

2 packages (1/4 ounce each)
   active dry yeast
2 cups warm water (110° to 115°)
1/2 cup sugar
2 teaspoons salt
1/4 cup butter or margarine,
   softened
1 egg
6-1/2 to 7-1/2 cups all-purpose flour
1 egg yolk
2 tablespoons water
Coarse salt, optional

In a large bowl, dissolve yeast in warm water. Add sugar, salt, butter and egg. Stir in 3 cups of flour; mix until smooth. Add enough additional flour to make a stiff dough. Cover bowl tightly with foil; refrigerate for 2-24 hours. Punch dough down and divide in half. On a lightly floured surface, cut each half into 16 equal pieces. Roll each piece into a 20-in. rope. Shape into the traditional pretzel shape and place on a greased baking sheet. In a small bowl, combine egg yolk and water; brush over the pretzels. Sprinkle with salt if desired. Cover and let rise in a warm place until doubled, about 25 minutes. Bake at 400° for 15 minutes or until brown. **Yield:** 32 pretzels.

Quick & Easy

NUTTY RHUBARB MUFFINS

Mary Kay Morris, Cokato, Minnesota

3/4 cup packed brown sugar
1/2 cup buttermilk or sour milk
1/3 cup vegetable oil
1 egg, beaten
1 teaspoon vanilla extract
2 cups all-purpose flour
1/2 teaspoon baking soda
1/2 teaspoon salt
1 cup diced rhubarb
1/2 cup chopped nuts
TOPPING:
1/4 cup packed brown sugar
1/4 cup chopped nuts
1/2 teaspoon ground cinnamon

In a small mixing bowl, combine brown sugar, buttermilk, oil, egg and vanilla; mix well. Set aside. In a medium mixing bowl, combine flour, baking soda and salt. Add egg mixture; stir just until combined. Fold in rhubarb and nuts. Spoon the batter into 12 greased muffin cups. Mix together topping ingredients; sprinkle over tops of muffins. Bake at 375° for 20 minutes or until muffins test done. **Yield:** 1 dozen.

YOUR FAMILY will fall for this selection of hearty recipes! Serve up a Texas-size helping of spicy lasagna and a thick slice of homemade rye bread. For a sweet conclusion, Cranberry Betty and a plate of chewy oatmeal pecan cookies are sure to please.

AUTUMN FAVORITES.
Clockwise from the top: **Chewy Pecan Cookies** (recipe on page 182), **Overnight Swedish Rye Bread** (recipe on page 165), **Cranberry Betty** (recipe on page 221) and **Texas-Style Lasagna** (recipe on page 81).

OVERNIGHT SWEDISH RYE BREAD

Caroline Carr, Lyons, Nebraska

(PICTURED AT LEFT)

2 packages (1/4 ounce *each*)
  active dry yeast
1/2 cup warm water (110° to 115°)
1 teaspoon sugar
4 cups warm milk (110° to 115°)
1 cup molasses
1 cup packed brown sugar
1 cup vegetable oil
1 cup quick-cooking oats
2 tablespoons grated orange
  peel
1 tablespoon salt
1 teaspoon fennel seed
1 teaspoon aniseed
1 teaspoon caraway seed
2 cups rye flour
11 to 12 cups all-purpose flour

In a large mixing bowl, dissolve yeast in water; stir in sugar and let stand for 5 minutes. Add milk, molasses, brown sugar, oil, oats, orange peel, salt, fennel, aniseed, caraway, rye flour and 6 cups of all-purpose flour. Add enough remaining all-purpose flour to form a soft but sticky dough. Cover and let rise in a warm place overnight. Punch dough down. Turn onto a floured board; knead until smooth and elastic, about 6-8 minutes. Shape into four loaves. Place in greased 9-in. x 5-in. x 3-in. loaf pans. Cover and let rise until doubled, about 1 hour. Bake at 350° for 35-45 minutes. Remove from the pans to cool on wire racks. **Yield:** 4 loaves.

STRAWBERRY RHUBARB COFFEE CAKE

Dorothy Morehouse, Massena, New York

(PICTURED ON PAGE 202)

FILLING:
3 cups sliced fresh *or* frozen
  rhubarb (1-inch pieces)
1 quart fresh strawberries,
  mashed
2 tablespoons lemon juice
1 cup sugar
1/3 cup cornstarch
CAKE:
3 cups all-purpose flour
1 cup sugar
1 teaspoon baking powder
1 teaspoon baking soda
1/2 teaspoon salt
1 cup butter *or* margarine, cut
  into pieces
1-1/2 cups buttermilk
2 eggs
1 teaspoon vanilla extract

TOPPING:
1/4 cup butter *or* margarine
3/4 cup all-purpose flour
3/4 cup sugar

In a large saucepan, combine rhubarb, strawberries and lemon juice. Cover and cook over medium heat about 5 minutes. Combine sugar and cornstarch; stir into saucepan. Bring to a boil, stirring constantly until thickened; remove from heat and set aside. In a large bowl, combine flour, sugar, baking powder, baking soda and salt. Cut in butter until mixture resembles coarse crumbs. Beat buttermilk, eggs and vanilla; stir into crumb mixture. Spread half of the batter evenly into a greased 13-in. x 9-in. x 2-in. baking dish. Carefully spread filling on top. Drop remaining batter by tablespoonfuls over filling. For topping, melt butter in a saucepan over low heat. Remove from heat; stir in flour and sugar until mixture resembles coarse crumbs. Sprinkle over batter. Lay foil on lower rack to catch any juicy fruit spillovers. Place coffee cake on middle rack; bake at 350° for 40-45 minutes. Cool in pan. Cut into squares. **Yield:** 16-20 servings.

APPLE DANISH

Sandy Lynch, Decatur, Illinois

PASTRY:
3 cups all-purpose flour
1/2 teaspoon salt
1 cup shortening
1 egg yolk
1/2 cup milk
FILLING:
6 cups sliced peeled apples
1-1/2 cups sugar
1/4 cup butter *or* margarine,
  melted
2 tablespoons all-purpose flour
1 teaspoon ground cinnamon
GLAZE:
1 egg white, lightly beaten
1/2 cup confectioners' sugar
2 to 3 teaspoons water

In a mixing bowl, combine flour and salt; cut in shortening until mixture resembles coarse crumbs. Combine egg yolk and milk; add to flour mixture. Stir just until dough clings together. Divide dough in half. On a lightly floured surface, roll half of dough into a 15-in. x 10-in. rectangle; transfer to a greased 15-in. x 10-in. x 1-in. baking pan. Set aside. In a bowl, toss together filling ingredients; spoon over pastry in pan. Roll out remaining dough to another 15-in. x 10-in. rectangle. Place over filling. Brush with egg white. Bake at 375° for 40 minutes or until golden brown. Cool on a wire rack. Combine the confectioners' sugar and enough water to achieve a drizzling con-

sistency. Drizzle over warm pastry. Cut into squares. Serve warm or cold. **Yield:** 20-24 servings.

CRANBERRY MUFFINS

Dorothy Bateman, Carver, Massachusetts

(PICTURED ON PAGE 180)

1 cup cranberries, quartered
8 tablespoons sugar, *divided*
1-3/4 cups all-purpose flour
2-1/2 teaspoons baking powder
1/4 teaspoon salt
1 egg
3/4 cup milk
1/3 cup vegetable oil
1 teaspoon grated lemon peel,
  optional
Cinnamon sugar

Sprinkle cranberries with 2 tablespoons sugar; set aside. Sift remaining sugar, flour, baking powder and salt into large mixing bowl. In separate bowl, beat egg, milk and oil. Make a hole in center of dry ingredients; pour in liquid ingredients. Stir only until mixed; do not overmix. Add berries and lemon peel. Fill greased standard or extra-large muffin cups with mixture. Sprinkle tops of muffins with cinnamon sugar. Bake at 400° about 18 minutes for standard-size muffins or about 22 minutes for extra-large muffins. **Yield:** 12 standard-size or 6 extra-large muffins.

MEXICAN CORN BREAD

Donna Hypes, Ramona, California

1 cup yellow cornmeal
1 cup all-purpose flour
1 tablespoon baking powder
1 teaspoon salt
2 tablespoons sugar
1 cup buttermilk
1 egg, beaten
1 can (8-3/4 ounces) cream-style
  corn
Dash hot pepper sauce
1/4 cup bacon drippings, melted
1/4 cup minced green onions
  with tops
1/2 cup shredded cheddar cheese

Combine first five ingredients in a large mixing bowl; set aside. In another bowl, combine buttermilk and egg; add corn and remaining ingredients. Pour over dry ingredients and stir just until blended. *Do not overmix.* Pour batter into a greased 8-in. square baking pan. Bake at 400° for 35 minutes or until bread tests done. Cool 5 minutes before cutting into squares. Serve warm or cold. **Yield:** 9 servings.

MAKING meals just like Mom used to prepare is easy when these mouth-watering dishes accompany your favorite main course. Mother's Rolls are fabulous fresh from the oven. Cheese and nuts are special additions to steamed cauliflower. And Molded Cranberry Salad and Raisin Pie are the perfect ending to wonderful meals.

MEMORIES OF MOM.
Clockwise from top left: **Mother's Rolls** (recipe on page 167), **Raisin Pie** (recipe on page 210), **Cauliflower with Almonds** (recipe on page 124) and **Molded Cranberry Salad** (recipe on page 54).

MOTHER'S ROLLS

Patricia Baxter, Great Bend, Kansas

(PICTURED AT LEFT)

   2 packages (1/4 ounce *each*)
     active dry yeast
   1 cup warm water (110° to 115°)
 1/3 cup sugar
   2 teaspoons salt
 1/3 cup shortening, melted and
     cooled
   1 egg, beaten
1-1/2 cups warm milk (110° to 115°)
   7 to 7-1/2 cups all-purpose flour

In a large mixing bowl, dissolve yeast in water. Add sugar, salt, shortening, egg, milk and 3 cups flour. Stir until mixture has a spongy texture. Let rest for 10 minutes. Mix in enough of the remaining flour to form a soft dough. Turn out onto a lightly floured board; knead until smooth and elastic, about 8-10 minutes. Place in a greased bowl, turning once to grease top. Cover and let rise until doubled, about 1 hour. Punch dough down. Turn out onto a lightly floured surface and divide in thirds. Let rest for 5 minutes. Grease 36 muffin cups. Divide each third of dough into 36 pieces. Shape each piece into a ball, pulling edges under to make a smooth surface. Arrange three balls, smooth side up, in each muffin cup. Cover and let rise until almost doubled, about 30 minutes. Bake at 375° for 12-15 minutes or until golden brown. **Yield:** 3 dozen.

HONEY-WHEAT SUNFLOWER BREAD

Lillian Wittler, Wayne, Nebraska

 This tasty dish uses less sugar, salt and fat. Recipe includes *Diabetic Exchanges.*

   2 cups water (120° to 130°)
2-3/4 to 3-1/4 cups all-purpose *or*
     bread flour
   2 packages (1/4 ounce *each*)
     active dry yeast
   1 tablespoon sugar
   2 cups whole wheat flour
   1 cup old-fashioned oats
 1/3 cup instant dry milk powder
 1/4 cup butter *or* margarine,
     melted and cooled
 1/4 cup honey
   2 teaspoons salt
   1 cup unsalted sunflower seeds

In a mixing bowl, combine the water, 2 cups all-purpose or bread flour, yeast and sugar. Beat on low speed for 3 minutes. Cover and let rise in a warm place until doubled, about 30 minutes. (Mixture will be spongy.) Stir in whole wheat flour, oats, milk powder, butter, honey and salt; mix

well. Stir in sunflower seeds and as much of the remaining all-purpose or bread flour as needed. Turn onto a lightly floured surface and knead until smooth and elastic, about 6-8 minutes. Shape into a ball. Place in a greased bowl; turning once to grease top. Cover and let rise until doubled, about 30-45 minutes. Punch down and divide in half. Cover and let rest 10 minutes. Shape into two loaves; place in two greased 8-in. x 4-in. x 2-in. loaf pans. Cover and let rise until doubled, about 30 minutes. Bake at 375° for 20 minutes. Cover with foil; bake 15 minutes longer. Remove from pans and cool on wire racks. **Yield:** 2 loaves (16 slices each). **Diabetic Exchanges:** One serving (one slice, prepared with margarine) equals 1 fat, 1 starch; also, 121 calories, 162 mg sodium, trace cholesterol, 18 gm carbohydrate, 4 gm protein, 4 gm fat.

MIRACLE ROLLS

Nell Bass, Macon, Georgia

(PICTURED ON PAGE 128)

   3 packages (1/4 ounce *each*)
     active dry yeast
 1/2 cup warm water (110° to 115°)
   5 cups self-rising flour
 1/4 cup sugar
   1 teaspoon baking soda
   1 cup shortening
   2 cups warm buttermilk (110°
     to 115°)

Dissolve yeast in warm water; set aside. In a large mixing bowl, combine flour, sugar and baking soda. Cut in shortening with a pastry blender until mixture resembles coarse meal. Stir in yeast mixture and buttermilk; mix well. Turn out onto a lightly floured surface; knead lightly a few times. Roll to a 1/2-in. thickness. Cut with a 2-1/2-in. biscuit cutter. Place on lightly greased baking sheets. Cover and let rise in a warm place for about 45 minutes. Bake at 400° for 10 minutes or until golden brown. **Yield:** about 4 dozen.

SOUR CREAM TWISTS

Kathy Floyd, Greenville, Florida

   1 package (1/4 ounce) active
     dry yeast
 1/4 cup warm water (110° to 115°)
   4 cups all-purpose flour
 3/4 teaspoon salt
 1/2 cup butter *or* margarine
 1/2 cup shortening

   2 eggs, lightly beaten
 1/2 cup sour cream
   3 teaspoons vanilla extract,
     divided
1-1/2 cups sugar
Red *or* green colored sugar

In a small bowl, dissolve yeast in water. Let stand 5 minutes. In a mixing bowl, stir together flour and salt. Cut in butter and shortening until particles are the size of small peas. Stir in eggs, sour cream, 1 teaspoon vanilla and the yeast mixture. Mix thoroughly (dough will be stiff and resemble pie pastry). Combine white sugar and remaining vanilla; lightly sprinkle 1/2 cup over a pastry cloth. Roll out half of the dough into a rectangle. Sprinkle with about 1 tablespoon of the sugar mixture plus some red or green colored sugar. Fold rectangle into thirds (fold one end of dough over center and fold other end over to make three layers). Give dough a quarter turn and repeat rolling, sugaring and folding two more times. Roll out into a 16-in. x 9-in. rectangle. Cut into 3-in. x 1-in. strips. Twist each strip two or three times. Place on chilled ungreased baking sheets. Repeat with remaining dough, sugar mixture and colored sugar. Bake at 375° for 15-20 minutes or until light golden brown. Immediately remove to wire racks. **Yield:** 8 dozen.

MASHED POTATO DOUGHNUTS

Florence Ladwig, Monroe, Wisconsin

   2 cups sugar, *divided*
   1 teaspoon salt
   1 teaspoon ground nutmeg
   1 teaspoon vanilla extract
 1/4 cup butter *or* margarine,
     softened
   1 cup cold mashed potatoes
   2 eggs, beaten
 2/3 cup milk
4-1/2 cups all-purpose flour
   1 tablespoon baking powder
 1/2 teaspoon ground cinnamon
Shortening *or* oil for deep-fat frying

In a mixing bowl, combine 1 cup sugar, salt, nutmeg, vanilla and butter. Add potatoes; mix well. Add eggs and milk; mix well. Stir in the flour and baking powder. Chill thoroughly. On a lightly floured board, roll out half the dough to 1/2-in. thickness. Cut into 4-in. x 1-1/2-in. strips; roll in flour and tie into knots. Preheat shortening or oil to 375°; fry doughnuts until golden on both sides, turning with a slotted spoon. Drain on paper towels. Repeat until all doughnuts are fried. Combine remaining sugar and cinnamon; roll the warm doughnuts in mixture. Serve immediately. **Yield:** about 2-1/2 dozen.

EMPIRE STATE MUFFINS

Beverly Collins, North Syracuse, New York

2 cups shredded unpeeled
apples
1-1/3 cups sugar
1 cup chopped cranberries
1 cup shredded carrots
1 cup chopped walnuts *or*
pecans
2-1/2 cups all-purpose flour
1 tablespoon baking powder
2 teaspoons baking soda
1/2 teaspoon salt
2 teaspoons ground cinnamon
2 eggs, lightly beaten
1/2 cup vegetable oil

In a large mixing bowl, combine apples
and sugar. Gently fold in cranberries, carrots and nuts. Combine dry ingredients;
add to mixing bowl. Mix well to moisten
dry ingredients. Combine eggs and oil;
stir into apple mixture. Fill 18 greased
muffin tins 2/3 full. Bake at 375° for 20-25
minutes. Cool 5 minutes before removing from tins. **Yield:** 18 muffins.

KRIS KRINGLE STAR BREAD

Marilyn Kidder, Fruitland, Idaho

FILLING:
1 cup chopped walnuts *or*
filberts
1/3 cup honey
1/4 cup sugar
1/2 cup chopped maraschino
cherries, blotted dry
BREAD:
1 cup warm water (110° to 115°)
1/2 cup sugar
1 teaspoon salt
2 packages (1/4 ounce *each*)
active dry yeast
2 eggs, beaten
1/2 cup butter *or* margarine,
softened
4-1/2 to 5 cups all-purpose flour
Confectioners' sugar icing

In a small bowl, combine filling ingredients. Set aside. In a mixing bowl, combine water, sugar and salt. Add yeast,
stirring until dissolved. Let stand for 5
minutes, then stir in eggs and butter.
Gradually add enough flour to form a
soft dough. Turn dough onto a floured
surface; knead until smooth and elastic, about 6-8 minutes. Place in a
greased bowl, turning once to grease
top. Cover and let rise in a warm place
until doubled, about 1 hour. Punch
down. Divide dough in half; roll each
half into a 14-in. circle. Transfer to two
greased baking sheets. Cut five slits
about 4 in. long into each circle. Place

a spoonful of filling in the middle of
each section, then spread a thin layer
of filling in the center of each star. Fold
the two outer edges of each section
over each other to form star points.
Pinch edges together to seal. Cover
and let rise in a warm place until doubled, about 30 minutes. Bake at 350°
for 25 minutes or until golden brown.
Frost while warm with a confectioners'
sugar icing. **Yield:** 2 breads.

CHERRY SWIRL
COFFEE CAKE

Charlene Griffin, Minocqua, Wisconsin

1-1/2 cups sugar
1/2 cup butter *or* margarine
1/2 cup shortening
1/2 teaspoon baking powder
1 teaspoon vanilla extract
1 teaspoon almond extract
4 eggs
3 cups all-purpose flour
1 can (21 ounces) cherry pie
filling
GLAZE:
1 cup confectioners' sugar
1 to 2 tablespoons milk

In a mixing bowl, blend the first seven ingredients on low speed. Increase to high
speed and whip for 3 minutes. Stir in
flour. Spread 2/3 of the batter over the
bottom of a greased 15-1/2-in. x 10-1/2-
in. x 1-in. jelly roll pan. Spread pie filling
over batter; drop remaining batter by tablespoonsful over all. Bake at 350° for 40
minutes or until golden. Meanwhile, combine glaze ingredients. Drizzle over cake
while warm. Cake is best if served immediately. **Yield:** 18-20 servings.

CHOCOLATE CHIP
PUMPKIN BREAD

Vicki Raboine, Kansasville, Wisconsin

1 cup packed brown sugar
1 cup sugar
2/3 cup butter *or* margarine,
softened
3 eggs
2-1/3 cups all-purpose flour
1-1/2 cups canned pumpkin
1/2 cup water
2 teaspoons baking soda
1 teaspoon ground cinnamon
1 teaspoon salt
1/2 teaspoon ground cloves
2 cups (12 ounces)
semisweet chocolate chips

In a mixing bowl, cream sugars, butter
and eggs. Add flour, pumpkin, water,

baking soda, cinnamon, salt and cloves.
Mix thoroughly. Fold in chocolate chips.
Pour into four greased and floured 6-in.
x 3-in. x 2-in. loaf pans. Bake at 350°
for 45 minutes or until breads test done.
Yield: 4 mini loaves.

BANANA BREAD

Irene Evans, Bradley, Illinois

2/3 cup sugar
1/3 cup shortening
2 cups all-purpose flour
2 teaspoons baking powder
1/4 teaspoon baking soda
1/4 teaspoon salt
1 cup mashed ripe bananas

*Note: This recipe does NOT contain eggs
or milk.* In a large bowl, cream sugar and
shortening for about 5 minutes (mixture
does not get smooth). Combine flour,
baking powder, baking soda and salt;
add to creamed mixture alternately with
bananas, beating after each addition
(the batter will be thick). Spoon into a
greased 9-in. x 5-in. x 3-in. loaf pan.
Bake at 350° for 40-45 minutes or until
bread tests done with a toothpick. Cool
in pan for 10 minutes before removing to
a wire rack. **Yield:** 1 loaf.

HONEY-NUT
BREAKFAST TWISTS

Holly Baird, Zurich, Montana

1 package (1/4 ounce) active
dry yeast
1/4 cup warm water (105° to 115°)
2 tablespoons sugar
1 teaspoon salt
2 tablespoons butter *or*
margarine, melted
1 cup (8 ounces) sour cream
1 egg
2-1/2 to 3 cups all-purpose flour
GLAZE:
1/3 cup packed brown sugar
3 tablespoons butter *or*
margarine, melted
3 tablespoons honey, warmed
3 tablespoons heavy cream
FILLING:
1/3 cup butter *or* margarine,
softened
1/4 cup finely chopped nuts
1/4 cup honey

In a mixing bowl, combine yeast and water; let stand 5 minutes. Stir in sugar, salt and butter. Add sour cream and egg; beat until smooth. Add 1-1/2 cups flour; blend at low speed until moistened. Beat 3 minutes at medium speed, scraping bowl twice. By hand, stir in enough remaining flour to make a soft dough. Turn out onto a floured surface; knead until smooth and elastic, about 5 minutes. Place in a greased bowl, turning once to grease top. Cover and let rise in a warm place until doubled, about 1 hour. Combine glaze ingredients; spread evenly in a 13-in. x 9-in. x 2-in. baking dish; set aside. Punch dough down. Roll into a 24-in. x 9-in. rectangle. Combine filling ingredients; spread over dough. Fold dough lengthwise over filling, forming a 12-in. x 9-in. rectangle. Cut lengthwise into six 9-in. x 2-in. pieces. Twist each piece loosely and place over glaze in baking dish. Cover and let rise until doubled, about 1 hour. Bake at 350° for 25-30 minutes or until golden brown. Invert pan onto a large platter; let set 1 minute before removing. Serve warm or refrigerate overnight. **Yield:** 6 servings.

PUMPKIN CINNAMON ROLLS

Janet Wells, Hazel Green, Kentucky

2-3/4 to 3-1/4 cups all-purpose flour, *divided*
1 package (1/4 ounce) active dry yeast
1/2 cup solid-pack pumpkin
2/3 cup milk
2 tablespoons sugar
4 tablespoons butter *or* margarine, *divided*
1/2 teaspoon salt
1 egg, beaten
1/2 cup packed brown sugar
1 teaspoon ground cinnamon
CARAMEL FROSTING:
2 tablespoons butter *or* margarine
1/4 cup packed brown sugar
1 tablespoon milk
1/4 teaspoon vanilla extract
Dash salt
1/4 to 1/3 cup confectioners' sugar

In a mixing bowl, combine 1-1/2 cups flour and yeast; set aside. In a saucepan, heat and stir pumpkin, milk, sugar, 2 tablespoons butter and salt until warm (120°-130°) and butter is almost melted. Add to flour/yeast mixture along with egg. Beat on low speed for 30 seconds. Beat on high speed for 3 minutes. Stir in enough remaining flour to make a moderately stiff dough. Knead on a lightly floured surface until smooth and elastic, about 6-8 minutes. Place in a greased

bowl, turning once to grease top. Cover and let rise until doubled, about 1 hour. Roll into a 12-in. x 10-in. rectangle. Melt remaining butter; brush on dough. Combine brown sugar and cinnamon; sprinkle over dough. Roll dough, jelly roll style, starting with the longer side. Cut into 12 slices, 1 in. each. Place rolls, cut side down, in a greased 13-in. x 9-in. x 2-in. baking pan. Cover and let rise until doubled, about 30 minutes. Bake at 375° for 20-25 minutes or until golden brown. Cool on a wire rack. For frosting, melt butter in a saucepan; stir in brown sugar and milk. Cook and stir over medium-low heat for 1 minute. Stir in vanilla, salt and 1/4 cup confectioners' sugar; beat until well blended. Add more sugar, if necessary, to achieve desired consistency. Drizzle over rolls. **Yield:** 1 dozen.

RHUBARB PECAN MUFFINS

Mary Kubik, Lethbridge, Alberta

(PICTURED ON PAGE 208)

2 cups all-purpose flour
3/4 cup sugar
1-1/2 teaspoons baking powder
1/2 teaspoon baking soda
1 teaspoon salt
3/4 cup chopped pecans
1 egg
1/4 cup vegetable oil
2 teaspoons grated orange peel
3/4 cup orange juice
1-1/4 cups finely chopped rhubarb

In a large mixing bowl, combine flour, sugar, baking powder, baking soda, salt and nuts. In another bowl, combine egg, oil, orange peel and orange juice. Add to dry ingredients all at once and stir just until moistened. Stir in rhubarb. Fill 12 lightly greased muffin cups almost to the top. Bake at 375° for 25-30 minutes. **Yield:** 1 dozen.

SOUTHWESTERN SPOON BREAD

Aldine Fouse, Farmington, New Mexico

1 can (16-1/2 ounces) cream-style corn
1 cup yellow cornmeal
3/4 cup milk
1/3 cup vegetable oil
2 eggs, lightly beaten
1 teaspoon baking powder
1/2 teaspoon salt
1 can (4 ounces) chopped green chilies, drained
1 cup (4 ounces) shredded cheddar cheese

In a mixing bowl, stir together all ingredients except last two. Pour half the batter

into a greased 2-qt. baking dish. Sprinkle with chilies and cheese. Pour remaining batter over all. Bake at 375° for 45 minutes or just until set. Serve warm with a spoon. **Yield:** about 6-8 servings.

APPLE ZUCCHINI BREAD

Patti Dillingham, Scranton, Arkansas

4 cups all-purpose flour
1 tablespoon baking soda
1-1/2 teaspoons ground cinnamon
1/2 teaspoon ground nutmeg
1/4 teaspoon salt
5 eggs
1-1/2 cups vegetable oil
2 cups sugar
1 cup packed brown sugar
1 tablespoon vanilla extract
2 cups shredded unpeeled zucchini
1 cup shredded peeled apples
1-1/2 cups chopped pecans

In a large bowl, combine flour, baking soda, cinnamon, nutmeg and salt. In another bowl, beat eggs. Add oil, sugars and vanilla. Pour over dry ingredients; mix well. Stir in zucchini, apples and pecans (batter will be stiff). Spoon into three greased 8-in. x 4-in. x 3-in. loaf pans. Bake at 350° for 50-55 minutes or until done. Cool in pans for 10 minutes before removing to a wire rack to cool completely. **Yield:** 3 loaves.

APRICOT MUFFINS

Ann Chamberlain, Denver, Colorado

1 cup dried apricots, cut up
1 cup boiling water
1/2 cup butter *or* margarine
1 cup sugar
3/4 cup sour cream
2 cups all-purpose flour
1 teaspoon baking soda
1/2 teaspoon salt
1 tablespoon grated orange peel
1/2 cup chopped nuts
TOPPING:
1/4 cup sugar
1/4 cup orange juice

In a small bowl, combine apricots and water. Let stand 5 minutes. Drain well and set aside. In a large mixing bowl, cream butter and sugar until fluffy. Add sour cream and mix well. Combine dry ingredients and add to butter mixture. Mix on low only until combined. Fold in orange peel, nuts and apricots. Batter will be very stiff. Spoon into well-greased muffin cups, filling each cup almost to the top. Bake at 400° for 18-20 minutes or until done. Combine sugar and orange juice; dip tops of warm muffins in mixture. **Yield:** 12 muffins.

SPARKLING Almond Raspberry Stars, rich Fudge Puddles, buttery Whipped Shortbread, colorful Rainbow Cookies. No matter the shape or flavor, there's something special about baking, decorating and giving cookies…*especially* at Christmas. Here's a small sample of some of the best cookies being baked across the country.

BATCH OF BEAUTIES.
Clockwise from the top: **Almond Raspberry Stars**, **Fudge Puddles**, **Whipped Shortbread** and **Rainbow Cookies** (all recipes on page 171).

COOKIES & BARS

*Why not treat your family to some cookie-jar classics or
pan pleasures today? You'll be thanked mmm-many times over!*

WHIPPED SHORTBREAD

Jane Ficiur, Bow Island, Alberta

(PICTURED AT LEFT)

**3 cups butter (no substitutes),
softened
4-1/2 cups all-purpose flour
1-1/2 cups confectioners' sugar,
sifted
1-1/2 cups cornstarch
Nonpareils *and/or* halved candied
cherries**

Using a heavy-duty mixer, beat butter
on medium speed until light and fluffy.
Gradually add dry ingredients, beating
constantly until well blended. Dust hands
lightly with additional cornstarch. Roll
dough into 1-in. balls, dip in nonpareils
and place on ungreased cookie sheet.
Press lightly with a floured fork. To decorate with cherries, place balls on cookie sheet and press lightly with fork. Top
each with a cherry half. Bake at 300° for
20-22 minutes or until cookie is set but
not browned. **Yield:** 16-18 dozen.
Editor's Note: Yes, this recipe does call
for 1-1/2 cups cornstarch.

RAINBOW COOKIES

Mary Ann Lee, Marco Island, Florida

(PICTURED AT LEFT)

**1 can (8 ounces) almond paste
1 cup butter (no substitutes),
softened
1 cup sugar
4 eggs, *separated*
2 cups all-purpose flour
6 to 8 drops red food coloring
6 to 8 drops green food coloring
1/4 cup seedless red raspberry
jam
1/4 cup apricot jam
1 cup (6 ounces) semisweet
chocolate chips**

Grease the bottoms of three matching
13-in. x 9-in. x 2-in. baking pans (or re-
use one pan). Line the pans with waxed
paper; grease the paper. Place almond
paste in a large mixing bowl; break up
with a fork. Cream with butter, sugar
and egg yolks until light, fluffy and

smooth. Stir in flour. In another mixing
bowl, beat egg whites until soft peaks
form. Fold into dough, mixing until thoroughly blended. Divide dough into three
portions (about 1-1/3 cups each). Color
one portion with red food coloring and
one with green; leave the remaining
portion uncolored. Spread each portion
into the prepared pans. Bake at 350°
for 10-12 minutes or until edges are
light golden brown. Invert onto wire
racks; remove waxed paper. Place
another wire rack on top and turn over.
Cool completely. Place green layer on
a large piece of plastic wrap. Spread
evenly with raspberry jam. Top with
uncolored layer and spread with apricot
jam. Top with pink layer. Bring plastic
wrap over layers. Slide onto a cookie
sheet and set a cutting board or heavy,
flat pan on top to compress layers.
Refrigerate overnight. The next day,
melt chocolate in a double boiler.
Spread over top layer; allow to harden.
With a sharp knife, trim edges. Cut into
1/2-in. strips across the width; then cut
each strip into 4-5 pieces. Store in airtight containers. **Yield:** about 8 dozen.

ALMOND
RASPBERRY STARS

Darlene Weaver, Lebanon, Pennsylvania

(PICTURED AT LEFT)

**3/4 cup butter *or* margarine,
softened
1/2 cup confectioners' sugar
1 teaspoon vanilla extract
1/2 teaspoon almond extract
1-3/4 cups plus 2 tablespoons
all-purpose flour
2 tablespoons finely chopped
almonds
1 tablespoon sugar
1/2 teaspoon ground cinnamon
1 egg white, lightly beaten
1/3 cup raspberry jam**

In a mixing bowl, cream the butter and
confectioners' sugar until light and
fluffy. Add extracts and beat until well
mixed. Stir in flour. Shape into a ball;
cover and chill for 15 minutes. On a
lightly floured board, roll dough to a 1/4-
in. thickness. Cut into about 72 stars,
half 2-1/2 in. and half 1-1/2 in. Combine
almonds, sugar and cinnamon. Brush

small stars with egg white and immediately sprinkle with cinnamon/sugar mixture. Leave large stars plain. Bake on
ungreased cookie sheets at 350° for 10
minutes (small stars) to 12 minutes
(large stars) or until the tips just begin to
brown. Cool on wire racks. To assemble, spread enough jam over large star
to cover the center. Top with a small
star. Press lightly; jam should show
around edge of small star. Let jam set
before storing. **Yield:** about 3 dozen.

FUDGE PUDDLES

Kimarie Maassen, Avoca, Iowa

(PICTURED AT LEFT)

**1/2 cup butter *or* margarine,
softened
1/2 cup creamy peanut butter
1/2 cup sugar
1/2 cup packed light brown sugar
1 egg
1/2 teaspoon vanilla extract
1-1/4 cups all-purpose flour
3/4 teaspoon baking soda
1/2 teaspoon salt
FUDGE FILLING:
1 cup (6 ounces) milk chocolate
chips
1 cup (6 ounces) semisweet
chocolate chips
1 can (14 ounces) sweetened
condensed milk
1 teaspoon vanilla extract
Chopped peanuts**

In a mixing bowl, cream butter, peanut
butter and sugars; add egg and vanilla.
Stir together flour, baking soda and
salt; add to creamed mixture. Mix well.
Chill for 1 hour. Shape into 48 1-in. balls.
Place in lightly greased mini-muffin tins.
Bake at 325° for 14-16 minutes or until
lightly browned. Remove from oven and
immediately make "wells" in the center
of each by lightly pressing with a melon
baller. Cool in pans for 5 minutes, then
carefully remove to wire racks. For filling, melt chocolate chips in a double
boiler over simmering water. Stir in milk
and vanilla; mix well. Using a small
pitcher or pastry bag, fill each shell with
filling. Sprinkle with peanuts. (Leftover
filling can be stored in the refrigerator
and served warm over ice cream.)
Yield: 4 dozen.

FRUITCAKE COOKIES

Hazel Staley, Gaithersburg, Maryland

(PICTURED ON PAGE 12)

6 cups chopped pecans
(about 1-1/2 pounds)
2 cups graham cracker crumbs
1-1/2 cups raisins
1-1/4 cups chopped candied
cherries (about 1/2 pound)
1-1/4 cups chopped candied
pineapple (about 1/2 pound)
4-1/2 cups miniature marshmallows
1/2 cup evaporated milk
1/4 cup butter *or* margarine
1-1/2 cups flaked coconut

In a large bowl, combine pecans, cracker crumbs, raisins, cherries and pineapple. In a large saucepan, combine marshmallows, milk and butter. Cook over low heat, stirring constantly, until melted. Pour over pecan mixture and mix well. Shape into 1-in. balls and roll in the coconut, washing your hands frequently. **Yield:** 7-8 dozen.

> **A NUTTY IDEA.** To quickly chop any kinds of nuts, spread out the nuts on a paper towel and cover with another paper towel. Roll over the towel with a rolling pin. This way you can "chop" a whole bag of nuts at a time. The paper towel also helps soak up some of the oil.

CHOCOLATE CLUSTERS

Sara Ann Fowler, Illinois City, Illinois

2 pounds white chocolate *or* almond bark
1 cup creamy *or* chunky peanut butter
2 cups salted dry roasted peanuts
3 cups pastel miniature marshmallows
4 cups crisp rice cereal

Melt white chocolate and peanut butter in microwave or double boiler, stirring often to mix well. Add all remaining ingredients; stir with wooden spoon to coat evenly. Drop by teaspoonful onto waxed paper. **Yield:** 11 dozen.

CARAMEL APPLE BARS

Carol Stuber, Osawatomie, Kansas

(PICTURED ON PAGE 63)

CRUST:
1/2 cup butter *or* margarine, softened
1/4 cup shortening

1 cup packed brown sugar
1-3/4 cups all-purpose flour
1 cup old-fashioned *or* quick-cooking oats
1 teaspoon salt
1/2 teaspoon baking soda
1/2 cup chopped pecans, optional
FILLING:
4-1/2 cups coarsely chopped peeled baking apples
3 tablespoons all-purpose flour
1 package (14 ounces) caramels
3 tablespoons butter *or* margarine

In a mixing bowl, cream butter, shortening and brown sugar until fluffy. Add flour, oats, salt and baking soda; mix well. Stir in pecans if desired. Set aside 2 cups. Press remaining oat mixture into the bottom of an ungreased 13-in. x 9-in. x 2-in. baking pan. For filling, toss apples with flour; spoon over the crust. In a saucepan, melt the caramels and butter over low heat; drizzle over apples. Top with the reserved oat mixture. Bake at 400° for 25-30 minutes or until lightly browned. Cool before cutting into bars. **Yield:** 15-20 servings.

 **Quick & Easy**

CONGO SQUARES

Darlene Cook, Mustang, Oklahoma

2/3 cup shortening
2-1/4 cups packed brown sugar
2-3/4 cups all-purpose flour
2-1/2 teaspoons baking powder
1/2 teaspoon salt
3 eggs, beaten
1 tablespoon vanilla extract
2 cups (12 ounces) semisweet chocolate chips
1 cup chopped nuts

In a saucepan, melt the shortening over medium heat. Stir in brown sugar. Cool slightly. Combine the flour, baking powder and salt; add gradually with eggs to the shortening mixture. Stir in the vanilla, chips and nuts (the batter will be very stiff). Spread into a greased and floured 12-in. x 9-in. x 2-in. baking pan. Bake at 350° for 25-30 minutes. Cut into squares while warm. **Yield:** about 48 bars.

FUDGY BROWNIES

Laura Katucki, Eagleville, Pennsylvania

(PICTURED ON PAGE 116)

1 cup butter *or* margarine, melted
3/4 cup baking cocoa
2 cups sugar
1-1/2 cups all-purpose flour
4 eggs
COCOA FROSTING:
2-1/2 cups confectioners' sugar
1/3 cup milk
1/4 cup butter *or* margarine, softened
3 tablespoons baking cocoa
2 teaspoons vanilla extract

In a mixing bowl, combine melted butter and cocoa. Mix in sugar and flour. Add eggs; mix well. Pour into a greased and floured 13-in. x 9-in. x 2-in. baking pan. Bake at 350° for 20-25 minutes. Meanwhile, for frosting, beat together all ingredients in a mixing bowl until smooth. Cool the brownies for 15 minutes before frosting. Cool completely. Cover with foil; freeze until firm. Serve frozen or thawed. **Yield:** 3 dozen. **Editor's Note:** Brownies are dense and resemble fudge.

DATE DELIGHTS

Helen Wolber, Brookville, Indiana

1 cup sugar
1/2 cup butter *or* margarine
1 egg
3/4 cup chopped dates
3/4 cup chopped pecans
2 cups crisp rice cereal
Confectioners' sugar

Combine sugar, butter, egg, dates and pecans in a heavy saucepan; bring to a boil, stirring thoroughly. Cook over medium heat until well blended, about 5 minutes. Remove from heat and stir in cereal. Cool. With buttered hands, roll into 1-in. balls; roll in confectioners' sugar. **Yield:** about 4 dozen.

HOLIDAY MACAROONS

Kristine Conway, Mogadore, Ohio

4 eggs
1-1/2 cups sugar
2/3 cup all-purpose flour
1/2 teaspoon baking powder
1/4 teaspoon salt
2 tablespoons butter *or* margarine, melted and cooled

1 teaspoon vanilla extract
5 cups flaked coconut
1 jar (10 ounces) maraschino
   cherries, drained and halved

In a mixing bowl, beat the eggs until foamy. Gradually add sugar, beating constantly until thick and pale yellow. Stir together dry ingredients; fold into egg mixture. Stir in butter, vanilla and coconut. Drop by teaspoonfuls onto greased and floured cookie sheets. Top with cherries. Bake at 325° for 10-13 minutes. **Yield:** about 6 dozen.

APPLE BUTTER COOKIES

Dorothy Hawkins, Springhill, Florida

1/4 cup butter *or* margarine,
   softened
1 cup packed brown sugar
1 egg
1/2 cup quick-cooking oats
1/2 cup apple butter
1 cup all-purpose flour
1/2 teaspoon baking soda
1/2 teaspoon baking powder
1/2 teaspoon salt
2 tablespoons milk
1/2 cup chopped nuts
1/2 cup raisins

In a mixing bowl, cream butter and sugar. Beat in egg, oats and apple butter. Combine dry ingredients; gradually add to creamed mixture along with the milk; beat until blended. Stir in nuts and raisins. Chill well. Drop by teaspoonfuls onto lightly greased cookie sheets. Bake at 350° for 15 minutes. **Yield:** about 2-1/2 dozen.

PEPPERMINT COOKIES

Donna Lock, Fort Collins, Colorado

2/3 cup butter-flavored shortening
1/4 cup sugar
1/4 cup packed brown sugar
1 egg
1-1/2 cups all-purpose flour
1/2 teaspoon baking powder
1/2 teaspoon salt
1/2 cup crushed peppermint
   candy

In a mixing bowl, cream shortening and sugars; beat in egg. Combine flour, bak-

ing powder and salt; stir into the creamed mixture. Fold in the candy. Drop by teaspoonfuls onto a greased cookie sheet. Bake at 350° for 10-12 minutes or until cookie edges just begin to brown. **Yield:** 3-1/2 dozen.

SPICED ALMOND COOKIES

Wanda Daily, Milwaukie, Oregon

(PICTURED ON BACK COVER AND PAGE 37)

1 cup butter *or* margarine,
   softened
1/2 cup shortening
1 cup packed brown sugar
1 cup sugar
2 eggs
4 cups all-purpose flour
2 teaspoons ground cinnamon
1 teaspoon baking soda
1 teaspoon salt
1 teaspoon ground cloves
1 teaspoon ground allspice
1 cup slivered almonds

In a mixing bowl, cream butter and shortening; beat in sugars until light and fluffy. Add eggs and beat well. Combine dry ingredients; stir into creamed mixture along with nuts. Shape into three 9-in. x 1-1/2-in. rolls; wrap in waxed paper. Chill 2-3 days for spices to blend. Slice cookies 1/4-in. thick and place on ungreased baking sheets. Bake at 350° for 12-14 minutes or until set. Remove cookies to a wire rack to cool. **Yield:** 7 dozen.

PEPPERY SNAPS

Joan Elbourn, Gardner, Massachusetts

1-1/4 cups all-purpose flour
1 cup whole wheat flour
1-1/2 teaspoons baking soda
1 teaspoon ground anise seed
1/2 teaspoon salt
1/2 teaspoon ground ginger
1/4 teaspoon pepper
1 cup packed light brown sugar
3 tablespoons light molasses
3/4 cup butter *or* margarine,
   softened
1 egg
Sugar

Combine first seven ingredients; set aside. In a mixing bowl, beat brown sugar, molasses, butter and egg. Stir in dry ingredients; mix well. Chill for 1 hour. Shape into 1-in. balls. Roll in sugar and place on ungreased cookie sheets. Bake at 350° for 10-13 minutes. Cool cookies about 1 minute before removing to wire racks. **Yield:** 6-7 dozen.

LEMON SNOWFLAKES

Linda Barry, Dianna, Texas

(PICTURED BELOW)

1 package (18-1/4 ounces)
   lemon cake mix with pudding
2-1/4 cups frozen whipped
   topping, thawed
1 egg
Confectioners' sugar

In a mixing bowl, combine cake mix, whipped topping and egg. Beat with electric mixer on medium speed until blended. Batter will be very sticky. Drop by teaspoonfuls into confectioners' sugar; roll lightly to coat. Place on ungreased cookie sheets. Bake at 350° for 10-12 minutes or until lightly brown. **Yield:** 5-6 dozen.

CRISP BUTTER COOKIES

Tammy Mackie, Seward, Nebraska

(PICTURED BELOW)

1/2 cup butter *or* margarine,
   softened
1 cup sugar
5 egg yolks
2 cups all-purpose flour
Colored sugar

In a mixing bowl, cream butter and sugar. Blend in egg yolks. Add flour, 1 cup at a time, beating well after each addition. Dough will be very stiff. On a well-floured board or pastry cloth, roll out dough to a 1/8-in. thickness. Using a pastry wheel or knife, cut into 2-1/2-in. squares, rectangles or diamonds. Place 1/2 in. apart on ungreased cookie sheets. Sprinkle with colored sugar. Bake at 375° for 7-8 minutes or until lightly browned. **Yield:** 6 dozen.

YOU'LL be out of the kitchen quick when you bake Crisp Butter Cookies, Lemon Snowflakes.

SANDBAKKELSE (SAND TARTS)

Karen Hoylo, Duluth, Minnesota

(PICTURED ON PAGE 122)

1 cup plus 2 tablespoons butter (no substitutes), softened
1 cup sugar
1 egg
1 teaspoon almond extract
1/2 teaspoon vanilla extract
3 cups all-purpose flour

In a mixing bowl, cream butter and sugar. Add egg and extracts. Blend in flour. Cover and chill for 1-2 hours or overnight. Using ungreased sandbakkelse molds, press about 1 tablespoon dough into each mold. Bake at 375° for 10-12 minutes or until cookies appear set and just begin to brown around the edges. Cool for 2-3 minutes in molds. When cool to the touch, remove cookies from molds. To remove more easily, gently tap with a knife and carefully squeeze it. **Yield:** about 8 dozen.

Quick & Easy

FLOURLESS PEANUT BUTTER COOKIES

Maggie Schimmel, Wauwatosa, Wisconsin

(PICTURED BELOW)

1 egg, beaten
1 cup sugar
1 cup creamy peanut butter

In a large bowl, mix all ingredients. Scoop level tablespoonfuls and roll into balls. Place on ungreased cookie sheet and flatten with a fork. Bake at 350° for about 18 minutes. Remove to a wire rack to cool. **Yield:** 2 dozen.

FAST FAVORITE. Flourless Peanut Butter Cookies don't ever stick around for very long!

LEMON-BUTTER SPRITZ COOKIES

Paula Pelis, Rocky Point, New York

2 cups butter (no substitutes), softened
1-1/4 cups sugar
2 eggs
Grated peel of 1 lemon
2 teaspoons lemon juice
1 teaspoon vanilla extract
5-1/4 cups all-purpose flour
1/4 teaspoon salt
Colored sugar

In a large mixing bowl, cream butter and sugar. Add the eggs, lemon peel, lemon juice and vanilla; mix well. Stir together flour and salt; gradually add to creamed mixture. Using a cookie press, shape into designs on ungreased cookie sheets. Sprinkle with colored sugar. Bake at 400° for 8-10 minutes or until lightly brown around the edges. **Yield:** about 12 dozen.

CRANBERRY NUT SWIRLS

Carla Hodenfield, Mandan, North Dakota

(PICTURED ON PAGE 107)

1/2 cup butter *or* margarine, softened
3/4 cup sugar
1 egg
1 teaspoon vanilla extract
1-1/2 cups all-purpose flour
1/4 teaspoon baking powder
1/4 teaspoon salt
1/2 cup finely ground cranberries
1/2 cup finely chopped walnuts
1 tablespoon grated orange peel
3 tablespoons brown sugar
2 teaspoons milk

In a large mixing bowl, combine first four ingredients. Beat until light and fluffy, scraping the bowl occasionally. Combine dry ingredients; add to the creamed mixture. Refrigerate at least 1 hour. In a small bowl, combine cranberries, walnuts and orange peel; set aside. On a lightly floured surface, roll dough into a 10-in. square. Combine brown sugar and milk; spread over the dough. Sprinkle with the cranberry mixture, leaving about a 1/2-in. edge at both ends of dough; roll up tightly, jelly-

roll style. Wrap with waxed paper; chill several hours or overnight. Cut roll into 1/4-in. slices and place on well-greased cookie sheets. Bake at 375° for 14-15 minutes or until edges are light brown. **Yield:** about 3-1/2 dozen.

KIPPLENS

Susan Bohannon, Kokomo, Indiana

2 cups butter *or* margarine, softened
1 cup sugar
5 cups all-purpose flour
2 teaspoons vanilla extract
2 cups chopped pecans
1/4 teaspoon salt
Confectioners' sugar

In a mixing bowl, cream butter and sugar; add flour, vanilla, pecans and salt. Mix well. Roll dough into 1-in. balls and place on ungreased cookie sheets. Bake at 325° for 17-20 minutes or until lightly browned. Cool cookies slightly before rolling them in confectioners' sugar. **Yield:** 12 dozen.

BETTER USE BUTTER. Some cookie recipes call for using butter only—not butter *or* margarine, as ordinarily. For best results with these recipes, don't substitute—even with a "light" butter product. (They can contain water and may not work correctly.)

WATERMELON COOKIES

A. Ruth Witmer, Stevens, Pennsylvania

3/4 cup butter *or* margarine, softened
3/4 cup sugar
1 egg
1/2 teaspoon almond extract
2-1/4 cups all-purpose flour
1/4 teaspoon salt
1/4 teaspoon baking powder
Red and green food coloring
Dried currants
Sesame seeds

In a mixing bowl, cream butter, sugar, egg and extract until light and fluffy. Combine flour, salt and baking powder; stir into creamed mixture and mix well. Remove 1 cup of dough; set aside. At low speed, beat in enough red food coloring to tint dough deep red. Roll into a 3-1/2-in.-long tube; wrap in plastic wrap and refrigerate until firm, about 2 hours. Divide 1 cup of reserved dough into two pieces. To one piece, add enough green food coloring to tint dough deep green. Do not tint remaining piece of dough. Wrap each piece separately in plastic wrap; chill until firm, about 1 hour. On a floured sheet of waxed paper, roll untinted dough into an 8-1/2-in. x 3-1/2-in. rectangle. Place red dough along short end of rectangle. Roll up and encircle red dough with untinted dough; set aside. On floured waxed paper, roll the green dough into a 10-in. x 3-1/2-in. rectangle. Place tube of red/untinted dough along the short end of green dough. Roll up and encircle tube with green dough. Cover tightly with plastic wrap; refrigerate at least 8 hours or overnight. Unwrap dough and cut into 1/8-in. slices. Place 1 in. apart on ungreased baking sheets. Lightly press dried currants and sesame seeds into each slice to resemble watermelon seeds. Bake at 375° for 6-8 minutes or until cookies are firm but not brown. While still warm, cut each cookie in half or into pie-shaped wedges. Remove to a wire rack to cool. **Yield:** 3 dozen.

CHOCOLATE BROWNIES

Becky Albright, Norwalk, Ohio

(PICTURED ON PAGE 190)

1-1/3 cups all-purpose flour
2 cups sugar
3/4 cup baking cocoa
1 teaspoon baking powder
1/2 teaspoon salt
1/2 cup chopped nuts
2/3 cup cooking oil
4 eggs, slightly beaten
2 teaspoons vanilla extract

Combine flour, sugar, cocoa, baking powder, salt and nuts. Set aside. Combine oil, eggs and vanilla; add to dry ingredients. Do not overmix. Spread in a 13-in. x 9-in. x 2-in. baking pan. Bake at 350° for 20-25 minutes or until toothpick inserted in center comes out clean. **Yield:** about 24 brownies.

WINTER SQUASH SQUARES

Shirley Murphy, Jacksonville, Illinois

(PICTURED ON PAGE 133)

2 cups all-purpose flour
2 cups sugar
2 teaspoons baking powder
1 teaspoon baking soda
1/2 teaspoon ground cinnamon

1/8 teaspoon salt
4 eggs, beaten
2 cups mashed cooked winter squash
1 cup vegetable oil
CREAM CHEESE FROSTING:
1 package (3 ounces) cream cheese, softened
2 cups confectioners' sugar
1 teaspoon vanilla extract
6 tablespoons butter *or* margarine, softened
1 tablespoon milk

In a mixing bowl, combine flour, sugar, baking powder, baking soda, cinnamon and salt. Stir in eggs, squash and oil; mix well. Spread into a greased 15-in. x 10-in. x 1-in. baking pan. Bake at 350° for 25 to 30 minutes or until bars test done. Cool on a wire rack. Meanwhile, for frosting, beat together cream cheese, confectioners' sugar, vanilla and butter. Add milk; stir until smooth. Frost cooled cake. Cut into squares. **Yield:** 4 dozen.

OATMEAL VALENTINE COOKIES

Louise Carter, Shepherdstown, West Virginia

2-1/2 cups all-purpose flour
1 teaspoon baking powder
1/2 teaspoon salt
3/4 cup butter *or* margarine, softened
3/4 cup sugar
2 tablespoons milk
1 egg
1 teaspoon vanilla extract
1 cup rolled oats
Decorative red sugar, optional

Sift together flour, baking powder and salt. Place in a large mixing bowl along with butter, sugar, milk, egg and vanilla; beat until smooth. Stir in oats. On a floured board, roll the dough to 1/8-in. thickness. Cut into heart shapes; decorate with red sugar if desired. Bake on an ungreased cookie sheet at 375° for 15-18 minutes or until light golden brown. Remove from cookie sheet and cool on wire racks. **Yield:** 2-1/2 dozen 3-inch cookies.

DOUBLE CHOCOLATE CRUMBLE BARS

Germaine Stank, Pound, Wisconsin

(PICTURED ON PAGE 216)

BARS:
1/2 cup butter *or* margarine, softened
3/4 cup sugar

2 eggs
1 teaspoon vanilla
3/4 cup all-purpose flour
1/2 cup chopped pecans
2 tablespoons baking cocoa
1/4 teaspoon baking powder
1/4 teaspoon salt
TOPPING:
2 cups miniature marshmallows
1 package (6 ounces) semisweet chocolate chips
1 cup creamy peanut butter
1-1/2 cups crisp rice cereal

Cream butter and sugar; beat in eggs and vanilla. Set aside. Stir together flour, nuts, cocoa, baking powder and salt; stir into egg mixture. Spread in bottom of greased 13-in. x 9-in. x 2-in. baking pan. Bake at 350° for 15-20 minutes or until bars test done. Sprinkle marshmallows evenly on top; bake 3 minutes more. Cool. In small saucepan, combine chocolate chips and peanut butter; cook and stir over low heat until chocolate is melted. Stir in cereal. Spread mixture on top of cooled bars. Chill; cut into bars. Refrigerate. **Yield:** 3-4 dozen bars.

PUMPKIN BARS

Brenda Keller, Andalusia, Alabama

4 eggs
1-2/3 cups sugar
1 cup vegetable oil
1 can (16 ounces) pumpkin
2 cups all-purpose flour
2 teaspoons ground cinnamon
2 teaspoons baking powder
1 teaspoon baking soda
1 teaspoon salt
ICING:
1 package (3 ounces) cream cheese, softened
2 cups confectioners' sugar
1/4 cup butter *or* margarine, softened
1 teaspoon vanilla extract
1 to 2 tablespoons milk

In a mixing bowl, beat eggs, sugar, oil and pumpkin. Combine flour, cinnamon, baking powder, baking soda and salt; gradually add to pumpkin mixture and mix well. Pour into an ungreased 15-in. x 10-in. x 1-in. baking pan. Bake at 350° for 25-30 minutes. Cool completely. For icing, beat cream cheese, sugar, butter and vanilla in a small mixing bowl. Add enough of the milk to achieve desired spreading consistency. Spread over bars. **Yield:** 2 dozen.

> **SQUASH SUB.** Winter squash can be substituted for pumpkin in most cookie, pie and bread recipes. Hubbard and banana squash work especially well.

DON'T LET the festive flair of these home-baked goodies stop you from making them throughout the year! Children will love to help with Molasses Spice Cutouts and Vanilla-Butter Sugar Cookies. Welcome unexpected guests with a plate of cheery Holly Wreaths. Or just keep some on hand for anytime nibbling.

COOKIE JAR JOYS.
Clockwise from lower left: **Finnish Pinwheels** (recipe on page 178), **Molasses Spice Cutouts** (recipe on page 178), **Eggnog Logs** (recipe on page 178), **Italian Sprinkle Cookies** (recipe on page 178), **Cherry Mocha Balls** (recipe on page 178), **Vanilla-Butter Sugar Cookies** (recipe on pages 179), **Miniature Christmas Fruitcakes** (recipe on page 198), and **Holly Wreaths** (recipe on page 179).

FINNISH PINWHEELS
Ilona Barron, Ontonagon, Michigan
(PICTURED ON PAGE 176)

FILLING:
- 1/2 pound pitted prunes, chopped
- 1/2 pound pitted dates, chopped
- 1 cup boiling water
- 2 tablespoons sugar
- 1 tablespoon butter *or* margarine

PASTRY:
- 3 cups all-purpose flour
- 1 cup sugar
- 2 teaspoons baking powder
- 1/2 teaspoon salt
- 1 cup butter
- 1 egg, beaten
- 3 tablespoons half-and-half cream
- 1 teaspoon vanilla extract

Confectioners' sugar, optional

In a saucepan, combine prunes, dates, water and sugar. Cook over low heat, stirring constantly, until thickened. Remove from the heat and stir in butter. Cool. Meanwhile, in a mixing bowl, sift together flour, sugar, baking powder and salt. Cut in butter as for a pie pastry. Blend in egg, cream and vanilla. Form into two balls. Place one ball at a time on a floured board and roll to a 1/8-in. thickness. Cut into 2-in. squares. Place on ungreased cookie sheets. Make 1-in. slits in corners (Fig. 1). Place 1/2 teaspoon filling in the center of each square. Bring every other corner up into center to form a pinwheel and press lightly (Fig. 2). Repeat with remaining dough and filling. Bake at 325° for 12 minutes or until the points are light golden brown. Sprinkle with confectioners' sugar if desired. **Yield:** about 7 dozen.

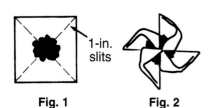

Fig. 1   Fig. 2

1-in. slits

MOLASSES SPICE CUTOUTS
Doris Heinen, St. Cloud, Minnesota
(PICTURED ON PAGE 176)

- 1 cup butter *or* margarine, softened
- 1-1/2 cups sugar
- 1 cup light molasses
- 1/2 cup cold coffee
- 6 cups all-purpose flour
- 2 teaspoons baking soda
- 1 teaspoon salt
- 1/2 teaspoon ground nutmeg
- 1/4 teaspoon ground cloves

ICING (optional):
- 1 envelope unflavored gelatin
- 3/4 cup cold water
- 3/4 cup sugar
- 3/4 cup confectioners' sugar
- 3/4 teaspoon baking powder
- 1/2 teaspoon vanilla extract

Colored sugar *or* nonpareils

Decorator icing, optional

In a mixing bowl, cream butter and sugar; beat in molasses and coffee. Stir together flour, baking soda, salt and spices; add to molasses mixture and mix well. Chill dough 1-2 hours or until easy to handle. If needed, add a little additional flour before rolling. On a lightly floured surface, roll dough to a 1/4-in. thickness. Cut with holiday cutters dipped in flour. Place on ungreased baking sheets. Bake at 350° for 12-15 minutes. Cool on wire racks. For icing, if desired, combine gelatin and water in a small saucepan. Let stand for 5 minutes to soften. Add sugar. Heat and stir over very low heat until the gelatin and sugar dissolve. Transfer to a mixing bowl. Add confectioners' sugar; beat until foamy. Add baking powder and vanilla; beat until very thick, about 10 minutes. Frost cookies by inverting them and quickly swirling the tops in the icing; decorate with colored sugar or nonpareils. For traditional gingerbread men, use decorator icing to add features as desired. **Yield:** about 7-8 dozen (2-1/2-in. cookies).

EGGNOG LOGS
Kim Jordan, Dunsmuir, California
(PICTURED ON PAGE 177)

- 1 cup butter *or* margarine, softened
- 3/4 cup sugar
- 1-1/4 teaspoons ground nutmeg
- 1 egg
- 2 teaspoons vanilla extract
- 1/2 to 1 teaspoon rum extract
- 3 cups all-purpose flour

FROSTING:
- 1/4 cup butter *or* margarine, softened
- 3 cups confectioners' sugar, *divided*
- 1 teaspoon vanilla extract
- 1/2 to 1 teaspoon rum extract
- 2 tablespoons light cream

Ground nutmeg

In a mixing bowl, cream butter and sugar. Add the nutmeg, egg and extracts; mix thoroughly. Stir in flour. If neces-sary, chill dough for easier handling. On a lightly floured surface, shape dough into 1/2-in.-diameter rolls; cut each into 3-in.-long pieces. Place 2 in. apart on ungreased baking sheets. Bake at 350° for 15 minutes or until lightly browned. Cool on wire racks. For frosting, cream butter until light and fluffy. Add 2 cups sugar and extracts; mix well. Beat in cream and remaining sugar. Frost cookies. With tines of a small fork, make lines down the frosting to simulate bark. Sprinkle with nutmeg. **Yield:** 4-1/2 dozen.

CHERRY MOCHA BALLS
Jeana Crowell, Whitewater, Kansas
(PICTURED ON PAGE 177)

- 1 cup butter (no substitutes), softened
- 1/2 cup sugar
- 4 teaspoons vanilla extract
- 2 cups all-purpose flour
- 1/4 cup baking cocoa
- 1 tablespoon instant coffee granules
- 1/2 teaspoon salt
- 1 cup finely chopped pecans
- 2/3 cup chopped red candied cherries

Confectioners' sugar

In a mixing bowl, cream butter. Gradually add sugar and vanilla; beat until light and fluffy. Stir together flour, cocoa, coffee and salt; gradually add to creamed mixture. Mix well. Stir in pecans and cherries. Chill dough for ease of handling if necessary. Shape into 1-in. balls and place on ungreased cookie sheets. Bake at 350° for 15 minutes or until cookies are set. Cool on wire racks. Dust with confectioners' sugar. **Yield:** about 6 dozen.

ITALIAN SPRINKLE COOKIES
Gloria Cracchiolo, Newburgh, New York
(PICTURED ON PAGE 177)

- 6 eggs
- 5 cups all-purpose flour
- 2 cups confectioners' sugar
- 2 tablespoons plus 1-1/2 teaspoons baking powder

1 cup shortening, melted
1 tablespoon almond extract
1-1/2 teaspoons lemon extract
GLAZE:
1/2 cup warm milk
1 teaspoon almond extract
1 teaspoon vanilla extract
1 box (1 pound) confectioners' sugar
Colored sprinkles (jimmies)

Using a heavy-duty electric mixer on high speed, beat eggs until light and foamy, about 5 minutes. Set aside. In another mixing bowl, stir together flour, sugar and baking powder; gradually add shortening and extracts until a bead-like texture is formed. Gradually add beaten eggs (dough will be stiff). Roll dough into 1-in. balls. Place on ungreased baking sheets. Bake at 350° for 12 minutes. The tops of the cookies will not brown, but the bottoms should brown slightly. For glaze, combine milk and extracts in a large bowl. Add sugar; whisk until all lumps are dissolved and the glaze is smooth. As soon as cookies are removed from the oven, quickly immerse two or three at a time into the glaze. Remove with a slotted spoon or fingers. Place cookies on wire racks to drain. Quickly top with sprinkles. Let dry 24 hours before storing in airtight containers. **Yield:** about 7 dozen.

TRY SPRAYING your beaters with non-stick cooking spray before mixing cookie and cake batters to prevent clumping.

VANILLA-BUTTER SUGAR COOKIES

Cindy Ettel, Hutchinson, Minnesota

(PICTURED ON PAGE 177)

1-1/2 cups sugar
1-1/2 cups butter (no substitutes), softened
2 eggs
2 tablespoons vanilla extract
4 cups all-purpose flour
1 teaspoon salt
1 teaspoon baking soda
1 teaspoon cream of tartar
FROSTING:
1-1/2 cups confectioners' sugar
3 tablespoons butter, softened
1 tablespoon vanilla extract
1 tablespoon milk
Food coloring, optional
Colored sugar

In a mixing bowl, combine sugar and butter; beat until creamy. Add eggs and vanilla; beat well. Stir together dry ingredients; gradually add to creamed mixture until completely blended. Chill for

30 minutes. On a lightly floured surface, roll dough to a 1/4-in. thickness. Cut with holiday cutters dipped in flour. Using a floured spatula, transfer cookies to ungreased baking sheets. Bake at 350° for 10-12 minutes. Cool on wire racks. For frosting, combine sugar, butter, vanilla and milk; beat until creamy. Thin with additional milk to desired spreading consistency if necessary. Add a few drops of food coloring if desired. Spread frosting over cookies and decorate with colored sugar. **Yield:** 7 dozen (2-1/2-in. cookies).

HOLLY WREATHS

Dee Lien, Longmont, Colorado

(PICTURED ON PAGE 176)

1 cup butter (no substitutes), softened
1 package (3 ounces) cream cheese, softened
1/2 cup sugar
1 teaspoon vanilla extract
2 cups all-purpose flour
Green cherries, cut into thin slices
Cinnamon red-hot candies
Frosting and decorator gel

In a mixing bowl, cream butter and cream cheese. Add sugar; blend well. Stir in vanilla. Gradually beat in flour. Using a cookie press fitted with star tip, form dough into 2-1/2-in. wreaths on ungreased baking sheets. Bake at 375° for 10-12 minutes or until set but not brown. Cool on wire racks. Decorate wreaths with green cherry "leaves" and cinnamon candy "berries" attached with a drop of frosting. Add bows with decorator gel. **Yield:** about 3 dozen.

APPLE HARVEST SQUARES

Maxine Heaney, Providence, Rhode Island

1-1/2 cups all-purpose flour
1/2 teaspoon salt
1 cup sugar, *divided*
1/2 cup butter *or* margarine
4 cups sliced peeled apples
2 tablespoons lemon juice
1 teaspoon ground cinnamon
1 egg, lightly beaten
1/3 cup evaporated milk
1 teaspoon vanilla extract
3/4 cup chopped nuts
1-1/3 cups flaked coconut

In a bowl, combine flour, salt and 1/3 cup sugar. Cut in butter until the mixture resembles fine crumbs; press into the bottom of a greased 13-in. x 9-in. x 2-in. baking pan. Arrange the apple slices on top of crumbs; sprinkle with lemon juice. Combine 1/3 cup sugar with cinnamon; sprinkle over apples. Bake at 375° for 20 minutes. Meanwhile, in a small bowl, combine remaining sugar with the rest of the ingredients. Spoon over baked apples; bake for another 20 minutes or until golden brown. Cut into squares while still warm. **Yield:** about 20 servings.

CINDY'S CHOCOLATE CHIP COOKIES

Cindy Utter, Jacksonville, Illinois

(PICTURED BELOW)

1 cup butter *or* margarine, softened
1 cup shortening
1 cup sugar
2 cups packed light brown sugar
2 teaspoons vanilla extract
4 eggs
4-1/2 cups all-purpose flour
2 teaspoons baking soda
2 teaspoons salt
2 cups (12 ounces) semisweet chocolate chips
1 cup chopped pecans

In a large mixing bowl, cream butter, shortening, sugars and vanilla. Beat in eggs. Combine dry ingredients; add to creamed mixture. Stir in chocolate chips and nuts. Drop by tablespoonfuls onto greased baking sheets. Bake at 350° for 10-12 minutes or until lightly browned. **Yield:** 9 dozen.

WITH traditional Chocolate Chip Cookies (recipe above), you can delight your cookie lovers.

FOR a supper that says "sincerely yours", treat your loved ones to these cherished recipes. Start the meal with refreshing Mixed Greens with Blue Cheese Dressing, along with pleasantly tart Cranberry Muffins. Savor the creamy sauce on the Saucy Chicken Casserole, then satisfy sweet tooths with several of Mom's Soft Sugar Cookies!

STRAIGHT FROM THE HEART.
Clockwise from top left: **Mom's Soft Sugar Cookies** (recipe on page 181), **Mixed Greens with Blue Cheese Dressing** (recipe on page 42), **Cranberry Muffins** (recipe on page 165), **Saucy Chicken Casserole** (recipe on page 76).

MOM'S SOFT SUGAR COOKIES

Arnita Schroeder, Hoagland, Indiana

(PICTURED AT LEFT)

1-3/4 cups sugar
1 cup butter (no substitutes), softened
3/4 teaspoon salt
4 egg yolks
2 eggs
1 teaspoon baking soda
2 tablespoons hot water
1 cup (8 ounces) sour cream
4 cups all-purpose flour
1 teaspoon baking powder
1/2 teaspoon nutmeg
Granulated *or* colored sugar
Walnut halves, optional

In a large mixing bowl, cream sugar, butter, salt, yolks and whole eggs. Dissolve baking soda in hot water; add, with sour cream, to butter mixture. In separate bowl, sift together flour, baking powder and nutmeg; add to egg mixture. Dough will be sticky. Cover and chill several hours or overnight. Roll chilled dough on a well-floured surface. Cut into 2-1/2-in. round or decorative shapes. Sprinkle with granulated or colored sugar. Top plain round cookies with a walnut half if desired. Bake at 350° for 8-10 minutes or until cookies are set but not browned. Remove cookies to wire rack to cool. **Yield:** about 7-1/2 dozen cookies.

SOUR CREAM APPLE SQUARES

Nancy Wit, Fremont, Nebraska

2 cups all-purpose flour
2 cups packed brown sugar
1/2 cup butter *or* margarine, softened
1 cup chopped nuts
2 teaspoons ground cinnamon
1 teaspoon baking soda
1/2 teaspoon salt
1 cup (8 ounces) sour cream
1 teaspoon vanilla extract
1 egg, beaten
2 cups chopped peeled apples
Whipped cream, optional

In a mixing bowl, combine flour, brown sugar and butter; blend at low speed until crumbly. Stir in the nuts. Press about 2-3/4 cups into the bottom of an ungreased 13-in. x 9-in. x 2-in. baking pan. To the remaining crumb mixture, add cinnamon, baking soda, salt, sour cream, vanilla and egg. Beat until thoroughly combined. Stir in apples. Spoon evenly over bottom layer. Bake at 350° for 35-40 minutes or until cake tests done. Cool on a wire rack. Cut into squares. Garnish with whipped cream if desired. **Yield:** 12-15 servings.

BANANA OATMEAL COOKIES

Yvonne Miller, Chenango Forks, New York

1 cup sugar
1 cup butter-flavored shortening
2 eggs
1 teaspoon vanilla extract
2 cups all-purpose flour
1 teaspoon baking soda
1 teaspoon ground cloves
1 teaspoon ground cinnamon
3 medium bananas, mashed
2 cups quick-cooking oats
1 cup (6 ounces) semisweet chocolate chips

In a large bowl, cream sugar, shortening, eggs and vanilla. Combine flour, baking soda, cloves and cinnamon; add to creamed mixture. Stir in bananas, oats and chocolate chips. Drop by rounded teaspoonfuls onto greased cookie sheets. Bake at 375° for 10-12 minutes. Immediately remove cookies to wire racks to cool. **Yield:** about 4 dozen.

> **TOASTED OATS.** For extra-crunchy and flavorful oatmeal cookies, toast the oats before adding to your batter. Spread the oats in a shallow pan and let them toast while heating the oven for baking.

ICED BROWNIES

Goldie Hanke, Tomahawk, Wisconsin

1 cup sugar
1/2 cup butter *or* margarine, softened
4 eggs
1 can (16 ounces) chocolate-flavored syrup
1 cup all-purpose flour
1/2 cup chopped nuts
ICING:
1-1/4 cups sugar
6 tablespoons butter *or* margarine
6 tablespoons milk *or* light cream
1 teaspoon vanilla extract
1 cup (6 ounces) semisweet chocolate chips

In a mixing bowl, cream sugar and butter. Add eggs, one at a time, beating well after each addition. Add syrup and flour; mix well. Stir in nuts. Pour into a greased 13-in. x 9-in. x 2-in. baking pan. Bake at 350° for 30-35 minutes or until top springs back when lightly touched. Cool slightly. Meanwhile, for icing, combine sugar, butter and milk in a small saucepan. Cook and stir until mixture comes to a boil. Reduce heat to medium and cook for 3 minutes, stirring constantly. Remove from the heat; stir in vanilla and chocolate chips until chips are melted. (Mixture will be thin.) Immediately pour over brownies. Cool completely before cutting. **Yield:** about 3 dozen.

SPICED OATMEAL COOKIES

Loretta Pakulski, Indian River, Michigan

1 cup shortening
2 cups packed brown sugar
2 eggs
2 tablespoons milk
2-1/2 cups all-purpose flour
2 cups old-fashioned oats
1 teaspoon baking soda
1 teaspoon salt
1 teaspoon ground cinnamon

In a mixing bowl, cream shortening and brown sugar. Add eggs and milk; mix well. Combine flour, oats, baking soda, salt and cinnamon; add to the creamed mixture. Drop by rounded teaspoonfuls 2 in. apart onto lightly greased cookie sheets. Bake at 350° for 12-15 minutes or until done. **Yield:** 4 dozen.

AUNT IONE'S ICEBOX COOKIES

Jenny Hill, Meridianville, Alabama

6 cups all-purpose flour
1-1/2 teaspoons baking powder
1 teaspoon baking soda
1 teaspoon ground nutmeg
1 teaspoon ground cinnamon
2 cups butter *or* margarine, softened
1 cup sugar
1 cup packed brown sugar
3 eggs
1 teaspoon vanilla extract
1 teaspoon lemon extract
2 cups chopped nuts

Sift together first five ingredients; set aside. In a mixing bowl, cream butter and sugars. Add eggs, vanilla and lemon extract; beat well. Add dry ingredients; mix well. Stir in nuts. Divide dough into four parts and shape into 1-1/2-in. x 11-in. rolls. Wrap in foil and chill overnight. Slice cookies 3/8-in. thick. Bake on greased cookie sheets at 350° for about 10 minutes. **Yield:** about 17 dozen.

POOR MAN'S COOKIES

Georgia Perrine, Bremerton, Washington

2 cups rolled oats
1 cup packed brown sugar
1/2 cup sugar
1 cup all-purpose flour
1/4 teaspoon salt
1 teaspoon baking soda
1/4 cup hot water
1/2 cup shortening, melted and cooled
1 teaspoon vanilla extract

In a mixing bowl, combine oats, sugars, flour and salt. In a separate bowl, combine soda and water; stir into oats mixture along with shortening and vanilla. Roll into walnut-size balls. Place on greased cookie sheets. Bake at 350° for 10 minutes or until golden brown. Remove from the oven; allow to stand 2 minutes before removing to a wire rack to cool. **Yield:** about 3-1/2 dozen.

PEANUT CHOCOLATE CHIP COOKIES

Jodie McCoy, Tulsa, Oklahoma

(PICTURED ON PAGE 217)

2 cups all-purpose flour
2 teaspoons baking powder
1/2 teaspoon salt
1 cup butter *or* margarine, softened
1 cup sugar
1 cup packed brown sugar
2 eggs
1 teaspoon vanilla
1 cup creamy peanut butter
1 cup Spanish peanuts
1 cup (6 ounces) semisweet chocolate chips

Combine dry ingredients; set aside. Cream margarine and sugars; add eggs and vanilla and beat until fluffy. Blend in peanut butter. Gradually add dry ingredients. Stir in peanuts and chocolate chips. Drop by teaspoonfuls onto greased cookie sheet. Bake at 350° for about 8 minutes. **Yield:** 7-8 dozen.

CHEWY PECAN COOKIES

Janice Jackson, Haleyville, Alabama

(PICTURED ON PAGE 164)

1 cup butter *or* margarine, softened
1 cup sugar
3/4 cup packed brown sugar
3 eggs
1/4 cup milk
1 teaspoon vanilla extract

2-1/4 cups all-purpose flour
1 tablespoon ground cinnamon
1 teaspoon baking soda
1 teaspoon salt
1 teaspoon pumpkin pie *or* apple pie spice
2 cups quick-cooking oats
2 cups raisins
1-1/2 cups chopped pecans

In a large mixing bowl, beat butter, sugars, eggs, milk and vanilla. Combine dry ingredients; add to creamed mixture and mix well. Stir in oats, raisins and nuts; mix well. Drop by tablespoonfuls onto greased baking sheets. Bake at 350° for 10-12 minutes or until light golden brown. Remove from baking sheets to cool on wire racks. **Yield:** 5-6 dozen.

FRUITCAKE SQUARES

Lana Rulevish, Ashley, Illinois

6 tablespoons butter *or* margarine, melted
4 cups vanilla wafer crumbs
3/4 cup halved candied green cherries
3/4 cup halved candied red cherries
1/2 cup chopped candied pineapple
3/4 cup chopped dates
1 cup pecan halves
1 can (14 ounces) sweetened condensed milk
1 teaspoon vanilla extract

Pour melted butter in a 15-in. x 10-in. x 1-in. baking pan. Sprinkle evenly with vanilla wafer crumbs. Arrange cherries, pineapple, dates and pecans evenly over the crumbs; press down gently. Combine milk and vanilla; pour over fruit. Bake at 350° for 20-25 minutes. **Yield:** about 6 dozen.

DOUBLE ORANGE COOKIES

Pamela Kinney, Irving, Texas

4 cups all-purpose flour
1 teaspoon baking powder
1 teaspoon baking soda
1/2 teaspoon salt
1-1/2 cups sugar
1 cup butter *or* margarine, softened
1 cup (8 ounces) sour cream
2 eggs
1 can (6 ounces) orange juice concentrate, thawed, *divided*
2 tablespoons grated orange peel

FROSTING:
1 package (3 ounces) cream cheese, softened
1 tablespoon butter *or* margarine, softened

2 cups confectioners' sugar
1 tablespoon grated orange peel
2 tablespoons milk

Combine flour, baking powder, baking soda and salt; set aside. In a large mixing bowl, cream sugar and butter until fluffy. Add sour cream and eggs. Beat until well blended. Reserve 1 tablespoon orange juice concentrate for frosting. Add the remaining concentrate with dry ingredients to the creamed mixture; mix well. Stir in orange peel. Drop by rounded tablespoonfuls onto lightly greased cookie sheets. Bake at 350° for about 10 minutes or until edges just begin to brown. Remove from the cookie sheets and allow to cool on a wire rack before frosting. For frosting, combine reserved orange juice concentrate and remaining ingredients in a small mixing bowl and beat until smooth. Spread a small amount over each cookie. **Yield:** about 7 dozen 2-1/2-inch cookies.

OATMEAL COOKIES

Diane Maughan, Cedar City, Utah

1 cup packed brown sugar
2 eggs
1/2 cup milk
3/4 cup vegetable oil
1 teaspoon vanilla extract
2 cups all-purpose flour
1 teaspoon baking soda
1 teaspoon salt
1 teaspoon ground cinnamon
1 teaspoon ground nutmeg
2 cups old-fashioned oats
1/2 cup semisweet chocolate chips
1/2 cup raisins

In a mixing bowl, combine brown sugar, eggs, milk, oil and vanilla; mix well. Combine flour, baking soda, salt, cinnamon and nutmeg; stir into batter. Stir in oats, chocolate chips and raisins. Let stand for 5-10 minutes. Drop by teaspoonfuls onto greased baking sheets. Bake at 350° for 10-12 minutes or until lightly browned. Remove immediately to wire racks. **Yield:** 3-1/2 dozen.

CHEWY DATE PINWHEELS

Naomi Cross, Goshen, Indiana

(PICTURED ON PAGE 190)

FILLING:
1-1/2 cups chopped dates
1 cup sugar
1 cup water
1/2 cup chopped pecans
COOKIE:
1 cup butter *or* margarine
2 cups packed brown sugar

1/2 cup sugar
3 eggs
4-1/2 cups all-purpose flour
1 teaspoon salt
1 teaspoon baking soda
1 teaspoon cinnamon

In a saucepan, combine dates, sugar and water. Cook over medium heat, stirring constantly, until thick, about 8 minutes. Add nuts; cool. Meanwhile, cream butter and sugars. Add eggs, one at a time, beating well after each addition. Combine flour, salt, baking soda and cinnamon. Add gradually to butter mixture. Divide dough and roll on a lightly floured surface to a rectangle 1/4-in. thick. Spread with half the date filling and roll up jelly-roll style. Wrap with plastic wrap. Repeat with remaining dough and filling. Chill dough rolls overnight. Before baking, remove plastic wrap and cut dough into 1/2-in. slices. Place on greased cookie sheets 2 in. apart. Bake at 375° for about 12 minutes. Cool on wire racks. **Yield:** about 4 dozen.

PEANUT BUTTER OATMEAL COOKIES

Linda Fox, Soldotna, Alaska

1-1/2 cups shortening
1-1/2 cups peanut butter
2 cups packed brown sugar
3 eggs
2 teaspoons vanilla extract
3 cups quick-cooking oats
2 cups whole wheat flour
2 teaspoons baking soda
1 teaspoon salt

In a mixing bowl, cream shortening and peanut butter. Add brown sugar, eggs and vanilla; mix well. Combine oats, flour, baking soda and salt; add to the creamed mixture and mix well. Drop by rounded teaspoonfuls onto ungreased baking sheets. Flatten with a fork. Bake at 350° for 12 minutes or until done. **Yield:** 6 dozen.

PRALINE COOKIES

Melody Sroufe, Wichita, Kansas

1/2 cup butter *or* margarine, softened
1-1/2 cups packed brown sugar
1 egg
1 teaspoon vanilla extract
1-1/2 cups all-purpose flour
1-1/2 teaspoons baking powder
1/4 teaspoon salt
1 cup pecans, coarsely chopped
ICING:
1 cup packed brown sugar
1/2 cup heavy cream
1 cup confectioners' sugar

In a mixing bowl, cream the butter and brown sugar. Add egg and vanilla; mix well. Combine flour, baking powder and salt; add to creamed mixture. Mix well. Cover and chill until dough is easy to handle, about 1 hour. Form into 1-in. balls; place 2 in. apart on greased baking sheets. Flatten cookies slightly with fingers; sprinkle each with 1 teaspoon pecans. Bake at 350° for 10 minutes. Cool on wire racks. Meanwhile, for icing, combine the brown sugar and cream in a saucepan. Cook over medium-high heat until sugar dissolves and mixture comes to a boil, stirring constantly. Remove from the heat; blend in confectioners' sugar until smooth. Drizzle over cookies. **Yield:** 4 dozen.

TOASTED OATMEAL COOKIES

Marilyn Krueger, Milwaukee, Wisconsin

3/4 cup butter *or* margarine
2-1/2 cups rolled oats
3/4 cup all-purpose flour
1 teaspoon baking soda
1 cup packed brown sugar
2 eggs, beaten
1 teaspoon vanilla extract
1/2 cup salted peanuts, coarsely chopped

In a large skillet over medium heat, melt butter until lightly browned. Add oats, stirring constantly until golden, about 8-10 minutes. Remove from the heat; cool. Combine flour and baking soda; set aside. In a large mixing bowl, beat brown sugar, eggs and vanilla until light. Stir in dry ingredients, oats and peanuts until well blended. Let stand for 15 minutes. Drop by rounded teaspoonfuls onto greased cookie sheets. Bake at 375° for 10 minutes or until golden. Remove to wire rack to cool. **Yield:** 3-1/2 dozen.

ZUCCHINI-RAISIN COOKIES

Margie Wampler, Butler, Pennsylvania

1/2 cup shortening
1 cup sugar
1 egg
1 cup shredded peeled zucchini
2 cups all-purpose flour
1 teaspoon baking soda
1 teaspoon ground cinnamon
1/2 teaspoon baking powder
1/2 teaspoon salt
1/2 teaspoon ground nutmeg
1/4 teaspoon ground cloves
1 cup raisins

In a mixing bowl, cream shortening and sugar. Add egg; beat well. Stir in zucchini; set aside. Combine flour, baking soda, cinnamon, baking powder, salt,

nutmeg and cloves. Add to zucchini mixture; stir until thoroughly combined. Stir in raisins. Drop by rounded teaspoonfuls 2 in. apart on greased baking sheets. Bake at 375° for 12-15 minutes or until golden brown. Cool on pans for 2 minutes before removing to a wire rack. Cookies are cake-like. **Yield:** 3 dozen.

FROSTED SPICE COOKIES

Debbie Hurlbert, Howard, Ohio

(PICTURED BELOW)

1 cup butter *or* margarine, softened
1 cup sugar
1 cup molasses
1 egg
1 cup sour milk*
6 cups all-purpose flour
1 tablespoon baking powder
1 teaspoon baking soda
1 teaspoon ground cinnamon
1 teaspoon ground ginger
1/2 teaspoon salt
1 cup chopped walnuts
1 cup golden raisins
1 cup chopped dates
FROSTING:
3-3/4 cups confectioners' sugar
1/3 cup orange juice
2 tablespoons butter *or* margarine, melted

In a large mixing bowl, cream butter and sugar. Add molasses, egg and milk; mix well. Combine the flour, baking powder, baking soda, cinnamon, ginger and salt; gradually add to creamed mixture. Stir in walnuts, raisins and dates. Chill for 30 minutes. Roll dough out on a lightly floured surface to 1/4-in. thickness. Cut with a 2-1/2-in. cutter. Place on greased baking sheets. Bake at 350° for 12-15 minutes. Cool completely. For frosting, beat all ingredients in a small bowl until smooth. Frost cookies. (*To sour milk, add 1 tablespoon vinegar to milk and let stand for 5 minutes.) **Yield:** 5-6 dozen.

WANT TO ADD some spice to your life? Why not bake a batch of old-fashioned Spice Cookies?

SOUR CREAM RAISIN SQUARES

Leona Eash, McConnelsville, Ohio

(PICTURED ON PAGE 162)

1 cup butter *or* margarine, softened
1 cup packed brown sugar
2 cups all-purpose flour
2 cups quick-cooking oats
1 teaspoon baking powder
1 teaspoon baking soda
1/8 teaspoon salt

FILLING:
4 egg yolks
2 cups (16 ounces) sour cream
1-1/2 cups raisins
1 cup sugar
1 tablespoon cornstarch

In a mixing bowl, cream the butter and brown sugar. Beat in flour, oats, baking powder, baking soda and salt (mixture will be crumbly). Set aside 2 cups; pat remaining crumbs into a greased 13-in. x 9-in. x 2-in. baking pan. Bake at 350° for 15 minutes. Cool. Meanwhile, combine filling ingredients in a saucepan. Bring to a boil; cook and stir constantly for 5-8 minutes. Pour over crust; sprinkle with reserved crumbs. Return to oven for 15 minutes. **Yield:** 12-16 servings.

CHERRY SQUARES

Ann Fabian, Tilley, Alberta

FILLING:
2 cans (16 ounces *each*) tart red cherries
3/4 cup sugar
5 tablespoons cornstarch
1/4 teaspoon salt
1 tablespoon butter *or* margarine
1/2 teaspoon almond extract
Several drops red food coloring

BASE:
1 package (1/4 ounce) active dry yeast
2/3 cup warm milk (110° to 115°)
1 cup butter *or* margarine
3-1/2 cups all-purpose flour
2 tablespoons sugar
1/2 teaspoon salt
5 egg yolks, beaten

TOPPING:
1/4 cup butter *or* margarine, softened
1-1/2 cups confectioners' sugar
2 tablespoons half-and-half cream
1/2 teaspoon almond extract
3/4 cup chopped nuts

Drain cherries; reserve 1 cup of the juice. Set aside. In a saucepan, combine sugar, cornstarch and salt. Stir in cherry juice. Cook and stir over medium-high heat until bubbly. Cook and stir 1 minute more. Remove from heat; stir in butter, extract, food coloring and cherries. Set aside to cool. Dissolve yeast in warm milk. Let stand 5 minutes. Cut butter into flour, sugar and salt. Add yeast mixture and egg yolks; mix thoroughly. If needed, add additional flour to make a soft dough. Turn dough out onto a lightly floured surface and knead 10 times. Divide dough in half. Roll half the dough into a 17-in. x 11-in. rectangle. Carefully transfer to a greased 17-1/2-in. x 11-1/2-in. x 1-in. baking pan. Spread cooled cherry filling over dough. Roll out second portion of dough to 17-in. x 11-in. rectangle. Carefully place over cherry filling. Press edges together to seal. Cover and allow to rise in a warm place until doubled, about 30 minutes. Bake at 350° about 25 minutes or until golden brown. Cool. Combine topping ingredients except nuts and spread over uncut surface. Top with nuts and cut into squares. **Yield:** 24 squares.

HAYSTACKS

Starrlette Howard, Ogden, Utah

1 package (6 ounces) butterscotch chips
1/2 cup peanut butter
1 can (3 ounces) chow mein noodles
1 cup miniature marshmallows

Melt butterscotch chips and peanut butter in the top of a double boiler. Fold in the chow mein noodles, then marshmallows. Drop by teaspoonfuls onto greased waxed paper. Cool. **Yield:** 2 dozen.

PECAN PIE BARS

Carolyn Custer, Clifton Park, New York

2 cups all-purpose flour
1/2 cup confectioners' sugar
1 cup butter *or* margarine, softened
1 can (14 ounces) sweetened condensed milk
1 egg

1 teaspoon vanilla extract
Pinch salt
1 package (6 ounces) toffee-flavored chips
1 cup chopped pecans

In a mixing bowl, combine flour and sugar. Cut in butter until mixture resembles coarse meal. Press firmly into a greased 13-in. x 9-in. x 2-in. baking dish. Bake at 350° for 15 minutes. Meanwhile, in another bowl, beat milk, egg, vanilla and salt. Stir in toffee chips and pecans; spread evenly over baked crust. Bake for another 20-25 minutes or until lightly browned. Cool, then refrigerate. When thoroughly chilled, cut into bars. Store in the refrigerator. **Yield:** 4 dozen.

SUGAR COOKIES

Helen Wallis, Vancouver, Washington

1/2 cup butter (no substitutes), softened
1/2 cup shortening
1 cup sugar
1 egg
1 teaspoon vanilla extract
2-1/4 cups all-purpose flour
1/2 teaspoon baking powder
1/2 teaspoon baking soda
Additional sugar

In a mixing bowl, cream butter, shortening and sugar. Add egg and vanilla; mix well. Combine flour, baking powder and baking soda; gradually add to the creamed mixture. Shape into 1-in. balls. Roll in sugar. Place on greased cookie sheet; flatten with a glass. Bake at 350° for 10-12 minutes. **Yield:** 5 dozen.

> **YOU CAN AVOID** the crumbling of chilled cookie dough when you slice it by first warming the blade of your knife with hot water and then wiping it dry. When the blade cools, warm it again the same way.

WASHBOARD COOKIES

John Cas Roulston, Stephenville, Texas

1/2 cup butter *or* margarine, softened
1 cup packed dark brown sugar
1 egg
1/2 teaspoon baking soda
1 tablespoon hot water
1 teaspoon vanilla extract
1-3/4 cups all-purpose flour
Sugar

In a mixing bowl, cream butter, brown sugar and egg. Stir together baking soda and water; add to creamed mixture. Add vanilla and flour; mix well. Shape into walnut-sized balls. Place on greased cookie sheets; flatten with a fork that has been dipped in water. Sprinkle with sugar. Bake at 325° for 15-20 minutes or until edges begin to brown. Cool on waxed paper. **Yield:** 3-1/2 dozen.

> **A REAL SOFTIE.** If your stored cookies have gotten too crisp for your liking, put them in a plastic bag with a piece of bread. The next day you'll have soft cookies again.

Quick & Easy

DOUBLE CHOCOLATE BROWNIES

Flo Burtnett, Gage, Oklahoma

1 egg beaten
1 box (21-1/2 ounces) fudge brownie mix
1/4 cup vegetable oil
1/4 cup cold coffee
1/4 cup water
1 cup white chocolate chips *or* coarsely chopped almond bark
3/4 cup chopped walnuts

Place egg, brownie mix, oil, coffee and water in a large mixing bowl. Mix with a spoon until just moistened, about 50 strokes. Stir in chocolate and nuts. Spread in a greased 13-in. x 9-in. x 2-in. baking pan. Bake 30 minutes at 350°. Cool in pan. **Yield:** 36 brownies.

HOLIDAY SHORTBREAD COOKIES

Erma Hiltpold, Kerrville, Texas

5 cups all-purpose flour
1 cup sugar
1/2 teaspoon salt
2 cups cold butter (no substitutes)

In a large mixing bowl, combine flour, sugar and salt. Cut in butter until mixture resembles fine crumbs. Pat into an ungreased 15-in. x 10-in. x 1-in. baking pan. Prick all over with a fork. Bake at 325° for 35 minutes or until center is set. Cool for 10-15 minutes. Cut into small squares. Continue to cool to room temperature. **Yield:** 5 dozen.

SOUTHERN TEA CAKES

Mary Singletary, Converse, Louisiana

1 cup shortening
1-3/4 cups sugar

2 eggs
1/2 cup milk
1/2 teaspoon vanilla extract
3 cups self-rising flour

In a mixing bowl, cream together shortening and sugar. Beat in eggs. Add milk and vanilla; beat well. Stir in flour; mix well. Drop by tablespoonfuls 2-1/2-in. apart onto greased cookie sheets. Bake at 350° for 15-20 minutes. **Yield:** about 3 dozen.

LEMON FILBERT TEA BARS

Cathee Bethel, Philomath, Oregon

(PICTURED ON PAGE 156)

1/2 cup butter *or* margarine, softened
1 cup plus 2 tablespoons all-purpose flour, *divided*
1/4 cup confectioners' sugar
2 eggs
1 cup sugar
1/2 cup ground toasted filberts
2 tablespoons lemon juice
1 teaspoon grated lemon peel
1/2 teaspoon baking powder
Additional confectioners' sugar

In a mixing bowl, combine butter, 1 cup flour and confectioners' sugar. Press into the bottom of an 11-1/2-in. x 7-1/2-in. baking pan. Bake at 350° for 10 minutes. Combine the remaining ingredients except additional confectioners' sugar. Pour over the crust; bake for 20 minutes. Cool. Cut into squares and sprinkle with confectioners' sugar. **Yield:** about 15 bars.

COCONUT CHERRY SQUARES

Mildred Schwartzentruber, Tavistock, Ontario

1-3/4 cups flaked coconut
1-1/2 cups all-purpose flour
1/2 cup butter *or* margarine, softened
1/2 cup sugar
1 can (21 ounces) cherry pie filling

In a mixing bowl, combine first four ingredients. Press half the mixture into the bottom of a greased 9-in. x 9-in. baking pan. Top with the pie filling and sprinkle with remaining crumb mixture. Bake at 375° for 40 minutes or until golden brown. **Yield:** 9 servings.

SWISS CHOCOLATE BARS

Margaret Jelinek, Wrentham, Massachusetts

(PICTURED BELOW)

2 cups all-purpose flour
2 cups sugar
1 teaspoon baking soda
1/2 teaspoon salt
2 eggs, beaten
1/2 cup sour cream
1 cup water
1/2 cup butter *or* margarine
1-1/2 squares (1-1/2 ounces) unsweetened chocolate
FROSTING:
4 cups confectioners' sugar
1/2 cup butter *or* margarine
1/3 cup milk
1-1/2 squares (1-1/2 ounces) unsweetened chocolate
1 teaspoon vanilla extract
Pecan halves

In a large bowl, combine flour, sugar, baking soda and salt. In a small bowl, combine eggs and sour cream. In a saucepan, cook and stir water, butter and chocolate just until melted. Stir into dry ingredients. Add sour cream mixture and mix well. Pour into a greased 15-in. x 10-in. x 1-in. baking pan. Bake at 375° for 25 minutes or until bars test done. Cool 30 minutes. Meanwhile, for frosting, place confectioners' sugar in a large mixing bowl. Combine butter, milk and chocolate in a saucepan. Cook and stir just until mixture boils. Add to sugar; beat until smooth. Stir in vanilla. Allow to stand for 5 minutes. Spread over warm bars. Top with pecan halves. Cool before cutting into bars. **Yield:** about 3 dozen.

HARD-TO-RESIST BARS. Swiss Chocolate Bars' chewy texture make for excellent eating.

WHO COULD resist a slice of this wonderfully moist cake
spread with a scrumptious cream cheese frosting?
A perfect dessert choice for Mother's Day, a birthday or
any special occasion, this delicious cake
will likely take top honors in your household!

SLICE OF LIFE.
Zucchini Carrot Cake (recipe on page 187).

CAKES & TORTES

After just one taste, you'll agree these attractive, tempting morsels take the cake—any way you slice them!

ZUCCHINI CARROT CAKE

Mary Spill, Tierra Amarilla, New Mexico
(PICTURED AT LEFT)

4 eggs
2 cups sugar
1-1/3 cups vegetable oil
2-1/2 cups all-purpose flour
2 teaspoons baking soda
2 teaspoons baking powder
2 teaspoons ground cinnamon
1 teaspoon ground cloves
1 teaspoon ground allspice
1 teaspoon ground ginger
1/2 teaspoon ground nutmeg
1 teaspoon salt
2 cups finely shredded carrots
2 cups finely shredded zucchini
1 cup coarsely chopped pecans
    or walnuts
FROSTING:
1 package (8 ounces) cream
    cheese, softened
1/2 cup butter *or* margarine,
    softened
5 cups confectioners' sugar
2 teaspoons vanilla extract
Whole *or* chopped pecans *or*
    walnuts for garnish, optional

In a large mixing bowl, beat eggs and sugar until frothy. Gradually beat in oil. Combine dry ingredients; add to batter. Beat 4 minutes. Stir in carrots, zucchini and nuts. Pour into three greased 9-in. baking pans. Bake at 350° for about 35 minutes or until top springs back when lightly touched. Cool 5 minutes before removing from pans. Cool thoroughly on a wire rack. For frosting, beat cream cheese and butter in a large mixing bowl until smooth. Add sugar and vanilla. Continue beating until sugar is dissolved. Spread between the layers and over the top and sides of the cake. Garnish with whole or chopped nuts if desired. **Yield:** 12-14 servings.

APPLE CAKE WITH BUTTERMILK SAUCE

Donni Way, Plattsburgh, New York

3 cups all-purpose flour
1 teaspoon baking soda

1 teaspoon ground cinnamon
1/2 teaspoon salt
3 eggs
2 cups sugar
1-1/4 cups vegetable oil
1/4 cup orange juice
1 teaspoon vanilla extract
2 cups chopped unpeeled apples
1 cup chopped walnuts
1 cup flaked coconut
BUTTERMILK SAUCE:
1 cup sugar
1/2 cup butter *or* margarine
1/2 cup buttermilk
1/2 teaspoon baking soda

Whipped cream, optional

Combine flour, baking soda, cinnamon and salt; set aside. In a large mixing bowl, beat eggs. Add sugar, oil, orange juice and vanilla. On low speed, blend in flour mixture. Fold in apples, walnuts and coconut. Pour into a greased and floured 10-in. tube pan. Bake at 325° for 1-1/4 hours or until the cake tests done. Invert cake onto a large plate or platter. Deeply puncture the top of the warm cake with a skewer or pick. In a small saucepan, bring all sauce ingredients to a boil, stirring frequently. Immediately spoon 1-1/4 cups of sauce slowly over the top of the cake, then pour the remainder down the sides. Cool. Serve with whipped cream if desired. **Yield:** 16 servings.

CLASSIC CHOCOLATE CAKE

Betty Follas, Morgan Hill, California
(PICTURED ON PAGE 29)

2/3 cup butter *or* margarine,
    softened
1-2/3 cups sugar
3 eggs
2 cups all-purpose flour
2/3 cup baking cocoa
1-1/4 teaspoons baking soda
1 teaspoon salt
1-1/3 cups milk
Confectioners' sugar *or* favorite
    frosting

In a mixing bowl, cream butter and sugar until fluffy. Add eggs, one at a time, beating well after each addition. Combine flour, cocoa, baking soda and salt; add to creamed mixture alternately with milk,

beating until smooth after each addition. Pour batter into a greased and floured 13-in. x 9-in. x 2-in. baking pan. Bake at 350° for 35-40 minutes or until cake tests done. Cool on a wire rack. When cake is cool, dust with confectioners' sugar or frost with your favorite frosting. **Yield:** 12-15 servings.

EASY RHUBARB DESSERT

Deb Jesse, Storm Lake, Iowa

1 package (18-1/2 ounces)
    yellow cake mix
5 cups diced fresh or frozen
    rhubarb
1 cup sugar
1 cup heavy cream

Mix cake as instructed on package. Pour batter into a greased 13-in. x 9-in. x 2-in. baking pan. Spread rhubarb over batter. Sprinkle with sugar; pour cream over top. Do not mix. Bake at 350° for 35-40 minutes or until cake tests done. **Yield:** 12-16 servings.

ANGEL FOOD CAKE

Lucille Proctor, Panguitch, Utah

1-1/2 cups egg whites (about 1
    dozen), room temperature
1-1/2 teaspoons cream of tartar
1-1/2 teaspoons vanilla extract
1/2 teaspoon almond extract
1/4 teaspoon salt
1 cup sugar
1 cup confectioners' sugar
1 cup all-purpose flour

In a mixing bowl, beat egg whites, cream of tartar, extracts and salt at high speed. While beating, gradually add sugar; beat until sugar is dissolved and mixture forms stiff peaks. Combine confectioners' sugar and flour; gradually fold into the batter, 1/4 cup at a time. Gently spoon mixture into an *ungreased* 10-in. tube pan. With a metal spatula or knife, cut through the batter to break large air pockets. Bake at 350° for about 35 minutes or until cake springs back when lightly touched. Immediately invert cake in pan to cool completely. When cool, remove from pan. **Yield:** 16 servings.

CREAM POUND CAKE

Marguerite Bubon, Charlton, Massachusetts

(PICTURED AT RIGHT)

**6 eggs
2-3/4 cups sugar
1 teaspoon vanilla extract
3 cups all-purpose flour
1 tablespoon baking powder
1/4 teaspoon salt
1 pint heavy cream**

In a mixing bowl, beat eggs at high speed for 5 minutes or until pale yellow. Gradually beat in sugar and vanilla, mixing until sugar is dissolved. Combine flour, baking powder and salt; add to batter alternately with cream. Pour into a greased 10-in. tube pan. Bake at 350° for 60-70 minutes or until cake tests done. Cool in pan 15 minutes before removing to a wire rack to cool completely. **Yield:** 12-16 servings.

Quick & Easy

CRUMB CAKE

Verna Hofer, Mitchell, South Dakota

**2 cups all-purpose flour
1-1/3 cups sugar
2/3 cup butter *or* margarine, softened
1/2 teaspoon salt
1 teaspoon baking soda
1 teaspoon ground cinnamon
1/2 teaspoon ground cloves
1 egg, beaten
1 cup buttermilk
1/2 cup semisweet chocolate chips
1/2 cup chopped nuts**

In a mixing bowl, combine flour, sugar, butter and salt until crumbly. Set aside 1 cup. Stir baking soda, cinnamon and cloves into the remaining crumb mixture. Add egg and buttermilk; mix well. Pour into a greased 13-in. x 9-in. x 2-in. baking pan. Sprinkle with reserved crumb mixture; top with chocolate chips and nuts. Bake at 350° for 30 minutes or until the cake tests done. Cool on a wire rack. **Yield:** 12-16 servings.

GREAT-GRANDMA'S LEMON CAKE

Glenda Stokes, Florence, South Carolina

**1 cup butter (no substitutes), softened
3 cups sugar
5 eggs, *separated*
1 tablespoon finely shredded lemon peel**

**3 tablespoons lemon juice
4 cups all-purpose flour
1/2 teaspoon baking soda
1 cup milk
Confectioners' sugar**

In a mixing bowl, cream butter; gradually add sugar, beating well. In a small mixing bowl, beat egg yolks until thick and lemon-colored. Add to creamed mixture and mix well. Stir in lemon peel and juice. Combine flour and baking soda; add alternately with milk, stirring well after each addition. Beat egg whites until stiff; fold into batter. Pour into two well-greased 9-in. x 5-in. x 3-in. loaf pans. Bake at 325° for 65-70 minutes or until cakes test done. Cool on wire rack for 10 minutes. Remove from pans to cool completely. Dust tops with confectioners' sugar. **Yield:** 2 cakes (24 servings).

ADAMS COUNTY APPLE CAKE

Gretchen Berendt, Carroll Valley, Pennsylvania

**3 cups all-purpose flour
1 tablespoon baking powder
2 cups plus 5 tablespoons sugar, *divided*
1 cup vegetable oil
4 eggs
1/3 cup orange juice
1/2 teaspoon salt
2-1/2 teaspoons vanilla extract
4 medium baking apples, peeled and thinly sliced
2 teaspoons ground cinnamon
Confectioners' sugar, optional**

In a mixing bowl, combine flour, baking powder, 2 cups of the sugar, oil, eggs, orange juice, salt and vanilla. Beat until thoroughly combined. In another bowl, toss apples with cinnamon and remaining sugar. Spread one-third of batter in a greased 10-in. tube pan. Cover with half of the apples. Repeat layers. Spoon remaining batter over top. Bake at 350° for 1 hour and 30 minutes or until cake tests done. Cool in pan for 20 minutes before removing to a wire rack to cool completely. Just before serving, dust with confectioners' sugar if desired. **Yield:** 12-16 servings.

HOT MILK CAKE

Suzanne Coleman, Rabun Gap, Georgia

(PICTURED ON PAGE 86)

**1/2 cup milk
3/4 cup all-purpose flour
1 teaspoon baking powder
1/4 teaspoon salt
3 eggs, room temperature**

**1 cup sugar
1 teaspoon vanilla extract
TOPPING:
1 cup shredded coconut
1/2 cup chopped pecans
1/3 cup packed brown sugar
2 tablespoons butter *or* margarine, softened
2 tablespoons milk**

Scald milk; set aside. Combine flour, baking powder and salt; set aside. In a mixing bowl, beat eggs until thick and lemon-colored. Gradually add sugar, blending well. On low speed, alternately mix in milk, dry ingredients and vanilla. Pour batter into a greased 10-in. cast-iron skillet. Bake at 350° for 25-30 minutes or until the cake springs back when lightly touched. Remove cake and preheat broiler. Combine all topping ingredients and sprinkle over cake. Broil 5 inches from the heat until topping bubbles and turns golden brown. Serve warm. **Yield:** 8 servings.

HERE'S A QUICK FROSTING IDEA. Place a solid chocolate-mint wafer on top of each cupcake after removing a batch from the oven. After it has softened, a wafer can be spread over the entire top or left as it is.

COCONUT FRUITCAKE

Lorraine Groh, Ferryville, Wisconsin

(PICTURED ON PAGE 13)

**2 cups all-purpose flour
1 teaspoon baking powder
1 teaspoon salt
1 pound chopped fruitcake mix
1-1/2 cups flaked coconut
1 cup golden raisins
1 cup chopped nuts
1/2 cup butter *or* margarine, softened
1 cup sugar
3 eggs, beaten
1 teaspoon lemon extract
1/2 cup orange juice
Additional candied fruit *or* nuts, optional**

In a large bowl, combine flour, baking powder and salt. Add fruitcake mix, coconut, raisins and nuts; mix well. In a mixing bowl, cream butter and sugar. Add eggs and extract; mix well. Stir in the flour mixture alternately with orange juice. Pack into a greased 10-in. tube pan lined with waxed paper. Bake at 250° for 2 to 2-1/2 hours or until cake tests done. Cool for 10 minutes. Loosen edges with a sharp knife. Remove from pan to cool completely on a wire rack. Garnish with candied fruit or nuts if desired. **Yield:** 12-16 servings.

ENTERTAINING is easy with this menu. Start with a
quick Salmon Spread appetizer and Asparagus Leek Soup.
Get ready for raves when you slice meaty helpings of
Italian Sausage and Spinach Pie. And for dessert, folks will love to
dig into moist Cream Pound Cake topped with
fresh fruit and whipped cream.

SATURDAY-NIGHT SPECIALS.
Clockwise from the top: **Cream Pound Cake** (recipe on page
188), **Italian Sausage and Spinach Pie** (recipe on page 77),
Asparagus Leek Soup (recipe on page 20) and
Salmon Spread (recipe on page 7).

EVERYONE loves dessert—and who could resist one of the deluxe recipes pictured here? You'll want to frequently dig into these cakes, cookies, bars, puddings and more. They're sweetly suited to serve at church potlucks, reunions, parties, the end of a meal… wherever dessert lovers are gathered!

SWEET TOOTH SATISFACTION.
Clockwise from lower left: **Saucy Mocha Pudding** (recipe on page 207), **Chewy Date Pinwheels** (recipe on page 182), **Chocolate Brownies** (recipe on page 175), **Sour Cream Pound Cake** (recipe on page 192), **Steamed Holiday Pudding** (recipe on page 207), **Old-Fashioned Rice Custard** (recipe on page 207), **Strawberry Shortcake** (recipe on page 207) and **Date Nut Torte** (recipe on page 192).

SOUR CREAM POUND CAKE
Karen Conrad, East Troy, Wisconsin

(PICTURED ON PAGE 191)

- 1 cup butter (no substitutes), softened
- 3 cups sugar
- 6 eggs
- 1 cup (8 ounces) sour cream
- 2 teaspoons vanilla extract
- 1/4 teaspoon baking soda
- 3 cups all-purpose flour
- Confectioners' sugar, optional

In a mixing bowl, cream butter and sugar. Add eggs, one at a time, beating well after each addition. Combine sour cream, vanilla and baking soda. Add alternately with the flour to the butter mixture. Mix well. Pour batter into a greased and floured tube pan. Bake at 325° for 80 minutes or until cake tests done. Cool in pan for 15 minutes before removing to a rack. Sprinkle with confectioners' sugar before serving if desired. **Yield:** about 16 servings.

Quick & Easy

DATE NUT TORTE
June Hovland, Rochester, Minnesota

(PICTURED ON PAGE 191)

- 2 eggs
- 1/2 cup sugar
- 1/2 cup packed brown sugar
- 2/3 cup all-purpose flour
- 1 teaspoon baking powder
- 1/4 teaspoon salt
- 1 cup chopped walnuts
- 1 cup chopped dates
- Whipped cream

In a mixing bowl, beat eggs. Gradually add sugars and beat until well mixed. Combine flour, baking powder and salt; Stir into egg mixture just until moistened. Stir in nuts and dates. Pour into a greased 8-in. x 8-in. baking pan. Bake at 350° for 30 minutes. Torte top will be crusty and the inside chewy. Cut into squares and serve with a dollop of whipped cream. **Yield:** 9 servings.

PRUNE CAKE
Betty Satterfield
Robbinsville, North Carolina

- 2 cups all-purpose flour
- 1-1/2 cups sugar
- 1 teaspoon baking soda
- 1 teaspoon ground nutmeg
- 1 teaspoon ground allspice
- 1 teaspoon ground cinnamon
- 1/2 teaspoon salt
- 1 cup vegetable oil

- 1 cup buttermilk
- 2 eggs, beaten
- 1 cup chopped cooked prunes, drained
- 1 cup chopped nuts

BUTTERMILK GLAZE:
- 1 cup sugar
- 1/2 cup butter *or* margarine
- 1/2 cup buttermilk
- 1 tablespoon light corn syrup
- 1/2 teaspoon baking soda

In a large mixing bowl, combine first seven ingredients. Add oil, buttermilk and eggs; mix well. Fold in prunes and nuts. Pour into a greased 13-in. x 9-in. x 2-in. baking pan. Bake at 325° for 40-45 minutes or until cake tests done. Remove from oven and punch holes in top of cake with a wooden skewer or pick. Immediately combine glaze ingredients in a saucepan. Bring to a boil and boil for 2 minutes, stirring constantly; pour hot glaze over warm cake. Cool in pan. **Yield:** 12-16 servings.

HOT FUDGE PUDDING CAKE
Martha Fehl, Brookville, Indiana

(PICTURED ON PAGE 216)

PUDDING CAKE:
- 1 cup all-purpose flour
- 1 cup baking cocoa
- 1 cup sugar
- 2 teaspoons baking powder
- 1/4 teaspoon salt
- 1/2 cup milk
- 2 tablespoons shortening, melted
- 1 teaspoon vanilla
- 1 cup broken pecans *or* walnuts

SAUCE:
- 1-1/2 cups brown sugar
- 5 tablespoons baking cocoa
- 1-3/4 cups hot water

Combine flour, cocoa, sugar, baking powder and salt. Stir in milk, shortening and vanilla (mixture will be very stiff). Blend in nuts. Spread mixture in 8- or 9-in. square pan. To make sauce, sprinkle brown sugar and cocoa over batter; pour hot water over all. Bake at 350° for 45 minutes. Serve warm with scoop of vanilla ice cream. **Yield:** 8-10 servings.

CRAN-ORANGE DELIGHT
Joyce Gee, Blytheville, Arkansas

(PICTURED ON PAGE 105)

- 1 package (18-1/4 ounces) yellow cake mix
- 1-1/3 cups orange juice
- 1/3 cup vegetable oil
- 3 eggs

- 1 teaspoon rum flavoring, optional

FROSTING:
- 1 carton (12 ounces) cranberry-orange sauce
- 1 package (3.4 ounces) instant vanilla pudding mix
- 2/3 cup orange juice
- 1 carton (8 ounces) frozen whipped topping, thawed
- Sliced almonds, optional

In a mixing bowl, beat the first five ingredients until smooth. Pour into two greased and floured 9-in. cake pans. Bake at 350° for 25-30 minutes or until the cakes test done. Cool in pans for 15 minutes before removing to a wire rack. For frosting, combine cranberry-orange sauce, pudding mix and orange juice in a mixing bowl. Fold in whipped topping. Split cooled cakes in half horizontally. Spread frosting between layers and over the top and sides of cake. Garnish with almonds if desired. Store in the refrigerator. **Yield:** 10-14 servings.

BLACK FOREST TORTE
Glatis McNiel, Constantine, Michigan

- 1-1/3 cups all-purpose flour
- 1-3/4 cups sugar
- 1-1/4 teaspoons baking soda
- 1/4 teaspoon baking powder
- 2/3 cup butter *or* margarine
- 4 squares (1 ounce *each*) unsweetened chocolate
- 1-1/4 cups water
- 1 teaspoon vanilla extract
- 3 eggs

CHOCOLATE FILLING:
- 2 bars (4 ounces *each*) German sweet chocolate, *divided*
- 3/4 cup butter *or* margarine
- 1/2 cup chopped pecans

CREAM FILLING:
- 2 cups heavy cream
- 1 tablespoon confectioners' sugar
- 1 teaspoon vanilla extract

In a mixing bowl, combine flour, sugar, baking soda and baking powder. In a saucepan, melt butter and chocolate; cool. Pour chocolate mixture, water and vanilla into flour mixture. Beat on low for 1 minute, then on medium for 2 minutes. Add eggs, one at a time, beating well after each. Divide batter among two 9-in. round pans that have been greased, floured and lined with waxed paper. Bake at 350° for 25-30 minutes or until cakes test done. Cool in pans 10 minutes. Remove to a wire rack. For chocolate filling, melt 1-1/2 bars of German chocolate over low heat. Stir in butter and nuts. Watching closely, cool filling just until it reaches spreading consistency. For cream filling, whip cream with sugar and vanilla until stiff peaks form. To assemble, slice cooled cake layers in half horizontally. Place one bottom layer on a serving platter; cover with half of the chocolate filling. Top with a second cake layer; spread on half of the cream filling. Repeat layers. Grate remaining German chocolate; sprinkle on the top. Refrigerate until serving. **Yield:** 12-16 servings.

FRESH PEAR CAKE

Frances Lanier, Metter, Georgia

3 eggs
2 cups sugar
1-1/2 cups vegetable oil
3 cups all-purpose flour
2 teaspoons ground cinnamon
1 teaspoon salt
1 teaspoon baking soda
1-1/2 cups finely chopped peeled pears (about 2 medium)
1 teaspoon vanilla extract
1-1/4 cups confectioners' sugar
2 tablespoons milk

In a mixing bowl, beat eggs on medium speed. Gradually add sugar and oil; beat thoroughly. Combine flour, cinnamon, salt and baking soda; add to egg mixture and mix well. Stir in pears and vanilla. (The batter will be stiff.) Spoon into a greased and floured 10-in. tube pan. Bake at 350° for 60-65 minutes or until cake tests done. Let cool in pan 10 minutes before inverting onto a serving plate. In a small bowl, combine the confectioners' sugar and milk; beat until smooth. Drizzle over warm cake. Cool completely. **Yield:** 14-16 servings.

CARROT CAKE

Melanie Habener, Santa Maria, California

3 eggs, beaten
3/4 cup vegetable oil
3/4 cup buttermilk
2 cups sugar
2 teaspoons vanilla extract
2 cups all-purpose flour
2 teaspoons ground cinnamon
2 teaspoons baking soda
1/2 teaspoon salt
1 can (8 ounces) crushed pineapple, undrained

2 cups grated carrots
1 cup raisins
1 cup chopped nuts
1 cup flaked coconut
CREAM CHEESE FROSTING:
1/2 cup butter *or* margarine, softened
1 package (8 ounces) cream cheese, softened
1 teaspoon vanilla extract
1 box (16 ounces) confectioners' sugar
2 tablespoons heavy cream

In a mixing bowl, combine eggs, oil, buttermilk, sugar and vanilla; mix well. Combine flour, cinnamon, baking soda and salt; stir into egg mixture. Stir in pineapple, carrots, raisins, nuts and coconut. Pour into a greased and floured 13-in. x 9-in. x 2-in. baking pan. Bake at 350° for 50-55 minutes or until cake tests done. *Do not overbake.* Remove to a wire rack to cool. In another mixing bowl, combine all frosting ingredients; beat until creamy. Spread on cooled cake. **Yield:** 12-16 servings.

CHERRY PINEAPPLE CAKE

Elaine De Rue, Hilton, New York

2 cans (16 ounces *each)* pitted tart red cherries, drained
1 can (20 ounces) crushed pineapple in syrup, undrained
1/3 cup finely chopped walnuts
1 package (18-1/4 ounces) white cake mix (without pudding)
1/2 cup butter *or* margarine, melted
Whipped cream, optional

Spread cherries and pineapple with syrup over the bottom of an ungreased 13-in. x 9-in. x 2-in. baking pan. Top with nuts. Sprinkle dry cake mix over all. Pour butter evenly over cake mix. Bake at 350° for 1 hour. Cool. Invert onto a serving plate. Cut into squares. Top with whipped cream if desired. **Yield:** 12-15 servings.

BUTTER PECAN CAKE

Virginia Gentry, Sutherlin, Virginia

3 tablespoons butter *or* margarine, melted
1-1/3 cups chopped pecans
2/3 cup butter *or* margarine, softened
1-1/3 cups sugar
2 eggs
2 cups all-purpose flour
1-1/2 teaspoons baking powder
1/4 teaspoon salt

2/3 cup milk
1-1/2 teaspoons vanilla extract
BUTTER PECAN FROSTING:
3 tablespoons butter *or* margarine, softened
3 cups confectioners' sugar
3 tablespoons milk
3/4 teaspoon vanilla extract

Pour melted butter into a baking pan. Stir in pecans. Toast at 350° for 10 minutes. Set aside to cool. In a mixing bowl, cream butter and sugar until light and fluffy. Add eggs, one at a time, beating well after each addition. Combine flour, baking powder and salt; add to creamed mixture alternately with milk, beginning and ending with dry ingredients. Stir in vanilla and 1 cup toasted pecans. Pour batter into two greased and floured 8-in. round cake pans. Bake at 350° for 30-35 minutes or until the cakes test done. Cool in pans 5 minutes. Remove from pans and cool thoroughly on a wire rack. Meanwhile, for frosting, cream butter and sugar. Add milk and vanilla, beating until light and fluffy. Add additional milk if needed. Stir in remaining toasted pecans. Spread between the layers and over the top and sides of the cake. **Yield:** 12 servings.

PECAN-CHOCOLATE CHIP POUND CAKE

Ruth Ann Vernon, Hobe Sound, Florida

(PICTURED ON PAGE 44)

2-3/4 cups sugar
1-1/4 cups butter, (no substitutes) softened
5 eggs
1 teaspoon almond extract
3 cups all-purpose flour
1 teaspoon baking powder
1/4 teaspoon salt
1 cup milk
1 cup mini semisweet chocolate chips
1 cup chopped pecans

In a large mixing bowl, beat sugar, butter *(must be very soft but not melted)*, eggs and almond extract on low just until mixed. Beat on high for 5 minutes, scraping bowl occasionally. In a separate bowl, combine flour, baking powder and salt. On low speed, add flour mixture alternately with milk, mixing just until blended. Fold in chocolate chips. Sprinkle pecans in the bottom of a greased and floured 10-in. tube pan. Carefully pour batter over pecans. Bake at 325° for 1 hour and 40 minutes or until cake tests done. Cool 20 minutes in pan before removing to a wire rack to cool completely. **Yield:** 16-20 servings.

SPECIAL gatherings deserve extra-special food…
like the hearty spread pictured here! If you're cooking for a crowd,
these buffet-style dishes will bring family and friends back to
the table for "just a little more". Get the party rolling with
Pineapple Pecan Cheese Ball, then enjoy Hot Italian
Roast Beef Sandwiches and Grandma's Potato Salad. For a
delightful dessert, serve slices of luscious California Lemon Pound Cake.

CELEBR-ATE-TION!
Clockwise from top right: **California Lemon Pound Cake**
(recipe on page 195), **Pineapple Pecan Cheese Ball** (recipe on
page 10), **Hot Italian Roast Beef Sandwiches** (recipe
on page 39) and **Grandma's Potato Salad**
(recipe on page 55).

CALIFORNIA LEMON POUND CAKE

Richard Killeaney, Spring Valley, California

(PICTURED AT LEFT)

- 1 cup butter *or* margarine, softened
- 1/2 cup shortening
- 3 cups sugar
- 5 eggs
- 3 cups all-purpose flour
- 1 teaspoon salt
- 1/2 teaspoon baking powder
- 1 cup milk
- 1 tablespoon lemon extract
- 1 tablespoon grated lemon peel

GLAZE:
- 1 to 1-1/4 cups confectioners' sugar
- 1/4 cup butter *or* margarine, softened
- 2 tablespoons lemon juice
- 1 teaspoon grated lemon peel

In a large mixing bowl, cream butter, shortening and sugar until light and fluffy. Add eggs, one at a time, beating well after each addition. Combine flour, salt and baking powder; gradually add to creamed mixture alternately with the milk. Mix well after each addition. Add lemon extract and peel. Mix on low until blended. Pour into a greased fluted tube pan. Bake at 350° for 70 minutes or until cake tests done. Turn out onto a rack to cool. For glaze, combine all ingredients and drizzle over cooled cake. **Yield:** 22 servings.

AMAZING CORN CAKE

Sallie Volz, Ypsilanti, Michigan

- 1 can (17 ounces) cream-style corn
- 1/2 cup packed brown sugar
- 3/4 cup sugar
- 3 eggs
- 1 cup vegetable oil
- 1 tablespoon baking powder
- 2-1/4 cups all-purpose flour
- 1 teaspoon baking soda
- 1 teaspoon salt
- 1 teaspoon ground cinnamon
- 1/2 cup raisins
- 1/2 cup chopped nuts

CARAMEL FROSTING:
- 4 tablespoons butter *or* margarine
- 1/2 cup packed brown sugar
- 1/4 cup milk
- 2 to 3 cups sifted confectioners' sugar

In a mixing bowl, combine corn and sugars. Add eggs and oil; beat until well blended. Combine dry ingredients; add

to batter and mix well. Stir in raisins and nuts. Pour into a greased 13-in. x 9-in. x 2-in. baking pan. Bake at 350° for 30-35 minutes or until cake tests done. Cool thoroughly. For frosting, bring butter and brown sugar to a boil over medium heat. Remove from the heat. Stir in milk. Stir in confectioners' sugar unti frosting is desired consistency. Frost cooled cake. **Yield:** 12-15 servings.

OLD-FASHIONED RHUBARB CAKE

Marilyn Homola, Hazel, South Dakota

- 1/2 cup butter *or* margarine, softened
- 1-1/4 cups sugar, *divided*
- 1 egg
- 1 cup buttermilk
- 1 teaspoon vanilla extract
- 2 cups all-purpose flour
- 1 teaspoon baking soda
- 1/2 teaspoon salt
- 2 cups chopped rhubarb
- 1/2 teaspoon ground cinnamon

MILK TOPPING:
- 1-1/2 cups milk
- 1/3 cup sugar
- 1 teaspoon vanilla extract

In a mixing bowl, cream butter and 1 cup sugar. Add egg; beat well. In a second bowl, combine buttermilk and vanilla; set aside. Combine flour, baking soda and salt; add alternately with buttermilk/vanilla to the creamed mixture. Stir in rhubarb. Spread into a greased 13-in. x 9-in. x 2-in. baking pan. Combine the remaining sugar with cinnamon; sprinkle over batter. Bake at 350° for 35 minutes or until cake tests done. For topping, combine all ingredients; pour over individual squares. **Yield:** 12 servings.

STICKY SITUATION? A cake plate sprinkled with powdered sugar will prevent the cake from sticking when you serve it later. It also adds a little extra sweetness.

PINEAPPLE SHEET CAKE

Kim Miller Spiek, Sarasota, Florida

CAKE:
- 2 cups all-purpose flour
- 2 cups sugar
- 2 eggs
- 1 cup chopped nuts
- 2 teaspoons baking soda
- 1 teaspoon vanilla extract
- 1/2 teaspoon salt

- 1 can (20 ounces) crushed pineapple in heavy syrup, undrained

CREAM CHEESE ICING:
- 1 package (8 ounces) cream cheese, softened
- 1 box (16 ounces) confectioners' sugar
- 1/2 cup butter *or* margarine, softened
- 1 teaspoon vanilla extract
- 1/2 cup chopped nuts

In a large mixing bowl, combine cake ingredients. Mix until smooth. Pour into a greased 15-in. x 10-in. x 1-in. baking pan. Bake at 350° for 35 minutes. Cool. Meanwhile, for icing, combine cream cheese, confectioners' sugar, butter and vanilla in a small mixing bowl. Beat until smooth. Spread over cake and sprinkle with nuts. **Yield:** about 24 servings. **Editor's Note:** Yes, there is no shortening in this cake.

STRAWBERRY CREAM CAKE ROLL

Laura Hagedorn, Fort Branch, Indiana

- 4 eggs
- 1 teaspoon vanilla extract
- 3/4 cup sugar
- 3/4 cup sifted cake flour
- 1 teaspoon baking powder
- 1/4 teaspoon salt
- Confectioners' sugar

CREAM FILLING:
- 1 cup whipping cream
- 1/4 cup sugar
- 1/2 teaspoon vanilla extract
- 2 cups fresh *or* frozen strawberries, cut up
- Confectioners' sugar
- Additional whole strawberries
- Whipped cream, optional

In a mixing bowl, beat eggs with vanilla on high speed with an electric mixer for 5 minutes or until lemon-colored. Gradually add sugar, beating until dissolved. Combine flour, baking powder and salt; fold gently into egg mixture just until combined. Pour into a greased and waxed paper-lined jelly roll pan. Spread batter evenly over pan. Bake at 375° for 10-12 minutes or until light brown. Turn out onto a cloth that has been sprinkled with confectioners' sugar. Peel off paper from cake; roll up cloth and cake. Cool. For filling, whip cream, sugar and vanilla. Unroll cake and spread filling over it; sprinkle with strawberries. Roll up the cake again and chill 2 hours before serving. Sprinkle with confectioners' sugar; garnish with strawberries and additional whipped cream if desired. **Yield:** 10 servings.

THE PLETHORA of palate-pleasing dishes on this page
proves that cheese is a family favorite in a variety of recipes.
Celebrate this dairy product with cheese-based main dishes...
rich cheesy desserts...refreshing salads...deliciously crusty breads...
even a satisfying cheese chowder.

CHEESE REALLY PLEASES.
Clockwise from lower left: **Black Bottom Cupcakes** (recipe on page 198),
Savory Cheddar Bread (recipe on page 154), **Fresh Fruit/Cheese Pie**
(recipe on page 207), **Lemon Streusel Cake** (recipe on page 198),
Cheese/Pepper Soup (recipe on page 31), **Mozzarella Pasta Salad**
(recipe on page 55), **Raspberry Cream Cheese Coffee Cake**
(recipe on page 150) and **Cheesy Fish Fillets**
with Spinach (recipe on page 72).

BLACK BOTTOM CUPCAKES

Julie Briceland, Windsor, Pennsylvania

(PICTURED ON PAGE 196)

FILLING:
- 1 package (8 ounces) cream cheese, softened
- 1/3 cup sugar
- 1 egg
- 1/8 teaspoon salt
- 1 cup (6 ounces) semisweet chocolate chips

CUPCAKES:
- 1-1/2 cups all-purpose flour
- 1 cup sugar
- 1/4 cup baking cocoa
- 1 teaspoon baking soda
- 1/2 teaspoon salt
- 1 egg
- 1 cup water
- 1/3 cup vegetable oil
- 1 tablespoon vinegar
- 1 teaspoon vanilla

TOPPING:
Sugar
Chopped almonds, optional

Combine cream cheese, sugar, egg and salt in a small mixing bowl; blend until smooth. Stir in chips; set aside. Sift together flour, sugar, cocoa, baking soda and salt. Add egg, water, oil, vinegar and vanilla; beat until well combined. Fill paper-lined muffin tins half full with chocolate batter. Drop a heaping teaspoon of cheese mixture in center of batter of each cupcake. Sprinkle with sugar and chopped almonds if desired. Bake at 350° for 25 minutes. Cool. Refrigerate any leftovers. **Yield:** 20-24 cupcakes.

LEMON STREUSEL CAKE

Karla Hecht, Brooklyn Park, Minnesota

(PICTURED ON PAGE 197)

- 1/2 cup butter *or* margarine
- 1 package lemon cake mix with pudding
- 3/4 cup milk
- 2 eggs

FILLING:
- 1/4 cup sugar
- 1 package (8 ounces) cream cheese, softened
- 1 tablespoon lemon juice
- 1 teaspoon grated lemon rind

TOPPING:
- 1/2 cup chopped walnuts

Cut butter into cake mix until crumbly; remove 1 cup mixture for topping. To remaining mixture, add milk and eggs; beat on high with mixer for 2 minutes. Pour into greased and floured 13-in. x 9-

in. x 2-in. pan; set aside. Cream together sugar, cream cheese, lemon juice and rind; blend well. Drop by teaspoonfuls onto the batter and spread across batter to edges of pan. Add nuts to reserved crumb mixture; sprinkle over batter. Bake at 350° for 30-35 minutes or until cake is light golden brown. Store in refrigerator. **Yield:** 12 servings.

PLUM UPSIDE-DOWN CAKE

Robert Fallon, Sayville, New York

- 7 tablespoons butter *or* margarine, *divided*
- 3/4 cup sugar, *divided*
- 3 to 4 plums, pitted and thinly sliced
- 1 egg
- 1 cup all-purpose flour
- 1/4 teaspoon salt
- 1 teaspoon baking powder
- 1/3 cup milk
- 1 teaspoon vanilla extract

Place 1 tablespoon butter in a 9-in. round baking pan. Put pan in a preheated 350° oven to melt. Remove from oven and sprinkle with 1/3 cup sugar. Arrange plum slices in a circular pattern over sugar. Bake for 10 minutes. Meanwhile, cream the remaining butter with remaining sugar; beat in the egg. Combine flour, salt and baking powder. Add to the creamed mixture alternately with milk and vanilla, beating until smooth. Spread evenly over plums. Bake for 30 minutes or until cake tests done. Remove from the oven and immediately invert onto a large serving platter. Serve warm. **Yield:** 6-8 servings.

Quick & Easy

CHOCOLATE CHERRY CAKE

Lois Valley, Morgan Hill, California

CAKE:
- 1 package (18-1/4 ounces) fudge cake mix
- 1 can (21 ounces) cherry pie filling
- 2 eggs, beaten
- 1 teaspoon almond extract

FROSTING:
- 1 cup sugar
- 1/3 cup milk
- 5 tablespoons butter *or* margarine
- 1 cup semisweet chocolate chips

In a mixing bowl, stir together all cake ingredients. Pour into a greased 13-in. x 9-in. x 2-in. baking pan. Bake at 350° for 30 minutes or until cake tests done. Meanwhile, in a saucepan, mix sugar, milk and butter. Bring to a boil and boil

for 1-1/2 minutes. Remove from the heat and stir in chocolate chips until melted. Pour over hot cake. Frosting will harden as it cools. **Yield:** 15-20 servings.

BUTTERMILK POUND CAKE

Gracie Hanchey, De Ridder, Louisiana

- 1 cup butter (no substitutes), softened
- 3 cups sugar
- 4 eggs
- 3 cups all-purpose flour
- 1/4 teaspoon baking soda
- 1 cup buttermilk
- 1 teaspoon vanilla extract
Confectioners' sugar, optional

In a mixing bowl, cream butter and sugar. Add eggs, one at a time, beating well after each addition. Combine flour and baking soda; add alternately with the buttermilk and beat well. Stir in vanilla. Pour into a greased and floured 10-in. fluted tube pan. Bake at 325° for 1 hour and 10 minutes or until cake tests done. Cool in pan for 15 minutes before removing to a wire rack to cool completely. If desired, dust with confectioners' sugar. **Yield:** 16-20 servings.

MINIATURE CHRISTMAS FRUITCAKES

Libby Over, Phillipsburg, Ohio

(PICTURED ON PAGE 177)

- 1/2 cup light molasses
- 1/4 cup water
- 1 teaspoon vanilla extract
- 1 box (15 ounces) raisins
- 1 pound candied fruit, chopped
- 1/2 cup butter *or* margarine, softened
- 2/3 cup sugar
- 3 eggs
- 1 cup plus 2 tablespoons all-purpose flour
- 1 teaspoon ground cinnamon
- 1 teaspoon ground nutmeg
- 1/4 teaspoon baking soda
- 1/4 teaspoon ground allspice
- 1/4 teaspoon ground cloves
- 1/4 cup milk
- 1 cup chopped nuts

In a saucepan, combine molasses, water and vanilla; add raisins and bring to a boil. Reduce heat and simmer for 5 minutes. Remove from heat and stir in fruit; cool. Meanwhile, in a mixing bowl, cream butter and sugar. Add the eggs, one at a time, beating well after each addition. Stir together dry ingredients; add to creamed mixture alternately with milk. Stir in fruit mixture; mix well. Fold in nuts. Spoon into paper-lined miniature muffin tins, filling almost to the top. Bake at 325° for 22-24 minutes or until cakes test done. Cool on wire racks. Store in airtight containers. **Yield:** about 6 dozen.

CRANBERRY UPSIDE-DOWN CAKE

Doris Heath, Bryson City, North Carolina

(PICTURED ON PAGE 144)

1/2 cup butter *or* margarine
2 cups sugar, *divided*
1 can (16 ounces) whole-berry cranberry sauce
1/2 cup coarsely chopped pecans
3 eggs, *separated*
1/3 cup orange juice
1 cup all-purpose flour
1 teaspoon baking powder
1/4 teaspoon salt

Melt butter in a 10-in. iron skillet. Add 1 cup sugar; cook and stir 3 minutes over medium heat. Remove from heat. Spoon cranberry sauce over butter mixture; sprinkle pecans over all. Set aside. In a mixing bowl, beat egg yolks until foamy. Gradually add remaining sugar; beat well. Blend in orange juice. Combine flour, baking powder and salt; add to egg mixture. Beat egg whites until stiff; fold into batter. Carefully spoon over topping in skillet. Bake at 375° about 30 minutes or until cake tests done. Cool 5 minutes in skillet; invert onto large serving plate. Serve warm. **Yield:** 10 servings.

APPLESAUCE CAKE

Kathie Grenier, Auburn, Maine

1 cup sugar
1/2 cup shortening
1-1/2 cups applesauce
2 tablespoons molasses
2 cups all-purpose flour
1 teaspoon baking soda
1 teaspoon ground cinnamon
1 teaspoon ground cloves
1/2 teaspoon salt
1 cup raisins

In a mixing bowl, cream the sugar and shortening. Beat in applesauce and molasses; set aside. Sift together flour, baking soda, cinnamon, cloves and salt; gradually add to batter, mixing well to moisten. Stir in raisins. Pour into a greased and floured fluted tube pan. Bake at 350° for 45 minutes or until

cake tests done. Cake will not rise to top of pan. After 10 minutes, remove cake from pan and cool on a wire rack. **Yield:** 8-10 servings.

OATMEAL CHOCOLATE CHIP CAKE

Luanne Thomson, Mannheim, Germany

1-3/4 cups boiling water
1 cup uncooked oatmeal
1 cup packed brown sugar
1 cup sugar
1/2 cup butter *or* margarine, softened
3 eggs
1-3/4 cups all-purpose flour
1 teaspoon baking soda
1 teaspoon baking cocoa
1/4 teaspoon salt
1 package (12 ounces) chocolate chips, *divided*
3/4 cup chopped walnuts

In a mixing bowl, pour water over oatmeal. Allow to stand 10 minutes. Add sugars and butter, stirring until the butter melts. Add eggs, one at a time, mixing well after each addition. Sift together flour, baking soda, cocoa and salt. Add to batter; mix well. Stir in half the chocolate chips. Pour into a greased 13-in. x 9-in. x 2-in. baking pan. Sprinkle top of cake with walnuts and remaining chips. Bake at 350° for about 40 minutes. **Yield:** 12 servings.

CENTER OF ATTENTION. To obtain nice, even layers when making a layer cake, spread the batter higher around the outside of the pan. (The center usually rises more.)

FRESH GRAPEFRUIT CAKE

Debbie Register, Youngstown, Florida

(PICTURED ON PAGE 102)

2/3 cup butter *or* margarine, softened
1-3/4 cups sugar
2 eggs
3 cups cake flour
2-1/2 teaspoons baking powder
1/2 teaspoon salt
1/2 cup fresh grapefruit juice
3/4 cup milk
1-1/2 teaspoons vanilla extract
1 teaspoon grated grapefruit peel
FROSTING:
2 egg whites
1-1/2 cups sugar
1/3 cup fresh grapefruit juice
1 tablespoon light corn syrup
1/8 teaspoon salt

2 teaspoons vanilla extract
1 tablespoon grated grapefruit peel

In a large mixing bowl, cream butter. Gradually add sugar; beat well. Add eggs, one at a time, beating well after each addition. Sift together flour, baking powder and salt; add to creamed mixture alternately with grapefruit juice, beginning and ending with flour mixture. Gradually add milk. Stir in vanilla and peel; mix well. Pour batter into 2 greased and floured 9-in. round cake pans. Bake at 350° for about 30 minutes or until a toothpick inserted in the center comes out clean. Cool in pans 10 minutes; remove to a wire rack to cool completely. For frosting, combine first five ingredients in the top of a double boiler. Beat at low speed with a portable electric mixer for 30 seconds. Place over boiling water; beat constantly at high speed 7 minutes or until stiff peaks form. Remove from the heat; add vanilla and grapefruit peel; beat 1-2 minutes or until frosting is thick enough to spread. Spread between layers and frost entire cake. **Yield:** 12-16 servings.

ROARING TWENTIES SPICE CAKE

Loretta Saltsganer, Denver, Colorado

1-1/2 cups water
1 cup sugar
1 cup raisins
1/2 cup shortening
1 teaspoon ground cinnamon
1 teaspoon ground nutmeg
1/2 teaspoon ground cloves
Pinch salt
1 teaspoon baking soda
1 tablespoon water
2 cups all-purpose flour
1 teaspoon baking powder
NUTMEG SAUCE:
1 cup water
1/2 cup sugar
2 tablespoons cornstarch
1 tablespoon butter *or* margarine
1 tablespoon lemon juice
1/4 teaspoon nutmeg

Combine first eight ingredients in a saucepan and bring to a boil. Boil 5 minutes; remove from heat. Dissolve baking soda in 1 tablespoon of water. Stir into raisin mixture along with flour and baking powder; mix well. Spread into a greased 8-in. x 8-in. baking pan. Bake at 350° for about 30 minutes or until a toothpick inserted in center of cake comes out clean. Meanwhile, combine sauce ingredients in a saucepan and cook over medium-low heat until thickened. Serve cake warm or room temperature with warm sauce. **Yield:** 9 servings.

FAMILY FAVORITES, like delicious Pork Stuffed with Corn Bread Dressing and aromatic Apricot-Glazed Sweet Potatoes, are sure-fire recipes for holiday meals. Cranberry Waldorf Salad will become your trademark salad. And the holidays wouldn't be the same without Christmas Special Fruitcake for dessert!

TRUE-BLUE MENU.
Clockwise from lower right: **Pork Stuffed with Corn Bread Dressing** (recipe on page 76), **Apricot-Glazed Sweet Potatoes** (recipe on page 127), **Christmas Special Fruitcake** (recipe on page 201) and **Cranberry Waldorf Salad** (recipe on page 58).

CHRISTMAS SPECIAL FRUITCAKE

Violet Cooper, Port Allegany, Pennsylvania
(PICTURED AT LEFT)

3 cups coarsely chopped Brazil nuts *or* other nuts (walnuts, pecans or hazelnuts)
1 pound pitted dates, coarsely chopped
1 cup halved maraschino cherries
3/4 cup all-purpose flour
3/4 cup sugar
1/2 teaspoon baking powder
1/2 teaspoon salt
3 eggs
1 teaspoon vanilla extract

In a mixing bowl, combine nuts, dates and cherries. In another bowl, stir together flour, sugar, baking powder and salt; add to nut mixture, stirring until nuts and fruit are well-coated. Beat eggs until foamy. Stir in vanilla; fold into nut mixture. Mix well. Pour into a greased and waxed paper-lined 9-in. x 5-in. x 3-in. loaf pan. Bake at 300° for 1 hour and 45 minutes. Cool 10 minutes in pan before removing to a wire rack. **Yield:** 24 servings.

CHOCOLATE MOCHA TORTE

Abby Slavings, Buchanan, Michigan

CAKE:
1/2 cup baking cocoa
1/2 cup boiling water
2-1/2 cups all-purpose flour
1-1/2 teaspoons baking soda
1/2 teaspoon salt
1-3/4 cups sugar
2/3 cup butter *or* margarine, softened
2 eggs
1 teaspoon vanilla extract
1 cup buttermilk
FILLING:
5 tablespoons all-purpose flour
1 cup milk
1 cup sugar
1 cup butter *or* margarine, softened
1/2 teaspoon instant coffee granules
2 teaspoons water
1 teaspoon vanilla extract
2 teaspoons baking cocoa
1 cup chopped pecans
FROSTING:
1/2 cup shortening
1/4 cup butter *or* margarine, softened
2-1/2 tablespoons evaporated milk

1 tablespoon boiling water
1-1/2 teaspoons vanilla extract
Dash salt
1 pound sifted confectioners' sugar, *divided*
Pecan halves, optional

For cake, make a paste of cocoa and water. Cool and set aside. Sift together flour, baking soda and salt; set aside. In a large mixing bowl, cream the sugar and butter. Add eggs and vanilla. Blend in cocoa mixture. Add flour mixture alternately with the buttermilk. Blend until smooth. Pour into two greased and floured 9-in. cake pans. Bake at 350° for 35 minutes or until cake tests done. Remove from pans and cool on a wire rack. For filling, cook flour and milk in a saucepan over low heat, stirring constantly, until thick. Cool. Meanwhile, cream sugar and butter until light. Dissolve coffee in water; add with vanilla, cocoa and milk mixture to creamed mixture. Beat until fluffy, about 5 minutes. Fold in nuts. Split each cake layer in half. Divide filling into thirds and spread between layers. For frosting, cream shortening and butter. Add milk, water, vanilla, salt and half the sugar. Beat well. Add remaining sugar and beat until smooth and fluffy. Spread over top and sides of cake. Garnish with pecan halves if desired. **Yield:** about 16 servings.

CHOCOLATE ZUCCHINI SHEET CAKE

Charlene Gledhill, Richfield, Utah

2 cups sugar
1 cup vegetable oil
3 eggs
2-1/2 cups all-purpose flour
1/4 cup baking cocoa
1 teaspoon baking soda
1/4 teaspoon baking powder
1/4 teaspoon salt
1/2 cup milk
2 cups shredded fresh zucchini
1 tablespoon vanilla extract
FROSTING:
1/2 cup butter *or* margarine
1/4 cup baking cocoa
6 tablespoons evaporated milk
1 pound (4 cups) confectioners' sugar
1 tablespoon vanilla extract

In a large mixing bowl, combine sugar and oil. Add eggs, one at a time, beating well after each addition. Combine flour, cocoa, baking soda, baking powder and salt; gradually add to the egg mixture alternately with the milk. Stir in the zucchini and extract. Pour into a greased 15-in. x 10-in. x 1-in. baking pan. Bake at 375° for 25 minutes or until cake tests done. While cake is baking, combine all

frosting ingredients. Mix until smooth. Spread frosting over cake while hot. Cool on wire rack. **Yield:** 20 servings.

COUNTRY POPPY SEED CAKE

Laurie Mace, Los Osos, California

1/4 cup poppy seeds
1 package (5-1/4 ounces) instant vanilla pudding mix
1 package (18-1/4 ounces) white cake mix (without pudding)
1/2 cup cooking oil
4 eggs
1 cup water
1 teaspoon almond extract
2 tablespoons sugar
1/2 teaspoon ground cinnamon
GLAZE:
1/2 cup confectioners' sugar
1/4 teaspoon vanilla extract
1 to 2 teaspoons milk

In a large mixing bowl, combine poppy seeds, pudding and cake mix. Add oil, eggs, water and almond extract. Blend with an electric mixer on low speed until dry ingredients are moistened. Increase speed to medium and mix for 2 minutes. Combine sugar and cinnamon; sprinkle into a greased fluted tube pan. Pour batter into pan and bake at 325° for about 1 hour or until cake tests done. Allow cake to cool 10 minutes before removing to a cooling rack. Combine glaze ingredients and drizzle over cooled cake. **Yield:** 12-16 servings.

WHOLE WHEAT GINGERBREAD

Patricia Habiger, Spearville, Kansas

1 cup molasses
3/4 cup honey
3/4 cup vegetable oil
3 eggs
3 cups whole wheat flour
1 tablespoon baking powder
1 teaspoon salt
1-1/2 teaspoons ground cinnamon
1-1/2 teaspoons ground cloves
1 teaspoon ground ginger
2 cups milk
Whipped cream

In a large mixing bowl, beat molasses, honey, oil and eggs until well mixed. Combine dry ingredients and add alternately with the milk to the egg mixture. Pour batter into a greased 13-in. x 9-in. x 2-in. baking pan. Bake at 350° for 45-50 minutes or until a toothpick inserted in the center comes out clean. Serve warm or at room temperature with chilled whipped cream. **Yield:** 12-15 servings.

PIES and desserts are the perfect ending to your country meals—
especially when they're made with sweet and tangy rhubarb!
Get ready…your gang will gobble up tasty Rhubarb Crumble and
Rhubarb Cherry Pie. And you may as well start copying the recipes for
Rhubarb Dumplings and Strawberry Rhubarb Coffee Cake…
you're bound to be asked for them!

PIEPLANT PLEASURES.
Clockwise from the top: **Strawberry Rhubarb Coffee Cake**
(recipe on page 165), **Rhubarb Dumplings**,
Rhubarb Crumble and **Rhubarb Cherry Pie**
(all three recipes on page 203).

PIES & DESSERTS

For a tasty finale to your down-home dinners, serve up palate-pleasing pies, puddings, candies...and more!

RHUBARB CRUMBLE

Linda Enslen, Schuler, Alberta

(PICTURED AT LEFT)

3 cups sliced fresh *or* frozen
  rhubarb (1/2-inch pieces)
1 cup cubed peeled apples
1/2 to 1 cup sliced strawberries
1/3 cup sugar
1/2 teaspoon ground cinnamon
1/2 cup all-purpose flour
1 teaspoon baking powder
1/4 teaspoon salt
4 tablespoons butter *or* margarine
2/3 cup packed brown sugar
2/3 cup quick-cooking oats
Vanilla ice cream, optional

Combine rhubarb, apples and strawberries; spoon into a greased 8-in. square baking dish. Combine sugar and cinnamon; sprinkle over rhubarb mixture. Set aside. In a bowl, combine flour, baking powder and salt. Cut in butter until mixture resembles coarse crumbs. Stir in brown sugar and oats. Sprinkle over rhubarb mixture. Bake at 350° for 40-50 minutes or until lightly browned. Serve warm or cold with a scoop of ice cream if desired. **Yield:** 6-8 servings.

RHUBARB DUMPLINGS

Elsie Shell, Topeka, Indiana

(PICTURED AT LEFT)

SAUCE:
1-1/2 cups sugar
1 tablespoon all-purpose flour
1/2 teaspoon ground cinnamon
1/4 teaspoon salt
1-1/2 cups water
1/3 cup butter *or* margarine
1 teaspoon vanilla extract
Red food coloring, optional
DOUGH:
2 cups all-purpose flour
2 tablespoons sugar
2 teaspoons baking powder
1/4 teaspoon salt
2-1/2 tablespoons cold butter *or* margarine
3/4 cup milk

FILLING:
2 tablespoons butter *or* margarine, softened
2 cups finely chopped fresh *or* frozen rhubarb
1/2 cup sugar
1/2 teaspoon ground cinnamon

In a saucepan, combine sugar, flour, cinnamon and salt. Stir in water; add butter. Bring to a boil; cook and stir 1 minute. Remove from heat. Add vanilla and, if desired, enough food coloring to tint sauce a deep pink; set aside. For dough, in a medium bowl, combine flour, sugar, baking powder and salt. Cut in butter until mixture resembles coarse crumbs. Add milk and mix quickly. Do not overmix. Gather dough into a ball and roll out on a floured surface into a 12-in. x 9-in. rectangle. Spread with softened butter; arrange rhubarb on top. Combine sugar and cinnamon; sprinkle over rhubarb. Roll up from the long side and place on a cutting board, seam side down. Cut roll into 12 slices. Arrange slices, cut side up, in a greased 13-in. x 9-in. x 2-in. baking dish. Pour sauce over. Bake at 350° for 35-40 minutes or until golden brown. **Yield:** 12 servings.

RHUBARB CHERRY PIE

Eunice Hurt, Murfreesboro, Tennessee

(PICTURED AT LEFT)

3 cups sliced fresh *or* frozen rhubarb (1/2-inch pieces)
1 can (16 ounces) pitted tart red cherries, drained
1-1/4 cups sugar
1/4 cup quick-cooking tapioca
4 to 5 drops red food coloring, optional
Pastry for double-crust pie (9 inches)

In a mixing bowl, combine first five ingredients; let stand for 15 minutes. Line a 9-in. pie plate with pastry; add filling. Top with a lattice crust; flute the edges. Bake at 400° for 40-50 minutes or until the crust is golden and filling is bubbling. **Yield:** 8 servings.

> **EASY AS PIE.** If it's difficult to put your pie crust into your pan, simply roll dough back onto your rolling pin. Then just put it over the pan, unroll it and shape into pan.

BLUEBERRY AND PEACH COBBLER

Laura Jansen, Battle Creek, Michigan

1/2 cup water
2 tablespoons sugar
2 tablespoons brown sugar
1 tablespoon cornstarch
1 tablespoon lemon juice
2 cups peeled sliced fresh peaches
1 cup blueberries
TOPPING:
1 cup all-purpose flour
1/4 cup sugar
1-1/2 teaspoons baking powder
1/2 teaspoon salt
1/2 cup milk
1/4 cup butter *or* margarine, softened

In a saucepan, combine first five ingredients. Bring to a boil, stirring until thick. Add fruit and pour into a 2-qt. baking dish. For topping, combine flour, sugar, baking powder and salt in a mixing bowl. Stir in milk and butter. Spread over fruit mixture and bake at 375° for 50 minutes or until topping is golden brown and tests done. Serve warm. **Yield:** about 6 servings.

BLUSHING APPLE CREAM PIE

Marny Eulberg, Wheat Ridge, Colorado

1 cup sugar
3/4 cup heavy cream
1/4 cup all-purpose flour
2 tablespoons red cinnamon candies
2 tablespoons vinegar
1/2 teaspoon ground cinnamon
4-1/2 cups thinly sliced peeled baking apples
Pastry for double-crust pie (9 inches)

In a mixing bowl, combine first six ingredients; mix well. Add apples and stir gently to mix. Pour into a pastry-lined pie plate. Roll out remaining pastry to fit top of pie. Cut slits in top crust; place over apples. Seal and flute edges. Bake at 400° for 50 minutes or until pastry is golden and apples are tender. **Yield:** 8 servings.

CHOCOLATE DESSERT WAFFLES

Carol Ann Reed, Salisbury, Missouri

(PICTURED AT RIGHT)

1/4 cup baking cocoa
1-1/2 cups cake flour
2 teaspoons baking powder
1/4 teaspoon salt
1/2 cup shortening
1 cup sugar
2 eggs, *separated*
1/2 cup milk
1/2 teaspoon vanilla extract
Vanilla ice cream
Chocolate sauce
Fresh raspberries

Combine cocoa, flour, baking powder and salt; set aside. In a mixing bowl, cream shortening and sugar until fluffy. Add egg yolks. Mix well. Add dry ingredients alternately with the milk. Mix until dry ingredients are moistened. Stir in vanilla. Beat egg whites until stiff and gently fold into the batter. Preheat waffle maker and bake waffles according to manufacturer's directions. Serve waffles warm or room temperature with ice cream, warmed chocolate sauce and fresh raspberries. **Yield:** 6-8 servings.

CHERRY CRISP

Carole Schlender, Burrton, Kansas

(PICTURED ON PAGE 159)

PASTRY:
1/4 teaspoon salt
1/2 cup packed brown sugar
1 cup all-purpose flour
1/2 cup butter *or* margarine
FILLING:
1 cup sugar
1/4 cup cornstarch
1 cup cherry juice
4 cups pitted tart red cherries
Few drops red food coloring, optional
TOPPING:
1-1/2 cups quick-cooking rolled oats
1/2 cup packed brown sugar
1/4 cup all-purpose flour
5 tablespoons butter *or* margarine, melted

To make pastry, combine salt, brown sugar and flour in a mixing bowl. Cut in butter. Press into a 2-qt. or 11-in. x 7-in. baking dish. Bake at 350° for 15 minutes. For filling, combine sugar and cornstarch in a saucepan. Stir in juice. Cook over medium heat until thick, stirring constantly. Fold in cherries and food coloring, if desired. Pour over baked crust. Combine all topping ingredients; sprinkle over filling. Bake for 20-25 min-

utes or until golden brown and bubbly around edges. **Yield:** 6-8 servings.

OZARK MOUNTAIN BERRY PIE

Elaine Moody, Clever, Missouri

(PICTURED ON PAGE 156)

1 cup sugar
Dash salt
1/4 cup cornstarch
1/2 teaspoon ground cinnamon, optional
1 cup blueberries
1 cup strawberries
3/4 cup blackberries
3/4 cup red raspberries
1/2 cup water
2 tablespoons lemon juice
2 tablespoons butter *or* margarine
Pastry for a double-crust pie (9 inches)

In a saucepan, combine sugar, salt, cornstarch, and cinnamon if desired. Stir in berries. Add water and lemon juice. Cook over medium heat just to the boiling point. Pour into pie shell; dot with butter. Top with a lattice or full crust. If using a full crust, cut slits in the top, brush with milk and sprinkle with sugar. Bake at 350° for about 45 minutes or until the crust is golden. **Yield:** 8 servings.

CHERRY CHEESECAKE TARTS

Mary Lindell, Sanford, Michigan

(PICTURED ON PAGE 159)

1 package (10 ounces) frozen puff pastry shells
2 packages (3 ounces *each*) cream cheese, softened
1/4 cup confectioners' sugar
1/2 teaspoon almond extract
1 can (21 ounces) cherry pie filling
Additional confectioners' sugar

Bake pastry shells according to package directions. Meanwhile, in a mixing bowl, beat cream cheese, sugar and extract. With a fork, carefully remove

the circular top of each baked shell and set aside. Remove any soft layers of pastry inside shells and discard. Divide the cheese filling among the shells; place on a baking sheet. Return to the oven and bake 5 minutes. Cool. Just before serving, fill each shell with pie filling. Top with reserved pastry circles. Dust with additional confectioners' sugar. **Yield:** 6 servings.

CHERRY/RHUBARB COBBLER

Mary Ann Earnest, Effingham, Illinois

(PICTURED ON PAGE 159)

FILLING:
1 can (21 ounces) cherry pie filling
3 cups chopped rhubarb
1 cup sugar
4 tablespoons butter *or* margarine
CRUST:
1/2 cup shortening
1 cup sugar
1 egg
1 cup all-purpose flour
1 teaspoon baking powder
1/2 cup milk

Spread fruit in a 13-in. x 9-in. x 2-in. baking pan. Sprinkle with sugar and dot with butter. For crust, cream shortening and sugar in a mixing bowl. Add egg and beat well. Set aside. Combine flour and baking powder; add alternately with milk to creamed mixture. Pour over fruit; bake at 350° for 50-60 minutes. **Yield:** about 12 servings.

FROZEN CHOCOLATE PIE

Bonnie Scott, McLouth, Kansas

1 package (3 ounces) cream cheese, softened
1/2 cup sugar
1 teaspoon vanilla extract
1/3 cup baking cocoa
1/3 cup milk
1 carton (8 ounces) frozen whipped topping, thawed
1 pastry shell (9 inches), baked
Chocolate curls *or* chips, optional

In a mixing bowl, beat cream cheese, sugar and vanilla until smooth. Add cocoa alternately with milk; mix well. Fold in whipped topping. Pour into pie shell. Freeze for 8 hours or overnight. If desired, garnish with chocolate curls or chips. Serve directly from the freezer (pie does not need to be thawed to cut). **Yield:** 6-8 servings.

FEAST your eyes on this irresistible dessert...
crunchy chocolate waffles crowned by a
scoop of ice cream, fresh raspberries and
warmed chocolate sauce. One taste and you'll agree—
waffles aren't just for breakfast anymore!

LOVE AT FIRST BITE.
Chocolate Dessert Waffles
(recipe on page 204).

IN RURAL Kentucky, where I grew up during the '20s, most families lived on isolated farms. One of the most exciting social events for everyone was the annual pie supper, a fund-raiser held to make money for the school.

Single girls would fill a decorated box with a picnic lunch or pie. The boxes would be auctioned to the men and boys, then the winning bidders shared the goodies with the girl who'd brought them.

I attended my first pie supper in 1928, and I was filled with dread. My best friend, Wilma, and I were taking pies, and we both had a crush on Walter Lewis from our third-grade class. Whose pie would he choose?

Work of Art

Only hours before the event, I ran home from school to try to get out of it. I found Mama in the kitchen. "Come see your pie," she said. Topped with a fluffy white meringue and drizzled with melted brown sugar, Mother's famous butterscotch creation sat on the table like a work of art.

I asked Mama to take the pie to the supper, but she shook her head. "Only single girls take pies. And you worked so hard to decorate your box."

"But Mama, what if nobody bids on my pie? Or what if it's somebody I don't want to eat with?"

"Maybe your daddy will buy it," she laughed.

My fear grew as we left the house. Trudging up to the school auditorium, I half-wished I'd trip on a step and drop that pie.

Wait Almost Over

I scanned the room and saw Wilma, looking as gloomy as I did. Then, taking my seat by Mama, I caught Walter's eye... and he winked at me! At that moment, I knew he'd bid on my pie, and my fears were lifted.

Every box the auctioneer picked

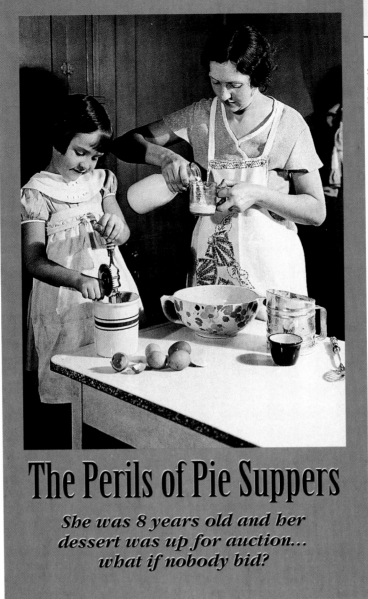

The Perils of Pie Suppers

She was 8 years old and her dessert was up for auction... what if nobody bid?

By Betty Vaught, Somerset, Kentucky

up brought him closer to mine. Most went for a quarter, but my older brother had to pay $5 for his sweetheart's pie—his high school buddies bid up the price on him.

Finally the auctioneer picked up my red-ruffled box. "What am I offered for this luscious pie?" he barked. Silence followed. There was no bid.

Moment of Panic

My heart was in my throat until our neighbor, Mr. McLaughlin, spoke up: "25¢."

Seeing the look on my face, Walter realized it was my pie and turned red with embarrassment. "I bid 50¢," he croaked.

Daddy looked at me and was about to bid, but I shook my head "no". I knew Walter didn't have much money to bid.

Then Mr. McLaughlin topped Walter's bid ...and Walter's father jumped in, taking up the challenge for his son.

Heads turned from one side of the room to the other as the two men bid back and forth. The price mounted by dimes, quarters and half-dollars.

"Sold!"

Finally, Mr. Lewis made a bid of $20 that went unchallenged. Everyone clapped as Walter and I took our $20 dessert to the back of the room.

I was feeling pretty proud...until I learned that the high bid wasn't because of my beauty or charm. As Walter's dad took a big bite of our pie, I heard him tell Dad, "Nope, that McLaughlin and I don't get along at all. Why, I'd pay $50 before I'd let him outbid me!"

After all these years, I don't recall who bid on Wilma's pie. But it was at least a week before she spoke to me.

As for Walter and me, at 8 years old, we were too young to date. But we started sitting together at church and school events. Eventually, in high school, we did date...but none of those dates were as memorable as that first pie supper.

MERINGUE MEMORIES. Reader's school made some dough when one of her mother's wonderful pies like the one at left was sold at her first pie supper.

OLD-FASHIONED RICE CUSTARD

Shirley Leister, West Chester, Pennsylvania

(PICTURED ON PAGE 191)

1/2 cup uncooked long grain rice
4 cups milk, *divided*
1/4 cup butter *or* margarine
3 eggs
3/4 cup sugar
1 teaspoon vanilla extract
1/4 teaspoon salt
1/2 teaspoon ground nutmeg

In the top of a double boiler, combine rice and 2 cups milk. Cook, stirring occasionally, over boiling water until rice is tender and most of the milk has evaporated, about 45 minutes. Stir in butter. Beat eggs; blend in sugar, vanilla, salt and remaining milk. Stir into the hot rice mixture. Pour into a lightly greased 2-qt. casserole and top with nutmeg. Bake at 350° for 50 minutes or until firm. **Yield:** 6-8 servings.

PEANUT BUTTER FUDGE

Frances Castor, Lapel, Indiana

1 cup packed brown sugar
1 cup sugar
1/2 cup milk
5 large marshmallows
1 jar (12 ounces) creamy peanut butter

In a heavy 2-qt. saucepan, combine the sugars, milk and marshmallows. Bring to a boil over medium heat, stirring until the sugar dissolves and marshmallows melt. Remove from the heat; stir in peanut butter. Pour into a buttered 8-in. square baking pan. Cool. When firm, cut into squares. **Yield:** 3 dozen pieces.

FRESH FRUIT/CHEESE PIE

Jody Steinke, Nekoosa, Wisconsin

(PICTURED ON PAGE 196)

CRUST:
1 cup walnuts, chopped
3/4 cup all-purpose flour
1/2 cup butter *or* margarine, softened
1/2 cup packed light brown sugar
1/2 teaspoon vanilla extract
FILLING:
4 cups fresh fruit (peaches, nectarines, strawberries, raspberries, banana, kiwifruit, blueberries or pineapple)
1 cup plain yogurt

1 cup small-curd cottage cheese
1/2 cup (8 ounces) unsweetened crushed pineapple, drained
1/4 cup unsweetened shredded coconut

In a medium bowl, blend nuts, flour, butter, brown sugar and vanilla with a fork. Press evenly into a buttered 9-in. pie plate. Bake at 350° for 10-15 minutes or until lightly browned. Cool on wire rack. Cut fruit(s) of choice into bite-size pieces; layer on crust. In blender, mix yogurt and cottage cheese until smooth; add pineapple and blend to desired consistency. Pour mixture over fruit. Sprinkle with coconut. Chill several hours before serving. Decorate with any combination of fruit slices. **Yield:** 12 servings.

STEAMED HOLIDAY PUDDING

Bernadean Bichel, Woodbine, Georgia

(PICTURED ON PAGE 191)

PUDDING:
1/2 cup light molasses
1/2 cup hot water
2 teaspoons baking soda
1-1/2 cups all-purpose flour
2 cups fresh *or* frozen cranberries
1/2 teaspoon salt
SAUCE:
1 cup sugar
1 teaspoon cornstarch
Dash salt
1 cup heavy cream
1/2 cup butter *or* margarine
1 teaspoon vanilla extract

In a mixing bowl, combine all pudding ingredients in order given. Pour into a well-greased 4-cup pudding mold. Place in a deep kettle on a rack. Fill kettle with boiling water to 1-in. depth; cover kettle and boil gently. Replace water as needed. Steam about 1 hour or until pudding tests done. Let stand 5 minutes before removing from mold. Meanwhile, prepare sauce by combining sugar, cornstarch and salt in a saucepan. Add cream and butter. Cook and stir over medium heat until mixture begins to boil. Boil for about 1 minute. Remove from the heat and stir in vanilla. Serve pudding and sauce warm. **Yield:** 6-8 servings.

SAUCY MOCHA PUDDING

Kathy Koch, Smoky Lake, Alberta

(PICTURED ON PAGE 190)

SAUCE:
1/4 cup baking cocoa
1/2 cup sugar
1/2 cup packed brown sugar
1-1/2 cups hot strong coffee
CAKE:
1/3 cup butter *or* margarine
2/3 cup sugar
1 egg
1/2 teaspoon vanilla extract
1 cup all-purpose flour
1-1/2 teaspoons baking powder
1/4 teaspoon salt
1/3 cup milk
Ice cream *or* whipped cream, optional

In a saucepan, combine all sauce ingredients and keep warm. Meanwhile, in a large mixing bowl, beat butter, sugar, egg and vanilla until light and fluffy. Combine flour, baking powder and salt; add alternately with milk to the egg mixture. Spread into a greased 8-in. square baking pan. Pour sauce over the batter. Do not stir. Bake at 350° for 45-50 minutes or until the cake tests done. When finished, the cake will float in the hot mocha sauce. Serve warm with ice cream or whipped cream if desired. **Yield:** about 9 servings.

EASY STRAWBERRY SHORTCAKE

Janet Becker, Anacortes, Washington

(PICTURED ON PAGE 191)

2/3 cup sugar
1/4 cup shortening
1 egg
1 teaspoon vanilla extract
1-1/2 cups all-purpose flour
2 teaspoons baking powder
1/4 teaspoon salt
1/2 cup milk
Whipped cream
1-1/2 quarts fresh *or* frozen strawberries, sliced

In a mixing bowl, cream sugar and shortening. Add egg and vanilla; beat well. Combine flour, baking powder and salt and add alternately with milk to the creamed mixture. Spread in a greased 9-in. square baking pan. Bake at 350° for 20-25 minutes. Cool on wire rack. Cut into 9 servings. Split each serving horizontally and fill with whipped cream and strawberries. Replace top of cake; garnish with more berries and a dollop of whipped cream. Serve immediately. **Yield:** 9 servings.

FOR THOSE with a sweet tooth, dessert is the focal point of a meal! So when you aim to please the dessert lovers in your family, make sure you have plenty of tasty Almond Rhubarb Pastry on hand. They'll delight in Cream Cheese Rhubarb Pie and love the taste of light, refreshing Berry Rhubarb Fool.

EVERYTHING'S COMING UP ROSY.
Clockwise from lower left: **Spiced Rhubarb** (recipe on page 147), **Cream Cheese Rhubarb Pie** (recipe on page 210), **Rhubarb Pecan Muffins** (recipe on page 169), **Berry Rhubarb Fool** (recipe on page 210), **Rhubarb Chutney** (recipe on page 146), **Rosy Rhubarb Salad** (recipe on page 49), **Rhubarb Pork Chop Casserole** (recipe on page 81) and **Almond Rhubarb Pastry** (recipe on page 210).

CREAM CHEESE RHUBARB PIE

Beverly Kuhn, Orwell, Ohio

(PICTURED ON PAGE 208)

1/4 cup cornstarch
1 cup sugar
Pinch salt
1/2 cup water
3 cups sliced fresh *or* frozen rhubarb (1/2-inch pieces)
1 unbaked pie shell (9 inches)
TOPPING:
1 package (8 ounces) cream cheese, softened
2 eggs
1/2 cup sugar
Whipped cream
Sliced almonds

In a saucepan, combine the cornstarch, sugar and salt. Add water; stir until thoroughly combined. Add rhubarb. Cook, stirring often, until mixture boils and thickens. Pour into the pie shell; bake at 425° for 10 minutes. Meanwhile, for topping, beat cream cheese, eggs and sugar until smooth. Pour over pie. Return to oven; reduce heat to 325°. Bake for 35 minutes or until set. Cool. Chill several hours or overnight. Garnish with whipped cream and sliced almonds. **Yield:** 8 servings.

ALMOND RHUBARB PASTRY

Lois Dyck, Coaldale, Alberta

(PICTURED ON PAGE 209)

PASTRY:
3 cups all-purpose flour
1 tablespoon baking powder
1 teaspoon salt
1 cup shortening
2 eggs, beaten
1/4 to 1/3 cup milk, *divided*
FILLING:
6 cups chopped fresh *or* frozen rhubarb
1-1/2 cups sugar
1/4 cup quick-cooking tapioca
TOPPING:
1/2 cup butter *or* margarine
3/4 cup sugar
2 tablespoons milk
1/2 teaspoon vanilla extract
1 cup slivered almonds

Combine flour, baking powder and salt; cut in shortening as for pie pastry. Mix eggs and 1/4 cup milk; add to dry ingredients and stir with a fork just until dough clings together. Add some or all of remaining milk if necessary. Shape into a ball. Divide in half. On a floured surface, roll half of dough into a 17-in. x 12-in. rectangle. Transfer to a greased 15-in. x 10-

in. x 1-in. baking pan. Combine filling ingredients; sprinkle over dough in pan. Roll out remaining dough into a 15-in. x 10-in. rectangle. Place over filling. Fold bottom edge of dough over top layer of dough; press edges together to seal. For topping, in a saucepan, melt butter; add sugar and milk. Bring to a gentle boil; boil 2-3 minutes, stirring constantly. Remove from heat; stir in vanilla. Spread over pastry. Sprinkle almonds on top. Bake at 400° for 20 minutes; reduce heat to 300°. Bake 30-40 minutes longer or until golden brown. Serve warm or cold. **Yield:** 16-20 servings.

BERRY RHUBARB FOOL

Cheryl Miller, Fort Collins, Colorado

(PICTURED ON PAGE 208)

3 cups sliced fresh *or* frozen rhubarb (1-inch pieces)
1/3 cup sugar
1/4 cup orange juice
Pinch salt
1 cup heavy cream
1 pint fresh strawberries, halved
Fresh mint leaves

In a saucepan, combine rhubarb, sugar, orange juice and salt. Bring to a boil. Reduce heat; cover and simmer for 6-8 minutes or until rhubarb is tender. Cool slightly. Pour into a blender container; cover and blend until smooth. Chill. Just before serving, whip cream until stiff peaks form. Fold rhubarb mixture into cream until lightly streaked. In chilled parfait glasses, alternate layers of cream mixture and strawberries. Garnish each serving with a strawberry and a sprig of mint. **Yield:** 6 servings.

Quick & Easy

CHOCOLATE CHERRY DESSERT

Cherry Turner, Eunice, Louisiana

26 chocolate wafer cookies, crushed
1/4 cup butter *or* margarine, melted
1 cup (8 ounces) sour cream
1 package (3.9 ounces) instant chocolate pudding mix
3/4 cup milk
1 can (21 ounces) cherry pie filling

In a mixing bowl, combine wafer crumbs with butter. Press into the bottom of an 8-in. square baking pan. Place in freezer for 10 minutes. In another mixing bowl, combine sour cream, pudding and milk; beat on low for 1-1/2 minutes. Spread over crust. Spoon pie filling on

top. Cover and refrigerate until ready to serve. **Yield:** 9 servings.

RAISIN PIE

Patricia Baxter, Great Bend, Kansas

(PICTURED ON PAGE 166)

1 cup sugar
2-1/2 tablespoons all-purpose flour
1-1/2 cups cold water
2 cups raisins
1/2 teaspoon salt
1/2 teaspoon ground cinnamon
1 tablespoon butter *or* margarine
Pastry for double-crust pie (9 inches)

In a saucepan, stir together sugar and flour. Add water and mix well. Stir in raisins, salt and cinnamon; cook and stir over medium heat until bubbly. Cook and stir 1 minute more. Remove from heat and stir in butter. Pour into a pastry-lined pie plate. Top with lattice crust, or cover with top crust and cut slits for steam to escape. Bake at 375° for about 45 minutes or until crust is golden brown. **Yield:** 6-8 servings.

> **BERRY SMART.** Fresh cranberries are much easier to grind in a food processor or grinder if you freeze them first. Allow ground berries to drain well before using.

CRANBERRY WALNUT TART

Beverly Mix, Missoula, Montana

(PICTURED ON PAGE 145)

TART SHELL:
1 cup all-purpose flour
1/3 cup sugar
Dash salt
5 tablespoons butter *or* margarine
1 egg, lightly beaten
1/2 tablespoon water, optional
FILLING:
1/2 cup sugar
1/2 cup light corn syrup
2 eggs, lightly beaten
2 tablespoons butter *or* margarine, melted
1 teaspoon grated orange peel
1 cup walnut halves
1 cup fresh *or* frozen cranberries

In a large bowl, combine flour, sugar and salt. With a pastry blender, cut in butter until mixture resembles very coarse crumbs. Add egg and stir lightly with fork just until mixture forms a ball, adding the water if necessary. Wrap in waxed paper and refrigerate at least 1 hour. Grease a 9-in. fluted tart pan with removable bottom. Press chilled pastry into the bottom and up the sides of pan. Line pastry shell with foil and top with an empty pie plate to prevent shrinkage. Bake at 375° for 10 minutes. Remove foil and empty pie plate and bake another 5 minutes. Cool. Meanwhile, for filling, combine sugar, syrup, eggs, butter and peel in a large bowl; set aside. Place walnuts and cranberries in bottom of tart; pour sugar mixture into pan. Bake for 30-35 minutes or until crust is golden, edge of filling is firm and center is almost set. Cool on wire rack. Chill until serving. Store leftovers in the refrigerator. **Yield:** 12 servings.

OLD-FASHIONED COCONUT PIE

Barbara Smith, Franklin, Georgia

1/4 cup all-purpose flour
1 cup sugar
Dash salt
2 cups milk
3 egg yolks, beaten
1-1/2 teaspoons vanilla extract
1-1/4 cups flaked coconut, *divided*
1 pastry shell (9 inches), baked
MERINGUE:
3 egg whites
6 tablespoons sugar

In a saucepan, combine flour and sugar; add salt, milk and egg yolks. Mix well. Cook over medium heat, stirring constantly, until mixture is thickened and bubbly. Reduce heat; cook and stir 2 minutes more. Remove from the heat; stir in vanilla and 1 cup coconut. Pour hot filling into pie shell. For meringue, beat egg whites in a mixing bowl until soft peaks form. Gradually beat in sugar until mixture forms stiff glossy peaks and sugar dissolves. Spread meringue over hot filling. Sprinkle with remaining coconut. Bake at 350° for 12-15 minutes or until golden. Cool. Store in the refrigerator. **Yield:** 6-8 servings.

CHOCOLATE ECLAIRS

Janet Davis, Murfreesboro, Tennessee

1/2 cup butter or margarine
1 cup water
1 cup all-purpose flour
1/4 teaspoon salt
4 eggs
FILLING:
1 package (5.1 ounces) instant vanilla pudding mix
2-1/2 cups cold milk
1 cup whipping cream
1/4 cup confectioners' sugar

1 teaspoon vanilla extract
CHOCOLATE ICING:
2 squares (1 ounce *each*) semisweet chocolate
2 tablespoons butter *or* margarine
1 cup confectioners' sugar
2 to 3 tablespoons hot water

In a saucepan, combine butter and water. Bring to a rapid boil, stirring until the butter melts. Reduce heat to low; add flour and salt. Stir vigorously until mixture leaves the sides of the pan and forms a stiff ball. Remove from heat. Add eggs, one at a time, beating well after each addition. With a tablespoon or a pastry tube fitted with a No. 10 or larger tip, spoon or pipe dough into 4-in.-long x 1-1/2-in.-wide strips on a greased cookie sheet. Bake at 450° for 15 minutes. Reduce heat to 325°; bake 20 minutes longer. Cool on a wire rack. For filling, combine pudding mix and milk; mix according to package directions. In another bowl, whip the cream until soft peaks form. Beat in sugar and vanilla; fold into pudding. Fill cooled shells. (Chill remaining pudding for another use.) For icing, melt chocolate and butter in a saucepan over low heat. Stir in sugar. Add hot water until icing is smooth and reaches desired consistency. Cool slightly. Spread over eclairs. Chill until serving. **Yield:** 8-9 servings.

CREAMY PEAR PIE

Kathryn Gross, Fontanelle, Iowa

4 cups sliced peeled pears
1/3 cup sugar
2 tablespoons all-purpose flour
1 cup (8 ounces) sour cream
1/2 teaspoon vanilla extract
1/2 teaspoon lemon extract
1/2 teaspoon almond extract
1 unbaked pastry shell (9 inches)
TOPPING:
1/4 cup all-purpose flour
2 tablespoons butter *or* margarine, melted
2 tablespoons brown sugar

In a large bowl, toss pears with sugar and flour. Combine sour cream and extracts; add to pear mixture and mix well. Pour into pie shell. In a small bowl, mix topping ingredients until crumbly. Sprinkle over pears. Bake at 400° for 10 minutes. Reduce heat to 350°; bake 45 minutes more or until the pears are tender. **Yield:** 6-8 servings.

RASPBERRY ALMOND TORTE

Dana Pratt, De Land, Illinois

1-1/3 cups all-purpose flour
1 teaspoon baking powder
1 cup sugar, *divided*
1 cup butter or margarine, *divided*
3 eggs, *divided*
1/2 cup raspberry jam, *divided*
1 cup ground almonds
1/2 teaspoon almond extract
1/2 cup confectioners' sugar
2 to 2-1/2 teaspoons lemon juice

In a mixing bowl, combine flour, baking powder and 1/3 cup sugar. Cut in 1/2 cup butter until fine crumbs form. Beat 1 egg; add to mixing bowl and stir until dry ingredients are moistened. Press dough evenly into bottom and up the sides of a 9-in. x 1-1/2-in. tart pan with removable bottom. Spread 1/4 cup of jam over dough. Cover with plastic wrap and chill. Meanwhile, cream together remaining sugar and butter; stir in almonds and extract. Add remaining eggs, one at a time, beating well after each addition; spoon filling over jam. Bake at 350° for 50 minutes. Cool in pan, then carefully remove sides from pan. Spread remaining jam on top. Combine confectioners' sugar and lemon juice; drizzle over the top. **Yield:** 10-12 servings.

STRAWBERRY RHUBARB CRUMB PIE

Paula Phillips, East Winthrop, Maine

1 egg
1 cup sugar
2 tablespoons all-purpose flour
1 teaspoon vanilla extract
3/4 pound fresh rhubarb, cut into 1/2-inch pieces (about 3 cups)
1 pint fresh strawberries, halved
1 unbaked pastry shell (9 inches)
TOPPING:
3/4 cup all-purpose flour
1/2 cup packed brown sugar
1/2 cup quick-cooking *or* rolled oats
1/2 cup butter *or* margarine

In a mixing bowl, beat egg. Beat in sugar, flour and vanilla; mix well. Gently fold in rhubarb and strawberries. Pour into pie shell. For topping, combine flour, brown sugar and oats in a small bowl; cut in butter until crumbly. Sprinkle over fruit. Bake at 400° for 10 minutes. Reduce heat to 350°; bake for 35 minutes or until golden brown and bubbly. **Yield:** 8 servings.

THESE recipes prove that everyday ingredients can be turned into sensational desserts in a snap! It's no wonder that they'll appeal to you and your family. Now you can enjoy lip-smacking desserts whenever you like.

DELIGHTFUL DESSERTS!
Clockwise from the bottom: **Family Cheesecake Squares**, **Strawberry Cream Puffs**, **Butter Pecan Ice Cream** and **Grandma's Chocolate Meringue Pie** (all recipes on page 213).

BUTTER PECAN ICE CREAM
Patricia Simms, Dallas, Texas
(PICTURED AT LEFT)

TOASTED NUTS:
- 3 tablespoons butter *or* margarine, melted
- 3/4 cup chopped pecans
- 1/8 teaspoon salt
- 1 tablespoon sugar

ICE CREAM:
- 1/2 cup packed brown sugar
- 1/4 cup sugar
- 2 tablespoons cornstarch
- 2 eggs, beaten
- 1/3 cup maple-flavored pancake syrup
- 2-1/2 cups milk
- 1 cup whipping cream
- 2 teaspoons vanilla extract

On a baking sheet, combine butter, pecans, salt and 1 tablespoon sugar; spread into a single layer. Roast at 350° for 15 minutes. Stir and roast 15 minutes longer. Cool. For ice cream, combine sugars, cornstarch, eggs and syrup in the top of a double boiler. Gradually add milk. Cook over boiling water until mixture thickens. Remove from the heat and chill for several hours or overnight. Stir in toasted nuts, cream and vanilla. Place in ice cream freezer and freeze according to manufacturer's directions. Allow to ripen in ice cream freezer or firm up in your refrigerator freezer an hour before serving. **Yield:** about 2 quarts.

STRAWBERRY CREAM PUFFS
Sherry Adams, Mt. Ayr, Iowa
(PICTURED AT LEFT)

- 1 cup water
- 1/2 cup butter *or* margarine
- 1 teaspoon sugar
- 1/4 teaspoon salt
- 1 cup all-purpose flour
- 4 eggs

CREAM FILLING:
- 2 pints fresh strawberries, sliced
- 1/2 cup sugar, *divided*
- 2 cups whipping cream

Confectioners' sugar
Additional sliced strawberries
Mint leaves

In a large saucepan, bring water, butter, sugar and salt to a boil. Add flour all at once and stir until a smooth ball forms. Remove from the heat and beat in eggs, one at a time. Continue beating until mixture is smooth and shiny. Make 10 cream puffs by dropping tablespoonfuls of dough 2 in. apart on a large ungreased cookie sheet. Bake at 400° for about 35 minutes or until golden brown.

Cool on a wire rack. For filling, combine berries and 1/4 cup sugar. Chill 30 minutes. Beat cream and remaining sugar until stiff. Just before serving, cut tops off puffs. Combine berries and cream mixture. Fill cream puffs and replace tops. Sprinkle with confectioners' sugar, and garnish with additional berries and mint leaves. **Yield:** 10 cream puffs.

FAMILY CHEESECAKE SQUARES
Loretta Ruda, Kennesaw, Georgia
(PICTURED AT LEFT)

CRUST:
- 1 package (4 ounces) active dry yeast
- 1/4 cup warm milk (105° to 110°)
- 1 tablespoon sugar
- 1 cup butter *or* margarine
- 2-1/2 cups all-purpose flour
- 1/2 teaspoon salt
- 4 egg yolks, slightly beaten

FILLING:
- 1 egg, *separated*
- 2 packages (8 ounces *each*) cream cheese, softened
- 1 cup sugar
- 1 teaspoon vanilla extract
- 1/2 cup chopped pecans

Dissolve yeast in warm milk; add sugar and set aside. In a large mixing bowl, cut butter into flour and salt as for pie crust. Add yolks and yeast mixture. Mix thoroughly. Divide dough into two parts. Roll each piece to fit a 13-in. x 9-in. x 2-in. baking pan. Place one piece in pan. For filling, beat yolk, cream cheese, sugar and vanilla until smooth. Spread over dough and cover with remaining dough. Press lightly to seal edges around pan. Brush top with slightly beaten egg white and sprinkle with nuts. Cover and allow to rise in a warm place 1-1/2 hours. Bake at 350° for 30-35 minutes or until lightly browned. Cut into squares to serve. **Yield:** 24 servings.

GRANDMA'S CHOCOLATE MERINGUE PIE
Donna Vest Tilley, Chesterfield, Virginia
(PICTURED AT LEFT)

- 3/4 cup sugar
- 5 tablespoons baking cocoa
- 3 tablespoons cornstarch
- 1/4 teaspoon salt
- 2 cups milk
- 3 eggs, *separated*
- 1 teaspoon vanilla extract
- 1 pastry shell (9 inches), baked

MERINGUE:
- 1/4 teaspoon cream of tartar
- 6 tablespoons sugar

In a saucepan, mix sugar, cocoa, cornstarch and salt; gradually add milk. Cook and stir over medium-high heat until thickened and bubbly. Reduce heat; cook and stir 2 minutes more. Remove from heat. Stir about 1 cup of the hot filling into the egg yolks. Return to saucepan and bring to a gentle boil. Cook and stir 2 minutes. Remove from the heat and stir in vanilla. Pour *hot* filling into pie crust. For meringue, immediately beat egg whites with cream of tartar until soft peaks form. Gradually add sugar and continue to beat until stiff and glossy. Spread evenly over hot filling, sealing meringue to pie crust. Bake at 350° for 12-15 minutes or until golden. **Yield:** 8 servings.

MAPLE CREAM PIE
Emma Magielda, Amsterdam, New York
(PICTURED ON PAGE 97)

CRUST:
- 1 cup all-purpose flour
- 1/4 teaspoon salt
- 3 tablespoons butter *or* margarine
- 3 tablespoons lard
- 2 to 3 tablespoons milk

FILLING:
- 1-3/4 cups milk, *divided*
- 1/4 cup cornstarch
- 3/4 cup plus 1 tablespoon maple *or* maple-flavored syrup, *divided*
- 1/4 teaspoon salt
- 2 egg yolks
- 2 tablespoons butter *or* margarine
- 1 cup whipping cream
Sliced almonds, toasted

Combine the flour and salt in a mixing bowl. Cut in butter and lard until mixture resembles a coarse meal. Sprinkle in milk, 1 tablespoon at a time, mixing until flour is moistened. Shape into a ball. Roll out on a lightly floured surface. Place in a 9-in. pie plate. Trim and flute edges. Prick the bottom and sides with a fork. Bake at 450° for 12-15 minutes or until lightly browned. Cool. For filling, blend together 1/4 cup milk and cornstarch in a saucepan. Gradually stir in remaining milk, 3/4 cup of the syrup and salt. Cook over medium heat, stirring constantly, until mixture comes to a boil. Remove from the heat. Stir about 1/4 cup of the hot mixture into the yolks; return all to the saucepan. Cook, stirring constantly, until thickened and bubbly. Remove from the heat; stir in butter. Cool thoroughly, stirring frequently. Meanwhile, whip cream until stiff. Fold 1 cup into cooled filling; spoon into prepared pie crust. Fold remaining syrup into remaining cream; frost top of pie. Chill for several hours. Garnish with toasted almonds. **Yield:** 8 servings.

AN IMMEDIATE HIT. Try tangy Raspberry/Lime Pie—it's a fun-to-make fruity dessert.

Quick & Easy

RASPBERRY/LIME PIE

Jane Zempel, Midland, Michigan

(PICTURED ABOVE)

   1 can (14 ounces) sweetened
      condensed milk
1/2 cup lime juice
   1 container (8 ounces) frozen
      whipped topping, thawed
Few drops red food coloring,
   optional
   1 cup fresh raspberries
   1 graham cracker pie crust
      (9 inches), baked and cooled
Raspberries for garnish
Fresh mint for garnish

In a mixing bowl, stir together milk and lime juice. Mixture will begin to thicken. Mix in whipped topping and food coloring if desired. Gently fold in raspberries. Spoon into pie crust. Chill. Garnish with additional raspberries and mint. **Yield:** 8 servings.

GRANDMA'S BREAKFAST FRUIT

Ethelyn Aanrud, Amherst Junction, Wisconsin

   3 large cooking apples, peeled
      and thickly sliced
1/2 cup pitted prunes
3/4 cup raisins
   1 orange, peeled and sectioned
   3 cups plus 3 tablespoons
      water, *divided*
1/2 cup sugar
1/2 teaspoon ground cinnamon
   2 tablespoons cornstarch

In a saucepan, combine apples, prunes, raisins, orange and 3 cups water. Bring to a boil; reduce heat and simmer 10 minutes. Stir in sugar and cinnamon. Combine cornstarch and remaining water; stir into saucepan. Bring to a boil, stirring constantly. Cook for 2 minutes. Chill. Store in the refrigerator for up to 1 week. **Yield:** 6-8 servings.

 Quick & Easy

ANGEL FOOD TORTE

Mary Lee Thomas, Logansport, Indiana

   1 prepared angel food cake
Red food coloring, optional
   1 container (16 ounces) frozen
      whipped topping, defrosted
   2 cups fresh or frozen
      blueberries, raspberries or
      sliced strawberries

Slice cake into thirds horizontally. If desired, tint the topping pink with a few drops of food coloring. Spread each layer with topping and 1 cup fruit (well drained, if frozen). Reassemble layers and spread remaining topping over entire cake. Chill until ready to serve. **Yield:** 12 servings.

PUMPKIN TRIFLE

Melody Hurlbut, St. Agatha, Ontario

(PICTURED ON PAGE 125)

   2 to 3 cups prepared crumbled
      unfrosted spice cake, muffins
      or gingerbread
   1 can (16 ounces) pumpkin
      (about 2 cups)
   1 teaspoon ground cinnamon
1/4 teaspoon ground nutmeg
1/4 teaspoon ground ginger
1/4 teaspoon ground allspice
2-1/2 cups cold milk
   4 packages (3.4 ounces *each*)
      instant butterscotch
      pudding mix
   2 cups whipping cream
Maraschino cherries, optional

Set aside 1/4 cup of cake crumbs for top. Divide remaining crumbs into four portions; sprinkle one portion into the bottom of a trifle bowl or 3-qt. serving bowl. In a large mixing bowl, combine pumpkin, spices, milk and pudding mixes; mix until smooth. Spoon half into the serving bowl. Sprinkle with a second portion of crumbs. Whip cream until stiff; spoon half into bowl. Sprinkle with a third portion of crumbs. Top with the remaining pumpkin mixture, then last portion of crumbs and remaining whipped cream. Sprinkle the reserved crumbs on top, around the edge of the bowl. Place cherries in the center if

desired. Cover and chill at least 2 hours before serving. **Yield:** 12-15 servings.

CARAMEL CUSTARD

Linda McBride, Austin, Texas

(PICTURED ON PAGE 105)

1-1/2 cups sugar, *divided*
   6 eggs
   2 teaspoons vanilla extract
   3 cups milk

In a heavy saucepan over low heat, cook and stir 3/4 cup sugar until melted and golden. Pour into eight 6-oz. custard cups, tilting to coat bottom of cup; let stand for 10 minutes. In a large bowl, beat eggs, vanilla, milk and remaining sugar until combined but not foamy. Pour over caramelized sugar. Place the cups in two 8-in. square baking pans. Pour boiling water in pans to a depth of 1 in. Bake at 350° for 40-45 minutes or until a knife inserted near center comes out clean. Remove from pans to cool on wire racks. To unmold, run a knife around rim of cup and invert onto dessert plate. Serve warm or chilled. **Yield:** 8 servings.

> **DELICIOUS DESSERT.** For a fast, delicious berry trifle, layer yellow pound cake, fresh or frozen berries, vanilla pudding and whipped cream. Chill until ready to serve.

BLACKBERRY DUMPLINGS

Liecha Collins, Oneonta, New York

(PICTURED ON PAGE 44)

   1 quart fresh *or* frozen
      (loose-pack) blackberries
   1 cup plus 1 tablespoon sugar,
      divided
3/4 teaspoon salt, *divided*
1/2 teaspoon lemon extract
1-1/2 cups all-purpose flour
   2 teaspoons baking powder
1/4 teaspoon ground nutmeg
2/3 cup milk
Cream *or* whipped cream, optional

In a Dutch oven, combine the blackberries, 1 cup sugar, 1/4 teaspoon salt and lemon extract. Bring to a boil; reduce heat and simmer for 5 minutes. Meanwhile, in a mixing bowl, combine flour, baking powder, nutmeg and remaining sugar and salt. Add milk; stir just until mixed. (Dough will be very thick.) Drop by tablespoonfuls into six mounds onto hot blackberry mixture; cover tightly and simmer for 15 minutes or until a toothpick inserted in a dumpling comes out clean. Spoon into serving dishes. Serve with cream or whipped cream if desired. **Yield:** 6-8 servings.

MAPLE-GLAZED APPLE PIE

Patricia Putnam, Lakeland, Florida

(PICTURED ON PAGE 57)

**Pastry for double-crust pie
 (9 inches)**
   6 cups thinly sliced peeled
     apples, *divided*
  1/2 cup sugar
  1/4 cup packed brown sugar
  1/2 cup crushed gingersnaps
  1/2 teaspoon ground cinnamon
  1/2 cup chopped walnuts *or*
     pecans
  1/4 cup butter *or* margarine,
     melted
  1/4 cup maple syrup

Line a 9-in. pie pan with the bottom crust. Place half of the apples in the crust; set aside. In a mixing bowl, combine sugars, gingersnaps, cinnamon, nuts and butter; sprinkle half over apples in crust. Top with remaining apples and sugar mixture. Roll out remaining pastry to fit top of pie. Cut a few slits in the top and place over apples; seal. Cover loosely with foil and bake at 375° for 35 minutes. Meanwhile, bring syrup to a gentle boil in a small saucepan. Remove pie from oven; remove foil and brush hot syrup over pie and into vents. Return pie to oven and bake, uncovered, 20 minutes longer. Serve warm. **Yield:** 8 servings.

PINEAPPLE SHERBET

Barbara Libkie, Roswell, New Mexico

  1 quart buttermilk
  1 can (20 ounces) crushed
     pineapple, drained
1-1/3 cups sugar
  1/2 cup chopped walnuts
  1 teaspoon vanilla extract

In a bowl, combine all ingredients; mix well. Cover and freeze for 1 hour. Stir; return to freezer for at least 2 hours before serving. **Yield:** 6-8 servings.

CHOCOLATE CHEWS

Donna Rhodes, Huntingdon, Pennsylvania

  1/4 cup butter *or* margarine
  1/2 cup dark corn syrup
  6 tablespoons baking cocoa
  1/2 teaspoon vanilla extract
3-1/4 cups confectioners' sugar,
     divided
  3/4 cup nonfat dry milk powder

In a saucepan, melt butter over medium heat. Stir in corn syrup and cocoa; bring to a boil. Remove from the heat; stir in vanilla, 2 cups confectioners' sugar and milk powder. (Mixture will be stiff.) Turn out onto a surface lightly dusted with confectioners' sugar. Knead in remaining confectioners' sugar; knead 3-4 minutes longer or until stiff. Divide into four pieces and roll each into an 18-in. rope. Cut into 3/4-in. pieces. Wrap each candy in cellophane or waxed paper. Store in refrigerator. **Yield:** 8 dozen.

MOM'S LEMON CUSTARD PIE

Jeannie Fritson, Kearney, Nebraska

  1 cup sugar
  1 tablespoon butter *or*
     margarine, softened
  3 tablespoons all-purpose flour
  1/8 teaspoon salt
  2 eggs, *separated*
  1 cup milk
  1/4 cup fresh lemon juice
Peel of 1 medium lemon
  1 unbaked pastry shell (9 inches)
Whipped cream, optional

Using a spoon, cream sugar and butter in a bowl until well mixed. Add flour, salt, egg yolks and milk; mix well. Add lemon juice and peel; mix well. Set aside. In a small bowl, beat egg whites until stiff peaks form; gently fold into lemon mixture. Pour into pie shell. Bake at 325° for 1 hour or until lightly browned and a knife inserted in center comes out clean. Cool. Garnish with whipped cream if desired. Store in the refrigerator. **Yield:** 6-8 servings.

BIRD'S NEST PIE

Jeannine Bates, Wauseon, Ohio

  4 to 5 medium apples, peeled
     and sliced
  2 cups all-purpose flour
  1 cup sugar
  1/2 teaspoon baking soda
  1/2 teaspoon cream of tartar
  1 cup sour milk*
  1 egg
TOPPING:
  1/4 cup sugar
  1/2 teaspoon ground cinnamon
  1/4 teaspoon ground nutmeg

Divide apples evenly between two greased 9-in. pie plates; set aside. In a mixing bowl, combine flour, sugar, baking soda, cream of tartar, sour milk and egg; mix well. Divide batter and pour over apples. Bake at 350° for 25-30 minutes or until pies are lightly browned and test done. Invert onto serving plates (so apples are on the top). Combine all topping ingredients; sprinkle over apples. Serve warm. (*To sour milk, place 1 tablespoon white vinegar in a measuring cup; add enough milk to equal 1 cup. Let stand for 5 minutes.) **Yield:** 12 servings.

APPLE DUMPLINGS

Marjorie Thompson, W. Sacramento, California

1-1/2 cups sugar, *divided*
  2 cups water
  4 tablespoons butter *or*
     margarine, *divided*
  1/2 teaspoon ground cinnamon,
     divided
Pastry for double-crust pie (9 inches)
  6 small to medium apples,
     peeled and cored

In a saucepan, combine 1 cup sugar, water, 3 tablespoons butter and 1/4 teaspoon cinnamon. Bring to a boil; boil for 3 minutes. Remove from the heat and set aside. Roll pastry into a 21-in. x 14-in. rectangle; cut into six 7-in. squares. Place one apple in the center of each square. Combine the remaining sugar and cinnamon; spoon into center of apples. Dot with remaining butter. Moisten edges of pastry; fold corners to the center atop apple. Pinch to seal. Place in an ungreased 12-in. x 8-in. x 2-in. baking dish. Pour syrup mixture around apples. Bake at 375° for 45 minutes or until pastry is golden brown and apples are tender. Serve warm. **Yield:** 6 servings.

FRESH RASPBERRY PIE

Deanna Richter, Elmore, Minnesota

CRUST:
1-1/2 cups graham cracker
     crumbs (about 20 squares)
  3 tablespoons sugar
  1/3 cup butter *or* margarine,
     melted
FILLING:
  24 large marshmallows
  1/3 cup milk
  2/3 cup whipping cream, whipped
**Few drops red food coloring,
    optional**
  2 cups fresh raspberries, *divided*

Combine crust ingredients. Press into a 9-in. pie plate; chill. Meanwhile, heat marshmallows and milk in a saucepan over low heat until smooth. Cool. Fold in cream and food coloring if desired. Spoon half into the crust. Top with half the raspberries. Repeat layers. Chill until firm, about 3 hours. **Yield:** 8 servings.

RICH and soothing, chocolate is one of life's little rewards. So, celebrate any day by sampling these delectable delights. From cookie jar favorites to traditional candies…classic cakes to very impressive pies, you'll savor the taste of each and every one.

CHOCK-FULL OF CHOCOLATE.
Clockwise from top left: **Double Chocolate Crumble Bars** (recipe on page 175), **Hot Fudge Sauce** (recipe on page 147), **Peanut Chocolate Chip Cookies** (recipe on page 182), **Chocolate Mousse Pie** (recipe on page 218), **Buckeye Candy** (recipe on page 218), **German Chocolate Pie** (recipe on page 218), **Chocolate Ice Cream Pie** (recipe on page 218) and **Hot Fudge Pudding Cake** (recipe on page 192).

CHOCOLATE MOUSSE PIE

Sheryl Goodnough, Eliot, Maine

(PICTURED ON PAGE 217)

4 ounces semisweet chocolate
1/3 cup milk, *divided*
2 tablespoons sugar
1 package (3 ounces) cream
cheese, softened
1 carton (8 ounces) whipped
topping
Peppermint flavoring to taste *or* flavor
of choice, optional
1 chocolate wafer crust (8 inches)

Heat chocolate and 2 tablespoons milk in medium saucepan over low heat, stirring until chocolate is melted. Set aside. Beat sugar into cream cheese; add remaining milk and chocolate mixture. Beat until smooth. Fold chocolate mixture into the whipped topping; blend until smooth. Add peppermint flavoring to taste if desired. Spoon filling into pie crust or springform pan. Freeze until firm, about 4 hours. Store any leftovers in freezer. **Yield:** 1 pie.

GERMAN CHOCOLATE PIE

Crystal Allen, Homer, Illinois

(PICTURED ON PAGE 217)

1 package (4 ounces) German
sweet chocolate
1/4 cup butter *or* margarine
1 can (12 ounces) evaporated
milk
1-1/2 cups sugar
3 tablespoons cornstarch
1/8 teaspoon salt
2 eggs
1 teaspoon vanilla
1 deep dish pastry shell
(9 inches), unbaked
1-1/2 cups coconut
1 cup pecans, chopped

Melt chocolate and butter over low heat; remove from heat. Blend in milk; set aside. Mix together sugar, cornstarch and salt. Beat in eggs and vanilla. Blend in chocolate mixture; pour into pie shell. Combine coconut and nuts; sprinkle on top of chocolate mixture. Bake at 375° for 45 minutes. **Yield:** 1 pie.

BUCKEYE CANDY

Bev Spain, Bellville, Ohio

(PICTURED ON PAGE 217)

CANDY:
1/2 cup butter *or* margarine,
softened

1-3/4 cups (18 ounces) creamy
peanut butter
1 teaspoon vanilla
About 1 pound confectioners' sugar
CHOCOLATE COATING:
1 package (12 ounces)
semisweet chocolate chips
1 tablespoon shortening

Cream butter, peanut butter and vanilla; add enough confectioners' sugar until proper consistency is reached. Roll candy into 1-inch balls and place on wax paper-lined cookie sheet. Melt chips and shortening in top of double boiler; keep warm over low heat. Using a toothpick, dip each ball covering about three-fourths of candy. (Peanut butter needs to show for an authentic buckeye.) Return candy to sheet to cool. **Yield:** 8 dozen.

CHOCOLATE ICE CREAM PIE

Bill Hughes, Dolores, Colorado

(PICTURED ON PAGE 216)

2 pints vanilla ice cream
1 box (3 ounces) instant
chocolate fudge pudding mix
1 box (6 ounces) instant French
vanilla pudding mix
2 cups extra heavy whipping
cream
1/2 cup coffee-flavored liqueur
4 ounces vanilla yogurt
6 ounces (6 squares)
unsweetened chocolate, grated
2 chocolate wafer pie shells
(8 inches *each*)
Additional whipped cream and
chocolate curls

Melt ice cream; set aside. In a separate bowl, blend the puddings with whipping cream and liqueur. Mix with electric mixer until stiff. Add mixture to melted ice cream, stirring to blend. Blend in yogurt and grated chocolate. Pour into pie shells or into springform pans and freeze until firm. Garnish with additional whipped cream and chocolate curls if desired. **Yield:** 2 pies.

CRANBERRY SHERBET

Heather Clement, Indian River, Ontario

(PICTURED ON PAGE 145)

1 bag (12 ounces) fresh *or*
frozen cranberries
2-3/4 cups water, *divided*
2 cups sugar
1 envelope unflavored gelatin
1/2 cup orange juice

In a saucepan, combine cranberries and 2-1/2 cups of water. Bring to a boil; cook gently until all the cranberries have popped, about 10 minutes. Remove from heat; cool slightly. Press mixture through a sieve or food mill, reserving juice and discarding skins and seeds. In another saucepan, combine cranberry juice and sugar; cook over medium heat until the sugar dissolves. Remove from the heat and set aside. Combine gelatin and remaining 1/4 cup water; stir until softened. Combine cranberry mixture, orange juice and gelatin; mix well. Pour into a 2-qt. container; freeze 4-5 hours or until mixture is slushy. Remove from freezer; beat with electric mixer until sherbet is a bright pink color. Freeze until firm. **Yield:** about 6 cups.

CARE FOR CRANBERRIES. Don't wash cranberries before storing—just put them in a freezer bag and freeze. As you need them, remove from the bag, rinse and cut up.

PEACHY ANGEL FOOD DESSERT

Lois Walters, Beaconsfield, Iowa

1 prepared angel food cake
2 envelopes (1.3 ounces *each*)
whipped topping mix
2 packages (3 ounces *each*)
cream cheese, softened
1 cup confectioners' sugar
1 can (21 ounces) peach *or*
cherry pie filling

Tear cake into bite-size pieces; set aside. Prepare whipped topping according to package directions; set aside. In a large mixing bowl, beat cream cheese and confectioners' sugar; fold in whipped topping. Add cake pieces; stir gently to coat evenly. Spoon into a 13-in. x 9-in. x 2-in. baking pan. Top with pie filling. Chill until ready to serve. **Yield:** 12 servings.

PRALINE PEACH COBBLER

Maithel Martin, Kansas City, Missouri

(PICTURED ON PAGE 162)

1-1/2 cups plus 2 teaspoons sugar,
divided
2 tablespoons cornstarch
1 teaspoon ground cinnamon
1 cup water
8 cups sliced peeled fresh
peaches
2 cups self-rising flour*

1/2 cup shortening
1/2 cup buttermilk
3 tablespoons butter *or* margarine, melted
1/4 cup packed brown sugar
1 cup chopped pecans

In a saucepan, mix 1-1/2 cups sugar, cornstarch, cinnamon and water; stir until smooth. Add peaches; cook and stir until thickened and bubbly. Cook and stir for 2 minutes more. Pour into a lightly greased 13-in. x 9-in. x 2-in. baking dish; set aside. In a bowl, combine flour and remaining sugar; cut in shortening until mixture resembles coarse crumbs. Add buttermilk and stir just until moistened. If needed, add additional buttermilk, 1 tablespoon at a time, until dough clings together. Turn onto a floured surface; knead gently 6-8 times. Roll into a 12-in. x 8-in. rectangle. Combine butter, brown sugar and pecans; spread over the dough to within 1/2 in. of edges. Starting with long side roll up jelly-roll style. Cut into 12 pieces, 1 in. each. Place on top of the peach mixture. Bake at 400° for 25-30 minutes or until golden brown. **Yield:** 12 servings. (*If self-rising flour is not available, substitute 2 cups all-purpose flour, 1 tablespoon baking powder and 1 teaspoon salt.)

SOUTHERN BREAD PUDDING

D. Darlene Knight, Bethany, Oklahoma

1/2 cup raisins
1/2 cup hot water
4 eggs
2 cups milk
3/4 cup sugar, *divided*
1 teaspoon vanilla extract
8 slices French bread (1/2 inch thick)
Butter *or* margarine, softened
1 teaspoon ground cinnamon
BUTTER SAUCE:
1/2 cup butter (no substitutes)
1 cup sugar
1/2 cup plus 2 tablespoons heavy cream

Place raisins in a small bowl; pour water over. Let stand for about 10 minutes to soften; drain. In a mixing bowl, beat eggs. Add milk, 2/3 cup sugar, vanilla and raisins. Pour half into a greased 13-in. x 9-in. x 2-in. baking dish. Butter both sides of bread; arrange in a single layer over egg mixture. Cover with remaining egg mixture. Combine cinnamon with remaining sugar; sprinkle on top. Bake at 350° for 30 minutes or until a knife inserted in center comes out clean. Meanwhile, for sauce, melt butter in a saucepan. Add sugar; cook and

stir over medium heat for 10 minutes. Remove from the heat and gradually stir in cream. Return to the heat; cook and stir 8-10 minutes longer or until thickened and golden-colored. Serve warm over a slice of bread pudding. **Yield:** 8 servings.

APPLE CRISP

Gertrude Bartnick, Portage, Wisconsin

(PICTURED ON PAGE 70)

1 cup all-purpose flour
3/4 cup rolled oats
1 cup packed brown sugar
1 teaspoon ground cinnamon
1/2 cup butter *or* margarine, softened
4 cups chopped peeled apples
1 cup sugar
2 tablespoons cornstarch
1 cup water
1 teaspoon vanilla extract
Vanilla ice cream, optional

In a mixing bowl, combine first four ingredients. Cut in butter until crumbly. Press half into a greased 2-1/2-qt. baking dish or a 9-in. square baking pan. Cover with apples. In a saucepan, combine sugar, cornstarch, water and vanilla; cook and stir until thick and clear. Pour over apples. Sprinkle with remaining crumb mixture. Bake at 350° for about 1 hour or until the apples are tender. Serve warm, with ice cream if desired. **Yield:** 8 servings.

CRUMB-TOPPED RHUBARB

Betty Combs, De Smet, South Dakota

3 cups diced fresh *or* frozen rhubarb
1/2 cup sugar
1 tablespoon all-purpose flour
1 teaspoon ground cinnamon
1/8 teaspoon salt
TOPPING:
6 tablespoons all-purpose flour
1/2 cup packed brown sugar
1/2 cup quick-cooking *or* rolled oats
6 tablespoons butter *or* margarine, softened

In a mixing bowl, combine rhubarb, sugar, flour, cinnamon and salt. Spoon into a greased 12-in. x 8-in. x 2-in. baking dish; set aside. Combine flour, brown sugar and oats. Cut in butter until crumbly; sprinkle over rhubarb mixture. Bake at 350° for 40 minutes or until lightly browned and bubbly. **Yield:** 6-8 servings.

HASTE MAKES CAKES! These tempting angel food treats (recipe below) fly from start to finish.

Quick & Easy

CHERRY ANGEL DELIGHT

Ida Wing, Cape Cod, Massachusetts
(PICTURED ABOVE)

1 large prepared angel food cake
1 can (21 ounces) cherry pie filling
1 package (3.4 ounces) instant vanilla pudding mix
1-1/2 cups cold milk
1 cup (8 ounces) sour cream

Cut or tear cake into 1/2-in. pieces to measure 8 cups. Place half the cake cubes in a 9-in. square baking pan. Reserve 1/3 cup of pie filling; spread remaining filling over cake. Top with remaining cake cubes. Combine the pudding mix, milk and sour cream. Spoon over cake. Cover and chill. To serve, cut into squares and top with reserved cherries. **Yield:** 9 servings.

CHERRY ICE CREAM

Carol Dale, Greenville, Texas

6 eggs
1-1/2 cups sugar
1-1/2 cups milk
1 can (21 ounces) cherry pie filling
1 quart cream
1 can (14 ounces) sweetened condensed milk
1 tablespoon vanilla extract
1 teaspoon almond extract

In a mixing bowl, beat the eggs and sugar until thick and lemon-colored. Scald milk; slowly pour into egg mixture, stirring constantly, until sugar is dissolved. Cool. Chop the cherries by hand or in a food processor. Combine cherries with egg mixture and all remaining ingredients. Freeze in an ice cream maker. **Yield:** about 1 gallon.

FAMILY and friends will think you slaved over a hot stove preparing Stuffed Crown Roast of Pork—but it's actually easy to put together. And everyone will savor rich Fudge Truffle Cheesecake and fruity Fluffy Cranberry Delight.

EASY AND ELEGANT.
Clockwise from top: **Fudge Truffle Cheesecake**, **Fluffy Cranberry Delight** (both recipes on page 221) and **Stuffed Crown Roast of Pork** (recipe on page 84).

FUDGE TRUFFLE CHEESECAKE

S.E. Sanborn, Perry, Michigan

(PICTURED AT LEFT)

CRUST:
1-1/2 cups vanilla wafer crumbs
1/2 cup confectioners' sugar
1/3 cup baking cocoa
1/3 cup butter *or* margarine, melted
FILLING:
3 packages (8 ounces *each*)
 cream cheese, softened
1 can (14 ounces) sweetened
 condensed milk
2 cups (12 ounces) semisweet
 chocolate chips, melted
4 eggs
2 teaspoons vanilla extract
Whipped cream and additional
 chocolate chips, optional

Combine all crust ingredients and press onto the bottom and 2 in. up the sides of a 9-in. springform pan; chill. For filling, beat cream cheese in a large mixing bowl until fluffy. Gradually add milk; beat until smooth. Add melted chips, eggs and vanilla; mix well. Pour into crust. Bake at 300° for 1 hour and 5 minutes. (Center will still jiggle slightly.) Cool for 15 minutes. Carefully run a knife between crust and sides of pan. Cool for 3 hours at room temperature. Chill overnight. Just before serving, remove sides of pan. Garnish with whipped cream and chocolate chips if desired. **Yield:** 12-16 servings.

FLUFFY CRANBERRY DELIGHT

Ruth Bolduc, Conway, New Hampshire

(PICTURED AT LEFT)

4 cups cranberries
1-1/2 cups sugar
3/4 cup water
1 envelope plain gelatin
1/4 cup lemon juice
2 tablespoons orange juice
1-1/2 cups whipping cream
3 tablespoons confectioners'
 sugar
1 teaspoon vanilla extract

In a saucepan, bring cranberries, sugar and water to a boil. Reduce heat and cook until berries burst. Strain through a food mill or sieve into a large bowl. Add gelatin, lemon juice and orange juice. Cool until mixture coats the back of a spoon. In a small bowl, whip cream until soft peaks form. Add confectioners' sugar and vanilla; whip until stiff peaks

---

form. Fold into cranberry mixture. Chill until set. **Yield:** 8-10 servings.

CRANBERRY BETTY

Leona Cullen, Melrose, Massachusetts

(PICTURED ON PAGE 164)

4 cups soft bread crumbs
6 tablespoons butter *or*
 margarine, *divided*
5 cups sliced peeled baking
 apples (4 to 5 large)
1 cup packed brown sugar
3/4 teaspoon ground nutmeg
2 cups fresh *or* frozen
 cranberries
LEMON SAUCE:
1/2 cup sugar
1 tablespoon cornstarch
Pinch salt
1 cup water
1 teaspoon grated lemon peel
2 tablespoons lemon juice
2 tablespoons butter *or*
 margarine

In a skillet, brown the bread crumbs in 3 tablespoons butter. Place half the apples in a greased 8-in. square baking dish. Combine the brown sugar and nutmeg; sprinkle half over apples. Top with half of the bread crumbs. Dot with half of the remaining butter. Place the cranberries on top. Layer with remaining apples, brown sugar mixture, bread crumbs and butter. Cover and bake at 350° for 45 minutes. Uncover and bake 15-20 minutes more or until fruit is tender. For lemon sauce, combine sugar, cornstarch and salt in a saucepan; add water and lemon peel. Bring to a boil; cook 2 minutes or until thick. Remove from the heat; stir in lemon juice and butter until melted. Serve over warm Cranberry Betty. **Yield:** 6-8 servings.

APPLE ROLY-POLY

Megan Newcombe, Cookstown, Ontario

(PICTURED ON PAGE 60)

1-3/4 cups all-purpose flour
1/4 cup sugar
4 teaspoons baking powder
1/2 teaspoon salt
1/4 cup shortening
1/4 cup butter *or* margarine
2/3 cup sour cream
FILLING:
1/4 cup butter *or* margarine,
 softened
1 cup packed brown sugar
2 teaspoons ground cinnamon
6 medium Granny Smith apples,
 peeled, cored and coarsely
 shredded (about 5 cups)

TOPPING:
2-1/2 cups water
2 tablespoons brown sugar
1 teaspoon ground cinnamon
1/2 cup light cream

In a mixing bowl, combine flour, sugar, baking powder and salt. Cut in shortening and butter until crumbly. Add sour cream and blend until a ball forms. Roll out on a floured surface into a 15-in. x 10-in. rectangle. Spread with softened butter; sprinkle with remaining filling ingredients. Roll up, jelly-roll style, starting with the long side. Cut into 12 slices. Place slices, cut side down, in a 13-in. x 9-in. x 2-in. baking pan. For topping, combine water, brown sugar and cinnamon in a saucepan. Bring to a boil; remove from the heat. Stir in the cream. Carefully pour hot topping over dumplings. Bake, uncovered, at 350° for 35 minutes or until bubbly. (Center will jiggle when dumplings are hot out of the oven but will set as dumplings stand for a few minutes.) Serve warm. **Yield:** 12 servings.

SQUASH CUSTARD PIE

Mary Kelly, Hopland, California

(PICTURED ON PAGE 133)

1 cup mashed cooked winter
 squash
1 cup whipping *or* heavy cream
1 cup sugar
3 eggs, lightly beaten
1 teaspoon ground ginger
1 teaspoon ground cinnamon
1/2 teaspoon ground nutmeg
Dash salt
1 unbaked pastry shell (9 inches)
Whipped cream *or* topping

In a mixing bowl, combine all ingredients except for the pie pastry and additional whipped cream. Pour into the pastry; bake at 375° for 10 minutes. Reduce heat to 350°; bake for 45 minutes or until set. Cool on a wire rack. Chill. Serve with a dollop of whipped cream. **Yield:** 8 servings.

QUICK CHOCOLATE MOUSSE

Elsie Shell, Topeka, Indiana

1 can (14 ounces) sweetened
 condensed milk
1 package (3.9 ounces) instant
 chocolate pudding mix
1 cup cold water
1 cup whipping cream, whipped

In a large mixing bowl, combine milk, pudding mix and water. Beat until well mixed. Chill for 5 minutes. Fold in whipped cream. Spoon into individual serving dishes. **Yield:** 4-6 servings.

SWEET juicy oranges, tart lemons and other citrus fruits add zest to a variety of tangy recipes. You can count on citrus around the clock—including breakfast muffins…luncheon salads…magnificent main courses…delectable desserts…and more!

CITRUS STARS.
Clockwise from lower left: **Zesty Lemon Curd** (recipe on page 147), **Mexican Carnitas** (recipe on page 36), **Lemon/Orange Ice** (recipe on page 224), **Orange Mini Muffins** (recipe on page 152), **Orange Lemonade** (recipe on page 17), **Lemon Custard in Meringue Cups** (recipe on page 224), **Citrus-Baked Cornish Hens** (recipe on page 76) and **Orange and Red Onion Salad** (recipe on page 58).

LEMON/ORANGE ICE

Karen Zwieg, Lowry, Minnesota

(PICTURED ON PAGE 222)

Juice of 6 lemons
Juice of 7 oranges
3-1/2 cups sugar
1 pint whipping cream
1 quart whole milk

In a large bowl, combine juices, sugar, cream and milk. Mix well. Pour mixture into an ice cream freezer and freeze according to manufacturer's directions. Serve immediately for a soft consistency or place in refrigerator/freezer. **Yield:** 2 quarts.

LEMON CUSTARD IN MERINGUE CUPS

Marie Frangipane, Eugene, Oregon

(PICTURED ON PAGE 223)

3 eggs, *separated*
1/2 teaspoon vinegar
1/4 teaspoon vanilla extract
1/4 teaspoon salt, *divided*
2 cups sugar, *divided*
1/3 cup cornstarch
1-1/2 cups water
1 tablespoon grated lemon peel
6 tablespoons fresh lemon juice
2 tablespoons butter *or* margarine
Sweetened whipped cream

In a mixing bowl, combine egg whites, vinegar, vanilla and 1/8 teaspoon salt. Beat until soft peaks form. Gradually add 1 cup sugar; continue beating until stiff peaks form. Cover baking sheet with plain brown paper. Spoon egg white mixture into eight mounds on paper. Shape into cups with a spoon. Bake at 300° for 35 minutes. Turn oven off; let shells dry in oven at least 1 hour with the door closed. Remove shells from paper. When thoroughly cooled, store in an airtight container. For custard, combine cornstarch and remaining salt and sugar. Add water and mix well. Cook and stir until thick and bubbly, about 2 minutes. Beat egg yolks; add a small amount of hot mixture. Return to saucepan. Cook and stir 2 minutes longer. Remove from the heat; blend in lemon peel, juice and butter. Chill. Just before serving, fill meringue shells with custard and top with whipped cream. **Yield:** 8 servings.

BUTTERNUT APPLE CRISP

Michele Van Dewerker, Roseboom, New York

(PICTURED ON PAGE 73)

3/4 cup packed brown sugar, *divided*
2 tablespoons lemon juice
1 teaspoon ground cinnamon
1/2 teaspoon salt
3 to 4 cups peeled sliced uncooked butternut squash (about 1-1/2 pounds)
1 can (20 ounces) apple pie filling
1/2 cup all-purpose flour
1/2 cup quick-cooking oats
6 tablespoons butter *or* margarine, softened

Combine 1/2 cup brown sugar, lemon juice, cinnamon, salt, squash and pie filling. Spoon into 10-in. x 6-in. x 2-in. greased baking dish. Cover and bake at 375° for 30 minutes. Combine remaining ingredients until crumbly. Sprinkle over squash mixture. Bake, uncovered, about 45 minutes longer or until squash is tender. Serve warm. **Yield:** 8 servings.

WRINKLE REDUCTION. To avoid wrinkled skins on apples when baking them for a dessert, cut a few slits in the skin to allow for expansion.

GOLDEN LEMON GLAZED CHEESECAKE

Betty Jacques, Hemet, California

(PICTURED ON PAGE 102)

CRUST:
2-1/2 cups graham cracker crumbs (30 crackers)
1/4 cup sugar
10 tablespoons butter *or* margarine, melted
FILLING:
3 packages (8 ounces *each*) cream cheese, softened
3 eggs
1-1/4 cups sugar
3 tablespoons fresh lemon juice
1 teaspoon vanilla extract
1 tablespoon grated lemon peel
GLAZE:
1 lemon, sliced paper-thin
3 cups water, *divided*
1 cup sugar
2 tablespoons plus 2 teaspoons cornstarch
1/3 cup fresh lemon juice

For crust, combine all ingredients and press into the bottom and 2 in. up the

sides of a 9-in. springform pan. Bake at 350° for 5 minutes. Cool. In a mixing bowl, beat cream cheese at medium-high speed until smooth. Add eggs, one at a time, beating well after each addition. Gradually add sugar, then lemon juice and vanilla. Mix well. Fold in lemon peel; pour into crust. Bake at 350° for 40 minutes. Cool to room temperature; refrigerate until thoroughly chilled, at least 4 hours. For the glaze, remove any seeds from lemon slices. Reserve 1 slice for garnish; coarsely chop remaining slices. Place in a saucepan with 2 cups water. Bring to a boil; simmer, uncovered, for 15 minutes. Drain and discard liquid. In a saucepan, combine sugar and cornstarch; stir in remaining water, lemon juice and lemon pulp. Bring to a boil, stirring constantly, and boil 3 minutes. Chill until cool, stirring occasionally. Pour over cheesecake and garnish with reserved lemon slice. Chill until ready to serve. **Yield:** 16 servings.

ANGEL FOOD CANDY

Shelly Matthys, New Richmond, Wisconsin

(PICTURED ON PAGE 142)

1 cup sugar
1 cup dark corn syrup
1 tablespoon vinegar
1 tablespoon baking soda
1 pound chocolate almond bark, melted

In a heavy saucepan, combine sugar, corn syrup and vinegar. Cook over medium heat, stirring constantly, until sugar dissolves. Cook without stirring until the temperature reaches 300° (hard crack stage) on a candy thermometer. Do not overcook. Remove from the heat and quickly stir in baking soda. Pour into a buttered 13-in. x 9-in. x 2-in. baking pan. Do not spread candy; mixture will not fill pan. When cool, break into bite-size pieces. Dip into melted chocolate; place on waxed paper until the chocolate is firm. Store candy tightly covered. **Yield:** 1-1/2 pounds.

LITTLE GIRL PIES

Pat Nofsinger, Charlotte, North Carolina

CRUST:
1 cup sugar
1/2 cup shortening
1 egg
1/2 cup milk
1 teaspoon vanilla extract
3-1/2 cups all-purpose flour
4 teaspoons baking powder
1/2 teaspoon salt

FILLING:
- 1/2 cup sugar
- 1 tablespoon cornstarch
- 1/2 cup water
- 1 cup raisins

In a mixing bowl, cream sugar and shortening. Add egg, milk and vanilla; mix well. Combine dry ingredients; add to creamed mixture and beat well. Chill. Meanwhile, for filling, combine sugar and cornstarch in a saucepan. Add water; stir to dissolve. Add raisins; cook and stir until mixture comes to a boil and thickens, about 3 minutes. Set aside to cool. Divide chilled dough into thirds. Roll one-third out on a lightly floured board to 1/8-in. thickness. Cut into 3-in. circles. Using a thimble, cut small holes in the center of half of the circles. Place 1 teaspoon filling on solid circles; top each with a circle that has a hole. Pinch edges together to seal. Repeat with remaining dough and filling. Bake on ungreased cookie sheets at 375° for 15-17 minutes or until lightly browned. **Yield:** 2 dozen cookies.

PRALINE CHEESECAKE

Jane Owens, Winona, Mississippi

- 1-1/2 cups graham cracker crumbs
- 3 tablespoons sugar
- 3 tablespoons butter *or* margarine, melted
- 3 packages (8 ounces *each*) cream cheese, softened
- 3/4 cup packed brown sugar
- 2 tablespoons all-purpose flour
- 3 eggs
- 2 teaspoons vanilla extract
- 1/2 cup chopped pecans, toasted

Whipped cream
Whole pecans

Combine cracker crumbs, sugar and butter. Press into the bottom of a 9-in. springform pan. Bake at 350° for 10 minutes. Set aside. Meanwhile, beat cream cheese until smooth in a large mixing bowl. Gradually add brown sugar and flour. Add eggs, one at a time, beating well after each addition. Add vanilla. Stir in chopped pecans. Pour into crust; bake at 350° for 40-45 minutes or until golden brown. Cool 20 minutes. Refrigerate overnight. Just before serving, garnish with whipped cream and pecans. **Yield:** 12-16 servings.

FRESH PEACH CRISP

Wilma Beller, Hamilton, Ohio

- 6 fresh peaches (about 1-1/2 pounds), sliced
- 1/4 cup sugar
- 2 teaspoons lemon juice

- 1/8 teaspoon almond extract
- 3/4 cup all-purpose flour
- 3/4 cup packed brown sugar
- 1/4 teaspoon salt
- 1/3 cup butter or margarine

Arrange peaches in a lightly greased 2-qt. baking dish. Combine sugar, lemon juice and almond extract; drizzle over peaches. In a small mixing bowl, combine flour, brown sugar and salt; cut in butter with a pastry blender until mixture is crumbly. Sprinkle over the peaches. Bake, uncovered, at 350° for 40-50 minutes or until peaches are tender. **Yield:** 8 servings.

RHUBARB CUSTARD PIE

Lucile Proctor, Panguitch, Utah

- 3 eggs
- 3 tablespoons milk
- 2 cups sugar
- 3 tablespoons quick-cooking tapioca

Pastry for double-crust pie (9 inches)
- 4 cups diced rhubarb
- 2 teaspoons butter *or* margarine

Light cream, optional
Cinnamon-sugar, optional

In a mixing bowl, beat eggs lightly; blend in milk. Combine sugar and tapioca; stir into egg mixture. Place bottom pastry in a pie plate; add the rhubarb. Pour egg mixture over rhubarb. Dot with butter. Cover with top pastry. Make slits in top for steam to escape. If desired, brush pastry with light cream. Bake at 425° for 15 minutes; reduce heat to 350°. Bake 35-40 minutes longer or until lightly browned. Sprinkle with cinnamon-sugar if desired. Cool on a wire rack. Store in the refrigerator. **Yield:** 6-8 servings.

BROWNIE PUDDING

Barbara Chamberlain, Lawrenceville, Georgia

SAUCE:
- 1-1/2 cups boiling water
- 1/2 cup packed brown sugar
- 1/4 cup baking cocoa

CAKE:
- 1 cup all-purpose flour
- 1/2 cup sugar
- 1/4 cup baking cocoa

- 1-1/2 teaspoons baking powder
- 1/4 teaspoon salt
- 1 egg, beaten
- 1/3 cup milk
- 2 tablespoons butter *or* margarine, melted
- 1 teaspoon vanilla extract
- 1/2 cup semisweet chocolate chips

Whipped cream *or* vanilla ice cream

In a saucepan, combine sauce ingredients and keep warm. In a mixing bowl, combine flour, sugar, cocoa, baking powder and salt. In a small bowl, combine egg, milk, butter and vanilla; add to dry ingredients and stir until moistened. Fold in chocolate chips. Pour into a greased 1-1/2-qt. baking dish. Pour warm sauce over batter. Do not stir. Bake at 350° for 35-40 minutes or until cake is firm and floats in sauce. Let rest 10 minutes. Serve warm with whipped cream or ice cream. **Yield:** 8-10 servings.

QUICK RICE PUDDING

Betty Greene, Holland, Michigan

(PICTURED BELOW)

- 1 package (3.4 ounces) instant vanilla pudding mix
- 2 cups cold milk
- 1 cup cold cooked rice
- 1/2 cup raisins

Whipped topping
Maraschino cherries

In a mixing bowl, combine pudding mix and milk; beat for 1-2 minutes until well blended. Stir in rice and raisins. Spoon pudding into individual bowls. Chill. Garnish with whipped topping and a cherry. **Yield:** 6 servings.

CREAMY CONCOCTION. Simple-to-prepare Quick Rice Pudding pleases kids of all ages!

DOWN-HOME country cooking begins with a meaty main course—like this tender pork roast with a sweet and spicy rub. Old-fashioned potato pancakes and cool, creamy cucumber salad are unforgettable side dishes. And for a deliciously different dessert, you'll want to try authentic Babka (or noodle pudding).

FOND FEAST.
Clockwise from the bottom: **Country Potato Pancakes** (recipe on page 126), **Spiced Pork Roast with Applesauce Glaze** (recipe on page 87), **Sour Cream Cucumber Salad** (recipe on page 47) and **Babka** (recipe on page 227).

BABKA
(NOODLE PUDDING)

Lydia Robotewskyj, Franklin, Wisconsin

(PICTURED AT LEFT)

1 pound egg noodles *or* spaghetti
1/2 cup butter *or* margarine, melted
10 eggs
3/4 cup milk
1 cup sugar
Cherry, apricot *or* strawberry preserves

Cook noodles in boiling salted water until almost done; drain. Place in a mixing bowl with butter; toss to coat. In a separate bowl, beat eggs, milk and sugar until well blended. Combine with noodles. Pour into a greased 13-in. x 9-in. x 2-in. baking dish. Bake at 350° for about 35 minutes or until puffy and noodles begin to brown at edges. Cut into squares and serve hot or cold with fruit preserves. **Yield:** 12 servings.

STRAWBERRY
ANGEL DESSERT

Mrs. J. Jelen, Minneota, Minnesota

1 envelope unflavored gelatin
3/4 cup cold water
1/2 cup sugar
1 package (10 ounces) frozen sliced strawberries, thawed
1 carton (8 ounces) frozen whipped topping, thawed
5 cups angel food cake cubes
Fresh strawberries, optional
Fresh mint, optional

In a saucepan, combine gelatin and cold water; let stand 5 minutes to soften. Heat and stir over low heat just until gelatin dissolves. Remove from the heat; add sugar. Stir until dissolved. Stir in undrained strawberries. Chill until partially thickened. Fold in whipped topping. Place cake cubes in a mixing bowl; pour strawberry mixture over cake and mix gently. Pour into an ungreased 8-in. square baking dish. Chill until firm. Garnish with fresh strawberries and mint if desired. **Yield:** 9 servings.

PATRIOTIC DESSERT

Flo Burtnett, Gage, Oklahoma

1 cup all-purpose flour
1 cup finely chopped pecans
1/2 cup butter *or* margarine, softened

1 cup confectioners' sugar
1 package (8 ounces) cream cheese, softened
1 carton (8 ounces) frozen whipped topping, thawed, *divided*
1 package (5.1 ounces) instant vanilla pudding mix
1-1/2 cups cold milk
1/2 cup fresh blueberries
3 cups fresh strawberries, halved

Combine flour, pecans and butter. Press into the bottom of an ungreased 13-in. x 9-in. x 2-in. baking pan. Bake at 350° for 20 minutes. Cool. In a mixing bowl, cream sugar and cream cheese. Fold in half of the whipped topping; mix until smooth. Spread over crust. In another mixing bowl, beat pudding and milk until smooth. Spread over cream cheese layer. Cover with remaining whipped topping. Decorate with blueberries and strawberries to resemble a flag, using blueberries as stars and strawberries as stripes. Chill at least 1 hour before serving. **Yield:** 12-15 servings.

UPSTATE CHOCOLATE
PEANUT BUTTER PIE

Kim Scott, Byron, New York

1 cup sugar
6 tablespoons all-purpose flour
1/2 teaspoon salt
2 cups milk
3 egg yolks, beaten
1 teaspoon vanilla extract
2 tablespoons creamy peanut butter
1 ounce semisweet chocolate, melted
1 graham cracker crust (9 inches), baked and cooled
Whipped cream
Chopped peanuts

In the top of a double boiler, over hot but not boiling water, combine sugar, flour and salt. Slowly add milk and cook 10 minutes, stirring constantly. Pour a little hot milk mixture into the egg yolks. Immediately add egg yolk mixture to double boiler. Cook 4 minutes, stirring constantly. Stir in vanilla. Cool about 10 minutes. Divide mixture in half. To one half add peanut butter; stir well. To the remaining half add the melted chocolate. Allow mixtures to cool completely. Fill pie crust first with peanut butter mixture, then chocolate layer. Chill before serving. Top with whipped cream and nuts. **Yield:** 8 servings.

RHUBARB CRUMB TART

Rebecca Gairns, Prince George, British Columbia

CRUST:
1 cup all-purpose flour
3 tablespoons confectioners' sugar
1 teaspoon baking powder
1/3 cup butter *or* margarine
1 egg, beaten
4 teaspoons milk
FILLING:
3 cups diced raw rhubarb
1 package (3 ounces) strawberry-flavored gelatin
TOPPING:
1 cup sugar
1/2 cup all-purpose flour
1/3 cup butter *or* margarine

Preheat oven to 350°. For crust, mix flour, confectioners' sugar and baking powder in a medium bowl. Cut in butter until mixture resembles coarse crumbs. Add egg and milk; stir until a ball forms. Pat into a greased 11-in. x 7-in. x 2-in. baking pan. Place rhubarb in crust. Sprinkle gelatin over rhubarb. In a small bowl, mix topping ingredients together until crumbly. Sprinkle over rhubarb mixture. Bake at 350° for 45-50 minutes. Allow to cool until firm. **Yield:** 12-15 servings.

RAISIN/DATE
BREAD PUDDING

Dawn Green, Hopkins, Michigan

(PICTURED ON PAGE 52)

4 cups milk
5 cups day-old bread cubes
1 cup sugar
8 eggs, beaten
1/2 cup butter *or* margarine, melted
1/4 cup chopped dates
1/4 cup raisins
1 teaspoon vanilla extract
1/2 teaspoon ground cinnamon
Dash salt
Dash ground nutmeg
Additional sugar, cinnamon and nutmeg, optional
Whipped cream, optional

In a large bowl, pour milk over bread. Add sugar, eggs, butter, dates, raisins, vanilla, cinnamon, salt and nutmeg; stir to mix well. Pour into a greased 13-in. x 9-in. x 2-in. baking dish. If desired, sprinkle top with additional sugar, cinnamon and nutmeg. Bake at 350° for 55 minutes or until golden brown and a knife inserted near the center comes out clean. Serve warm with whipped cream if desired. **Yield:** 10-12 servings.

CHERRY BERRY PIE

Mamie Palmer, Sault Sainte Marie, Michigan

(PICTURED ON PAGE 136)

1 can (16 ounces) pitted red cherries
1 package (10 ounces) frozen red raspberries
3/4 cup sugar
3 tablespoons cornstarch
3 tablespoons butter *or* margarine
1/4 teaspoon almond extract
1/4 teaspoon red food coloring
Pastry for double-crust pie (9 inches)

Drain cherries and raspberries; reserve 1-1/4 cups juice and set fruit aside. In a saucepan, combine sugar and cornstarch; gradually stir in juice. Cook and stir over medium heat until the mixture begins to boil. Cook and stir 2 minutes longer. Remove from the heat; stir in butter, extract and food coloring. Gently fold in fruit. Cool slightly. Pour filling into pie crust and top with a lattice crust. Bake at 375° for 45 minutes or until bubbly. Cool. **Yield:** 8 servings.

FROZEN ICE CREAM DELIGHT

Sue Bracken, State College, Pennsylvania

2-1/2 cups cream-filled chocolate cookie crumbs, *divided*
1/2 cup butter *or* margarine, melted
1/2 cup sugar
1/2 gallon chocolate, coffee *or* vanilla ice cream, softened
CHOCOLATE SAUCE:
2 cups confectioners' sugar
2/3 cup semisweet chocolate chips
1 can (12 ounces) evaporated milk
1/2 cup butter *or* margarine
1 teaspoon vanilla extract

1-1/2 cups salted peanuts
1 carton (8 ounces) frozen whipped topping, thawed

Combine 2 cups cookie crumbs with butter and sugar. Press into the bottom of a 13-in. x 9-in. x 2-in. baking pan. Freeze for 15 minutes. Spread ice cream over crumbs; freeze until firm, about 3 hours. Meanwhile, combine first four sauce ingredients in a saucepan; bring to a boil. Boil for 8 minutes. Remove from the heat and stir in vanilla; allow to cool to room temperature. Spoon sauce over ice cream; sprinkle with nuts. Freeze until firm. Spread whipped topping over nuts and sprinkle with remaining cookie crumbs. Freeze at least 3 hours before serving. Can be stored in the freezer for up to a week. **Yield:** 12-16 servings.

PRAIRIE APPLE CRUNCH

Florence Palmer, Paris, Illinois

6 large baking apples, peeled and sliced
1/2 cup sugar
1/2 teaspoon ground cinnamon
1/2 teaspoon ground nutmeg
Dash salt
1 cup packed brown sugar
1 cup all-purpose flour
1/2 cup butter *or* margarine, melted
Cream, optional

Place apples in a greased 12-in. x 7-1/2-in. x 2-in. baking dish. Sprinkle with the sugar, cinnamon, nutmeg and salt. Combine brown sugar, flour and butter; sprinkle over apple mixture. Bake at 350° for 40-45 minutes or until apples are tender. Serve warm or at room temperature, with cream if desired. **Yield:** 10-12 servings.

COCONUT CREAM PIE

Vera Moffitt, Oskaloosa, Kansas

3/4 cup sugar
3 tablespoons all-purpose flour
1/8 teaspoon salt
3 cups milk
3 eggs, beaten
1-1/2 cups flaked coconut, toasted, *divided*
1 tablespoon butter *or* margarine
1-1/2 teaspoons vanilla extract
1 pastry shell (9 inches), baked

In a medium saucepan, combine sugar, flour and salt. Stir in milk; cook and stir over medium-high heat until thickened and bubbly. Reduce heat; cook and stir 2 minutes longer. Remove from the heat; gradually stir about 1 cup of hot mixture into beaten eggs. Return all to saucepan; cook and stir over medium heat until nearly boiling. Reduce heat; cook and stir about 2 minutes more. Do not boil. Remove from the heat; stir in 1 cup coconut, butter and vanilla. Pour into pie shell; sprinkle with remaining coconut. Chill for several hours before serving. Refrigerate leftovers. **Yield:** 6-8 servings.

STRAWBERRY ICE CREAM

Kimberly Whitham, Moscow, Kansas

6 tablespoons all-purpose flour
3 cups sugar, *divided*
1 teaspoon salt
6 eggs
4 cups milk
1-1/2 pints strawberries, hulled
2 tablespoons lemon juice
4 cups half-and-half cream
2 tablespoons vanilla extract
Red food coloring

In a heavy saucepan and using a whisk, combine flour, 2 cups sugar and salt. Beat in eggs and milk until well blended. Cook over medium heat, stirring constantly, until mixture thickens and coats a spoon (about 45 minutes). Do not boil. Cover with plastic wrap. Allow to cool for at least 2 hours. Meanwhile, in a medium bowl and using a potato masher, crush berries with lemon juice and remaining sugar. Let stand for 1 hour. Pour cream, vanilla, food coloring, egg mixture and berry mixture into an ice cream freezer. Freeze according to manufacturer's directions. **Yield:** 3 quarts.

OUT OF WHIPPING CREAM? Add sliced bananas to the white of an egg; then beat until stiff. Use this creamy concoction anywhere you'd use whipping cream.

INDIVIDUAL CHERRY CHEESECAKES

Marian Platt, Sequim, Washington

24 vanilla wafer cookies
2 packages (8 ounces *each*) cream cheese, softened
3/4 cup sugar
2 eggs
1 teaspoon vanilla extract
1 can (21 ounces) cherry pie filling
Whipped topping

Place one cookie each in the bottom of 24 greased muffin cups. In a mixing bowl, beat cream cheese and sugar until smooth. Add eggs and vanilla; beat well. Divide filling into each muffin cup. Bake at 375° for 20 minutes. Chill before removing from cups. To serve, top each cheesecake with pie filling and a spoonful of whipped topping. **Yield:** 24 servings.

GLAZED PEACH PIE

Trudy Dunn, Dallas, Texas

1 cup sugar
1/4 cup cornstarch
Dash salt
Dash ground nutmeg
2 tablespoons water
1 tablespoon lemon juice
2-1/2 cups pureed peeled fresh peaches
1 pastry shell (9 inches), baked
3-1/2 cups sliced peeled fresh peaches

In a saucepan, combine sugar, cornstarch, salt and nutmeg. Stir in water, lemon juice and pureed peaches. Cook over medium heat, stirring constantly, about 5 minutes or until mixture is thickened. Pour all but 1/2 cup of glaze into the pie shell. Top with sliced peaches and brush with reserved glaze. Chill for at least 3 hours. **Yield:** 8 servings.

GRAMMY GILMAN'S RAISIN PIE

Ruth Bolduc, Conway, New Hampshire

1 cup sugar
3 tablespoons all-purpose flour
1-1/2 cups cold water
1 cup raisins
1 tablespoon butter or margarine
1 tablespoon vinegar
Pastry for double-crust pie (8 inches)

In a saucepan, combine sugar and flour. Add all remaining ingredients except crust; cook over medium heat, stirring constantly, until thickened. Pour into a prepared shell. Cut several slits in top crust and position over filling. Seal. Bake at 400° for about 45 minutes or until golden. **Yield:** 6 servings.

LUSCIOUS LEMON PIE

Mary Wharton, Shreve, Ohio

1 cup sugar
3 tablespoons cornstarch
Dash salt
1 cup milk
3 egg yolks, slightly beaten
1/3 cup lemon juice
1/4 cup butter

Grated peel of 1 lemon
1 cup (8 ounces) sour cream
1 pastry shell (9 inches), baked
TOPPING:
2/3 cup whipping cream
2 tablespoons confectioners' sugar
1/8 teaspoon almond flavoring, optional

In the top of a double boiler, combine sugar, cornstarch and salt. Stir in milk, egg yolks and lemon juice. Cook and stir over boiling water until thickened and bubbly. Cook and stir 3 minutes longer. Remove from the heat and stir in butter and lemon peel. Cool, stirring occasionally. When mixture is room temperature, stir in sour cream. Pour into shell and refrigerate several hours or overnight. For topping, whip cream until thick; beat in sugar and almond flavoring if desired. Continue to beat until stiff. Spread or pipe with pastry bag on pie before serving. **Yield:** 6-8 servings.

GRANDMA BUELAH'S APPLE DUMPLINGS

Jenny Hughson, Mitchell, Nebraska

Pastry for double-crust pie
6 small cooking apples, peeled and cored
1/3 cup sugar
2 tablespoons half-and-half cream
3/4 cup maple or maple-flavored syrup, warmed

On a floured surface, roll out pastry to an 18-in. x 12-in. rectangle. Cut into six 6-in. squares. Place an apple on each square. Combine sugar and cream; spoon into apple center. Moisten edges of pastry; fold up the corners to center and pinch to seal. Place on an ungreased 13-in. x 9-in. x 2-in. baking pan. Bake at 450° for 15 minutes. Reduce heat to 350° and continue baking until done, about 30 minutes. Baste dumplings with syrup twice during last 30 minutes. Serve warm. **Yield:** 6 servings.

APPLE CHERRY COBBLER

Eleanore Hill, Fresno, California

(PICTURED ON PAGE 40)

1 egg, beaten
1/2 cup sugar

1/2 cup milk
2 tablespoons vegetable oil
1 cup all-purpose flour
2-1/4 teaspoons baking powder
1 can (21 ounces) apple pie filling
1 can (21 ounces) cherry pie filling
1 tablespoon lemon juice
1 teaspoon vanilla extract
TOPPING:
1/3 cup packed brown sugar
3 tablespoons all-purpose flour
1 teaspoon ground cinnamon
2 tablespoons butter or margarine, softened

In a bowl, combine first four ingredients. Combine flour and baking powder; add to egg mixture and blend well. Pour into a greased 13-in. x 9-in. x 2-in. baking pan. Combine pie fillings, lemon juice and vanilla; spoon over batter. For topping, combine all ingredients; sprinkle over filling. Bake at 350° for 40-45 minutes or until bubbly and cake tests done. If necessary, cover edges with foil to prevent over-browning. **Yield:** 12-16 servings.

MAPLE SUGAR PUMPKIN PIE

Martha Boudah, Essex Center, Vermont

1 can (16 ounces) solid-pack pumpkin
1 cup sugar
1 cup milk
2 tablespoons maple syrup
2 tablespoons all-purpose flour
1 tablespoon butter or margarine, softened
1/2 teaspoon ground cinnamon
1/2 teaspoon ground nutmeg
1/2 teaspoon ground ginger
2 eggs
1 unbaked pastry shell (9 inches)
Whipped cream, optional

In a mixing bowl combine all ingredients except last two. Pour into the pie shell. Bake at 425° for 15 minutes. Reduce heat to 350° and continue baking for about 45 minutes or until a knife inserted near the center comes out clean. Cool to room temperature. Refrigerate. Garnish with whipped cream if desired. **Yield:** 8 servings.

FROM spicy salsa to deep-dish pie, cherries add a delicious touch of color to tables across the country. And the dishes shown here will brighten up meals from breakfast to dinner—and right on through dessert.

BRIGHT IDEAS.
Clockwise from lower left: **Northwest Cherry Salsa** (recipe on page 143), **Creamy Cherry Cheesecake** (recipe on page 232), **Cherry/Almond Ham Glaze** (recipe on page 146), **Easy Cherry Fruit Soup** (recipe on page 24), **Cherry Cinnamon Dessert Ring** (recipe on page 232), **Cherry/Nut Breakfast Rolls** (recipe on page 154), **Cherry Chewbilees** (recipe on page 232) and **Deep-Dish Cherry Pie** (recipe on page 232).

CREAMY CHERRY CHEESECAKE

Julie Sibley, Kenai, Alaska

(PICTURED ON PAGE 230)

CRUST:
- 1-1/2 cups graham cracker crumbs (21 squares)
- 1/4 cup sugar
- 6 tablespoons butter *or* margarine, melted

FILLING:
- 2 packages (8 ounces *each*) cream cheese, softened
- 2 eggs
- 1/2 cup sugar
- 1 teaspoon vanilla extract

SOUR CREAM TOPPING:
- 1 cup (8 ounces) sour cream
- 1/4 cup sugar
- 1 teaspoon vanilla extract

CHERRY TOPPING:
- 1/2 cup sugar
- 2 tablespoons cornstarch
- 1 can (16 ounces) pitted tart red cherries, juice drained and reserved
- 1 teaspoon lemon juice

Few drops red food coloring

Combine all crust ingredients. Press onto the bottom and one-third the way up the sides of a 9-in. springform pan. Set aside. For filling, beat cream cheese until smooth. Add eggs, sugar and vanilla; beat until smooth. Pour into prepared crust. Bake at 375° for 20 minutes. Remove from oven; cool 15 minutes. Meanwhile, combine all sour cream topping ingredients. Spread over filling. Bake at 475° for 10 minutes. Cool to room temperature; cover and chill 10-12 hours. For cherry topping, combine sugar and cornstarch in a saucepan; blend in the cherry juice. Heat, stirring constantly, until thickened. Remove from heat; stir in lemon juice, food coloring and cherries. Cool 5 minutes. Spread on top of cheesecake; chill 2 hours. **Yield:** 10 servings.

CHERRY CHEWBILEES

Debbi Smith, Crossett, Arkansas

(PICTURED ON PAGE 231)

CRUST:
- 1-1/4 cups all-purpose flour
- 1/2 cup packed brown sugar
- 1/2 cup butter-flavored shortening
- 1 cup chopped walnuts, *divided*
- 1/2 cup flaked coconut

FILLING:
- 2 packages (8 ounces *each*) cream cheese, softened
- 2/3 cup sugar

- 2 eggs
- 2 teaspoons vanilla extract
- 2 cans (21 ounces *each*) cherry pie filling

In a bowl, combine flour and brown sugar; cut in shortening until fine crumbs form. Stir in 1/2 cup nuts and coconut. Reserve 1/2 cup crumb mixture for topping. Press remaining mixture into the bottom of a greased 13-in. x 9-in. x 2-in. baking pan. Bake at 350° for 12-15 minutes or until lightly browned. Meanwhile, for filling, beat cream cheese, sugar, eggs and vanilla in a mixing bowl until smooth. Spread over the hot crust. Bake 15 minutes. Spread pie filling on top. Combine remaining nuts and reserved crumbs; sprinkle over cherries. Bake 15 minutes more. Cool. Refrigerate until serving. **Yield:** 20 servings.

CHERRY CINNAMON DESSERT RING

Catherine Aitken, Courtenay, British Columbia

(PICTURED ON PAGE 231)

- 3 cups fresh *or* frozen pitted dark sweet cherries
- 3-1/4 cups water, *divided*
- 1 cup sugar
- 2 cinnamon sticks
- 1 teaspoon almond extract
- 2 envelopes unflavored gelatin

Sweetened whipped cream

In a saucepan, combine cherries with 3 cups of water, sugar and cinnamon. Bring to a boil; reduce heat, cover and simmer 15 minutes. Remove from the heat. Remove cinnamon sticks and stir in extract. Set aside. Place remaining water in a saucepan. Sprinkle gelatin over water; let stand 1 minute. Heat until dissolved. Stir into cherry mixture and mix well. Refrigerate until mixture begins to thicken, stirring occasionally to distribute cherries evenly. Spoon into a 5-1/2-cup ring mold. Refrigerate until set, about 3-4 hours. Turn onto a serving platter. Serve with whipped cream. **Yield:** 20 servings.

DEEP-DISH CHERRY PIE

Lillian Heston, Warren, New Jersey

(PICTURED ON PAGE 231)

- 6 cups pitted tart red cherries
- 3/4 cup sugar
- 3/4 cup packed brown sugar
- 3 tablespoons cornstarch
- 1 teaspoon almond extract

Few drops red food coloring, optional

Dash salt

- 3 to 4 tablespoons butter *or* margarine

CRUST:
- 1-1/2 cups all-purpose flour
- 1 tablespoon sugar
- 1/2 teaspoon salt
- 1/2 teaspoon ground nutmeg
- 1/2 cup plus 2 tablespoons shortening
- 4 to 5 tablespoons ice water

Milk *or* cream
Additional sugar

In a large mixing bowl, combine cherries, sugars, cornstarch, extract, food coloring if desired and salt. Place in a greased 1-1/2-qt. to 2-qt. casserole. Dot with butter. Set aside. For crust, combine flour, sugar, salt and nutmeg. Cut in shortening. Add water, a little at a time, until a dough forms. Do not overmix. Roll out on a floured surface to fit the top of the casserole. Place on top of the cherries, pressing against the sides of the dish. Cut decorative designs or slits in center of crust. Brush with milk or cream and sprinkle with sugar. Bake at 350° for 1 hour or until crust is golden brown. Cool at least 15 minutes before serving. **Yield:** 8-10 servings.

SPEEDY APPLE CRISP

Lucy Euvrard, Okena, Ohio

- 5 to 6 cups peeled sliced cooking apples
- 1/3 cup butter *or* margarine
- 3/4 cup packed brown sugar
- 1/2 cup all-purpose flour
- 1/2 cup rolled oats
- 1/2 to 1 teaspoon cinnamon

Spread apples in a 9-in. square baking pan. Cut butter into remaining ingredients until the mixture resembles coarse crumbs. Sprinkle over apples. Bake at 375° for 30-35 minutes or until apples are tender and topping is golden. Serve warm. **Yield:** 6-8 servings.

FRUIT PIZZA

Doris Sather, Eleva, Wisconsin

CRUST:
- 1/2 cup butter *or* margarine
- 1/2 cup shortening
- 1 cup sugar
- 1 egg
- 1 teaspoon vanilla extract
- 2 cups all-purpose flour
- 1/2 teaspoon cream of tartar
- 1/2 teaspoon baking soda
- 1/4 teaspoon salt

CREAM FILLING:
- 2 packages (8 ounces *each*) cream cheese, softened

1 cup confectioners' sugar
1 carton (8 ounces) frozen whipped topping, thawed

GLAZE:
1 cup pineapple juice
1 cup orange juice
2 tablespoons cornstarch
1-1/2 cups fresh raspberries
2 kiwifruit, peeled and sliced
2 bananas, sliced
1 pint fresh strawberries, hulled and sliced

In a mixing bowl, cream butter, shortening and sugar. Add egg and vanilla. Combine dry ingredients; blend into creamed mixture. Press dough into a 14-in. or 16-in. pizza pan. Bake at 350° for 8-10 minutes or until light golden brown. Cool. For the filling, whip cream cheese until smooth; add sugar and whipped topping. Spread over crust. For glaze, combine juices with cornstarch; cook and stir until thickened. Reserve 1/2 cup; spread remaining warm glaze over filling. Arrange fruit over glaze and brush reserved glaze over fruit. Chill until ready to serve. **Yield:** 12 servings. **Editor's Note:** If making a day ahead, substitute another seasonal fruit for bananas.

CHOCOLATE COCONUT CREAM PIE

Nancy Reichert, Thomasville, Georgia

1 unbaked pastry shell (9 inches)
2/3 cup sugar
1/3 cup cornstarch
1/4 teaspoon salt
3 cups milk
3 egg yolks
1 tablespoon butter *or* margarine
2 teaspoons vanilla extract
1/2 cup flaked coconut

CHOCOLATE LAYER:
3 tablespoons baking cocoa
3 tablespoons sugar
2 tablespoons milk

MERINGUE:
3 egg whites
1/4 teaspoon cream of tartar
6 tablespoons sugar

Bake pie pastry; cool. Meanwhile, in a saucepan, combine sugar, cornstarch and salt; stir in milk. Cook and stir over medium-high heat until thickened and bubbly. Reduce heat; cook and stir 2 minutes more. Remove from the heat. Beat egg yolks lightly. Stir a little of the hot mixture into the yolks; return all to saucepan. Bring to a gentle boil. Cook and stir 2 minutes more. Remove from the heat. Stir in butter and vanilla. Pour 1-1/2 cups mixture into small bowl; add coconut to bowl and set aside. Com-

bine chocolate layer ingredients; blend into remaining mixture in saucepan. Return to heat; cook and stir until mixture begins to boil. Remove from the heat; spread 1 cup over bottom of pie crust. Top with coconut mixture and finish with remaining chocolate mixture. For meringue, beat egg whites with cream of tartar until foamy. Gradually add sugar, beating until stiff peaks form. Spread over hot filling, sealing to edges of pie crust. Bake at 350° for 12-15 minutes or until lightly browned. Cool to room temperature; chill several hours before serving. **Yield:** 8 servings.

PERFECT APPLE PIE

Wilma Beller, Hamilton, Ohio

2 cups all-purpose flour
2 teaspoons sugar
1-1/4 teaspoons salt
2/3 cup vegetable oil
3 tablespoons milk
6 to 7 tart baking apples
3/4 to 1 cup sugar
2 tablespoons all-purpose flour
1/2 to 1 teaspoon ground cinnamon
Dash ground nutmeg
Dash salt
2 tablespoons butter *or* margarine

In a 9-in. pie plate, sift together flour, sugar and salt. In a measuring cup, whip oil and milk; pour over flour mixture. Mix with a fork until the dry ingredients are moistened. Remove 1/3 cup; press remaining crumbs evenly over the bottom and sides of pie plate. Set aside. Pare, core and slice apples. Combine sugar, flour, cinnamon, nutmeg and salt; toss with apples. Fill the pie crust with apple mixture. Dot with butter. Sprinkle reserved crumbs over apples. Bake at 400° for 50 minutes or until apples are tender and crust is golden. **Yield:** 8 servings.

BUTTERY BLUEBERRY COBBLER

Marjorie Green, South Haven, Michigan

2 cups fresh or frozen blueberries
1 tablespoon lemon juice
1-1/2 cups sugar, *divided*
1/2 cup butter *or* margarine
1 cup all-purpose flour
2 teaspoons baking powder
1/2 teaspoon salt
3/4 cup milk

1 egg, beaten
Whipped cream or topping

In a saucepan, combine berries, lemon juice and 1/2 cup sugar. Bring to a boil; remove from the heat. Set aside. Put butter in a 12-in. x 7-in. baking pan; place in oven until butter melts. In a small mixing bowl, combine remaining sugar with flour, baking powder, salt, milk and egg. Pour over melted butter. Do not stir. Spoon reserved berry mixture over batter. Do not stir. Bake at 350° for 40-45 minutes or until golden brown. Serve at room temperature with whipped cream or topping. **Yield:** 10-12 servings.

STRAWBERRY RHUBARB ICE CREAM PIE

Connie Fleck, Fort Atkinson, Wisconsin

(PICTURED BELOW)

1 quart vanilla ice cream, softened
1 graham cracker crust (9 inches)
1-1/2 cups sliced fresh *or* frozen rhubarb (1/2-inch pieces)
1/2 cup sugar
1 tablespoon cornstarch
1 tablespoon water
1 pint fresh strawberries, sliced

Spoon ice cream into crust; freeze. Meanwhile, in a saucepan over medium heat, cook rhubarb and sugar, stirring occasionally, until sugar dissolves and mixture boils. Combine cornstarch and water; stir into saucepan. Cook until thickened, stirring constantly. Cook 2 more minutes. Cool. Fold in berries; chill. Spread over ice cream. Let stand 10 minutes at room temperature before cutting. **Yield:** 8 servings.

BEAT THE HEAT. Strawberry Rhubarb Ice Cream Pie makes plain ice cream extraordinary.

MEALS IN MINUTES

In this chapter, country cooks share 18 simple, satisfying meals that can be prepared in 30 minutes or less.

A WEEKLY FAMILY FAVORITE

AS an ex-farm girl, Jean Brenneman of Cedar Rapids, Iowa enjoys trying out different recipes she comes across in various publications.

As the mother of an active toddler, however, with a part-time job outside the home to boot, she sometimes needs to improvise on her own! That's where the "Meal in Minutes" Jean shares here originated.

"After our daughter arrived, our schedule became much more hectic, leaving me little time to prepare elaborate meals," she notes. "I developed this meal so I could have dinner ready within 30 minutes of getting home from work. Then I can enjoy the evening with my family.

"The recipes all came from different sources. But they blended well when I put them together. In fact, my husband says that he *loves* this meal—even though I've been known to serve it as often as once a week!"

When she's not scurrying to make up time in the kitchen, Jean relaxes with reading or cross-stitching.

Give her speedy supper a try at your place the next time your cooking has to be extra quick. You never know...if your hungry crew is like Jean's, you may have a new favorite your family will ask for even when meal-making time *isn't* tight!

PARMESAN NOODLES

8 ounces wide noodles
2 tablespoons butter *or* margarine
1/4 teaspoon garlic powder
1/4 cup grated Parmesan cheese
2 tablespoons minced fresh parsley

Cook noodles according to package directions; drain. Place in a bowl. Immediately add remaining ingredients and toss well. **Yield:** 4 servings.

MARINATED ITALIAN CHICKEN

4 boneless skinless chicken breasts
1/2 cup Italian salad dressing

Place chicken breasts in a shallow pan; pour dressing over. Marinate for 15 minutes. Place chicken on rack of a broiler pan. Broil for 5-7 minutes on each side or until juices run clear. **Yield:** 4 servings.

SWEDISH CREAM

1 package (3.4 ounces) instant vanilla pudding mix
1-1/2 cups cold milk
1 cup plain yogurt
1/8 teaspoon almond extract
2 to 3 cups fresh strawberries, raspberries *or* blueberries

In a mixing bowl, whisk together first four ingredients. Place berries in dessert cups and top with cream mixture, or layer berries and cream in parfait glasses. **Yield:** 4-6 servings.

...toes are browned, about 5-7 min-...s. Top with cheese. Cover and ...ove from the heat; let stand for sev-... minutes. Sprinkle with parsley ...re serving. **Yield:** 4 servings.

LEMON PEPPER STEAK

4 T-bone *or* New York strip
    steaks (1 inch thick)
...on pepper to taste

...nkle steaks with lemon pepper. Broil ...preheated broiler 3-4 in. from the ... for 5-7 minutes per side or until ...steaks reach desired doneness.
...: 4 servings.

ALMOND PEACH SUNDAE

1 can (16 ounces) sliced peaches
1 tablespoon cornstarch
2 teaspoon ground cinnamon
4 teaspoon ground nutmeg

1/2 teaspoon almond extract
1/4 cup slivered almonds
Vanilla ice cream

Drain peaches and place the liquid in a saucepan. Stir in cornstarch, cinnamon and nutmeg. Cook and stir over medium-high heat until thickened, about 2-3 minutes. Stir in extract, almonds and peaches. Heat through. Serve warm over ice cream. **Yield:** 4-6 servings.

CITRUS BROCCOLI TOSS

2 tablespoons butter *or*
    margarine
1 package (10 ounces) frozen
    cut broccoli, thawed
1-1/2 teaspoons grated orange peel
1-1/2 teaspoons grated lemon peel
Salt and pepper to taste

In a skillet, melt butter over medium heat. Saute broccoli until crisp-tender. Sprinkle with orange and lemon peel, salt and pepper, then toss to coat. Heat through. **Yield:** 4 servings.

Cheese and Onion Potatoes cook up crispy to a pretty golden brown...and—talk about saving time—the potatoes don't even need peeling! Citrus Broccoli Toss has a nice tangy taste, and Almond Peach Sundae is a refreshing, no-fuss finish to a filling meal.

So why not sample this down-home dinner tonight? Lois guarantees it'll be a hit with your family.

CHEESE AND ONION POTATOES

1/4 cup butter *or* margarine
4 medium unpeeled red
    potatoes, sliced 1/4 inch thick
2 tablespoons dried minced
    onion
Pepper to taste
1/3 cup shredded cheddar cheese
Chopped fresh parsley

In a skillet, melt butter over medium-high heat. Add potatoes, onion and pepper; toss to coat. Cover and cook, stirring occasionally, until potatoes are tender, about 10 minutes. Uncover; cook until

A Bushel of Fantastic Flavor

HARVESTTIME has always been "hurry-up time" for South Dakota farm wife Gretchen Kuipers of Platte. Now, her growing family's made the pace at that time of year even a faster one!

"We have two small boys and they keep me on the move all day long," she remarks. "Most days, I have little time for cooking. So I've come to rely on recipes that can be prepared in 30 minutes or less."

One such three-course standby meal Gretchen's cooked up in her own kitchen not only is quick as can be, it gives tried-and-true ground beef a tasty new zing.

"My Stroganoff Sandwich can easily be prepared at a moment's notice,"
reports Gretchen. "I often serve it to my husband as a hearty main dish when he comes in from working in the field late in the afternoon.

"The spinach salad's also speedy to prepare—plus, you can substitute other greens for the spinach if you like. Finally, my fruit salad is a convenient dessert all year-round. Our kids *love* it!"

To learn why, try Gretchen's imaginative menu at your house. You're sure to harvest hurrahs…in a hurry!

STROGANOFF SANDWICH

    1 pound lean ground beef
    1/4 cup chopped onion
    1 teaspoon Worcestershire
      sauce
    1/4 teaspoon garlic powder
    Salt and pepper to taste
    1 can (4 ounces) sliced
      mushrooms, drained
    1 cup (8 ounces) sour cream
    Butter *or* margarine, softened
    1 loaf French bread, cut in half
      lengthwise
    2 medium tomatoes, thinly sliced
    1 medium green pepper, cut
      into rings
    1 cup (4 ounces) shredded
      cheddar cheese

In a skillet, brown beef with onion. Drain. Season with Worcestershire sauce, garlic powder, salt and pepper. Remove from the heat and stir in mushrooms and sour cream; set aside. Butter the cut surface of the bread. Place it with the buttered side up on a baking sheet; broil until light golden brown. Reset oven to 375°. Spread bread with ground beef mixture. Top with the tomatoes, pepper rings and cheese. Bake for 5 minutes or until the cheese melts. Serve immediately. **Yield:** 6-8 servings.

BACON SPINACH SALAD

    6 bacon strips
    6 cups torn spinach leaves
    1/2 small head iceberg lettuce, torn
    1 bunch green onions, thinly
      sliced
    1/2 cup vegetable oil
    1/4 cup vinegar
    1 tablespoon sugar
    1 teaspoon salt
    1 teaspoon dry mustard

In a skillet, cook bacon until crisp. Drain, crumble and set aside. Place greens and onions in a salad bowl; refrigerate until serving. Combine all remaining ingredients in a jar and shake until well mixed. Just before serving, pour dressing over greens. Toss well to coat. Add bacon and toss. **Yield:** 6-8 servings.

TROPICAL FRUIT DESSERT

    1/2 cup plain *or* vanilla yogurt
    1 tablespoon frozen orange
      juice concentrate
    2 kiwifruit, peeled and sliced
    2 bananas, sliced
    1 can (11 ounces) mandarin
      oranges, drained
    Shredded coconut

In a small bowl, combine yogurt and orange juice concentrate. Place fruit in individual dessert bowls. Drizzle each serving with yogurt sauce. Sprinkle with coconut. **Yield:** 6 servings.

TOSS THIS TOGETHER TONIGHT!

THE RANCH Gail Jenner helps her husband run outside Etna, California really has time on its side—four generations of the family have raised cattle there!

With three active children however, time too often is what she *doesn't* have when meals must be made. So Gail's become somewhat of an "expert" at expeditious dishes!

"I love to cook and host fancy dinner parties," she says. "But when my schedule is hectic, planning is everything. To save time, I frequently prepare several meals at once I can simply defrost when I need them."

This menu, though, doesn't require even a moment of advance work.

"My spaghetti's good for feeding ranch hands—or guests who arrive on short notice." Gail says. "It uses ingredients that are always on hand.

"The cool, crisp salad's also simple to prepare. And by rubbing the bowl with fresh garlic, I can easily add an extra tangy touch!

"To finish off the meal, I put together my sundae. It's one I adapted from a more complicated recipe to fit my need for a quick dessert."

Gail's meal goes from stovetop to tabletop in less than 30 minutes. Try it in your kitchen when time's fleeting…or whenever you want to surprise your family with a new treat!

IF YOU OPEN a large package of bacon but only use a few slices, place the other pieces side by side on a cookie sheet and freeze. Then store frozen slices in a plastic zipper-type freezer bag and remove and thaw as needed.

SPAGHETTI WITH EGGS AND BACON

  8 ounces spaghetti
1/2 pound bacon
  4 eggs, beaten
1/2 cup grated Parmesan cheese
1/2 cup light cream
Additional Parmesan cheese

Cook spaghetti according to package directions. Meanwhile, cook bacon; drain and crumble, then set aside. Combine eggs, Parmesan cheese and cream in a small mixing bowl. Drain spaghetti and return to cooking pan. Stir in egg mixture. Quickly toss and cook until egg mixture is done and coats spaghetti. Stir in bacon and serve immediately with additional Parmesan cheese. **Yield:** 4 servings.

TOSSED ITALIAN SALAD

  1 garlic clove, peeled
  6 cups assorted salad greens
1/2 cucumber *or* zucchini, thinly sliced
  1 large tomato, cut into wedges
Italian salad dressing

Rub the inside of a salad bowl with the garlic. Add the greens, cucumber or zucchini and tomato. Just before serving, toss with enough salad dressing to coat. **Yield:** 4 servings.

FLORENTINE SUNDAE

  1 can (8 ounces) pineapple slices, drained
  1 quart orange *or* lemon frozen sherbet
Grated semisweet chocolate
Chopped nuts
Flaked coconut

Place a pineapple slice in the bottom of four dessert dishes. Top with a scoop or two of sherbet. Sprinkle with grated chocolate, nuts and coconut. Serve immediately. **Yield:** 4 servings.

TIMELESS CLASSIC ENTREE

WHEN Dawn Supina of Edmonton, Alberta has to make tracks in the kitchen, she has time on her side... twice.

"The main course for my favorite 'Meal in Minutes' is actually a classic old dish that my father used to make years ago," Dawn details. "I eventually added the caraway to give it a robust taste. You can add a little bit of leftover meat, too, if you like."

Dawn's dish is "timeless"—or just about so—in another way besides!

"It's so quick and easy to prepare that it can be made at the last minute if necessary," she notes. "I keep all of the ingredients on hand just in case.

"My husband and our two children like this meal for lunch or for a light supper. So do I! I'm not a 'gourmet' cook, just a very basic one."

Outside the kitchen, this Canadian cook tends to her flower garden. After drying, Dawn uses her floral harvest in wreaths and arrangements.

The other courses in her "Meal in Minutes" make a pleasing arrangement themselves. The speedy salad is a nice fresh one with ingredients that can be varied based on availability. And the cool, creamy dessert couldn't be quicker or easier. Why not see for yourself sometime soon?

HEARTY CHEESE 'N' TOAST

  1 tablespoon butter *or* margarine
  1 tablespoon all-purpose flour
2/3 cup milk
  1 teaspoon Worcestershire sauce
1/2 teaspoon dry mustard
  1 teaspoon whole caraway seeds
Pepper to taste
  2 cups (8 ounces) shredded sharp cheddar cheese
  4 to 6 slices white *or* whole wheat bread, toasted
  4 to 6 slices cooked turkey, chicken, beef *or* ham, optional
Chopped fresh parsley

In a saucepan, melt butter over medium-high heat. Stir in flour to form a smooth paste. Gradually stir in milk. Cook and stir until the mixture is smooth and thickened. Add the Worcestershire sauce, mustard, caraway and pepper. Stir until well blended. Add the cheese; cook and stir over low heat until melted. Cut toast diagonally and place on individual plates. If desired, top each with a slice of meat. Spoon cheese sauce over meat and toast. Sprinkle with parsley. Serve immediately. **Yield:** 4 servings.

QUICK ITALIAN SALAD

  1 head romaine lettuce, torn
  1 medium tomato, cut into wedges
1/2 medium cucumber, sliced
  1 small red onion, chopped
1/2 cup cubed mozzarella cheese
1/4 cup sliced ripe olives
Bottled Italian dressing

Toss the first six ingredients in a large salad bowl. Pour dressing over all and toss lightly to coat. Serve immediately. **Yield:** 4 servings.

> **BUYING BERRIES.** When purchasing fresh raspberries, look for deep red color and fruit that is slightly firm to the touch.

SWEET AND CREAMY RASPBERRIES

  1 pint fresh raspberries
Light cream
Confectioners' sugar
Fresh mint, optional

Place raspberries in individual bowls. Just before serving, pour cream over each serving. Sprinkle with sugar; garnish with mint if desired. **Yield:** 4 servings.

FIRE UP THE GRILL!

WITH all the plates to fill whenever her family comes visiting, Johnnie McLeod of Bastrop, Louisiana easily could end up spending *hours* cooking.

Instead, she satisfies her clan of 14 with this quick-to-fix menu. It goes from start to "Soup's on!" in only 30 minutes—letting Johnnie relax and enjoy her company outside the kitchen!

"An easy meal like this is just what I need," she confirms.

The tasty main course of Johnnie's "Meal in Minutes" has an extra advantage built in—the burgers can be prepared ahead, then refrigerated till it's time to barbecue them.

The corn goes right on the grill with the burgers. And the slaw and fudgy dessert are fast food at its finest also.

Sound good to you, too? Don't hesitate then! Serve this speedy supper to your family without delay...even if you *aren't* cooking for a crowd tonight.

ROAST CORN ON THE COB

    6 ears fresh sweet corn
    6 tablespoons butter *or*
      margarine
    6 ice cubes
Salt and pepper to taste
Additional butter *or* margarine,
  optional

Remove husk and silk from corn. Place each ear of corn on a piece of aluminum foil. Add 1 tablespoon butter and 1 ice cube. Wrap securely, twisting ends to make handles for turning. Place corn on grill. Cook for 25 minutes, turning once. Season with salt and pepper, and additional butter if desired. **Yield:** 6 servings.

CABBAGE SLAW

    1 medium head cabbage
      (about 2-1/2 pounds)
    1 carrot
    1 cup mayonnaise
    2 tablespoons milk
    2 tablespoons vinegar
    3 tablespoons sugar
    1 teaspoon salt

    1/2 to 1 teaspoon pepper
    1/2 to 1 teaspoon celery seed

In a food processor or by hand, coarsely chop the cabbage and carrot. In a small bowl, combine the mayonnaise, milk, vinegar, sugar, salt, pepper and celery seed. Stir into the cabbage mixture. Chill until serving. **Yield:** 6 servings.

STUFFED BACON BURGERS

1-1/2 pounds ground beef
    1 envelope (1 ounce) dry onion
      soup mix
  1/4 cup water
    6 slices (1 ounce *each*) process
      American cheese
    6 bacon strips
    6 hamburger buns, toasted

In a bowl, combine ground beef, soup mix and water; mix well. Shape into 12 thin patties. Place a cheese slice on six of the patties. Cover each with another patty. Pinch edges to seal. Wrap a strip of bacon around each; fasten with a wooden toothpick. Grill for 8-10 minutes, turning once, or until burgers reach desired doneness. Remove toothpicks. Serve on buns. **Yield:** 6 servings.

FUDGE BROWNIE PIE

    1 cup sugar
  1/2 cup butter *or* margarine,
      melted
    2 eggs
  1/2 cup all-purpose flour
  1/3 cup baking cocoa
  1/4 teaspoon salt
    1 teaspoon vanilla extract
  1/2 cup chopped pecans
Whipped cream, optional
Strawberries, optional

In a mixing bowl, beat sugar and butter. Add eggs; mix well. Add flour, cocoa and salt. Stir in vanilla and nuts. Pour into a greased 9-in. pie pan. Bake at 350° for 25-30 minutes or until almost set. Serve with whipped cream and strawberries if desired. **Yield:** 6 servings.

FRESH FISH IN A FLASH

TWO busy youngsters and a split-shift job as a waitress leave Denise Blackman little time on weeknights for making the meals she serves her own family. That's why Denise counts on a helpful husband …and on "Meals in Minutes" menus!

"With my changeable work schedule, I need recipes that are quick to fix and easy enough for my husband to prepare when I have to work in the evening," declares Denise.

Fast doesn't rule out fresh ingredients, however. Denise prefers using them whenever possible. And, on weekends, she loves to cook more complicated dishes.

The meal pictured here is a favorite with the Blackman family. It features fresh salmon—a seafood that's a mealtime mainstay in Denise's home area of Port Cartier, Quebec. (If fresh salmon isn't readily available where you live, Denise assures other fish varieties will also work well.)

Enjoy summer's garden greens in a crisp salad crowned with creamy blue cheese dressing. And take advantage of plentiful seasonal squash and tiny red potatoes for the speedy and delicious vegetable side dish.

But be sure to save room for dessert —fresh berries topped with a dollop of orangy whipped cream are a perfect ending to an extra-easy meal that goes from start to finish in a snap!

BLUE CHEESE DRESSING

1/4 cup crumbled blue cheese
3/4 cup sour cream, *divided*
2 tablespoons vegetable oil
1 tablespoon lemon juice
1 to 1-1/2 teaspoons Worcestershire sauce, optional
Salt and pepper to taste

In a small bowl, mash blue cheese with a fork. Add 2 tablespoons sour cream; beat until smooth. Stir in all remaining ingredients. Serve over mixed greens. **Yield:** 1 cup.

FISH FILLETS IN GARLIC BUTTER

2 tablespoons butter *or* margarine
2 small garlic cloves, minced
4 fish fillets (about 6 ounces *each*) salmon *or* whitefish *or* cod
1/4 cup thinly sliced green onion
Lemon wedges

In a skillet, melt butter over medium heat. Saute garlic 1 minute. Place fish over garlic, cover and cook over low heat 3 minutes. Carefully turn fish; sprinkle with onions. Cover and continue to cook until fish flakes easily with a fork, about 2-3 minutes. Squeeze lemon over fish. Serve immediately. **Yield:** 4 servings.

SUMMER SQUASH AND POTATO SAUTE

2 tablespoons butter *or* margarine
2 medium summer squash, sliced
2 small red potatoes, thinly sliced
Minced fresh parsley
Salt and pepper to taste

In a skillet, melt butter over medium heat. Saute squash and potatoes until tender. Sprinkle with parsley, salt and pepper to taste. **Yield:** 4 servings.

STRAWBERRIES ROMANOFF

1 quart fresh strawberries, hulled
1/2 cup confectioners' sugar
1 cup whipping cream
1/4 cup orange juice

Sprinkle strawberries with sugar. Cover and refrigerate 15-20 minutes. Just before serving, whip cream until stiff. Gently stir in orange juice. Fold in berries, or serve individually in bowls topped with the flavored cream. **Yield:** 4-6 servings.

Warm Up With Chili

PASTORS don't work "regular" hours. So pastors' wives—like Judy King of Johnstown, Pennsylvania—can't always count on regular mealtimes.

When committee meetings or visits to parishioners keep her husband past suppertime, Judy relies on recipes like the ones featured here for satisfying, speedy meals. She also finds "Meals in Minutes" menus handy when she's called on to feed neighbors or friends who occasionally need a helping hand.

"I'm basically a scratch cook," Judy says. "But making fast and easy meals during the week seems to fit our schedules better. On weekends and for special occasions, I like to take my time and prepare big meals."

Whether she's preparing a meal in minutes or a more elaborate dinner, Judy credits her mom as her original inspiration in the kitchen.

"I developed my Pronto Chili recipe through trial and error," she admits. "Using tomato paste was born out of necessity when I ran out of canned tomato sauce one day! My family agrees the result was unbeatable."

Judy recommends corn bread as a satisfying accompaniment to her chili. "Originally, I baked it in muffin tins — but, to save time, I switched to a baking pan." A speedy banana cream dessert makes a cool, refreshing finish after the spicy main course.

Next time the clock's ticking too fast in *your* kitchen, try Judy's quick, hearty chili supper—it'll warm body and soul!

CORN BREAD

1-1/2 cups all-purpose flour
3/4 cup cornmeal
2 tablespoons sugar
2 teaspoons baking powder
1/4 teaspoon salt
1 cup milk
1 egg, beaten
4 tablespoons butter *or* margarine, melted

Combine the first five ingredients. Add milk, egg and butter; stir until dry ingredients are moistened. Pour batter into a greased 8-in. x 8-in. baking pan. Bake at 400° for 20-25 minutes or until golden brown and a wooden pick inserted in center of bread comes out clean. Serve warm. **Yield:** 9 servings.

PRONTO CHILI

1 pound ground beef
1 small onion, chopped
1 can (6 ounces) tomato paste plus 2 cans water
2 teaspoons chili powder
1 teaspoon salt
1/2 teaspoon cumin, optional
1/4 teaspoon black pepper
1 to 2 tablespoons brown sugar
1 can (16 ounces) kidney beans, rinsed and drained
Shredded cheddar cheese

In a saucepan, brown beef and onion. Drain fat. Stir in all remaining ingredients *except* cheese; cover and simmer 20 minutes. Top each serving with cheese. **Yield:** 4 servings.

BANANA CREAM PARFAIT

1 package (3-1/2 ounces) instant banana pudding
2 cups cold milk
1/2 cup graham cracker crumbs
2 medium ripe bananas, sliced
Whipped cream
4 maraschino cherries, optional

Prepare pudding according to package directions, using the 2 cups cold milk. Sprinkle 1 tablespoon graham cracker crumbs into each of four parfait or dessert glasses. Top crumbs with 1/4 cup prepared pudding and *half* of the banana slices. Repeat layers of crumbs, pudding and banana slices. Top each dessert with a dollop of whipped cream and garnish with a cherry, if desired. **Yield:** 4 servings.

A Busy Cook's Speedy Supper

HER JOB in a school cafeteria kept hundreds of hungry youngsters fed… but sometimes had Betty Claycomb of Alverton, Pennsylvania too tired to fix fancy meals for her family.

So, with a husband and two children of her own at home, Betty turned to "Meals in Minutes" for help!

"Meat loaf was always a favorite," she relates. "But it took too long to bake. So I devised a stove-top version that didn't require heating up the oven."

As a matter of fact, it sounds from chatting with her that Betty may need "Meals in Minutes" more now than ever! "Since retiring, I've been compiling recipes from family and friends into cookbooks," she reports. "I also write a weekly recipe column for a small newspaper in the area."

As you can see in the photo below, Betty's speedy meal includes a rich tomato sauce. So, while the meat loaves are cooking, you'll likely want to boil pasta to accompany them. At the same time, prepare the dilled cucumbers—a light, refreshing side dish.

The meal's topped off with a fruit and cream treat. "I use canned fruit cocktail with fresh bananas in winter," Betty notes. "In summer, we enjoy the fresh berries of the season."

Whatever the season, you'll find her meat loaf meal is a tasty time-saver.

DILLED CUCUMBERS

2 medium cucumbers, peeled and thinly sliced
1/2 teaspoon salt
1/2 cup sour cream
1 tablespoon lemon juice
2 tablespoons finely chopped green onion
1/8 teaspoon pepper
1/4 teaspoon sugar
1/2 teaspoon dried dill weed

In a small bowl, toss cucumbers with salt. Allow to stand for 10 minutes. Meanwhile, combine all remaining ingredients. Drain cucumbers and combine with sour cream mixture. Chill until ready to serve. **Yield:** 6 servings.

INDIVIDUAL MEAT LOAVES

1 egg, beaten
1 cup soft bread cubes
1/4 cup milk
1-1/2 teaspoons onion salt
1 teaspoon dried parsley flakes
Dash pepper
1-1/2 pounds lean ground beef
6 sticks (2-1/2 inches x 1/2 inch *each*) cheddar *or* mozzarella cheese
SAUCE:
2 cans (15 ounces *each*) tomato sauce
1/2 cup chopped onion
1 tablespoon dried parsley flakes
1/2 teaspoon dried oregano
1/4 teaspoon garlic salt

In a mixing bowl, combine first six ingredients. Mix in beef. Divide into six portions. Shape each portion around a cheese stick and form into a loaf. Set aside. In a large skillet, combine all sauce ingredients. Add loaves and spoon sauce over each. Cover and bring to a boil. Reduce heat to simmer; cook until done, about 20 minutes. **Yield:** 6 servings.

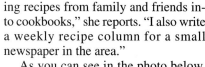

FRUIT AND CREAM DESSERT

2 cans (17 ounces *each*) chunky fruit cocktail, drained
2 bananas, sliced
1 teaspoon lemon juice
1/4 cup maraschino cherries
1-1/2 cups whipped topping
3/4 cup sour cream

In a bowl, combine fruit cocktail, bananas, lemon juice and cherries. In another bowl, combine the whipped topping and sour cream. Refrigerate both bowls until ready to serve. To serve, spoon fruit into individual serving bowls; top with cream mixture. **Yield:** 6 servings.

SLOPPY JOES ARE JUST RIGHT

YEARS AGO, as a newlywed, Alpha Wilson of Roswell, New Mexico was already adept at making minutes count in the kitchen.

"I was raised on a farm," she explains. "When the chores ran late, my mom and I had to come up with quick and hearty meals. Later, I often used those recipes for my own family."

Nowadays, she's retired. But Alpha still relies on "Meals in Minutes" menus to make time for her favorite activities. When she's not walking her two dogs or tending to her many plants, she's an avid quilter—last year, she painstakingly restored *seven* heirlooms.

Alpha and her husband, Thomas, also like to pack their camper and head for parts unknown. On the road as well as at home, they'll often enjoy the Barbecue Beef Sandwiches that she shares here. Alpha likes serving the sandwiches with her crunchy stuffed celery and pretty pepper salad. For dessert, her peach crisp's always in season.

STUFFED CELERY STALKS

  1 package (3 ounces) cream cheese, softened
  2 tablespoons creamy peanut butter
  1 tablespoon light cream
1-1/2 teaspoons minced onion
  1/4 teaspoon curry powder
  4 celery stalks, cut into 3-inch pieces
  1/4 cup chopped salted peanuts

In a small bowl, blend first five ingredients. Stuff into celery pieces; sprinkle with peanuts. Chill until serving. **Yield:** 6-8 servings.

PEPPER SALAD

  1 green pepper, thinly sliced
  1 sweet red pepper, thinly sliced
  1 pound fresh mushrooms, sliced
  3 tablespoons vinegar
  1/4 cup vegetable oil
  1/2 teaspoon salt

   Dash pepper
   Dash garlic powder, optional

In a bowl, toss peppers and mushrooms. Combine all remaining ingredients and toss with vegetables. Cover and refrigerate until serving. **Yield:** 6-8 servings.

BARBECUE BEEF SANDWICHES

  1 tablespoon butter *or* margarine
  1 pound lean ground beef
  1/2 cup chopped onion
  1 medium green pepper, chopped
  3/4 cup ketchup
  1/4 cup water
  1 tablespoon sugar
  2 tablespoons prepared mustard
  1 tablespoon vinegar
Salt and pepper to taste
Hamburger buns

In a skillet, melt butter over medium-high heat. Brown the beef, onion and green pepper. Add all remaining ingredients except buns. Simmer, uncovered, 15 minutes. Serve on buns. **Yield:** about 6 servings.

SPICY PEACH CRISP

  1 can (29 ounces) sliced peaches, well drained
  1/2 cup rolled oats
  1/2 cup packed brown sugar
  1/4 cup all-purpose flour
  1/4 teaspoon ground cinnamon
  1/4 teaspoon ground nutmeg
  1/4 teaspoon ground allspice
  1/4 cup butter *or* margarine
Cream *or* ice cream

Arrange peaches in an 8-in. x 8-in. pan. In a small bowl, combine oats, sugar, flour and spices. Cut in butter until coarse crumbs form; sprinkle over peaches. Bake at 400° for 15-20 minutes. Serve warm with cream or ice cream. **Yield:** 6-8 servings.

SCRUMPTIOUS SUMMER SPREAD

AS a home economics teacher, she helps others learn to make the most of minutes in the kitchen. And, with a growing family of her own, Nancy Brown of Janesville, Wisconsin has plenty of practical experience!

"The secret is planning," Nancy notes. "On weekends, I work out the menus for the week ahead…and often I roast a chicken or ham so I'll have leftovers for quick meals later."

A little leftover ham makes a fast, filling meal when she prepares her Ham and Cheese Frittata, featured here. "I also frequently add fresh herbs and zucchini," Nancy shares.

Gardening's a favorite activity for Nancy, who counts herself lucky to have the summers off to enjoy it. Her home is always decorated with bouquets of fresh flowers, plus Nancy dries flowers and herbs for basket arrangements and wreaths.

An afternoon gardening or crafting still leaves time for this 30-minute meal, however. "Fresh tomatoes add a flavorful touch, and the dessert can include fruit in season," she advises. "Kids just love that treat."

Likely, you'll love Nancy's menu, too. It might even leave *you* more time for gardening!

PARMESAN TOMATOES

- 2 large tomatoes
- 3 tablespoons dry bread crumbs
- 2 tablespoons grated Parmesan cheese
- 2 tablespoons butter *or* margarine, melted
- 1/2 teaspoon dried basil *or* 1 tablespoon snipped fresh basil
- 1/2 teaspoon chopped fresh parsley

Dash pepper

Remove stems from the tomatoes and halve crosswise. Place, cut side up, in a small baking dish. Combine all remaining ingredients; sprinkle over tomato tops. Bake at 375° for 15 minutes or until heated through. **Yield:** 4 servings.

TOMATO TIP: Refrigerating a tomato ruins its fabulous flavor. So be sure to store them at room temperature.

HAM AND CHEESE FRITTATA

- 2 tablespoons butter *or* margarine
- 1/2 cup sliced fresh mushrooms
- 1/2 cup chopped sweet red *or* green pepper
- 1/4 cup sliced green onions
- 6 eggs
- 2 tablespoons water
- 1/2 cup diced cooked ham
- 1 cup (4 ounces) shredded cheddar cheese

In a skillet, melt butter over medium heat. Saute mushrooms, pepper and onions until tender. In a mixing bowl, beat eggs with water until foamy; stir in ham. Pour over the vegetables. Let eggs set on the bottom, then lift the edges to allow any uncooked egg to flow underneath. Cover and cook until the eggs are set, about 3 minutes. Sprinkle with cheese and cut into wedges to serve. **Yield:** 4 servings.

GLAZED FRUIT DESSERT

- 1 package (3.4 ounces) instant vanilla pudding mix
- 1 can (20 ounces) pineapple chunks in natural juice, liquid drained and reserved
- 1 can (11 ounces) mandarin oranges, drained
- 2 bananas, sliced

Whipped topping

In a mixing bowl, combine pudding and pineapple juice. Stir until thickened. Fold in pineapple, oranges and bananas. Refrigerate until serving. Garnish with a dollop of whipped topping. **Yield:** 6 servings.

YOU'LL TASTE SWEET SUCCESS

AS a busy professional dietitian, Janice MacLeod of Roanoke, Virginia appreciates quick-meal menus that are hearty *and* wholesome.

Her Orange-Glazed Pork Tenderloins with Quick Baked Potatoes combine both traits tastily—they can satisfy a man-sized appetite, but are suitable for calorie-conscious folks, too. And they can be ready in just 30 minutes!

"I fix the potatoes first, since they take the longest time to cook," Janice explains. "Potatoes are a good source of carbohydrate, and—if you prefer—with this recipe they don't need gravy or sour cream. They're also pretty on the plate."

While the potatoes cook, Janice prepares the tenderloins in a sweet/tart sauce. "Pork tenderloin is perfect for a quick meal," she points out, "and it's nearly as lean as chicken. I use non-stick cookware and a minimum of oil for browning."

Steamed fresh vegetables complete the meal. A year-round favorite for its appealing color and natural good taste is broccoli. "I squeeze some fresh lemon juice over it just before serving," Janice says.

For a refreshing dessert, Janice uses frozen fruits to make a soft sherbet—also in seconds! These three delicious recipes will fast become your family's favorites.

CREAMY PEACH SHERBET

    2 cups frozen, unsweetened peach slices*, partially thawed
1/2 cup plain nonfat yogurt
    2 tablespoons orange juice concentrate
    2 tablespoons sugar *or* 1 to 2 packets sweetener
Freshly grated nutmeg to taste (1/8 to 1/4 teaspoon)
    1 teaspoon vanilla extract

In a food processor or blender, pulse/chop peaches. Add remaining ingredients; blend until creamy. May be served immediately or stored in the freezer until serving time. **Yield:** 4 servings (3/4 cup each). (*Other frozen fruits may be substituted for peaches.)

ORANGE-GLAZED PORK TENDERLOINS

    8 slices lean pork tenderloin cutlets (1/4 inch thick)
    2 teaspoons vegetable oil
Freshly ground black pepper to taste
    1/4 teaspoon garlic powder
    2 tablespoons Worcestershire sauce
    4 tablespoons orange juice concentrate
    4 green onions, sliced
Orange slices, optional

Heat oil in a heavy, nonstick skillet. Brown pork on both sides; sprinkle with pepper and garlic powder. Continue cooking pork while combining Worcestershire sauce and orange juice concentrate. Pour sauce over meat; sprinkle with green onions and cook over low heat until sauce is thick and glazed. Serve with fresh orange slices, if desired. **Yield:** 4 servings.

QUICK BAKED POTATOES

    4 large baking potatoes, scrubbed
    2 to 3 tablespoons butter *or* margarine, melted
Paprika
Salt to taste
    3 tablespoons grated Parmesan cheese

Cut the potatoes in half lengthwise. Brush each cut half with butter; sprinkle with paprika, salt and cheese. Place cut side down on an oiled cookie sheet. Bake at 350° for 25-30 minutes or until potatoes are fork tender. **Yield:** 4 servings.

MEAL-MAKING'S A FAMILY AFFAIR

HER HUSBAND and two teenagers happily help out in the kitchen, making mealtimes easier for Carol Dalke of Elk Creek, Montana. With many "Meals in Minutes" menus, quick cooking's catching on with the whole family!

"I have a long commute to my job, so I don't have as much time to spend in the kitchen as I'd like," Carol explains. "Now, my husband cooks more, and the children are pitching in, too. Our son loves to make omelets in the morning, while our daughter is putting her 4-H training to good use."

Such kitchen cooperation means Carol still has the time to participate as a 4-H leader and an Extension home-maker and to enjoy an occasional hunting and fishing trip with her whole family.

Her Minute Steaks Parmesan utilizes a popular cut of meat, prepared with a new twist. "My family loves the Italian sauce and the zesty cheese flavor," she says. "While the steaks are cooking, I prepare the fruit sauce to serve on ice cream for dessert. It can be served warm if there isn't time to chill it beforehand," she adds.

Carol continues the meal preparation by tossing the salad ingredients and cooking the corn. "Just before serving, I brush the hot corn with the honey-butter sauce. It's delicious!"

Whether or not you have extra helpers in your kitchen, you'll want to try Carol's meal soon. It might even help you "recruit" some assistants—in a hurry!

HONEY BUTTERED CORN

4 ears fresh *or* frozen corn
1/3 cup butter *or* margarine
1 tablespoon honey
3/4 teaspoon seasoned salt

Cook corn until tender. Meanwhile, melt butter; stir in honey and salt. Brush corn with butter mixture. **Yield:** 4 servings.

MINUTE STEAKS PARMESAN

1 egg white, lightly beaten
2 teaspoons water
Dash pepper
1/2 cup finely crushed saltine crackers
1/2 cup grated Parmesan cheese
4 cube steaks (about 4 ounces *each*)
2 tablespoons butter *or* margarine
1 can (8 ounces) pizza sauce

In a shallow bowl, combine egg white, water and pepper. Set aside. On a plate, combine cracker crumbs and cheese. Dip each cube steak into the egg mixture, then coat with the cracker/cheese mixture. In a large skillet, melt butter; brown steaks on both sides. Top with pizza sauce and simmer for 3-5 minutes. Garnish with remaining crumb mixture. Serve immediately. **Yield:** 4 servings.

ITALIAN SALAD BOWL

1 bunch leaf lettuce, torn into bite-size pieces
8 cherry tomatoes, halved
8 fresh mushrooms, sliced
4 radishes, sliced
1 small zucchini, thinly sliced
1/2 yellow, red *or* green pepper, thinly sliced
1/4 cup shredded mozzarella cheese
Italian salad dressing to taste

In a large salad bowl, toss all ingredients. Serve immediately. **Yield:** 4 servings.

PEACH MELBA DESSERT

2 cups sliced peeled fresh *or* frozen peaches
2 cups fresh *or* frozen raspberries
3/4 cup sugar
2 tablespoons water
Vanilla ice cream

In a saucepan, bring peaches, raspberries, sugar and water to a boil. Reduce heat and simmer 5 minutes. Chill, if desired. Serve over ice cream. **Yield:** about 8 servings.

Your 'Posse' Will Savor Stew!

EVEN in sunny Arizona, the pace slows somewhat during winter, permitting busy cooks a bit more time to prepare elaborate meals.

Still, there are days when minutes matter at mealtime. When they do, Michel Karkula of Chandler is all set to serve up a satisfying spread!

"Years ago, I relied on recipes I could fix fast for my growing family," she relates. "Today, when the children and grandchildren come to visit, I still use some of them."

One such "old friend" in Michel's kitchen is hearty Posse Stew, which can be called into action in a hurry from the pantry and easily expanded.

Also finished in minutes are spicy, moist Pumpkin Muffins. They can be prepared with little fuss from a biscuit mix, canned pumpkin and spices.

For dessert, Michel's tapioca and banana pudding—served either warm or cold—brims with old-fashioned taste (make it ahead, if you like).

Next time *you* have one of those "need-to-feed-'em-fast" days, turn to Michel's menu for the solution. Your family will be quick to thank you!

> **COME OUT ON TOP.** For evenly rounded tops on your muffins every time, only grease muffin cups on the bottom and 1/2-inch up the sides.

PUMPKIN SPICE MUFFINS

- 1/2 cup canned pumpkin
- 1/2 cup milk
- 1 egg
- 2 cups biscuit mix
- 1/4 cup sugar
- 1/2 teaspoon ground nutmeg
- 1/2 teaspoon ground cinnamon
- 1/2 teaspoon ground ginger

STREUSEL TOPPING:
- 2 tablespoons sugar
- 1 tablespoon biscuit mix
- 1/4 teaspoon ground cinnamon
- 2 teaspoons butter *or* margarine, softened

In a mixing bowl, combine pumpkin, milk and egg with a fork. Combine dry ingredients; add to mixing bowl and stir just until moistened. Spoon into 12 well-greased muffin cups. Combine streusel ingredients; sprinkle over muffins. Bake at 400° for 15 minutes or until golden brown. Serve warm. **Yield:** 1 dozen.

POSSE STEW

- 1 pound ground beef *or* turkey
- 1 medium onion, diced
- 1 can (16 ounces) tomatoes, undrained
- 1 can (15 ounces) chili beans, undrained
- 1 can (4 ounces) diced green chilies, undrained
- 1 can (15-1/2 ounces) hominy, drained
- 1 can (16 ounces) whole kernel corn, drained
- Salt and pepper to taste
- 1 tablespoon cornstarch, optional
- 1/4 cup water, optional

In a skillet, brown ground meat and onion; drain. Stir in tomatoes, beans, chilies, hominy and corn; season with salt and pepper. For a thicker stew, combine cornstarch and water, then stir into stew. Cook and stir until thickened. **Yield:** 4-6 servings.

BANANA TAPIOCA PUDDING

- 2-3/4 cups milk
- 3 tablespoons quick-cooking tapioca
- 1/3 cup sugar
- 1 egg, lightly beaten
- 1 teaspoon vanilla extract
- 2 bananas, sliced

In a saucepan, combine milk, tapioca, sugar and egg; let stand 5 minutes. Cook and stir over medium heat until mixture comes to a full boil; remove from heat. Stir in vanilla and bananas. Cool for 20 minutes. Serve warm or cold. **Yield:** 6 servings.

HEARTY PASTA IS INVITING

WHEN unexpected guests come for dinner, country cooks can count on quick meals. But when those guests are hungry teenagers, the fare had better be fast *and* filling!

Janet Roehring of Marble Falls, Texas shares just that sort of specialty here. "I came up with this menu when one of our sons arrived home unannounced from college with a couple of friends," she relates. "I offered them a home-cooked meal, and they jumped at the idea.

"I simply sorted through some of my tried-and-true recipes and combined them in short order. Happily, the entire concoction was an instant success...to this day, it's known in our family as '*the meal*'!"

It's still getting a workout at the Roehring home with Janet's three other college-age youngsters and their pals regularly dropping in at mealtime. "But that's okay with us," she assures. "It's always 'open house' here for our children and their friends. That's the way we want it.

"And when we moved our 'open house' to a new home on a 40-acre cattle ranch a few years back, this fast menu saw even more use," adds Janet.

You'll appreciate Janet's quick, hearty Pasta and Sausage Bake anytime. The accompanying bean salad is a snap to put together. As for dessert, a prepared pie crust and frozen strawberries assure you'll be serving the entire meal in under 30 minutes.

You don't have to wait for unexpected guests either...enjoy this tasty, timely meal tonight!

SPEEDY BEAN SALAD

- 3/4 cup sugar
- 2/3 cup vinegar
- 1/3 cup vegetable oil
- 1 teaspoon salt
- Dash pepper
- 1 can (15 ounces) garbanzo beans, rinsed and drained
- 1 can (15-1/2 ounces) kidney beans, rinsed and drained
- 1 can (15 ounces) great northern beans, rinsed and drained
- 1/2 medium onion, chopped
- 1/2 cup chopped green pepper

In a bowl, combine sugar, vinegar, oil, salt and pepper. Stir in all remaining ingredients. Let marinate until serving time. **Yield:** 6 servings.

PASTA AND SAUSAGE BAKE

- 1 pound Italian sausage, cut into 1/4-inch slices
- 1 jar (15 ounces) spaghetti sauce
- 8 ounces mostaccioli, cooked and drained
- 1/3 cup grated Parmesan cheese
- 1 package (4 ounces) shredded mozzarella cheese

In a skillet, brown sausage. Drain. In a greased 2-qt. baking dish, combine sausage, sauce, mostaccioli and Parmesan cheese. Top with mozzarella cheese. Bake at 350° for 15-20 minutes or until heated through. **Yield:** 4-6 servings.

SPARKLING STRAWBERRY PIE

- 2 packages (3 ounces *each*) regular *or* sugar-free raspberry *or* strawberry-flavored gelatin
- 2 cups boiling water
- 3 to 4 cups frozen whole strawberries
- 1 pastry shell (8 *or* 9 inches), baked
- Whipped topping

In a mixing bowl, dissolve gelatin in water. Add frozen berries and allow to set a few minutes to thicken. When partially set, spoon into pie shell. Refrigerate. Garnish with whipped topping. **Yield:** 6 servings.

A MEAL WITH KID APPEAL

BETWEEN RAISING a toddler of her own and caring for a neighbor's child on weekdays, Joanne Schlabach of Shreve, Ohio doesn't have many seconds to spare. So it's no wonder this busy mom and sitter is always searching for fast menus that also have "kid appeal".

"I rely on recipes that can be prepared ahead and held until the children are settled and all set to eat," Joanne reports. "Pizza Burgers are one of their favorites. My husband also enjoys them."

In fact, the menu she shares here is truly a family affair. The zesty main dish came from her mother-in-law, the salad is from her own mother, and the dessert's from her grandmother.

From those ladies, Joanne also inherited a love of all kinds of cooking and baking. "On weekends, when I have a little more time, I prepare big meals from scratch," she says. Joanne finds time besides to garden, put up fruits and vegetables, sew and help work on projects around the house.

When a fast meal is in order, Joanne stirs up some of her Pizza Burgers (an Italian-style sloppy joe). "You can make the filling ahead and reheat it when you're ready to serve," she notes.

While the filling simmers, Joanne prepares the crunchy layered salad. Then the refreshing lemon dessert is mixed in minutes and chilled while she and the children eat.

Joanne's finished-in-a-jiffy menu will please everyone in your family—kids (of all ages) included!

PIZZA BURGERS

    1 pound lean ground beef
    1 can (15 ounces) pizza
      sauce
    1 teaspoon dried oregano
    1/2 medium onion
    1/2 medium green pepper
    1 ounce sliced pepperoni
    6 hamburger buns, split
    1/2 cup shredded Mozzarella
      cheese
    1/2 cup sliced fresh mushrooms

In a skillet, brown ground beef. Drain. Stir in sauce and oregano. In a food processor, chop onion, pepper and pepperoni; add to beef mixture. Simmer 20-25 minutes. Spoon mixture onto buns. Top with cheese and mushrooms. Serve immediately. **Yield:** 6 servings.

LAYERED LETTUCE SALAD

    1 cup mayonnaise
    3 tablespoons grated
      Parmesan cheese
    2 tablespoons sugar
    1 medium head lettuce, torn
      into bite-size pieces
    1 medium head cauliflower,
      broken into florets
    1 bunch broccoli, broken into
      florets
    1 medium red onion, thinly
      sliced
    1/2 cup bacon bits

In a small bowl, stir together first three ingredients for dressing; set aside. Layer remaining ingredients in a large salad bowl. Pour on dressing; refrigerate. Toss just before serving. **Yield:** 6-8 servings.

ADD COLOR to salads with onion rings marinated in leftover green pickle or beet pickle juice. Chill rings in liquid for 24 hours or more before using.

LEMON PIE

    1 can (14 ounces) sweetened
      condensed milk
    1/2 cup lemon juice
    1 carton (8 ounces) frozen
      whipped topping, thawed
    Few drops yellow food coloring,
      optional
    1 graham cracker crust (8 *or* 9
      inches)

In a medium bowl, combine milk and juice. Let stand a few minutes. Stir in whipped topping. Add food coloring if desired. Spoon into crust. Chill until firm. **Yield:** 6 servings.

Skillet Specialty In a Snap

ALTHOUGH her four children are grown and gone, Peggy Langen of Lanconia, New Hampshire hasn't put away her "Meals in Minutes" menus.

"This quick Chicken and Potato Saute is a family favorite I've relied on for 30 years," Peggy says. "These days, the kids still request it whenever they visit—even when we're not in a hurry for a meal!"

The pace may have slowed some at her place, but the need for speedy meals hasn't. She and her husband enjoy the many outdoor sports available in the New England area, such as swimming, skiing, biking and hiking.

"We still have a very active lifestyle, so fast meals are important. Chicken breasts are perfect. They're done quickly but taste like they've been cooking for hours."

During summer months, when fresh vegetables are abundant, Peggy serves either a zucchini and peppers saute or boiled corn on the cob. Both complement the chicken in color and flavor.

For dessert, she tops a refreshing raspberry and cantaloupe mixture with a chilled cranberry/almond sauce. (This treat can be enjoyed during winter months by substituting frozen rasperries and melon balls for fresh.)

Try Peggy's easy, delicious meal soon...and use the time you save for some outdoor activity of your own!

CHICKEN AND POTATO SAUTE

1/4 cup butter *or* margarine
4 to 6 boneless chicken breast halves
1 medium onion, sliced
1 garlic clove, minced
2 tablespoons all-purpose flour
1/2 teaspoon dried thyme, optional
Salt and pepper to taste
1 chicken bouillon cube
1 cup hot water
1 can (16 ounces) whole potatoes, drained
1/4 cup red wine *or* water
Snipped fresh parsley

In a large skillet, melt butter over medium heat. Saute chicken until browned on both sides. Add onion and garlic; cook about 5 minutes. In a small bowl, combine flour and seasonings. Dissolve bouillon in water and stir into flour mixture; pour over chicken. Cover; simmer 20 minutes. Add potatoes and wine or water; heat through. Sprinkle with parsley. **Yield:** 4-6 servings.

GARDEN MEDLEY

2 tablespoons butter *or* margarine
2 medium zucchini, cut into julienne strips
1 sweet red pepper, cut into julienne strips
1 green pepper, cut into julienne strips
1 yellow pepper, cut into julienne strips
1/2 teaspoon seasoned salt
Dash pepper

In a skillet, melt butter over medium heat. Saute vegetables until crisp-tender. Season with salt and pepper. **Yield:** 4-6 servings.

CANTALOUPE AND RASPBERRY MELBA

1/2 cup cranberry juice cocktail
1 tablespoon sugar
2 teaspoons cornstarch
1/4 teaspoon almond extract
3 cups cantaloupe cubes *or* balls
1 cup raspberries
Mint leaves, optional

In a saucepan, blend juice, sugar and cornstarch. Cook and stir over medium heat until mixture is thickened. Stir in extract. Cool. When ready to serve, combine cantaloupe and raspberries in individual bowls. Top with cranberry sauce and a mint garnish if desired. **Yield:** 4-6 servings.

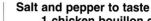

EASY—YET ELEGANT—ENTREE

AT WORK, home economist Lorene Frohling sometimes spends *hours* preparing food.

But on days like that, she has to rush through meal making in her own Waukesha, Wisconsin kitchen. And that's when Lorene looks for delicious dishes to feed her family in *30 minutes or less*.

"My job involves 'food styling'," Lorene explains. "The foods I prepare are photographed for magazines or cookbooks, so they need to look picture perfect. With a pasta dish, for example, I arrange every strand of pasta with an attractive curl.

"Believe me, after doing that for hours on end, I want my own meal to look good and taste great without a lot of fuss. So, I prepare this quick-and-easy meal often. But my family doesn't complain. Everyone loves this hearty meat-and-potatoes meal. And I know you will, too!"

Lorene begins by washing and slicing the new potatoes and getting them in the oven immediately. While the potatoes bake, she prepares and seasons the tenderloin slices and assembles the sauce ingredients.

In season, one of Lorene's favorite vegetables is asparagus…either steamed or microwaved. Dessert is a delicious combination of berries, sherbet and a topping of warmed marmalade…a colorful dish to a fine-looking feast!

You can count on Lorene's speedy, stylish standby to be flavorful and to look "picture perfect" besides!

TENDERLOIN DIANE

1 pound beef tenderloin, cut
   into 8 slices
Salt to taste
Freshly ground black pepper to taste
1 teaspoon dry mustard
2 tablespoons butter *or*
   margarine
2 tablespoons sliced
   green onion
1 tablespoon lemon juice
2 teaspoons Worcestershire
   sauce

Sprinkle one side of tenderloin slices with salt, pepper and *half* of the dry mustard. Pound the seasonings into meat. Repeat on the other side. In a large skillet, melt butter on medium-high heat; add meat slices in a single layer. Cook for 2 minutes on each side for medium-rare doneness. Remove to a heated serving platter. To pan juices in skillet, add the green onion, lemon juice and Worcestershire sauce. Cook and stir for 1 minute. Spoon sauce over meat. **Yield:** 4 servings.

NEW POTATOES WITH DILL

1 pound new potatoes,
   unpeeled
2 tablespoons butter *or*
   margarine
1 teaspoon fresh dill *or*
   1/2 teaspoon dried dill
1/2 teaspoon seasoned salt

Wash potatoes; cut into 3/8-in.-thick slices. In a 12-in. x 7-1/2-in. x 2-in. baking dish, arrange potatoes in thin layer. Dot with butter; sprinkle with dill and salt. Cover and bake at 425° for 25 minutes or until tender, stirring after 15 minutes. **Yield:** 4 servings.

BLUEBERRY-ORANGE CUPS

1/3 cup orange marmalade
1 pint orange sherbet
1 cup fresh blueberries

Heat marmalade over low heat until melted. Scoop sherbet into 4 dessert dishes; top with blueberries. Spoon warm marmalade over all. **Yield:** 4 servings.

FREEZE FRESH blueberries in a single layer on a tray, then transfer them into freezer containers. That way, you can easily remove only as much as you need…and capture the fantastic flavor of fresh fruit.

PICNIC PLEASERS.
Clockwise from the bottom: Honey Barbecued
Spare Ribs, Crunchy Cheese Potatoes, Summer
Salad with Golden Dressing and Blueberry Pudding
with Lemon Cream Sauce (all recipes on page 253).

MY MOST MEMORABLE MEAL

In this chapter, 16 cooks across the country share recipes for— and memories of—their most treasured meal.

WHEN Belle Kemmerer of Stanfordville, New York wants to "set off some fireworks", she relies on this tried-and-true summer favorite.

"As a child, I enjoyed this wonderful meal at my grandmother's home every Fourth of July," Belle recalls. Now Belle carries on her grandmother's tradition in her own family.

"Everyone is pleased whenever I serve these dishes," Belle shares. "Much of the meal can be prepared ahead of time. That way, the cook can enjoy the holiday, too." She adds, "Many of my friends have asked for these recipes, and my church included them in its cookbook."

Belle guarantees this mouth-watering combination will put some real "bang" into *any* get-together!

BLUEBERRY PUDDING WITH LEMON CREAM SAUCE

"This dessert is so good that I make it often during blueberry season."

LEMON CREAM SAUCE:
- 2 teaspoons cornstarch
- 1/2 cup sugar
- 2/3 cup water
- 2 tablespoons lemon juice
- 1 cup heavy cream

PUDDING:
- 2 cups all-purpose flour
- 1-1/2 cups sugar
- 2 teaspoons baking powder
- 1/2 teaspoon salt
- 1/2 teaspoon ground nutmeg
- 3/4 teaspoon ground cinnamon
- 2/3 cup butter *or* margarine
- 2 eggs
- 3/4 cup milk
- 2 cups fresh blueberries, washed and drained

In a small saucepan, combine the cornstarch and sugar. Stir in water; cook and stir until thickened and clear. Remove from the heat; stir in lemon juice. Cool. In a mixing bowl, whip the cream; fold cooled mixture into cream. Cover and refrigerate until ready to use. For pudding, combine dry ingredients in another mixing bowl. Cut in butter with a pastry blender until particles are the size of small peas. Add eggs and milk and

TRUE BLUE MENU COMES THROUGH

beat on low until thoroughly combined. Spread into a greased 9-in. square baking pan. Sprinkle berries over batter. Bake at 350° for 50-55 minutes or until cake tests done. Serve warm or cold with Lemon Cream Sauce. **Yield:** 9 servings.

SUMMER SALAD WITH GOLDEN DRESSING

"This dressing's touch of curry gives vegetables a tangy taste."

- 1 package (16 ounces) frozen French-style green beans, cooked and drained *or* 1 can (14-1/2 ounces) French-style green beans, drained
- 1/2 cup sliced celery
- 1/2 cup sliced unpeeled cucumber
- 4 radishes, sliced
- 4 medium tomatoes, cut into wedges

Lettuce leaves

DRESSING:
- 1 hard-cooked egg, chopped
- 1 tablespoon instant minced onion
- 1/4 cup vinegar
- 1/2 cup vegetable oil
- 1/2 teaspoon salt
- 1/8 teaspoon curry powder

In a bowl, lightly toss green beans with celery, cucumber and radishes. Chill. Arrange tomatoes on a lettuce-lined platter. Fill center with vegetables. Combine dressing ingredients; just before serving, pour over salad. **Yield:** 8 servings.

CRUNCHY CHEESE POTATOES

"These delicious, easy-to-prepare potatoes live up to their crunchy name!"

- 1 cup (8 ounces) sour cream
- 1/2 cup milk
- 1 tablespoon minced chives
- 1/2 teaspoon salt
- 1/4 teaspoon pepper
- 6 medium potatoes, peeled and sliced 1/4 inch thick
- 1 cup (4 ounces) shredded sharp cheddar cheese
- 1/2 cup finely crushed cornflakes

Additional minced chives, optional

In a large bowl, combine sour cream, milk, chives, salt and pepper. Add potatoes and mix thoroughly. Spread in a 15-in. x 10-in. x 1-in. baking pan. Combine cheese and cornflakes; sprinkle over potatoes. Bake at 350° for 50-60 minutes or until potatoes are tender. Sprinkle with additional chives if desired. **Yield:** 6-8 servings.

HONEY BARBECUED SPARE RIBS

"The honey-and-oil glaze seals in the tender goodness of these flavorful ribs as they bake."

- 3 pounds pork spare ribs *or* pork loin back ribs
- 3 tablespoons lemon juice
- 2 tablespoons honey
- 2 tablespoons vegetable oil
- 1 tablespoon soy sauce
- 1 tablespoon instant minced onion
- 1 teaspoon paprika
- 1 teaspoon salt
- 1/2 teaspoon dried oregano
- 1/8 teaspoon garlic powder

Cut spare ribs into serving-size pieces. Place ribs, bone side down, on a rack in a shallow roasting pan. Cover and roast at 350° for 1 hour. Drain. Combine all the remaining ingredients in a bowl; brush some of the glaze on ribs. Roast, uncovered, 30-45 minutes longer or until meat is tender, brushing occasionally with remaining glaze. **Yield:** 4 servings.

REUNION RECIPES.
Clockwise from the bottom:
Best-Ever Meat Loaf, Green Bean Casserole,
Cocoa Cola Cake and Dinner Rolls
(all recipes on page 255).

NOT MANY meals recall the past as well as this one from Anna Baker of Blaine, Washington. Although it's full of old-fashioned feeling, it's as popular today as ever!

"My home's known as the 'Do Drop Inn'," relates Anna. "I'm delighted with that—the door's always open and no one needs an invitation to come by and enjoy 'Grandma Baker's goodies'."

And, while family members and friends rate *all* of Anna's dishes as delicious, they readily agree the one she shares here—the meal that she serves at her family's annual reunion—is surely her best. "The combination of aromas that comes from the kitchen while I'm preparing it is so familiar," explains Anna, "that everyone always knows what's cooking!"

In addition to the delicious dishes pictured here, Anna completes the meal with a large batch of scalloped potatoes, fresh corn on the cob and a big green salad.

HER MEAL IS PICTURE PERFECT

DINNER ROLLS

"The aroma of baked bread makes any house seem so inviting! My family loves the fragrance of these rolls as they bake and has come to expect them whenever I make a special meal."

- 2 packages (1/4 ounce *each*) active dry yeast
- 1/2 cup warm water (100° to 115°)
- 1/3 cup plus 1 teaspoon sugar, *divided*
- 1-1/4 cups warm milk (110° to 115°)
- 1/2 cup butter *or* margarine, melted and cooled
- 1-1/2 teaspoons salt
- 2 eggs, beaten
- 6 to 6-1/2 cups all-purpose flour
- Additional melted butter *or* margarine, optional

In a large bowl, dissolve yeast in warm water with 1 teaspoon sugar. Add milk, butter, salt, remaining sugar, eggs and 3 cups flour; beat until smooth. Stir in enough remaining flour to form a soft dough. Turn out onto a floured surface; knead until smooth and elastic, about 6-8 minutes, adding additional flour as needed. Place in a greased bowl, turning once to grease top. Cover and let rise in a warm place until doubled, about 1 hour. Punch dough down, then turn out onto a lightly floured board. Divide dough in half. Divide each half into 12 pieces. Shape each piece into a ball; place in two greased 13-in. x 9-in. x 2-in. baking pans. Cover and let rise until doubled, about 30 minutes. Bake at 375° for 20-

25 minutes or until golden brown. Lightly brush with melted butter if desired and serve warm. **Yield:** 2 dozen.

GREEN BEAN CASSEROLE

"This has always been one of my favorite 'convenience dishes' because it can be prepared ahead and refrigerated until ready to bake."

- 2 cans (10-3/4 ounces *each*) condensed cream of mushroom soup, undiluted
- 1 cup milk
- 2 teaspoons soy sauce
- 1/8 teaspoon pepper
- 2 packages (16 ounces *each*) frozen whole *or* cut green beans, cooked and drained
- 1 can (6 ounces) french fried onions, *divided*

In a mixing bowl, combine soup, milk, soy sauce and pepper. Gently stir in beans. Spoon half of the mixture into a 12-in. x 8-in. x 2-in. baking dish. Sprinkle with half of the onions. Spoon remaining bean mixture over the top. Bake at 350° for 30 minutes or until heated through. Sprinkle with remaining onions. Return to oven for 5 minutes or until the onions are brown and crispy. **Yield:** 10 servings.

COCOA COLA CAKE

"I GET a great response every time I serve this cake, and I'm forever sharing this recipe! The unusual ingredients make it moist and delectable."

- 2 cups all-purpose flour
- 2 cups sugar
- 1 teaspoon baking soda
- 1 cup butter *or* margarine
- 3 tablespoons baking cocoa

- 1 cup cola
- 1/2 cup buttermilk
- 2 eggs, beaten
- 1 teaspoon vanilla extract
- 1 cup miniature marshmallows

ICING:
- 1/2 cup butter *or* margarine
- 2 to 3 tablespoons baking cocoa
- 6 tablespoons cola
- 3-1/4 cups confectioners' sugar
- 1 cup coarsely chopped nuts

In a mixing bowl, combine the flour, sugar and baking soda; set aside. In a saucepan, bring butter, cocoa and cola to a boil; stir into dry ingredients. Stir in buttermilk, eggs, vanilla and marshmallows; mix well. Pour into a greased 13-in. x 9-in. x 2-in. baking pan. Bake at 350° for 35 minutes or until cake tests done. For icing, combine butter, cocoa and cola in a saucepan; bring to a boil. Remove from heat; stir in confectioners' sugar and mix well. Spread over hot cake. Sprinkle with nuts. Cool before cutting. **Yield:** 8-10 servings.

BEST-EVER MEAT LOAF

"The combination of onion, carrot, parsley and cheese—plus the tomato-mustard topping—makes this meat loaf unusually colorful."

- 2 eggs
- 2/3 cup milk
- 3 slices bread, torn into pieces
- 1/2 cup chopped onion
- 1/2 cup grated carrot
- 1 cup (4 ounces) shredded cheddar *or* mozzarella cheese
- 1 tablespoon chopped fresh parsley *or* 1 teaspoon dried parsley
- 1 teaspoon salt
- 1 teaspoon dried basil, thyme *or* sage, optional
- 1/4 teaspoon pepper
- 1-1/2 pounds lean ground beef

TOPPING:
- 1/2 cup tomato sauce
- 1/2 cup packed brown sugar
- 1 teaspoon prepared mustard

In a large bowl, beat eggs. Add milk and bread; let stand a few minutes or until the bread absorbs the liquid. Stir in the onion, carrot, cheese, herbs and seasonings. Add beef; mix well. In a shallow baking pan, shape beef mixture into a 7-1/2-in. x 3-1/2-in. x 2-1/2-in. loaf. Bake at 350° for 45 minutes. Meanwhile, combine topping ingredients. Spoon some of the topping over meat loaf. Bake for about 30 minutes longer or until no pink remains, occasionally spooning some of the remaining topping over loaf. Let stand 10 minutes before serving. **Yield:** 6 servings.

DOWN-ON-THE-FARM DINNER.
Clockwise from the top:
Strawberry Shortcake, Crispy Lemon-
Fried Chicken, Pennsylvania Dutch
Cucumbers and Red Potato Salad.
(all recipes on page 257).

"SUMMER has always been my favorite season," admits Shirley Helfenbein of Lapeer, Michigan. "Working hard on the small farm where I grew up meant hearty appetites...and lots of farm-fresh food satisfied them!

"We had a cow to provide rich, creamy dairy products. And I vividly recall the fresh berries, sweet corn and little red potatoes that made such *wonderful* weekday meals."

Shirley recalls, "Of course, the highlight of each summer week was Sunday supper after church. That was our big meal of the day. Fried chicken was the traditional main course, and all the vegetables were fresh from our garden.

"Over the years, I've added corn on the cob topped with my home-churned butter to this already magnificent menu," she adds. One taste and you'll see why Shirley and her family love this Sunday dinner standby so much.

STRAWBERRY SHORTCAKE

(ALSO PICTURED ON FRONT COVER)

"I can still taste the sweet juicy berries piled over warm biscuits and topped with a dollop of fresh whipped cream. My father added even more indulgence by first buttering his biscuits."

- 2 cups all-purpose flour
- 2 tablespoons sugar
- 1 tablespoon baking powder
- 1/2 teaspoon salt
- 1/2 cup cold butter *or* margarine
- 1 egg, beaten
- 2/3 cup light cream
- 1 cup whipping cream
- 2 tablespoons confectioners' sugar
- 1/8 teaspoon vanilla extract
Additional butter *or* margarine
- 1-1/2 quarts fresh strawberries, sliced

In a bowl, combine flour, sugar, baking powder and salt. Cut in butter until mixture resembles coarse crumbs. In a small bowl, combine egg and light cream; add all at once to the crumb mixture and stir just until moistened. Spread batter into a greased 8-in. round baking pan, slightly building up around the edges. Bake at 450° for 16-18 minutes or until golden brown. Remove from pan and cool on a wire rack. In a mixing bowl, beat whipping cream, confectioners' sugar and vanilla until soft peaks form; set aside. Just before serving, split cake crosswise in half; butter bottom layer. Spoon half of the strawberries over bottom layer. Spread with some of the whipped cream. Cover

SUMMER MEAL HAS APPEAL

with top cake layer. Top with remaining berries and whipped cream. Cut into wedges. **Yield:** 6-8 servings.

RED POTATO SALAD

"I remember digging small red potatoes from the soft warm soil, then gently pushing the plants back into the ground and reminding them to keep on making more potatoes. The new potatoes we brought home were made into this fresh salad."

- 3/4 cup sour cream
- 1/2 cup mayonnaise *or* salad dressing
- 2 tablespoons herb *or* white vinegar
- 1-1/2 teaspoons salt
- 1 teaspoon celery seed
- 6 medium red potatoes (about 2 pounds), peeled, cooked and cubed
- 3/4 cup sliced green onions
- 1/3 cup radish slices
- 1/4 cup chopped celery
- 3 to 4 hard-cooked eggs, chopped

In a small bowl, combine sour cream, mayonnaise, vinegar, salt and celery seed; set aside. In a large bowl, combine potatoes, green onions, radishes, celery and eggs. Add dressing and toss lightly. Cover and chill. **Yield:** 6-8 servings.

CRISPY LEMON-FRIED CHICKEN

"THIS IS my husband's favorite chicken dish. He loves it done very crispy and well-browned. The steps of soaking the chicken pieces in salted lemony

water and re-crisping are the secrets to this recipe."

- 2 broiler-fryer chickens (2 to 3 pounds *each*), cut up *or* 16 pieces of chicken
- 3-1/2 teaspoons salt, *divided*
Juice of 1 medium lemon
- 1 cup all-purpose flour
- 1 teaspoon paprika
- 1/8 teaspoon pepper
Cooking oil
- 2 tablespoons water

Place chicken in a large bowl; add 3 teaspoons of salt, lemon juice and enough water to cover chicken. Soak in refrigerator overnight. Drain thoroughly. In a paper bag, combine flour, paprika, pepper and remaining salt. Toss chicken pieces in flour mixture; shake off excess. Heat about 1/2 in. of oil in a large skillet. When hot, carefully add chicken and brown lightly on all sides, about 20 minutes. Reduce heat. Add water; cover and cook until tender, about 20 minutes. Uncover and cook until chicken is crisp, about 10 minutes. **Yield:** 6-8 servings.

PENNSYLVANIA DUTCH CUCUMBERS

"Settling in Pennsylvania, my mom's family adopted some of the cooking and customs of the Pennsylvania Dutch. This is a Dutch dish Mom loved, and today it's my favorite fresh vegetable dish...the blend of cucumbers and tomatoes is wonderful!"

- 3 to 4 small cucumbers
- 1 teaspoon salt
- 1 medium onion, thinly sliced into rings
- 1/2 cup sour cream
- 2 tablespoons vinegar
- 1 tablespoon chopped fresh chives
- 1/2 teaspoon dried dill seed
- 1/4 teaspoon pepper
Pinch sugar
Lettuce leaves, optional
Sliced tomatoes, optional

Peel cucumbers; slice paper-thin into a bowl. Sprinkle with salt; cover and refrigerate for 3-4 hours. Rinse and drain cucumbers. Pat gently to press out excess liquid. Combine cucumbers and onion in a large bowl; set aside. In a small bowl, combine sour cream, vinegar, chives, dill seed, pepper and sugar. Just before serving, add dressing to cucumbers and toss. If desired, arrange lettuce and tomatoes in a serving bowl and spoon cucumbers into the middle. **Yield:** 6 servings.

ST. PATTY'S DAY MAINSTAY.
Clockwise from the bottom:
Corned Beef and Cabbage, Beet Relish,
Irish Soda Bread and Emerald Isle Cake
(all recipes on page 259).

"YOU don't need to be Irish to get into the spirit of St. Patrick's Day," assures Evelyn Kenney of Trenton, New Jersey, "especially at mealtime!

"I like St. Patrick's Day because it's not a 'gift-giving' holiday," Evelyn explains. "Instead, family members and friends can relax and focus on old-fashioned hospitality."

What makes this holiday extra-special for Evelyn's family is the Irish meal she has served for years on the day for "the wearin' of the green." Along with corned beef and cabbage, there are sauces and beet relish, Irish soda bread and a glazed cake that's right from old Erin's Isle!

Today, Evelyn's children and grandchildren share this mouth-watering meal with their own friends and family. These tasty recipes are bound to become a St. Patrick's Day tradition in your home, too.

CELEBRATE HOLIDAY IN GOOD TASTE

CORNED BEEF AND CABBAGE

"This traditional Irish dish is perfect not only for St. Patrick's Day, but any time of year."

      1 corned beef brisket (4 to 6 pounds)
      2 tablespoons brown sugar
      2 to 3 bay leaves
     16 to 24 small potatoes, peeled
      8 to 12 carrots, halved
      1 large head cabbage, cut into wedges
Minced fresh parsley, optional
HORSERADISH SAUCE:
      3 tablespoons butter *or* margarine
      2 tablespoons all-purpose flour
      1 to 1-1/2 cups cooking liquid (from brisket)
      1 tablespoon vinegar
      1 tablespoon sugar
      1/4 cup horseradish
SOUR CREAM AND MUSTARD SAUCE:
      1 cup (8 ounces) sour cream
      2 tablespoons Dijon mustard
      1/4 teaspoon sugar

Place brisket in a large Dutch oven; cover with water. Add brown sugar and bay leaves. (If a spice packet is enclosed with the brisket, add it also.) Bring to a boil. Reduce heat; cover and simmer for 2 hours. Add potatoes and carrots. Return to boiling. Reduce heat; cover and simmer 30-40 minutes or until meat and vegetables are just tender. If your Dutch oven is not large enough for cabbage to fit, remove potatoes and carrots and keep warm (they can be returned to cooking liquid and heated through before serving). Add cabbage; cover and cook about 15 minutes or until tender. Discard bay leaves. Remove cabbage and meat. If making Horseradish Sauce, strain and remove about 1-1/2 cups cooking liquid. Let meat stand a few minutes. Slice meat across the grain. Serve with Horseradish Sauce or Sour Cream and Mustard Sauce. Garnish with parsley if desired. **Yield:** 8-12 servings.

Horseradish Sauce: In a small saucepan, melt butter. Blend in flour. Add 1 cup cooking liquid; stir until smooth. Add vinegar, sugar and horseradish. Cook and stir over medium heat until thickened and bubbly. Adjust seasoning with additional vinegar, sugar or horseradish if needed. Thin sauce if necessary with the remaining cooking liquid. **Yield:** about 1-1/2 cups.

Sour Cream and Mustard Sauce: Combine all ingredients in a small bowl. Mix until well blended. **Yield:** 1 cup.

IRISH SODA BREAD

"Some people consider bread to be the most important part of a meal...and this bread just might satisfy such folks!"

      4 cups all-purpose flour
      1/4 cup sugar
      1 teaspoon salt
      1 teaspoon baking powder
      1 teaspoon baking soda
      1/4 cup butter *or* margarine
      3 to 4 tablespoons caraway seeds
      2 cups raisins
  1-1/3 cups buttermilk
      1 egg, beaten
Milk

In a mixing bowl, combine flour, sugar, salt, baking powder and baking soda. Cut in butter until mixture resembles coarse meal. Stir in caraway seeds and raisins. Combine buttermilk and egg; stir into dry ingredients just until moistened. Turn out onto a floured surface and knead lightly until smooth. Shape dough into a ball and place in a greased baking pan. Pat into a 7-in. round loaf. Cut a 4-in. cross about 1/4 in. deep on top to allow for expansion. Brush top with milk. Bake at 375° for 1 hour or until golden brown. **Yield:** 1 loaf.

EMERALD ISLE CAKE

"This cake is simple to make and provides the perfect finish for an Irish meal."

      1/2 cup butter *or* margarine, softened
      1 cup sugar
      2 eggs
      1 teaspoon vanilla extract
  1-3/4 cups all-purpose flour
      2 teaspoons baking powder
      1/2 teaspoon salt
      1/2 cup milk
GLAZE:
      1 cup confectioners' sugar
      1 to 2 tablespoons milk *or* Irish whiskey
Green food coloring, optional
Slivered almonds, optional

In a mixing bowl, cream butter and sugar. Add eggs, one at a time, beating well after each addition. Blend in vanilla. Combine flour, baking powder and salt; add alternately with the milk. Beat until smooth. Spread into a greased 9-in. square baking pan. Bake at 350° for 40 minutes or until cake tests done. For glaze, combine confectioners' sugar and milk or whiskey; stir until smooth and fairly thin. If desired, add 1 to 2 drops of food coloring and stir until well blended. Spread glaze over warm cake. Sprinkle with almonds if desired. **Yield:** 9-12 servings.

Quick & Easy

BEET RELISH

"Served with corned beef and cabbage, this relish provides an interesting combination of flavors."

      2 cups coarsely shredded cooked beets
      2 tablespoons chopped red onion
      2 tablespoons red wine vinegar
      1 teaspoon sugar
      2 tablespoons Dijon mustard
      3 tablespoons vegetable oil
Salt and pepper to taste

Combine all ingredients in a small bowl and blend well. Chill thoroughly. **Yield:** about 2 cups.

PACKED WITH PRODUCE.
Clockwise from the bottom:
Pork Chops with Corn Dressing, Rhubarb
Pinwheels, Old-Fashioned Applesauce and
Wilted Lettuce (all recipes on page 261).

"THE SUNDAY suppers my mother served back on our family farm were always memorable meals," recalls Doris Natvig of Jesup, Iowa.

"Practically all our food was home-grown. We raised our own livestock, so choice pork and beef were readily available. And Mother's vegetable garden yielded a variety of fresh produce all summer long. Mother had a knack for turning ordinary foods into delectable works of art.

"I can remember me and my sister going to the garden on summer afternoons to pick enough vegetables for our supper. Later on, we'd gather the remaining vegetables for canning or freezing. In fall, we also picked an assortment of apples from Mother's trees to enjoy in pies!

"This is the meal Mother fixed most often for Sunday dinner—and all the recipes are her originals. I was thrilled when she passed them on to me. Now I make these foods for my own family. I know your friends and family will be delighted to see them appear on *your* table."

WILTED LETTUCE

"When we were kids, my sister and I would prepare the freshly picked lettuce for this salad, rinsing it several times and carefully drying it. As we did so, we quibbled about the portions we'd each have. Somehow, it seems she always managed to get more!"

- **4 bacon strips, cut up**
- **1/4 cup vinegar**
- **2 tablespoons water**
- **2 green onions with tops, sliced**
- **2 teaspoons sugar**
- **1/4 teaspoon salt**
- **1/4 teaspoon pepper**
- **8 to 10 cups torn leaf lettuce**
- **1 hard-cooked egg, chopped**

In a skillet, cook bacon until crisp. Remove from the heat. Stir in vinegar, water, onions, sugar, salt and pepper; stir until sugar is dissolved. Place lettuce in a salad bowl; immediately pour dressing over and toss lightly. Garnish with eggs. Serve immediately. **Yield:** 6 servings.

OLD-FASHIONED APPLESAUCE

"We had all kinds of apple trees in the yard when I was growing up, so I don't

know for sure which ones Mother liked best for applesauce. (Today I use Cortlands.) I do know that her applesauce was very white. The secret, she said, was to keep the apples in salt water while she peeled them so that they wouldn't darken."

- **4 pounds cooking apples**
- **1 cup water**
- **1 cinnamon stick *or* 1/2 teaspoon cinnamon extract**
- **1/2 to 1 cup sugar**

Peel, core and quarter the apples. In a Dutch oven, bring apples, water and cinnamon to a boil. Reduce heat; cover and simmer 10-15 minutes or until apples are tender. Remove from the heat. Add sugar to taste and stir until dissolved. If you used a cinnamon stick, remove and discard. Mash apples with a potato masher until desired texture is reached. Serve warm or chilled. **Yield:** 6 cups.

PORK CHOPS WITH CORN DRESSING

"My mother's wonderful corn dressing recipe goes so well with pork chops, making them especially moist and tender. This main dish takes very little time to prepare, and it's a winner every time."

- **2 eggs, beaten**
- **2 cans (15 ounces *each*) cream-style corn *or* 1 can cream-style corn and 1 can (15-1/4 ounces) whole kernel corn, drained**
- **1/4 cup butter *or* margarine, melted**
- **1/3 cup chopped celery**
- **2 tablespoons chopped pimiento**
- **4 slices white bread, cubed (about 2 cups)**
- **1/2 teaspoon paprika**
- **1/2 teaspoon salt**
- **1/2 teaspoon pepper**
- **4 to 6 pork chops (about 1 inch thick)**
- **Additional paprika and salt**

In a mixing bowl, combine eggs, corn, butter, celery, pimiento, bread cubes, paprika, salt and pepper. Spoon into a greased 13-in. x 9-in. x 2-in. baking pan. Arrange pork chops over dressing. Sprinkle with additional paprika and salt. Cover and bake at 350° for 30 minutes. Uncover and bake 30 minutes longer or until the chops are done. **Yield:** 4-6 servings.

RHUBARB PINWHEELS

"I love to make this colorful, tart-tasting dessert in the spring, just as Mother always did. As soon as the fresh rhubarb is long enough to pick, I make sure this special dish makes an appearance on our table."

DOUGH:
- **2 cups all-purpose flour**
- **1 tablespoon sugar**
- **4 teaspoons baking powder**
- **1/2 teaspoon salt**
- **1/3 cup shortening**
- **1 egg, beaten**
- **1/2 cup milk**

FILLING:
- **2 tablespoons butter *or* margarine, melted**
- **1 cup sugar**
- **3 to 4 cups diced fresh *or* frozen rhubarb**

SYRUP:
- **1-1/2 cups water**
- **1 cup sugar**
- **Few drops red food coloring, optional**
- **Cream, optional**

In a mixing bowl, sift together dry ingredients. Cut in shortening until mixture resembles coarse crumbs. Combine egg and milk; add to crumb mixture, stirring just until moistened. Turn out onto a floured surface. Roll into a 12-in. x 10-in. rectangle. Brush dough with melted butter; sprinkle with sugar and top with rhubarb. Carefully roll up dough, jelly-roll style, starting with the shorter side. Cut into 1-in. slices. Reshape the slices as needed to form round pinwheels. Place in a 13-in. x 9-in. x 2-in. baking dish. For syrup, bring water and sugar to a boil in a saucepan. Cook and stir until sugar dissolves. Stir in food coloring if desired. Carefully pour hot syrup over pinwheels. Bake at 400° for 30 minutes or until golden brown. Serve warm with cream if desired. **Yield:** 12 servings.

A TASTE OF ITALY.
Clockwise from the lower right:
Italian Garlic Toast, Green Garden Salad,
Auntie Ann's Eggplant Relish and Stuffed
Manicotti (all recipes on page 263).

"SOME OF MY happiest childhood memories are of visits to my Auntie Ann's little ranch house," recalls Cookie Curci-Wright of San Jose, California. "She welcomed us anytime and treated us to delicious meals.

"Visits with Auntie Ann continue to remain an important part of my life," she notes. "Her words are always filled with happy thoughts to brighten my day, and her cooking is just wonderful!

"Through the years, I've savored her home cooking with an enthusiasm and appetite that remain unchanged.

"Auntie Ann served her delicious manicotti, garlic toast, salad and eggplant relish at a surprise birthday party for me years ago. Every recipe speaks of our Italian heritage."

With these simple satisfying dishes, Cookie proves that serving flavorful fare to your family and friends is easy.

 **Quick & Easy**

ITALIAN GARLIC TOAST

"Every Italian meal must have its garlic bread, and this recipe is not only delicious but also attractive."

- 1 unsliced loaf (1-1/2 pounds) French bread
- 1/2 cup butter *or* margarine, melted
- 1/4 cup grated Romano *or* Parmesan cheese
- 2 garlic cloves, minced *or* 1/2 teaspoon garlic powder
- 1/2 teaspoon dried oregano

Paprika

Slice bread lengthwise; place with cut side up on a large baking sheet. In a small bowl, combine butter, cheese, garlic and oregano; brush onto cut surfaces of bread. Sprinkle with paprika. Broil about 4 in. from heat for 2-3 minutes or until lightly toasted. Cut crosswise into 3-in. pieces to serve. **Yield:** 8-10 servings.

AUNTIE ANN'S EGGPLANT RELISH

"This is my favorite of Auntie Ann's dishes and one I enjoy making!"

- 1 medium eggplant, peeled and cubed
- 1 medium onion, chopped
- 1 celery rib, chopped
- 1 cup chopped fresh mushrooms

A BIRTHDAY TO REMEMBER

- 1 green *or* sweet red pepper, chopped
- 1 cup pitted ripe olives, sliced
- 4 garlic cloves, minced
- 1 can (8 ounces) tomato sauce
- 1/2 cup water
- 1 teaspoon dried oregano
- 1/2 teaspoon salt
- 2 tablespoons ketchup
- 2 teaspoons red wine vinegar
- 1 teaspoon sugar, optional

Few drops hot pepper sauce

In a Dutch oven, combine the first 11 ingredients; mix well. Bring to a boil. Reduce heat; cover and simmer for 20 minutes or until vegetables are tender. Stir in the ketchup, vinegar, sugar if desired and hot pepper sauce. Cook, uncovered, about 5 minutes longer or until slightly thickened. Cool. **Yield:** 10-12 servings (about 6 cups).

STUFFED MANICOTTI

"The aroma of this delicious dish baking in the oven brings back many warm and tasty memories!"

SPAGHETTI SAUCE:
- 1 medium onion, chopped
- 1/2 green pepper, chopped
- 2 garlic cloves, minced
- 3 tablespoons olive oil
- 1 can (29 ounces) tomato sauce
- 3/4 cup water
- 3/4 cup dry red wine *or* water
- 1 teaspoon dried oregano
- 1/2 teaspoon dried basil
- 1/2 teaspoon salt
- 1/4 teaspoon pepper

MANICOTTI:
- 1-1/2 pounds ground beef
- 1/2 medium onion, finely chopped
- 2 garlic cloves, minced
- 1 package (10 ounces) frozen chopped spinach, thawed

- 3/4 cup grated Parmesan cheese, *divided*
- 3 eggs, beaten
- 1 teaspoon dried oregano
- 1/2 teaspoon salt
- 1/4 teaspoon pepper
- 1 package (8 ounces) manicotti, cooked and drained
- 3/4 cup shredded mozzarella cheese

In a saucepan, saute onion, green pepper and garlic in olive oil until tender. Stir in all remaining sauce ingredients; bring to a boil. Reduce heat; cover and simmer for 1 hour, stirring occasionally. Uncover; simmer 10-15 minutes longer or until as thick as desired. Meanwhile, for manicotti, cook beef, onion and garlic in a skillet until the meat is browned and onion is tender. Drain; cool slightly. Squeeze spinach thoroughly to remove excess water; add to the skillet with 1/2 cup Parmesan cheese, eggs, oregano, salt and pepper. Mix well. Refrigerate 1-1/2 cups of the sauce (makes 4 cups) for another recipe. Pour 1 cup of the remaining sauce into a 13-in. x 9-in. x 2-in. baking dish. Stuff manicotti with the meat mixture; arrange over the sauce. Pour another 1-1/2 cups of sauce on top. Sprinkle with the mozzarella and remaining Parmesan. Bake, uncovered, at 350° for 25-30 minutes or until heated through. **Yield:** 7 servings.

 **Quick & Easy**

GREEN GARDEN SALAD

"This dressing enhances any kind of greens with a special flavor."

DRESSING:
- 3/4 cup olive oil
- 1/2 cup red wine vinegar
- 2 tablespoons lemon juice, optional
- 2 teaspoons grated Parmesan cheese
- 1 teaspoon dried oregano
- 1/2 teaspoon sugar
- 1/4 teaspoon salt
- 1/4 teaspoon pepper

SALAD:
- 8 to 10 cups torn salad greens
- 1 red onion, sliced into rings
- 1 cucumber, peeled and sliced
- 2 to 3 tomatoes, cut into wedges
- 1 green pepper, sliced into rings

In a jar or bottle with tight-fitting lid, combine all the dressing ingredients; shake well. Chill. Just before serving, combine greens, onion, cucumber and tomatoes in a large salad bowl. Pour desired amount of dressing over salad; toss to mix. Top with the green pepper rings. **Yield:** 8-10 servings (1-1/3 cups dressing).

FROM MOM'S RECIPE BOX.
Clockwise from the lower right:
Hearty Ham Loaf, Strawberry Glaze Pie,
Golden Dinner Rolls and Cauliflower
Au Gratin (all recipes on page 265).

A RECIPE BOX can hold all sorts of treasures and that's exactly how Colleen Demuth looks at the one she received from her mother.

"Going through its contents brings back many memories," says Colleen, who lives in the small town of Le Mars, Iowa. "There are recipes from my grandmothers and my parents that were always family favorites, and they're favorites with my family, too!

"I enjoy pulling out the much-used recipe box for when one or all of our eight children—and *their* own families —visit," she adds. "Everyone requests a different dish, so we're always cooking up some wonderful treat!"

These four recipes take Colleen back to her roots, reviving fond memories of the days when she was growing up in Nebraska. Colleen's mother would serve meals on Desert Rose china—just as you see it served here.

"These recipes are very easy to make," Colleen notes. "Even the rolls are, although anyone who has made bread knows it does take a little more time and effort. But one taste makes it all worth it."

Colleen assures that you'll frequently reach for these recipes…year after year!

STRAWBERRY GLAZE PIE

"Strawberries are one of my favorite fruits. So, when they're in season, we go out to the strawberry farms to pick our own berries for this pie—and a delicious one it is!"

 6 cups fresh whole
  strawberries, hulled, *divided*
 1 cup sugar
 3 tablespoons cornstarch
 3/4 cup water
Few drops red food coloring,
 optional
 1 pastry shell (9 inches), baked
Whipped cream

Mash 1 cup strawberries; set aside. In a saucepan, combine sugar and cornstarch; stir in water and mashed berries. Bring to a boil, stirring constantly. Stir in food coloring, if desired. Cook and stir 3 minutes more. Cool for 10 minutes. Spread about 1/3 cup glaze over bottom and sides of pie shell. Halve remaining strawberries; arrange in shell. Spoon remaining glaze over berries. Chill 1-2 hours. Just before serving, garnish with whipped cream. Pie is best served the day it's made. **Yield:** 6-8 servings.

SUPPER STOOD TEST OF TIME

CAULIFLOWER AU GRATIN

"Nebraska, where I grew up, is a farming state, and we always had lots of vegetables at our table. Topping cauliflower with cheddar cheese makes this dish a real winner."

 1 large head cauliflower, broken
  into florets (about 6 cups)
 1/4 cup butter *or* margarine,
  divided
 1/2 cup diced onion
1-1/2 cups (6 ounces) shredded
  cheddar cheese
 1 cup (8 ounces) sour cream
 1/4 teaspoon salt
 1/2 cup dried bread crumbs

In a large saucepan, cook cauliflower in boiling salted water for 10 minutes. Drain well. Combine cauliflower with 2 tablespoons butter, onion, cheese, sour cream and salt. Spoon into a 1-1/2-qt. casserole. Melt remaining butter and toss with bread crumbs. Sprinkle over the cauliflower mixture. Bake at 350° for 30 minutes or until heated through. **Yield:** 10-12 servings.

> **JUST WHITE!** To keep cauliflower white while cooking, add 1/2 teaspoon sugar to the water.

GOLDEN DINNER ROLLS

"My father's mother passed this recipe down to me. It's an unbelievably easy way to make rolls. And the recipe makes a delicious bread, too."

 2 packages (1/4 ounce *each*)
  active dry yeast
 1 cup warm water (110° to 115°)

 1/2 cup sugar
 1 teaspoon salt
 1 cup milk
 1/2 cup shortening
 3 eggs, beaten
 6 to 6-1/2 cups unbleached
  flour

Dissolve yeast in warm water. Place sugar and salt in large mixing bowl. Set aside. Heat and stir milk and shortening until shortening melts (120°-130°). Add to mixing bowl along with eggs and yeast mixture. Stir in 1 cup of flour at a time to form a soft dough. Turn onto a floured board; knead until smooth and elastic. Place in a large greased bowl, turning once to grease top. Cover and let rise in a warm place until doubled, about 1 hour. Punch dough down. Turn out onto a lightly floured surface. Shape into desired rolls or loaves. Place on greased baking sheets or in bread pans. Cover and let rise until nearly doubled, about 30 minutes. Bake rolls at 375° for 15-18 minutes or until golden. Bake loaves at 375° for about 30 minutes or until bread tests done. Remove from pans and cool on wire racks. **Yield:** 36 rolls or 2 loaves.

HEARTY HAM LOAF

"This recipe comes from my father's side of the family. The sauce makes the meat especially flavorful. It's a simple dish to prepare, which makes it ideal for any occasion."

1-1/2 pounds ground ham
 1 pound ground pork
 1/8 teaspoon pepper
 2 eggs, beaten
 1 cup milk
 1 cup coarsely crushed soda
  crackers (about 22)
BASTING SAUCE:
 1/2 cup packed brown sugar
 1/4 cup water
2-1/2 tablespoons vinegar
 1 teaspoon dry mustard

Combine first six ingredients; form into an 8-1/2-in. x 4-1/2-in. x 2-1/2-in. loaf. Bake at 350° for about 80 minutes or until thermometer reaches 170°. Meanwhile, combine sauce ingredients in a saucepan; bring to a boil. Boil for 2 minutes. Baste loaf with sauce occasionally after first 10 minutes of baking. **Yield:** 10-12 servings.

BOUNTIFUL BREAKFAST.
Clockwise from the top right:
Strawberry Muffins, Fresh Fruit Bowl, Night-Before
Casserole and Aunt Edith's Baked Pancake
(all recipes on page 267).

THE SAVORY smells and tantalizing tastes of a magnificent meal can bring back a surge of magical memories. Marion Kirst of Troy, Michigan harks back to the carefree summers of her childhood each time she prepares the delightful morning meal that her Aunt Edith served to Marion's family during the late 1930's.

"When school let out in the spring, my younger brother and I would get to spend a relaxing week at Aunt Edith and Uncle Tom's in Chicago," Marion recalls.

"It seemed the week always ended too soon, and our parents would arrive on Saturday evening to take us back home on Sunday morning," she says. "To send us on our way, Aunt Edith made this mighty breakfast that I've never forgotten.

"Breakfast began with sweet Strawberry Muffins—a favorite of my younger brother. Served with bacon and sausage, 'The Big Pancake' defied description!

"Bite-sized pieces of melon, slightly sweetened with corn syrup, and other fruit complemented the meal. And to be sure there was more than enough food, Aunt Edith made an egg casserole as a backup.

"I still use Aunt Edith's recipes—especially for brunches. They always remind me of my kind and generous aunt and uncle. They opened new worlds to us and provided us with fond memories that will be with us forever."

Now, you can create your own memories with these hearty down-home dishes.

AUNT EDITH'S BAKED PANCAKE

"I always enjoyed watching my aunt bake this confection to perfection in her huge iron skillet. Sprinkled with powdered sugar, this crispy, golden-brown treat was delightful to the eye—and to the palate!"

   3 eggs
1/2 teaspoon salt
1/2 cup all-purpose flour
1/2 cup milk
   2 tablespoons butter *or*
     margarine, softened
Confectioners' sugar
Lemon wedges

In a mixing bowl, beat eggs until very light. Add salt, flour and milk; beat well.

MEMORABLE MORNING MENU

Thoroughly rub bottom and sides of a 10-in. cast-iron or heavy skillet with butter. Pour batter into skillet. Bake at 450° for 15 minutes. Reduce heat to 350° and bake 5 minutes more or until set. Remove pancake from skillet and place on a large hot platter. Dust with confectioners' sugar and garnish with lemon. Serve immediately. **Yield:** 4-6 servings.

FRESH FRUIT BOWL

"The crowning glory to my aunt's breakfast table was this delightful bowl of fresh fruit. The assorted colors provided the perfect accent to her antique dishes and white linen tablecloth."

  8 to 10 cups fresh melon cubes
  1 to 2 tablespoons white corn
    syrup
  1 pint fresh strawberries
  2 cups fresh pineapple chunks
  2 oranges, sectioned
Fresh mint leaves, optional

In a large bowl, combine melon cubes and corn syrup. Cover and refrigerate overnight. Just before serving, stir in remaining fruit. Garnish with fresh mint leaves if desired. **Yield:** 3-4 quarts.

STRAWBERRY MUFFINS

"These luscious oven treats are sweet and flavorful because they're made with lots of strawberry jam. They have a feathery texture and are very good when served either hot or cold."

  2 cups all-purpose flour
  1 cup sugar
  1 teaspoon baking soda

  1 teaspoon ground cinnamon
  1 teaspoon ground nutmeg
1/2 teaspoon salt
  2 eggs, beaten
1/2 cup vegetable oil
1/2 cup buttermilk
1/2 cup strawberry jam

In a mixing bowl, stir together flour, sugar, baking soda, cinnamon, nutmeg and salt; make a well in the center. Combine eggs, oil and buttermilk; pour all at once into the well. Stir just until dry ingredients are moistened. Do not overmix. Gently fold in jam (a few lumps will remain). Place in well-greased or paper-lined muffin tins. Bake at 375° for 20 minutes. **Yield:** 18 muffins.

NIGHT-BEFORE CASSEROLE

"This bread, egg and cheese combination came out of her oven light and puffy, and your fork easily glided through it. Even still, there was body and substance in each delicious mouthful."

  12 slices white bread, crusts
    removed
  6 to 8 tablespoons butter *or*
    margarine, softened
  6 slices deluxe American
    cheese
  6 slices boiled *or* baked ham
Prepared mustard
  4 eggs, beaten
3-1/3 cups milk, *divided*
    1 can (10-3/4 ounces) cream of
     mushroom soup, undiluted
Dash Worcestershire sauce
Chopped fresh parsley

Spread bread with butter. Place six slices, buttered side up, in the bottom of a greased 13-in. x 9-in. x 2-in. baking pan. Top each bread slice with a slice of cheese and ham. Brush with mustard. Place the remaining bread slices, buttered side up, over mustard. Beat eggs and 3 cups milk; pour over all. Cover and refrigerate overnight. Bake at 300° for 1 hour. Let stand 5 minutes before serving. Meanwhile, heat soup, Worcestershire sauce and remaining milk; keep warm. To serve, garnish casserole with parsley and pass the mushroom sauce. **Yield:** 12 servings.

FOND FEAST.
Clockwise from the top right:
Zwieback Rolls, German Meatballs,
Glazed Carrots and Apple Cake
(all recipes on page 269).

"I GREW UP in a German Mennonite family," relates Iona Redemer of Calumet, Oklahoma. "It was customary to invite friends or relatives to our home for Sunday dinner. Those days were special occasions, so the guests were served this memorable meal. It's one I learned to *love*.

"When I pull out these recipes today, fond memories of my grandmother and mother—who handed them down through our family—come flooding back to me," Iona shares.

"Maybe this meal is so dear because I often helped Mother prepare parts of it," she continues. "We began by baking zwieback (a delicious bread) on Saturday. I can still smell the mouthwatering aroma that filled Mother's kitchen…what a wonderful way to anticipate a house full of guests the next day! The rest of the menu included robust German meatballs, sweet glazed carrots and homemade apple cake."

Of course, you don't have to wait for Sunday to make this flavorful feast!

ZWIEBACK ROLLS

"Fresh zwieback is baked in many German Mennonite homes to serve to friends who might drop in, or for the weekly Sunday dinner known as Faspa. Instead of butter, we served jelly with our zwieback. Cold sliced meats and cheeses were delicious with these tasty rolls, too!"

 This tasty dish uses less sugar, salt and fat. Recipe includes *Diabetic Exchanges.*

- 1 package (1/4 ounce) active dry yeast
- 1/4 cup warm water (110° to 115°)
- 1-3/4 cups milk, scalded
- 1/2 cup shortening
- 1/4 cup sugar
- 2 teaspoons salt
- 5 to 6 cups all-purpose flour

Dissolve yeast in warm water; set aside. In a large mixing bowl, combine milk and shortening; stir to melt shortening. When cool, add sugar and salt. Stir in yeast mixture and 3 cups flour; beat well. Add enough of the remaining flour to form a soft dough. Turn out onto a lightly floured board; knead until smooth and elastic, about 6-8 minutes. Place dough in a greased bowl, turning once to grease top. Cover and let rise in a warm place until doubled, about 1 hour. Punch down dough and divide into fourths. Divide three of the pieces into eight pieces each; shape into

HONOR HERITAGE WITH HEARTY MEAL

smooth balls and place on greased baking sheets. Divide the fourth piece of dough into 24 small balls. Make an indentation in the top of each larger ball; press one small ball atop each larger ball. Cover and let rise in a warm place until doubled, about 45 minutes. Bake at 375° for 20-25 minutes or until golden brown. **Yield:** 2 dozen. **Diabetic Exchanges:** One serving (prepared with skim milk) equals 1-1/2 starch, 1 fat; also, 142 calories, 201 mg sodium, trace cholesterol, 23 gm carbohydrate, 3 gm protein, 4 gm fat.

GERMAN MEATBALLS

"This was one of our favorite main dishes. Since we raised our own pork and beef, the meat we used was always freshly ground. For a little variety, these meatballs can be cooked with a sweet cream gravy or steamed with tomatoes —but we prefer them with homemade sauerkraut."

- 1 pound ground beef
- 1/2 pound ground pork
- 1/2 cup finely chopped onion
- 3/4 cup fine dry bread crumbs
- 1 tablespoon snipped fresh parsley
- 1-1/2 teaspoons salt
- 1/8 teaspoon pepper
- 1 teaspoon Worcestershire sauce
- 1 egg, beaten
- 1/2 cup milk
- 2 to 3 tablespoons vegetable oil
- 1 can (27 ounces) sauerkraut, undrained
- 1/3 to 1/2 cup water, optional
- Additional snipped parsley

In a mixing bowl, combine first 10 ingredients; shape into 18 meatballs, 2 in. each. Heat the oil in a skillet; brown the meatballs. Remove meatballs and drain

fat. Spoon sauerkraut into skillet; top with meatballs. Cover and simmer for 15-20 minutes or until meatballs are done. Add water if necessary. Sprinkle with parsley. **Yield:** 6 servings.

 Quick & Easy

GLAZED CARROTS

"The sweet taste of the glaze not only enhances these carrots, but it is very compatible with the rest of the meal. Another great thing about this vegetable dish is that it adds a nice colorful touch to the table. Whenever Mom fixed this dish, friends and family were never disappointed!"

- 9 to 12 medium carrots (about 1-1/2 pounds)
- 4 tablespoons butter *or* margarine
- 1 to 2 tablespoons lemon juice
- 2 tablespoons brown sugar

Peel carrots and cut in half lengthwise. Boil in salted water until tender; drain well. Melt butter in a heavy skillet; add lemon juice and brown sugar and stir until mixture thickens. Add carrots; stir until well glazed and heated through. **Yield:** 6 servings.

APPLE CAKE

"Apples were plentiful in our area, so they were the staple of many of the desserts served at our table. This apple recipe was one of my mom's favorites. Today, it reigns supreme in our family as the choice dessert. Warm or cold, it's a treat every time!"

- 3 tablespoons butter *or* margarine, softened
- 1 cup sugar
- 1 egg, beaten
- 1 cup all-purpose flour
- 1/2 teaspoon ground cinnamon
- 1/2 teaspoon ground nutmeg
- 1/2 teaspoon salt
- 1 teaspoon baking soda
- 3 cups diced peeled apples
- 1/4 cup chopped nuts
- 1 teaspoon vanilla extract
- Whipped cream *or* ice cream

In a mixing bowl, cream butter, sugar and egg. Stir together dry ingredients; add to creamed mixture (batter will be very thick). Stir in the apples, nuts and vanilla. Spread into a greased 8-in. square baking pan. Bake at 350° for 35-40 minutes or until cake tests done. Serve warm or cold with whipped cream or ice cream. **Yield:** 9 servings.

SENTIMENTAL MEAL.
Clockwise from the top left:
Lettuce with Cream Dressing, Country Ham and
Potatoes and Fried Green Tomatoes
(all recipes on page 271).

"THIS MEAL stands out the most among my childhood memories because it seems to speak of my area of the country," explains Helen Bridges of Washington, Virginia.

"When I was 11, our family moved from the city to an old farm. My parents worked hard to make that farm a very cozy place, and I grew up to love the country," Helen recalls.

"My treasured memories are entwined with the big country kitchen in our old farmhouse. My mom cooked some *absolutely delicious* meals in that kitchen on her cast-iron wood stove.

"Mom often prepared this fabulous meal featuring ham and potatoes, fried green tomatoes and lettuce with tasty dressing," Helen adds. "Now when I serve these dishes—with old-fashioned Nutmeg Sauced Apples—it takes me back to that farm and happy days."

COUNTRY HAM AND POTATOES

"The browned potatoes pick up the tasty flavor of the ham. And piled on the platter surrounding the slices of ham, they are the perfect addition to make this entree very attractive."

2 to 3 tablespoons butter *or* margarine
2 pounds fully cooked sliced ham (about 1/2 inch thick)
1-1/2 pounds potatoes, peeled, quartered and cooked
Snipped fresh parsley

In a large heavy skillet, melt butter over medium-high heat. Brown ham on both sides. Move ham to one side of the skillet; brown potatoes in the drippings. Sprinkle potatoes with parsley. **Yield:** 6 servings.

FRIED GREEN TOMATOES

"With its crisp crust, moistened slightly with the pan gravy, I savor the flavor of this delicately sauteed vegetable. Mom made these to perfection—no

SOUTHERN COOKING AT ITS BEST

wonder why this is my favorite part of the meal."

1 tablespoon brown sugar
1 cup all-purpose flour
4 to 6 medium green tomatoes, sliced 1/2 inch thick
1 egg, beaten
1/4 cup milk
1 cup seasoned dry bread crumbs
3 tablespoons butter *or* margarine
1 tablespoon cooking oil

Combine sugar and flour; place on a shallow plate. Dip both sides of each tomato slice into the mixture. Combine the egg and milk. Dip each tomato slice; then dip into the bread crumbs. In a skillet, heat butter and oil over medium-high heat. Fry tomatoes until brown on both sides, but firm enough to hold their shape. **Yield:** about 6 servings.

 Quick & Easy

LETTUCE WITH CREAM DRESSING

"This simple salad is one of my mom's original recipes. The sweet-sour combination and the tang of the onion seems to convince people there is some secret ingredient!"

8 cups torn leaf *or* iceberg lettuce
1/2 cup sugar
1/4 cup vinegar
1/3 to 1/2 cup light cream *or* sour cream

2 to 3 tablespoons sliced green onions

Place lettuce in a large bowl. In a small bowl, stir together sugar, vinegar and light cream or sour cream until sugar dissolves and dressing is smooth. Stir in green onion. Just before serving, pour dressing over lettuce; toss lightly. **Yield:** 6 servings.

APPLE STORAGE. You'll find that apples will store for a longer period if they don't touch each other too much. To prevent bruising, try not to stack them on each other.

NUTMEG SAUCED APPLES

(PICTURED BELOW)

"This dessert may be old-fashioned—the recipe comes from a 1883 cookbook—but the slightly sweet flavor appeals to people of all generations."

6 medium tart baking apples, peeled, cored and halved
1/3 cup water
4 teaspoons sugar
4 teaspoons all-purpose flour
1/2 teaspoon ground nutmeg
1-1/2 cups light cream

Place apples in a 13-in. x 9-in. x 2-in. baking dish; add water. Bake, covered, at 350° for 30-40 minutes or until tender. Remove from the oven and keep warm. In a small saucepan, combine sugar, flour and nutmeg. Stir in cream. Cook and stir over medium heat until thickened and bubbly. Cook 2 minutes longer. Remove from the heat. Serve warm over apples. **Yield:** 6 servings.

APPLE A DAY. Keep hunger away by serving up oven-baked Nutmeg Sauced Apples!

GOLDEN OLDIES.
Clockwise from the top:
Cheesecake Pie, Stuffed Green Peppers,
Four-Bean Salad and Orange
Corn Muffins (all recipes on page 273).

AFTER marrying a tall Kansas farmer with broad shoulders and a hearty appetite, Hope Huggins of Santa Cruz, California quickly learned that it took an awful lot of cooking to fill him up. But she was up to the challenge!

Luckily, Hope learned how to cook long before she got married. By age 7, she was already baking four loaves of bread at a time in her family's old wood-burning range.

"I learned from my mother and grandmother, and making some of those same recipes now takes me back to those times," Hope says. "I can still see Grandmother putting her hand inside the range to make sure the temperature was just right."

Hope's husband and the rest of her family think her tasty stuffed peppers are just right, too. That's why Hope selected that family favorite as part of one of her best meals. Also included are a tangy four-bean salad, orange corn muffins and her favorite dessert, a lemony cheesecake pie.

Just the aroma of these dishes will make you recall the love *your* mother and grandmother put into cooking. Your family will savor every bite!

STUFFED GREEN PEPPERS

"For a change of pace, I like to add bouillon to the pan when the peppers are baking. It also steams them a little. If I'm making chicken or turkey with the peppers, I use chicken bouillon; if I'm making beef, then I use beef bouillon. You'll love the added flavor."

    5 to 6 medium green peppers
    3/4 cup uncooked brown rice
    1 pound lean ground beef
    1 medium onion, chopped
    1 can (8 ounces) tomato sauce
    1/4 teaspoon dried basil
    1/4 teaspoon dried oregano
    1/4 teaspoon dried thyme
    1/2 teaspoon salt
Pepper to taste
    1/2 teaspoon instant beef
        bouillon granules

Remove tops and seeds from peppers. In a large kettle, bring water to a boil; cook peppers for 5 minutes. Remove

FAMILY FAVORITE IS SURE TO SATISFY

and drain. Cook rice according to package directions. In a skillet, brown beef and onion. Drain. Add tomato sauce, herbs, salt, pepper and bouillon; cook 5 minutes. Stir in rice. Stuff peppers with the beef/rice mixture. Place upright in a shallow baking dish or casserole. Bake at 375° for 15-20 minutes. **Yield:** 5-6 servings.

CHEESECAKE PIE

"A friend gave me this recipe, and I love it so much! The secret is in the baking—I just let it barely show little bubbles on the surface before I take it out of the oven."

    1-1/4 cups graham cracker crumbs
        (about 18 squares)
    1/3 cup butter *or* margarine,
        melted
    2 packages (8 ounces *each*)
        cream cheese, softened
    1/2 cup sugar
    2 eggs
    1 teaspoon vanilla extract
    1/2 teaspoon finely grated
        lemon peel
TOPPING:
    1 cup (8 ounces) sour cream
    2 tablespoons sugar
    1/2 teaspoon vanilla extract
Additional lemon peel, optional
Mint leaves, optional

Combine crumbs and butter. Firmly press into the bottom and up the sides of a 9-in. pie plate. Chill. In a small mixing bowl, blend cream cheese, sugar, eggs and vanilla. Stir in lemon peel. Pour into prepared crust; bake at 325° for 25 minutes. Remove from oven. Cool 5 minutes. Meanwhile, in a small bowl, combine sour cream, sugar and vanilla. Spread over pie; bake 5 additional minutes. Cool to room tempera-

ture, then refrigerate at least 5 hours. Garnish with additional lemon peel and mint leaves if desired. **Yield:** 6-8 servings.

ORANGE CORN MUFFINS

"This recipe has been in my recipe box for years. If I don't have any orange on hand, I'll sometimes make lemon corn muffins by substituting lemon peel for orange peel."

    1 cup yellow cornmeal
    1 cup all-purpose flour
    1/3 cup sugar
    4 teaspoons baking powder
    1/4 teaspoon salt
    1 egg, beaten
    1 cup milk
    1/4 cup vegetable oil
    1 tablespoon grated orange
        peel

In a mixing bowl, combine cornmeal, flour, sugar, baking powder and salt. In another bowl, combine egg, milk, oil and orange peel. Add to cornmeal mixture, stirring just until ingredients are combined. Fill greased muffin tins 2/3 full. Bake at 425° for 15 minutes or until lightly brown. Remove from the tins and serve warm. **Yield:** 12 muffins.

FOUR-BEAN SALAD

"My mother gave me this recipe. It actually was a three-bean salad, but I added the garbanzo beans (also known as chick-peas). This dish goes over big at potlucks."

    1 can (16 ounces) green beans,
        drained
    1 can (16 ounces) wax beans,
        drained
    1 can (16 ounces) garbanzo
        beans, rinsed and drained
    1 can (16 ounces) kidney
        beans, rinsed and drained
    1/4 cup slivered green pepper
    8 green onions, sliced
    3/4 cup sugar
    1/2 cup cider vinegar
    1/4 cup vegetable oil
    1/2 teaspoon salt

In a large salad bowl, combine all of the beans, green pepper and onions. In a small bowl, combine remaining ingredients; stir until the sugar dissolves. Pour over bean mixture. Cover and refrigerate overnight, stirring several times. **Yield:** 10-12 servings.

A GIFT FROM THE HEART.
Clockwise from the top right:
English Muffin Bread, Polish Apple Pancakes,
Sunshine Baked Eggs and Fresh
Fruit Salad (all recipes on page 275).

EVERY mother should be treated like royalty on Mother's Day, and Jane Zielinski feels like a queen when her family serves this annual May brunch in her honor.

Jane's family, which now numbers 11, has gathered for years at her home in Rotterdam Junction, New York to present Mom with this most memorable meal.

"It not only honors me, but my mother, too, since two of the recipes are hers," Jane informs.

"When our family knew Mom was whipping up Polish Apple Pancakes," explains Jane, "we'd eagerly wait for the first batch to come hot off the griddle. And her fruit salad has been a classic treat for generations.

"To complement Mom's menu items, I often prepare English Muffin Bread and keep one loaf in the freezer for a quick and easy treat," she adds.

The recipe for simple-to-prepare Sunshine Baked Eggs was created by Jane's son-in-law, Mark Wilson, who loves to cook. Mark's not afraid to experiment in the kitchen, either, and the whole family loves all of his delicious results.

"Sitting down to this fabulous spread and spending time with family is the greatest gift the kids could ever give me," says Jane. These recipes will help you mark any special occasion very tastefully!

A MOTHER'S DAY BRUNCH

SUNSHINE BAKED EGGS

"My-son-in-law loves to cook, and he experimented with my old standby recipe for eggs by adding cottage cheese and crushed pineapple. It turned out to be so delicious we make eggs like this all the time!"

    1 pound sliced bacon
    14 eggs
1-1/3 cups cottage cheese
    1 can (8 ounces) crushed
        pineapple, drained
    1 teaspoon vanilla extract
Chopped fresh parsley, optional

In a skillet, cook bacon until crisp; drain and discard all but 2 tablespoons drippings. Crumble bacon. In a large bowl, lightly beat eggs; add bacon and drippings, cottage cheese, pineapple and vanilla. Pour into a greased 11-in. x 7-in. x 2-in. baking dish. Bake, uncovered, at 350° for 40-45 minutes or until a knife inserted near center comes out clean.

Let stand for 5 minutes before serving. If desired, garnish with parsley. **Yield:** 8 servings.

POLISH APPLE PANCAKES

"My mom used to make these wonderful pancakes for me as an after-school snack. She'd simply put a sprinkle of confectioners' sugar on top. What a delicious treat!"

    1 cup all-purpose flour
    1 tablespoon sugar, optional
1/2 teaspoon salt
    1 egg
    1 cup milk
    1 tablespoon vegetable oil *or*
        melted shortening
    5 medium apples, peeled and
        thinly sliced
Confectioners' sugar, optional

In a bowl, combine flour, sugar if desired and salt. In another bowl, lightly beat egg; add milk and oil. Add to dry ingredients and stir until smooth. Fold in apples. Pour batter by 1/2 cupfuls onto a lightly greased hot griddle and spread to form a 5-in. circle. Turn when bubbles form. Cook the second side until golden brown and apples are tender. Sprinkle with confectioners' sugar if desired. **Yield:** 14-16 pancakes.

Quick & Easy

FRESH FRUIT SALAD

"We grow our own strawberries, so our table usually features an abundance of this fruit. We gather other favorite fruits at the store and blend them with our berries for a refreshing, colorful

breakfast salad. I serve the dressing on the side, so people can take as much as they want."

    4 cups fresh strawberries,
        halved
    2 cups fresh blueberries
    2 to 3 kiwifruit, peeled and sliced
    2 bananas, sliced
    2 cups seedless grapes, halved
    1 carton (8 ounces) plain *or*
        vanilla yogurt
    2 teaspoons lemon juice
    1 teaspoon sugar
1/2 teaspoon vanilla extract

In a large salad bowl, combine strawberries, blueberries, kiwi, bananas and grapes. In a small bowl, combine yogurt, lemon juice, sugar and vanilla; mix well. Serve with fruit. **Yield:** 8-10 servings.

ENGLISH MUFFIN BREAD

"Many years ago, a good friend gave me her mother's recipe for this delightful bread, and I've made it ever since. It's perfect for a hearty breakfast, especially when smothered with your favorite jam."

    5 cups all-purpose flour, *divided*
    2 packages (1/4 ounce *each*)
        active dry yeast
    1 tablespoon sugar
    2 teaspoons salt
1/4 teaspoon baking soda
    2 cups warm milk (120° to 130°)
1/2 cup warm water (120° to 130°)
Cornmeal

In a large mixing bowl, combine 2 cups flour, yeast, sugar, salt and baking soda. Add warm milk and water; beat on low speed for 30 seconds, scraping bowl occasionally. Beat on high for 3 minutes. Stir in remaining flour (batter will be stiff). *Do not knead.* Grease two 8-1/2-in. x 4-1/2-in. x 2-1/2-in. loaf pans. Sprinkle pans with cornmeal. Spoon batter into the pans and sprinkle cornmeal on top. Cover and let rise in a warm place until doubled, about 45 minutes. Bake at 375° for 35 minutes or until golden brown. Remove from pans immediately and cool on wire racks. Slice and toast. **Yield:** 2 loaves.

STAR-SPANGLED SPECIALTIES.
Clockwise from the top right:
Homemade Bread, Fried Chicken,
Chocolate Nut Brownies and Mama's
Potato Salad (all recipes on page 277).

WHEN Sandra Anderson was growing up in Arnold, Nebraska in the 1950's, the Fourth of July was one of the biggest holidays of the year.

A picnic outing with several families to a nearby river made it a *big* celebration. Traditions were so well-established back then that the menu for the picnic remained the same.

"Everybody who came brought the same foods each year," remembers Sandra, who now lives in New York City. "But I always thought Mama's was the best. She made potato salad the same way *her* mother made it.

"Mama also served the best fried chicken ever, accompanied by homemade bread-and-butter sandwiches. She topped off the meal with a big pan of brownies and a gallon jar of fresh lemonade."

Sandra adds, "I can still remember swimming in that river, enjoying these great foods and ending the day watching fireworks in the clear country sky."

You're bound to create fireworks of your own when you present this menu at your next family picnic.

HOMEMADE BREAD

"We baked at least two batches of bread each week for our family of six. Nothing tasted as good as Mama's home-churned sweet butter spread on this oven-fresh bread."

 This tasty dish uses less sugar, salt and fat. Recipe includes *Diabetic Exchanges*.

>   2 packages (1/4 ounce *each*)
>   active dry yeast
> 4-1/2 cups warm water (110° to 115°)
>   6 tablespoons sugar
>   2 tablespoons salt
>   1/4 cup shortening, melted and
>   cooled
>   12 to 12-1/2 cups all-purpose
>   flour, *divided*

In a large mixing bowl, dissolve yeast in water. Add sugar, salt and shortening; stir until dissolved. Add half the flour; beat until smooth and the batter sheets with a spoon. Mix in enough remaining flour to form a soft dough that cleans the bowl. Turn onto a floured board. Knead 8-10 minutes or until smooth and elastic. Place in a greased bowl, turning once to grease top. Cover and allow to rise in a warm place until doubled, about 1-1/2 hours. Punch dough down. Cover and let rise again for 30 minutes. Divide dough into four parts and shape into loaves. Place in four greased 9-in. x 5-in. x 3-in.

PICNIC FARE WITH FESTIVE FLAIR

loaf pans. Cover and let rise in a warm place until doubled, about 30-45 minutes. Bake at 375° for 30-35 minutes or until golden brown. Remove from pans and allow to cool on wire racks. **Yield:** 4 loaves. **Diabetic Exchanges:** One serving (one slice) equals 1 starch; also, 93 calories, 70 mg sodium, 0 mg cholesterol, 18 gm carbohydrate, 3 gm protein, 1 gm fat.

MAMA'S POTATO SALAD

"This old-fashioned potato salad recipe doesn't have many ingredients, so it isn't as colorful as many that you find nowadays. But just taste it and see if it isn't one of the best potato salads you've ever eaten!"

>   3 to 3-1/2 pounds potatoes
>   (about 10 medium)
>   6 hard-cooked eggs
>   1 medium onion, finely chopped
>   1/2 cup mayonnaise
>   1/2 cup evaporated milk
>   3 tablespoons vinegar
>   2 tablespoons prepared mustard
>   1/4 cup sugar
>   1 teaspoon salt
>   1/4 teaspoon pepper
> **Additional hard-cooked eggs, sliced**
> **Paprika**

In a large kettle, cook potatoes in boiling salted water until tender. Drain and cool. Peel potatoes; cut into chunks. Separate egg yolks from whites. Set yolks aside. Chop whites and add to potatoes with onion. In a small bowl, mash yolks. Stir

in mayonnaise, milk, vinegar, mustard, sugar, salt and pepper. Pour over potatoes; toss well. Adjust seasonings if necessary. Spoon into a serving bowl. Garnish with egg slices and paprika. Chill until serving. **Yield:** 12 servings.

 Quick & Easy

CHOCOLATE NUT BROWNIES

"These brownies were enjoyed by everyone at our family's Fourth of July picnic. Mama always said that they didn't need frosting because they were the richest brownies around. And I think you'll agree!"

>   2/3 cup shortening
>   2 cups sugar
>   4 eggs
>   1 teaspoon vanilla extract
>   3/4 cup baking cocoa
> 1-1/2 cups all-purpose flour
>   1 teaspoon baking powder
>   1/2 teaspoon salt
>   1 cup chopped nuts, *divided*

In a mixing bowl, beat shortening, sugar, eggs and vanilla just until smooth. Combine dry ingredients; stir into batter. Fold in half the nuts. Spread into a greased 13-in. x 9-in. x 2-in. baking pan. Sprinkle remaining nuts on top. Bake at 350° for 20-25 minutes or until brownies pull away from the sides of the pan. Cool on wire rack. Cut into squares. **Yield:** 2 dozen.

FRIED CHICKEN

"Back when we used farm-fresh ingredients, our foods didn't need much embellishment to make them look and taste better. We prepared our chickens the day before and cooked them simply."

> 1-1/2 cups all-purpose flour
> 1-1/2 teaspoons salt
>   1/2 teaspoon pepper
>   1/2 teaspoon garlic powder
>   1 broiler-fryer chicken (2-1/2 to
>   3 pounds), cut up
> **Shortening**

In a bowl, combine first four ingredients. Wash and dry chicken; coat pieces in flour mixture. In a skillet, melt shortening to 1/2-in. depth over medium-high heat. Fry chicken (in batches if necessary) in hot shortening until golden brown on all sides. Return all chicken to pan; cover and cook over low heat until chicken is done, about 30 minutes. **Yield:** about 8 servings.

COMFORTING FOOD.
Clockwise from the top left:
Anise Cookies, Meatball Minestrone,
Baked Rigatoni and Marinated
Vegetables (all recipes on page 279).

"CHILDHOOD dinners at Aunt Carmella's house in Chicago are vivid in my mind," says Esther Perea, now of Van Nuys, California. "I can still smell the wonderful aromas from her kitchen.

"Oftentimes, I would try to snatch a taste of something as it cooked, but Aunt Carmella would shoo me away. 'Help me set the table and then we'll eat,' she'd promise. I soon became the fastest table setter in the family!"

"I always liked to watch her cook and bake," Esther says, "but she never measured anything. She would add a pinch of this, a cup or so of that. Just when I thought I had the right amounts written down, I'd catch her adding a little more of this or that!

"Years and numerous attempts later I finally came close to her recipes! Whenever I want a trip back in time, I reach for this menu."

MEATBALL MINESTRONE

"Just thinking about this simmering soup gets me hungry for some!"

    1 pound ground beef
    1 egg, beaten
    1/2 cup chopped onion
    1/4 cup dry bread crumbs
    1 teaspoon salt
    1/4 teaspoon pepper
    1 can (15 ounces) tomato sauce
2-1/2 cups water
    1 can (15-1/2 ounces) kidney
        beans with liquid
    1/2 teaspoon dried oregano
    1/4 teaspoon dried thyme
    1 cup sliced celery
    1/4 cup uncooked elbow macaroni
    1/4 cup chopped fresh parsley

In a mixing bowl, combine beef, egg, onion, crumbs, salt and pepper. Shape into 30 1-in. balls. In a large saucepan, brown meatballs on all sides. Drain excess fat. Add remaining ingredients except macaroni and parsley; cover and simmer 20 minutes. Add macaroni; simmer 10 minutes or until tender. Stir in parsley. **Yield:** about 2 quarts.

BAKED RIGATONI

"This recipe calls for rigatoni, but you can substitute just about any pasta, especially mostaccioli."

    2 tablespoons cooking oil
    1 medium onion, chopped
    1 small green pepper, diced
    1 can (28 ounces) whole
        tomatoes, cut up

A TASTE
TRIP DOWN
MEMORY LANE

    1 can (8 ounces) tomato sauce
    1 can (6 ounces) tomato paste
3/4 cup water
    1 jar (4-1/2 ounces) sliced
        mushrooms, undrained
    3 garlic cloves, minced
    1 bay leaf
    2 teaspoons sugar
    1 teaspoon oregano
1-1/2 teaspoons salt
    1/4 teaspoon pepper
    1/4 cup chopped fresh parsley
    1 pound rigatoni
    2 tablespoons butter *or*
        margarine
    2 eggs, beaten
    1 carton (15 ounces) ricotta
        cheese
    1/2 cup grated Parmesan cheese
Additional Parmesan cheese

In a large skillet, heat oil over medium-high. Cook onion and green pepper until tender. Add tomatoes, sauce, paste, water, mushrooms, herbs and seasonings. Simmer, uncovered, for 30 minutes. Remove bay leaf. Cook rigatoni according to package directions; drain and toss with butter. Mix eggs, ricotta and Parmesan cheese. Stir into rigatoni mixture and spoon into a 13-in. x 9-in. x 2-in. baking dish. Top with tomato mixture; bake at 350° for 30-40 minutes or until heated through. Sprinkle with additional Parmesan cheese. **Yield:** 8-10 servings.

MARINATED VEGETABLES

"This recipe proves that a blend of vinegar and garlic can be strong but subtle, too."

    14 whole fresh mushrooms
Boiling water
    1 eggplant, peeled and cut into
        strips
    1 can (13-3/4 ounces) artichoke
        hearts, drained and halved
    1 sweet red pepper, sliced

    1 green pepper, sliced
    1 sweet yellow pepper, sliced
    1 jar (4 ounces) chopped
        pimientos, drained
    1 can (6 ounces) pitted ripe olives
        or 1 cup Italian black olives
DRESSING:
    1/3 cup tarragon wine vinegar
    2 tablespoons olive oil
2-1/3 cups vegetable oil
    2 garlic cloves, minced
    1 teaspoon salt
    1/2 teaspoon pepper
    2 tablespoons lemon juice
    1/2 teaspoon dry mustard
    1/4 teaspoon paprika
1-1/2 tablespoons Italian seasoning
    1/4 cup grated Parmesan cheese

In a saucepan, cook the mushrooms in boiling water for 1 minute. Drain. In a large salad bowl, combine all vegetables; set aside. Combine all dressing ingredients and pour over vegetables. Stir gently. Cover and refrigerate 8 hours or overnight. Stir occasionally. **Yield:** about 10 cups.

ANISE COOKIES

"I remember walking into my aunt's house and I'd almost swoon when I smelled these cookies baking."

2-1/2 cups all-purpose flour
    3 teaspoons baking powder
1-1/2 teaspoons crushed anise seed
    3/4 teaspoon salt
    1/4 teaspoon ground cinnamon
    1/4 teaspoon ground nutmeg
    1/2 cup butter, softened
    1 cup sugar, *divided*
1-1/4 teaspoons vanilla extract
    2 eggs
    1 cup blanched almonds,
        toasted and finely chopped
    2 teaspoons milk

Combine flour, baking powder, anise seed, salt, cinnamon and nutmeg; set aside. In a separate bowl, cream butter and 3/4 cup sugar until fluffy. Beat in vanilla and eggs. Stir in almonds and flour mixture. Line a baking pan with foil. Divide the dough in half and mold into two 12-in. x 2-in. rectangles on the foil. Smooth the surface of each rectangle; then brush with milk and sprinkle with remaining sugar. Bake at 375° for 20 minutes or until golden brown and firm to the touch. Remove from the oven and reduce heat to 300°. Lift rectangles with foil onto a wire rack; cool 15 minutes. Place rectangles on a cutting board; slice 1/2 in. thick crosswise on the diagonal. Place slices, cut side down, on baking sheets. Bake 10-12 minutes longer. Turn oven off, leaving cookies in oven to cool with door ajar. Store cookies in airtight containers. **Yield:** 3-1/2 dozen.

HOMEGROWN MEMORIES.
Clockwise from the top left:
Carrot Casserole, Vegetable Medley
Salad, Rhubarb Crunch and Ham Loaf
(all recipes on page 281).

"GOING to Grandma and Grandpa's house was always a treat, but my most special memories are of the bountiful meal Grandma served on Easter Sunday," recalls Esther Mishler of Hollsopple, Pennsylvania.

"We'd go to sunrise services and then Sunday school. Later, all the relatives would gather for a fun-filled day.

"Nearly everything on the table was grown right there on the farm. In addition to fresh-from-the-oven bread, these four dishes in particular were my favorites when I was growing up.

"Happily, my husband and our children are of the same opinion nowadays," admits Esther. "At their request, I serve this meal every Easter…in addition to several times throughout the year." They're sure to become winners with your family, too!

VEGETABLE MEDLEY SALAD

"My grandparents tended a big garden and grew and canned all their own vegetables. Grandma always had the ingredients on hand for this salad, and I think she was happy to have a recipe that she could make well ahead when planning that big Easter dinner."

- 1 medium head cauliflower, broken into florets and blanched
- 1 medium onion, sliced into rings
- 1 can (16 ounces) green beans, drained
- 1 can (16 ounces) wax beans, drained
- 1 can (16 ounces) lima beans, drained
- 1 can (16 ounces) kidney beans, rinsed and drained
- 4 sweet pickles, sliced
- 3 carrots, sliced and blanched
- 1-1/2 cups vinegar
- 3/4 cup water
- 1/2 cup sweet pickle juice, optional
- 2 cups sugar
- 1 teaspoon salt
- 1/2 teaspoon ground turmeric
- 1/4 teaspoon dry mustard

In a large bowl, combine cauliflower, onion, all of the beans, pickles and carrots. In a medium saucepan, bring remaining ingredients to a boil. Boil for 2 minutes, stirring occasionally. Pour over vegetables; stir gently. Cover and chill overnight. Stir again; drain before serving. **Yield:** 12-18 servings.

HAM LOAF

"I copied this recipe exactly the way Grandma had written it in her worn cookbook. The only difference today is that I can't get home-smoked ham like those Grandpa used to cure in his old-fashioned smokehouse. But that never matters to hungry folks at the table—Grandma's recipe is a winner every time!"

- 2 eggs
- 1 cup milk
- 1 cup dry bread crumbs
- 1/4 teaspoon pepper
- 1-1/2 pounds ground fully cooked ham
- 1/2 pound ground pork

GLAZE:
- 1/3 cup packed brown sugar
- 1/4 cup vinegar
- 1/2 teaspoon dry mustard
- 2 tablespoons water

In a large bowl, beat the eggs; add milk, bread crumbs and pepper. Add ham and pork; mix well. In a shallow baking pan, shape meat mixture into a loaf, about 8 in. x 4 in. x 2-1/2 in. Insert a meat thermometer. Bake at 350° for 30 minutes. Meanwhile, combine glaze ingredients. Spoon over loaf. Continue baking until the thermometer reaches 170°, about 40 minutes longer, basting occasionally with glaze. **Yield:** 8 servings.

RHUBARB CRUNCH

"Rhubarb was one of the first crops Grandma gathered from her garden in spring. She told us kids her rhubarb sauce was a good tonic for whatever ailed us, but we much preferred the delicious dessert she served after Easter dinner. This Rhubarb Crunch was so delicious with fresh cream skimmed from the top of some milk."

- 1 cup all-purpose flour
- 3/4 cup rolled oats
- 1 cup packed brown sugar
- 1 teaspoon ground cinnamon
- 1/2 cup butter *or* margarine, melted
- 4 cups sliced fresh *or* frozen rhubarb

TOPPING:
- 1 cup sugar
- 2 tablespoons cornstarch
- 1 cup water
- 1 teaspoon vanilla extract

Few drops red food coloring, optional

In a large bowl, combine flour, oats, brown sugar, cinnamon and butter; mix until crumbly. Press half of the mixture into an ungreased 9-in. square baking pan. Cover with rhubarb. For topping, combine sugar and cornstarch in a small saucepan; add water. Cook and stir until thickened and bubbly. Cook and stir 2 minutes more. Remove from the heat. Stir in vanilla and food coloring if desired. Pour over the rhubarb. Top with the remaining crumb mixture. Bake at 350° for 50-60 minutes or until bubbly. **Yield:** 8-10 servings.

CARROT CASSEROLE

"Some of us grandchildren didn't like cooked carrots, but we all dug into this Carrot Casserole. Maybe that was because it tastes more like a stuffing than a vegetable dish. Whatever the reason, we kids forgot we were eating carrots whenever we enjoyed this casserole."

- 1 pound carrots, sliced
- 2 eggs
- 1/2 cup chopped onion
- 1 cup chopped celery
- 1 tablespoon chopped fresh parsley
- 3/4 cup butter *or* margarine, melted
- 1 teaspoon salt
- 8 cups cubed day-old bread

In a saucepan, cover carrots with water and cook until very tender. Drain and mash. In a large bowl, beat eggs; add onion, celery, parsley, butter and salt. Stir in carrots. Add bread cubes and mix well. Pour into a greased 2-qt. baking dish. Bake, uncovered, at 350° for 30-40 minutes or until set. **Yield:** 8-10 servings.

SATISFYING STAPLES.
Clockwise from the top:
Creamed Potatoes, Green Beans with
Bacon, Cheese Biscuits and Daddy's Sunday
Roast (all recipes on page 283).

MARY LEWIS of Memphis, Tennessee fondly remembers the Sunday dinner that became a delicious tradition at her childhood home.

"The cornerstone of the meal was Daddy's roast," she recalls. "My big, jovial father was truly a meat-and-potatoes man.

"Once, he commemorated our family's collective appetite for such hearty fare by designing a make-believe 'coat of arms'—a family crest with a big roast beef at its center!

The succulent side dishes of potatoes, green beans and cheese biscuits were always served with the traditional roast beef."

"Mostly, though, I remember that Daddy had a knack for making dinnertime fun," she relates. "Every plate was served with his abundant love…and of course, Mom's delectable dishes." Mary makes these dishes often—and every bite brings back fond recollections of her father and the fun he brought to her life.

GREEN BEANS WITH BACON

"My mother was from North Carolina, and she preferred green pole beans to green snap beans. I've found that either is delicious in this recipe, as long as the beans are fresh. Mother also brought with her from North Carolina the custom of chopping and 'mounding' the beans before serving—a touch that makes them even more special."

**1-1/2 pounds green beans, cut into 1-inch pieces
6 bacon strips
Pepper and seasoned salt to taste**

In a covered saucepan, cook beans in a small amount of water for 20-25 minutes or until tender. Drain. Meanwhile, in a skillet, cook bacon until crisp. Remove bacon, reserving drippings. Crumble bacon and set aside. Add beans to drippings; sprinkle with pepper and seasoned salt. Heat through. Add crumbled bacon and toss. Serve immediately. **Yield:** 8 servings.

CREAMED POTATOES

"We always had mashed potatoes with our roast beef, only we called them 'creamed' potatoes, a cloud-like delight

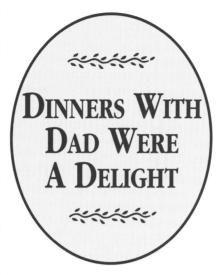

DINNERS WITH DAD WERE A DELIGHT

crowned with golden-brown gravy from the roast! Any kind of potato will do…the secret to making them light and fluffy is in the whipping!"

**3-1/2 to 4 pounds potatoes, peeled and quartered
1/4 cup butter *or* margarine
1 ounce cream cheese, softened
1/3 to 2/3 cup evaporated milk *or* heavy cream
Salt and pepper to taste**

Cook the potatoes in boiling salted water until tender; drain. Add butter, cream cheese and 1/3 cup milk or cream. Whip potatoes with electric mixer on low speed or mash with a potato masher, adding remaining milk or cream as needed to make potatoes light and fluffy. Season with salt and pepper. **Yield:** 8-10 servings.

> **STORING SPUDS.** The best place to store most fresh potatoes is in a cool, dark, well-ventilated place. However, you should refrigerate new potatoes whenever possible.

DADDY'S SUNDAY ROAST

"Daddy was a close friend of the local butcher, Mr. Mason, who always saved the preferred cut for his best customer! To please Daddy, that roast had to be big enough so he could count on leftovers for cold beef sandwiches the following week."

**1 boneless beef rump roast (5 to 6 pounds)
1/2 cup cider vinegar
Salt and pepper to taste
1 cup water
GRAVY:
1/2 cup all-purpose flour**

**1 cup cold water
1 teaspoon browning sauce
Salt and pepper to taste**

Place roast in a deep roasting pan, fat side up. Puncture meat with tenderizing tool or meat fork; pour vinegar over. Let stand at room temperature for 15 minutes. Sprinkle roast with salt and pepper. Add water to the pan. Cover and bake at 400° for 3-1/2 hours or until meat is tender, adding additional water if needed. About 15 minutes before roast is done, uncover to brown the top. Remove roast from the pan and keep warm; skim fat from pan juices. Measure the juices, adding water if needed to equal 3 cups. Mix flour and cold water until smooth; stir into pan juices. Cook and stir until thickened and bubbly. Cook and stir 1 minute more. Stir in browning sauce. Season with salt and pepper. Serve gravy with roast. **Yield:** 10-12 servings.

CHEESE BISCUITS

"The bread at this meal sometimes varied, but we loved Mother's cheese biscuits best. Although the biscuit bowl was always filled to the top, there never seemed to be enough. The cheddar cheese gives these biscuits an unforgettable flavor, and buttermilk makes them especially light."

**1-2/3 cups all-purpose flour
2 teaspoons baking powder
1/2 teaspoon salt
1/4 teaspoon baking soda
1/4 cup shortening
1 cup (4 ounces) shredded cheddar cheese
3/4 cup buttermilk**

In a mixing bowl, combine flour, baking powder, salt and baking soda. Cut in shortening until the mixture resembles coarse crumbs. Stir in cheese. Add buttermilk; stir just until dough clings together. On a lightly floured surface, knead dough lightly until easy to handle. Roll into a 12-in. circle. Cut into eight wedges. Begin at wide end of wedge and roll toward point. Place biscuits, point side down, on a greased baking sheet. Bake at 450° for 12-14 minutes or until golden brown. Serve warm. **Yield:** 8 biscuits.

INDEX

✓ Denotes recipes that are lower in sugar, salt and fat, and are evaluated for diabetics.

⊕ Denotes Quick & Easy recipes.